Victor Wilkerson

PUBLISHING FUNDAMENTALS: UNSTRUCTURED FRAMEMAKER 8

About the Authors

Sarah S. O'Keefe is founder and president of Scriptorium Publishing Services, Inc. The company provides technical publishing services to high-tech companies, including outsourced documentation solutions, technical training, and consulting. Sarah is an experienced FrameMaker trainer; her background includes technical writing, technical editing, production editing, and extensive online help development with various help authoring tools. Currently, she works as a consultant to assist companies in implementing structured authoring, single sourcing, and other publishing solutions. Sarah resides in Durham, North Carolina. In her spare time, she likes to cook.

Sheila A. Loring is a senior technical consultant for Scriptorium Publishing Services near Research Triangle Park, North Carolina. During her many years at Scriptorium, Sheila has designed FrameMaker templates, written technical documentation, and designed systems to produce and repurpose XML. Sheila has also created conversion processes and converted large libraries of unstructured files from Word or FrameMaker to structured FrameMaker. Sheila and Sarah previously collaborated on a WebWorks Publisher book. In her alternate reality, Sheila enjoys photography and reading.

Terry Smith is a technical consultant who recently returned to Scriptorium Publishing after ten years. A longtime FrameMaker zealot, Terry is a founding member of the North Carolina FrameMaker Users Network (NC-FUN, now an STC-Carolina special interest group). Terry enjoys woodcarving and working in silver.

Lydia K. Wong has worked in technical communications for more than 15 years. She is a technical consultant and technical trainer at Scriptorium Publishing Services. A FrameMaker ACE and Certified Technical Trainer (CTT), Lydia teaches FrameMaker and XML publishing courses for Scriptorium. Before coming to Scriptorium, Lydia documented user interface guidelines and Windows development components. She founded the API technical writing Yahoo group in 2001, and she has made presentations at local and regional STC and FrameMaker users' group meetings. Lydia enjoys spending time with her husband, two sons, and dog.

Publishing Fundamentals: Unstructured FrameMaker 8

Sarah S. O'Keefe
Sheila A. Loring
Terry Smith
Lydia K. Wong

Publishing Fundamentals: Unstructured FrameMaker 8

ISBN-10: 0-9704733-4-6
ISBN-13: 978-0-9704733-4-9

Written and composed in Adobe® FrameMaker®, this book contains material adapted from *Publishing Fundamentals: FrameMaker 7* (ISBN 978-0-9704733-3-2).

Cover design: Sean Byrne

CONTENTS

Part IV: Building Books

ACKNOWLEDGMENTS

The entire staff of Scriptorium Publishing contributed to this book. Some took on extra work so that the people assigned to the book could focus on writing. Others contributed software testing, content verification, or technical reviews. And by the time you read this, several people have ensured that your order was processed and shipped.

In addition to the people whose names appear on the cover of the book, the following individuals made major contributions to the content:

- Karen Brown, who provided proofreading and sanity checking
- Alan Pringle, who provided his usual eagle-eyed technical editing along with coordination of the print production process

We appreciate everyone's efforts in completing this book.

Sarah O'Keefe & Sheila Loring
May 2008

INTRODUCTION

Welcome to *Publishing Fundamentals: Unstructured FrameMaker 8.* Adobe's FrameMaker software is the industry leader in technical publishing, and the release of version 8 continues that tradition. FrameMaker automates mundane but essential tasks, such as maintaining running headers and footers and updating tables of contents. It offers an easy path to producing multiple output formats, including print, Portable Document Format (PDF), and several other online formats.

This book shows new users how to use unstructured FrameMaker, which is the traditional FrameMaker user interface, to streamline their publishing workflows and greatly improve efficiency and productivity. For current users, we have provided complete coverage of the new features in version 8 and perhaps some new tips for older features.

In addition to writing about FrameMaker, we practice what we preach. Most of the documents we write are created in FrameMaker. The book you are holding was itself produced in FrameMaker version 8.

This book is part of a two-volume set documenting FrameMaker 8. The second volume, *Publishing Fundamentals: Structured FrameMaker 8* (ISBN 978-0-9704733-5-6), explains how to set up a structured authoring environment. The structured FrameMaker user interface has additional features that are required to produce well-formed, valid Extensible Markup Language (XML) files in FrameMaker.

What's New in FrameMaker 8

Version 8 contains some significant changes, including the following:

- **Unicode support.** By far the most momentous improvement is support for the Unicode text encoding standard. In practice, Unicode support means that you can produce documents in Russian, Greek, Turkish, and other languages that use non-Latin alphabets. Right-to-left languages, such as Hebrew and Arabic, are not supported. You can add Unicode text in the body of your document, and you can also use Unicode characters throughout FrameMaker—in the names of tags, within markers, in hypertext links, and in the find/change dialog box.

  You can copy and paste special characters into your text or into dialog boxes from Unicode-compliant applications such as the Windows Character Map utility, Microsoft Word, or FrameMaker itself.

  You can export and import Unicode content to and from other applications. PDF files created from FrameMaker can include Unicode within bookmarks, comments, file information, and so on. Third-party conversion tools that support Unicode can produce the correct symbols in HTML or other online outputs from FrameMaker 8 files without the need for complex character mapping.

  FrameMaker has new dictionaries to support spell-checking and hyphenation for more languages, and it has new system variables to support Japanese date formats.

  There is a new MIF 8 format that supports Unicode features. You can save back to the MIF 7 format if you need to open your FrameMaker 8 content in FrameMaker 7 or earlier. In past versions of FrameMaker, you could open MIF files created in later versions, and new features would be ignored when you opened the MIF in the earlier version of FrameMaker. With FrameMaker 8, you must save back to MIF 7 because earlier versions have no understanding of Unicode.
- **Track Text Edits.** You can turn on Track Text Edits to see the text changes in the document. Colors and strikethrough lines highlight the changes. You can accept or reject specific changes, and you can preview the original and final document states.
- **Enhanced conditional text features.** You can now build expressions to handle complex conditional-text filtering. In previous versions, you could only set a particular condition to either show or not show. Now you have the option to use expressions instead to create combinations of conditions and Boolean operators. For example, you could build an expression that shows just the text that has both the Windows and Product1 conditions applied.

  FrameMaker 8 displays a mix of the condition colors when two or more conditions are applied; mixed conditions were displayed as magenta in previous versions. You can define a new color from the Add Condition Tag dialog box without defining the color first in a separate step.

  You can also rename conditions. Any conditions or expressions that use the old name are updated to use the new name.

- **Rich media support for 3D and Flash Files.** You can import 3D models (U3D format) or Flash movies (SWF or FLA) the same way you import other graphics. When you use Save As PDF to generate an Adobe PDF file, the 3D or Flash files are embedded into the PDF file. Users can then manipulate the 3D objects and play the Flash movies in the PDF file.

  For 3D objects, you can change the default view, rendering mode, background color, and lighting within FrameMaker. You do not need to have the application that created the 3D objects.
- **HTTP paths for graphics.** You can specify an http path instead of a folder to include graphics by either copying or by reference.
- **Import of Office 2007 content.** You can import content from Microsoft® Word 2007 and Microsoft Excel 2007.
- **Adobe PDF Creation Add-On.** The Adobe PDF Creation Add-On is a version of Acrobat Distiller that runs in the background when you select Save As PDF. It generally works the same as the regular Acrobat Distiller program that is included as part of Acrobat Professional or Acrobat 3D (and that was previously included with FrameMaker). Using the add-on, you cannot create PDF files from applications other than FrameMaker as you can with the regular Acrobat Distiller program, nor can you set up folders that Acrobat Distiller watches and processes on a schedule. You can use the predefined job options or create your own.
- **Inclusion in Adobe Technical Communication Suite.** While the Adobe Technical Communication Suite isn't a feature of FrameMaker, the suite's existence affects FrameMaker users. You can purchase FrameMaker 8 by itself or as part of the Adobe Technical Communication Suite that includes four products: FrameMaker, RoboHelp (for creating online output), Captivate (for creating product demos that are saved in Flash), and Adobe Acrobat 3D (the Acrobat version with the most features). The price of the suite is tempting if you need Acrobat Professional or better (which you probably do), or if you are considering authoring in FrameMaker and converting to online formats using RoboHelp.

Who Should Read This Book

The information in this book will be useful for both new and long-time FrameMaker users. The book is the first third-party reference that explains unstructured FrameMaker from top to bottom. It details basics, such as creating a document, importing formats from one file to another, and applying paragraph tags. In more advanced sections, this reference describes how to create templates, build books, use modular text, and insert hypertext commands.

In short, there's something in this book for every user. Beginners will find a wealth of information, organized in order of increasing complexity. Advanced users may want to skip the first few parts and focus on the second half of the book.

What's in This Book

This rather large book is divided into several parts to help you find your way around. You'll notice that each part has a handy thumb tab to help find the part you need.

Part I, Getting Started with FrameMaker

Part I is intended mainly for new users. It provides an overview of FrameMaker's features and interface. All users should probably read Chapter 2, which describes several different workflows that include FrameMaker.

Part I includes the following chapters:

- Chapter 1, "Why FrameMaker?," offers an overview of FrameMaker's features. It describes some of the features that make FrameMaker unique and explains how you can use them to automate common publishing tasks. This chapter is intended for users who are new to FrameMaker and need an explanation of why FrameMaker makes sense for technical publishing projects.
- Chapter 2, "Establishing a Workflow in FrameMaker," describes the typical publishing workflow and examines how FrameMaker fits into that workflow. It also includes an overview of how to set up a single-sourcing workflow that lets you publish to multiple output formats. If you are starting with a clean slate and can configure your workflow however you want, read this chapter to get an idea of the possibilities.
- Chapter 3, "Creating Your First Document," explains how to create a new document and open existing documents. It also describes the document window, toolbars, and status bar. Finally, it explains how to configure preferences to suit your workflow. Read this chapter if you are not familiar with the FrameMaker interface.

Part II, Creating and Manipulating Text

Part II explains the word processing features of FrameMaker and how to add and manipulate text, tables, and other items in your documents. This part includes basic information, such as how to apply a paragraph tag, but it also covers more advanced topics, such as how to create a paragraph tag and set up autonumbering. New users will want to read at least the first half of each chapter to learn about each feature; more advanced users will probably focus on the latter half of each chapter.

Part II includes the following chapters:

- Chapter 4, "Word-Processing Features," describes how to type text into FrameMaker. It also explains how to import text from other applications. Generally, FrameMaker users write directly in FrameMaker. This chapter will be helpful to new users who are not yet familiar with basic text manipulation in FrameMaker. For more advanced users, the importing section provides detailed information about how to import content from Microsoft Word files successfully.

- Chapter 5, "Formatting Text with Paragraph Tags," begins with an explanation of paragraph-level style sheets and how to apply them. It also provides a detailed explanation of how to create and modify paragraph tags.
- Chapter 6, "Formatting Text with Character Tags," shows you how to apply and create character-level style sheets. In FrameMaker, character-level and paragraph-level style sheets are stored in separate locations. Characters tags are used in several other features, such as cross-references and variables, to provide formatting; this chapter also explains those relationships.
- Chapter 7, "Understanding Table Design," explains how to create tables and modify their formatting. Like paragraphs, tables have style sheets, and this chapter describes how to set up table styles.
- Chapter 8, "Cross-References," describes how to create pointers from one section of a document to another. FrameMaker automatically maintains and updates these references as pagination in the document changes.
- Chapter 9, "Storing Content in Variables," details how to use variables to store and format bits of reused text, such as the title of a book or a product name. It also describes how to use system variables to automate running headers and footers, page numbers, and "continued" labels in tables.

Part III, Controlling Page Layout

The chapters in Part III describe managing blocks of text and positioning them on your pages. This part also includes discussions about importing graphics created in other applications and creating graphics in FrameMaker.

Part III includes the following chapters:

- Chapter 10, "Understanding Master Pages," explains how to set up master pages to determine the page layout in a file, and it shows how to apply and import page layout definitions.
- Chapter 11, "Understanding Text Flows," describes how to create and connect blocks of text, or text flows. This information is especially helpful for template designers, who need to understand how to position text blocks on a page and how text blocks are connected and disconnected.
- Chapter 12, "Importing Graphic Content," explains anchored frames, which serve as containers for most graphics. It also describes how to import graphics and rich media files from other applications.
- Chapter 13, "FrameMaker's Graphics Tools," describes how to use FrameMaker's built-in graphics tools to create art.

Part IV, Building Books

You can create a book file to hold a collection of files that make up a larger document. Among these files, you can include automated tables of contents and index files, which are explained in this part.

Part IV includes the following chapters:

- Chapter 14, "Setting Up Book Files," describes how to set up and modify book files. It explains how to control chapter, page, and other numbering from the book and how to perform global (bookwide) updates on your content.
- Chapter 15, "Creating Tables of Contents," explains how to choose items for inclusion in a table of contents and how to format those items.
- Chapter 16, "Creating Indexes," explains how to create the markers that become index entries and how to format the generated index.
- Chapter 17, "Creating Other Generated Files," describes some of the less well-known generated files. You can, for example, create a list of fonts used in a document, or a list of imported graphics. Several variations on the standard index are also available.

Part V, Creating Output

In Part V, you learn how to create print, PDF, and online formats, and you learn about managing color.

Part V includes the following chapters:

- Chapter 18, "Print and PDF Output," provides detailed information about printing FrameMaker files and creating PDF files. It explains how to configure your system for successful PostScript printing and provides some information about Acrobat Distiller settings.
- Chapter 19, "Producing Online Output," describes how to use FrameMaker's rudimentary built-in HTML and XML converters, and it also describes the tools and processes for using third-party tools to create robust HTML and online help from unstructured FrameMaker. (If you need to produce full-blown XML, you need structured FrameMaker.)
- Chapter 20, "Color Output," explains how FrameMaker handles color output and describes how to set up colors in your document.

Part VI, Advanced Techniques

Part VI covers a variety of advanced topics, including template design, conditional text, hypertext, and WebDAV use with FrameMaker.

Part VI includes the following chapters:

- Chapter 21, "Setting Up Conditional Text," explains how to create two (or more) versions of a document in a single file. The conditional text feature is an important part of most single-sourcing environments.
- Chapter 22, "Creating Interactive Content with Hypertext," describes how to link documents, create popups, and insert hotspots into graphics with hypertext commands. Many hypertext commands are translated when you convert to HTML or PDF output.
- Chapter 23, "Writing Equations," tells you how to create and format equations in your documents.
- Chapter 24, "Maker Interchange Format," explains Maker Interchange Format (MIF), which is a text-based markup language that describes FrameMaker files. MIF files can be useful for global changes that aren't easily implemented through the FrameMaker interface. It's also widely used as an intermediate format when converting to and from FrameMaker format. FrameMaker files saved back to MIF 7 format can be opened in earlier versions of FrameMaker.
- Chapter 25, "Creating Modules with Text Insets," provides information about FrameMaker's text importing feature. You can create small text fragments and import them into larger documents to create modular documentation.
- Chapter 26, "Templates," pulls together information about many different features. It describes interactions among different components and provides some tips for designing useful templates.
- Chapter 27, "Sharing and Managing Files Using WebDAV," describes FrameMaker's support for version control and content management through WebDAV. WebDAV software (www.webdav.org) runs on any web server and is accessed via http protocol, so you can store files anywhere and access them over the Internet. This allows you to set up a version control system for authors in many different locations. The "DAV" in WebDAV actually stands for "Distributed Authoring and Versioning."

Part VII, Appendixes

The following appendixes are included:

- Appendix A, "Resources," offers a list of FrameMaker-related resources, including a list of utilities.
- Appendix B, "Building Blocks," provides a comprehensive lists of the building blocks you use to create tags and formats in FrameMaker.
- Appendix C, "Customizing maker.ini," describes the file where FrameMaker settings are stored and some settings you may want to modify.

Conventions Used in This Book

Some of the text in this book uses special formatting to help indicate emphasis or keystrokes. The text conventions as are follows:

Convention	Example	Meaning
SMALL CAPS	■ press the TAB key ⋆ ESC O P D ⋆ ESC SHIFT-F L K	Indicates keystrokes. If a keyboard shortcut (such as ESC O P D) contains no hyphens, press each key individually. When keys are joined by hyphens, press the joined keys at the same time; for example, SHIFT-F means to type a capital letter F.
Italics	*single sourcing*	Indicates a defined term, a book title, a placeholder, or text that requires emphasis.
Bold	if you type **2**	Indicates text you type or terms that are being defined in a list.
Courier	`<$paratext>`	Indicates building block strings or output (for example, Maker Interchange Format output).
Arrow (➤)	File ➤ Open	Indicates selecting a menu and menu choice (select the File menu, then select the Open menu choice).

Mistakes Were Made...

We've tried to make this book as accurate as possible. However, there's the possibility that we were, well, wrong about something. Some features in FrameMaker may have changed (or bugs may have been fixed) since this book was published, too. For changes and errata, visit:

www.scriptorium.com/books/fm8

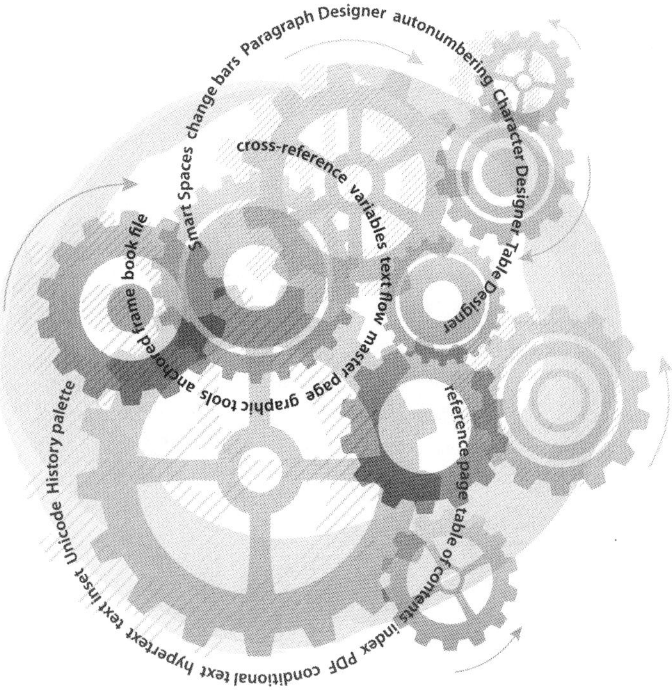

PART I

Getting Started with FrameMaker

CHAPTER 1

Why FrameMaker?

Adobe FrameMaker is the workhorse that technical communicators depend on year after year. FrameMaker is intended for creating complex documents, especially materials full of technical information, such as:

- Technical documentation—user guides, installation guides, system administration guides, reference guides, and training materials
- Dissertations and other long academic publications
- Nonfiction books, especially third-party documentation (including this book!)
- Legal and financial documents, such as prospectuses

If you're responsible for creating these and similar long, technical documents, your software requirements are quite different from someone who produces short, graphics-intensive documents such as brochures, newsletters, or annual reports. For technical publishing, stability and reliability are critical, especially as documents get longer. Having a document crash because it exceeds 100 pages or contains too many graphics or cross-references is unacceptable, especially in an environment where books of 200 or 2,000 pages are quite common. FrameMaker provides a stable, reliable environment in which to create and manage these types of documents.

Most likely, though, you're hoping for something more than an application that doesn't crash too often. FrameMaker includes many features that are important for anyone working with long documents in a graphical what-you-see-is-what-you-get (WYSIWYG) environment, shown in Figure 1-1.

Highlights of FrameMaker's strengths include the following:

- **Consistent, repeatable, and maintainable formatting.** FrameMaker's templates make it possible to create different documents with the same look and feel. You use template components to ensure that formatting is consistent from one document to another, and you can quickly copy updates from file to file. Instead of hours of manual reformatting, you apply the template across the document library, and FrameMaker changes formatting and repaginates the documents as necessary.
- **Complex document management.** Equations, variables for text, conditional text, and many other features help you create and maintain complex documents. Imported graphics are updated automatically when you change the referenced file.
- **Stability.** FrameMaker is a stable, reliable application. It does not spontaneously repaginate documents when you change print drivers or perform any of those other maneuvers that can be so frustrating in other applications.

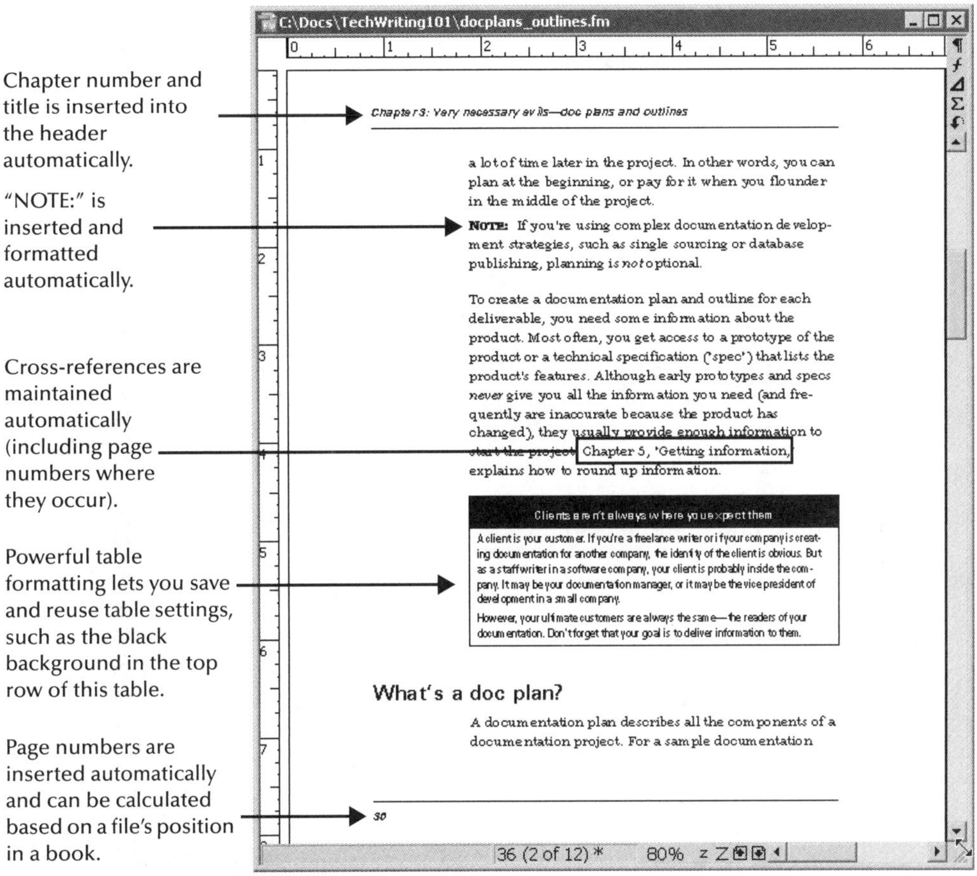

Figure 1-1. A typical page in FrameMaker

- **Long-document management.** FrameMaker provides very strong support for managing pagination, tables of contents, and indexes in books. This lets you process multivolume books, dozens of chapters, and thousands of pages without having to worry about the accuracy of volume, chapter, and page numbering. To rearrange the order of chapters in a book, you drag and drop the files to their new locations and then update the book. FrameMaker automatically changes the pagination to reflect the new order, changes the chapter numbers as necessary, and updates the table of contents and index.

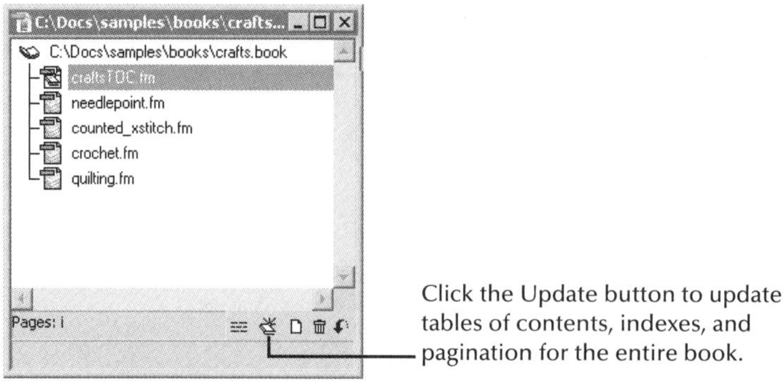

- **Cross-media publishing.** FrameMaker can serve as the engine or as a component of a very sophisticated publishing system, in which you create print, Portable Document Format (PDF), Extensible Markup Language (XML), Hypertext Markup Language (HTML), and various help formats from a single set of documents. This *single-source* publishing makes it possible to write content once and then publish information in several different media.

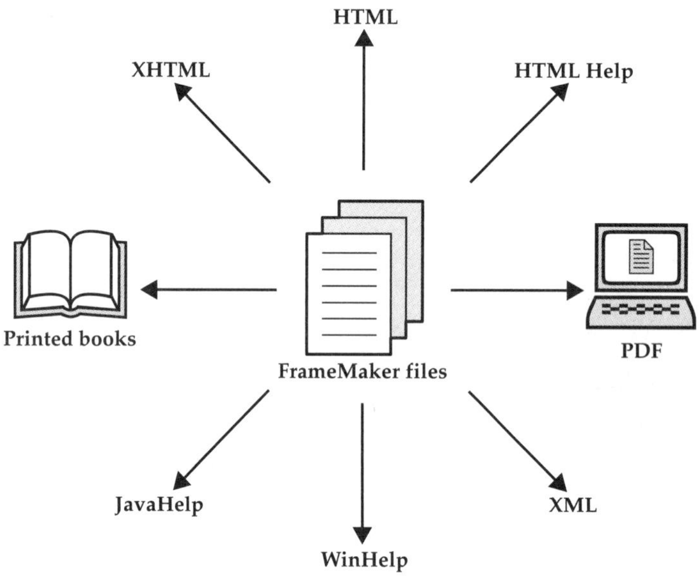

NOTE Structured FrameMaker is better for some of these outputs, especially XML.

- **Change management.** FrameMaker supports WebDAV, which lets you set up a version control system on a web server. Given a library of very large books, often with multiple authors collaborating on a single document, change management becomes a critical issue.

- **Cross-platform software.** FrameMaker is available for the Windows and UNIX platforms. Files are cross-platform compatible; for example, you can develop a file in FrameMaker for UNIX and open it in FrameMaker for Windows. No conversion is required, and FrameMaker can substitute for any unavailable fonts temporarily or permanently. The user interface is almost identical on the two platforms, so after you learn how to use FrameMaker for one platform, you can use it on the other. Furthermore, there is a full set of keyboard shortcuts available that works on both platforms.

NOTE This book provides information and instructions for the Windows platform; the examples shown are from Windows XP and Vista.

You'll find many superficial similarities between FrameMaker's feature set and other desktop publishing applications. Only FrameMaker, however, is *designed* for long-document publishing; its document-management features are robust and reliable. In some other applications, those features seem like afterthoughts and don't always work as they should. Highlights of FrameMaker's document-management features include the following:

- **Style sheets.** Most word processors and desktop publishing packages provide style sheets for paragraph formatting, but FrameMaker takes this concept much farther. A FrameMaker file includes style sheets for paragraphs, characters, tables, cross-references, variables, master pages, and several other items. These style sheets, or *tags,* are stored in catalogs, which can be imported from one file to another.
- **Books.** A book is a collection of files (chapters) in a particular sequence. FrameMaker manages the pagination and chapter numbering as information is added to and deleted from the book.
- **Cross-references.** Using cross-references, you create a pointer from one part of the book to another (for example, *see "Widgets" on page 13*). FrameMaker automatically updates the page numbers and heading information when content changes. In PDF and HTML, cross-references are preserved as hyperlinks.
- **Tables of contents.** You can automatically generate a list of major topics in the document. After making changes to a document, updating the table of contents automatically updates topic lists and page references.
- **Indexes.** You identify which terms to index by inserting markers in the documents. After that, the index is generated, sorted, and grouped automatically.

- **Tables.** Table support is very strong and includes the ability to save named table formats with settings for lines and shading.

Table 1-1. Being wired

Not wired	*Somewhat wired*	*Overly wired*
Computer	Computer	Computer
Modem	Broadband	Broadband, router, and wireless in-home network
Writes letters	Sends email	Sends email from more than four email accounts per day

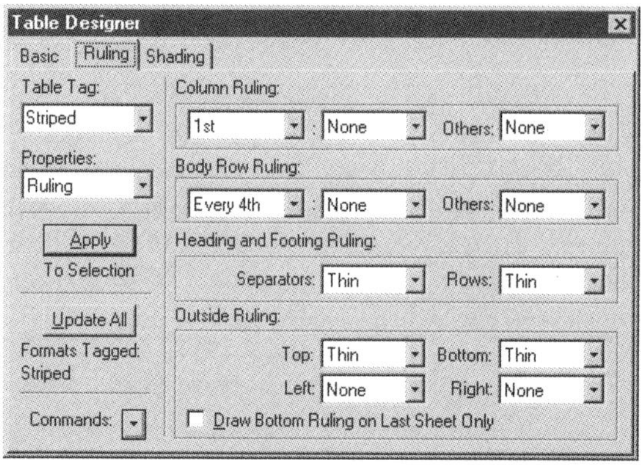

- **Graphics.** FrameMaker includes a solid set of graphic tools for creating graphics. You can also import external graphics and embed or link them into the document. Linked graphics are automatically updated in the FrameMaker file when the graphic changes.
- **Conditional text.** You can use conditional text to identify information that belongs to a specific version of a document (for example, instructor-only material in a training guide). You can then create document versions that include or exclude the tagged material. Conditional text is an important component of any single-sourcing strategy because it lets you identify information that should be excluded from some output (most commonly, you have "print-only" and "online-only" content).
- **Variables.** These are useful for items that can change frequently. For example, you can create a variable called ProductName and use it throughout the document wherever the product name is needed. If the product name changes, you change the value of the variable, which automatically changes every occurrence of the variable throughout the document.
- **Modular text.** You can create small files that contain chunks of content and then assemble the chunks into larger documents. Modular text lets you reuse chunks in different documents and maintain the information for both documents in a single file.

- **Equations.** FrameMaker includes an equation editor, which lets you create complex mathematical expressions.
- **Templates.** FrameMaker lets you save named style sheets as a template. In most desktop publishing applications, templates are limited to paragraph style sheets and master pages, but in FrameMaker, template items include paragraph tags, character tags (for formatting inside paragraphs, such as italics), tables, master pages (page layouts), cross-reference formats, variable names and definitions, conditional text tag names, custom elements for equations, and more.

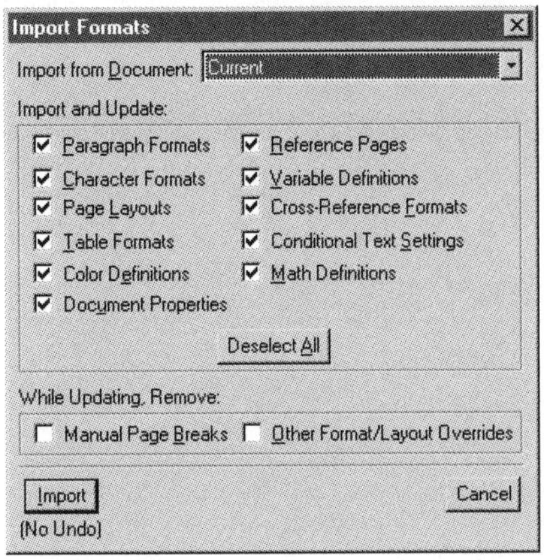

It's possible to use FrameMaker to create highly designed documents, such as annual reports and newsletters, where the layout changes on every page, and FrameMaker is also capable of handling full-color publications. However, FrameMaker's document-management features are much more useful in enforcing consistency across hundreds (or thousands) of pages.

FrameMaker is very good at...	FrameMaker isn't ideal for...
■ Enforcing consistency throughout documents ■ Handling long documents ■ Providing stability ■ Managing books, tables of contents, and indexes ■ Single sourcing/converting to other formats ■ Formatting tables ■ Importing and maintaining graphics ■ Creating graphics ■ Providing cross-platform compatibility	■ Performing word processing easily ■ Working in an environment with users who don't believe in using or templates in their documents ■ Creating artistic typography ■ Setting up complex, single-use layouts

FrameMaker won't solve all of your problems, but if you're looking for a reliable, industrial-strength publishing tool that produces consistent output, it is the software for you.

CHAPTER 2

Establishing a Workflow in FrameMaker

Setting up a publishing workflow requires you to organize the publishing process (which many have compared to the inner workings of a sausage factory—you *really* don't want to know the details) into discrete tasks. Fortunately, the high-level process is fairly standard:

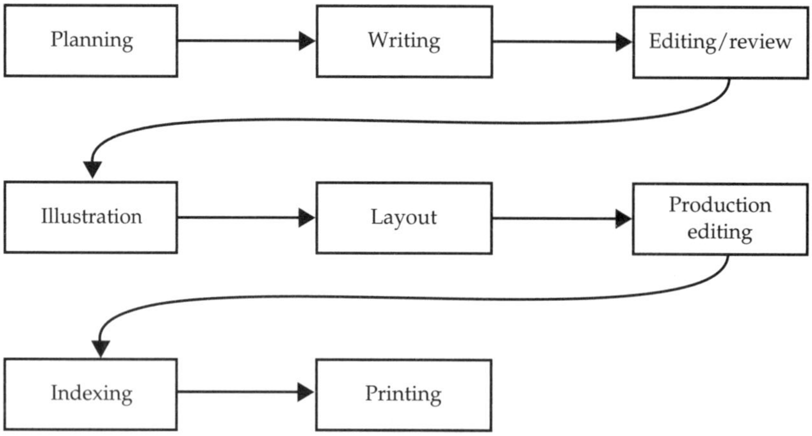

In some publishing workflows, these tasks are performed by different people using different tools. For example, the initial authoring is done in a word processor, and information is transferred from a word processor into a desktop publishing tool for formatting. Illustration is done in a separate graphics program. The index may be created in the desktop publishing tool ("embedded") or as a stand-alone file:

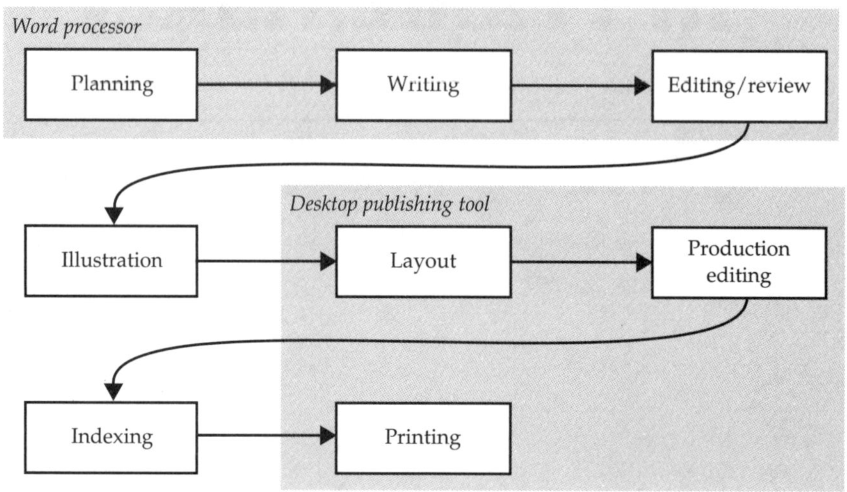

FrameMaker eliminates the need for a separate authoring tool by providing a comprehensive set of word processing tools. Most formatting is handled by applying paragraph styles, which writers can master fairly easily. Creating content directly in FrameMaker eliminates the layout step from your workflow because layout is done automatically as the author creates information. A production editor can review the files to finalize pagination, but the vast majority of the layout work is done by the time the file reaches the production stage.

As authors create information, they can add illustrations or other graphic objects. These might be created by a graphic artist, but there's no need to wait until after the manuscript review to insert them. This makes it possible for editors and reviewers to see text and graphics on the same page, just as the reader will see them in the final printed version.

NOTE It's possible to create content in an external word processor and then import information into FrameMaker, but the time and effort required to convert content makes it a less efficient option than doing all the development in FrameMaker.

The following illustration shows a typical FrameMaker-based workflow:

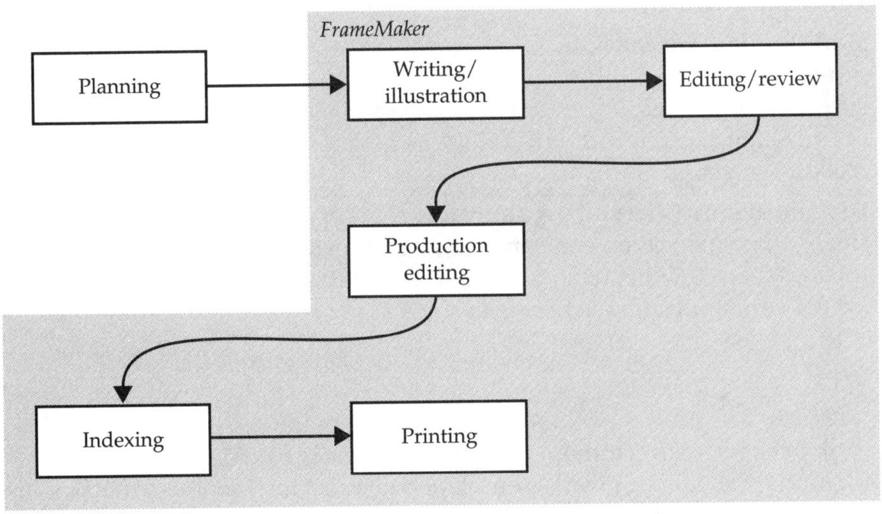

Planning

Given a tight deadline and limited resources, planning is often the first thing to go. However, a minimal amount of time invested at the beginning of the project will make the whole project much more efficient. For short, simple documents, the only thing required in planning might be to create a document template (or identify an existing template that will be used). There are three items that should be created during planning:

- Document templates (if they do not exist already)
- Document outline
- Documentation plan, which includes resources required, a preliminary schedule, a high-level description of the document to be created, and related project-management information

More complex projects make planning more critical—failing to address issues before development begins invariably results in more work (and rework) later. When the following factors are present in a project, even more up-front planning is required:

- **Cross-media publishing/single sourcing.** If the content being developed needs to be delivered in several different media (print, online, and so on), detailed planning is required to analyze the documents and map out how information is presented in each medium.
- **Complex document libraries.** If your document library will contain thousands (as opposed to hundreds) of pages of content, planning helps you to avoid redundancy and ensures that all needed topics are covered.
- **Multiple authors.** If multiple authors are working on different books (or portions of the same book), you need to coordinate to make sure that the finished product looks like a single book and not a collection of disjointed sections with different voices.
- **Modular documentation.** Setting up documents with "chunks" of content lets you reuse information instead of writing multiple versions of the same information. It does, however, require careful planning of the document organization, storage and retrieval of the modules, and authoring to ensure that modules are consistent.
- **Distributed or "virtual" workgroup.** A group of authors and editors in a single physical location can communicate informally (by shouting over cubicle walls). When content creators are in different locations all over the world, more formal communication is necessary.

Writing

In a FrameMaker workflow, authors write in FrameMaker, not in a separate word processor. Authors should be given a template and some instructions on how to use it. They should also be able to use certain FrameMaker features, such as cross-references, variables, and markers.

To ensure that writers can succeed in a new FrameMaker environment, it's important to provide some information about the new environment. With its emphasis on organization, templates, and tagging, FrameMaker is quite different from other word processor or desktop publishing tools. Authors must understand why tagging is so critical.

Some writers believe, "I'm a writer, not a publisher." Typically, this translates into disinterest or outright hostility toward templates and formatting rules. In a FrameMaker workflow, following the template is a requirement. Writers who cannot or will not follow templates create documents that will probably print adequately (because they look correct on screen), but the document cannot be reused or processed to produce other output in a single-sourcing environment. If your group includes such a writer, your options are as follows:

- **Education.** Explain to the writer why following the template is necessary. Show what happens when the template is not followed and how this completely destroys the automated workflow and the ability to produce other formats (such as HTML, XML, or help files) from the FrameMaker files.
- **Persuasion/coercion.** Ensure that there are consequences for not following the template. This approach could include requiring the writer to fix any errors that occur in the final output. Keep in mind, though, that a software-averse writer might not have the skills to correct problems, so additional training might be needed.
- **Cleaning up.** As a last resort, evaluate the writer's value to the organization. Is this person a particularly talented writer with specific knowledge that no one else shares? In that case, it might be worthwhile to assign a person to clean up the writer's files so that they conform to the template.

CAUTION It's been our experience that up to 10 percent of the writers moving from a word processing environment to a single-sourcing workflow will be unwilling or unable to follow strict template rules.

Illustration

Some authors create their own illustrations and other graphic objects, but many work with a graphic artist or technical illustrator. FrameMaker provides a basic set of graphic tools, which are adequate for simple line art or small flowcharts. To create more complex graphics, use a dedicated graphic package (such as Illustrator or Visio) and then import the graphic into FrameMaker. FrameMaker supports a wide variety of graphic formats, including PDF, EPS, TIFF, PNG, and GIF. When importing graphics, you can either create a link to the graphic (import by reference) or embed the graphic in the FrameMaker file (copying into the document). Although most organizations use the import-by-reference feature, each has advantages and disadvantages. These are discussed in detail in "Importing a Graphic" on page 308.

Editing/Reviewing

Instead of distributing FrameMaker files, which would require the reviewers to have access to FrameMaker, most organizations generate PDF files from the FrameMaker source files and use the PDF files for review. Reviewers can mark up changes on a paper copy or use Acrobat's online annotation tools. For an online review, one person initiates the review from Adobe Acrobat Professional or 3D, and the reviewers can mark up the file using the free Adobe Reader.

The inability for reviewers to edit files directly is a double-edged sword. Some reviewers prefer to go into the source files and make changes, but restricting access to these files makes it easier for authors to keep track of changes and control the information in the files. Furthermore, correcting their own errors makes it more likely that authors will learn from their mistakes and improve their writing over time.

Finally, there is the issue of reviewer accuracy. More than one well-intentioned reviewer has "corrected" information by sprinkling commas at random throughout a document. Using PDF files prevents these mishaps.

Technical editing and copy editing can be done directly in the FrameMaker files, perhaps with track text edits or change bars turned on. Paper copies or online Acrobat reviews provide much better audit trails for tracking changes.

Production Editing

During the production edit, the document is checked to ensure that each page is copyfitted; that is, the pages are filled with consistent amounts of text and graphics. Production editors also look for awkward line and page breaks, and they verify that headers and footers, cross-references, tables of contents and indexes, and front and back matter are set up correctly. Because FrameMaker automates many of these tasks, the main task of the production editor is to verify that the template was applied correctly—overrides to template formatting often cause problems elsewhere. For example, applying the wrong paragraph tag to a heading causes that heading to disappear from the table of contents.

Indexing

When indexing a book, there are two workflow options:

- **Embedded indexing.** The index is generated from markers that are inserted (embedded) into the document files.
- **Stand-alone indexing.** The index is generated in dedicated indexing software, and the resulting text is inserted into the document.

If you plan to make frequent, incremental updates to the content, creating an embedded index is probably the right choice because you can reuse markers and reduce the amount of work required to update the index. If the book is a one-time project, you might want to create a stand-alone index, especially if you plan to use a freelance indexer. In technical writing groups, embedded indexes are the standard; in publishing environments, stand-alone indexes are more common. Table 2-1 lists the advantages and disadvantages of each approach.

Printing

You can print documents from FrameMaker directly to a printer (such as your office laser printer), but most professional output is done by creating a PDF file, which is sent to a print vendor. In most cases, there's no need to give the print vendor your FrameMaker source files.

Printing and other outputs are described in detail in Part V, "Creating Output."

Embedded	Stand-Alone
Pro ■ Page numbers are automatically updated when content moves, including text expansion during translation. ■ You can reuse index markers when a document is revised, which can make revisions much faster. ■ Using the built-in indexing feature eliminates the cost of a separate tool. ■ Easier to learn than stand-alone indexing software.	**Pro** ■ Faster development of the index. ■ Powerful editing capabilities. You can make changes directly in the index and make global changes quickly. ■ Sort options are adequate and easy to use. ■ Cross-references (see and see also) are verified automatically. ■ Different view options are available for the index: standard alphabetical order, primary headings only, page order, chronological order (the order in which you created the index entries), and entries that contain specific keywords only.
Con ■ Creating markers is time consuming. ■ The indexer must have access to source files. ■ Editing the index is difficult and tedious. Global changes are very time consuming. ■ You cannot change the index perspective; only an alphabetical list is available. ■ Cross-references in the index (see and see also references) are not verified. ■ Sort options are limited.	**Con** ■ The document must be very close to finished before it can be indexed. ■ The indexer must type in all the page numbers, so they are hard-coded in the index. Hand-typed page numbers are subject to human error. ■ Dedicated software is expensive and has a significant learning curve. ■ Updated or translated documents usually have to be reindexed from scratch.

Thanks to Dick Evans of Infodex Indexing Services (infodex@mindspring.com) for his assistance in creating this list.

Table 2-1. Comparing Embedded and Stand-Alone Indexing

Single Sourcing

The term *single sourcing* refers to creating multiple outputs (for example, print, PDF files, and online help) or multiple documents (for example, a user's guide and an administrator's guide) from one set of files. Single-sourcing implementation can be simple; for example, a FrameMaker file that is both printed and converted to PDF. A more complex setup might involve a content repository from which you extract relevant information by keyword searches and then assemble and format the information for print or online help.

The basic premise of single sourcing is that you "write once, publish many." Because you write content once and then use automated tools to process the information for different output media, you save time and money.

NOTE Adobe defines multichannel publishing as "publishing from a single source to print, PDF, HTML, XML, and more." Many portions of their web site describe how tools, including FrameMaker, fit into multichannel publishing solutions.

For a single-sourcing project, the planning stage is absolutely essential. Each piece of content can be presented differently in each medium, and understanding these relationships before beginning the writing process is critical. To ensure that single sourcing succeeds, content must conform to templates—overrides and "custom" formatting are usually lost when converting from one format to another.

Aside from the increased emphasis on planning and standards, workflow is modified because additional output is generated in the last stage of the project. A number of FrameMaker add-on tools are available that convert your source files into other output media. For more information, see "Creating PDF Files" on page 467 and "Third-Party Tools for Online Output" on page 480.

NOTE If you want to produce XML, use structured FrameMaker. For more information, refer to *Publishing Fundamentals: Structured FrameMaker 8*.

Evaluating Workflow Options

Before embarking on a single-sourcing project, it can be helpful to review the pros and cons of different workflow options. If you need to deliver the same information in different media (for example, procedures in both a user's guide and in the online help), single sourcing will probably be the most efficient approach, but there are other options.

Parallel Development

In a parallel development process, all deliverables are created simultaneously. For example, one writer might create a user's guide in FrameMaker while another writer creates online help in a help authoring tool and yet another creates HTML in a web development tool.

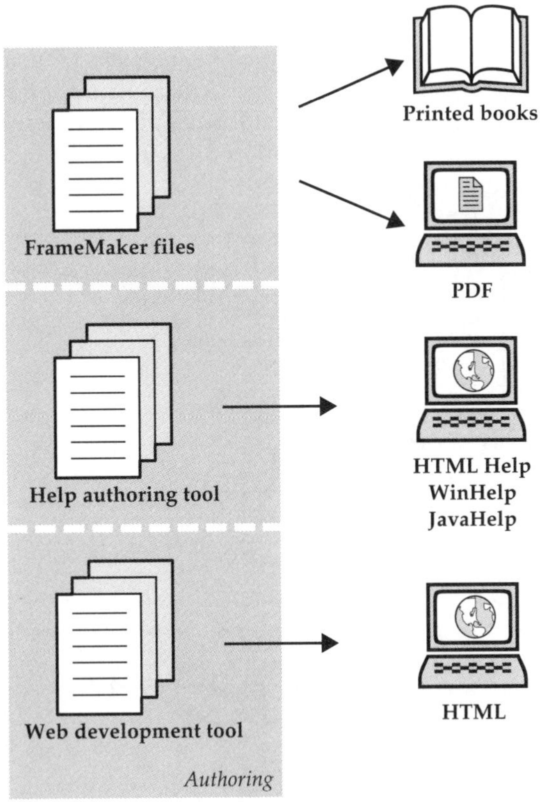

Parallel development has a few advantages:

- All deliverables are ready at the same time.
- Writers can specialize in print or online work and optimize the information for each deliverable.

Parallel development can be a good choice if the information in the deliverables is different. If, however, there is content overlap among the deliverables, there are a number of problems with this workflow:

- Because the same information is being created more than once, the workflow is very labor-intensive.
- Maintenance is problematic, and differences in terminology or even outright contradictions often creep into the documents. This confuses the readers.
- Transferring information from one tool to another is time consuming. Formatting is often lost, so you spend a lot of time cleaning up after conversion.

Parallel development makes sense when the information in the print and the online help does not overlap. But when there is significant overlap, parallel development is time consuming and inefficient.

Serial Development

Serial development could be considered a type of single sourcing. You write the information once and then convert it from one format to another. However, serial development typically involves copying the information from one format (for example, the print development tool) to another format (the help authoring tool) and then reworking the information to add formatting.

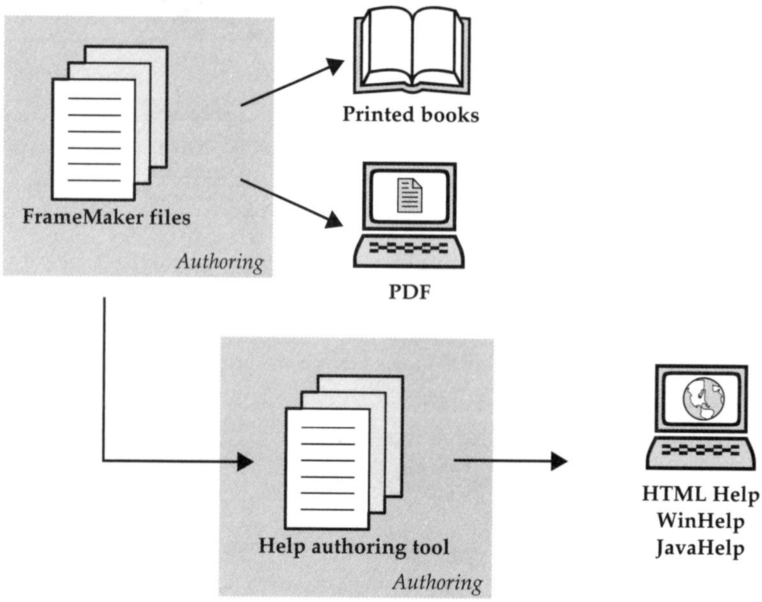

You could also create the help first and then move the information to FrameMaker to create the print and PDF versions.

Serial development has some advantages:

- Because the information is written once, information is consistent across all deliverables.
- The second deliverable is not created until the first deliverable is completed, so the information is finalized.
- Maintenance is simplified because you only convert once per release and do not have to maintain two sets of documentation.
- One writer can create the print output and then the help, so it's less expensive than having two writers working in parallel.

But there are some serious disadvantages:

- Serial development means that one deliverable will lag significantly behind the other. For example, the printed version might be ready three or four weeks before the online help. This leads to scheduling problems before a release because you have to build in several weeks for the conversion and reformatting process.

- Often, the print tool and the online help tool do not work well together, so formatting is lost when you transfer information from one tool to the other. The cleanup that's done in the second version must be repeated for each release (unless you keep the files and only put in the changes, in which case you've switched to a parallel development process).

Serial development can be viable if you need to transfer only a small amount of content from one deliverable to another. But large-scale manual conversion is incredibly tedious, and better options are available.

Modular Development

Single sourcing often focuses on creating multiple deliverables in different media, such as print and online help, from a single set of files. Modular development has a slightly different emphasis—creating multiple deliverables in the same medium and reusing overlapping content. For example, if two products share several features, it would be helpful to write about those features only once and reuse the information in both books. Modular development lets you create information that both products share and then reuse that information as needed.

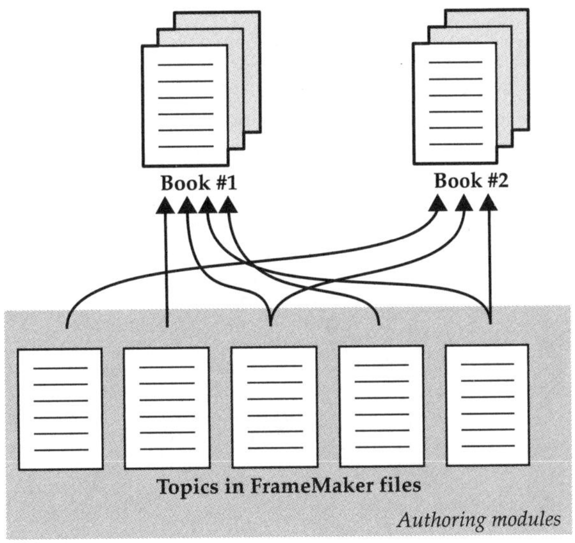

Authoring modules

To implement modular development in FrameMaker, you typically use text insets, which are discussed in Chapter 25, "Creating Modules with Text Insets." Alternatively, you might consider creating structured documents. For more information about modular documentation and structured documents, refer to *Publishing Fundamentals: Structured FrameMaker 8*.

When you reuse modules, you create multiple deliverables (books) from a single set of source files, but modular development does not necessarily include delivery of information in multiple media. Many (but not all) technical publishers use the term single sourcing only when they are producing different media from a single set of source files.

Database Publishing

Database publishing is used most often for directories or other highly structured content. The information that needs to be published is already stored as records in a database, so you extract information from the database, tag it as appropriate to format it, and create a FrameMaker file. Many databases are now XML-based, and you can extract XML-tagged information to use within FrameMaker. Also, a number of third-party applications, such as Miramo and PatternStream, can create FrameMaker or MIF files from database content.

Database publishing is best suited for working with highly structured information that's already in a database. Information that's output in a particular sequence (for example, alphabetical order for a list of doctors) works well in this environment. Documents that have a well-defined sequence (for example, a programmer's reference with an alphabetical list of commands) can also work well. Less regimented documents, such as user's guides, tutorials, and the like, do not work well in database publishing.

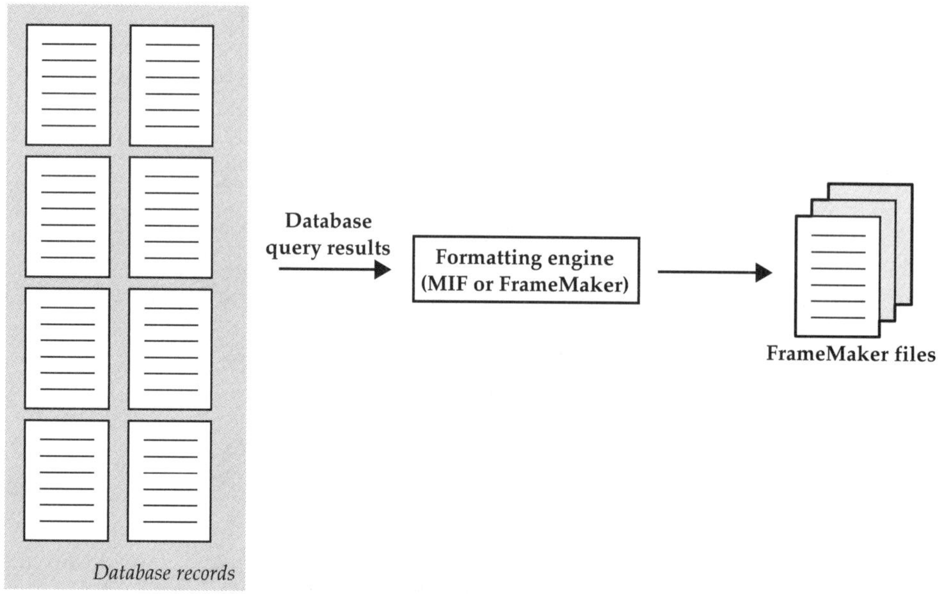

Traditionally, the database serves as the content repository, so you make changes to the information only in the database. The generated FrameMaker files might need formatting tweaks, but any changes you make in them are lost the next time you export from the database.

Single-Sourcing Workflows

If you are required to deliver the same content in multiple media, you should consider a single-sourcing approach. In this environment, FrameMaker can be used either as an authoring tool and content repository or solely as a print and PDF creation engine.

If you plan to use FrameMaker for authoring, you can export to other formats either via XML or by using third-party tools to convert from FrameMaker directly to the required format (such as HTML Help). FrameMaker also provides a built-in HTML converter, but it is appropriate only for very basic conversions of short documents.

NOTE If you want to produce XML, use structured FrameMaker. Refer to *Publishing Fundamentals: Structured FrameMaker 8*.

Creating HTML and Help with Third-Party Tools

Some very good third-party tools are available to create HTML and various help formats (JavaHelp, WinHelp, HTML Help, and so on) from FrameMaker files. These tools vary considerably in terms of their intent (stand-alone help authoring versus large-scale conversion), interface, pricing, and licensing. For some information, see "Third-Party Tools for Online Output" on page 480.

The following diagram shows a workflow that incorporates a third-party tool.

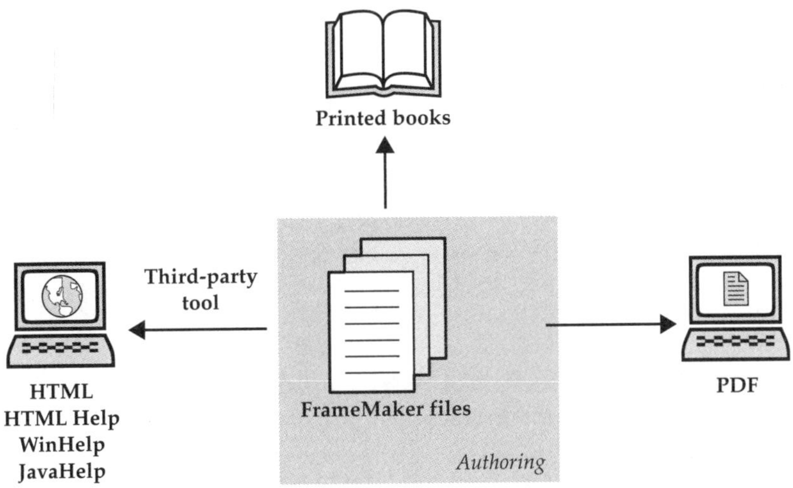

Structured Authoring and Single Sourcing

Structured authoring, which requires structured FrameMaker, provides different approaches to single sourcing. In one scenario, you import and export XML ("round-tripping"). This lets you author content either in FrameMaker or in XML. From the

FrameMaker files, you can produce printed books and PDF files. From the XML files, you can use Extensible Stylesheet Language Transform (XSLT) files to process the XML and produce HTML and online help formats.

In a second scenario, instead of using FrameMaker files as your content repository, you store information in XML. You can then open files in FrameMaker, edit them, and then save them back to XML. You could also use XML editors to modify the XML files and pull information into FrameMaker when you need to print or create a PDF file. In the latter case, you use FrameMaker as a print rendering engine, not as a content-development tool.

For an overview of structured authoring, see the following sections.

Structured FrameMaker In versions previous to FrameMaker 7, the structured and unstructured versions of FrameMaker were sold separately. FrameMaker+SGML (and its predecessor, FrameBuilder) are equivalent to structured FrameMaker, and unstructured FrameMaker is "regular" FrameMaker in these earlier versions. In versions 7 and 8, both unstructured and structured FrameMaker are delivered in a single product.

FrameMaker gives you the choice of working in a structured or unstructured authoring environment. (This book is for people using the unstructured FrameMaker interface.) Unstructured authoring means that you use paragraph and character tags to control formatting. With structured authoring, you define an allowable structure for your document, and FrameMaker automatically handles formatting based on the structure. In the structured authoring environment, you can create both structured and unstructured documents. In unstructured FrameMaker, though, you can create only unstructured documents.

Because you can enforce structure rules, structured FrameMaker gives a template designer more control over the author's workflow. However, setting up a structured FrameMaker template is significantly more challenging and more time consuming than creating an unstructured FrameMaker template. In the unstructured version, the template designer creates paragraph tags and other components that control the appearance of the document. For the structured version, the template designer must create a document that describes the structure of the document and then attach formatting information to each element in the structure.

Choosing Between Structured and Unstructured Workflows All of the features available in unstructured FrameMaker are also present in structured FrameMaker, but structured FrameMaker provides additional capabilities. There are some advantages and disadvantages to each type of document. Table 2-2 summarizes the differences between structured and unstructured FrameMaker.

Unstructured	Structured
Authoring	
Getting started in unstructured FrameMaker is faster and easier than working in structured FrameMaker. Unstructured documents are less restrictive for authors than structured documents, but document authors must remember to follow certain formatting rules (for example, "a heading must be followed by a lead-in paragraph"). Authors must apply paragraph tags and often use tags with similar names, such as Note, TableNote, and NoteContinued. Authors must learn which paragraph tag to use in which context.	The template enforces structuring rules. Authors are guided through the available elements. Authors choose elements; the template controls what formatting is applied, sometimes applying different formatting to the same element based on the context of the element. The guidance that structured documents provide to authors becomes more and more important in larger workgroups. Structured FrameMaker is common in large organizations, especially in the aerospace and telecommunications industries and in government organizations.
Template design	
Creating templates is easier in unstructured FrameMaker because you do not have to set up structured templates.	Creating structured document templates is quite challenging.
Single-source publishing	
You can export unstructured documents to other formats through a number of third-party tools.	You can publish to other formats through third-party tools, or use the SGML/XML conversion features and process that output.
Learning curve	
Moderate for document authors; high for template designers.	Low to moderate for document authors; very high for template designers.
Workflow	
Works well in small groups; more difficult to manage in large groups.	Requires additional up-front planning, but works well for large groups.

Table 2-2. Structured versus Unstructured FrameMaker

Unstructured	Structured
XML conversion	
Export only. No element hierarchy.	Import and export. Element hierarchy is preserved. If you need the ability to convert to and from XML, structured documents are a must.

Table 2-2. Structured versus Unstructured FrameMaker (Continued)

For detailed information about structured authoring, refer to *Publishing Fundamentals: Structured FrameMaker 8*.

Language Support

The user interface for FrameMaker is in several languages—English, French, German, or Japanese—but you can author content in many more languages. FrameMaker supports the Unicode text encoding standard, which is a character set that includes characters for all living languages. With Unicode support, elaborate workarounds are no longer necessary for authoring in Cyrillic languages, such as Russian.You can use Unicode content in document text and in all features including find/change, catalog tags, markers, and so on. You can import Unicode content from other applications and include Unicode content in PDF files and other FrameMaker outputs.

NOTE For details about the Unicode text encoding standard, go to www.unicode.org.

FrameMaker's Unicode support has limitations:

- No support for right-to-left languages such as Arabic.
- No support for complex scripts. For example, FrameMaker cannot support Thai, which uses different ligatures depending on which characters come before or follow after.

There are several things you must consider if you are going to author in multiple languages in FrameMaker:

- **Fonts.** When working with content in multiple languages, you need to install fonts for those specific languages or a Unicode font that includes all the characters you need. If you try to work with a language when you don't have a font installed to display that text or don't have the correct font applied to the text, the characters are replaced with placeholders such as question marks or gray boxes.

TIP Question marks, gray boxes, or incorrect glyphs may also be displayed, depending on the printer you have selected. To avoid the problem, select Adobe PDF in FrameMaker's print setup.

- **A way to enter text.** To type Unicode content, you can copy and paste from the Windows Character Map utility (or any from any Unicode application, including Microsoft Word or FrameMaker). However, to enter any significant amount of text, you need to configure your system to use either a language-specific keyboard, and then you use that keyboard to enter characters, or an Input Method Editor (IME), which is software that lets you insert characters phonetically that aren't on the keyboard. (IMEs are primarily used for authoring in Korean, Japanese, and Chinese.)

  If the characters look wrong after you paste text from Microsoft Word, a browser, or other application, select Edit➤Paste Special and select Unicode Text. The text is pasted into FrameMaker and maintains all the Unicode characters from the original source.

TIP To have FrameMaker automatically paste as Unicode text instead of plain text, change the paste order in maker.ini. See "Setting Clipboard Pasting Order" on page 681.

- **Dictionaries.** FrameMaker installs a number of dictionaries for spell-checking and hyphenating. You can still author in languages that don't have a dictionary provided, but FrameMaker won't spell-check or hyphenate the text.

CHAPTER 3

Creating Your First Document

To start working, you start FrameMaker and either create a new document or open an existing document. After you do that, you can start learning how to get around in the FrameMaker interface. This chapter explains how to start FrameMaker, create documents, and open them.

Starting FrameMaker

A shortcut for FrameMaker is installed in the Start menu after installation. Assuming that you installed FrameMaker in the default location, select Start➤Programs (or All Programs)➤Adobe➤FrameMaker 8➤Adobe FrameMaker 8 to start the program.

The first time you start FrameMaker, you are prompted to register the product. Next, you are prompted to select an interface.

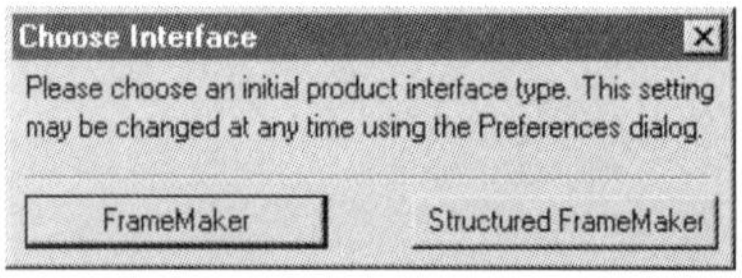

FrameMaker provides you with two operating modes: structured and unstructured. You can change this selection later if you need to.

Choose one of the following options:

- **FrameMaker** (unstructured): Starts the "vanilla," unstructured version of FrameMaker. Lets you work on unstructured documents without the structure features getting in the way. This book explains the unstructured interface.
- **Structured FrameMaker:** Starts the structured version of FrameMaker. Lets you create structured documents, import and export SGML and XML, and see the structure view. Refer to *Publishing Fundamentals: Structured FrameMaker 8.*

When you start FrameMaker, it does not automatically create a blank document. Instead, the Windows version displays the menu bar and no document. To begin working, you need to either create a new document or open an existing one.

Setting Up a New Document

When you create a new document, FrameMaker names the file Untitled1.fm (additional documents are named Untitled2.fm, Untitled3.fm, and so on). You can save the document with a more informative name.

There are several ways to create a new document:

- Exploring the standard templates, then choosing one of those templates
- Using a file as a template
- Creating a blank document
- Saving an existing file under a new name

Exploring the Standard Templates

For each of the default templates, FrameMaker includes a preview and a feature summary. This information helps you determine whether a particular template will meet your needs.

To examine the unstructured templates, follow these steps:

1. Select File➤New➤Document, press CTRL-N , or click the Document button on the Quick Access Bar. The New dialog box is displayed (Figure 3-1).

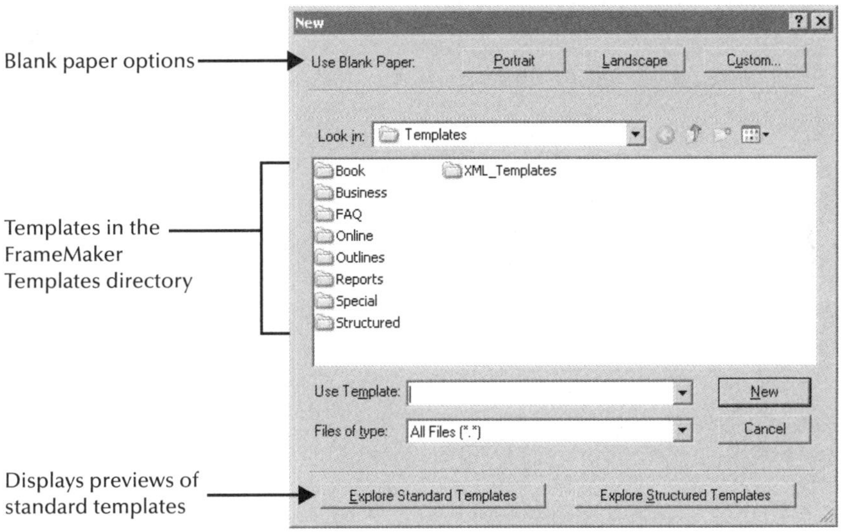

Figure 3-1. Creating a new document

2. Click the Explore Standard Templates button. A list of templates is displayed with previews.

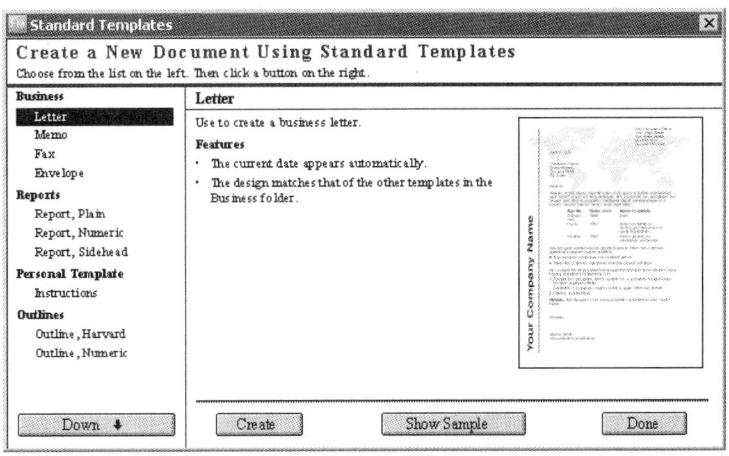

3. Click an item in the template list on the left to display a feature summary and preview for that template on the right. To see a sample document with placeholder text, click the Show Sample button.
4. To use a particular template, click the Create button. FrameMaker creates a new, untitled document by making a copy of the template file.

You can now save the document with an appropriate name and begin working.

Using a File as a Template

In addition to the standard templates, you can use any FrameMaker file as a template.

To use a file as a template, follow these steps:

1. Select File➤New➤Document, press CTRL-N , or click the New File button on the Quick Access Bar. The New dialog box is displayed (Figure 3-1 on page 31).
2. Select the template by doing one of the following:
   - To find a standard FrameMaker template, double-click a folder in the Look In window and then double-click the template. You can display a preview of FrameMaker's standard templates by clicking the Explore Standard Templates button.

TIP If you save a file in FrameMaker's template directory, that file will be displayed along with the standard FrameMaker templates. It will not, however, be listed when you explore templates.

   - To use another file as a template, navigate to the directory that contains the file and double-click the file.

   The new document is displayed.

When you create a new document from a template, FrameMaker makes a complete copy of the file. Any content in the original file is included in the new, untitled document. For documents that contain a lot of standard information (such as contracts), you can use this feature to your advantage.

Create a template file that includes standard information, perhaps with variables where information will change:

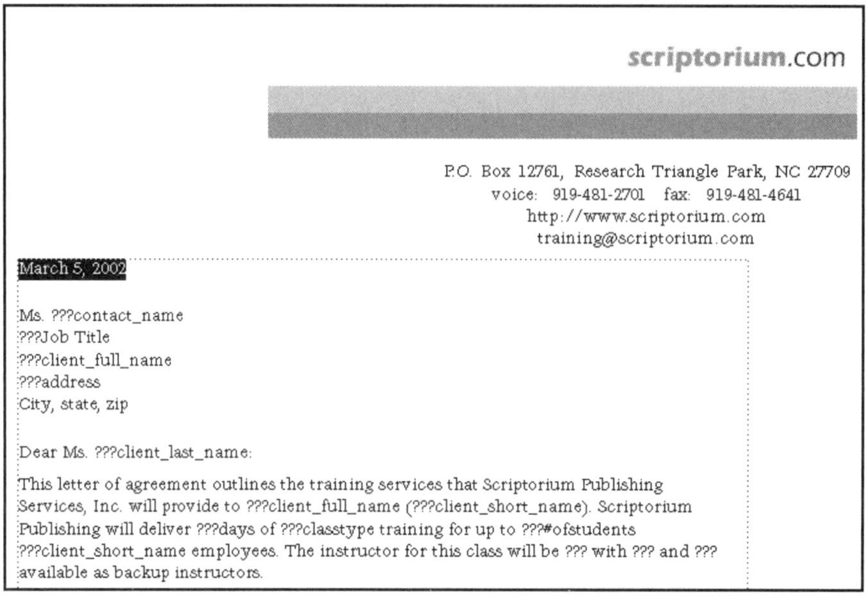

scriptorium.com

P.O. Box 12761, Research Triangle Park, NC 27709
voice: 919-481-2701 fax: 919-481-4641
http://www.scriptorium.com
training@scriptorium.com

March 5, 2002

Ms. ???contact_name
???Job Title
???client_full_name
???address
City, state, zip

Dear Ms. ???client_last_name:

This letter of agreement outlines the training services that Scriptorium Publishing Services, Inc. will provide to ???client_full_name (???client_short_name). Scriptorium Publishing will deliver ???days of ???classtype training for up to ???#ofstudents ???client_short_name employees. The instructor for this class will be ??? with ??? and ??? available as backup instructors.

For more information about variables, see Chapter 9, "Storing Content in Variables."

Creating a Blank Document

When you create a blank document, you can use a default portrait or landscape page, or you can create a custom page size.

To create a blank portrait or landscape document, follow these steps:

1. Select File➤New➤Document or press CTRL-N. The New dialog box is displayed (Figure 3-1 on page 31).
2. In the Use Blank Paper section, click the Portrait or Landscape button. The new document is displayed.

To create a document that uses a custom paper size, follow these steps:

1. Select File➤New➤Document or press CTRL-N. The New dialog box is displayed (Figure 3-1 on page 31).
2. In the Use Blank Paper section, click the Custom button. The Custom Blank Paper dialog box is displayed.

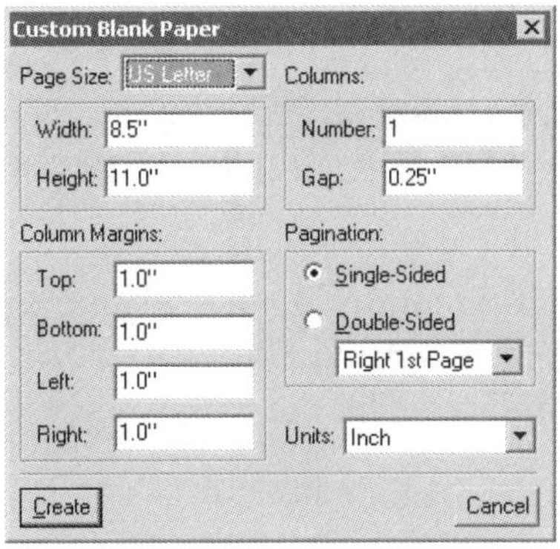

3. Click a paper size in the Page Size drop-down list:
   - **Custom:** You specify the page width and height.
   - **US Letter:** 8.5 inches wide by 11 inches tall
   - **US Legal:** 8.5 inches wide by 14 inches tall
   - **Tabloid:** 11 inches wide by 17 inches tall
   - **A3 Tabloid:** 29.7 cm wide by 42 cm tall
   - **A4 Letter:** 21 cm wide by 29.7 cm tall
   - **A5 Letter:** 14.8 cm wide by 21 cm tall
   - **B5 Letter:** 17.6 cm wide by 25 cm tall

TIP To change the measurement units (for example, from inches to picas), select a measurement unit in the Units drop-down list at the bottom right. FrameMaker automatically converts the current measurements into the new units.

4. Modify the margins as appropriate. Margins are measured from the edge of the page to the edge of the text area.
5. To create a document with equal-sized columns, specify the number of columns you want in the Columns area. The default is 1. The Gap measurement determines the amount of space between the columns. After you specify the columns and gap value, FrameMaker automatically creates even columns.
6. Set the pagination. Most books use double-sided pagination and start with a right first page. If you specify single-sided pagination, only one master page is created (called Right); if you specify double-sided pagination, two master pages are created (Left and Right). For details, see "Switching from Single- to Double-Sided Pages" on page 300.
7. Click the Create button. Your new document is displayed.

Using an Existing File

Instead of using a document as a template and creating a new file, you can save the template file with a new name to make a copy. To use an existing file, follow these steps:

1. Open a file that has the correct formats.
2. *(optional)* To delete the content in the file, highlight all the information in the file by selecting Edit➤Select All in Flow, then press the DELETE key.
3. Select File➤Save As and save the file with a new name.

You now have a new file and can begin editing it.

Opening, Saving, Closing, and Printing Documents

FrameMaker includes standard open, save, close, and printing commands:

- To open a file, select File➤Open, then locate the file you want.
- To close a file, select File➤Close.
- To save a file, select File➤Save, or select File➤Save As to save the file with a different name.
- To print a file, select File➤Print.

Files created in earlier versions of FrameMaker open in newer versions; for example, a file created in FrameMaker 7 opens in FrameMaker 8. However, you cannot open a version 8 FrameMaker file in earlier versions of FrameMaker. To move a file "back" to an earlier version of FrameMaker, save the file as Maker Interchange Format 7, then open the MIF file in the older version. You will lose features that are not supported in the older versions, but the files usually open cleanly. If you have authored in multiple languages or languages FrameMaker 8 now supports with Unicode, you will need to check your file carefully for changes.

TIP FrameMaker 8 also provides a Save As FrameMaker 7 feature, which lets you save files in FrameMaker 7 format directly instead of using MIF as an intermediate format. This feature could be useful if you are working in a mixed version 7/version 8 environment, but you will have to check your files carefully, especially if you use features unique to FrameMaker 8.

Understanding the Document Window

You view and edit your document in the document window. A dotted line indicates the area in which you can insert content. (If you do not see the dotted line, select View➤Borders to display it.)

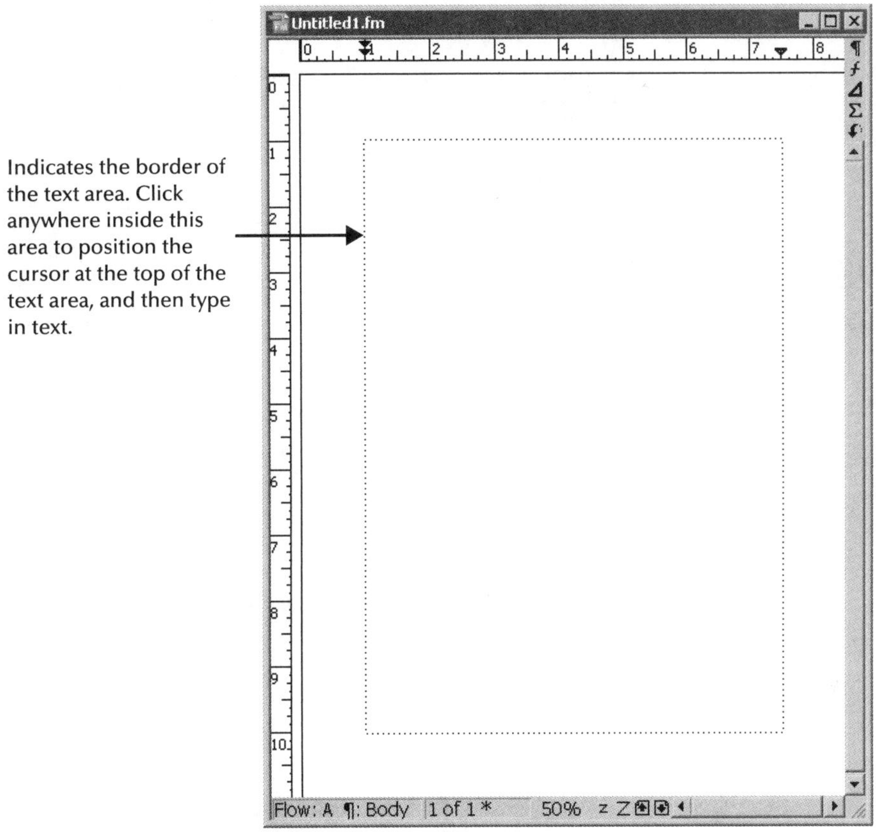

At the bottom of the document window, a status bar displays information about the current document. By looking at the status bar, you can find out the following information:

- Flow tag, paragraph tag, character tag, and conditional text tag for the currently selected item. (In structured documents, the element name is listed instead of the paragraph and character tags.)
- Current page number and total page count.
- Whether the file has been modified since you last saved it.
- The current percentage zoom at which the file is being displayed.

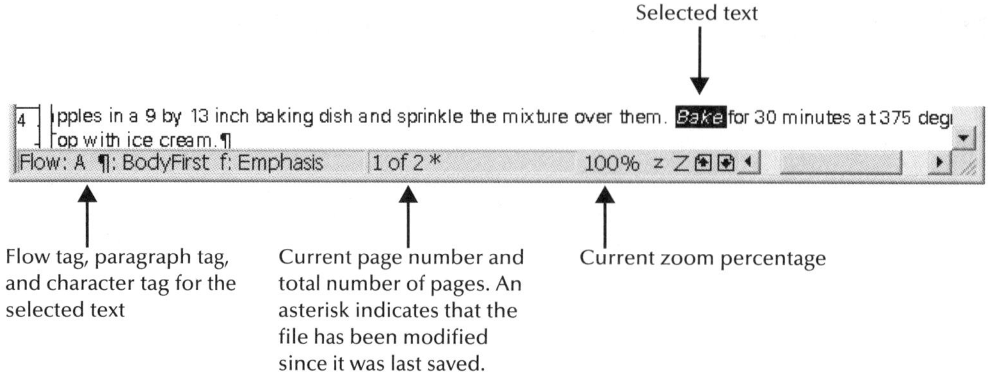

Changing the Zoom Settings

To change the size at which a document is displayed, you can zoom in or zoom out. The big and little Zs on the status bar let you zoom in or out one step at a time.

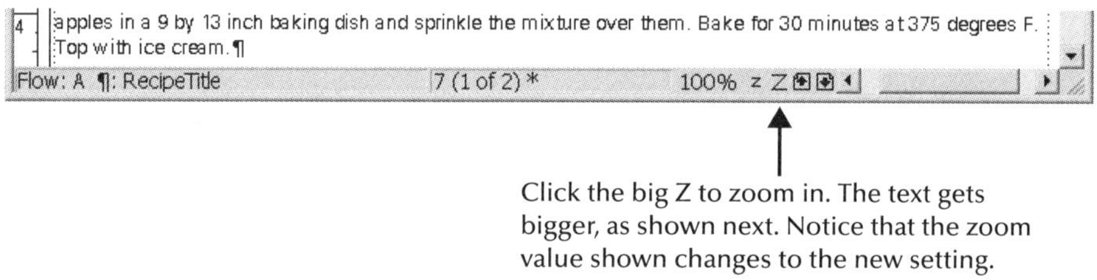

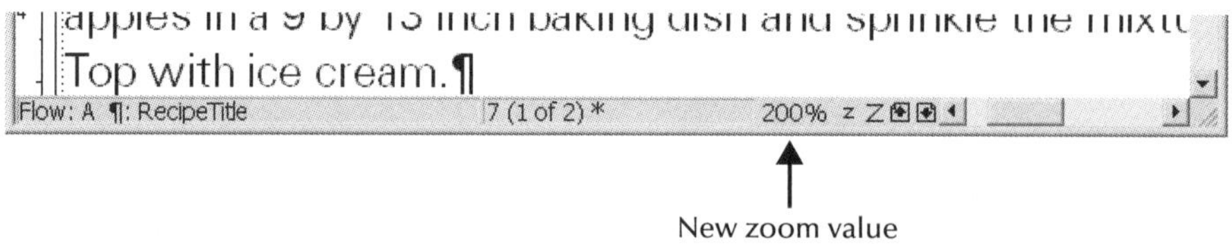

You can also use the zoom pop-up menu to change to a specific setting immediately. To change the zoom level through this menu, follow these steps:

1. Click on the zoom percentage to display the zoom pop-up menu.

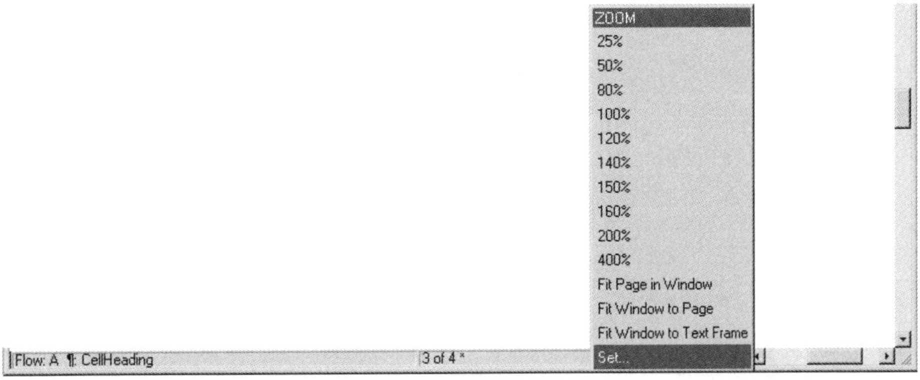

2. Click the zoom setting you want. The document is immediately changed to that zoom level.

FrameMaker provides ten zoom settings. You cannot add more settings, but you can change the provided settings to values anywhere between 25% and 1600%.

To change the available zoom settings, follow these steps:

1. Click on the zoom percentage to display the zoom pop-up menu.
2. Click the Set button. The Zoom Menu Options dialog box is displayed.

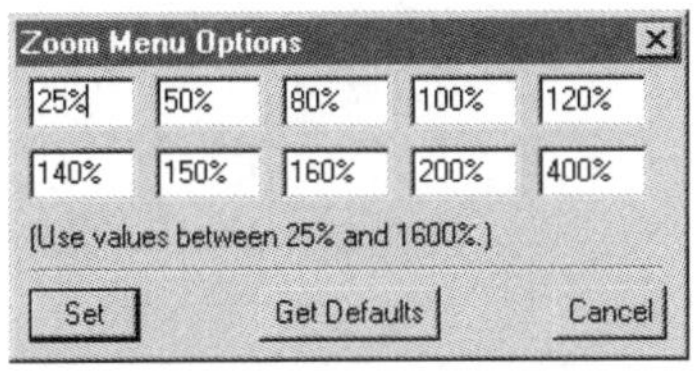

3. To change a setting, delete the existing number and type in a new one. You can insert them in any order, and you do not have to type in the percentage sign. For instance, in the preceding example, you can delete 25% and type in **250**. FrameMaker will automatically put the new 250% setting in the correct order.
4. Click the Set button to save your changes. To revert back to FrameMaker's default zoom settings, click the Get Defaults button.

The new settings are immediately shown in the zoom menu and are used when you click the zoom in and zoom out buttons.

Displaying Nonprinting Items in the Document Window

You can turn on and off the display of several items in the document window. They are as follows:

- **Borders.** With borders on, the edge of text frames, table cells, and the like are indicated with dotted lines.
- **Text Symbols.** With text symbols on, tabs, end-of-paragraph symbols, markers, and other nonprinting characters are displayed on screen.
- **Rulers.** With rulers on, measurements are shown on the top and right of the document window.
- **Grid Lines.** With grid lines on, a grid pattern is shown to help you align objects on the page.

The commands to toggle each of these options are in the View menu.

Borders, Text Symbols, Rulers, and Grid Lines off.

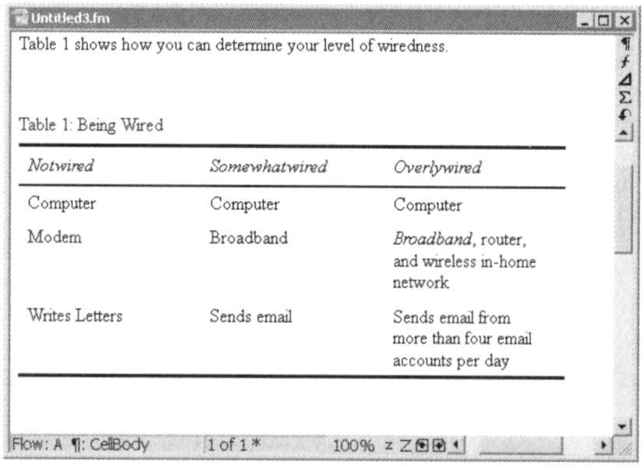

Borders on.
The dotted lines indicate the edge of the text area and the table cell boundaries.
Select View➤Borders to toggle borders.

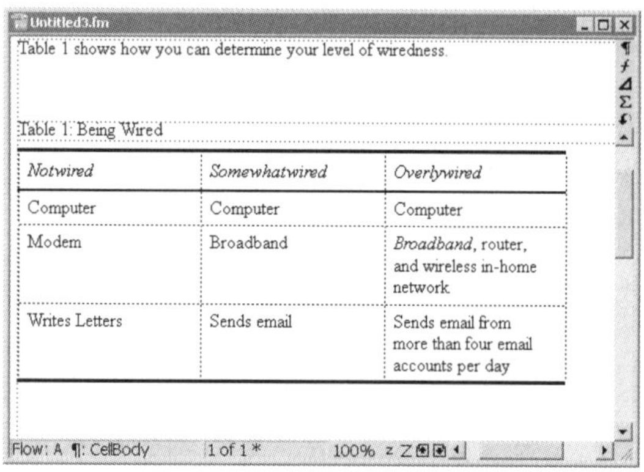

Borders and Text Symbols on. When text symbols are on, nonprinting symbols, such as tabs and end-of-paragraph symbols, are displayed. See Table 3-1 on page 42 for a list of text symbols.

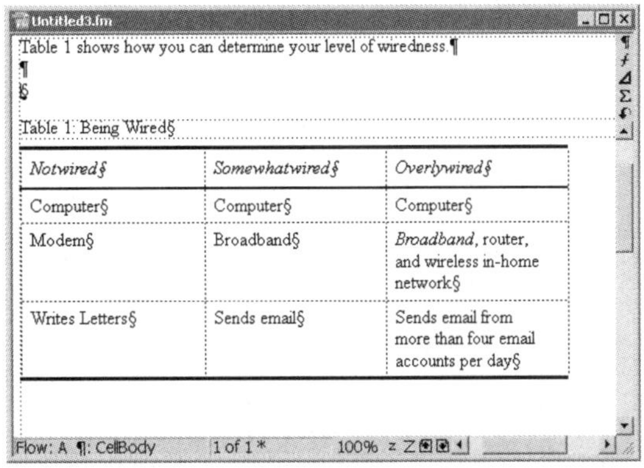

Rulers on.
Select View➤Rulers to toggle rulers. The measurement units used are determined by the view options you set. See "Changing View Options" on page 43.

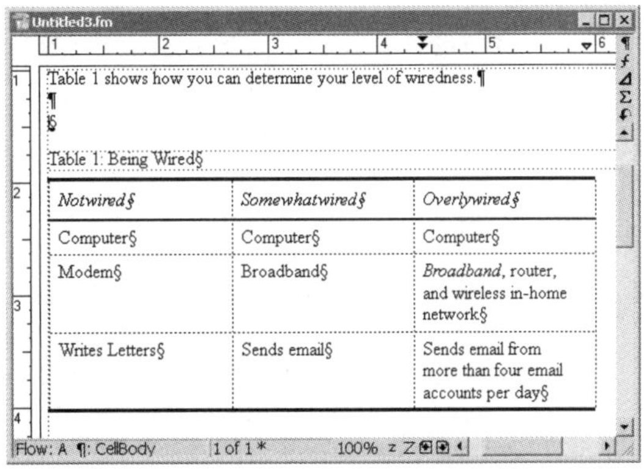

Grid Lines on.
Grid lines can help with aligning graphics or other objects.
Select View➤Grid Lines to toggle grid lines.

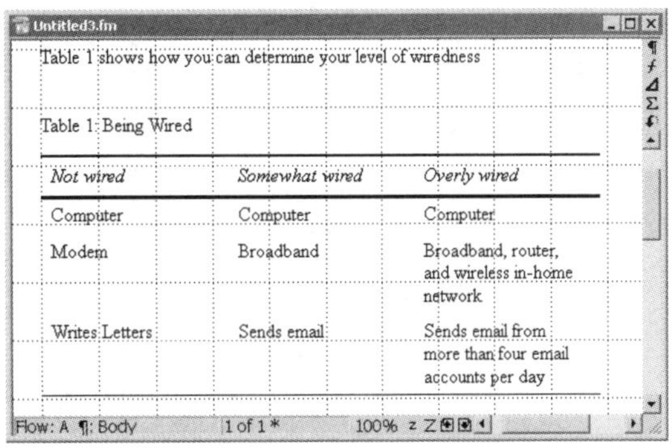

FrameMaker uses many different nonprinting symbols. Table 3-1 on page 42 lists them.

Symbol	Description
〉	**Tab.** Indicates a tab character. Keep in mind that tabs do not move text unless a tab stop is defined for that paragraph. For details, see "Setting Tab Stops" on page 115.
¶	**End of paragraph symbol.** Indicates the end of a paragraph. When you press ENTER to end a paragraph, FrameMaker inserts this symbol.
§	**End of flow symbol.** Indicates the end of the content in the current flow. As you add more content, the end of flow symbol always stays at the end of the text. You cannot remove this symbol.
〈	**Forced return.** Indicates a forced line break. Press SHIFT-ENTER to insert a forced return.
␣	**Hard space.** Indicates a nonbreaking space (inserted by pressing CTRL-SPACE), which does not allow a line break to occur at that location.
┬	**Discretionary hyphen.** Indicates a location at which the word can be hyphenated if necessary, in addition to the hyphenation points defined in the dictionary. Press CTRL-HYPHEN or ESC HYPHEN SHIFT-D to insert a discretionary hyphen. Discretionary hyphens are shown above the text: determine
—	**Suppress hyphen.** Indicates a location at which the word cannot be hyphenated, even if the dictionary allows hyphenation there. Press ESC N S to suppress hyphenation for a word and insert a suppress hyphen symbol. The suppress hyphenation symbol is displayed under the text: wire
⊥	**Anchor for table or anchored frame.** Indicates the location at which a table or anchored frame is anchored to a paragraph.

Table 3-1. Text Symbols

Symbol	Description
T	**Marker.** Indicates the location of a marker, which contains hidden, nonprinting text. Markers are used for several different features, including index entries. FrameMaker automatically inserts markers to manage cross-references and conditional text, so you should not delete a marker unless you are certain it isn't needed. Markers can occur anywhere in text, including in the middle of a word. (They are, however, usually easier to maintain if you put them at the beginning or end of a word.)

Table 3-1. Text Symbols (Continued)

Changing View Options

The view options let you set measurement units, page options, and more.

To change your view options, follow these steps:

1. Select View➤Options. The View Options dialog box is displayed.

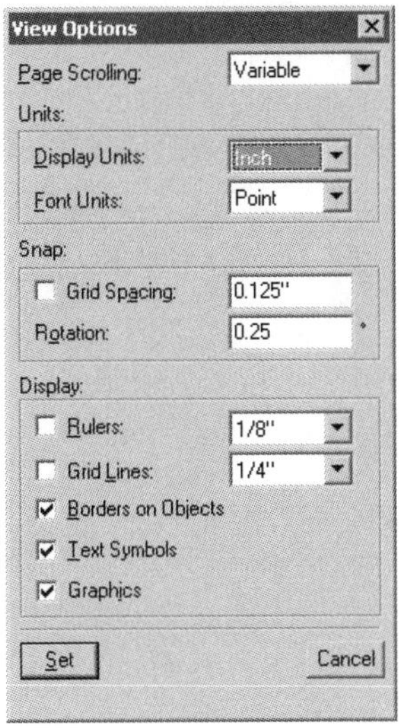

2. Set the page scrolling you want. Your choices are as follows:
   - **Vertical:** In the document window, pages scroll vertically. (This is standard behavior in most word processing and publishing applications.)
   - **Horizontal:** Pages scroll horizontally.

- **Facing Pages:** Pages are displayed in spreads, with the left and right pages displayed in the document window together.
- **Variable:** Pages are displayed depending on how the document is zoomed. If facing pages fit in the window, they are displayed; if not, pages scroll vertically.

3. Set the display units with the Display Units and Font Units drop-down lists. The font units are used for font size, leading, and space above and below paragraph. Display units are used for all other items.

TIP Refer to Chapter 13, "FrameMaker's Graphics Tools," for information about the grid and snap options.

4. In the Display section, check the items you want to display. Unchecking the Graphics check box results in all of your graphics turning into gray boxes temporarily. This can help speed up display of your file.
5. Click the Set button to save and apply your changes.

Button List

At the top-right corner of the document window, FrameMaker displays a series of buttons in a vertical column.

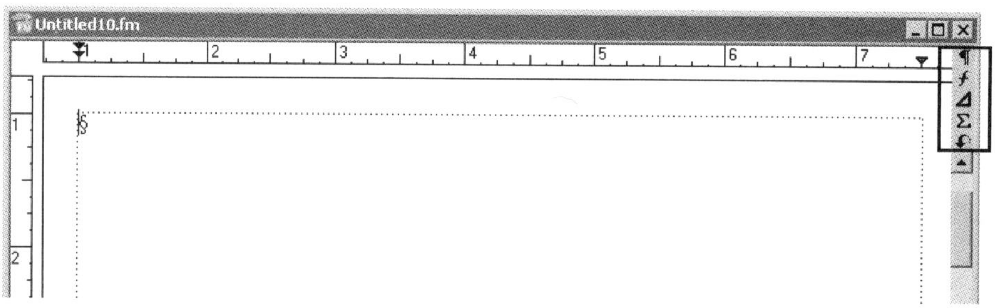

These buttons provide shortcuts to frequently used windows, such as the paragraph and character catalogs.

Button	Function
	**Paragraph Catalog:** Displays the paragraph catalog, which lets you apply paragraph tags to your content. For details, see Chapter 5, "Formatting Text with Paragraph Tags."
	**Character Catalog:** Lets you apply formatting within a paragraph. For details, see Chapter 6, "Formatting Text with Character Tags."
	**Graphic Toolbar:** Lets you create graphics with FrameMaker's graphics tools. For details, see Chapter 13, "FrameMaker's Graphics Tools."
	**Equation Editor:** Lets you create and modify equations. For details, see Chapter 23, "Writing Equations."
	**History Palette:** Lets you view the history of your changes and revert to before an earlier change. For details, see "Undoing and Redoing Changes" on page 62.

Toolbars

FrameMaker provides two toolbars at the top of the main window: the Quick Access Bar and the Formatting Bar. To toggle display of the toolbars, select View➤QuickAccess Bar and View➤Formatting Bar.

FrameMaker 8 also displays a tabs for the open files. You can click on a tab to move that file to the front of the working files. Clicking on a tab does not maximize a minimized file window. To toggle the display of the tabs, select View➤Tabbed Bar.

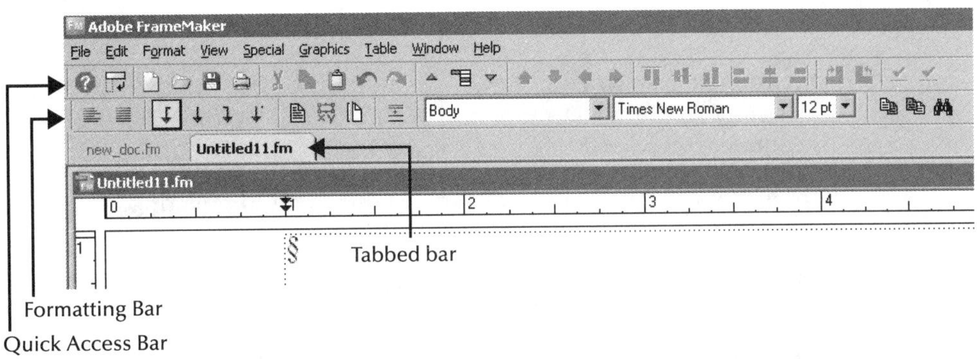

The Quick Access Bar is really four toolbars in one. The left side of the Quick Access Bar is always the same, but the information shown on the right changes when you click the up and down arrows in the middle of the bar. Table 3-2 on page 46 lists the buttons on the bar.

CAUTION The Plain, Bold, Italics, Underline, and Increase/Decrease Font Size buttons introduce untagged formatting. In general, you should avoid these buttons; use character tags instead. For details on character tags, see Chapter 6, "Formatting Text with Character Tags."

Button	Function
Common Toolbar (Left Side)	

	**Help:** Displays the online help.
	**Vertical QuickAccess Bar:** Click to display the toolbar as a vertical floating palette (shown at right) instead of a horizontal toolbar. You cannot create a horizontal floating palette. To return to the default horizontal toolbar, click this button again. Notice that on the vertical palette, the toolbar indicator goes from left to right instead of top to bottom. Closing the palette is equivalent to selecting View➤QuickAccess Bar; it removes the palette and the toolbar from the interface. 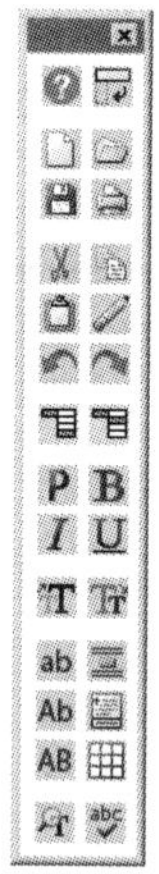
	**Document:** Displays the New Document dialog box. Equivalent to selecting File➤New➤Document. For details, see "Setting Up a New Document" on page 30.
	**Open:** Displays the Open dialog box. Equivalent to selecting File➤Open.
	**Save:** Saves the file. Equivalent to selecting File➤Save.
	**Print:** Displays the Print dialog box. Equivalent to selecting File➤Print.
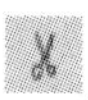	**Cut:** Deletes the selected content and puts it on the clipboard. Equivalent to selecting Edit➤Cut.

Table 3-2. Buttons on the Quick Access Bar

Button	Function
	**Copy:** Puts a copy of the selected content on the clipboard. Equivalent to selecting Edit➤Copy.
	**Paste:** Retrieves the information on the clipboard and inserts it into the document. Equivalent to selecting Edit➤Paste.
	**Undo:** Undoes the last action. Click multiple times to continue to undo previous actions in the Undo history.
	**Redo:** Performs the last action that was undone. Click multiple times to continue to perform actions that were previously undone.
Toolbar Navigation	
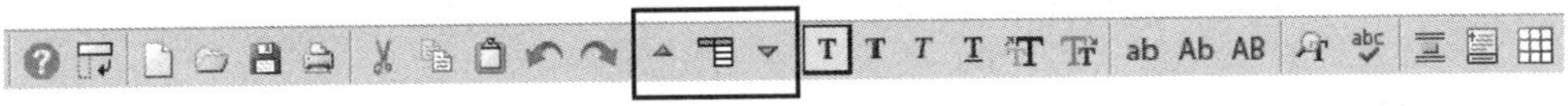	
	**Previous Toolbar:** Displays the previous set of toolbar buttons.
	**Toolbar Indicator:** Shows which of the four toolbars is currently being displayed.
	**Next Toolbar:** Displays the next set of toolbar buttons.
Toolbar One (Formatting Items) We recommend that you do not use this toolbar for any character formatting. Instead, always use character tags to adjust weight, angle, size and other character features.	

	**Plain:** Removes any bold, italic, or underlining from the selected text. Use character tags instead to avoid formatting overrides.
	**Bold:** Applies bold formatting to the selected text. Use character tags instead to avoid formatting overrides.
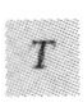	**Italic:** Applies italic formatting to the selected text. Use character tags instead to avoid formatting overrides.
	**Underline:** Adds underlining to the selected text. Use character tags instead to avoid formatting overrides.

Table 3-2. Buttons on the Quick Access Bar (Continued)

Button	Function
	**Increase Font Size:** Increases the font size of the selected text. Use character tags instead to avoid formatting overrides.
	**Decrease Font Size:** Decreases the font size of the selected text. Use character tags instead to avoid formatting overrides.
	**Lowercase:** Changes the selected text to all lowercase.
	**Initial Capital:** Changes the selected text to Initial Capitals (that is, first letter of each word is uppercase; the remainder is lowercase).
	**Uppercase:** Changes the selected text to UPPERCASE.
	**Find/Change:** Displays the find/change dialog box. For details about using the find/change feature, see page 67.
	**Check Spelling:** Displays the spell-checker. For details about spell-checking, see page 73.
	**Anchored Frame:** Inserts an anchored frame, which is used to place graphics. For details about anchored frames, see page 305.
	**Footnote:** Inserts a footnote. For details about footnotes, see page 97.
	**Insert Table:** Inserts a table. For details, see Chapter 7, "Understanding Table Design."
Toolbar Two (Graphics)	

	**Group:** Groups the selected objects. For details about grouping and ungrouping, see "Grouping" on page 363.
	**Ungroup:** Ungroups the selected objects. For details about grouping and ungrouping, see "Grouping" on page 363.
	**Bring to Front:** Puts the selected object on top of the object stack. For details about stacking, see "Layering Objects" on page 365.
	**Send to Back:** Puts the selected object at the bottom of the object stack. For details about stacking, see "Layering Objects" on page 365.

Table 3-2. Buttons on the Quick Access Bar (Continued)

Button	Function
	**Distribute:** Lets you space objects evenly. For details about distributing, see page 362.
	**Reshape:** Provides selection handles so that you can change the shape (not just the size) of the selected object. For details, see page 353.
	**Smooth:** Makes corners in the selected object curvy rather than sharp. For details, see page 355.
	**Unsmooth:** Makes corners in the selected object sharp rather than curvy. For details, see page 355.
	**Flip Up/Down:** Flips the selected object vertically. For details, see page 368.
	**Flip Left/Right:** Flips the selected object horizontally. For details, see page 368.
	**Scale:** Displays the Scale dialog box, where you can change the size of the selected object. For details about scaling, see "Resizing" on page 351.
	**Object Properties:** Displays the Object Properties dialog box, which provides information about the selected object, such as the height, width, location, and border. For details, see "Modifying Objects" on page 346.
	**Snap:** If selected, objects you move are snapped to a grid. For details, see "Working with Grids" on page 343.
	**Gravity:** If selected, objects are attracted to each other, which makes it easier to align them. For details, see page 351.

Toolbar Three (More Graphics)

Button	Function
	**Move Up:** Nudges the selected object up. Equivalent to ALT-UP ARROW.
	**Move Down:** Nudges the selected object down. Equivalent to ALT-DOWN ARROW.

Table 3-2. Buttons on the Quick Access Bar (Continued)

Button	Function
	**Move Left:** Nudges the selected object to the left. Equivalent to ALT-LEFT ARROW.
	**Move Right:** Nudges the selected object to the right. Equivalent to ALT-RIGHT ARROW.
	**Align Top:** Aligns the selected objects to the top edge of the last-selected object. For details about alignment, see page 360.
	**Align Horizontal Center:** Aligns the selected objects to the middle of the last-selected object. For details about alignment, see page 360.
	**Align Bottom:** Aligns the selected objects to the bottom edge of the last-selected object. For details about alignment, see page 360.
	**Align Left:** Aligns the selected objects to the left edge of the last-selected object. For details about alignment, see page 360.
	**Align Vertical Center:** Aligns the selected objects to the center of the last-selected object. For details about alignment, see page 360.
	**Align Right:** Aligns the selected objects to the right edge of the last-selected object. For details about alignment, see page 360.
	**Rotate Clockwise:** Rotates the selected object clockwise in 15-degree increments. For details about rotating objects, see page 366.
	**Rotate Counterclockwise:** Rotates the selected object counterclockwise in 15-degree increments. For details about rotating objects, see page 366.
	**Make Line Solid:** Sets a solid line for lines and object borders.
	**Make Line Dashed:** Sets a dashed line for lines and object borders.

Toolbar Four (Tables)

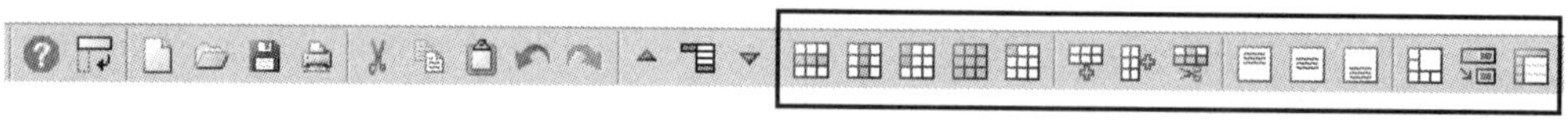

Button	Function
	**Select Row:** Selects the current table row.
	**Select Column:** Selects the current column, including any heading rows.

Table 3-2. Buttons on the Quick Access Bar (Continued)

Button	Function
	**Select Column Body Cells:** Selects the current column, but not any of the heading rows.
	**Select Table:** Selects the entire table.
	**Move Insertion Point to Top Left Cell:** Positions the cursor in the top left cell of the table.
	**Add Row Below:** Adds a row below the current row.
	**Add Column to Right:** Adds a column to the right of the current column.
	**Remove Row or Column:** If an entire row or column is selected, that row or column is deleted. If only a few cells in a row or column are selected, nothing is deleted.
	**Align Top:** Aligns the contents of the current cell to the top of the cell.
	**Align Middle:** Aligns the contents of the current cell to the middle of the cell.
	**Align Bottom:** Aligns the contents of the current cell to the bottom of the cell.
	**Straddle:** If two or more cells are selected, they are straddled (merged) into a single cell.
	**Shrinkwrap Column Width:** The current column is adjusted to the width of its contents.
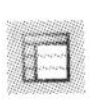	**Custom Ruling and Shading:** Displays the Custom Ruling & Shading dialog box. For details about applying custom ruling and shading, see page 177.

Table 3-2. Buttons on the Quick Access Bar (Continued)

Understanding File Configuration and Preferences

FrameMaker files normally use the .fm extension. FrameMaker book files (more on those in Chapter 14, "Setting Up Book Files") normally use .book or .bk.

A FrameMaker document file is self-contained; it includes all of the formatting or structure information needed to display and print the content. Unlike some other applications, FrameMaker files do not refer to a separate template file; the template information is embedded in each individual document file.

When you add graphics to a document, you can either link or embed the graphic. When you link (import by reference) a graphic, you insert a pointer from the FrameMaker file to the graphic. This pointer is basically just a file name and path, so it's very small. If you embed (copy into document) a graphic, you insert the entire graphic into the FrameMaker file, so the FrameMaker file grows accordingly.

To prevent two people from working on the same file simultaneously, FrameMaker provides a feature called network file locking. If network file locking is active, opening a file creates a .lck file ("lock" file, *not* "ick" file). If a second person attempts to open the locked file, FrameMaker displays an error message:

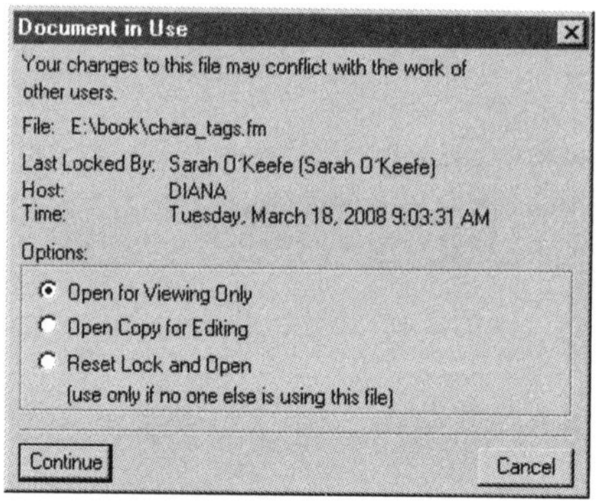

You have three choices:

- **Open for Viewing Only:** Opens a read-only version of the file. You cannot make any changes to this file.
- **Open Copy for Editing:** Creates an untitled copy of the file. You can make changes in this file.
- **Reset Lock and Open:** Removes the lock and lets you edit the file. Use this option only when you are certain that nobody else is using the file (for example, if your computer crashed and left incorrect locking information on the server).

To activate network file locking, follow these steps:

1. Select File➤Preferences➤General. The Preferences dialog box is displayed (Figure 3-2).
2. Check the Network File Locking check box.
3. Click the Set button to save your change.

REMEMBER Network file locking is turned on by default when you install FrameMaker. Keep in mind, though, that each user must have network file locking activated in their copy of FrameMaker.

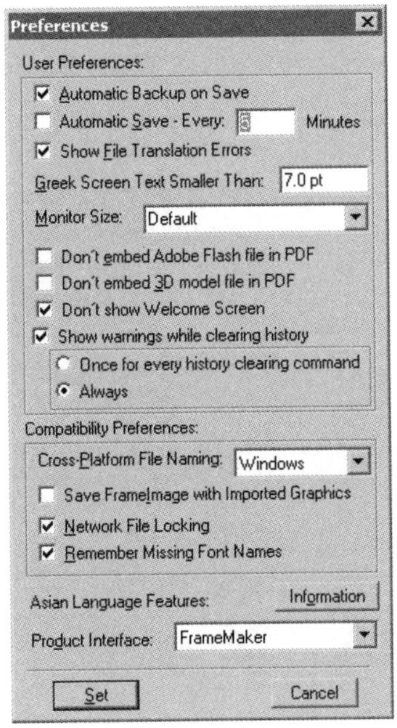

Figure 3-2. Use the Preferences dialog box to set file locking, backup settings, and other options.

In a larger group (or if you have people working on the files who are not on the same network), the basic file security provided by file locking may not suffice. If this is the case, you can use WebDAV. FrameMaker supports file check-in and check-out on a WebDAV server. See Chapter 27, "Sharing and Managing Files Using WebDAV," for details. You can also use source control systems to manage FrameMaker files.

Handling Missing Fonts

To display text, FrameMaker uses fonts that are installed on your system. When you open a file, any missing fonts are identified and listed in the console window. By default, FrameMaker performs only a temporary font replacement. You might have a situation where authors' computers are missing several fonts that are required to print documents correctly, but the final production computers have the licensed fonts installed. In this scenario, you want FrameMaker to keep track of the missing fonts and replace them only while the file is being edited on the authors' side. When the file is opened on production computers with the appropriate fonts, it contains the correct formatting. The font that FrameMaker displays for missing fonts is specified in the maker.ini file. To change the substitution font, see "Changing the Substitution Fonts" on page 682.

In some cases, you may want permanent font substitution. You might, for example, receive a file from another company, which uses fonts that you do not have and don't plan to install. In that case, you probably want to get rid of the fonts so that you don't get the missing fonts message every time you open the file.

CAUTION If some characters in your FrameMaker file are displayed as boxes, question marks, or other strange characters, the missing font may be a Unicode font that has characters that cannot be displayed in the font that FrameMaker is substituting. In this case, make sure you have a font that can display all the characters correctly before you allow FrameMaker to permanently substitute a different font.

To toggle your missing font setting, follow these steps:

1. Select File➤Preferences➤General. The Preferences dialog box is displayed (Figure 3-2 on page 53).
2. Check or uncheck the Remember Missing Font Names check box.
3. Click the Set button to save your change.

To remove missing fonts from a file, follow these steps:

1. In the Preferences dialog box, turn off Remember Missing Font Names as described in the preceding steps.
2. Open the problem file.
3. Save the file. The missing fonts are replaced with the fonts specified in the maker.ini file. See "Changing the Substitution Fonts" on page 682.
4. *(optional, but recommended)* Return to the Preferences dialog box and turn on Remember Missing Font Names.

The fonts are now removed from the file.

Organizing Directories and Files

Although many companies establish rules about how to store files and set up directories to manage content, a surprising number do not. If you need to set up a new organization for your documentation library, this section provides some suggestions on how best to manage the files.

The first principle of organizing documents is that a book should have its own directory. Moving the directory (and any associated subdirectories) should move all of the contents of the book. For instance, you can set up a directory organization for a book that includes the book file, chapter files, and graphics in a simple organization:

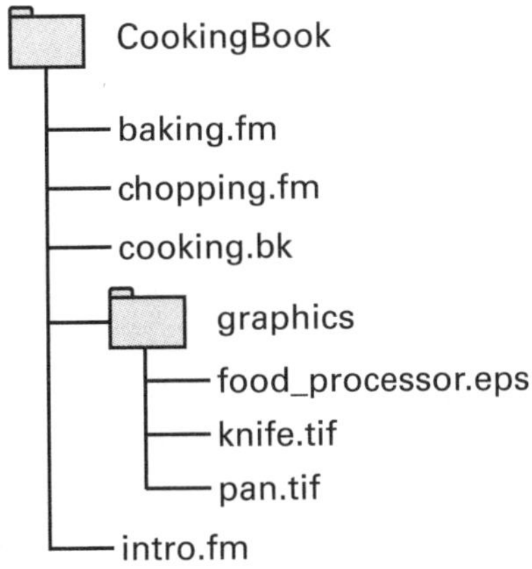

We recommend against naming chapters by their numbers; for example, chap01.fm, chap02.fm, and so on. If you move chapters around, you will either have a big renaming job or chapters whose file names don't match their numbers. Instead, name chapters by subject: production_editing.fm, workflow.fm, and so on.

Putting referenced graphics in a subdirectory makes it easier to keep track of them and to separate the graphics from the FrameMaker content files. Creating subdirectories for each chapter can be appealing when you have lots and lots of graphics, but again, avoid naming these directories by chapter number because of the naming mismatch that will occur if you rearrange chapters. For longer books, consider using a prefix for each chapter so that the graphics sort nicely into chapter groups.

Files that are reused across chapters and especially across books present a problem. Consider creating a special "shared" folder in the book folder or one level up from the book folder if you want to share across different books. Keep in mind, though, that you must remember to send the shared folder in addition to the book folder if you ship the files to someone who cannot access them from your network.

File Naming Conventions

You can open a FrameMaker file created on one platform's version of FrameMaker in the other platform. For example, if you create a file in FrameMaker for UNIX, you can open that file in Windows FrameMaker without any trouble.

REMEMBER The version numbers have to match; you cannot open a FrameMaker 8 file in FrameMaker 7 unless you go through Maker Interchange Format 7 (MIF 7) or save to FrameMaker 7 format—see page 36.

To ensure that files transfer seamlessly from one platform to another, you need to use file names that work on all platforms. Here are some common tips that will help you create well-behaved file names (the platform that requires the limitation is listed in parentheses):

- Do not use spaces in file names (UNIX).
- Do not use slashes or backslashes in file names (UNIX, Windows).
- Use a file-name extension (.fm or .book) to ensure files are recognized by the application and the operating system (Windows).

FrameMaker provides a preferences setting to help you create compatible file names. If you attempt to create a file with a name that will not work on the target platform, a warning message is displayed.

To set cross-platform file naming, follow these steps:

1. Select File➤Preferences➤General. The Preferences dialog box is displayed (Figure 3-2 on page 53).
2. In the Cross-Platform File Naming drop-down list, click the platform to which you plan to send the files. For example, if you're working under Windows but will need to use the files on the UNIX platform, click UNIX.
3. Click the Set button to save your change.

The next time you save a file, FrameMaker will check the file name for compatibility with the platform specified in the preferences. If any problems are detected, an error message is displayed:

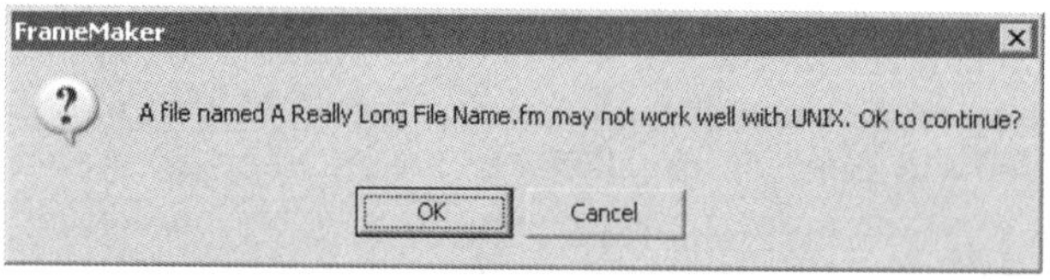

Click the OK button to save the file with the incompatible name. Click the Cancel button to return to the Save dialog box and specify a different name.

Saving File Information with XMP

You can save file information, such as the author, keywords, and title, along with your file. This information is saved as *metadata,* or information about the document. The file information you save is stored in a special format called Extensible Metadata Platform, or XMP. XMP allows you to view metadata without opening the file. You could, for example, define some file information and save your FrameMaker file. An XMP-compatible application or browser can access the XMP data stored for your FrameMaker file, even if the FrameMaker application is not available.

If you make a PDF file from your document, the file information you specify can also be viewed in Adobe Reader.

To set up file information, follow these steps:

1. Open the file or book for which you want to save file information.
2. Select File➤File Info. The File Info dialog box is displayed.

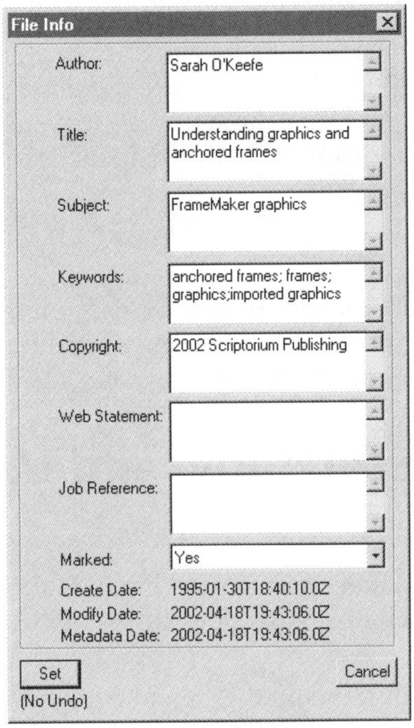

3. Type in the information you want to save. You can fill in any or all of the available fields.
4. Click the Set button to save your changes with this file.

After setting file information, the data you provided is included as XMP metadata when you save the file.

For more details about XMP, consult Adobe's web site (www.adobe.com/products/xmp/).

Setting Automatic Backup and Save Features

FrameMaker provides two complementary features that save files automatically:

- **Automatic save.** While you work in FrameMaker, a backup file (.auto) is created periodically. If you exit FrameMaker normally, the file is deleted. However, if your system crashes (which means you didn't have a chance to close FrameMaker properly), the file is preserved. When you reopen the file you were working on, FrameMaker offers to open the .auto file, which might contain more recent information.

- **Automatic backup.** When you save the working file, a .backup.fm file is created. Backup files reside in the same directory as the working file.

To set your file backup options, follow these steps:

1. Select File➤Preferences➤General. The Preferences dialog box is displayed (Figure 3-2 on page 53).
2. To set automatic backup, check the Automatic Backup on Save check box.
3. To set automatic saving, check the Automatic Save check box, then specify the interval at which you want the file saved. (The default is 5 minutes.)
4. Click the Set button to save your changes.

NOTE Sometimes, FrameMaker saves a crash recovery file (.recover) when a crash occurs. That file might contain more up-to-date information than the .auto or .backup files. We recommend that you inspect both the .recover and the .auto and .backup files to identify which one is most current.

Switching Between Structured and Unstructured Interfaces

To switch between structured and unstructured FrameMaker, you must choose the new interface, close FrameMaker, and reopen it.

NOTE To find out more about structured FrameMaker, refer to *Publishing Fundamentals: Structured FrameMaker 8*.

To change interfaces, follow these steps:

1. Select File➤Preferences➤General. The Preferences dialog box is displayed (Figure 3-2 on page 53).
2. In the Product Interface drop-down list, select the interface you want to switch to.
3. Save all your open files.
4. Exit FrameMaker.
5. Restart FrameMaker. The product is started and displays the interface you selected.

PART II

Creating and Manipulating Text

CHAPTER 4

Word-Processing Features

FrameMaker provides full-featured word processing, including standard features such as search and replace. FrameMaker also provides FrameMaker-specific options, such as searching for paragraph tags or cross-references. However, unlike some word processors you might have used, FrameMaker does not offer onscreen spell-check highlighting (such as red underscores) or drag-and-drop editing.

Standard Word-Processing Features

FrameMaker's word-processing features work much like those found in typical word-processing programs. Using the Undo and Redo feature, you can remove or re-create multiple changes. Using the History menu choice, you can display a change history and revert to before a change. You can insert special characters like nonbreaking spaces, em dashes, or arrows. Using the Find/Change feature, you can find and replace words, paragraph tags, and other components. The Spelling Checker locates misspelled words, extra spaces, unusual punctuation, and other irregularities. The Thesaurus helps you find synonyms, antonyms, and other information about specific words.

Undoing and Redoing Changes

FrameMaker lets you undo or redo changes you have made in a document. In addition, FrameMaker tracks your changes in a History palette, from which you can display a list of changes and revert to a specific change. Certain actions will clear the change history for the document; FrameMaker can display a warning whenever you are about to perform an action that clears the history.

Undoing or Redoing an Action

You can undo or redo changes in the order in which you made them. For example, if you added text, applied a paragraph tag, and then added more text, you could undo the last text you typed and then undo the paragraph tag.

If you want to undo or redo changes, do the following:

- If you want to undo one or more of your most recent changes, select Edit➤Undo, click the Undo Typing button, or press CTRL-Z as many times as needed to remove the changes you want.

- If you want to redo one or more of your recent changes, select Edit➤Redo, click the Redo button, or press SHIFT-CTRL-Z as many times as needed to redo the changes you want.

Displaying the History Palette

You can display the History palette and select a change to which to revert. The change history is tracked for each open file in its own History palette. If you want to undo multiple changes, using the History is faster than performing multiple Undo and Redo commands.

To display the palette and revert to a specific change, follow these steps:

1. Select Edit➤History or press CTRL-K or ESC E H. The History palette is displayed.

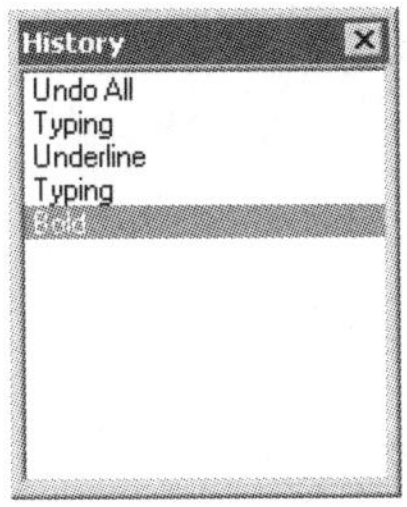

2. Select a change from the list. For example, in the history shown in the previous illustration, choosing the first "Typing" entry would remove the Bold, Typing, and Underline changes.

   To undo every change in the history, select Undo All from the top of the list.

NOTE Clicking a change in the history reverts that item and all the changes that followed.

Your document reverts to the change you chose. The History palette displays changes that have been removed with asterisks, indicating you can select Redo to restore those changes, or you can select one in the palette to restore that change and any preceding changes. After you perform additional actions that change the document, the Redo history is cleared.

Setting Options for History Warnings

When you perform certain tasks in FrameMaker, such as saving a file, FrameMaker clears the change history, and from that point you can no longer undo or redo changes.

By default, FrameMaker displays a warning whenever you are about to perform an action that clears the change history.

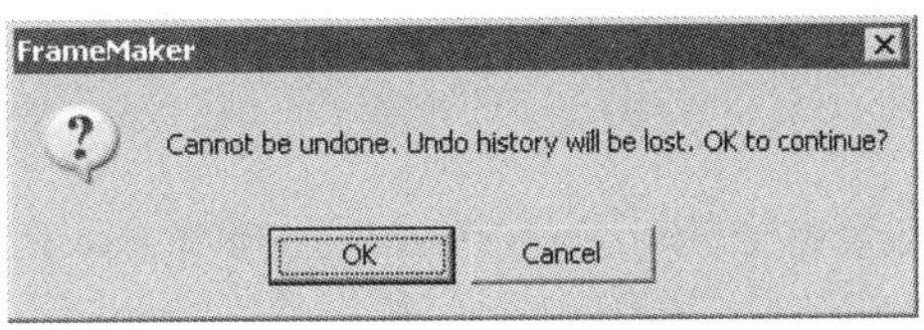

You can specify when FrameMaker displays this warning or you can turn the warning off. To change this setting, follow these steps:

1. Select File➤Preferences➤General. The Preferences dialog box is displayed.

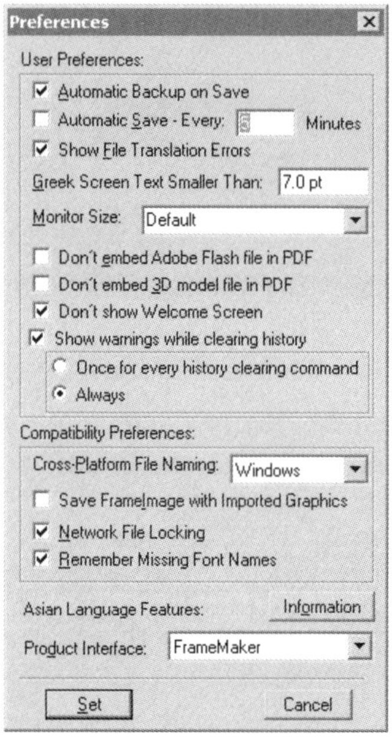

2. Do one of the following:
   - To turn off clear history warnings, uncheck the Show warnings while clearing history check box.
   - To display warnings the first time in each FrameMaker session that you perform an action that clears the history, select the Once for every history clearing command option under the Show warnings while clearing history check box.
   - To display warnings every time you perform an action that clears the history, select the Always option under the Show warnings while clearing history check box.
3. Click the Set button to save your change.

TIP To help understand which actions clear the change history, consider displaying all warnings when you first start to use FrameMaker. After you are familiar with those actions, you can turn off the warnings.

For a complete list of actions that can be undone and ones that clear the change history, see the FrameMaker online help.

Inserting Special Characters

When you are creating content, you often have to use characters that are not on the keyboard, such as em dashes, special spaces, or dingbats. This section describes working with special characters in FrameMaker. If you have questions about how to enter a particular character, see the *Adobe FrameMaker 8 Character Sets* online manual in the Documents folder in your FrameMaker installation folder.

NOTE If you are working with content you created in FrameMaker version 7 or earlier, you should read the section "Support for FrameMaker 7.x Character Sets" in the *Adobe FrameMaker 8 Character Sets* online manual.

Using the Symbols Toolbar List

FrameMaker 8 provides an icon in the Formatting toolbar to add these commonly used special characters:

- Bullet (•)
- Plus/minus (±)
- Double dagger (‡)
- Ellipsis (…)
- En dash (–)
- Em dash (—)
- Register (®)
- Copyright (©)
- Trademark (™)
- Cent (¢)
- Pound (£)
- Yen (¥)

To insert one of these characters, select it from the drop-down list displayed after you click the Symbols icon. If you need to insert a special character not in this list, use one of the other methods described in the following sections.

You can customize the list to include other symbols by modifying the menus.cfg file, as described in the *Adobe FrameMaker Customizing (Windows)* online manual. You will find this manual in the Documents folder in your FrameMaker installation folder.

NOTE At the time this book was written, the *Customizing Windows* manual had not been updated from FrameMaker 7, but the instructions should still apply.

Third-party tools that let you add menus of symbols are also available. ToolbarPlus Express from Microtype offers a preconfigured drop-down list of different special characters and other interface enhancements. You can create your own custom list of symbols (and many other items, too) with Auto-Text from Silicon Prairie Software. For details, see Appendix A, "Resources."

Pasting from the Windows Character Map Utility

You can find special characters using the Windows Character Map utility provided with Windows. When you have found a special character in the Windows Character Map utility, you can copy and paste the character into FrameMaker, or you can use the map to find its associated code.

If you copy and paste the character from the Windows Character Map utility, you must be sure to use the same font in FrameMaker to display the character as you used for choosing the character in the Windows Character Map utility. For example, if you select a special character from the Windows Character Map utility using the Symbol font, the text in FrameMaker must also use the Symbol font, or your character will not be correct.

To use the Windows Character Map utility, follow these steps:

1. In Windows, select Start➤Programs (or All Programs)➤Accessories➤System Tools➤Character Map. The Character Map dialog box is displayed.

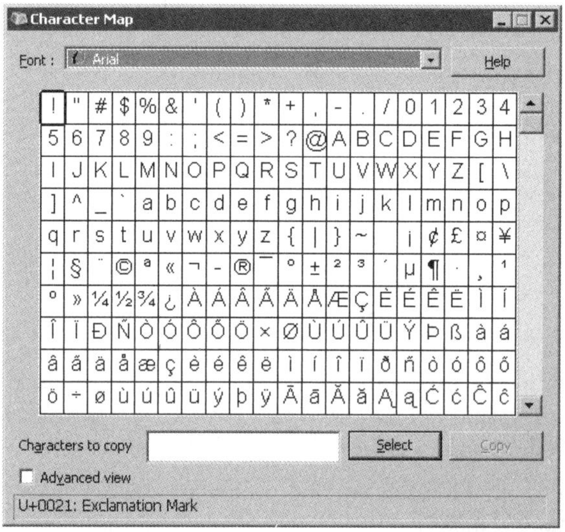

2. Select the font you are using from the Font drop-down list. This should match the font for your paragraph or character tag in FrameMaker.
3. From the character table, select the character to insert in FrameMaker.
4. Click Select, and then Copy.
5. In FrameMaker, select Edit➤Paste.

   If question marks or gray boxes are displayed instead of the correct characters in the pasted text, you are copying and pasting Unicode characters, so use paste special. Select Edit➤Paste Special, select Unicode Text, then click OK.

   To have FrameMaker automatically paste as Unicode text instead of plain text, change the paste order in maker.ini. See "Setting Clipboard Pasting Order" on page 681.

Using Keyboard Sequences

FrameMaker provides keyboard sequences for typing some special characters. Often, the keyboard sequences are complex. For example, to type an em dash, you type CTRL-Q SHIFT-Q. (That is, press and hold CTRL, then press Q, release those keys, then press and hold SHIFT, then press Q.)

All of the keyboard sequences that FrameMaker provides are documented in the *Adobe FrameMaker 8 Character Sets* online manual.

NOTE If you are familiar with keyboard sequences and have used them in previous versions of FrameMaker, you should read the sections "Support for FrameMaker 7.x character sets" and "Unsupported keyboard shortcuts for the Symbol and Dingbats character set in FrameMaker 8" in the *Adobe FrameMaker 8 Character Sets* online manual.

Typing ANSI Codes

You can type a special character by typing its ANSI code using your numeric keypad. The ANSI codes that FrameMaker supports are documented in the *Adobe FrameMaker 8 Character Sets* online manual.

To type the ANSI code, follow these steps:

1. Press the NUM LOCK key on your keyboard to use the numeric keypad, if it is not already turned on.
2. Press and hold down the ALT key and type the ANSI code on the keyboard for the special character, including the leading zero.

Searching and Replacing

The Find/Change feature lets you search for text strings, paragraph tags, variable names, broken cross-references, and other items. You can search selected text, the current document, or an entire book. Suppose that you create a variable for your document title after you typed the title in several places. You can search for the places where you typed the document title and replace the title with the variable.

There are several ways to customize your search:

- **Consider Case:** Finds text capitalized like the search item. If you search for *island*, FrameMaker skips the capitalized word *Island*.
- **Whole Word:** Finds the exact words and skips all instances where the text is part of a larger word. If you search for *object*, FrameMaker finds *object* and skips *objective*, *objects*, and *objectification*.
- **Use Wildcards:** Lets you use special characters in place of one or more unspecified characters. Table 4-1 describes how to use each wildcard.

<table>
<tr><th>Wildcard</th><th>Description</th><th>Example</th></tr>
<tr><td>*</td><td>Placeholder for zero or more characters.</td><td>s*n finds sin, son, soon, and sullen.</td></tr>
<tr><td>?</td><td>Placeholder for any single character except for spaces and punctuation.</td><td>s?n finds sin, sun, and sandal.</td></tr>
<tr><td>|</td><td>Placeholder for one or more spaces and punctuation characters.</td><td>gh|the|wo finds through the woods.</td></tr>
<tr><td>[ ]</td><td>Placeholder for one or more characters you type between the square brackets.</td><td>s[ai]ng finds sang and sing.</td></tr>
<tr><td>[^]</td><td>Excludes the characters in brackets from the search.</td><td>s[^i]ng finds sang, song, and sung, but not sing.</td></tr>
<tr><td>^</td><td>Placeholder for the beginning of a line. Not applicable with the Whole Word option.</td><td>^si finds sing and single only at the beginning of a line.</td></tr>
<tr><td>$</td><td>Placeholder for the end of a line. This is especially useful for finding text that you do not want to break across lines. Not applicable with the Whole Word option.</td><td><i>Mr.$ finds Mr. at the end of a line. If you search for $ed, FrameMaker finds the end of a line followed by ed on the next line.</td></tr>
</table>

Table 4-1. Using Wildcards in a Search

- **Find Backward:** Searches the selection, document, or book starting at the cursor location and moving towards the beginning of the document.
- **Clone Case:** Matches the case of the original item in the replacement. For example, if you type "President" in the search field and "leader" in the replace field and do not check Clone Case, then FrameMaker replaces "President" with "leader." With Clone Case checked, "President" is replaced with "Leader."
- **Look in:** Searches the current document, selected text, or an entire book. The Book option is available only if a book that contains the current file is open in FrameMaker.

FrameMaker can find items other than just text. You pick an item to search for—marker text or an unresolved cross-reference, for example—from a list.

Searching for an Item

To find and change an item in a document, follow these steps:

1. You can search a book, a document, or selected text. Do one of the following:
   - To search a document, click anywhere in the document's text.
   - To search a specific section of text, select that text.
   - To search a book, open the book. You can start your search from the book window or inside a file that belongs to that book. To search only specific files in the book, select them by CTRL-clicking the files you want.
2. Select Edit➤Find/Change. The Find/Change dialog box is displayed (Figure 4-1).

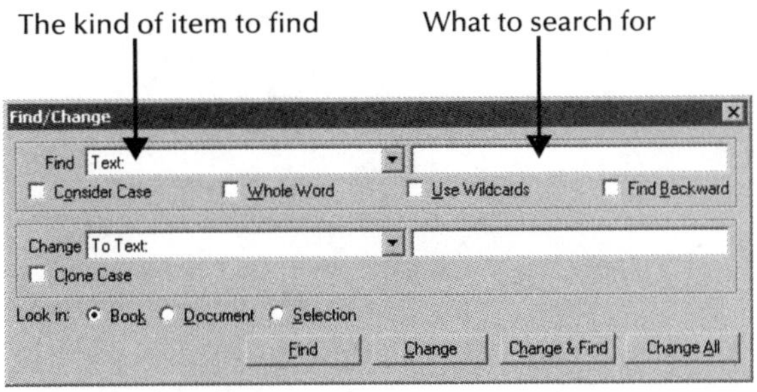

Figure 4-1. Searching FrameMaker documents

3. In the Find drop-down list, click the item you want to find. Items followed by an ellipsis (...) will display a dialog box in which you select additional options. Items followed by colons (:) require that you type in additional search information in the Find field. Table 4-2 on page 70 describes the search options.

Search for...	To find...
Text:	Text you type or paste in the Find field.
Character Format...	Text that uses the specified character formatting. When you select Character Format, the Find Character Format dialog box is displayed, which lets you specify which formatting properties you want to search for. FrameMaker will find italicized characters, including those italicized by a character tag. 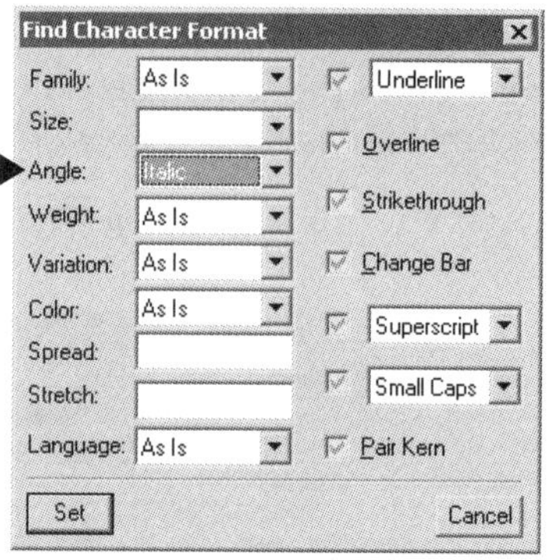 When you click As Is in the Size drop-down list, the setting defaults to the size of the font at the insertion point. If a specific font setting (such as size) is specified in the dialog box, to remove it you must delete the font setting or click As Is in the drop-down list. To set the Spread and Stretch properties to As Is, delete the information shown in the fields. To set the pair kerning to As Is, check the Pair Kern check box once. The gray check mark, as shown in the preceding example, indicates the As Is setting.
Paragraph Tag:	The paragraph tag name you specify in the Find field.
Character Tag:	The character tag name you specify in the Find field.
Any Marker	Any type of marker, such as hypertext markers, index markers, cross-reference markers, and so on.
Marker of Type:	Markers of the type you specify in the Find field.
Marker Text:	Markers of any type that contain the text you specify in the Find field.

Table 4-2. Search Criteria

Search for...	To find...
Any Cross-Reference	Any cross-reference.
Cross-Reference of Format:	Cross-references that use the cross-reference format you specify in the Find field.
Unresolved Cross-Reference	Unresolved (broken) cross-references.
Any Text Inset	Any text inset.
Unresolved Text Inset	Unresolved (broken) text insets.
Any Publisher	Not used in FrameMaker 8 (formerly used on Macintosh only).
Any Variable	Any variable.
Variable of Name:	A variable that matches the name you specify in the Find field.
Any Rubi	Rubi characters. Rubi are pronunciation cues for Japanese characters.
Anchored Frame	Any anchored frame.
Footnote	Any footnote.
Any Table	Any table.
Table Tag:	Tables that use the table tag you specify in the Find field.
Conditional Text:	Conditional text. When you select this option, the Find Conditional Text dialog box is displayed. Set the condition tags to match the conditional text you want to find, then click the Set button. 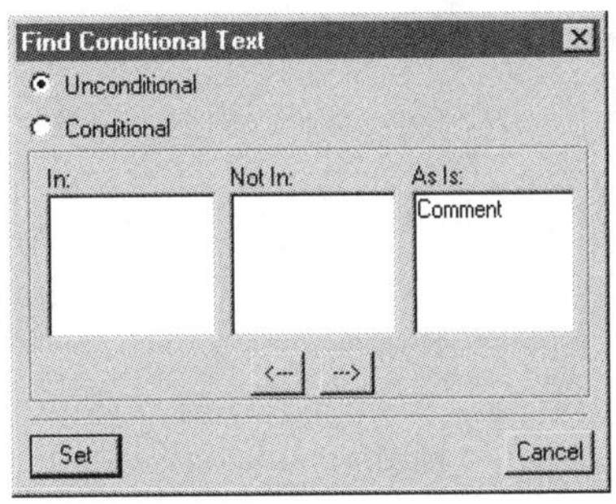
Automatic Hyphen	Hyphens inserted by FrameMaker's hyphenation utility.
Text & Character Formats on Clipboard	Text or character formatting you've copied from the FrameMaker document.

Table 4-2. Search Criteria (Continued)

4. *(optional)* To limit the search, check any of the Consider Case, Whole Word, Use Wildcards (only if searching for text), or Find Backward check boxes.
5. To indicate the scope of the search, click the Book, Document, or Selection radio button in the Look in section. (If the book file is displayed, and you want to search only some of its files, then select those files and choose Selection, not Book.)
6. Click the Find button or press ENTER to begin the search. FrameMaker highlights the first match in your document, book, or selection.
7. Click the Find button to search for the next occurrence.

CAUTION Don't press ENTER to search for the next occurrence. After you click the Find button, the focus is on the page instead of the dialog box, so you'll delete the highlighted word and insert a carriage return if you do so.

Replacing an Item

To replace the item you've found, follow these steps:

1. Click a replacement method in the Change drop-down list.
   - **To Text:** Replaces the found item with the text you type in the Change field.
   - **To Character Format:** Displays the Change to Character Format dialog box, which looks similar to the Character Designer. Click the properties you want in the drop-down lists, then click the Set button.
   - **By Pasting:** Replaces the found item with the contents of the clipboard (which can be formatted text or special copied items such as paragraph or conditional text formats).
2. After FrameMaker finds the item you searched for, do one of the following to replace the item:
   - To change only the first match, click the Change button.
   - To change the first match and find the next one, click the Change & Find button.
   - To change all matches, click the Change All button. Click the OK button to replace all matches. If you searched across a book, the item is replaced throughout the book.

Spell-Checking

The language setting in paragraph and character tags tells FrameMaker which dictionary to use when spell-checking (and hyphenating) the text. Don't assign a language if you don't want FrameMaker to spell-check the text. For example, users often set the language in a Code paragraph tag to None to skip spell-checking computer code.

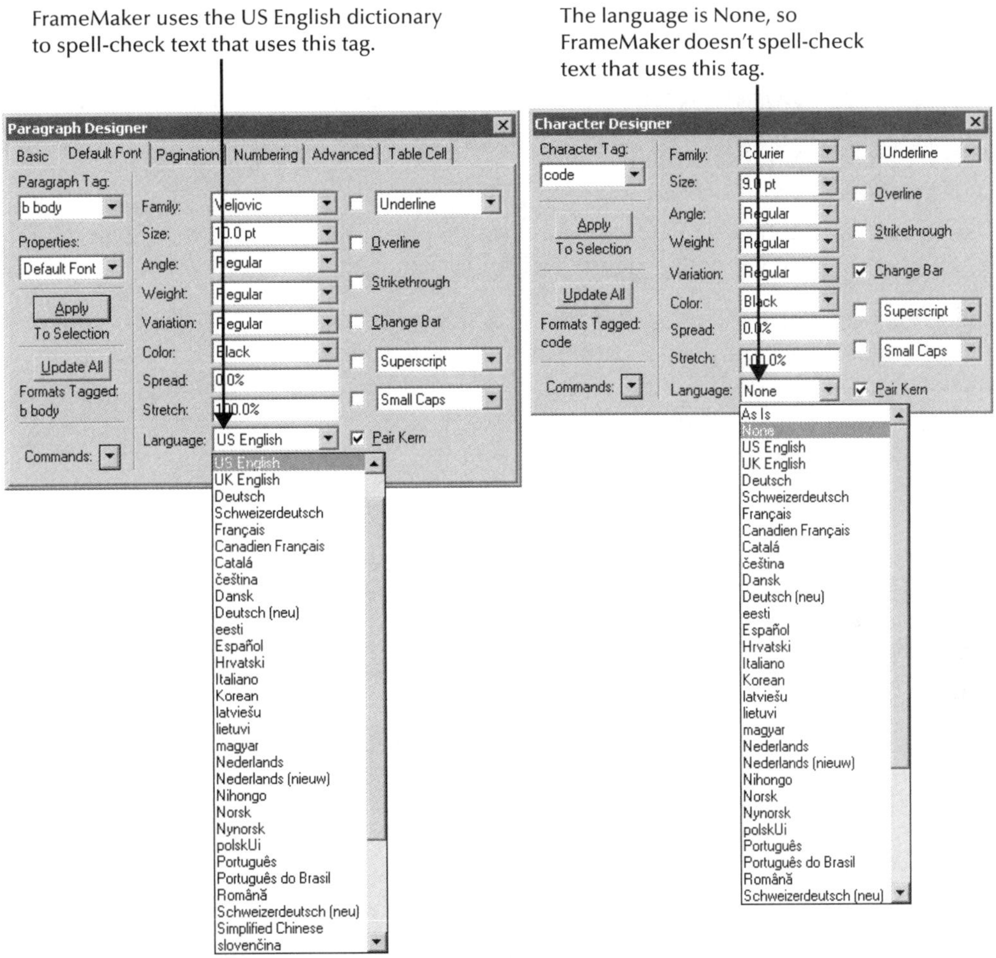

Figure 4-2. FrameMaker spell-checks using the dictionary for the tag's language

FrameMaker spell-checks using four dictionaries:

- **Main dictionary.** The primary dictionary installed with the program. FrameMaker provides main dictionaries in several languages. You pick the language in paragraph and character tags.

- **Personal dictionary.** The dictionary of words added during a spell-check. You click the Learn button in the Spelling Checker to add words to this dictionary. FrameMaker also lets you create additional personal dictionaries to use, for example, in different types of documents—a financial dictionary for annual reports or a computer dictionary for user's guides. Coworkers can merge your personal dictionary with their personal dictionaries.
- **Document dictionary.** The dictionary embedded in the document. You add words that are correct in the current document but not in other contexts by clicking the Allow in Document button in the Spelling Checker dialog box. This dictionary is part of the FrameMaker document, not a separate file like the other dictionaries. As a result, anyone who spell-checks the document has access to the same dictionary, even if the document is opened on another computer. You can write this dictionary to a separate file and clear the dictionary.
- **Site dictionary.** A dictionary containing terms specific to your company, for example, and generally maintained by a system administrator.

When you spell-check, FrameMaker looks for misspelled words and items you select in the Spelling Checker options. Extra spaces, straight quotes, repeated words, and unusual punctuation are among the options you can choose. See "Spelling Checker Options" on page 76 for details.

To spell-check, follow these steps:

1. Display the item you want to spell-check by doing one of the following:
   - Position your cursor in the page or document you want to spell-check.
   - Display the book file you want to spell-check. To spell-check specific chapters, CTRL-click each chapter.
2. Select Edit➤Spelling Checker. The Spelling Checker dialog box is displayed.

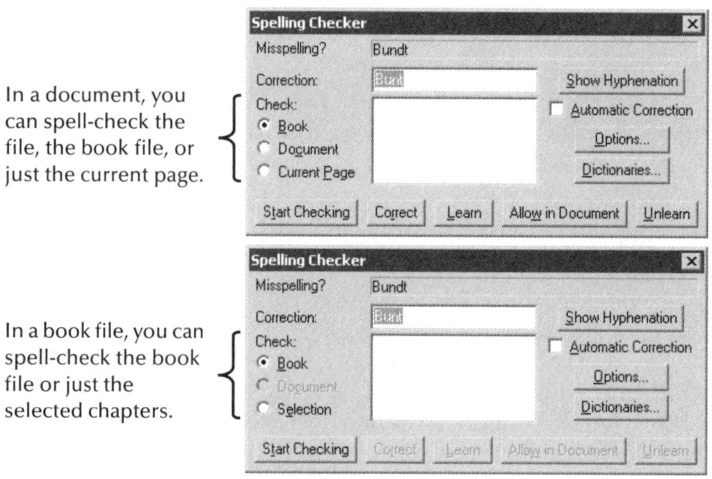

Figure 4-3. Displaying the Spelling Checker

3. In the Check section, indicate the item you want to spell-check by doing one of the following:
   - In a document, click the Book, Document, or Current Page radio button. (The Book radio button is not available if the book file isn't open.)
   - In a book file, click the Book or Selection radio button. (The Document radio button is not available at the book level.)
4. To start spell-checking, click the Start Checking button, or press ENTER. When FrameMaker finds a misspelled word, possible corrections are displayed. The closest match is displayed in the Correction field. The remaining possibilities are displayed in the list beneath the Correction field.

NOTE If no misspellings are found, "Spelling OK" is displayed in the upper-left corner of the Spelling Checker dialog box.

5. Do one of the following:
   - To correct the word, either click the Correct button to accept the first suggested word, double-click another word in the list, or type in the correct word in the Correction field, then click the Correct button. The word on the page is updated.
   - To add the word to the current document dictionary, click the Allow in Document button. The word won't be flagged again in the current document.
   - To add the word to your personal dictionary, click the Learn button. The word won't be flagged again in any document you spell-check. See "Modifying Your Personal Dictionary" on page 77 for details.

TIP When the correct spelling is displayed in the Correction field, check the Automatic Correction check box to replace other occurrences of that misspelling automatically as you spell-check. FrameMaker won't prompt you each time the Spelling Checker finds the word. You can undo the automatic corrections by clicking the Dictionaries button in the Spelling Checker, clicking the Clear Automatic Corrections check box in the Dictionary Functions dialog box (Figure 4-4 on page 77), and then clicking the OK button.

   - To skip the word, click the Start Checking button or press ENTER. You can't add the spell-check options (extra spaces, straight quotes, repeated words, and so on) to the dictionary, so you should skip a straight quote if you need it in the document. FrameMaker will find skipped items, however, each time you spell-check the document.

Spelling Checker Options

The Spelling Checker options let you include additional items in a spell-check. By default, FrameMaker checks for repeated words, two consecutive punctuation marks of several types, straight quotes, extra spaces, and spaces before and after specific characters. Single words, all uppercase words, words containing a period, and words with digits are ignored.

To modify the Spelling Checker defaults, do the following:

1. Click the Options button in the Spelling Checker. The Spelling Checker Options dialog box is displayed.

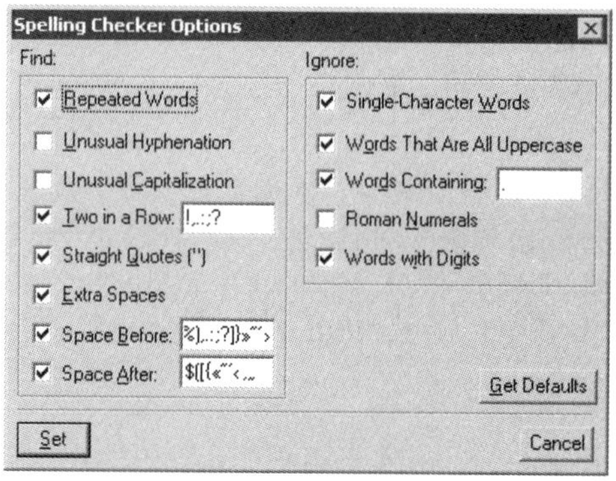

2. Change the options. Table 4-3 describes the options.

Item	Example
Find	
Repeated Words	the the
Unusual Hyphenation	unu-sual
Unusual Capitalization	cRazY
Two in a Row	Why??
Straight Quotes	"happy"
Extra Spaces	party time
Spaces Before and Spaces After	(howling)
Ignore	
Single-Character Words	a

Table 4-3. Spell-Check Options

Item	Example
Words That Are All Uppercase	OLE
Words Containing	window.pane
Roman Numerals	ii
Words with Digits	555-TIME

Table 4-3. Spell-Check Options (Continued)

3. Click Set.

After you modify the Spelling Checker options, you can spell-check the document using the new guidelines. To do so, click the Dictionaries button in the Spelling Checker (Figure 4-4 on page 77), click the Mark All Paragraphs for Rechecking check box in the Dictionary Functions dialog box, and click the OK button.

NOTE You cannot add items to the dictionary that the Spelling Checker looks for, such as repeated words or extra spaces. If you want to skip these items, modify the Spelling Checker options and spell-check again.

Modifying Your Personal Dictionary

FrameMaker updates your personal dictionary when you click the Learn and Unlearn buttons. You can also create new personal dictionaries, merge another dictionary into yours, save unknown words to a separate file, and stop using your personal dictionary.

To modify your personal dictionary or create a new one, follow these steps:

1. Click the Dictionaries button in the Spelling Checker dialog box. The Dictionary Functions dialog box is displayed (Figure 4-4).

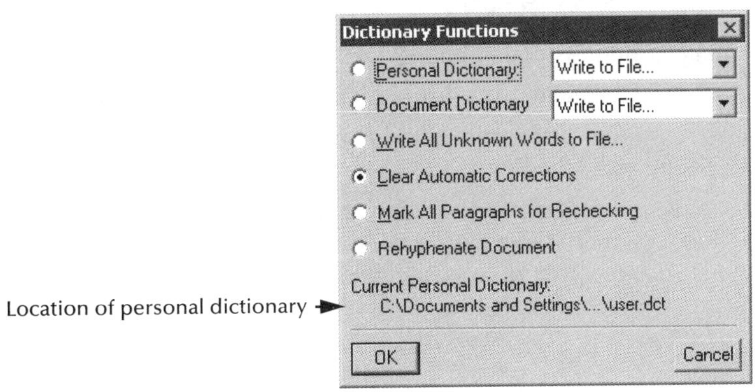

Figure 4-4. Displaying dictionary options

2. In the Personal Dictionary drop-down list, do one of the following:
   - To export your personal dictionary to a text file, click Write to File, then click the OK button. The Write Personal Dictionary to File dialog box is displayed. Type the name of the dictionary in the File name field, then click the Save button. The text file is created.
   - To switch personal dictionaries, click Change Dictionary, then click the OK button. The Use File for Personal Dictionary dialog box is displayed. Click the file you want to use, then click the Use button. The name of the new personal dictionary is displayed.
   - To add entries from another dictionary to your dictionary, click Merge from File, then click the OK button. The Merge File into Personal Dictionary dialog box is displayed. Click the file you want to merge into your dictionary, then click the Merge button. The dictionaries are merged.
   - To stop using your personal dictionary, click Set to None, then click the OK button. The name of your current personal dictionary is no longer displayed in the Dictionary Functions dialog box. (If you click the Learn or Unlearn button without a personal dictionary selected, FrameMaker warns that you need to select the personal dictionary and try again.)

Modifying the Document Dictionary

FrameMaker updates the document dictionary when you click the Allow in Document button during a spell-check. You can also remove entries, merge another document dictionary into the current one, and save the dictionary to a separate file.

TIP To edit the document dictionary by hand, save your FrameMaker document as a Maker Interchange Format (MIF) file, and then open the MIF file in a text editor. The words you allowed in the document are in the Dictionary section. See Chapter 24, "Maker Interchange Format," for details about MIF files.

To modify the document dictionary, follow these steps:

1. Click the Dictionaries button in the Spelling Checker dialog box. The Dictionary Functions dialog box is displayed (Figure 4-4 on page 77).
2. In the Document Dictionary drop-down list, do one of the following:
   - To remove all entries from the document dictionary, click Clear, then click the OK button. The words are removed from the document dictionary.
   - To merge another document dictionary with the current document dictionary, click Merge from File, then click the OK button. The Merge File into Document Dictionary dialog box is displayed. Click the document

dictionary you want to merge with your dictionary, then click the Merge button. The files are merged.

- To export the document dictionary from your FrameMaker document to a separate text file, click Write to File, then click the OK button. The Write Document Dictionary to File dialog box is displayed. Type the name of the dictionary in the File name field, then click the Save button. The dictionary file is created.

TIP You can merge the exported document dictionary with your personal dictionary. See "Modifying Your Personal Dictionary" on page 77 for details.

Customizing Hyphenation

Dictionaries don't just contain lists of words; they also show how words are hyphenated. FrameMaker shows the hyphenation points when you click the Show Hyphenation button in the Spelling Checker. For example, the following dictionary entries suggest hyphenation for three words:

```
fire-wall
gray-scale
hy-per-link
```

When you install FrameMaker, dictionaries for different languages and the corresponding hyphenation files are also installed. For example, the *hyphens.itl* file contains hyphenation points for popular Italian words. If you don't like the hyphenation, you correct the hyphenation in the Spelling Checker and click the Learn button. The main dictionary is updated.

Paragraph tags also determine how words are hyphenated:

- **Language:** On the Default Font sheet of the Paragraph Designer, you select a language for the paragraph tag, and FrameMaker uses the corresponding hyphenation file.
- **Hyphenation parameters:** On the Paragraph Designer's Advanced sheet, you turn hyphenation off or on and specify how words are broken across lines. For example, the CellBody paragraph style shown in the following illustration limits the shortest prefix and suffix to three characters each. See "Advanced Sheet" on page 125 for details.

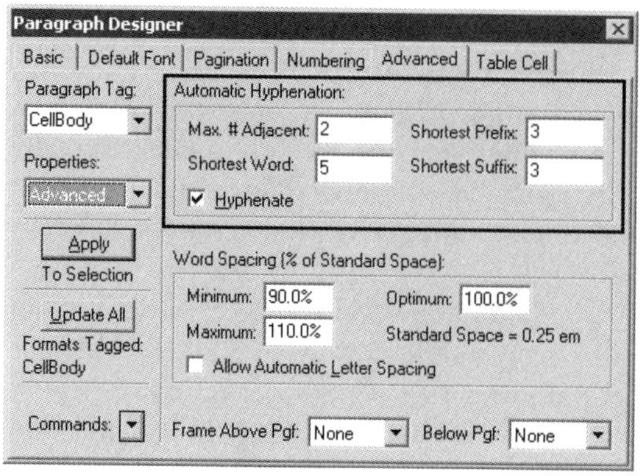

The paragraph tag hyphenation settings take precedence over the hyphenation points. For example, suppose the word *paper* is hyphenated as *pa-per.* According to the predefined hyphenation, the word breaks after the two-letter prefix *pa-*. If the paragraph tag requires at least a three-character prefix, *paper* moves to the next line, and FrameMaker doesn't use the predefined hyphenation.

Paragraph tag allows a two-character prefix at the end of the line. → We subscribe to the local pa-
per, *The News and Observer.*

Paragraph tag requires a three-character prefix, so the word "paper" moves to the next line. Also, the word "Observer" isn't hyphenated due to prefix and suffix rules. → We subscribe to the local
paper, *The News and*
Observer.

To display and modify hyphenation, follow these steps:

1. Select Edit➤Spelling Checker. The Spelling Checker is displayed (Figure 4-3 on page 74).
2. Type a word in the Correction field, then click the Show Hyphenation button. The hyphenation points are displayed.
3. To change the hyphenation, modify the word in the Correction field, then click the Learn button. (To remove all hyphenation from a word, type a hyphen before the word, as in **-paper**.) The hyphenation points are updated in your personal dictionary.
4. *(optional)* To update hyphenation throughout the document after you correct hyphenation points, follow these steps:
   a. Click the Dictionaries button in the Spelling Checker. The Dictionary Functions dialog box is displayed (Figure 4-4 on page 77).
   b. Click the Rehyphenate Document radio button.
   c. Click the OK button. The hyphenation in your document is updated.

TIP To edit hyphenation by hand, open your personal dictionary in a text editor and type the hyphens where you want them.

Hyphenation Shortcuts

In addition to using the Spelling Checker and paragraph tags to control hyphenation, you can insert symbols in specific words.

- **Prevent hyphenation.** To prevent a word from hyphenating at all, insert the suppress hyphenation symbol at the beginning of the word. If you choose, you can insert the symbol where the word breaks. Press ESC N S to insert the symbol. In a variable or cross-reference format, type \+ where you want to prevent hyphenation.
- **Prevent hyphenation at the end of the line.** To prevent a word from hyphenating at the end of a line, insert a nonbreaking hyphen before the hyphen at the end of the line. Press ESC HYPHEN H to insert the symbol.
- **Force hyphenation.** To force a hyphen to display in a specific location, insert a discretionary hyphen where you want the word to break. Press CTRL-D or ESC HYPHEN SHIFT-D.

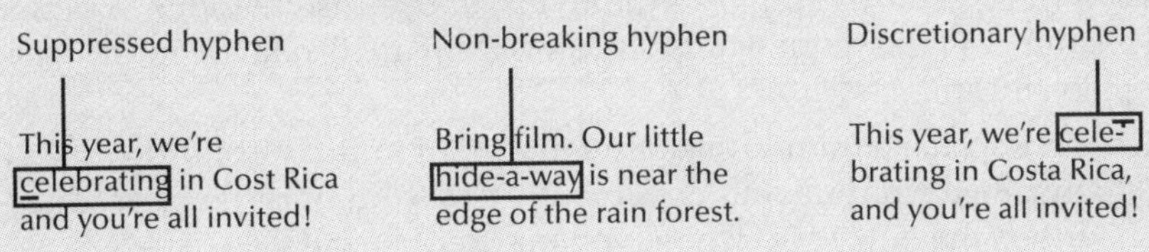

Thesaurus

FrameMaker's Thesaurus identifies the part of speech, synonyms, antonyms, and related words for the selected word or phrase. The Thesaurus isn't as comprehensive as a traditional thesaurus. You might not find an entire word, but you can try to find the root word.

To use the Thesaurus, follow these steps:

1. Do one of the following:
   - If the word doesn't occur in the document or you haven't selected it, select Edit➤Thesaurus. The Thesaurus Look Up dialog box is displayed. Type the word in the Word field, then click the Look Up button. You can also search for the word in a different language by clicking an item in the Language drop-down list. FrameMaker provides a dictionary and associated thesaurus for each of its fully supported languages. See the FrameMaker online help for a list of fully supported languages.

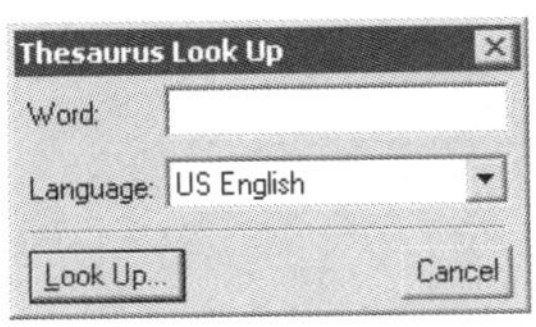

- To look up a word in the document, select the word, then select Edit➤Thesaurus.

The word, definition, and corresponding entries are displayed in the Thesaurus dialog box.

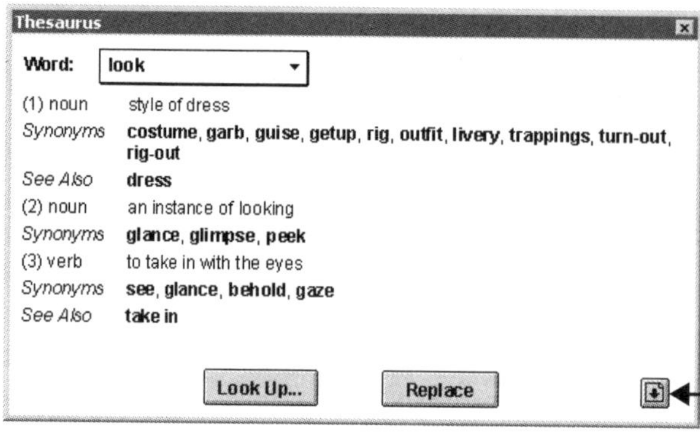

Click the arrow to display the next page of definitions.

2. Click a word in the Synonyms, Antonyms, or See Also sections to explore its meaning. The last ten words you looked up are displayed in the Word drop-down list.
3. Click the Replace button to substitute the word in the Word drop-down list for the highlighted word in your document. (The word must be highlighted, or you'll insert the new word where you inserted the cursor.)

Configuring Default Text Options

Though paragraph tags determine most formatting, FrameMaker lets you specify document defaults to fine-tune the display of text. For example, the Smart Spaces option allows only one consecutive space in the document. When you turn on Smart Quotes, quotes you type are curly. (Quotes you typed before turning on Smart Quotes are still straight quotes.) You can also prevent line breaks after certain characters and specify size and spacing for superscript, subscript, and small caps characters.

You modify text options in an individual file or book file. Because FrameMaker considers the default text options part of the document properties, you can also import the document properties into another FrameMaker file, and the text options are updated. Select Format➤Document➤Text Options to display and change these default text options (Figure 4-5).

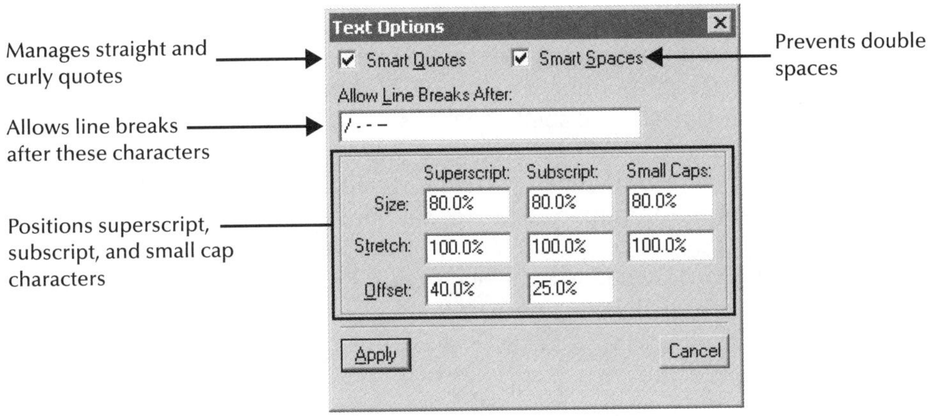

Figure 4-5. Modifying text options

Smart Quotes

When you type single and double quotes, the Smart Quotes option ensures that the quotes are curly instead of straight. For example, instead of typing:

' and "

you type:

‘ and “

In some typeface families, curly quotes are more curved than curly. The previous example shows curly quotes in the Palatino typeface. Notice that the quotes look more angled than curved. In the Times New Roman typeface, however, the quotes are curly, as shown in the following sentence:

> “Hurry up,” cried the impatient customer.

The Spelling Checker can find straight quotes and replace them with curly quotes. This feature is particularly helpful when you import another type of file into FrameMaker. For example, in an imported Microsoft Word document, you need to run the Spelling Checker to find and correct straight quotes. Although FrameMaker catches most of the straight double quotes, it skips over some of the straight single quotes. You need to find and correct the skipped quotes by hand.

Smart Quotes are enabled by default. To turn off smart quotes, follow these steps:

1. In an individual file or book file, select Format➤Document➤Text Options. The Text Options dialog box is displayed (Figure 4-5).
2. Uncheck the Smart Quotes check box, then click the Apply button. Your changes are saved in the document.

When Smart Quotes are enabled, you can still type straight quotes, by typing ESC CTRL-' for a single quote, and ESC SHIFT-' for double quotes.

Smart Spaces

Smart Spaces prevent you from typing more than one space in a row. This feature provides consistent spacing throughout a document. Although the Smart Spaces text option isn't enabled by default, the spell-checker's Extra Spaces is enabled by default. That means that FrameMaker automatically searches for extra spaces during a spell-check, which is especially handy when you import documents of other formats into FrameMaker. For example, an imported Microsoft Word document may have extra spaces after periods. Extra spaces may also have been inserted instead of tabs to position words. When you spell-check the document, FrameMaker finds the extra spaces and replaces them with a single space.

To enable Smart Spaces, follow these steps:

1. In an individual file or book file, select Format➤Document➤Text Options. The Text Options dialog box is displayed (Figure 4-5 on page 83).
2. Check the Smart Spaces check box, then click the Apply button. In any new text, you are prevented from typing two spaces in a row. To remove extra spaces from the existing information, you need to spell-check with the Extra Spaces option checked.

NOTE If you turn off Smart Spaces, you need to modify the Spelling Checker options to disable checking for extra spaces. See "Spelling Checker Options" on page 76 for more information.

Restricting Line Breaks

You can force special characters and spaces to move to the next line or prevent them from doing so. By default, line breaks are permitted after the following characters:

- **Forward slash.** /
- **Dash.** -
- **En dash.** –
- **Em dash.** —

These characters are displayed in the Allow Line Breaks After field of the Text Options dialog box (Figure 4-5 on page 83). When you modify characters in the field, FrameMaker instantly updates line breaks in the document.

Line break permitted after em dash → Which fruit do you prefer—
apples or oranges?

Line break not permitted after em dash → Which fruit do you
prefer—apples or oranges?

For information about typing special characters in the dialog box, see "Entering Special Characters in Dialog Boxes" on page 629.

To configure line breaks, follow these steps:

1. In an individual file or book file, select Format➤Document➤Text Options. The Text Options dialog box is displayed (Figure 4-5 on page 83).
2. Modify characters in the Allow Line Breaks After field, then click the Apply button. Your changes are applied to the document.

Formatting Superscripts, Subscripts, and Small Caps

The document text options determine the size, offset, and width for superscript, subscript, and small caps characters. When you change the defaults, FrameMaker changes how these characters are displayed across paragraph tags, character tags, footnotes, variables, and other components that include them. These settings apply to the entire document.

You can change the following properties:

- **Size.** The superscript, subscript, and small caps characters are a certain percentage smaller than the default paragraph or character formatting.
  To change the size of the characters throughout a document, you modify the percentage in the appropriate Size fields of the Text Options dialog box.

  Small caps are 80 percent shorter than the default font. → ADOBE FRAMEMAKER

  Small caps decreased to 60 percent of default font. → ADOBE FRAMEMAKER

- **Offset.** Superscript and subscript characters are displayed a certain percentage above or below the current line. To increase the offset, you increase the percentages in the Offset fields. To decrease the offset, you decrease the percentage as shown in the following example:

  40 percent offset → Adobe FrameMaker®

  30 percent offset → Adobe FrameMaker®

- **Width.** You can change the width of superscript, subscript, and small caps characters by modifying the Stretch fields. In the following example, the registration mark is displayed with a 100 percent stretch (the same size as the paragraph tag) and with an 80 percent stretch:

  100 percent stretch → Adobe FrameMaker®

  80 percent stretch → Adobe FrameMaker®

NOTE In the document text options, the stretch value applies only to superscript, subscript, and small caps characters. You can set the stretch in paragraph and character tags, but those settings are unrelated to the text options.

To change the superscript, subscript, and small caps settings, follow these steps:

1. In an individual file or book file, select Format➤Document➤Text Options. The Text Options dialog box is displayed (Figure 4-5 on page 83).
2. Do any of the following:
   - To change the size, stretch, or offset of superscript and subscript characters, type new percentages in the Size, Stretch, or Offset fields.
   - To change the size or stretch of small caps characters, type new percentages in the Small Caps fields.
3. Click the Apply button. The new settings are applied to the document.

Tracking Changes

You can track changes as they are made using the Track Text Edits tool. After the revisions are made, you can review the edits one at a time, accept all edits, or reject all edits. You can also keep track of changes in other ways in FrameMaker. The basic word count tells you the number of words in the document (see "Displaying the Word Count" on page 90). You might compare this number to the number of words in a previous version of the document. To show modified text on the page, you can turn on automatic change bars, which are displayed in the margin of the document when any change is made (see "Using Change Bars" on page 91). For more specific information, you can compare two versions of the same document or book (see "Comparing Documents and Books" on page 93).

Using the Track Text Edits Tool

FrameMaker lets you track text edits as you make them by highlighting inserted and deleted text. You can track revisions, then review the changes, and accept or reject edits. You can also preview the final document with the changes, or preview the original document as it was before changes were made.

If you have used a track changes tool in other software, you might expect features that are not available with the track text edits feature. For example, you cannot track changes by author, and dates of changes are not saved.

Figure 4-6 shows a FrameMaker file in which text edits are being tracked.

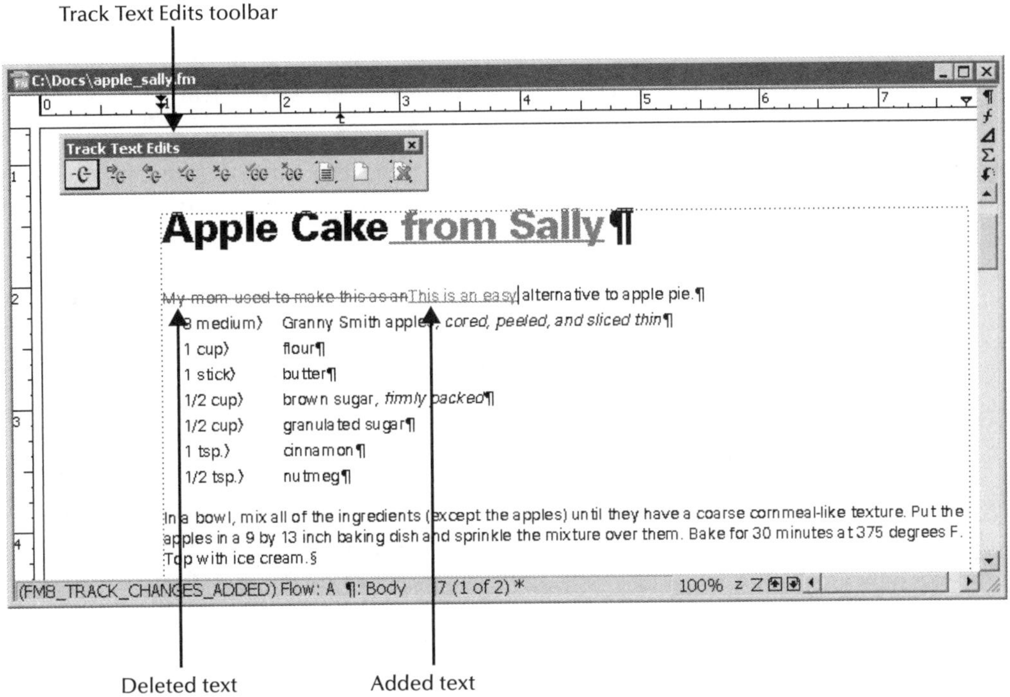

Figure 4-6. Tracking text edits

You can access the track text edits options either through the Special menu, or by using the Track Text Edits tool bar.

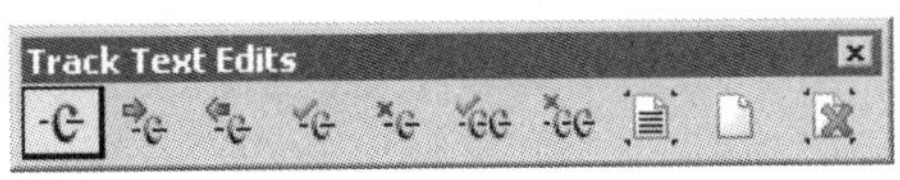

To display the Track Text Edits tool bar, select View➤Track Text Edit Bar. Table 4-4 lists the buttons on the bar.

Button	Function
	**Enable/Disable:** Turns track text editing on or off.
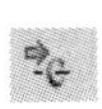	**Show Next:** Moves to and selects the next text edit.
	**Show Previous:** Moves to and selects the previous text edit.

Table 4-4. Buttons on the Track Text Edits toolbar

Button	Function
	**Accept Edit:** Accepts the selected edit and removes the track text edit display.
	**Reject Edit:** Rejects the selected edit, removes the changes, and removes the track text edit display.
	**Accept All:** Accepts all the edits in the current document and removes the track text edit display.
	**Remove All:** Removes all the edits in the current document and removes the track text edit display.
	**Preview Final:** Displays the current document with all the edits applied and no track text edit display.
	**Preview Original:** Displays the current document as it was before you began tracking text edits.
	**Preview Off:** Turns off the preview for the current document to display all text edits.

Table 4-4. Buttons on the Track Text Edits toolbar (Continued)

You cannot change the display settings for deleted and inserted text. Also, if you preview either the final or original document, and then make a change, the preview is turned off and FrameMaker displays all the edits again.

Although tracking uses a form of conditional text, you cannot control these highlights as with other conditional text in FrameMaker. You cannot turn on tracking for an entire book or import the setting across files. You must turn on tracking for each file in which you want to track changes.

If you find the visual highlighting of tracking text edits distracting, consider making backup copies of your original files, editing the files, and then using the comparison utility provided with FrameMaker. For instructions, see "Comparing Documents and Books" on page 93.

For more details about tracking text edits, see "More Information About Track Text Edits" on page 90.

Turning On Tracking

To turn on text edit tracking:

1. Select Special➤Track Text Edits➤Enable or click the Enable/Disable button on the Track Text Edits toolbar.

2. Start working in your document. As you make changes, the changes are highlighted as follows:
   - Inserted text is shown as green and underlined. It is also marked with the FM8_TRACK_CHANGES_ADDED condition, which is shown in the status bar.
   - Deleted text is displayed as red and underlined. It is also marked with the FM8_TRACK_CHANGES_DELETED condition, which is shown in the status bar.

Reviewing Edits

You can review each edit in a document and accept or reject it, or you can accept or reject all edits.

To review individual edits in a document:

1. Select Special➤Track Text Edits➤Show Next (or Show Previous), or click the Show Next or Show Previous button on the toolbar to select the next or previous text edit.
2. Do one of the following:
   - To accept the edit, select Special➤Track Text Edits➤Accept Edit, or click the Accept Edit button on the toolbar.
   - To reject the edit, select Special➤Track Text Edits➤Reject Edit, or click the Reject Edit button on the toolbar.

To accept or reject all edits in a document:

- Select Special➤Track Text Edits➤Accept All, or click the Accept All button on the toolbar to accept all edits.
- Select Special➤Track Text Edits➤Reject All, or click the Reject All button on the toolbar to reject all edits.

Previewing Changes

As you work, you might want to preview the document as it was originally or as it is with all of the text edits. For example, you might want to print both versions for someone to review. You can preview the final document with edits or the original, and then turn the preview off to return to displaying all edits:

- To preview the final document with all edits, Select Special➤Track Text Edits➤Preview Final, or click the Preview Final button on the toolbar.
- To preview the original document with no edits, select Special➤Track Text Edits➤Preview Original, or click the Preview Original button on the toolbar.
- To return to viewing all the text edits, select Special➤Track Text Edits➤Preview Off, or click the Preview Off button on the toolbar.

More Information About Track Text Edits

- Tracking is done with conditional text. For best results, choose colors other than red or green for regular conditional text display because these are the default colors used for deleted and inserted text. Also, if you add text marked as conditional while you are tracking changes, the FM8_TRACK_CHANGES_ADDED text condition is the one displayed. FrameMaker does not display a merged color to show the overlapping conditions.
- If you delete a table row, the text is deleted and not marked.
- You cannot track by author. Changes are always shown as they are made and retained until you accept or reject edits.
- When deletions are displayed in your document, the content is still considered part of the document. For example, if you create a table of contents, it will include all headings, including deleted headings. Unresolved cross references will also still appear. Therefore, when updating books or generating files, you might want to set all files to the Preview Final setting to hide any deleted content.
- If you have Smart Spaces turned on, and you delete a space, and then try to insert a space in front of it, FrameMaker will not insert the new space because it sees this as a double space.
- Because tracking in FrameMaker is not as robust as the tracking in Microsoft Word, you may not be satisfied with the results. Consider using the change bar or compare document features described in "Using Change Bars" on page 91 and "Comparing Documents and Books" on page 93.

Displaying the Word Count

FrameMaker's Word Count feature shows the number of words in a document. You might run a word count along with comparing documents to show the degree to which content has changed. Running a word count may also help you meet a specific word quota.

In the word count, items such as variables and cross-references are included; paragraph autonumbers (step or footnote numbers, for instance) and hidden conditional text are excluded.

To run a word count, follow these steps:

1. Select File➤Utilities➤Document Reports. The Document Reports dialog box is displayed.

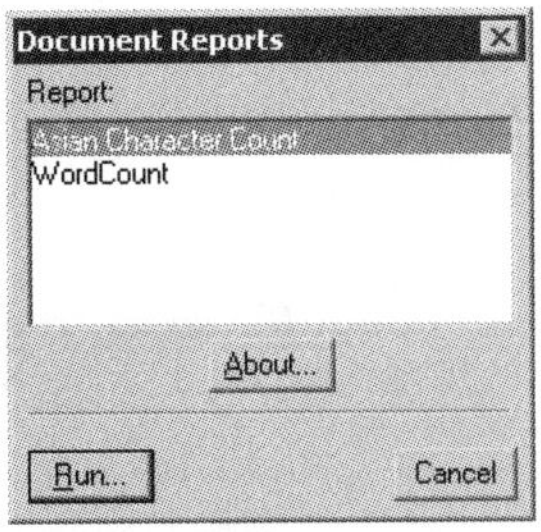

2. In the Report list, click Word Count, then click the Run button. The results are displayed.

3. Click the OK button to close the dialog box.

NOTE For Asian language documents, run an Asian Character Count instead of a word count. The number of single- and double-width characters is displayed.

Using Change Bars

Change bars help readers locate new material. When you modify a document, change bars are displayed in the margin on the line containing the change, even when you insert only a space. As a result, it's often difficult to decipher exactly what was changed. For instance, the following example shows change bars next to modified lines, but the exact changes are not apparent. You can determine only that information changed in lines 1, 2, and 4; but not in line 3.

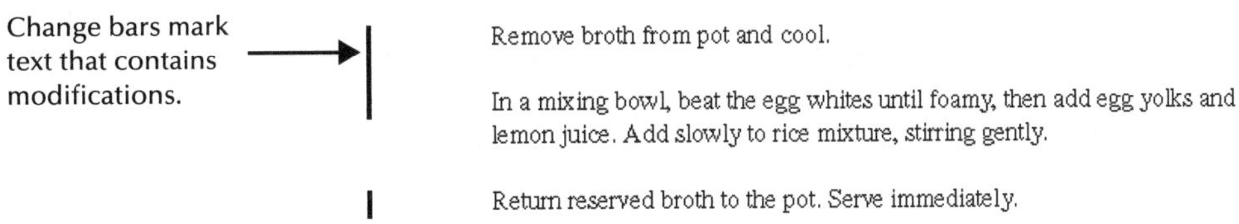

You can customize the color, position, and thickness of automatic change bars and their distance from the text column. These settings apply to the entire document, and you cannot define different change bars for individual editors. Character tags have a change bar option, but you must mark changes manually. You're also still limited to one change bar style.

To toggle and customize automatic change bars, follow these steps:

1. Select Format➤Document➤Change Bars. The Change Bar Properties dialog box is displayed.

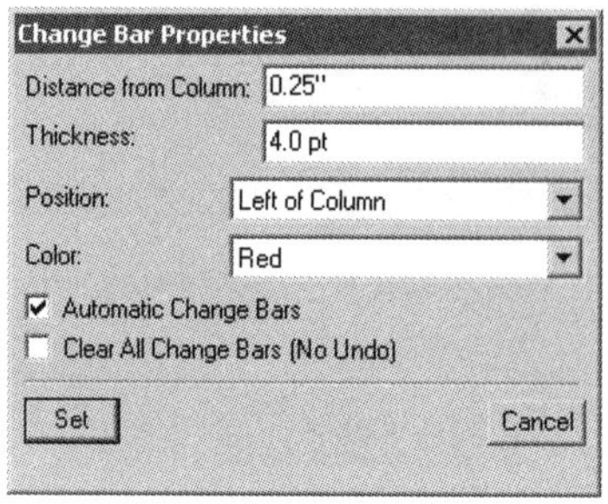

2. To change the space between the change bar and text column, type a new number in the Distance from Column field.
3. To change the size of the change bar, type a new width in the Thickness field.
4. To modify the change bar location, click a location in the Position drop-down list:
   - **Left of Column** *(single-sided document)*: Change bar is displayed in the left margin.
   - **Right of Column** *(single-sided document)*: Change bar is displayed in the right margin.
   - **Side Closer to Page Edge** *(double-sided document)*: Change bar is displayed in the left margin on a left page or in the right margin on a right page.
   - **Side Farther from Page Edge** *(double-sided document)*: Change bar is displayed in the right margin on a left page or in the left margin on a right page.
5. To change the color, click a color in the Color drop-down list. The colors defined in your document are displayed in the list. You can create new colors if needed. See Chapter 20, "Color Output," for details.
6. To remove all existing change bars from your document, check the Clear All Change Bars check box. All change bars are cleared from the document when you click the Set button.

CAUTION Clearing change bars also removes those applied by character tags. You cannot undo this command once change bars are removed. To be safe, save your document before you clear change bars, so you can revert to the saved file if necessary.

7. Check the Automatic Change Bars check box, then click the Set button.

Comparing Documents and Books

The Compare Documents feature lets you compare two versions of the same document or book to see what's changed. In a document comparison, FrameMaker analyzes the contents of matching flows and reports changes to items including the following:

- Text
- Variable definitions
- Marker contents
- Cross-reference formats and the location of cross-reference links
- Anchored frames
- Tables

In a book comparison, FrameMaker lists the modified book components in addition to the document components. For example, the modified items in each file are displayed, along with which files were inserted, modified, or deleted in the book.

There are two types of document comparison reports. In the *composite report,* a marked-up version of the newer document is displayed. The changes are marked with condition tags or special characters—you choose the style before running the report. The *summary report* is only a list of changes. (By default, this report is view-only. Press ESC SHIFT-F L K to make it editable.) FrameMaker lets you run just a summary report or both the composite and summary reports. You can also print and save the reports.

Figure 4-7 on page 94 shows samples of the reports.

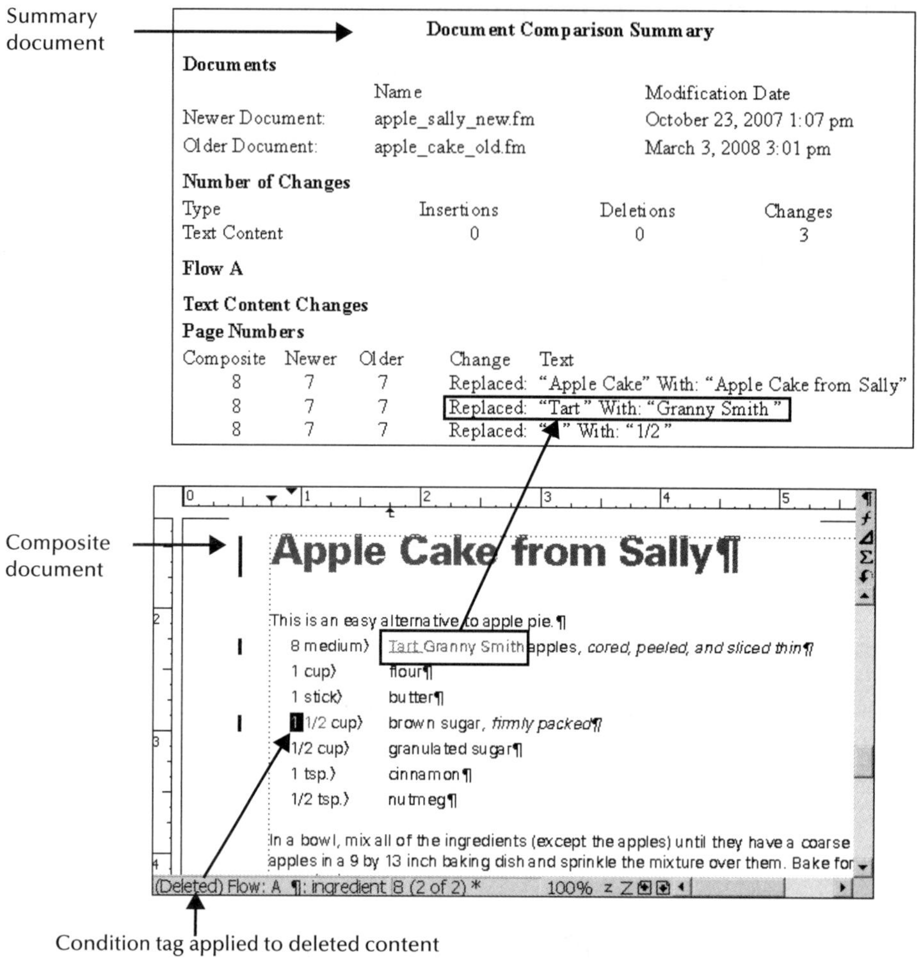

Figure 4-7. The summary and composite document comparison reports

To compare two versions of the same document, follow these steps:

1. Open the old version of the document you want to compare.
2. Open the new version of the document.
3. From the new document, select File➤Utilities➤Compare Documents. The Compare Documents dialog box is displayed.

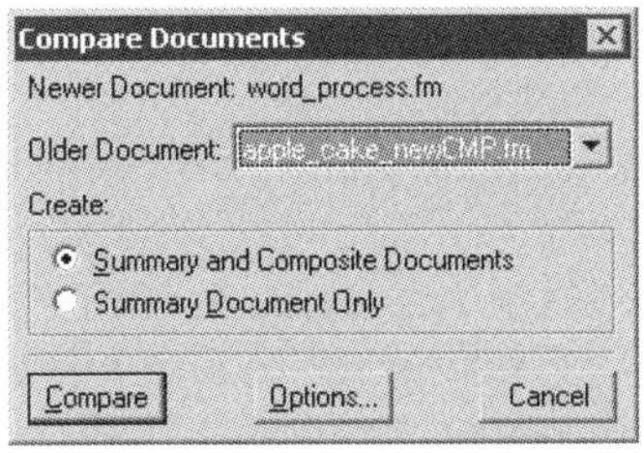

4. If several documents are open, click the name of the document you want to compare in the Older Document drop-down list.

CAUTION Comparing two completely different documents is possible, but it's usually pointless and might cause unexpected results. You compare documents to pinpoint the changes, and FrameMaker doesn't find changes in disparate documents!

5. Do one of the following:
   - Click the Summary and Composite Documents radio button to create both a summary of changes and the marked document.
   - Click the Summary Document Only radio button to create a list of changes.
6. *(optional)* Click the Options button to change the mark-up methods. The Comparison Options dialog box is displayed.

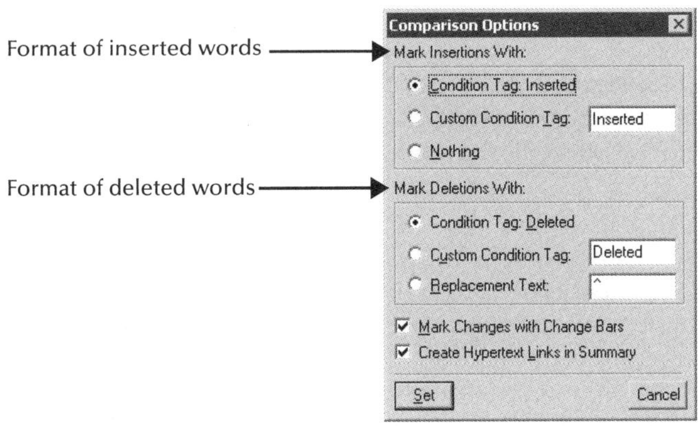

   - In the Mark Insertions With section, click one of the radio buttons to specify formatting for the inserted characters. The default setting applies a condition tag called Inserted, but you can type a new or existing condition in the Custom Condition Tag field or click the Nothing radio button to avoid marking insertions.
   - In the Mark Deletions With section, click one of the radio buttons to customize formatting for the deleted characters. You can assign the Deleted

condition, specify a different condition, or replace the deletion with text, such as "Deleted Text."

- To display change bars in the margin, check the Mark Changes with Change Bars check box.
- To link the changes in the summary document to the original document, check the Create Hypertext Links in Summary check box. You can CTRL-ALT-click a hyperlink to display the referenced document.

Click Set in the Comparison Options dialog box.

7. Click the Compare button. The document reports you chose are displayed.

To compare two versions of the same book file, follow these steps:

1. Open the old and new versions of the book file. The two book files must have identical names, and only chapter files with the same names are compared.
2. From the new book file, select File➤Utilities➤Compare Books. The Compare Books dialog box is displayed.
3. Click the name of the old book file in the Older Book drop-down list.
4. Click the Compare button. The documents you chose are displayed.

Working with Footnotes

Footnotes provide ancillary information at the bottom of the text column or below a table. Three factors affect the format of footnotes:

- **Numbering properties.** In the footnote properties of a book or stand-alone document, you set up the footnote number position, prefix or suffix, paragraph tag applied to the footnote, and maximum height. There are separate properties for main footnotes and table footnotes. If the document is in a book, you select the two properties in the book setup—the footnote format and the numbering options. The footnote format can be numeric, uppercase or lowercase alphabetic, uppercase or lowercase Roman numerals, or a custom format. Numbering options let you specify whether you want the footnote numbering to start over on each page, continue from a previous number, or read the footnote number from the file. You can also specify the starting footnote number for each document in the book. See "Managing Numbering" on page 386 for more information.
- **Footnote paragraph tag.** FrameMaker applies the paragraph tag you specify in the footnote properties to the footnote paragraph. The paragraph uses the Footnote border on the reference page as the frame above the paragraph. You might need to change the height of the frame to adjust spacing. You can also change the properties of the footnote border—for example, modify the line width or color. See "Placing Graphics Above and Below the Paragraph" on page 329 for more information on reference page graphics. Table footnotes and main footnotes can use different paragraph tags.

- **Paragraph tag for main text.** The paragraph tag applied at the location of the footnote number formats the number. If the main paragraph has a serif font, the footnote number is displayed in a serif font.

Figure 4-8 shows the pieces of a footnote.

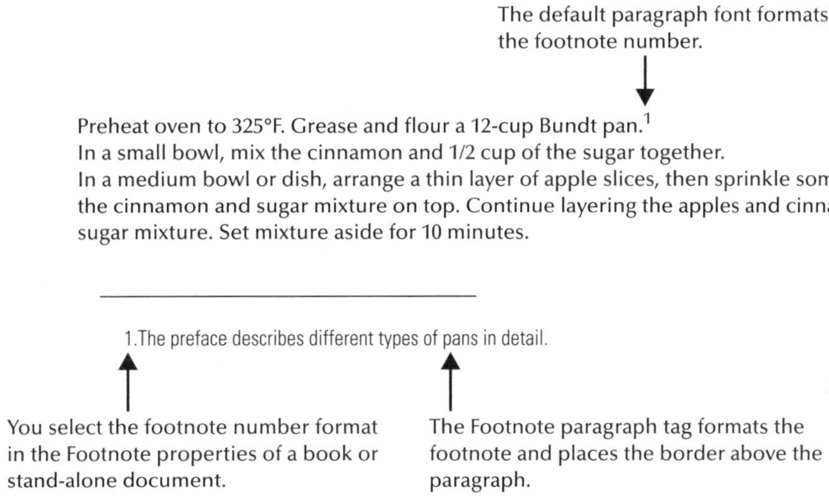

Figure 4-8. Factors affecting footnote formatting

Inserting Footnotes

When you insert a footnote, the number is displayed at the insertion point. Your cursor appears in a new footnote paragraph, which is located at the bottom of the text column (if your cursor is in the body text) or below the table (if your cursor is in a table).

Footnotes are displayed by their position in the body text or table, not by the order in which you insert the footnotes. For example, if you insert a footnote in the first paragraph and the third paragraph, and then insert one in the second paragraph, FrameMaker renumbers the footnote paragraphs.

FrameMaker does not split footnotes between two pages. For example, if there isn't enough room for the footnote paragraph on the current page, the entire paragraph moves to the next page. You can sometimes prevent this problem by manually adjusting the text frame so the footnote fits on the current page or by changing the maximum height of the footnote paragraph. See "Customizing Footnote Properties" on page 99 for details on increasing the maximum height.

The footnote paragraph can be displayed in the column or side head space, across all columns, or across all columns and side heads. If you're working in a multicolumn document, you must adjust the pagination settings in the footnote paragraph tag accordingly. See "Modifying Paragraph Tags" on page 112 for details.

To insert a footnote, follow these steps:

1. Position the cursor where you want the footnote number to be displayed, then select Special ➤ Footnote. The footnote number is displayed in the main text, and your cursor is displayed in the new footnote paragraph at the bottom of the column or below the table, depending on the type of footnote.
2. Type your footnote. The footnote is displayed in the document.

Using the Same Number for Several Footnotes

When you need to refer to the same footnote number in several places, you insert a cross-reference to the existing footnote. The following example shows the initial footnote in the first line and the cross-referenced footnote in the second line. The two references look the same because the footnote number in the second line uses a cross-reference format that applies the superscript automatically.

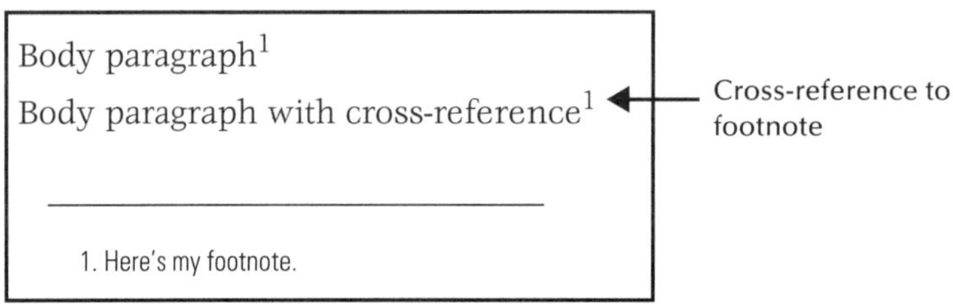

The font properties for the footnote number and cross-reference number are determined by the paragraph tag. For instance, if the footnote paragraph has a serif font and the cross-reference number is in a sans-serif paragraph, the two numbers won't match.

The following example shows the serif footnote number and a sans-serif number for the cross-reference:

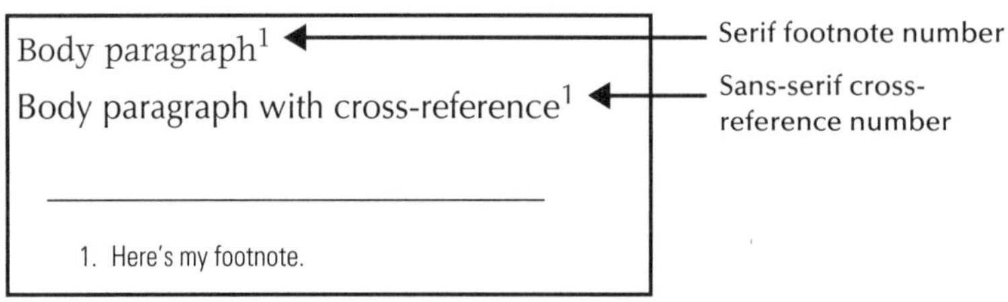

You can prevent this problem by creating a character tag for the cross-reference that specifies the font you want to use for the "imitation" footnotes. The character tag should also include a subscript or superscript property to match the style of the existing footnote. In the cross-reference format, you insert the character tag before the <$paranumonly> building block. The cross-reference format looks something like this:

```
<footnote><$paranumonly></>
```

To create a cross-reference to an existing footnote, follow these steps:

1. Create a character tag that matches the footnote paragraph tag's font properties and the style of the footnote number (superscript or subscript).
2. Create a cross-reference format that includes the character tag and <$paranumonly> building block.
3. Position the cursor where you want the cross-reference, then select Special➤Cross-Reference. The Cross-Reference dialog box is displayed.

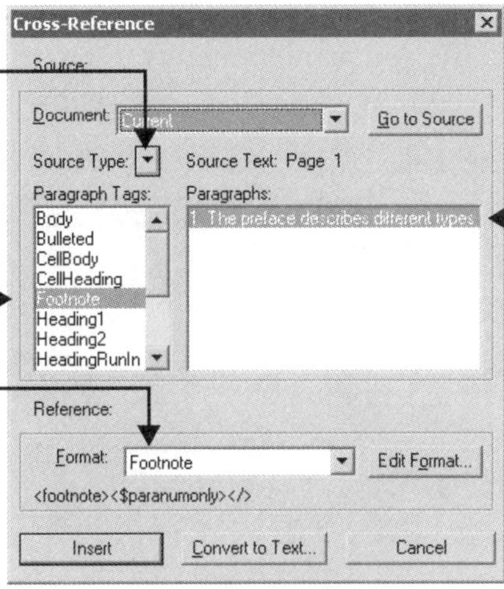

4. Click Paragraphs in the Source Type pop-up menu to display the paragraph tags.
5. In the Paragraph Tags section, click the footnote paragraph tag. The footnote paragraph is displayed in the Paragraphs section.
6. In the Paragraphs section, click the footnote paragraph.
7. In the Format drop-down list, click the footnote cross-reference format you created.
8. Click the Insert button. The cross-reference number is displayed in the text.

For more information on creating cross-reference formats, see "Setting Up Cross-Reference Formats" on page 198. See "Creating Character Tags" on page 149 for details on setting up a character tag.

Customizing Footnote Properties

FrameMaker lets you customize footnote formatting and numbering properties. The formatting properties, which you configure in individual files, consist of the footnote prefix or suffix, position of the number, paragraph tag applied to the footnote, and maximum height. You can import the formatting properties into other documents by importing the document properties. The numbering properties determine how footnotes are numbered in a book (or document) and the type of alphanumeric footnote character. If the document is in a book file, you set the number format in the book file setup. If not, you can change the number format in the document's numbering properties.

Modifying Footnote Formatting

To customize footnote formatting, follow these steps:

1. Open the file or book file you want to modify, then select Format➤Document➤Footnote Properties. The Footnote Properties dialog box is displayed.

Click the tab or drop-down list for the type of footnote you want to edit.

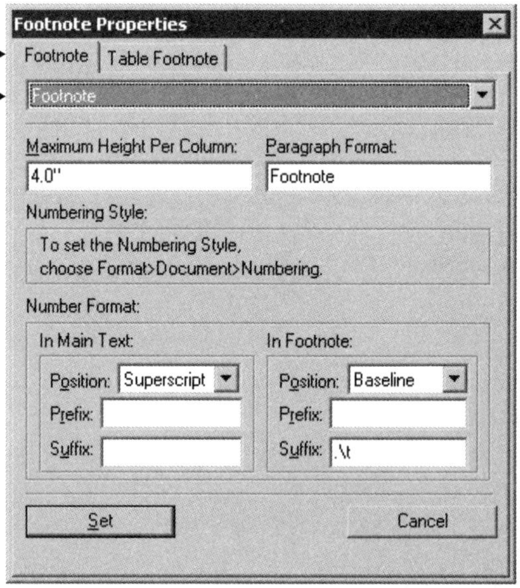

2. Click the Footnote or Table Footnote tab, depending on which type of footnote you need to modify. You can also click Footnote or Table Footnote in the drop-down list at the top.
3. *(standard footnote only)* To limit the height of the Footnote paragraph, type a number in the Maximum Height Per Column field.

NOTE In FrameMaker, you can specify the unit of measure used throughout the document—in paragraph tags, text frame properties, table tags, and so on. To change the unit of measure, select View➤Options and click a different item in the Display Unit drop-down list.

4. To change the paragraph tag applied to new footnotes, type the tag name in the Paragraph Format field. This setting does not change existing footnotes.

CAUTION If you misspell the paragraph tag name, FrameMaker applies the paragraph tag to new footnotes and considers the paragraph tag an override. In the status bar, the asterisk next to the misspelled paragraph tag indicates the override. You can either correct the paragraph tag in the footnote properties or create a new paragraph tag.

5. To change the format of the footnote character in the main text, do any of the following in the In Main Text section (or the In Cell section of table footnotes):
   - Click a position in the Position drop-down list. (Baseline aligns the character with the main text.)
   - To precede the footnote character with a specific character, type the character in the Prefix field. You can type special characters such as an em space (`\sm`) or en space (`\sn`). For more information about typing special characters in dialog boxes, see "Entering Special Characters in Dialog Boxes" on page 629.
   - To display a specific character after the footnote character, type the character in the Suffix field.
6. To change the format of the footnote character in the actual footnote, change settings in the In Footnote section. See the previous step for descriptions of each option.
7. Click the Set button. Your changes are applied to existing footnotes, except for the maximum height and paragraph tag settings, which are only applied to future footnotes.

Modifying the Footnote Numbering Properties in the Book File

To change the footnote numbering properties in a book file, follow these steps:

1. Open the book file, then select the files whose footnote properties you want to change. Press CTRL-A to select all files in the book; CTRL-click to select specific files.
2. Select Format➤Document➤Numbering. The Numbering Properties dialog box is displayed.

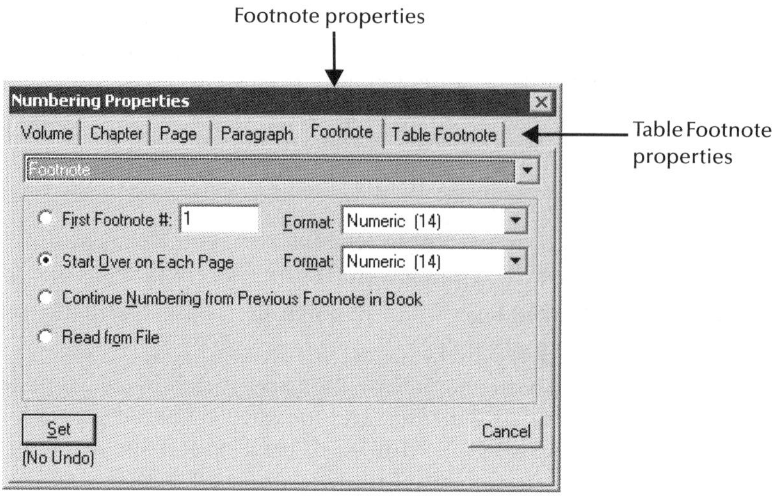

3. Click the Footnote or Table Footnote tab, or click a choice in the drop-down list, depending on the type of footnote you need to modify.
4. Do any of the following:
   - To specify the number of the first footnote in each file, type the number in the First Footnote # field.
   - To change the format of the first footnote, click an item in the Format drop-down list that is displayed next to the First Footnote # field. If you click Custom, the Custom Numbering dialog box is displayed. You change the numbering pattern for the footnotes here. According to the following example, FrameMaker assigns the asterisk to the first footnote, the dagger to the second footnote, and the double dagger to the third footnote in the document or book. These symbols are repeated if you have more than three footnotes. For more information on typing special characters in dialog boxes, see "Entering Special Characters in Dialog Boxes" on page 629.

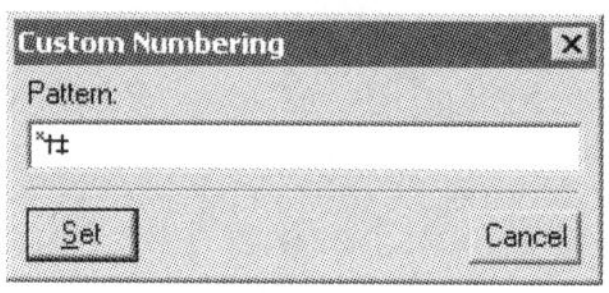

   - To restart footnote numbering on each page, click the Start Over on Each Page radio button, then click the numbering style from the Format drop-down list.
   - To continue numbering from the previous footnote, click the Continue Numbering from Previous Footnote in Book radio button.
   - To use the footnote numbering properties set up in the file, click the Read from File radio button.

CAUTION If the file- and book-level footnote properties differ, FrameMaker displays an Inconsistent Numbering Properties warning when you update the book. The warning explains that file-level numbering properties are ignored during the update.

5. Click the Set button. Your changes are applied to the selected files in the book.

Modifying the Footnote Numbering Properties in Standalone Documents

To modify footnote numbering in individual documents, follow these steps:

1. Select Format➤Document➤Numbering. The Numbering Properties dialog box is displayed.

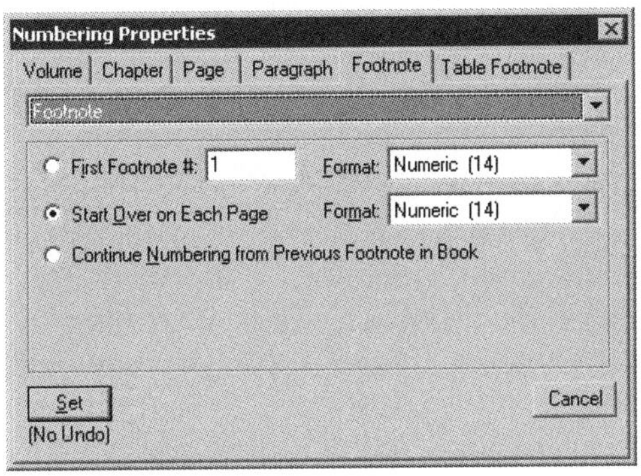

2. Click the Footnote or Table Footnote tab, or click a choice in the drop-down list, depending on the type of footnote you need to modify.
3. Change the properties as described in "Modifying the Footnote Numbering Properties in the Book File" on page 101, then click the Set button. Your changes are applied to the file.

Importing Text from Other Applications

FrameMaker provides filters that let you convert text from many applications into FrameMaker formats. (Importing graphic files is discussed separately; see Chapter 12, "Importing Graphic Content.") Depending on the source format, you may have several different options available for pulling text into FrameMaker, including the following:

- **Copying and pasting.** For some applications, you can open the source document, copy the information you want, and then switch to FrameMaker and paste it in. If you are pasting from Microsoft Word, select Edit➤Paste Special and select Unicode Text, RTF, or unformatted text. Otherwise, text is imported as an OLE object.

For best results, paste as Unicode Text when pasting from Microsoft Word.

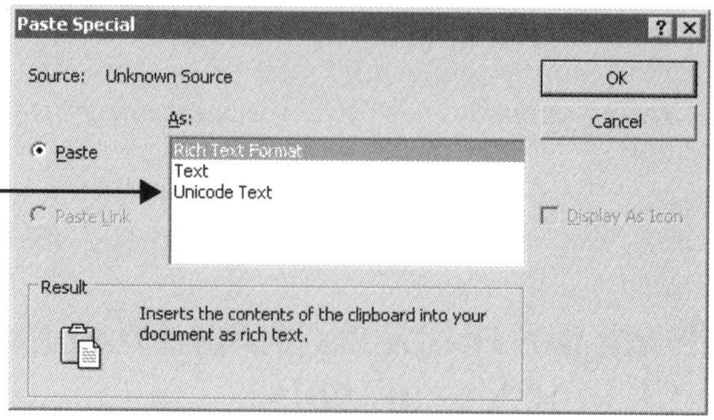

TIP If you pasted from Microsoft Word as Unicode text but there are still gray boxes or question marks appearing instead of the characters you expect, the font you are using in FrameMaker doesn't include the correct Unicode characters. Install the correct font to fix the problem.

To have FrameMaker automatically paste as Unicode text instead of plain text, change the paste order in maker.ini. See "Setting Clipboard Pasting Order" on page 681.

- **Opening the source document.** In FrameMaker, try selecting File➤Open and then opening the source document (such as a Word file). FrameMaker will filter the document and open it as a FrameMaker document. If FrameMaker does not automatically identify the file type, you are prompted to identify it.

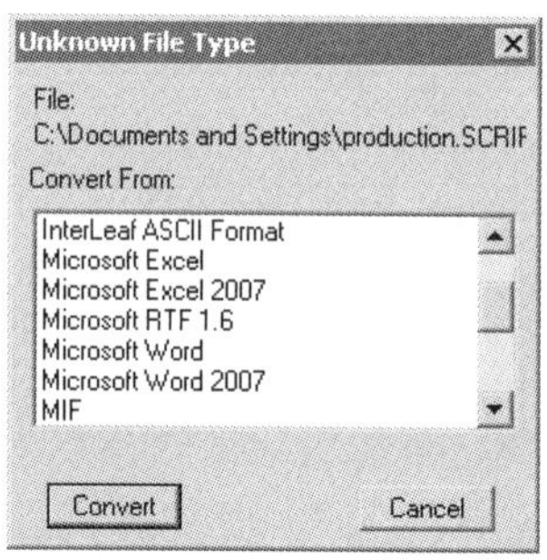

By default, all filters are installed with FrameMaker, but it's possible to exclude filters from the installation if you do a custom installation. If filters seem to be missing, check to see whether you can install more.

- **Creating an intermediate file.** For some applications, such as InDesign, direct import is not available. In most cases, though, you can export the file to an intermediate format (for example, InDesign offers RTF export), and import the intermediate file into FrameMaker. The resulting FrameMaker file usually requires major clean-up.

Whenever you import content from other applications, you might encounter issues with content such as table formatting, graphics, cross-references, and page layouts.

You might need to perform additional processing or formatting to move all the content into FrameMaker format.

The amount of additional processing varies depending on the source document and the program in which it was created. Try using one of the provided import filters first. If the results are not what you need, consider looking at a third-party tool such as Filtrix from Blueberry Software. For details, see Appendix A, "Resources."

For a detailed list of all available filters provided with FrameMaker, check the *Using Filters* online manual. You will find this manual in the Documents folder in your FrameMaker installation folder.

NOTE The *Using Filters* online manual had not been updated for FrameMaker 8 at the time this book was written.

FrameMaker can import Microsoft Word DOCX files as well as DOC and RTF files. Importing content from Microsoft Word is a relatively smooth process. Text usually converts reasonably well, and paragraph styles applied in Word show up in FrameMaker. Index entries are converted into FrameMaker index markers. The results of the conversion aren't perfect. Here are some things you need to do:

- Be sure to accept any revisions in Word *before* importing the document; otherwise, revisions may be displayed as FrameMaker conditional text.
- Graphics are converted, but results are often unusable. Remove graphics before conversion, and import the graphics directly into FrameMaker instead of attempting to convert them through the filter. If source files are unavailable, try saving the Word file as HTML and using the resulting PNG, GIF, or JPEG files, which are usually higher quality than the graphics that are produced during Word-to-FrameMaker conversion. You could also save the Word file as a PDF file and export the graphics from it using Adobe Acrobat Professional or 3D.
- Cross-references are converted as text, so you must re-create them.
- Tables are converted, but Word formatting is applied as overrides. Cleanup is required. Reapply a table format in FrameMaker and remove custom formatting, as described in Chapter 7, "Understanding Table Design." The TableCleaner plug-in from Carmen Publishing (www.frameexpert.com) is invaluable for reformatting tables easily.
- Apply your own master pages to fix the headers and footers.
- Master documents, which are Microsoft Word files that embed other Word files, are not converted. Convert the individual files and add them to a FrameMaker book file.

TIP After you import the Word file into FrameMaker, save it as MIF to remove hidden characters that can cause problems in FrameMaker. See Chapter 24, "Maker Interchange Format."

CHAPTER 5

Formatting Text with Paragraph Tags

FrameMaker provides several different ways to format text. *Paragraph tags* (equivalent to style sheets in other applications) let you save a group of formatting choices and apply them in one step. In a single, named paragraph tag (for example, "Body" or "ChapterTitle"), you can store information including font name and size, tabs, indents, lines above or below, and hyphenation settings. When you apply the Body paragraph tag to a paragraph, all of the stored settings are applied, which is much more efficient than assigning each item individually.

Efficiency, however, is only half the story. Using paragraph tags ensures that formatting is consistent across an entire document. Every time you apply the Body tag, FrameMaker assigns the same formatting. The result is that all of your body paragraphs use identical settings. In a two-page document, this is nice. In a 200-page document, it's critical. When you update the Body tag's settings, FrameMaker immediately updates every body paragraph in the document.

When you assign a paragraph tag, it's applied to the paragraph where the cursor is located or to the paragraph with selected text. (You do not have to select the entire paragraph.) Unlike some other applications, FrameMaker *will not* apply a paragraph tag to a portion of a paragraph (a few words or characters); paragraph tags are always applied to the entire paragraph. If you need to assign special formatting to a few words or characters within the paragraph, use character tags. These are discussed in Chapter 6, "Formatting Text with Character Tags."

Applying Paragraph Tags

Paragraph tags are listed in the paragraph catalog. To display it, click the paragraph catalog button in the upper-right corner of your document.

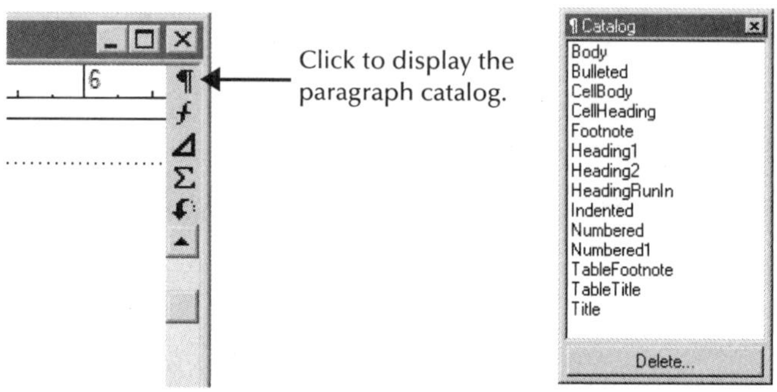

Using the Paragraph Catalog to Apply a Tag

To apply a paragraph tag using the paragraph catalog, follow these steps:

1. In the text, click in a paragraph or select a portion of the paragraph.

2. In the paragraph catalog, click a paragraph tag. The selected tag is applied to the current paragraph. The lower-left corner of the status bar shows the paragraph tag name.

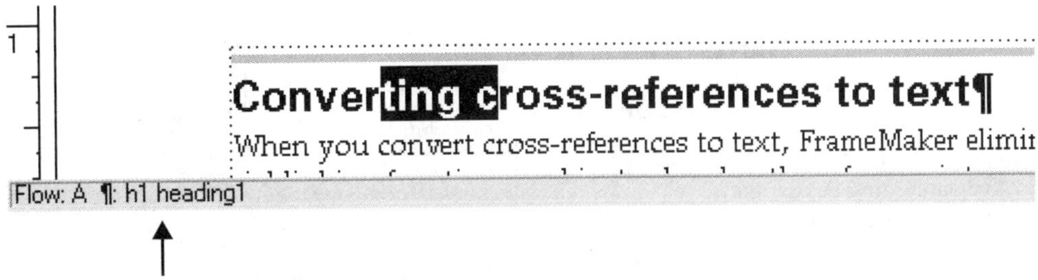

The paragraph tag for the selected paragraph is shown in the status bar.

FrameMaker provides other ways to apply paragraph tags, including:

- Using the Formatting Bar
- Selecting a menu choice
- Using the right-click pop-up menu
- Using keyboard shortcuts

NOTE You can also use the Paragraph Designer to apply paragraph tags, but because you could inadvertently change the paragraph tag definition, this approach is not recommended.

Using the Formatting Bar

You can use the drop-down list on the Formatting Bar to apply paragraph tags. The list of tags is identical to the list in the paragraph catalog.

To apply paragraph tags using the Formatting Bar, follow these steps:

1. If the formatting toolbar is not visible, select View➤Formatting Bar to display it.
2. In the text, click in a paragraph.
3. In the Formatting Bar, click a paragraph tag in the drop-down list.

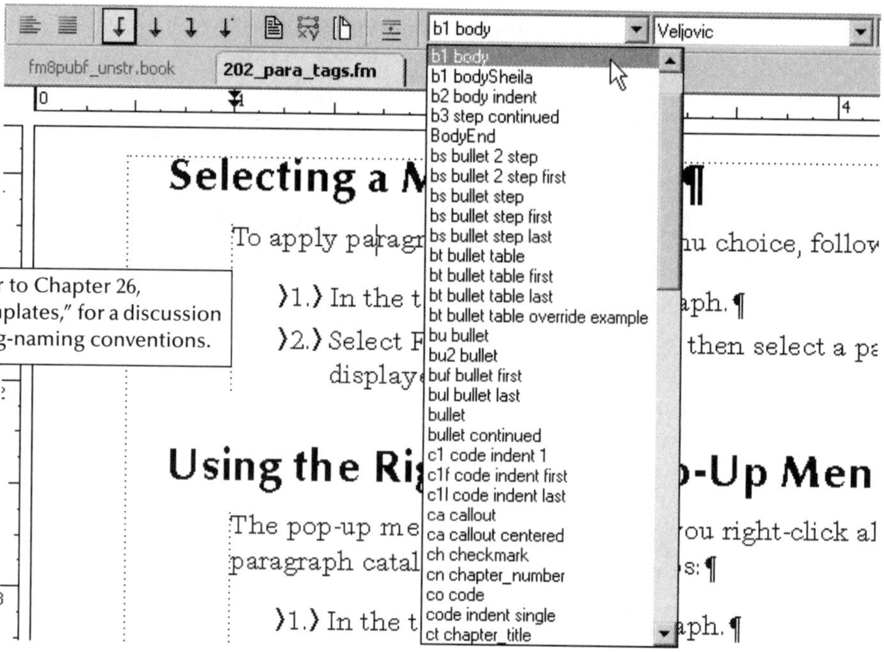

> Refer to Chapter 26, "Templates," for a discussion of tag-naming conventions.

Selecting a Menu Choice

To apply paragraph tags using a menu choice, follow these steps:

1. In the text, click in a paragraph.
2. Select Format➤Paragraphs, then select a paragraph tag from the list that is displayed in the submenu.

Using the Right-Click Pop-Up Menu

The pop-up menu displayed when you right-click also gives you a way to access the paragraph catalog. Follow these steps:

1. In the text, click in a paragraph.
2. Right-click to display the pop-up menu, select Paragraphs, then select a tag from the list that's displayed.

Using Keyboard Shortcuts

You can use keyboard shortcuts to assign paragraph tags. To do so, follow these steps:

1. In the text, click in a paragraph.
2. Press F9. Notice that the left side of the status bar changes color.

Use the arrow keys to scroll through the list of paragraph tags. Press ENTER to apply the tag you want.

3. Display the tag you want by doing any of the following:
   - Use the arrow keys to scroll through the list of available tags.
   - Type a letter to jump to that section of the paragraph catalog.
   - Type the first few letters of the tag name.
4. Press ENTER.

NOTE Some of the keys on your computer may be specially programmed. If so, one or more keyboard shortcuts may not work as described. Consult your system documentation for help.

Avoiding Formatting Overrides

FrameMaker's paragraph tagging gives you complete control over the appearance of the text in your document. When you change paragraph tag settings, FrameMaker automatically applies those changes to every instance of that paragraph in the entire document.

Formatting overrides occur when the tag settings are changed for a single paragraph. Overrides cause inconsistency in the document and make it much more difficult to maintain. When a paragraph has an override, the status bar usually indicates this with a star in front of the tag name.

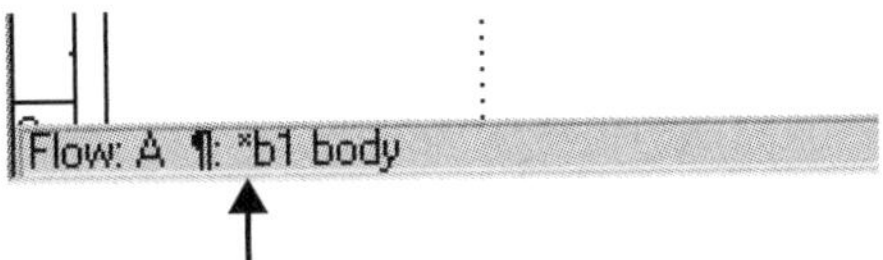

The star in the status bar indicates an override.

The fastest way to remove overrides is to reapply your template and tell FrameMaker to remove all formatting overrides (see "Importing Settings from a Template File" on page 615).

A better approach is not to introduce overrides at all. As long as you apply paragraph tags from the paragraph catalog, you won't have any overrides. Problems occur when you go into the Paragraph Designer and make changes "just this once" to customize the paragraph for a special formatting requirement. Applying font, font size, or font style attributes from the Format menu is an override; avoid these if at all possible. Similarly, assigning tabs by dropping them on the ruler creates overrides. You can make tabs part of the tag definition by setting the tab in the ruler and then clicking the Update All button in the Paragraph Designer. The Bold, Italics, and Underline buttons on the Formatting Bar are also overrides; use character tagging instead.

Modifying Paragraph Tags

Applying paragraph tags is useful, but it probably won't be long before you need to modify the tags. You can make changes in the Paragraph Designer.

CAUTION In many companies, templates are set up and maintained by a standards group or template guru (some have less complimentary names for this person). If you have an official template, you're probably not supposed to make changes to it—unless, of course, *you* are the template guru.

To make changes to an existing tag, follow these steps:

1. Display the Paragraph Designer (Figure 5-1) by selecting Format➤Paragraph➤Designer or by pressing CTRL-M or ESC O P D. You can also CTRL-click a paragraph tag in the paragraph catalog to display the Paragraph Designer for that tag.

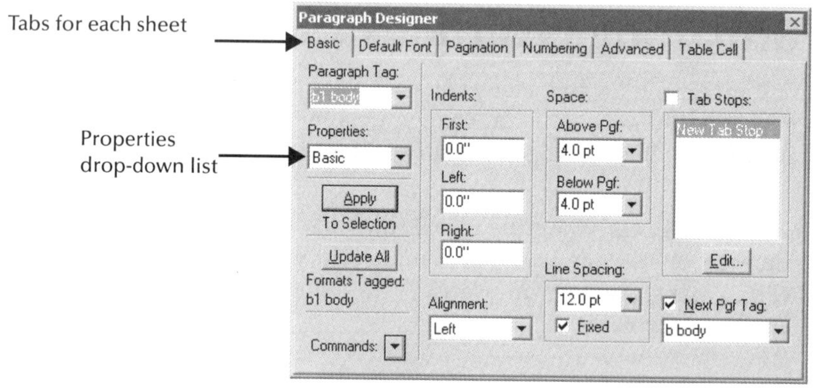

Figure 5-1. Paragraph Designer, Basic properties

2. For each of the six property sheets, change the properties as needed, then click the Update All button. You can move from sheet to sheet using the tabs at the top of the window or the Properties drop-down list.

   The Update All button applies your change to all of the existing paragraphs that use the current tag. It also saves the changes into the paragraph catalog, so that any paragraphs you create in the future will use the same formatting.

NOTE Clicking the Apply button instead of the Update All button creates an override, which is not recommended.

The following sections describe each setting in the Paragraph Designer.

Paragraph Designer Settings

Tag settings are stored in the Paragraph Designer's six property sheets. To navigate from one sheet to the next, click the tab at the top of the dialog box or select from the Properties drop-down list. The sheets are as follows:

- Basic
- Default Font
- Pagination
- Numbering
- Advanced
- Table Cell

Options Available on Every Sheet

The items on the left side of the Paragraph Designer are displayed on every sheet. Table 5-1 lists these properties.

Item	Description
Paragraph Tag drop-down list	Lists the paragraph tags defined in the catalog.
Properties drop-down list	Lists the paragraph properties (or sheets). You can also access the properties using the tabs across the top of the Paragraph Designer dialog box.
Apply button	Applies the changes you've made to the current selection. Use the Apply button only when you want to create an override.
Update All button	Applies the changes you've made to all paragraphs that use the current tag and updates the paragraph catalog. Use the Update All button whenever you want to make a global change.
Commands pop-up menu	Provides advanced commands, such as global updates (see "Updating Selected Paragraphs Globally" on page 131).

Table 5-1. Paragraph Designer Common Properties

Basic Sheet

The options on the Basic sheet (Figure 5-1 on page 112) let you control the paragraph's positioning, such as indents and space above and below the paragraph. You'll find additional positioning choices on the Pagination sheet. Table 5-2 describes the items on the Basic sheet.

Item	Description
Indents	All indents are measured from the edge of the text frame, not from the edge of the paper. (The text frame is represented by a dotted line surrounding the "live" area where you can insert text.) See "Setting Up Indentation" on page 117 for details. ▪ **First:** Sets a left indent for the first line of the paragraph. ▪ **Left:** Sets a left indent for the second and subsequent lines of the paragraph. This indent does not affect the first line. ▪ **Right:** Sets the right indent for each line of the paragraph.
Alignment	Sets the alignment—left, center, right, or justified—for the paragraph.
Space Above Pgf	Sets the amount of white space between the current paragraph and the preceding paragraph. To determine spacing between paragraphs, FrameMaker uses the larger of the space above the current paragraph or the space below the previous paragraph. They are *not* added together. The Space Above setting is ignored for a paragraph at the top of a page. If you need to move a paragraph down from the top of the page, either move the text frame down or use a graphic frame to provide spacing (see "Advanced Sheet" on page 125 for details).
Space Below Pgf	Sets the space below the paragraph.
Line Spacing	Sets the *leading*—the vertical space between lines inside the paragraph. When you change the font size (on the Default Font properties), the leading automatically changes (to about 15 percent more than the font size value), so set the font size before setting the line spacing.

Table 5-2. Basic Sheet

Item	Description
Fixed	When checked, this option sets line spacing from baseline to baseline. (The *baseline* is the bottom of a line of text, not including characters that drop below this invisible line. The letters g, p, q, and y are all *descenders;* they extend below the baseline.) If not checked, line spacing is adjusted to accommodate superscripts and subscripts. Compare the following two paragraphs: ■ This bullet uses fixed line spacing. Superscripts don't have much[1] of an effect. ■ In this bullet, line spacing is not fixed. The superscript does make a[1] difference here.
Tab Stops	Lets you set tab stops for the paragraph. In FrameMaker, paragraphs do not have tab stops by default. Until you add tab stops, pressing the TAB key in a paragraph has no effect. See the following section, "Setting Tab Stops," for details on how to control the tab settings.
Next Pgf Tag	Sets the default tag for the next paragraph tag. When you press ENTER to start a new paragraph, this choice determines what paragraph tag is set by default. For example, a Heading tag could default to Body as the next tag. You can change the Body tag to something else later. If you do not specify a setting for the next paragraph tag, FrameMaker uses the same tag as the current paragraph.

Table 5-2. Basic Sheet (Continued)

NOTE In FrameMaker, you can specify the unit of measure used throughout the document—in paragraph tags, text frame properties, table tags, and so on. To change the unit of measure, select View➤Options and click a different item in the Display Unit drop-down list.

Setting Tab Stops FrameMaker's tab stops are measured from the edge of the text frame, not the edge of the page. By default, paragraphs do not have any tab stops defined; until you create them, pressing the TAB key doesn't have any effect. (There are anecdotes about people replacing their keyboards to correct this problem because they didn't realize they needed to make a change in FrameMaker.)

To set up tab stops, follow these steps:

1. In the Paragraph Designer's Basic sheet, make sure that New Tab Stop is selected in the Tab Stops section. (If a specific tab location is selected, the following steps will change its position.)
2. Click the Edit button in the Tab Stops section to display the Edit Tab Stop dialog box.

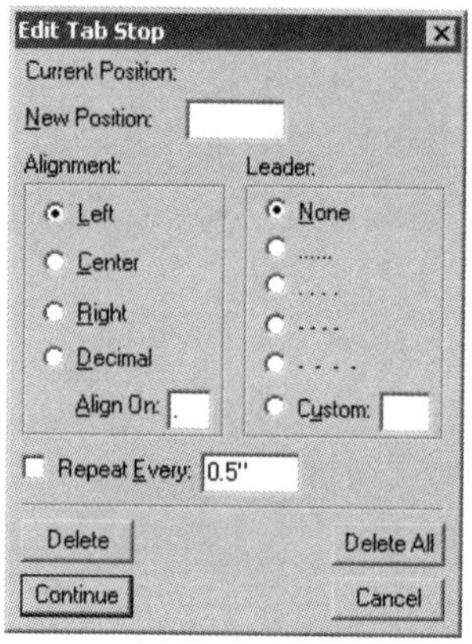

3. In the New Position field, type the position you want to use for the new tab stop.
4. In the Alignment section, specify one of the following:
   - **Left:** Text after the tab is left-aligned starting at the tab's position.
   - **Center:** Text after the tab is centered at the tab's position.
   - **Right:** Text after the tab is right-justified from the tab's position.
   - **Decimal:** Text after the tab is aligned so that the decimal point (a period by default in the English version) is aligned on the tab. To align based on a different character, type that character in the Align On field.
5. In the Leader section, specify whether you want any characters preceding the tab. Most often, you use "dot leaders" in tables of contents. To create a different leader, type the character or symbol in the Custom field.
6. If you want to create several tabs at once, specify at what increments you want to repeat the tab in the Repeat Every field.
7. Click the Continue button to set up the new tabs and return to the Paragraph Designer. If you made a mistake, double-click the tab, then click the Delete button in the Edit Tab Stop dialog box. (Or, click the Delete All button to delete every tab that's defined for this paragraph and start over.)
8. Click the Update All button to save your changes in the paragraph definition.

NOTE If you prefer to use the ruler to create tabs, set up the tab in the ruler at the top of the window (click and drag to position a tab on the ruler), display the Paragraph Designer, and then click the Update All button to save the tab in the paragraph definition.

Setting Up Indentation Getting your indents positioned correctly can be confusing because FrameMaker calculates indentation differently from most other applications. All indents are calculated from the edge of the text frame (not the edge of the page). The Left indent setting is applied only to the second and subsequent lines of a paragraph, never to the first paragraph—it uses the First indent setting. The following illustration shows a few examples of the interaction between the First and Left indent settings.

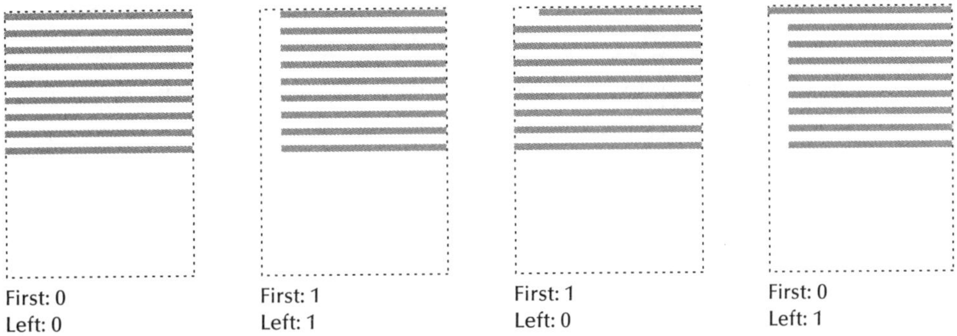

The Right indent always applies to all lines in the paragraph and is measured from the right side of the text frame.

Default Font Sheet

The Default Font sheet lets you specify font, font size, and other typographical controls. Table 5-3 on page 118 lists the Default Font sheet items.

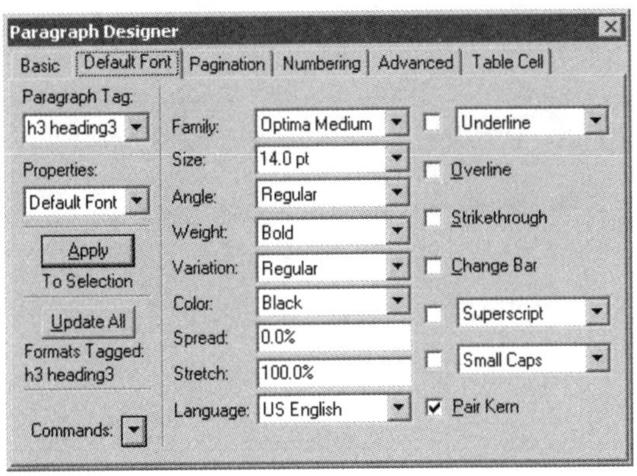

Item	Description
Family	Sets the overall typeface, such as Garamond, Palatino, Helvetica, or Times.
Size	Sets the size of the type. The smallest allowed value is 2 points.
Angle	Sets the angle, such as Italic or Oblique.
Weight	Sets the weight, such as Bold, Black, Medium, or Light.
Variation	Some fonts have variations available. These might be choices such as Small Caps or Expert Numbers.
Color	Sets the color of the text. The choices come from the color catalog. See Chapter 20, "Color Output," for information about how to add colors to the color catalog.
Spread	Adjusts the space between letters. The default is 0%. Increasing this value increases the space between letters; a negative value reduces the space between letters. Spread is similar to tracking in other applications.
Stretch	Adjusts the shape of the letters to the specified percentage. The default is 100% (normal shape). A stretch of 200% results in letters that are twice their normal width. A condensed or expanded font is usually a better choice than using the Stretch attribute.
Language	Sets the language of the current paragraph. This determines which dictionary is used when the paragraph is hyphenated or spell-checked. To prevent spell-checking, set the Language to None. This is useful for paragraphs that contain code samples.
Underline drop-down list	▪ **Underline:** Applies a line under the text. ▪ **Double Underline:** Applies a double line under the text. ▪ **Numeric Underline:** Similar to a regular underline, but spaced a little farther from the text.
Overline	Applies a line over the text.
Strikethrough	Applies a strikethrough line (a line through the middle of the text).

Table 5-3. Default Font Sheet

Item	Description
Change Bar	Applies a vertical line in the margin of the document. You can create automatic change bars; for details, see "Using Change Bars" on page 91.
Superscript Subscript	Sets text above the baseline. Sets text below the baseline.
Capitalization drop-down list	All of the capitalization choices change the appearance of the text but preserve the capitalization of the underlying text. For example, you can display the text as ALL CAPS, but a cross-reference would pick up the underlying capitalization (whatever the user typed). ■ **Small Caps:** The size of the small capital letters is set in the document's text options. For more information, see "Formatting Superscripts, Subscripts, and Small Caps" on page 85. ■ **Lowercase:** Sets the text in lowercase letters. ■ **Uppercase:** Sets the text in uppercase letters.
Pair Kern	Adjusts the spacing between each pair of letters to improve readability. In general, Pair Kern should be turned on for most paragraphs with the exception of paragraphs that use monospaced fonts (such as code examples).

Table 5-3. Default Font Sheet (Continued)

Pagination Sheet

The Pagination sheet sets the paragraph's position on the page. For example, you can set a particular paragraph to start at the top of a page. Table 5-4 on page 120 lists the Pagination sheet items.

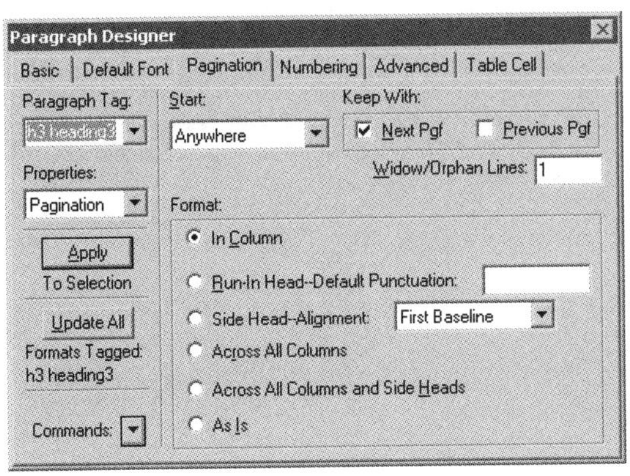

Item	Description
Start	Lets you set where on the page the paragraph begins. ■ **Anywhere:** Starts in the next available space, subject to the space above and below settings on the Basic sheet and any restrictions from the Widow/Orphan Lines or Keep With settings (described in the text that follows). ■ **Top of Column:** Starts at the top of the next column. (In a single-column document, this is the same as Top of Page.) ■ **Top of Page:** Starts at the top of the next page. ■ **Top of Left Page:** Starts at the top of the next left page. ■ **Top of Right Page:** Starts at the top of the next right page. (This setting is very common for chapter titles, which are often required to be on a right page.)
Keep With	Controls how the paragraph interacts with the preceding and following paragraphs. ■ **Next Pgf:** If checked, the current paragraph is attached to the next paragraph. Use this for headings that you want to keep on the same page as their introductory paragraphs. The Keep With setting forces at least the number of lines specified in the Widow/Orphan Lines setting to be placed on the same page as the next paragraph. ■ **Previous Pgf:** If checked, the current paragraph is attached to the previous paragraph.
Widow/ Orphan Lines	Sets the number of lines that can appear at the top or bottom of a page. For example, if you type **2**, the paragraph must always have at least two lines at the bottom of the page or at the top of the page.

Table 5-4. Pagination Sheet

Item	Description
Format	Determines the paragraph's general positioning in relation to the text column, side head, and following paragraph. See Figure 5-2 on page 122 for examples of each Format option. ■ **In Column:** Positions the paragraph in the main text column. ■ **Run-In Head:** Positions the paragraph so that the next paragraph starts on the same line. This is very useful for glossary entries and to save space for lower-level headings. In the Default Punctuation field, you can specify any default punctuation you want after the heading, such as a period. In this book, the fourth-level headings (such as "Setting Tab Stops" on page 115) use a run-in heading. The punctuation is set as an em space. ■ **Side Head:** Positions the paragraph so that it is on the same line as the following paragraph but in a separate column. You must define a side head area (discussed in Chapter 11, "Understanding Text Flows"). The drop-down list lets you choose how the side head is aligned in relation to the next paragraph: First Baseline, Top Edge, or Last Baseline. ■ **Across All Columns:** Positions the paragraph to span all text columns (but not the side head area). ■ **Across All Columns and Side Heads:** Positions the paragraph to span all available columns and the side head area. ■ **As Is:** The paragraph inherits the setting that was previously applied. This setting is useful only when you are performing global updates ("Setting Properties Across the Entire Paragraph Catalog" on page 130).

Table 5-4. Pagination Sheet (Continued)

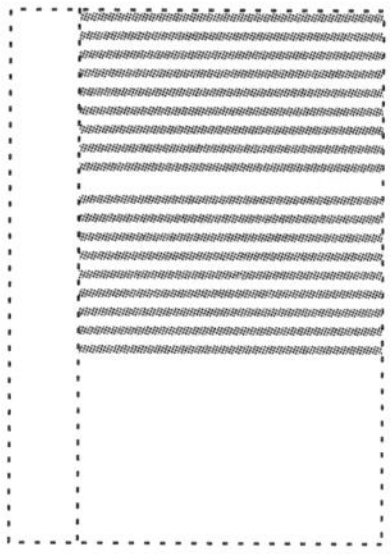

In Column. The paragraphs do not use the side head area on the left.

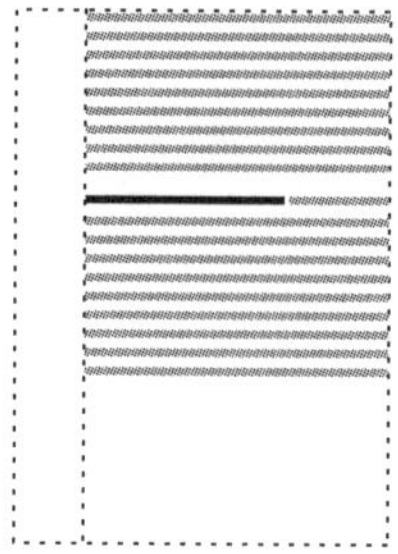

Run-In Head. The black paragraph is a run-in head. The following paragraph begins on the same line as the run-in head paragraph.

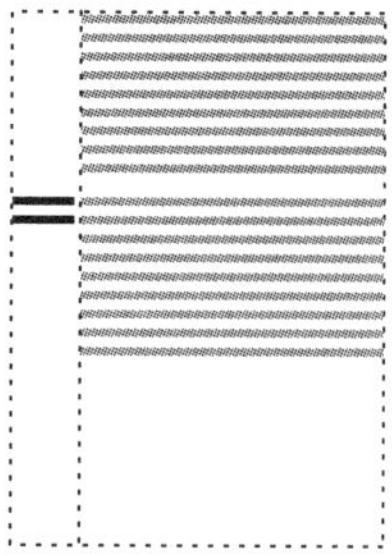

Side Head. The black paragraph is set as a side head. It flows in the side head area.

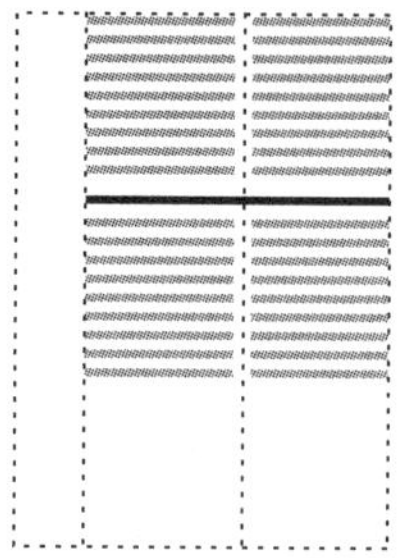

Across All Columns. The black paragraph is set across all columns. It flows across the two main columns but does not use the side head area.

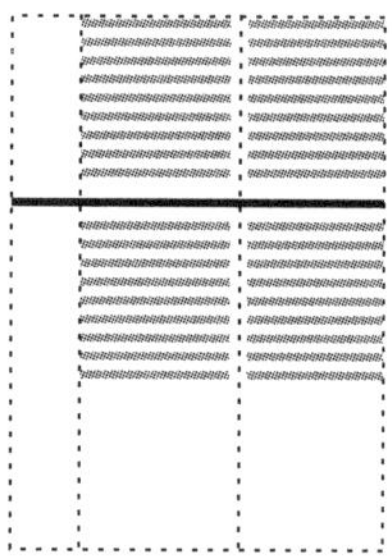

Across All Columns and Side Heads. The black paragraph is set across all columns and side heads. It flows across the two main columns and the side head area.

Figure 5-2. Understanding pagination format options

Numbering Sheet

The Numbering sheet lets you set up automatic numbering for your paragraph. This includes step numbers, chapter numbers, bullets, and repeated words (such as "Note:") at the beginning of a paragraph.

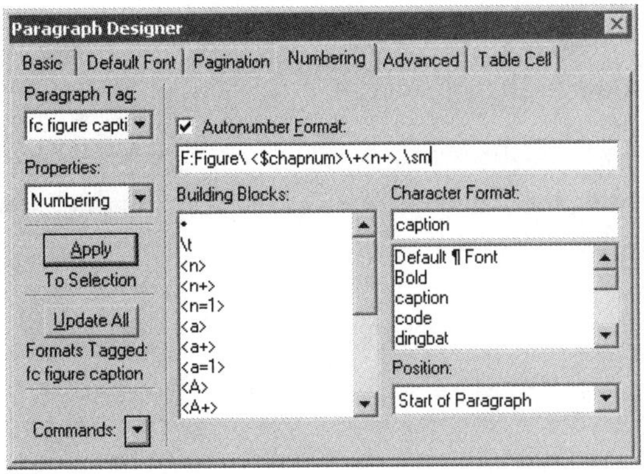

Table 5-5 describes the Numbering sheet items. Table 5-6 on page 124 lists the building blocks you can use in the Autonumber Format field.

Item	Description
Autonumber Format	Sets the definition of the numbering for the paragraph. The Autonumber Format check box determines whether the autonumbering definition (typed in the field that follows the check box) is used. See page 134 for a full discussion.
Building Blocks	Provides a list of building blocks that you can select to insert in the Autonumber Format field. See Table 5-6 for a description of each building block. You can also type the building blocks instead of selecting them from the list.
Character Format	Provides a list of character tags. The selected character tag is applied only to the autonumber for the paragraph. If the style you want isn't available, you must create a character tag to add it to the list. See Chapter 6, "Formatting Text with Character Tags," for details.
Position	Determines whether the autonumber occurs at the beginning or the end of the paragraph. Steps, bullets, and the like are normally at the beginning of the paragraph. You might use the end of paragraph position for a graphic "bug" that marks the end of a section. The autonumber is always right-aligned when positioned at the end of a paragraph.

Table 5-5. Numbering Sheet

Using counters, you can create several different types of numbering—numeric, alphabetic, and Roman. The counters come in groups of three, where the three members of each group have these functions:

- Display current value (for example, <n> or <a>)
- Increment counter and display new value (for example, <n+> or <a+>)
- Set counter (for example, <n=1> or <a=6>)

Name/Function	Counter	Description
Bullet	• or `\b`	Inserts a bullet.
Tab	`\t`	Inserts a tab. (You cannot use the TAB key inside a dialog box.) In the Basic sheet of the Paragraph Designer, specify tab position, type and leader, and the hanging indent. You define the actual numerical value of the tab in the Basic sheet (see "Setting Tab Stops" on page 115).
Hard space	`\ `	Type backslash-space to insert a nonbreaking space.
Displays the current value	`<n>`	Numeric value (1, 2, 3)
	`<a>`	Lowercase alphabetic value (a, b, c)
	`<A>`	Uppercase alphabetic value (A, B, C)
	`<r>`	Lowercase Roman value (i, ii, iii)
	`<R>`	Uppercase Roman value (I, II, III)
Increments by 1 and displays the new value	`<n+>`	Numeric value (1, 2, 3)
	`<a+>`	Lowercase alphabetic value (a, b, c)
	`<A+>`	Uppercase alphabetic value (A, B, C)
	`<r+>`	Lowercase Roman value (i, ii, iii)
	`<R+>`	Uppercase Roman value (I, II, III)
Sets to the specified value and displays that value	`<n=1>`	Numeric value (1, 2, 3)
	`<a=1>`	Lowercase alphabetic value (a, b, c)
	`<A=1>`	Uppercase alphabetic value (A, B, C)
	`<r=1>`	Lowercase Roman value (i, ii, iii)
	`<R=1>`	Uppercase Roman value (I, II, III)
Volume number	`<$volnum>`	Displays the current value of the volume number.
Chapter number	`<$chapnum>`	Displays the current value of the chapter number.

Table 5-6. Building Blocks for Autonumbering

Name/Function	Counter	Description
Placeholder counters	< >	Suppresses display of a counter but does not change its value. This building block has a space between the angle brackets. This counter was in common use in numbering series developed in FrameMaker version 5.5 or earlier.
Reset	< =0>	Suppresses display of a counter and resets counter to zero. This counter isn't listed as a building block; you have to type it in the Autonumber Format field. (A space precedes the equals sign.)

Table 5-6. Building Blocks for Autonumbering (Continued)

For more information on typing special characters in the Paragraph Designer, see "Entering Special Characters in Dialog Boxes" on page 629. See "Autonumbering Details" on page 134 for several examples of autonumbering.

Advanced Sheet

The Advanced sheet lets you set hyphenation controls, justification, and lines above or below the paragraph.

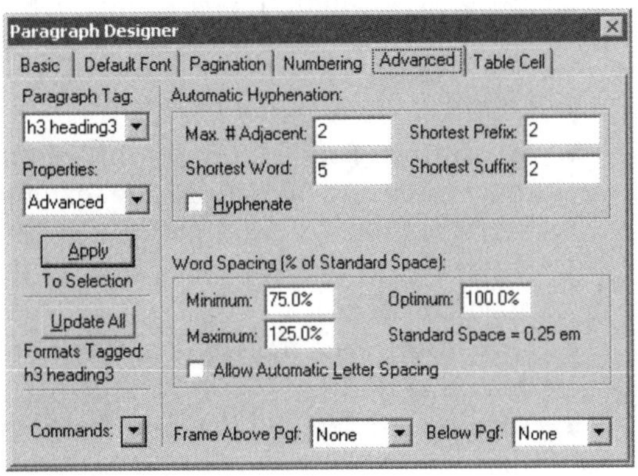

Table 5-7 on page 126 lists the Advanced sheet items.

Item	Description
Automatic Hyphenation	■ **Max. # Adjacent:** Sets the number of hyphens that can occur in consecutive lines in the paragraph. For example, 2 means that if you have two lines with hyphens at the end, the next line cannot be hyphenated. ■ **Shortest Prefix:** Sets the minimum number of letters for a hyphenated beginning fragment. For example, 3 means that the prefix must have at least three letters—"pre-fix" could be hyphenated, but "re-create" could not. ■ **Shortest Word:** Sets the minimum length of a hyphenated word. For example, 8 means that FrameMaker cannot hyphenate "pre-view." ■ **Shortest Suffix:** Sets the minimum number of letters for a hyphenated end fragment. For example, 5 means that FrameMaker cannot hyphenate "pre-tend."
Hyphenate	If checked, the paragraph is hyphenated. That is, if a word doesn't quite fit at the end of a line, FrameMaker may break it with a hyphen (for example, "acro-batic"). The locations where hyphens are allowed are called hyphenation points. Each language dictionary stores hyphenation points for its words, so if you check hyphenation, the processing is based on the language that's selected on the Default Font sheet for this paragraph. If no language is selected, the paragraph is not hyphenated.
Word Spacing	Word Spacing controls the changes FrameMaker can make when justifying text in a paragraph. ■ **Minimum:** Sets the minimum amount of word spacing that's allowed when justifying text and avoiding hyphenation. For example, 90% means that each space between words must be no smaller than 90 percent of a normal space. ■ **Optimum:** Sets the target amount of word spacing. The default is normally 100%. ■ **Maximum:** Sets the maximum amount of word spacing allowed.
Allow Automatic Letter Spacing	If checked, FrameMaker adds space between characters (not just words) when justifying text.

Table 5-7. Advanced Sheet

Item	Description
Frame Above Pgf	Lets you specify a graphic frame that's inserted above this paragraph. The graphic frames are stored on the reference pages. See "Placing Graphics Above and Below the Paragraph" on page 329 for details.
Below Pgf	Lets you specify a graphic frame that's inserted below this paragraph.

Table 5-7. Advanced Sheet (Continued)

Table Cell Sheet

The Table Cell sheet sets properties for paragraphs inside tables.

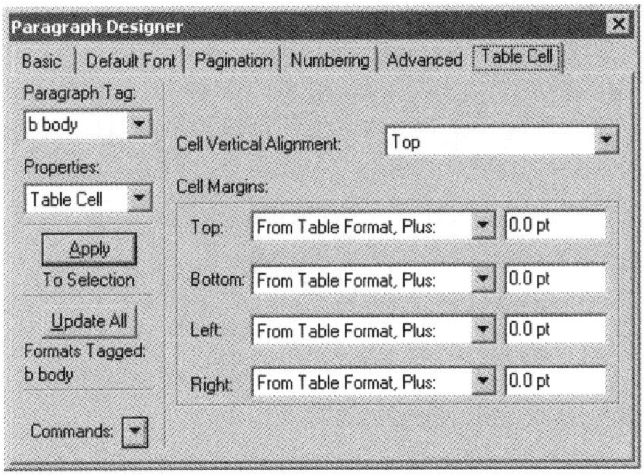

The cell margin properties interact with the default cell margins set in the Table Designer. You can either add to (or subtract from) the default margins in the Table Designer, or you can override the Table Designer's margins entirely with the settings in these paragraphs.

These properties affect only paragraphs in a table. Table 5-8 on page 128 lists the Table Cell sheet items.

Item	Description
Cell Vertical Alignment	Sets the vertical position of the paragraph in the table cell. The Top setting applies only to the first paragraph in a cell. The Bottom setting applies only to the last paragraph in a cell. The Left and Right settings are used for every paragraph.
Cell Margins (Top, Bottom, Left, Right)	Sets the cell margins, which are dependent on the location of the paragraph in the cell. You can add to the default margins (From Table Format, Plus), or you can completely ignore the default margins (Custom).

Table 5-8. Table Cell Sheet

Creating Paragraph Tags

The easiest way to create a new paragraph tag is to start with a tag that's close to what you need. If, for example, you want to create an indented paragraph, you could start with the Body tag—Body and Indent are probably identical except for the first and left indent settings.

To create a new paragraph tag, follow these steps:

1. Click in a paragraph that is similar to what you need (for example, the Body paragraph).
2. Display the Paragraph Designer.
3. Click the Commands button, then select New Format from the pop-up menu. The New Format dialog box is displayed.

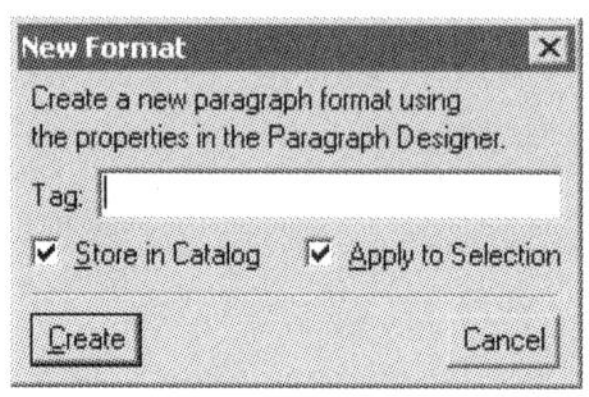

CAUTION By default, the Store in Catalog and Apply to Selection check boxes are checked. The latter is irrelevant unless you selected text before creating the tag. Do make sure that Store in Catalog is checked, or the tag will not be displayed in the paragraph catalog.

4. In the Tag field, type a name for the new paragraph tag (such as Indented). Verify that the Store in Catalog check box is checked. If you are using the

current paragraph as a template for your new tag (and thus you don't want to change the current paragraph), then uncheck the Apply to Selection check box.

5. Click the Create button. FrameMaker creates a new paragraph tag. At this point, the tag's definition is identical to the tag you started with.
6. In each sheet of the Paragraph Designer, make the needed changes. Click the Update All button before moving from one sheet to the next. If you forget, the Apply Changes dialog box is displayed.

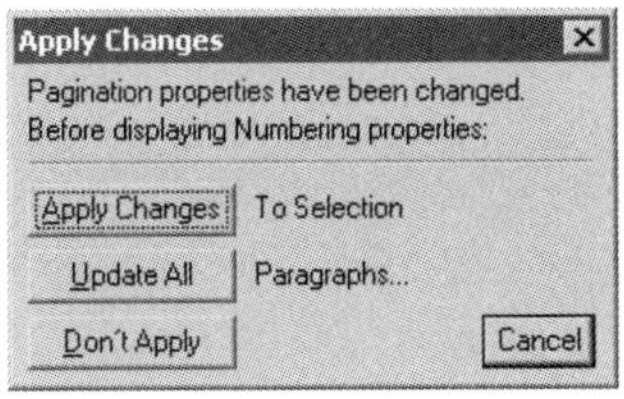

If the dialog box is displayed, do one of the following:

- Click the Apply Changes button to apply your changes to the current selection only. *This creates a formatting override.*
- Click the Update All button to update the paragraph definition and all of the tags that use it.
- Click the Don't Apply button to throw away your changes and go to the next sheet.
- Click the Cancel button to discard your changes and go back to the current sheet.

7. When you have finished, close the Paragraph Designer. The new paragraph tag is now available in the paragraph catalog.

TIP If you want to rename the current paragraph, you can use a slightly faster approach. In the Paragraph Designer, type the new tag name in the Tag Name field. Click the Apply button to display the New Format dialog box, then click the Create button. (If you click the Update All button, you rename the existing tag.)

Renaming Paragraph Tags

You can rename any paragraph tag. When you rename a paragraph tag, FrameMaker does the following:

- The original tag name (A) is changed to the new tag name (B).
- Tag A is removed from the paragraph catalog. Tag B appears in the paragraph catalog.
- All paragraphs that use tag A now use tag B.

NOTE You can also make a copy of an existing paragraph tag. In this case, the old tag is retained in the paragraph catalog. For details, see "Creating Paragraph Tags" on page 128.

To rename a paragraph tag, follow these steps:

1. Display the Paragraph Designer.
2. In the Paragraph Tag drop-down list, select the paragraph tag you want to rename.
3. In the Paragraph Tag field, type the new name of the paragraph tag.
4. Click the Update All button and confirm that you want to rename the tag.

All the paragraph tags are renamed for you. Notice that the old tag name is no longer available in the paragraph catalog.

NOTE The Global Update Options dialog box (Figure 5-3 on page 131) lets you accomplish the same thing, but it takes more steps.

Setting Properties Across the Entire Paragraph Catalog

Changing properties for a single paragraph tag is fairly quick, but if you need to make the same change for all of your paragraph tags, changing them one by one is tedious.

FrameMaker gives you a way of making global changes within your paragraph tags. For example, assume that your original files use GimzelFlopper as the official font, so all of your paragraph tags use GimzelFlopper. But now, the new corporate guidelines dictate that GimzelFlopper is no longer allowed. Instead, you need to switch to the new, official font MegaCorpo.

You could make this change by displaying each paragraph tag in turn, changing the font, and selecting the Update All button. But you can also do this with a global change, even though your paragraph tags use all sorts of different settings.

CAUTION This is not for the faint of heart. You might want to back up your file before trying this.

To change a paragraph property for all the tags in your document, follow these steps:

1. Display the Paragraph Designer. It doesn't matter which paragraph tag is selected.
2. Display the Default Font sheet.
3. Click the Commands button, then select Set Window to As Is from the pop-up menu. This sets all of the properties in the Default Font sheet to "use what's there." This is useful when you're trying to preserve conflicting settings in different paragraphs.

4. In the Family field, select MegaCorpo as your new font.
5. Click the Commands button, then select Global Update Options from the pop-up menu. The Global Update Options dialog box is displayed (Figure 5-3).
6. In the Use Properties in the Paragraph Designer section, click the Default Font Properties Only radio button. (This option changes depending on which sheet you started from. For example, if you had been on the Numbering properties when you selected Global Update Options, the option would be Numbering Properties Only instead of Default Font Properties Only.)
7. In the Update Paragraph Formats section, click the All Paragraphs and Catalog Entries radio button.

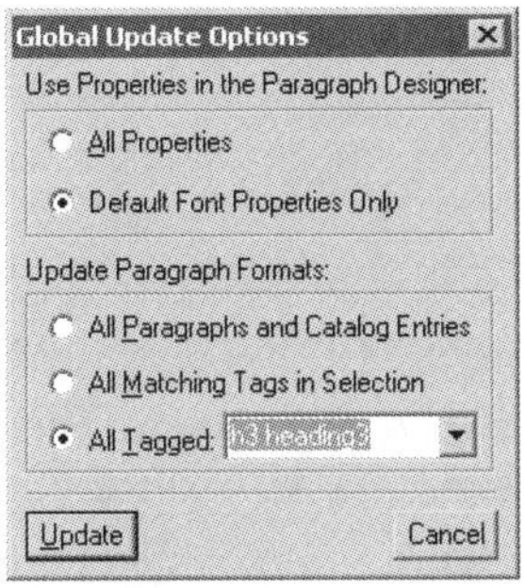

Figure 5-3. Updating paragraph tags globally

8. Click the Update button. Every paragraph tag in your document now uses the new font.

Updating Selected Paragraphs Globally

Instead of modifying all of the tags in the paragraph catalog, you can change specific paragraphs. To update several tags at once, use the All Matching Tags in Selection radio button in the Global Update Options dialog box (see Figure 5-3). Before you begin, set up several paragraphs in a row, and apply a paragraph tag you want to change to each paragraph. (The paragraphs can be empty.) Then, follow these steps to modify the tags globally:

1. Select the paragraphs you created. Every paragraph tag in this text will be changed, so you select only tags you want to change.
2. Display the Paragraph Designer. Notice that where the various paragraph tag settings conflict, the As Is setting is used.

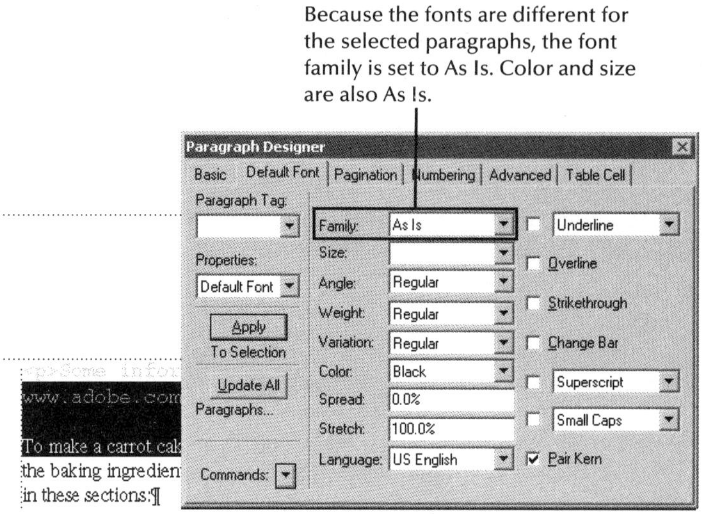

3. For each sheet of the Paragraph Designer, follow these steps to make changes:
   a. Modify the sheet as needed. If you want the paragraphs to retain different settings for an item, leave the As Is setting intact.
   b. Click the Commands button, then select Global Update Options from the pop-up list. This displays the Global Update Options dialog box, shown in Figure 5-3 on page 131.
   c. In the Use Properties in the Paragraph Designer section, select the current sheet only (for example, Default Font Properties Only).
   d. In the Update Paragraph Formats section, click the All Matching Tags in Selection radio button.

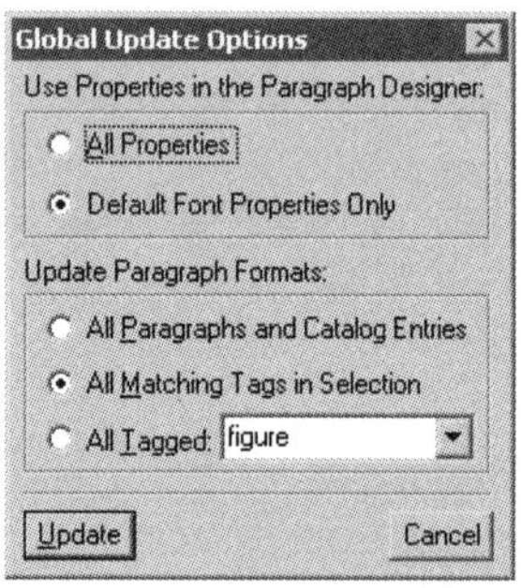

   e. Click the Update button.

Deleting Paragraph Tags

You can remove paragraph tags from the catalog. Those tags are no longer available for new paragraphs. However, any paragraph that uses the tag you deleted still has that tag applied to it—but now it's considered an override. After you delete the tag, apply a different tag to the leftover paragraphs. Alternatively, you can reassign a new tag to the paragraphs that use the tag you plan to delete. It's usually more efficient to apply the new tag before you delete a paragraph tag.

To delete paragraph tags, follow these steps:

1. Display the paragraph catalog.
2. Click the Delete button at the bottom of the paragraph catalog. The Delete Formats from Catalog dialog box is displayed.

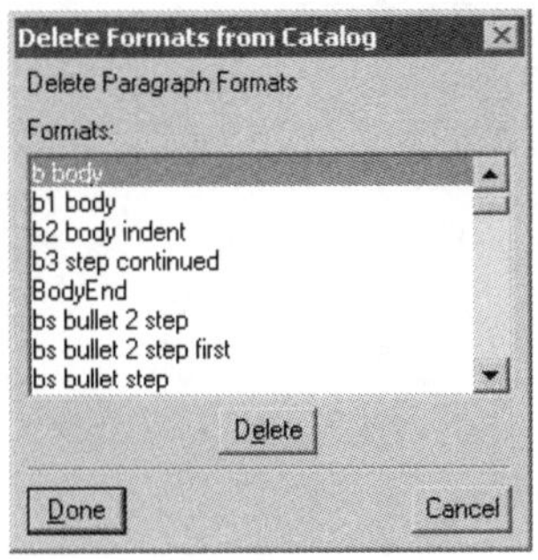

3. For each tag you want to delete, select the style, then click the Delete button. To delete all of the tags, press and hold ALT-E until all of the tags are gone.

CAUTION If you make a mistake, you must click the Cancel button and start over. There is no Apply button.

4. When you have finished, click the Done button.

When you delete paragraph tags from the paragraph catalog, the tags are not stripped from the paragraphs. As a result, you can have paragraphs that use tags that are no longer available in the paragraph catalog. However, these tags are now considered overrides (because they use a paragraph tag that's not available in the paragraph catalog). After removing the paragraph tag, you'll probably want to assign new names to those paragraphs (see "Creating New Formats" on page 134).

NOTE A number of third-party tools are available to help you find those overrides. In particular, you might want to look into the aptly named HuntOverrides. See Appendix A, "Resources," for more details about these and other add-on tools.

Creating New Formats

Every once in a while (and we hope this is a rare occurrence), you will inherit bad FrameMaker files. The files will be riddled with overrides; in fact, the paragraph and character overrides may be the rule and not the exception. In this case, you may want to identify all the overrides. FrameMaker provides a way to do this—select File➤Utilities➤Create & Apply Formats.

The Create & Apply Formats feature does the following for paragraph and character tags:

- If a tag is used by a paragraph or character but doesn't appear in the appropriate catalog, Create & Apply Formats adds it to the catalog.
- If a paragraph or character uses a tag that's in the catalog, but the tag is used with an override, Create & Apply Formats creates a new tag for that item and adds it to the catalog. The tag name is based on the original name, so if the tag was Code, then any new tags would be Code1, Code2, and so on.

After you create the new tags, you can rename them or apply the correct tags globally to remove the overrides.

Autonumbering Details

FrameMaker's autonumbering lets you set up automated numbering, such as step numbers and chapter numbers. But you can also use autonumbering for repeated text (Note:) or symbols (•) at the beginning or end of the paragraph. It's much more efficient to define a paragraph tag that automatically inserts these items because you don't have to type in the text over and over again or keep track of the last number used.

NOTE To strip off an autonumbering, you must apply a different (non-autonumbered) paragraph tag. You cannot select an autonumber or press BACKSPACE to delete it.

This section describes how to set up autonumbers with varying degrees of complexity. In some cases, the autonumbering in different paragraph tags interacts, so you have to set up several paragraph tags to get the effect you want.

Some of the examples build on concepts introduced in the early examples, so we recommend that you read this entire section through the first time.

Basic Autonumbering

As mentioned in "Numbering Sheet" on page 122, you use automated numbering for bullets and text-based formats, such as notes, cautions, and warnings. To set up these autonumbers, you insert the text you need in the Autonumbering Format field. When you apply the paragraph tag, the text is inserted automatically.

Bullets

FrameMaker includes a bullet in the list of building blocks. You can also use other characters, such as hyphens, em dashes, or wingdings, to create bullets.

To create a basic bullet, click the bullet building block, then click the tab (\t) building block to insert the following in the Autonumbering Format field:

```
•\t
```

Next, set up the Basic properties to allow for the tab and a left indent. The definition and the result are shown in the following illustration.

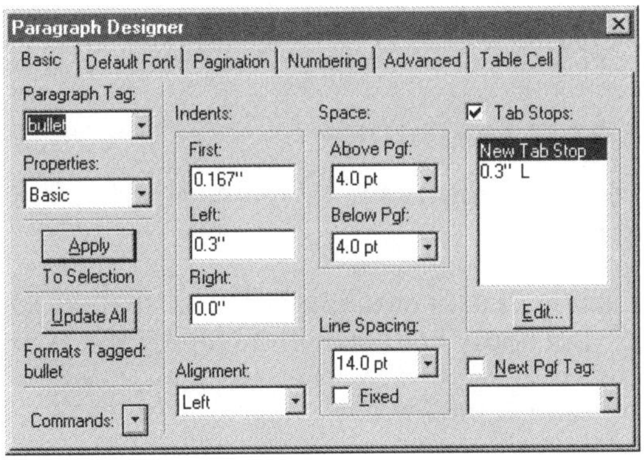

Typical information in a spec includes:

- Lists of menus and menu choices (software)
- Mock-ups of the interface (software)
- Illustrations of components (hardware)

The bullets are indented according to the settings on the Basic sheet.

For more information on typing special characters in the Paragraph Designer, see "Entering Special Characters in Dialog Boxes" on page 629.

Another way to set up bullets involves taking advantage of the character formatting that's available. You can, for example, create a character tag that applies the Zapf Dingbats or Wingdings font, and then use one of the dingbats or wingdings to make a special bullet (such as check marks, diamonds, or pointing hands). When you enter the character in the Autonumber Format field, no formatting is displayed. However, when you apply the paragraph tag to text, the character is displayed using the font from the character tag you selected in the Character Format field. See the example in Figure 5-4.

In this example, the 4 displays as a check mark in the document, because the "dingbat" character tag applies the Zapf Dingbat font to the autonumber.

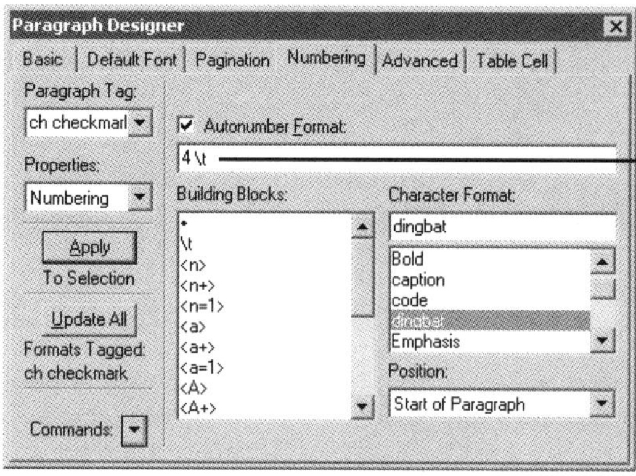

✔ This paragraph style uses a custom bullet.

Figure 5-4. Creating a Special Bullet

Notes, Cautions, and Warnings

You can set up notes and similar formats with autonumbering. For example, consider the following note format:

> **Note:** This is a note. It uses autonumbering so that you don't have to type in the word "Note:" and apply bold formatting every time you need a note.

It uses the following autonumbering format:

```
Note:\t
```

To add the bold formatting, apply a Bold character tag.

After setting the autonumbering, you'll need to set the appropriate indents for your note.

Numbered Steps (1, 2, 3 and a, b, c)

When you create step formats, you must tell FrameMaker when to increment (or count) steps and when to reset them to restart at 1. There are two ways of doing this:

- You can create two step formats: StepFirst and StepNext. StepFirst resets your steps to start at 1 and is always used for the first step in a series. StepNext is used for all subsequent steps.
- You can create a single step format, Step. In this approach, you must use another format, such as Body or Heading, to reset your step series.

Working with the Two-Step Format

The advantage of using StepFirst and StepNext is that you explicitly control how the steps are reset. The disadvantage is that you have to remember to reset the step list. And if you rearrange the steps, you may have to change the paragraph tag assignments to ensure that StepFirst is applied to only the first paragraph in the list of steps.

Paragraph Tag	Definition
StepFirst	S:<n=1>
StepNext	S:<n+>

The S: is called a series label. It tells FrameMaker that the counters in the two paragraph tags are interdependent. You can use any letter for a series label, but each series must have a unique series label. (For example, S for steps and F for figures.) Because of the series label, the <n=1> and <n+> counters affect each other. The result looks like this:

Paragraph Tag	Autonumber	Result
StepFirst	S:<n=1>	1
StepNext	S:<n+>	2
StepNext	S:<n+>	3
StepNext	S:<n+>	4
StepNext	S:<n+>	5
StepNext	S:<n+>	6
StepFirst	S:<n=1>	1
StepNext	S:<n+>	2

If you need second-level steps (a, b, c) in addition to the first-level numbered steps, you can set up two more tags, StepLetterA and StepLetterNext. Make sure that the new tags use a different series label.

Paragraph Tag	Definition
StepLetterA	T:<a=1>
StepLetterNext	T:<a+>

To set up similar numbering with Roman numerals, use the <r> and <R> building blocks for lowercase and uppercase Roman numerals.

Working with a Single Step Format

If you want to minimize the number of paragraph tags in your document, you can use a single step format. In this case, you need to use another paragraph tag to reset your steps. The disadvantage to this approach is that you must always have the separator paragraph (Body in the example) between your step lists. If this doesn't happen, the numbering won't work properly. Set up the paragraphs as shown here:

Paragraph Tag	Definition
Step	S:<n+>
Body	S:

Here, the Step tag is set to <n+>, increasing each time you use it. But the Body tag uses an empty autonumber definition with just a series label. This lets you take advantage of a little-known autonumbering feature: *When a counter is not listed in the definition, it is reset to zero.* If you prefer, you can write out the "reset to zero" for Body:

```
S:< =0>
```

The single-step approach relies on the fact that you do not plan to have two step lists without an intervening Body paragraph tag. You could use a similar approach for your substeps, but you would probably assign the reset function to the first-level steps.

Paragraph Tag	Definition
Step	S:<n+>
Body	S:
StepA	S:< ><a+>

To ensure that the Step tag resets the StepA tag, you must use the same series label for those tags. But at the same time, the StepA tag should not interact with the Step's numbering, so you have to insert a blank counter < > (with a space between the brackets) at the first position. This tells FrameMaker not to display a counter at that position but to preserve the value of that counter.

Incorporating Chapter and Volume Numbers

In FrameMaker version 6, Adobe introduced two new building blocks: <$chapnum> and <$volnum>. These are a departure from paragraph-based autonumbering. In effect, <$chapnum> and <$volnum> are *global* building blocks—they are available in autonumbers, cross-references, variables, and several other places. Within an autonumber, <$chapnum> returns the current value of the chapter number and <$volnum> returns the value of the volume or part number. These are normally set in your book file (see "Managing Numbering" on page 386 for details).

Unlike most other building blocks, you cannot change the value of <$chapnum> or <$volnum> (for example, <$chapnum+ > doesn't work). Furthermore, you can use them in several different autonumbering definitions that are *not* tied together with a series label.

If you need to reference the chapter number (for example, in your chapter title paragraph tag), you can use the following autonumber definition:

```
<$chapnum>
```

This will retrieve the value of <$chapnum>. The formatting (such as numeric or Roman) is determined at the book level in the Numbering dialog box (Format➤Document➤Numbering) in the Chapter sheet.

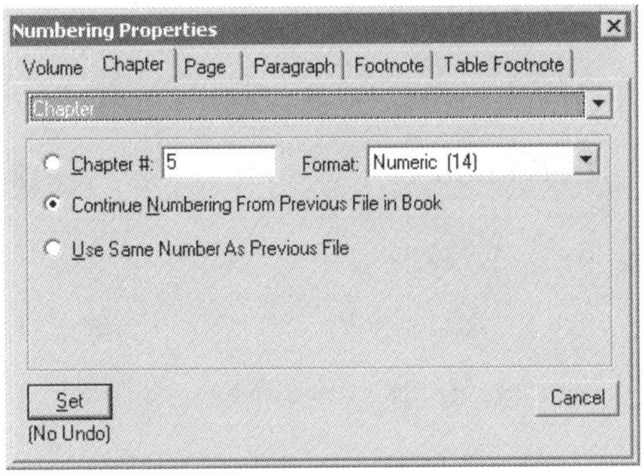

You can change this inside the file, but the book overrides the value set in the file. The rules for <$volnum> are the same; it uses the Volume sheet on the Numbering dialog box.

The example that follows shows how you can take advantage of <$chapnum> to set up independent figure, table, and example numbering that uses the chapter number.

NOTE This is a major change from earlier versions of FrameMaker (5.5.6 and earlier), which required all of these items to be in a single numbering series and led to very complicated numbering schemes.

Paragraph Tag	Definition	Result
ChapterTitle	<$chapnum>	1, 2, 3
FigureTitle	F:Figure\ <$chapnum>\+<n+>	Figure 1-1, Figure 1-2, Figure 1-3
TableTitle	U:Table\ <$chapnum>\+<n+>	Table 1-1, Table 1-2, Table 1-3
ExampleTitle	E:Example\ <$chapnum>\+<n+>	Example 1-1, Example 1-2, Example 1-3

The backslash-space sequence produces a nonbreaking space; backslash-plus produces a nonbreaking hyphen. Using these special characters prevents unattractive line breaks. The nonbreaking spaces and hyphens are also picked up by any cross-references to these items.

Creating Numbered Headings

Some documents require that you number your headings and perhaps even the body paragraphs. FrameMaker autonumbering can handle this situation for you. You use the higher-level headings to restart the lower-level headings. The following example shows a typical setup.

Paragraph Tag	Definition	Result
ChapterTitle	H:<$chapnum>	1, 2, 3
Heading1	H:<$chapnum>.<n+>	1.1, 1.2, 1.3, 1.4
Heading2	H:<$chapnum>.<n>.<n+>	1.1.1, 1.1.2, 1.1.3, 1.1.4
Body	H:<$chapnum>.<n>.<a+>	1.1.1.a, 1.1.1.b, 1.1.1.c, 1.1.1.d, 1.1.1.e

In this example, the ChapterTitle tag carries a series label because it resets the second counter in the Heading1 format to zero.

You might also want to set up numbered headings for an outline, as shown in the following example.

Paragraph Tag	Definition	Result
Heading1	`H:<R+>`	I, II, III, IV
Heading2	`H:<R>.<A+>`	I.A, I.B, I.C, I.D
Heading3	`H:<R>.<A>.<r+>`	I.A.i, I.A.ii, I.A.iii, I.A.iv
Heading4	`H:<R>.<A>.<r>.<n+>`	I.A.i.1, I.A.i.2, I.A.i.3, I.A.i.4

Marking the End of a Story

In many magazines, the end of a story is indicated by a small graphic "bug," which gives the reader a visual indication that the article is done. This is very helpful when the story jumps over pages of advertisements and the like. You can automate the insertion of this graphic by setting up a special paragraph tag for it. You might, for instance, create a paragraph tag called BodyEnd. In it, you could set up the autonumbering format to insert the graphic. You may need to apply a character tag to use a font such as Zapf Dingbats.

The BodyEnd style uses a small box to indicate the end of the story. ■

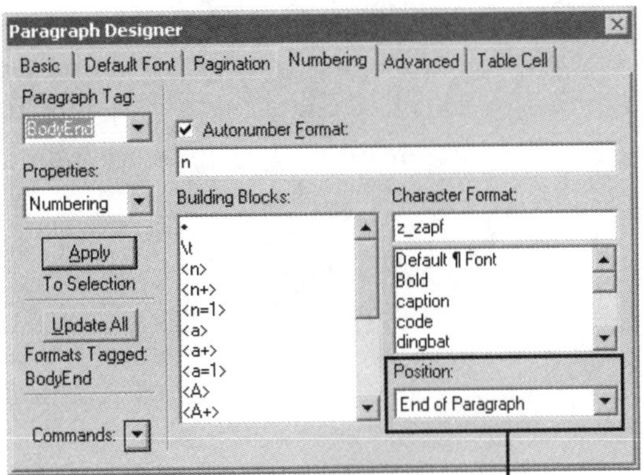

The autonumber is positioned at the end of the paragraph.

Formatting Ideas for Paragraph Tags

FrameMaker's Paragraph Designer offers some standard formatting and interesting customization options. Here are some ideas:

- **Inserting lines above or below a paragraph.** On the Advanced sheet, use the Frame Above and Frame Below settings to set lines or other graphics above or below your headings. If you don't like the provided lines, go to the reference pages and create your own graphic frames (see "Placing Graphics Above and Below the Paragraph" on page 329 for details).
- **Forcing headings to the top of a page.** On the Pagination sheet, use the Start drop-down list to specify that a particular heading must always start at the top of the page.
- **Formatting your glossary with run-in headings.** Use run-in headings (set on the Pagination sheet) for glossary terms; use body text for the definitions. Set the glossary term in bold. (This also makes it easier to cross-reference the glossary later because the term is in its own paragraph. If you use a single paragraph tag and bold the glossary term, you cannot pick up just the term in a cross-reference.)
- **Eliminating spell-checking.** For paragraphs that should not be spell-checked (such as code listings), set the Language to None on the Default Font sheet.
- **Stacking lines with negative line spacing.** On the Basic sheet, if you set the space below paragraph one to a negative number and the space above paragraph two to a negative number, you can force FrameMaker to write two paragraphs in the same location. You can use this to create some interesting effects, such as white text in a black box.
- **Invisible autonumbers.** Include an autonumber at the end of your paragraph, but set the autonumber on the Numbering sheet to be white text and tiny (2 points) using a character tag. When you reference the paragraph in a variable, cross-reference, or generated file, you can take advantage of the hidden autonumber to accomplish some interesting effects. (This is helpful if you have generated a table of contents and need to refer to an autonumber that isn't normally defined in the paragraph you're working with.)
- **Change bars.** For typing comments in a file, create a comment paragraph tag with the Change Bar property selected on the Default Font sheet.

CHAPTER 6

Formatting Text with Character Tags

FrameMaker distinguishes between paragraph-level and character-level formatting. Paragraph tags always format an entire paragraph. *Character tags* provide a way to format one or more characters inside the paragraph. For example, you can create formats for italicized, underlined, or bold text.

By applying character tags, you can quickly format text, but more importantly, you maintain consistency and make it easy to update your document. For example, suppose your new corporate style department bans boldface text from product documentation. The Menu Item character tag formats menu items in boldface text, so you change the weight property of the Menu Item character tag and update the tag's definition globally in the book.

You can easily reformat text that has a character tag applied.

For example, you can change the text from boldface to regular.

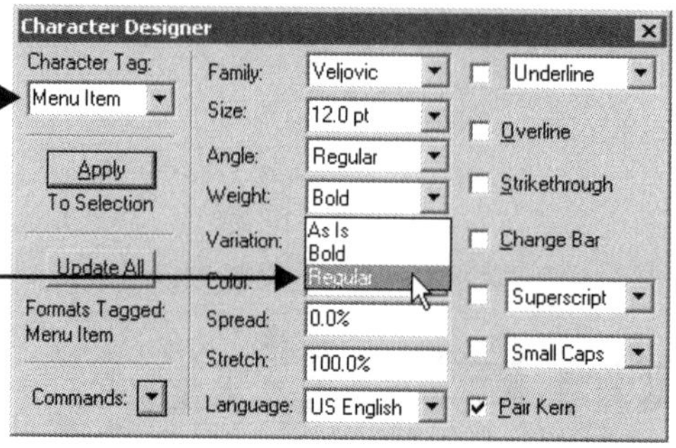

If you had used the Format menu (or B button) to emphasize menu items, you would have to scan your book for each bold menu item and manually remove the bold formatting.

Character tags also act as formatting building blocks for other FrameMaker features. Using character tags, you can assign color or other formatting to a portion of a cross-reference or a variable.

Applying Character Tags

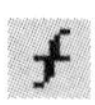

The *character catalog* lists the character tags in a document. To display the catalog, click the character catalog button in the upper-right corner of the FrameMaker window.

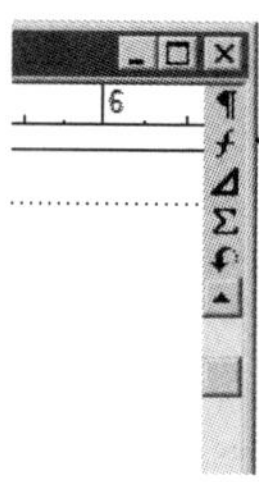

Click to display the character catalog.

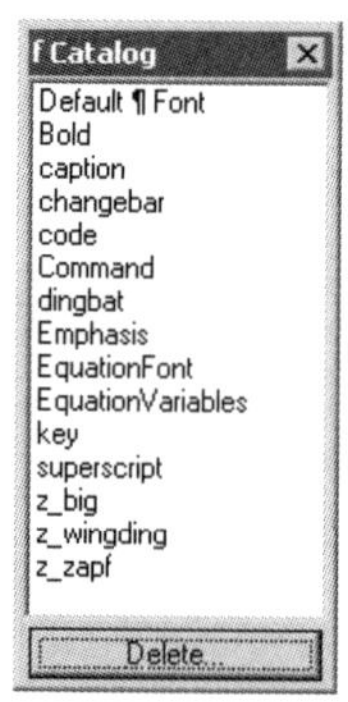

Although you can apply multiple character tags to achieve formatting effects, FrameMaker recognizes just the last tag. If, for example, you apply an italicized character tag and then apply a boldface tag, the text will most likely display as boldface, italicized text. FrameMaker, however, recognizes only the last character tag you applied. A better approach is to create a single character tag that combines both properties.

Using the Character Catalog to Apply a Tag

To apply a character tag through the character catalog, follow these steps:

1. Select the text you want to format.
2. In the character catalog, click a character tag. The character tag is applied to the selected text. In the status bar, the character tag name indicates that you applied the tag.

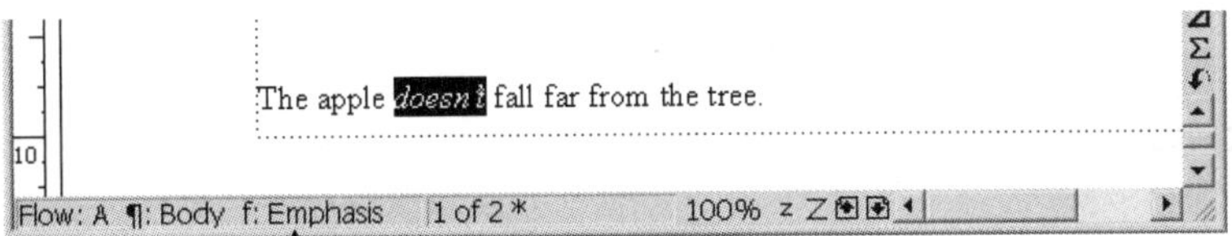

Name of character tag applied to selected text

FrameMaker provides other ways to apply a character tag, including:

- Selecting a menu choice
- Using the right-click pop-up menu
- Using keyboard shortcuts

NOTE You can also apply character tags by using the Character Designer, but this isn't recommended because you could accidentally modify the character tag definition.

Selecting a Menu Choice

To apply a character tag through a menu choice, follow these steps:

1. Select the text you want to format.
2. Select Format➤Characters, then select a character tag from the submenu.

Using the Right-Click Pop-Up Menu

The pop-up menu displayed when you right-click also gives you a way to apply a character tag. Follow these steps:

1. Select the text you want to format.
2. Right-click to display the pop-up menu, select Characters, and then select a tag from the list that's displayed.

Using Keyboard Shortcuts

To apply a character tag using a keyboard shortcut, follow these steps:

1. Select the text you want to format.
2. Press F8 or CTRL-8. The bottom-left of the status bar is highlighted.

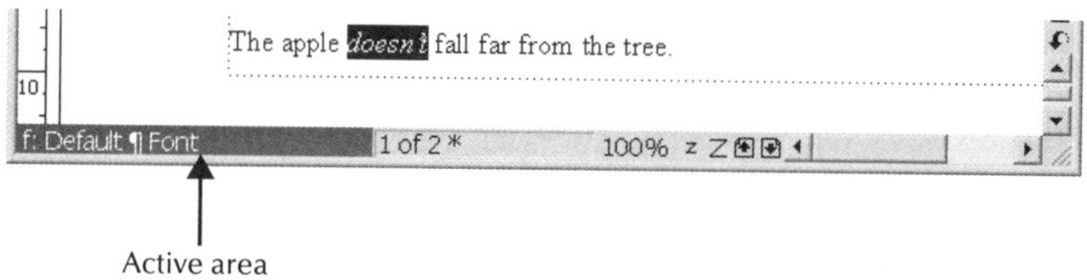

3. Display the character tag you want by doing any of the following:
   - Use the arrow keys to scroll through the list of available tags.
   - Type a letter to jump to that section of the character catalog.
   - Type the first few letters of the character tag name.
4. Press ENTER.

NOTE Some of the keys on your computer may be specially programmed. If so, one or more keyboard shortcuts may not work as described. Consult your system documentation for help.

Modifying Character Tags

In the Character Designer, you modify character tag properties, such as font size, color, and angle. When you save your changes, you update all character tags in the document at once. Content formatted by the updated character tag is automatically reformatted.

The Character Designer consists of the same choices as the Paragraph Designer's Default Font sheet. For a description of each item, see "Default Font Sheet" on page 117. The commands on the left side of the Character Designer also work very much like the commands in the Paragraph Designer.

To modify a character tag, follow these steps:

1. Display the Character Designer by selecting Format➤Characters➤Designer or by pressing CTRL-D or ESC O C D.
2. Select the character tag you want to modify in the Character Tag drop-down list.

The Menu Item character tag formats text as bold. The other properties are set to As Is because they're not needed.

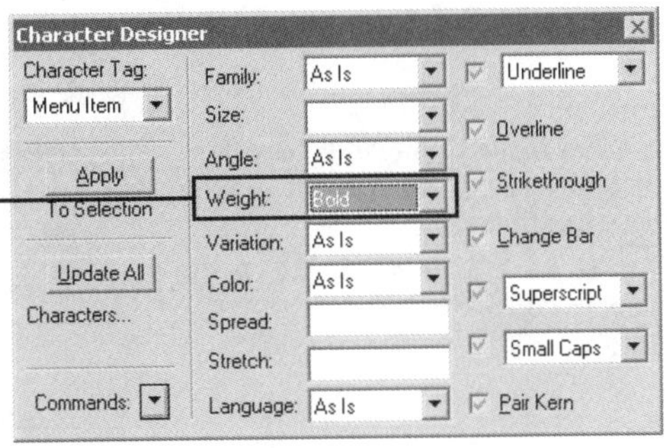

3. Select As Is for the properties you want determined by the *paragraph* tag. Font size is a good example. (After you set Size field to As Is, that field is blank.) In some templates, the body and table cell paragraph tags have different font sizes. If you want to emphasize something in a body paragraph and in a table cell, you don't want the character tag to control the font size. This would make the table cell text as large as the body paragraph text. For this reason, it's best to set font size to As Is. See the following section, "As Is Character Properties," for details.
4. Use the other drop-down lists and check boxes to change the properties you need.

NOTE If the color you need isn't listed, modify your document's color definitions (select View➤Color➤Definitions), and the new color will be displayed in the Character Designer. For details, see Chapter 20, "Color Output."

5. Click the Update All button to modify all instances of the character tag in your document.

As Is Character Properties

When you create a character tag, you don't use many properties in the Character Designer. For example, in an Emphasis character tag, you change the angle setting to Italics (or Oblique, depending on the font). The remaining properties—font family, font size, weight, variation, color, word spread, underline, and so on—come from the paragraph tag applied to the current paragraph. Using the As Is setting for the other properties saves time and helps you build character tags that format content properly.

Figure 6-1 illustrates the benefit of using As Is properties. Most properties have been modified in the first example, which improperly formats the text. In the second example, most properties except weight are set to As Is, so the text is formatted correctly. Most of the check boxes are grayed out, and the Size drop-down list is blank. This indicates that those properties have been set to As Is. You set check box properties to As Is by double-clicking the check box (if the check box is originally unchecked). When you click As Is in the Size drop-down list, the field is cleared. See the sidebar "Understanding Check Boxes in FrameMaker" on page 151 for more information.

Most properties in the Command character tag have been specified, so text formatted by the tag looks like this:

Type **Caution:\t** in the Autonumber Format field.

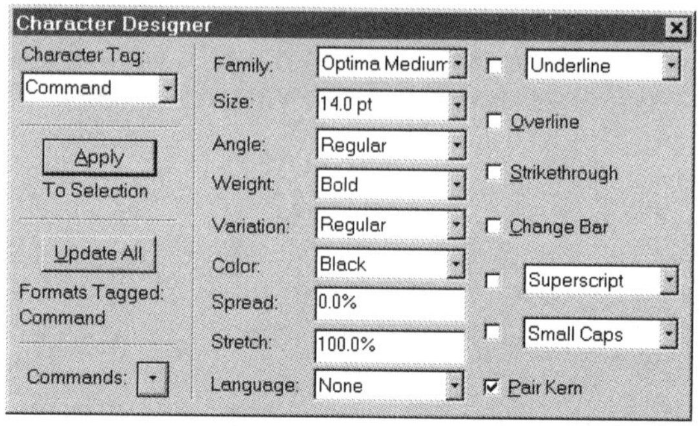

Most properties except the weight are set to As Is in this character tag. The text is now properly formatted.

Type **Caution:\t** in the Autonumber Format field.

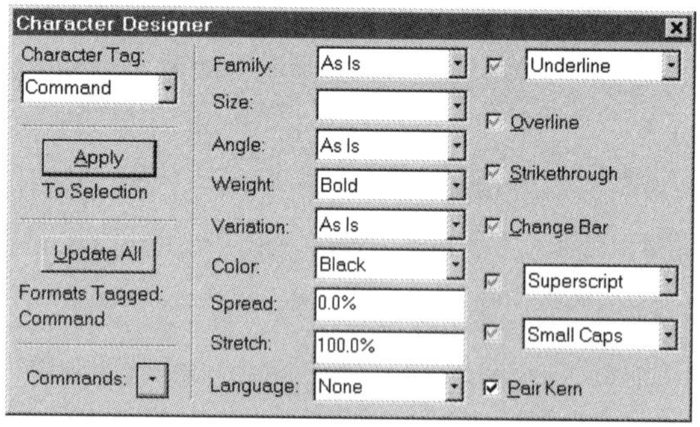

Figure 6-1. Using As Is properties

Avoiding Character Tag Overrides

When you modify a tag in the Character Designer and click the Apply button instead of clicking the Update All button, you create an override. A star is displayed next to the character tag name in the status bar. You also create an override by applying a character tag to an entire paragraph. Typically, if you need to change the style of the entire paragraph, you should create a new paragraph tag instead of applying a character tag.

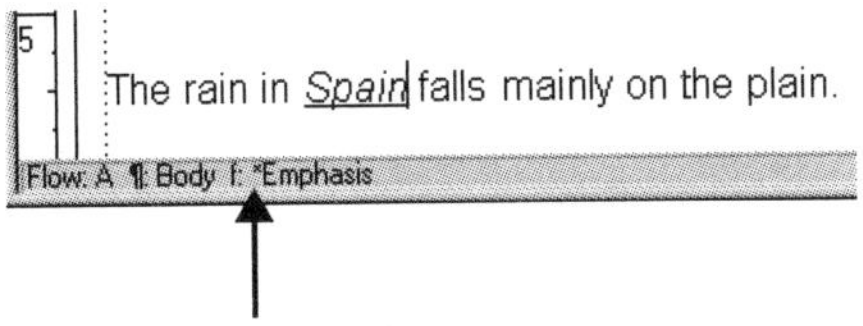

Star indicates the Emphasis character tag has been modified.

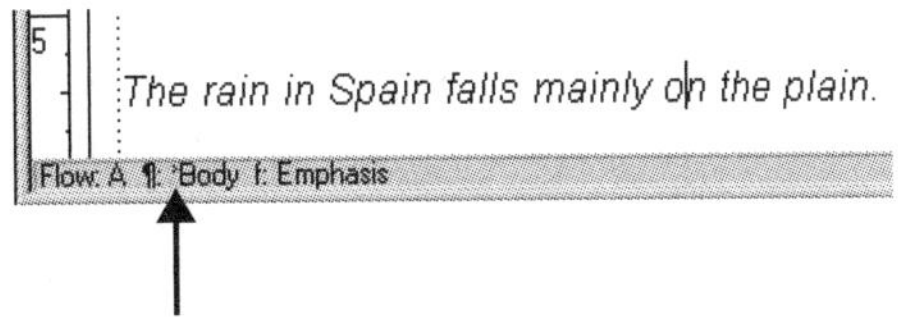

Star indicates the Emphasis character tag overrides the Body paragraph tag.

You remove character tag overrides by importing the template (see "Importing Settings from a Template File" on page 615) with the Remove Format Overrides option checked or by reapplying the character tag. To remove a paragraph tag override, apply the Default Paragraph Font character tag and reapply the paragraph tag.

Overrides defeat the goal of maintaining consistently formatted documents. Although FrameMaker provides ways to remove overrides, you should avoid creating them in the first place.

Creating Character Tags

In addition to modifying tags in the Character Designer, you also create them. When you create a character tag, it's best to follow a specific naming convention. Typically, you should name character tags based on their function rather than their style properties. For example, your template may include a character tag that formats computer commands with the Courier font. Instead of naming the tag Courier, you name it Command. If you decide later to format commands in bold, you can update the Command character tag without changing the tag name. If you had named the tag Courier, the character tag name would not describe the new property.

To create a character tag, follow these steps:

1. Display the Character Designer. The settings of the currently selected text (or of the text at the insertion point) are displayed.

CAUTION When you position the cursor in text formatted with a character tag, the Character Designer displays that character tag's name. However, the properties shown in the Character Designer are not necessarily that character tag's properties. Many character tags have items set to As Is, and those will not be reflected when you first display the Character Designer. Instead, you see the setting of the underlying paragraph tag. To see the actual settings, click the tag name again in the Character Tag drop-down list.

2. Click the Commands button, then select Set Window to As Is from the pop-up menu to reset the character properties. The As Is concept is discussed in more detail in "As Is Character Properties" on page 147.

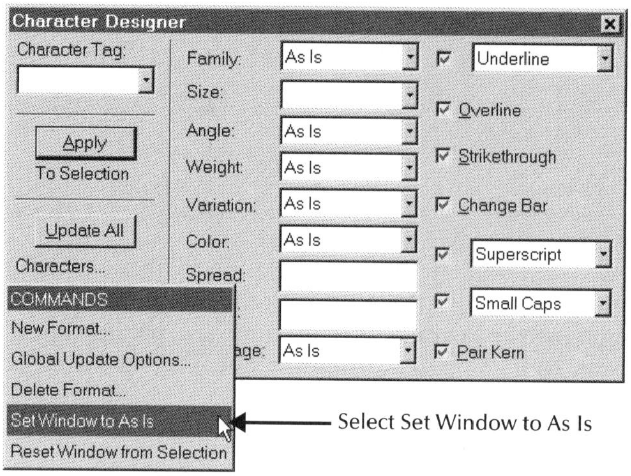

3. Click the Commands button, then select New Format from the pop-up menu. The New Format dialog box is displayed.

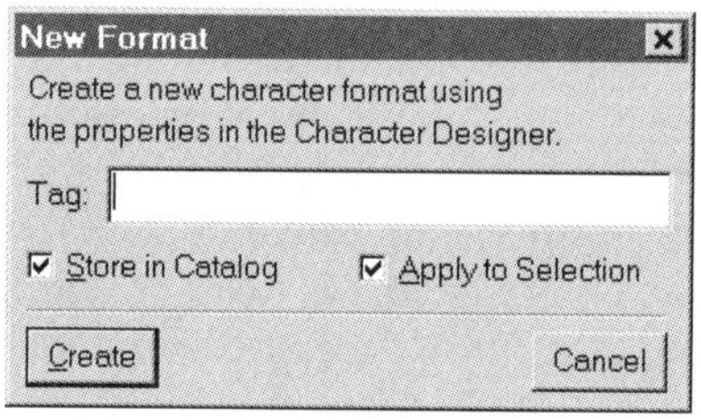

4. Type the name of your new tag in the Tag field, then click the Create button. The new tag is displayed in the character catalog.

CAUTION By default, the Store in Catalog and Apply to Selection check boxes are checked. The latter is irrelevant unless you selected text before creating the tag. Do make sure that Store in Catalog is checked, or the tag will not be displayed in the character catalog.

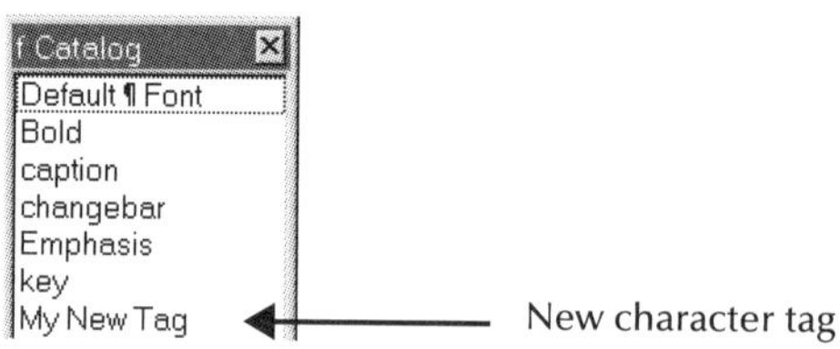

5. Change the properties as needed, then click the Update All button to save your changes. Notice that all of the As Is settings disappear again. To verify that the tag is set correctly, click its name in the Character Tag drop-down list again.

Understanding Check Boxes in FrameMaker

FrameMaker check boxes confuse many users. Most programs have only two settings for a check box—checked or unchecked. In FrameMaker, there are three values—checked, unchecked, and As Is, as illustrated below.

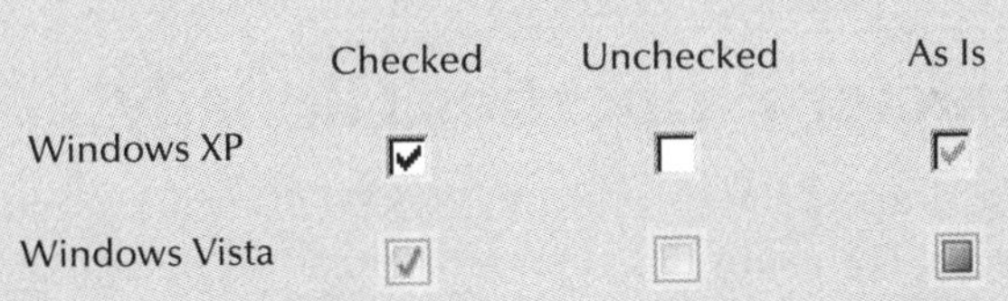

To clear the As Is setting, check the box once. To change the value from As Is to checked, check the box twice.

Renaming Character Tags

FrameMaker makes it easy to change the name of a character tag you've already created. For example, you may need to rename the Emphasis character tag Strong. After you rename Emphasis, the character tag name will change to Strong where you've applied it, and the previous tag name will no longer be displayed in the character catalog.

Renaming character tags also lets you globally assign a new character tag to text formatted by a deleted tag. When you select the formatted text, the deleted character tag name is still displayed in the status bar. You can "rename" the deleted tag in the Character Designer. This applies the new character tag where the deleted tag is applied in your document.

Caution When you rename a character tag, FrameMaker updates the catalog definition and the locations where you applied the tag; however, references to the old tag name (for example, in variables and cross-references) are not updated. You'll need to search for the old tag name in these components and change the name yourself.

To rename a character tag, follow these steps:

1. Display the Character Designer.
2. Click the tag you plan to rename from the Character Tag drop-down list. If you're renaming a deleted tag, select the text that was previously formatted by the tag. (The deleted tag name is marked in the status bar with a star.)
3. In the Character Tag field, type the new name over the existing name.

4. Click the Update All button. A confirmation dialog box is displayed.
5. Click the OK button. The renamed character tag is applied in your document and listed in the character catalog in place of the initial tag.

NOTE The Global Update Options dialog box also lets you rename a tag, but the method involves more steps. See the next section for details.

Updating Character Properties Globally

FrameMaker's global update feature provides several ways to modify more than one character tag at once. For example, you can replace all instances of magenta text with black text, apply a different character tag in place of the old one throughout the document, and more.

There are three global update options:

- **All Characters and Catalog Entries:** You can update specific properties in all character tags, paragraph tags, and text lines. Use this option if, for instance, you need to change the default font size in all tag definitions and text lines.
- **All Matching Tags in Selection:** You can modify character tags that have been applied to different words in a paragraph. For example, suppose the Menu Item character tag is applied to one word and the Command character tag is applied to a different word in the same paragraph. You can select the paragraph and remove bold formatting from both character tags.
- **All Tagged:** Applies a new character tag in place of the selected tag. For example, you can use this option to apply the Hyperlink character tag instead of the Underline character tag in an entire document.

Changing Specific Properties

You can instantly modify specific character properties in a document, whether the properties are in character tags, paragraph tags, or text lines. This is handy for removing color from all characters or only from selected character tags and changing the default font.

To modify selected properties, follow these steps:

1. Display the Character Designer.
2. Click the Commands button, then select Set Window to As Is from the pop-up menu. This resets all character properties.
3. Set the properties you want to update.
4. Click the Commands button, then select Global Update Options from the pop-up menu. The Global Update Options dialog box is displayed.

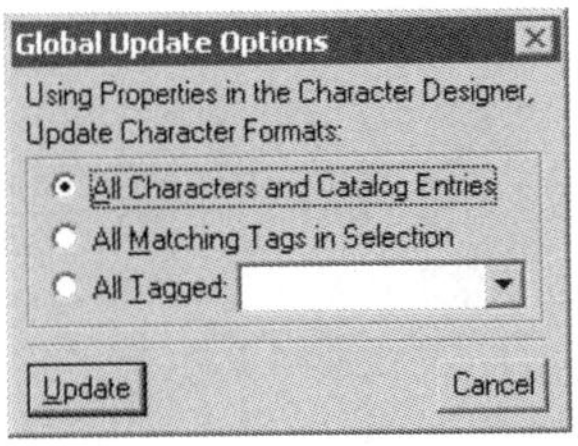

5. Do *one* of the following:
   - To update specific properties in *all* character tags, paragraph tags, and text lines, click the All Characters and Catalog Entries radio button. If you selected a tag name before performing this step, FrameMaker gives you the option to apply the tag to all characters in the document. Typically, you want to avoid this, so click the No button to update only the properties you changed.
   - To update specific properties in character tags applied to *selected text*, click the All Matching Tags in Selection radio button.
6. Click the Update button. FrameMaker globally makes the appropriate changes.

Reassigning a Character Tag Globally

FrameMaker provides a way to assign a new character tag in place of the selected tag. For example, you can swap each instance of the Button character tag with the Key character tag.

To reassign a character tag globally, follow these steps:

1. Display the Character Designer.
2. In the Character Tag drop-down list, click the tag name you want to apply.
3. Click the Commands button, then select Global Update Options from the pop-up menu. The Global Update Options dialog box is displayed.
4. Click the All Tagged radio button, then click the tag you want to replace from the drop-down list.
5. Click the Update button. A confirmation dialog box is displayed.
6. Click the OK button to update the tag.

Removing Character Tag Formatting

After you apply a character tag, you can remove the tag by selecting text and applying the Default Paragraph Font character tag. The text will be reformatted with the paragraph tag properties. If a character tag has been applied to an entire paragraph, you need to remove the character tag formatting and reapply the paragraph tag.

To remove character tag formatting from selected text, follow these steps:

1. Display the character catalog.
2. Select the text you want to reformat.
3. In the character catalog, click Default Paragraph Font. The text is reformatted with the original paragraph style. In the left status bar, the character tag name is no longer displayed. A star displayed next to the paragraph tag name indicates an override. See "Avoiding Character Tag Overrides" on page 148 for more information.

TIP Instead of using the character catalog, you can press F8 or CTRL-8 to activate the status bar and select Default Paragraph Font to remove the character formatting.

Deleting Character Tags

All character tags can be deleted from the character catalog except the Default Paragraph Font. When you delete a tag, the catalog is updated, but variables, cross-references, and other components can still refer to the deleted tag name. Deleting a tag also does not remove the character tag from text. The name of the deleted character tag is still displayed in the status bar, along with a star to indicate that it's an override. To prevent the override, globally replace each instance of the character tag you plan to delete with another tag. See "Reassigning a Character Tag Globally" on page 153 for details.

TIP If you delete the tag without globally applying another one, you can select the text formatted by the deleted tag and assign a new one in its place. For more information, see "Renaming Character Tags" on page 151.

To delete a character tag from the character catalog, follow these steps:

1. Display the character catalog.
2. Click the Delete button to display the Delete Formats from Catalog dialog box. You can also display the dialog box by clicking the Commands button in the Character Designer and selecting Delete Format from the pop-up menu.

Click the tag you want to delete.

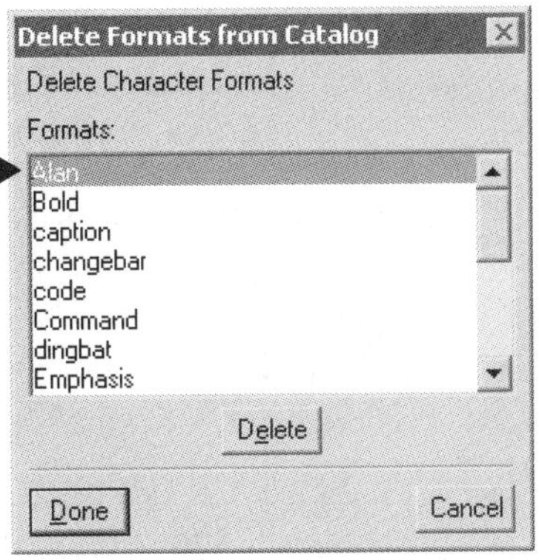

3. Click the tag you want to delete, then click the Delete button. To delete all character tags, press and hold ALT-E. This method quickly deletes the tags. You can delete tags from the paragraph catalog the same way.

CAUTION If you make a mistake, you must click the Cancel button and start over. There is no Apply button.

4. Click the Done button. The character tag you deleted is no longer displayed in the character catalog.

Additional Character Tags Tips

This chapter has covered applying character tags to text directly, but you can also format text in variables, cross references, autonumbered paragraphs, markers, and other FrameMaker components. Table 6-1 describes more advanced uses for character tags. You'll read more about each component in the corresponding chapter (for example, cross-references formats are discussed in the cross-reference chapter).

Item	Description
Variable	Create a book title variable and include a character tag to italicize the title. See Chapter 9, "Storing Content in Variables."
Autonumbered paragraph	Create a bullet character tag that uses the Wingdings font and use the character tag in the autonumber format of a bulleted paragraph tag. See "Autonumbering Details" on page 134.

Table 6-1. Character Tag Tips

Item	Description
Cross-reference format	Format cross-references as blue in a PDF file by inserting a blue character tag in the cross-reference format. Before you create a PDF file for printing, set the color in the blue tag to As Is. See "Formatting Cross-References" on page 201. You can achieve the same result by printing spot color to black, except that *all* color would print as black. Read more about spot color in Chapter 20, "Color Output."
Marker	Italicize *See Also* in an index entry by including a character tag in the index marker. See Chapter 16, "Creating Indexes."
Text line	Draw a text line using the Text Line feature in the Tools Palette and format the text with an italicized character tag. See Chapter 13, "FrameMaker's Graphics Tools."
Spell checker	Skip spell-checking for specific words by setting their language to "None" in a character tag. See Chapter 4, "Word-Processing Features."
Change bar	Mark text you modify with a change bar character tag instead of or in addition to relying on automatic change bars. See Chapter 4, "Word-Processing Features."
Reference page	Create highlighted page numbers for TOC entries in a PDF file by applying a blue character tag to <$pagenum> building blocks on the TOC reference page. See Chapter 15, "Creating Tables of Contents."
Hyperlink	Create a character tag with all properties set to As Is and apply to hyperlinks. The format marks the beginning and end of the hyperlink without modifying the character properties. See Chapter 22, "Creating Interactive Content with Hypertext."

Table 6-1. Character Tag Tips (Continued)

CHAPTER 7

Understanding Table Design

FrameMaker lets you define preformatted table formats using *table tags*. The table tags store formatting such as alignment, spacing, cell margins, pagination, ruling, shading, and the default number of columns and rows. When you need a table, you select a table tag and insert the table in your document. Table tags also store paragraph formatting, so when you insert a new table, the paragraph tags for text in the table are already applied to the table title and cells.

Table 7: Results of Annual Tri-City Dog Show

Ribbon	Dog Name	Breed
Red	Charlie Chan's Revival	Toy Poodle
Blue	Trixie the Trotter	Pomeranian
Purple	Island Girl Blanc	Maltese
Yellow	Jake's Nine Lives	Pointer
Judge R.C. Smith presided.		

The biggest advantage of table tags is that they help maintain consistency. If the corporate style guide changes or your department decides to redesign tables, you update the FrameMaker template and import the new table tag into your document. Tables tagged with the modified table tag are updated instantly. Some properties, however, do not change until you insert a new table. For example, if you update a table tag's default column width or number of rows, existing tables are not affected; the changes apply only to new tables.

Both table and paragraph tags provide default formatting for the underlying content. To emphasize text in a paragraph, you apply a character tag. This reformats the selected text without changing the paragraph tag. Similarly, you can modify a table without changing the default table design. Adding rows and columns, inserting a table title, shading specific cells, merging cells, modifying borders, and other reformatting can be done on a table-by-table basis. Some of these changes, such as adding rows and columns, can be saved in the table tag; others apply only to the selected table. For example, you can't save merged table cells or irregular ruling patterns in a table tag.

Inserting Tables

Tables consist of four basic components—the table title, heading rows, body rows, and footing rows. When you insert a table into your document, you specify the number and types of rows, the number of columns, and the table tag. You can make many modifications to the table—both inside and outside the Table Designer.

To insert a table, follow these steps:

1. Position your cursor where you want to put the table.
2. Select Table➤Insert Table. The Insert Table dialog box is displayed.

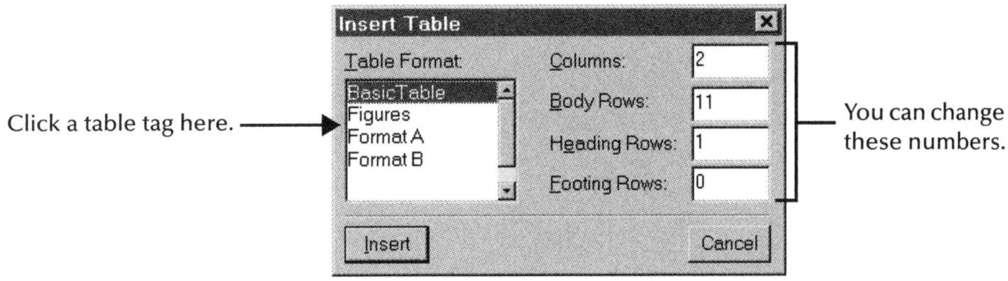

3. Click a table tag in the Table Format list.
4. In the fields on the right, type the number of rows and columns you want for the table. You can add three kinds of rows to a table:
   - **Heading row.** Contains the names of each column and repeats when the table breaks to the next page.
   - **Body row.** Displays main content.
   - **Footing row.** Includes text that repeats when the table breaks to the next page.
5. Click the Insert button. The table is displayed in your document.

With the FrameMaker text symbols displayed, you'll see an upside-down T (or table anchor) above the table. The anchor locks the table to the paragraph. As the paragraph fills the page, the table moves down. (Floating tables are a bit different. See "Basic Sheet" on page 164.)

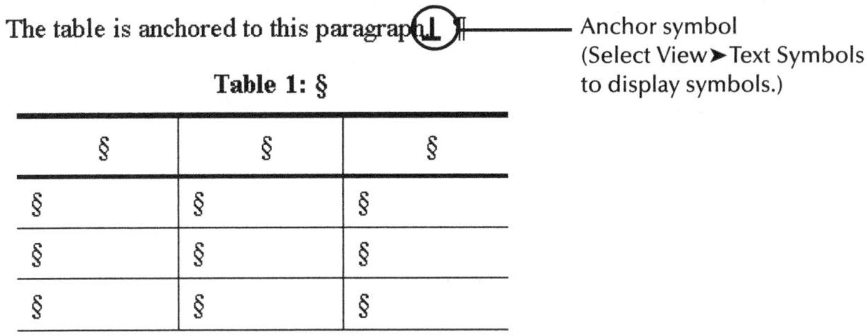

After you insert a table, you type text in the table cells and press the TAB key to move the cursor from cell to cell. The cursor moves horizontally to the end of the row and then to the first cell in the next row until reaching the end of the table. In some word processing programs, you can press the TAB key at the end of the table to add a row. In FrameMaker, when the cursor reaches the last cell in the last row, the cursor jumps to the table title (if the table has one) or the first cell of the table.

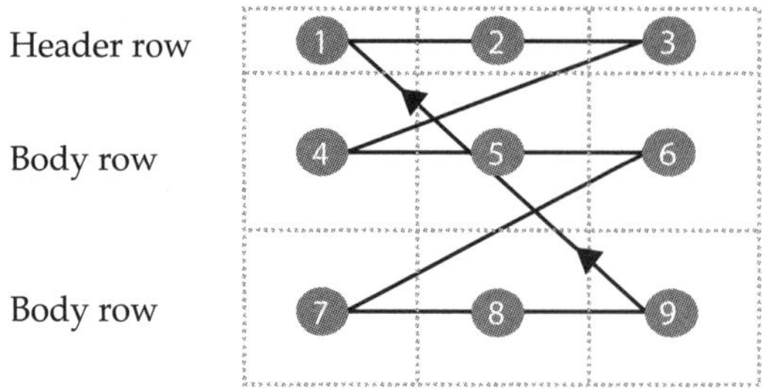

Inserting a tab in a table cell is also different. To insert a tab, position your cursor in the cell and press ESC TAB. The paragraph tag applied to the table cell must include a tab stop, or text will not appear to be after a tab; however, a tab is still inserted and you can see the tab symbol if you view text symbols.

Selecting Cells

Double-clicking a table cell selects the contents of the cell, not the actual table cell. The quickest way to select a table cell is by CTRL-clicking the cell you want to select. A small square, or *handle*, is displayed on the right border of the selected cell. You select and drag a handle to resize the selected column manually.

You can also select a cell by using the Object pointer in the Tools Palette or by pressing the left mouse button and dragging the cursor over the table cells.

Equipment§	Aisle Number§	Stock Number§
Lantern§	3D§	730-439H93§
Portable stove§	5A§	072-321C85§

Drag the handle to resize the column manually.

To select a row or column, you CTRL-click twice in a specific location. Typically, the border closer to your cursor before you select the cells determines whether the row or column is selected. If the cursor is closer to the left or right cell border, you select the row. If the cursor is closer to the top or bottom cell border, you select the column. Adding to the confusion, CTRL-click twice in the *middle* of the cell also selects the column. In addition, FrameMaker offers a table toolbar in the Quick Access Bar, from which you can select a column, a row, column body cells, or the whole table.

CTRL-click near the left or right border to select the cell.

English Setter	Sporting
Beagle	Hound
Poodle	Toy

English Setter	Sporting
Beagle	Hound
Poodle	Toy

CTRL-click near the left or right border twice to select the row.

English Setter	Sporting
Beagle	Hound
Poodle	Toy

English Setter	Sporting
Beagle	Hound
Poodle	Toy

CTRL-click near a top or bottom border twice to select the column.

English Setter	Sporting
Beagle	Hound
Poodle	Toy

English Setter	Sporting
Beagle	Hound
Poodle	Toy

Moving and Deleting Tables

You can move and delete tables by selecting the table anchor or selecting the table itself. The document symbols must be displayed for you to see anchors (select View➤Text Symbols), and anchors can be difficult to select. If there are two adjacent tables, the anchors may be stacked on top of one another on the same line. Cutting and pasting is easier, but both methods are described here.

NOTE If you don't select the entire table before cutting and pasting or selecting the anchor, a warning dialog box is displayed with the choice to leave the cells empty or to remove the cells. Click the Cancel button and start over.

To cut and paste a table to another paragraph, follow these steps:

1. Position your cursor in the table you want to move.
2. CTRL-click three times to select the table.
3. Press CTRL-X to cut the table.
4. Position the cursor where you want the table and press CTRL-V to paste the table.

To select the anchor to move the table, follow these steps:

1. Position your cursor next to the anchor. You might have to change the page magnification rate to 150 or 200 percent to see the anchor.
2. Press SHIFT-LEFT ARROW or SHIFT-RIGHT ARROW key to select the anchor until the table is highlighted. Keep in mind the following tips:
   - If you're moving a table that is above other tables, the two anchors may be stacked. They're on the same line but are displayed as one anchor. You'll need to position your cursor in the middle of the anchor, press the RIGHT ARROW key, and then press the SPACEBAR until the two anchors are separated.

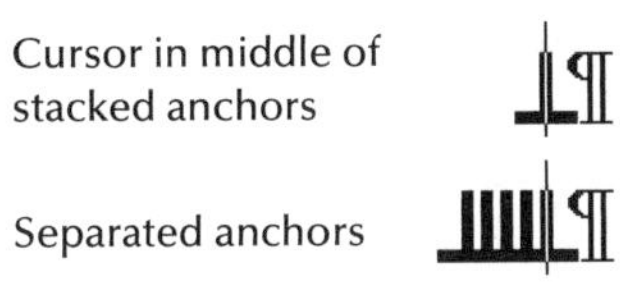

   - If you don't select the end of flow symbol with the table anchor, you'll leave an empty paragraph.
3. Press CTRL-X. The table is no longer displayed.
4. Position the cursor where you want the table and press CTRL-V. The table is displayed in the new location.

To delete a table, follow these steps:

1. Select the table.
2. Press the DELETE key, or select Edit➤Clear.
3. The table is deleted from the document.

Changing the Assigned Table Tag

You can apply table tags to existing tables. This lets you reformat the selected table with a different table tag. Unlike the paragraph and character catalogs, which can be displayed in separate palettes, the table catalog has no palette. Table tag names are displayed only in the Table Designer and when you insert a table.

To apply a table tag, follow these steps:

1. Place your cursor inside a table.
2. Display the Table Designer by pressing CTRL-T or ESC-SHIFT-F I T.
3. Click the new tag in the Table Tag drop-down list, then click the Apply button.

Table Tag drop-down list

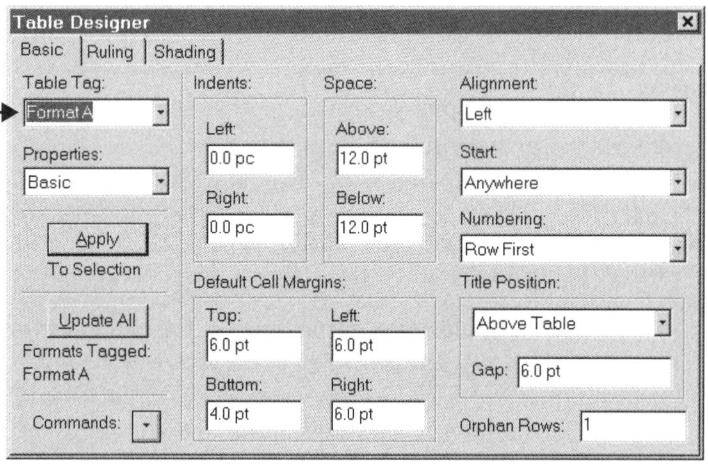

TIP If the table doesn't appear to be formatted by the table tag—the borders or colors are wrong, for instance—check the table's current settings, remove all custom formatting, and reapply the tag. See "Displaying and Removing Custom Ruling and Shading" on page 179 for details.

Modifying a Table Tag

Most table tag properties are configured in the Table Designer. When you make changes in the Table Designer and click the Update All button, two things happen—all tables of that type in the document are updated where you inserted them, and new tables of that type will have the new formatting. When you modify a table definition outside the Table Designer, the changes aren't applied throughout the document; they apply only to the selected table and to those you insert in the future using the modified tag.

In the Table Designer, you can change the following properties:

- Indents
- Space above and below the table
- Cell margins
- Vertical and horizontal table alignment
- Cell sequence for autonumbers
- Title position and gap
- Number of orphan rows
- Borders
- Shading

Outside the Table Designer, you can modify the following properties:

- Column width
- Number of columns and rows
- Types of columns (heading, body, footing)
- Paragraph tags applied to the table

NOTE If you make changes outside the Table Designer and don't click the Update All button in the Table Designer, those changes apply only to the selected table.

To modify a table tag in the Table Designer, follow these steps:

1. Insert a table and display the Table Designer.
2. Make changes on one of the sheets, then click the Update All button. Repeat for the other sheets. Your changes are saved in the table tag and applied to all existing tables of the same type.

NOTE Clicking the Apply button instead of the Update All button creates a formatting override. This isn't recommended because your changes are saved only in the current table, not in the table tag.

The following sections describe each setting in the Table Designer. For details on changing table tags outside the Table Designer, see "Customizing Tables Outside the Table Designer" on page 170.

Changing Table Designer Settings

The Table Designer has three property sheets. To view a sheet, click its tab or click the sheet in the Properties drop-down list. This section describes the sheets.

Basic Sheet

On the Basic sheet, you change spacing, pagination, numbering, orphan rows, and other properties.

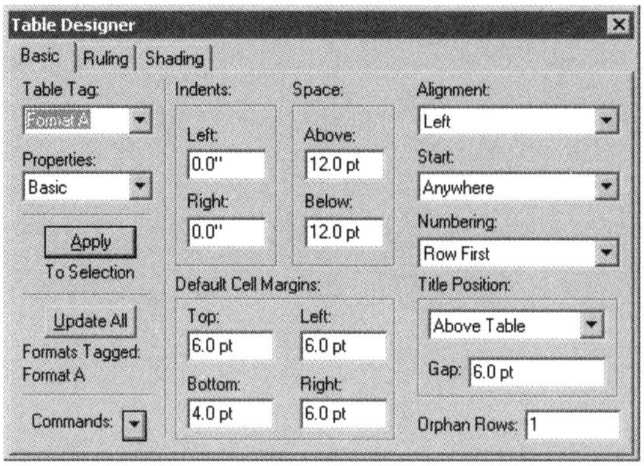

Table 7-1 describes the options.

Item	Description
Indents	Adds space between the left or right edge of the text frame and the table.
Spacing	Determines the room above the table title and below the last row. The paragraphs above and below the table also include spacing properties, so FrameMaker uses the larger of the two spaces; the sizes aren't added. For example, if the space above a table is set to 12 points and the space below the previous paragraph is set to 3 points, FrameMaker places the previous paragraph and the table title 12 points apart.
Default Cell Margins	Adds space inside each table cell. Interacts with settings in the Paragraph Designer Table Cell sheet, where you can customize table cell margins and alignment for a paragraph tag. (See "Table Cell Sheet" on page 127 for details.)

Table 7-1. Table Designer, Basic Sheet

Item	Description
Alignment	Horizontal position of table under the previous paragraph. Interacts with the paragraph's pagination settings. For example, in a paragraph that begins within the side head, a left-aligned table also stays in the side head. ■ **Left:** Aligns the table with the left side of the column. ■ **Right:** Aligns the table with the right side of the column. ■ **Center:** Places the table in the center of the text area. ■ **Side Closer to Binding:** Aligns the table closer to the bound edge of the page. ■ **Side Farther from Binding:** Aligns the table farther from the bound edge of the page.
Start	Positions the table vertically on the page. ■ **Anywhere:** Places the table wherever it fits on the page; table moves down with the anchored paragraph. ■ **Top of Column:** Places the table at the top of the next text column; same as Top of Page in one-column documents. ■ **Top of Page:** Moves the table to the top of the next page. ■ **Top of Left Page:** Places the table at the top of the next left page in a double-sided document. ■ **Top of Right Page:** Places the table at the top of the next right page in a double-sided document. ■ **Float:** Moves the table to the first text column that has room for the entire table. If you type text above the table and the table can't fit on the current page, the table floats to the next page, and text that was previously below the table might move above the table to fill in the space. Float is the only position that could potentially reorder the content around the table.

Table 7-1. Table Designer, Basic Sheet (Continued)

<table>
<tr><th>Item</th><th>Description</th></tr>
<tr><td>Numbering</td><td>Organizes autonumbered paragraphs either horizontally or vertically:
<ul><li>Row First: Numbers paragraphs horizontally, as in:</li></ul>
<table>
<tr><td>1. Go</td><td>2. Yield</td><td>3. Stop</td></tr>
<tr><td>4. Merge</td><td>5. Slow</td><td>6. Exit</td></tr>
<tr><td>7. Caution</td><td>8. School</td><td>9. Turn</td></tr>
</table>
<ul><li>Column First: Numbers paragraph vertically, as in:</li></ul>
<table>
<tr><td>1. Go</td><td>4. Yield</td><td>7. Stop</td></tr>
<tr><td>2. Merge</td><td>5. Slow</td><td>8. Exit</td></tr>
<tr><td>3. Caution</td><td>6. School</td><td>9. Turn</td></tr>
</table></td></tr>
<tr><td>Title Position and Gap</td><td>Positions the table title.
<ul><li>No Title: Indicates the table has no title.</li>
<li>Above Table: Displays the title above the table.</li>
<li>Below Table: Places the title below the table.</li></ul>
The gap is the space between the table and the table title. (Spacing in the table title paragraph itself does not apply.)</td></tr>
<tr><td>Orphan Rows</td><td>Indicates the number of table rows that must stay together when the table breaks across a page. To force the entire table to fit on the same page, specify up to 255 rows.</td></tr>
</table>

Table 7-1. Table Designer, Basic Sheet (Continued)

Ruling Sheet

The Ruling sheet contains border styles for rows, columns, heading and footing rows, and the outside edges of the table.

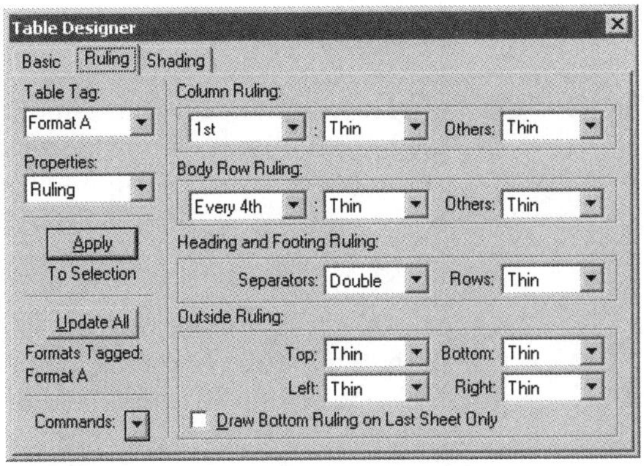

You can arrange borders in a variety of patterns. For example, the second column can have a thick border, and the other columns can have a thin border or no border at all. In rows, a medium ruling may separate every fifth row, and thin rulings may be used for the rest. The five default ruling styles—double, medium, thick, thin, and very thin—are defined in the custom ruling and shading properties of a document and are also displayed in the Table Designer. For details on creating, editing, and deleting ruling styles, see "Changing Ruling Options" on page 178. Table 7-2 describes the Ruling sheet.

<table>
<tr><th>Item</th><th>Description</th></tr>
<tr><td>Column Ruling</td><td>Specifies a unique border for the nth column and a repeating border for the remaining columns. Useful if the table cell headings are vertical instead of horizontal. The following table has a single ruling for the first column and no ruling for the others.
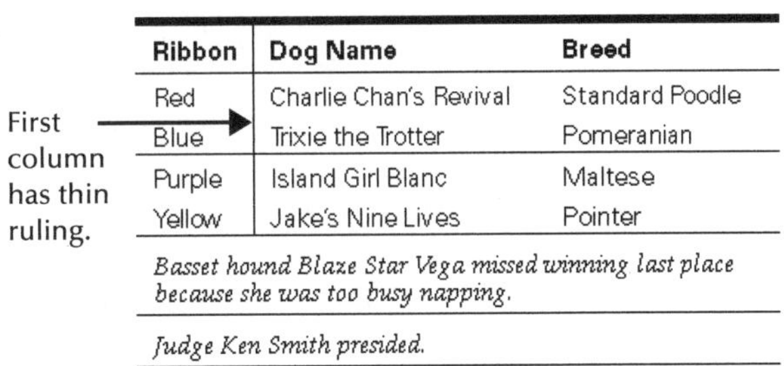
</td></tr>
<tr><td>Body Row Ruling</td><td>Specifies a repeating border for every nth body row and the same border for the remaining body rows. The previous table has a thin border for every second body row and no border for the others. (The last two rows are footing rows.)</td></tr>
</table>

Table 7-2. Table Designer, Ruling Sheet

Item	Description
Heading and Footing Ruling	Separates the heading and footing rows from the table and provides a border for multiple heading and footing rows. The previous table has a thin border for the separator and a thin border for the footing rows.
Outside Ruling	Specifies the outside border with an option to draw the bottom border only on the last sheet of a table (for tables that break across pages). The previous table has a medium top border, a thin bottom border, and no left or right borders.

Table 7-2. Table Designer, Ruling Sheet (Continued)

Shading Sheet

On the Shading sheet, you choose the color and shading amount for heading and footing rows and the body cells.

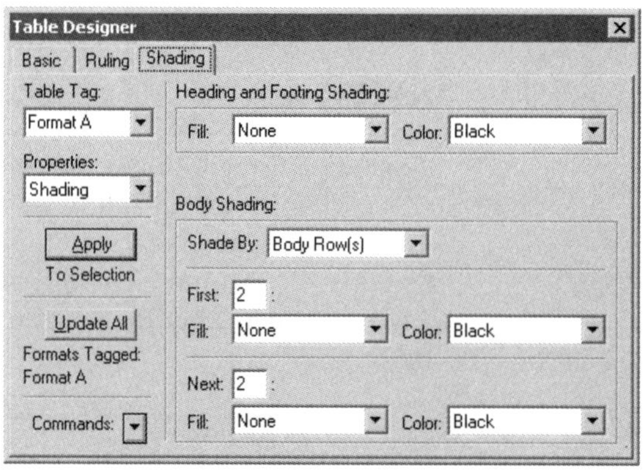

For example, your table can have a 30 percent blue heading row and alternate 10 percent yellow and white body rows. The fill percentages—3, 10, 30, 50, 70, 90, and 100—are defaults and cannot be modified. You *can* set up additional colors in the document's color definitions, and the color itself can have a tint. See Chapter 20, "Color Output," for details. Table 7-3 describes the Shading sheet.

Item	Description
Heading and Footing Shading	Applies fill percentage and color to *both* the heading and footing rows. The heading row of the following table shows a 100 percent black fill. If the table had a footing row, the row would have the same shading. 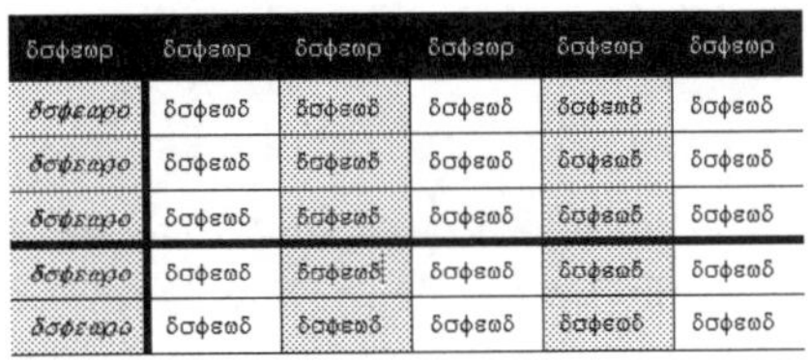
Body Shading	Applies fill percentage and color to *either* the rows or the columns and lets you define alternate shading for each row or column. The previous table is shaded by column with a 10 percent black fill.

Table 7-3. Table Designer, Shading Sheet

Globally Updating Table Tags

You can update table tag properties across the entire table catalog, just as you do with the paragraph and character tags. For example, you can change the body row ruling in all table definitions to None, and all tables in the document will be updated.

The global update options shown in the Table Designer sheet change depending on which sheet is displayed. If you click the Ruling sheet before displaying the Global Update Options dialog box, you have the option to change just the ruling properties. With the Shading sheet displayed, you have the option to change only the shading properties.

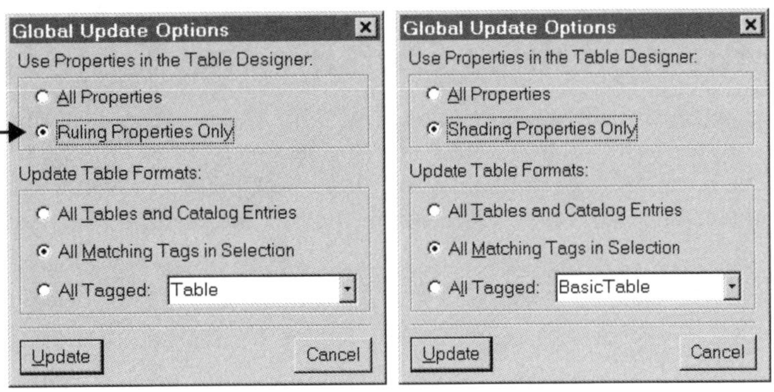

Global Update Options change depending on the Table Designer sheet you selected.

For more information about global updating, see "Setting Properties Across the Entire Paragraph Catalog" on page 130.

Creating a Table Tag

New table tags are based on existing tags—you must insert a table before creating a new tag.

To create a table tag, follow these steps:

1. Insert a table with the tag that looks closest to the table you want to create.
2. Display the Table Designer, then type a new name in the Table Tag field.
3. Click the Apply button. The New Format dialog box is displayed.

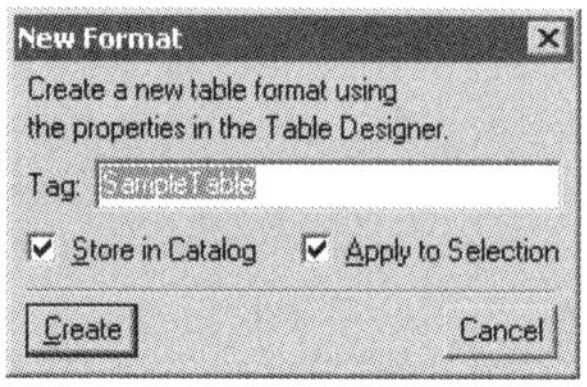

4. Verify the name you typed, then click the Create button. Your table format is displayed in the Table Designer.

CAUTION By default, the Store in Catalog and Apply to Selection check boxes are checked. Most of the time, you don't uncheck the Store in Catalog check box unless you don't want to use the new table format for other tables. Uncheck the Apply to Selection check box only if your cursor is in a table, but you don't want to apply the new tag to it.

5. Make changes on one of the Table Designer sheets, then click the Update All button to save your changes. Repeat for remaining sheets. (If you click the Apply button, the table definition is not updated. This creates a formatting override.)

Customizing Tables Outside the Table Designer

You can customize a table outside the Table Designer by applying paragraph tags to the text in the cells, adding and deleting columns or rows, and resizing columns. If you make such changes in a table and click the Update All button in the Table Designer, your changes are made to the current table and become the default properties for all future tables of that type.

NOTE Unlike changes you make in the Table Designer, changes you make to a table outside the Table Designer are not applied to existing tables of that type in the document except for the current table. If you click the Update All button in the Table Designer, however, the changes are applied to tables you insert in the future using the modified tag.

Adding and Deleting Rows and Columns

When your cursor is in a table and you click the Update All button, the table tag uses the number and location of rows and columns in that table as the default the next time you add a table of the same type. For example, if the current table consists of one heading row, five body rows, and two columns, those defaults are stored in the updated tag. When you insert a new table using the updated tag, the default row and column settings are included unless you change them in the Insert Table dialog box. You can, however, add rows and columns to an existing table and save your changes as the new defaults for that tag.

Although there's only one type of column, there are three types of rows:

- **Heading row.** Repeats column headings.
- **Body row.** Contains main content.
- **Footing row.** Repeats text at the bottom of the table.

Table on page 1

Genre	Artist
Opera	Maria Callas
Bluegrass	Ralph Stanley
Folk	Emmylou Harris
Country	Johnny Cash
Rock	Rolling Stones
Source: Guide for Music Aficionados, Franklin Press	

← Heading row

← Footing row

Table continued on page 2

Genre	Artist
Jazz	Sarah Vaughan
Blues	Albert King
Pop	Michael Jackson
Punk	The Ramones
Source: Guide for Music Aficionados, Franklin Press	

To change the number of rows and columns in a table, follow these steps:

1. Place your cursor in a table you want to modify.
2. Select Table➤Add Rows or Columns. The Add Rows or Columns dialog box is displayed.

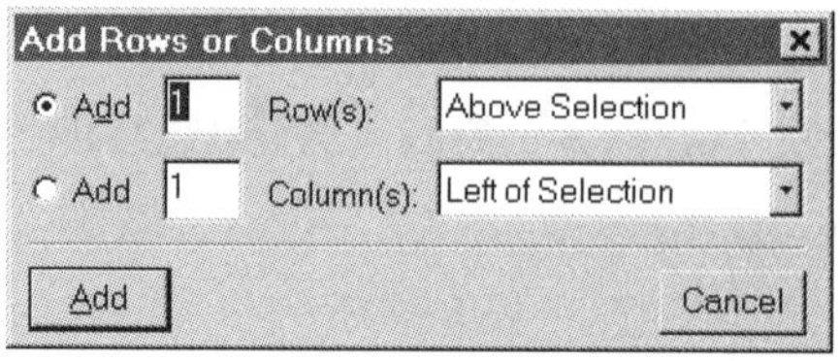

3. To add rows, type the number of rows in the Add field, then click the row location in the Row(s) drop-down list. You can also add a row below the current row by pressing CTRL-ENTER.
4. To add columns, type the number of columns in the Add field, then click the column location in the Column(s) drop-down list.
5. Click the Add button. You can click the Cancel button if you change your mind.
6. *(optional)* To save the current number of rows and columns as the default for this table tag, keep your cursor in the table, display the Table Designer, and click the Update All button.

To delete rows and columns, do the following:

1. Select the row or column you want to delete. If you select only one cell, you'll delete the contents of the cell, not the cell itself.
2. Press the DELETE key. The Clear Table Cells dialog box is displayed.

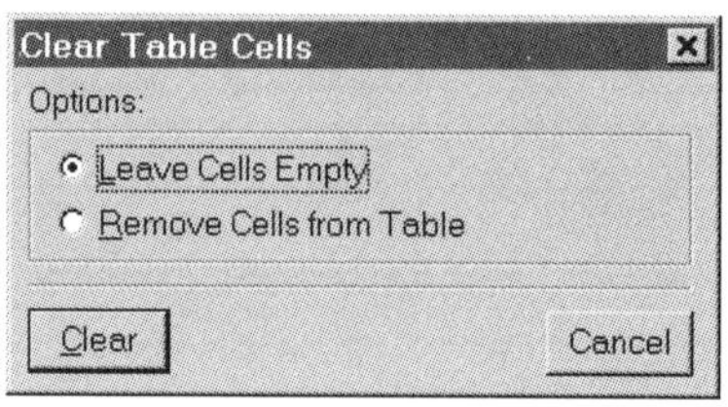

3. Click the Remove Cells from Table radio button to delete the cells, then click the Clear button. The row or column is removed from the table.

NOTE If you click the Leave Cells Empty radio button, the contents of the row or column are deleted, not the row or column.

4. *(optional)* Click the Update All button in the Table Designer to save your changes in the table tag. All new tables inserted using the modified tag will have the new number of rows and columns.

Resizing Columns

Table tags store default column widths. Each time you insert a particular table style, the columns are the same size from table to table. You can resize table columns either manually or by specifying a width. When you resize one column, the other columns remain the same size. This differs in other word processing programs, where table columns adjust to maintain the table width. To maintain the table width when you manually resize a column in FrameMaker, press SHIFT. The width of the column on the right is automatically adjusted to maintain the original table width.

Original column widths

Equipment	Aisle	Stock Number
Lantern	3B	730-439H93

Column 2 is resized while maintaining the table width.

Equipment	Aisle	Stock Number
Lantern	3B	730-439H93

The table widens when column 2 is resized without maintaining the table width.

Equipment	Aisle	Stock Number
Lantern	3B	730-439H93

After resizing a table, you can update the table tag to save the new default column widths. This updates the table tag but not tables already in the document.

Manually Resizing Columns

You can resize table columns manually and use the FrameMaker ruler as a guide. As you drag the column border, the ruler marking moves. If you turn on FrameMaker's snap feature, the border moves to the nearest ruler marking. This helps you precisely resize the columns. To drag the column border between markings, you need to turn snap off. Select Graphics➤Snap to toggle the snap feature. See "Working with Grids" on page 343 for details.

As you resize a table column, the width displayed in the status bar also changes. The dimensions reflect the width of all selected columns.

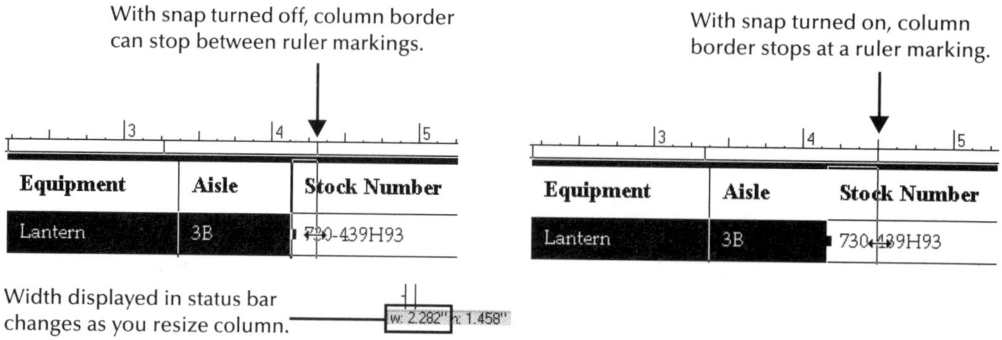

To resize columns manually, do the following:

1. In the column you want to resize, either CTRL-click twice to highlight the column or select a few cells in the column. The sizing arrow and handles are displayed.

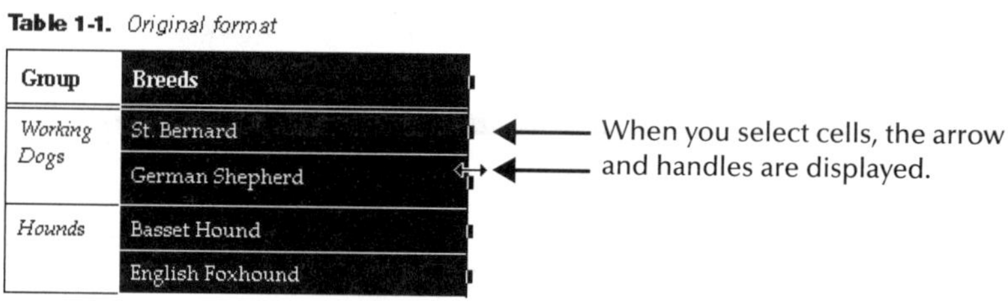

2. Select one of the handles and drag the column to the left or right. When the column is adjusted to the correct width, release the cell handles. The new column width is displayed.

NOTE FrameMaker always resizes the entire column. You cannot create a table with an irregular grid, except by straddling cells. For more information about straddling cells, see "Merging Table Cells" on page 180.

3. *(optional)* To save the current column widths as the default for this table tag, keep your cursor in the table, display the Table Designer, and click the Update All button. All new tables inserted using the modified tag will have the new column widths.

Specifying the Column Width

You can drag columns to resize them, or you can specify the column width as follows:

1. Select the column or columns you want to resize.

2. Select Table➤Resize Columns. The Resize Selected Columns dialog box is displayed.

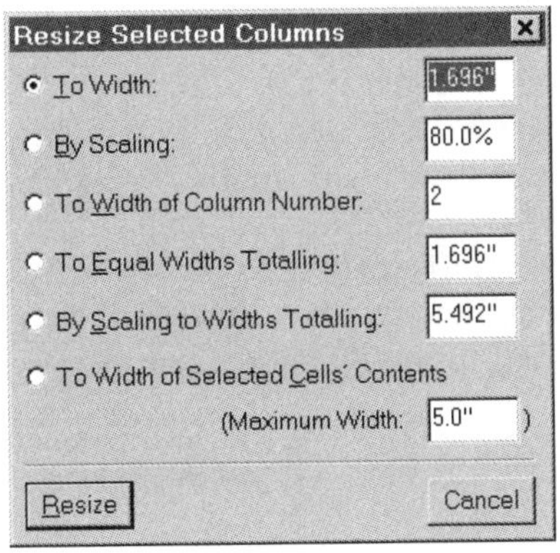

3. Type the appropriate measurement next to the method you want to use:
   - **To Width:** Type the column width. If you select two columns, each column is resized to the specified width.
   - **By Scaling:** Change the width by a specific percentage. For example, you can scale the selected column 200 percent to double the width.
   - **To Width of Column Number:** Match the column width to the specified column.
   - **To Equal Widths Totalling:** Resize two or more columns to equal a specific width.
   - **By Scaling to Widths Totalling:** Resize two or more columns a specific percentage while maintaining the original column proportions.
   - **To Width of Selected Cells' Contents:** Resize the cell to fit its contents.
4. Click the Resize button. The selected table columns are updated.
5. *(optional)* To save the current column widths as the default for this table tag, keep your cursor in the table, display the Table Designer, and click the Update All button. All new tables inserted using the modified tag will have the new the new column widths.

NOTE In FrameMaker, you can specify the unit of measure used throughout the document—in paragraph tags, text frame properties, table tags, and so on. To change the unit of measure, select View➤Options and click a different item in the Display Unit drop-down list.

Applying Paragraph Tags

Paragraph tags format the text in each table cell and in the table title. The typical FrameMaker template includes paragraph tags such as TableTitle, CellBody, CellHeading, and TableFooting, but you can use any paragraph tags you choose. The table tag definition stores a pattern based on the paragraph tags used for the first heading row, first body row, and first footing row. New tables include the paragraph tags stored from the table tag's pattern.

Only the paragraph tags applied to the first row of each row type—heading, body, and footing row—are stored in the table tag. If you apply different paragraph tags to each cell in a table, those tag settings are not saved in the table tag. For example, the following table on the left is consistently formatted—CellHeading is applied to the heading row, CellBody is applied to all body rows, and TableFooting is applied to the footing row. The table on the right is formatted inconsistently. Even though the CellBullet paragraph tags are applied in the second body row, these tags won't be saved in the table tag; the tags applied in the *first* body row are saved.

Consistent application of paragraph tags

Table 6: TableTitle

CellHeading	CellHeading	CellHeading
CellBody	CellBody	CellBody
CellBody	CellBody	CellBody
CellBody	CellBody	CellBody
TableFooting		

Inconsistent CellBullet tags aren't saved in the table tag.

Table 6: TableTitle

CellHeading	CellHeading	CellHeading
CellBody	CellBody	CellBody
• CellBullet	• CellBullet	CellBody
CellBody	CellBody	CellBody
TableFooting		

TIP You can insert tables that have complex formatting by selecting the table from your own customized menu created with the third-party tool, Auto-Text (www.siliconprairiesoftware.com). See Appendix A, "Resources" for more information.

To apply paragraph tags to cells in a table, follow these steps:

1. Put your cursor in a cell (or select several cells), then apply a paragraph tag.

NOTE Formatting overrides (indicated by the star displayed in the status bar by the paragraph tag name) are saved with the table tag. If you modify a paragraph tag in the table, be sure you avoid overrides by updating the paragraph tag definition.

2. *(optional)* To save the paragraph formatting in the table tag, display the Table Designer, then click the Update All button. The paragraph formatting is saved in the table tag.

Customizing Cell Ruling and Shading

FrameMaker's custom ruling and shading feature lets you apply ruling and shading to particular cells in a table, providing more flexibility than the Table Designer properties. You apply the formatting only when you need it (for example, to highlight important content). The following table cells have been reformatted with a 10 percent black fill and a medium border:

Equipment
Lantern
Portable stove
Sleeping bag
Tent

CAUTION By applying custom ruling and shading to table cells, you create a formatting override. Typically, you can remove overrides by reimporting the template with the Remove Layout/Format Overrides setting checked. To strip custom ruling and shading, however, you must remove the formatting manually (as explained later on page 179). Modifying tables outside the table tag makes it difficult to maintain consistency, so you should customize tables sparingly.

To apply custom ruling and shading, follow these steps:

1. Highlight the cells you want to format.
2. Select Table➤Custom Ruling & Shading. The Custom Ruling and Shading dialog box is displayed.

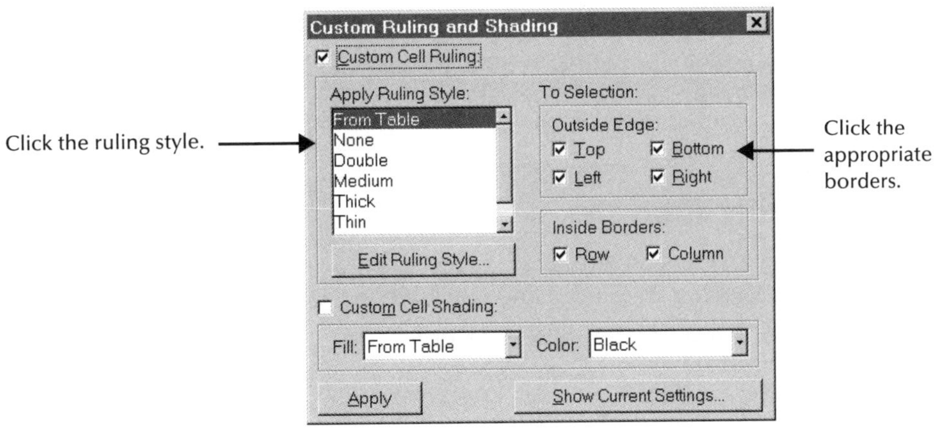

TIP When the cursor is inside a table, clicking the Set Fill Pattern, Set Pen Pattern, or Set Line Width button in the Tools palette displays the Custom Ruling and Shading dialog box.

3. To apply custom ruling, complete the following:
   a. Click a border style in the Apply Ruling Style list.
   b. *(optional)* If you do not want to change the custom cell shading when you change the ruling, uncheck the Custom Cell Shading check box.
   c. Click the cell borders you want to reformat in the To Selection section. The border types are displayed in the following table, which assumes that the entire table is selected.

Inside column border of selection

Outside edge

Genre	Artist
Opera	Maria Callas
Bluegrass	Ralph Stanley
Folk	Emmylou Harris
Country	Johnny Cash
Rock	Rolling Stones
Source: Guide for Music Aficionados, Franklin Press	

Inside row border of selection

4. To apply custom shading to selected cells, do the following:
   a. Click the type of shading in the Fill drop-down list. You can choose specific percentages or solid white.
   b. *(optional)* If you do not want to change the custom cell ruling when you change the shading, uncheck the Custom Cell Ruling check box.
   c. Click a color in the Color drop-down list (unless you set the fill to White, None, or As Is).
5. Click the Apply button. Your changes are made to the selected table cell or cells.

Changing Ruling Options

You can edit, create, and delete ruling styles, and the changes will be displayed in the Custom Ruling and Shading dialog box and the Table Designer.

To edit and create ruling styles, follow these steps:

1. *(optional)* Select the cells you need to format.
2. Select Table►Custom Ruling & Shading. The Custom Ruling and Shading dialog box is displayed.

3. In the Apply Ruling Style list, click the style you want to edit or base the new style on, then click the Edit Ruling Style button. The Edit Ruling Style dialog box is displayed.

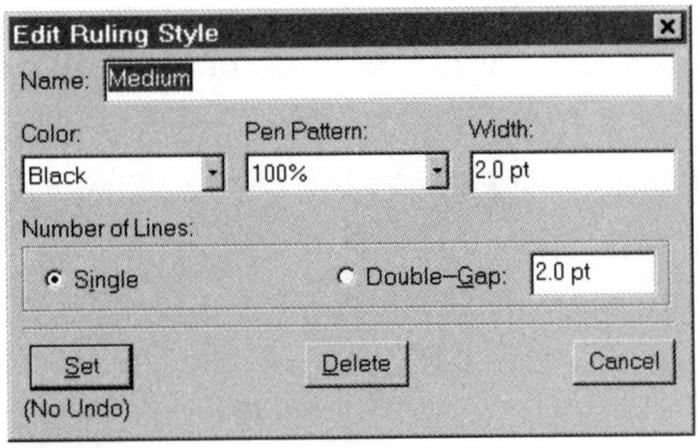

4. Change the appropriate properties:
   - Click a color in the Color drop-down list.
   - Click a fill percentage (or White) in the Pen Pattern drop-down list.
   - Type a new line width from .015 to 360 points in the Width field.
   - Click the Double–Gap radio button to create a double line and type the space between the lines (from .015 to 360 points).
5. If you're creating a new style, type a new name in the Name window.
6. Click the Set button. The ruling style is updated in the selected cells.

To delete a ruling style, follow these steps:

1. Display the Custom Ruling and Shading dialog box.
2. Click the style you want to delete, then click the Edit Ruling Style button.
3. Click the Delete button. If the ruling style is used in the document, a warning is displayed.
4. Click the OK button to confirm the change. The ruling style is removed from the Custom Ruling and Shading dialog box and from table cells to which you applied the border.

Displaying and Removing Custom Ruling and Shading

In addition to customizing table cells, you can also display and remove formatting properties for selected table cells. Showing the current settings indicates whether cells are formatted by the table tag or the custom ruling and shading properties. If table tag properties aren't displaying as you expect in a particular table, you can show the current settings through the Custom Ruling and Shading dialog box and reset the properties.

To display current table settings, follow these steps:

1. Select specific table cells to view their settings, or select the entire table to view all settings.
2. Display the Custom Ruling and Shading dialog box, then click the Show Current Settings button. The Current Selection's Settings dialog box is displayed.

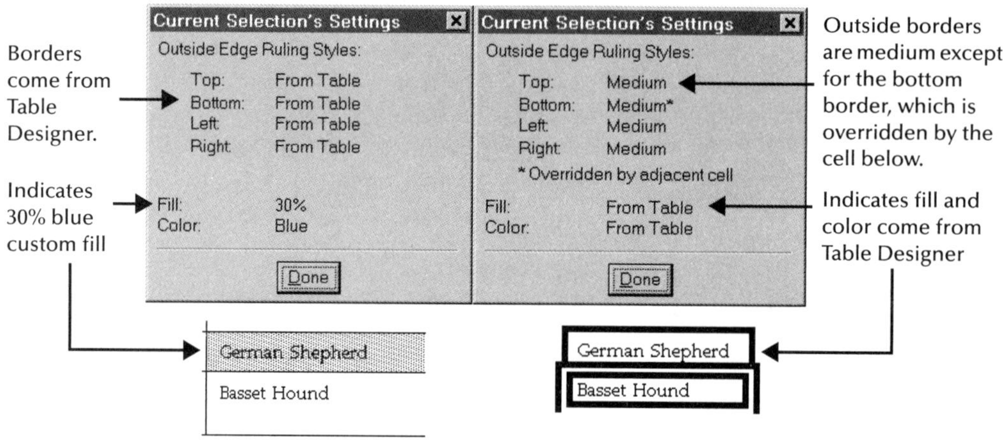

3. Click the Done button.

To restore table tag defaults, do the following:

1. Make sure the table cells are still selected, then display the Custom Ruling and Shading dialog box.
2. Check the Custom Cell Shading and Custom Cell Ruling check boxes.
3. In the Apply Ruling Style list, click From Table, then check all check boxes in the To Selection section.
4. In the Fill and Color drop-down lists under the Custom Cell Shading check box, click From Table.
5. Click the Apply button. The default borders and shading are restored.

TIP You might find this feature useful for tables imported from other applications. Restoring table tag defaults is a quick way to make a clean table with no overrides.

Merging Table Cells

You merge, or *straddle*, table cells to create one cell across two or more rows or columns. By straddling cells, you can modify the table design to display content more clearly. For instance, the following tables list two dog groups—working dogs and hounds—and two breeds for each group. Unless you know your dog breeds, the two blank cells in the Group column of Table A are confusing. Should the blank cells contain content or remain empty?

Table B (on the right) divides the space more efficiently. In the first column, the first and second body cells—and then the third and fourth body cells—have been straddled. Now it's evident that two breeds belong to each dog group.

NOTE Straddled table cells cannot break across pages. This can cause unsightly page breaks. When a straddled cell fills with text, the entire row moves to the next available page or text column. If you have this problem, it may be easier to use a different table design than to use straddled cells.

Table A

Group	**Breeds**
Working dogs	St. Bernard
	German Shepherd
Hounds	Basset Hound
	English Foxhound

Table B

Group	**Breeds**
Working dogs	St. Bernard
	German Shepherd
Hounds	Basset Hound
	English Foxhound

Displaying document borders makes it easier to see straddled cells.

Before straddling table cells, consider the following:

- You can straddle two or more heading rows, body rows, footing rows, and vertical cells; however, you cannot straddle across different types of rows—a body row with a footing row, for instance.
- In a table with straddled cells, you can sort by column, but you cannot sort the rows. For example, the breeds in Table B cannot be alphabetized until you unstraddle the rows in the Group column. You can, however, alphabetize the columns, which would place the Breeds column before the Group column.
- Display the document borders before straddling table cells (select View➤Borders). It's easier to see which cells you've selected.
- You cannot save straddled table cells in a table definition.

NOTE Though you can select Edit➤Undo to take back the previous action, save the file before you straddle table cells. If the results are not what you expected, you can select File➤Revert to Saved to restore the file to its previous state.

To straddle table cells, follow these steps:

1. Select the table cells you want to join.
2. Select Table➤Straddle. The straddled table cells appear as one cell.

Group	Breeds
Working dogs (two breeds are provided as examples)	St. Bernard
	German Shepherd

To unstraddle table cells, follow these steps:

1. Select the merged table cells.
2. Select Table➤Unstraddle. The merged cells are restored as separate cells. All text moves to the first unstraddled cell, which expands to accommodate the text.

The first unstraddled cell expands to accommodate the text.

Group	Breeds
Working dogs (two breeds are provided as examples)	St. Bernard
	German Shepherd

CAUTION If you straddle two cells that have text in each cell, then unstraddle the cells, the text remains in the first cell that was straddled. Be careful when straddling and unstraddling cells; check to make sure your text is in the appropriate cells when you have finished.

Rotating Table Cells

You can rotate table cells to change the direction in which content is displayed. For example, to prevent text in a heading row from wrapping, you could rotate the text vertically. The table cell expands vertically to display the line of text. The width of the rotated table cell, however, does not change. It is still determined by the column width.

FrameMaker rotates table cells in 90° increments. In the following Table A, the heading cells were rotated counterclockwise 90° to prevent text from wrapping.

Table A

Table 6: The Sweet Shack Inventory of Desserts

	War eho use A	War eho use B	War eho use C
Strawberry Pie	54	29	3
Angel Food Cake	32	94	43
Chocolate Mousse	5	23	382

→

Table B

Table 6: The Sweet Shack Inventory of Desserts

	Warehouse A	Warehouse B	Warehouse C
Strawberry Pie	54	29	3
Angel Food Cake	32	94	43
Chocolate Mousse	5	23	382

To rotate a table cell, follow these steps:

1. Select the cell or cells you want to rotate.
2. Select Graphics➤Rotate. The Rotate Table Cells dialog box is displayed.

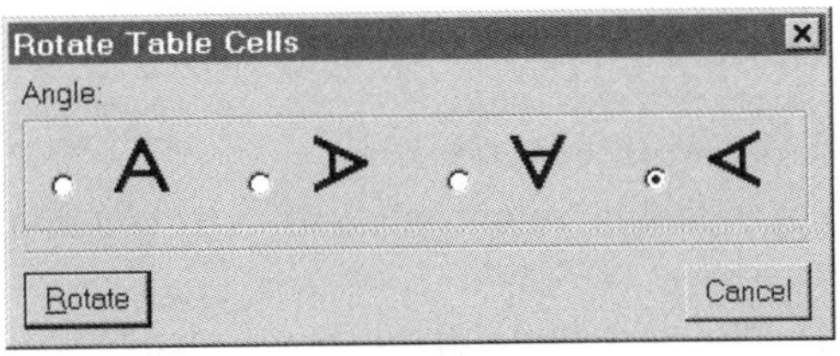

3. Click one of the radio buttons to indicate the direction you want to rotate the cell. To rotate text counterclockwise 90°, as shown in the previous table, click the last radio button.
4. Click the Rotate button. The text appears in the new orientation. If you make a mistake, you can select Edit➤Undo.

NOTE You can rotate only table cells this way; tables themselves are reoriented by applying a rotated master page. For details, see "Creating a Landscape Master Page" on page 251.

If you want to display text at an angle other than the four angles in the Rotate Table Cell dialog box, you can insert an anchored frame in the cell, and then put text inside the anchored frame and rotate that text. You can rotate this text at any angle. For more information, see "Rotating" on page 366. Note that if you save the file to HTML, the rotated text is saved as a graphic and not as text.

Sorting Table Data

FrameMaker can sort table data in a number of ways:

- **By row or column.** Sorted vertically (by row) or horizontally (by column). When sorting by row, you can sort specific rows or all rows in the table.
- **In ascending or descending alphanumeric order.** Sorted from A to Z and 1 to 9 (ascending), or Z to A and 9 to 1 (descending).
- **Considering case sensitivity.** If capitalization is considered, *snake* is sorted before *Snake.*
- **Second- and third-level sorting.** After sorting the table by the initial criterion, FrameMaker performs the second and third sorts. For example, FrameMaker can sort a table of university departments and courses in which departments are sorted first and then each course within the department is sorted.

CAUTION You cannot undo a table sort, so save the file before you begin. You can select File➤Revert to Saved to restore the original file if necessary.

You can sort a table that contains Unicode content, but note that the sorting performed is based on the locale setting of your system. (The locale is specified in the Control Panel in the Region and Language Options dialog box's Regional Options tab.) Make sure before you sort that your locale setting is the best match for your content to ensure correct sorting.

To sort a table, follow these steps:

1. Click in the table you want to sort.
2. To sort only part of the table, select those rows. If you do not select anything in the table, the entire table is sorted.
3. Select Table➤Sort. The Sort Table dialog box is displayed.

Group	Dog
Working Dog	Doberman Pinscher
Sporting	English Setter
Hound	Beagle
Terrier	Boston Terrier

Group	Dog
Hound	Beagle
Sporting	English Setter
Terrier	Boston Terrier
Working Dog	Doberman Pinscher

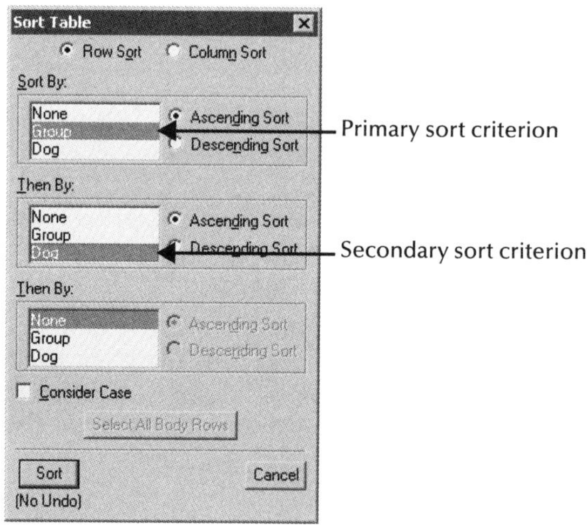

4. Click the Row Sort or Column Sort radio button to indicate the type of sort you want.
5. In the Sort By window, click the appropriate column or row you want to use to sort by.
   - To rearrange data by rows, specify the column to be sorted. In the preceding table, FrameMaker alphabetized the table rows by the Group column.
   - For a column sort, specify a row to sort on. If row one is empty, for example, specify row two.
6. Indicate whether the sort should be in ascending or descending order by clicking the appropriate radio button.
7. *(optional)* For secondary and tertiary sorting, change settings in the Then By sections. In the following table, rows in the first column were sorted first, followed by rows in the second column, then rows in the third column. For the

secondary sort, courses within each department are alphabetized. For the tertiary sort, course numbers in the third row were alphabetized within each department.

CAUTION If you click the None setting for the primary sort, you cannot change the secondary and tertiary sort options.

Table A

Department	Course	Number
Art History	Rothko	GT4901-F
Art History	Rothko	DS2031-S
English	Film Noir 101	AT8032-E
English	French Poetry	Z87322-N

For the secondary sort, courses within each department were sorted.

Table B

Department	Course	Number
Art History	Rothko	DS2031-S
Art History	Rothko	GT4901-F
English	Film Noir 101	AT8032-E
English	French Poetry	Z87322-N

For the tertiary sort, course numbers for the identical Rothko courses were sorted.

8. To consider the capitalization of words during the sort, check the Consider Case check box.
9. *(optional)* If you selected specific rows to sort and change your mind, click the Select All Body Rows button to highlight all rows in the table. This option is grayed out if you clicked in one cell instead of selecting rows.
10. Click the Sort button. The table data is rearranged to your specifications.

CAUTION Sorting a table that contains *cross-reference* markers deletes the markers and breaks the cross-references to them. The workaround is to prevent the problem is to change all of the cross-reference markers in the table to some other marker type you aren't using (such as the Author marker or perhaps a custom marker you create) before you sort the table. After you sort, change the markers back to cross reference markers. The easiest way to do change the marker types is to use MarkerTools (www.leximation.com). See Appendix A, "Resources" for more information. Of course, you may find it easier to fix any broken cross-references after sorting the table.

Deleting Table Tags

You can delete table tags in the Table Designer. Existing tables, however, are still formatted by the deleted tags. This is considered an override because tables that use a table tag that isn't included in the catalog can't be updated globally. Before deleting a table tag, you can assign a different tag to the tables globally, just as you can with paragraph and character tags. "Reassigning a Character Tag Globally" on page 153 describes the process. Another option is to add the tag back into the catalog, click the the table, open the Table Designer, and click Apply. Finally, you can apply a different tag to the table.

To delete a table tag, follow these steps:

1. Display the Table Designer.
2. Click the Commands button, then select Delete Format from the pop-up menu. The Delete Formats from Catalog dialog box is displayed.

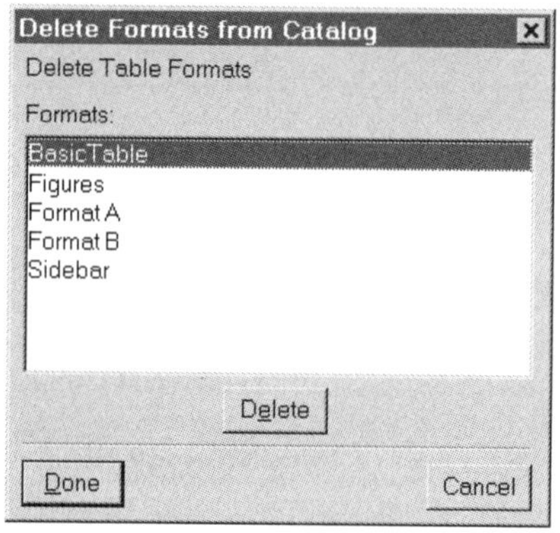

3. Click the tag you want to delete, then click the Delete button. To delete all table tags quickly, press and hold ALT-E.
4. Click the Done button. The tags are removed from the table catalog. If you click in a table still formatted by a deleted tag, the tag name is displayed in the Table Tag field but not in the drop-down list.

If you do find a table still formatted by a deleted tag, you have several options. You can globally rename the deleted tag. This applies the new table tag where the deleted tag is applied in your document. "Renaming Character Tags" on page 151 describes the process.

Creating Tables from Text

Instead of inserting an empty table and typing text into the cells, you can convert imported text files or existing text to tables. The pieces of text must be separated by one of the following:

- Tabs
- Two or more spaces
- Commas or another specific character
- Paragraphs

The following illustration shows text separated by all four methods and the table created by converting the data. The converted data is displayed identically despite the differences in the original formats.

Tabs	Spaces	Commas	Paragraphs
Fruit→Color¶	Fruit Color¶	Fruit,Color¶	Fruit¶
Pear→Green¶	Pear Green¶	Pear,Green¶	Color¶
Apple→Red¶	Apple Red¶	Apple,Red¶	Pear¶
Pomegranate→Purple¶	Pomegranate Purple¶	Pomegranate,Purple¶	Green¶
Banana→Yellow¶	Banana Yellow¶	Banana,Yellow¶	Apple¶
			Red¶
			Pomegranate¶
			Purple¶
			Banana¶
			Yellow§

Fruit	Color
Pear	Green
Apple	Red
Pomegranate	Purple
Banana	Yellow

After you convert text to a table, you can convert it back to paragraph format. This option lets you undo a table conversion or format text to import into other applications. See "Converting a Table to Text" on page 190 for details.

CAUTION Table conversion can be tricky, so consider saving your file or creating a backup copy before the table conversion. Although you can undo any mess you might create, it's safer not to rely on FrameMaker's undo feature.

To create a table from text, follow these steps:

1. Set up the text using one of the four methods.
2. Select the text, then select Table➤Convert to Table. The Convert to Table dialog box is displayed.

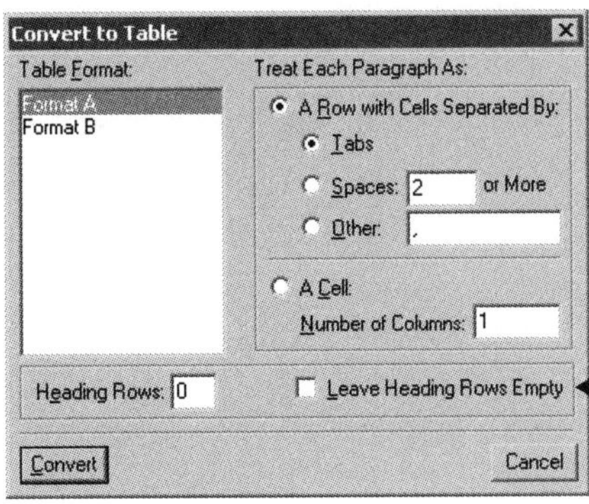

Check to create blank heading rows.

3. In the Table Format list, click a format for the table.
4. Click the radio button that describes how your text is currently formatted.
   - For text separated by tabs, click the Tabs radio button.
   - For text separated by spaces, click the Spaces radio button and type the number of spaces.

CAUTION Be careful when using spaces as delimiters. If the text you are converting to a table uses different amounts of space between columns, you can get unexpected results—especially if Smart Spaces is turned on. For more information, see "Smart Spaces" on page 84.

   - If another character (such as a comma) separates the text, click the Other radio button and type the character.
   - If the text is in paragraphs, click the A Cell radio button and type the number of columns you want in the table.
5. Define the heading row.
   - To type the column headings after the table is created, check the Leave Heading Rows Empty check box and type the number of heading rows you want in the Heading Rows field.
   - To convert existing text to column headings, type the number of heading rows and uncheck the check box.
   - To create a table with no heading, type **0** in the Heading Rows field. You can add a heading row later if you change your mind. See "Customizing Tables Outside the Table Designer" on page 170 for details.
6. Click the Convert button. The text is formatted with the selected table tag.

Converting data takes practice, so don't worry if your table doesn't convert correctly the first time. Undo your changes, or if you created a backup file, open the file and start over.

Handy Table Tags

Most FrameMaker documents include table tags with basic features such as heading rows and cell ruling. You can, however, use tables for other reasons, such as for displaying lists of interface buttons and labels, creating a warning paragraph with the graphic displayed, and more.

- **List of icons.** Insert a two-column borderless table with narrow cell margins. You apply paragraph tags and save them in the table tag. After inserting the table in your document, you can import the icons in the first column and type the icon names in the other column (as shown on the right).

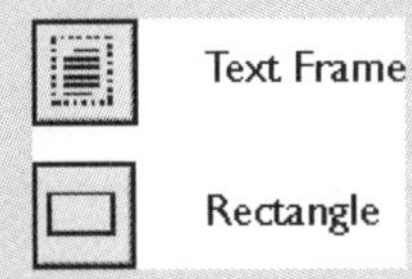

- **Warning paragraph.** Create a two-column, one-row table with the graphic inserted in the left column, and the warning paragraph tag applied to the right column. Add the warning graphic on the Reference page in a graphic frame named something like *Warning icon*. Create a 2-point font paragraph tag and specify *Warning icon* as the Frame Above Paragraph drop-down list. See "Placing Graphics Above and Below the Paragraph" on page 329 for details.
- **Figure table.** Insert an invisible one-cell table into which you import screen captures and graphics. Apply a figure caption paragraph tag to the table title section. Use this table to keep a floating graphic with the caption (otherwise, the caption floats away from the graphic, which is a bad thing).
- **Shaded sidebar.** For sidebars (such as this one), create a one-column, one-row table. For the borders, set all rulings to None. For the shading, specify a 100 percent fill for the second column using a custom color that is 15 percent black.

Converting a Table to Text

When you convert a table to text, the table content (including the title) is converted to separate paragraphs. The original paragraph tags are still applied to each paragraph. To convert a table to text, you specify conversion by row or column. Tables that read across must be converted by rows to display correctly in paragraph format. Tables that read down must be converted by columns. The following table was converted using both methods.

Dog	**Group**
English Setter	Sporting
Beagle	Hound
Boston Terrier	Terrier

Converted by rows	*Converted by columns*
Dog	**Dog**
Group	English Setter
English Setter	Beagle
Sporting	Boston Terrier
Beagle	**Group**
Hound	Sporting
Boston Terrier	Hound
Terrier	Terrier

To convert a table to text, follow these steps:

1. Select the table, then select Table➤Convert to Paragraphs. The Convert to Paragraphs dialog box is displayed.

2. Do one of the following:
   - To convert text horizontally, click the Row by Row radio button.
   - To convert text vertically, click the Column by Column radio button.
3. Click the Convert button. The table appears in the selected format. If necessary, you can undo the conversion by selecting Edit➤Undo.

Reformatting Word Tables

Converting Microsoft Word tables to FrameMaker can be tedious. When you open a Word document, FrameMaker assigns a new generic table tag called Table to all tables in the document, clears the table shading, and keeps the table borders. In addition, Word tables lack typical FrameMaker table components. For example, the repeating table rows in Word don't convert into FrameMaker heading rows.

You'll need to clean up imported Word tables by doing the following:

- **Assigning a table tag.** The FrameMaker-created Table table tag does not have any paragraph tags associated with it, nor any other table settings, such as a table title. Assign a table tag to have FrameMaker format the imported table.
- **Adding a heading row.** Heading rows in a Word document convert to body rows. You need to add a heading row to the table, copy or type the column headings into the heading row, and delete the former Word heading row.
- **Adding a table title.** In Word tables, the table title is a standard paragraph above the table; it isn't part of the table format. If your Word table has a title, you'll need to copy and paste the title above or below the converted table into the table title paragraph. If necessary, remove the title and its associated row from the current table or assign a table tag that doesn't include a title.
- **Fixing the borders and shading.** The Word table ruling settings are converted in FrameMaker; however, the shading settings are not. After you convert a table and apply a table tag, you may need to reset the ruling and shading properties to the tag's defaults. You can add custom ruling and shading after you apply the default settings (see "Displaying and Removing Custom Ruling and Shading" on page 179).
- **Assigning paragraph tags.** FrameMaker assigns paragraph tags from the Format A table tag to the converted Word table. If the paragraph tags contain overrides or don't exist in the document, you need to reapply the paragraph tags.

A third-party FrameMaker plug-in called TableCleaner automates these functions; it adds heading rows to tables and automates many other functions, such as applying paragraph tags and removing custom ruling and shading. You might also want to try a third-party tool called Filtrix, which imports different file types into FrameMaker. For details on these third-party tools, see Appendix A, "Resources."

Occasionally, FrameMaker may choke if you try to convert a document with table footnotes. An error dialog box displays the message "The filter encountered an error and could not complete the conversion." To prevent this problem, type the table footnote as regular text below the Word table and hard-code the footnote number in the table cell. You can create a real table footnote in the FrameMaker table after conversion.

CHAPTER 8

Cross-References

Cross-references refer readers to other parts of a document. Often, cross-references start with "see" or "refer to"; for example:

```
see page 217
refer to "All About Chocolate" on page 82
```

You could type these references, but setting them up with cross-references lets FrameMaker update the page numbers and referenced text for you automatically. This is much more efficient than checking all the references manually after the pagination is finally set for your document.

Another major advantage to using cross-references is that they become live hyperlinks when you convert the FrameMaker file to PDF, HTML, or other online formats. They are also live links in view-only FrameMaker documents.

When you set up a cross-reference, you create a pointer from the cross-reference to another location (Figure 8-1). FrameMaker calls this other location the "source"—the place where the information is coming from.

After you insert a cross-reference, the text is formatted as part of the current paragraph. Several default cross-references formats are provided, and you can create additional ones as necessary.

Cross-references look like the surrounding text, but they are treated differently in some cases:

- **You cannot edit cross-references as part of the text.** You can't even click inside the cross-reference text. When you click on text that's part of a cross-reference, FrameMaker selects the entire cross-reference. To change it, you must edit the cross-reference inside the Cross-Reference dialog box. This feature is very useful when you want to verify that a page reference is actually a cross-reference. Just click on it and see whether the entire reference is selected. If you can position the cursor in the text, then it's regular text. If the reference is selected as a block, then it's a cross-reference.

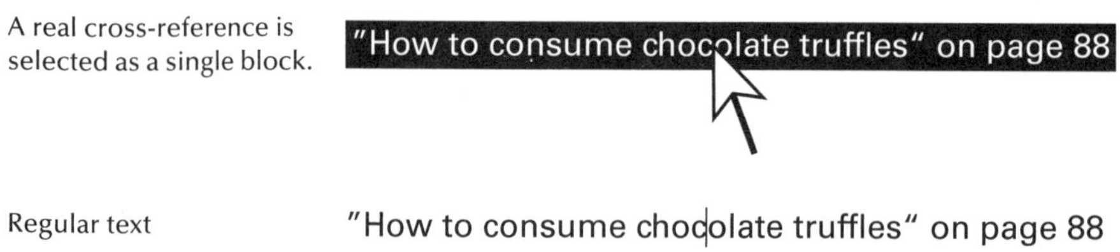

- **When searching for text, cross-references are ignored.** If, for example, you search for the word "page," none of the occurrences inside cross-references will match. The Find/Change dialog box does, however, give you the option of searching for cross-references, unresolved cross-references, or cross-references that use a specific format.

- **You can use cross-references as hyperlinks inside a regular FrameMaker document.** CTRL-ALT-click on the cross-reference, and it will take you to the cross-reference's source.

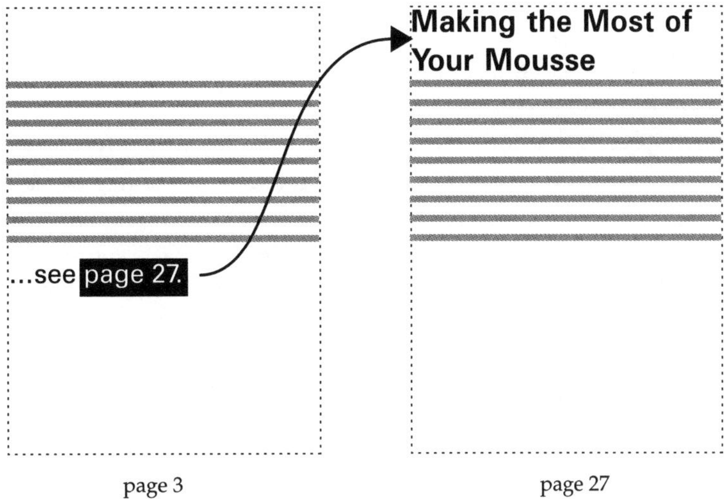

Figure 8-1. Cross-references create a pointer.

By default, cross-references are updated when you update a book file, open a file, save, or print. They are not, however, updated immediately when the file changes. For example, if you create a cross-reference to an item on page 17, then rearrange your file so that the referenced information moves to page 23, FrameMaker does *not* immediately update the reference to page 17. When you perform an update, the page number changes.

How Cross-References Really Work

When you create a cross-reference, FrameMaker inserts a marker at the source. The cross-reference itself points to the unique identifier in the source paragraph.

Inserting Cross-References

When you insert a cross-reference, you must define the link's source and specify the formatting. Paragraph-based cross-references are the most common; another alternative is spot cross-references.

Creating Paragraph-Based Cross-References

To create a paragraph-based cross-reference, follow these steps:

1. Open the file that contains the source paragraph. (Not necessary if you're creating a cross-reference within a single file.)
2. Locate the source paragraph that you want to point to. Make a note of its paragraph tag and what file it's in.
3. Position your cursor where you want to insert the cross-reference.
4. Select Special➤Cross-Reference. The Cross-Reference dialog box is displayed (Figure 8-2).
5. In the Document drop-down list, click the file that you are linking to. Notice that only currently open files are available in this list. If your file isn't open, click the Cancel button to exit this dialog box, open the file, and start over.
6. Select the Source Type button, then select Paragraphs from the pop-up menu.
7. In the Paragraph Tags list, click the paragraph tag you want. The right side of the dialog box displays the first few words of each occurrence of that paragraph tag.

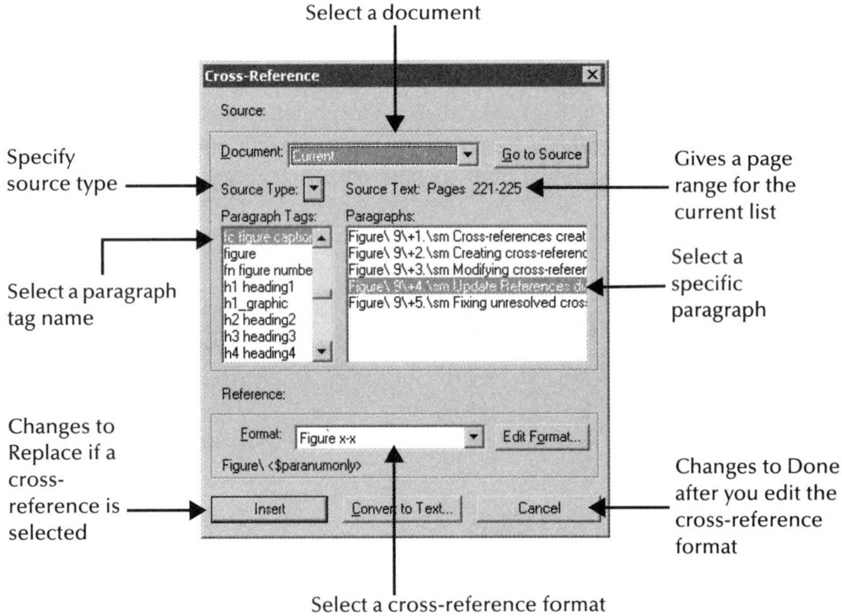

Figure 8-2. Creating cross-references

8. In the Paragraphs list, select the specific paragraph you want to point to. To help you locate the correct paragraph, an approximate page range for the items is displayed above the list.

9. In the Format drop-down list, click a cross-reference format. If the format you want isn't available, you can create a new one. See "Setting Up Cross-Reference Formats" on page 198.
10. Click the Insert button to insert the cross-reference.

NOTE If you selected some text or are modifying an existing cross-reference, you see a Replace button instead of an Insert button.

After inserting a cross-reference, you can double-click it to display the Cross-Reference dialog box and make changes (such as choosing a different format).

Creating Spot Cross-References

Spot cross-references let you point to a particular line in a paragraph. Paragraph references always point to the beginning of the paragraph, and when the paragraph is lengthy and splits across two pages, the information you're referencing can end up on a different page. To ensure that you point to the exact location where the information occurs, use a spot cross-reference. You create a marker and link the cross-reference to that marker.

To create a spot cross-reference, follow these steps:

1. Locate the spot that you want to link to and position your cursor there.
2. Select Special➤Marker. The Marker dialog box is displayed.

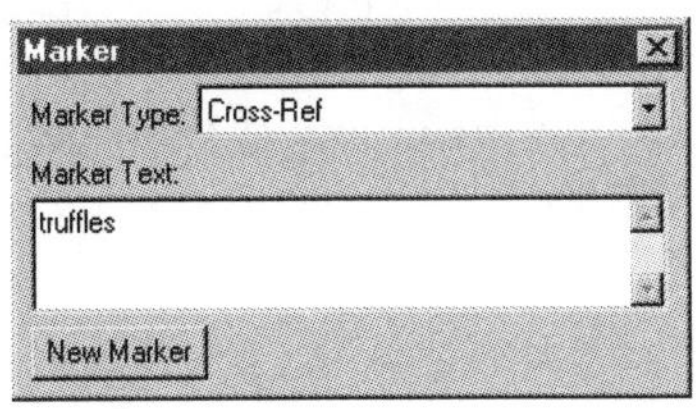

3. In the Marker Type drop-down list, click Cross-Ref.
4. In the Marker Text field, type a label for this cross-reference that is unique across the file. The label should be short and descriptive.
5. Click the New Marker button to save your changes. If you have text symbols turned on (View➤Text Symbols), you will see a marker symbol.
6. Leave the source document open and go to the document in which you want to create the cross-reference.
7. Position your cursor where you want to insert the reference.
8. Select Special➤Cross-Reference. The Cross-Reference dialog box is displayed (Figure 8-2).
9. In the Document drop-down list, click the file that you are linking to.

10. In the Source Type pop-up menu, click Cross-Reference Markers.
11. In the Cross-Reference Markers list, select the marker you created.

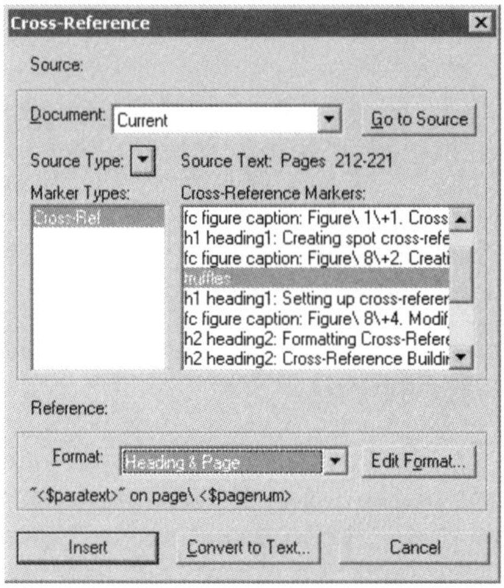

NOTE Whenever you create a paragraph-based cross-reference, FrameMaker automatically inserts Cross-Ref markers. You will see these in the cross-reference marker list. However, those markers usually include the paragraph tag name and the text of the paragraph; yours is shorter.

12. In the Format drop-down list, click a cross-reference format.

NOTE For spot cross-references, you usually want to select a format that displays just the page number and not the paragraph's text.

13. Click the Insert button to insert the cross-reference.

Setting Up Cross-Reference Formats

FrameMaker provides some default cross-reference formats, but you can also create your own new formats. To do so, you assemble a combination of text, character tags, and building blocks to create a cross-reference format. *Building blocks* are placeholders; they change for each cross-reference. For example, a cross-reference definition might read:

```
see page <$pagenum>
```

< $pagenum > is a building block; it is replaced with the page number of the source paragraph. The rest of the definition is text that doesn't change.

After you have created your cross-reference formats, you can import them into other documents or a book to make formats consistent across files.

To create a new cross-reference format, follow these steps:

1. Select Special➤Cross-Reference. The Cross-Reference dialog box is displayed (Figure 8-2 on page 196).
2. Click the Edit Format button. The Edit Cross-Reference Format dialog box is displayed (Figure 8-3).

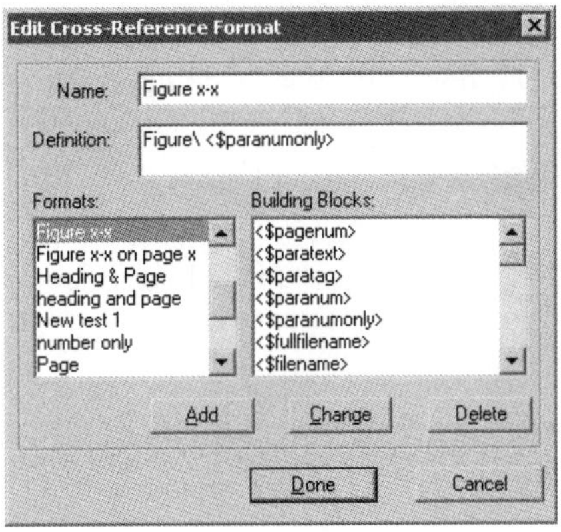

Figure 8-3. Modifying cross-reference formats

3. You can change an existing format or create a new one:
   - To change an existing format, click that format in the Formats list.
   - To create a new format, type the name for the new format in the Name field. The name is what you see when you're selecting a format for a new cross-reference (in the Format drop-down list; see Figure 8-2 on page 196), so the name should be descriptive. If you're creating a new Chapter cross-reference format, you might call it:

     ```
     Chapter "title"
     ```

4. In the Definition field, modify the existing definition as needed or create a new definition.

   Cross-references usually contain text (such as the word "page") and building blocks. You can select the building blocks from the list or type them in. You can also apply character formatting by inserting character tags, which are available at the bottom of the building block list. All building blocks begin with an angle bracket (<) and end with an angle bracket (>). Except for character tags, all building blocks begin with a dollar sign ($) after the opening angle bracket.

Refer to Table 8-1 on page 202 for a list of available building blocks. For the new Chapter cross-reference, the definition could look like this if you type the special characters instead of using copy and paste:

```
Chapter\ <$chapnum>, \`<$paratext>\'
```

NOTE A backslash followed by a space (\ ) creates a nonbreaking space. A backslash followed by a backtick (`) creates an opening curly quote. A backslash followed by a regular straight quote (\')creates a closing curly quote.

If you choose, you can copy and paste the curly quotes into the cross-reference definition instead; the resulting cross-reference will be the same:

```
Chapter\ <$chapnum>, "<$paratext>"
```

NOTE For more information about typing special characters in dialog boxes, see "Entering Special Characters in Dialog Boxes" on page 629.

5. To create a new format, click the Add button. To modify an existing format, click the Change button.

CAUTION If you select the Change button instead of Add, the original format is replaced with the one you just created. This means you renamed and redefined the cross-reference format you started with.

6. Click the Done button to return to the Cross-Reference dialog box. If the format you modified is already in use in your document, FrameMaker prompts you to update the existing cross-references. Click the OK button to update your cross-references.
7. In the Cross-Reference dialog box, click the Done button to close the dialog box and return to your document. (It appears in place of the Cancel button.)

Occasionally, you'll notice that the building block is displayed in your text instead of being replaced with the referenced information. This is usually caused by a typo in your definition; for example, using a building block with a missing bracket:

```
$paratext>
```

To correct the preceding problem, add the opening bracket in the format's definition. The building block should then be replaced with the correct information.

Formatting Cross-References

Inside the cross-reference definition, you can use character tags to create special formatting. Without character tags, the cross-reference will match the format of the surrounding paragraph.

One very common requirement is to create a cross-reference that is blue and underlined for hyperlinks. When you convert the FrameMaker file to a PDF file, users reading the PDF file can easily see where the links occur.

To create a blue, underlined cross-reference, follow these steps:

1. Create a character tag called hyperlink that applies blue and an underline. (For information on creating character tags, see page 149.)

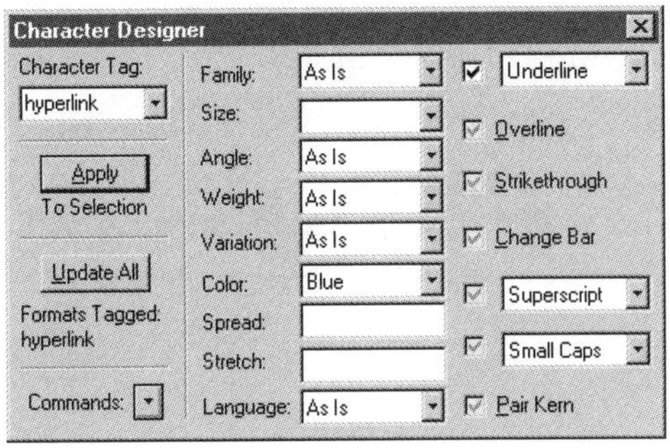

2. Select Special➤Cross-Reference. The Cross-Reference dialog box is displayed (Figure 8-2 on page 196).
3. Click the Edit Format button. The Edit Cross-Reference Format dialog box is displayed (Figure 8-3 on page 199).
4. In the Name field, type a name for the cross-reference format; for example:

   HeadingPDF

5. In the Definition field, insert the definition for the cross-reference format; for example:

   <hyperlink><$paratext></>

   In this example, <hyperlink> is the character tag that formats the cross-reference and </> (which is the abbreviation for <Default Para Tag>) ends the character tag.

6. Click the Add button to add the new format.
7. Click the Done button.
8. In the Cross-Reference dialog box, click the Done button. (It appears in place of the Cancel button.)

TIP You can use the third-party tool FrameMaker-to-Acrobat TimeSavers from Microtype (www.microtype.com) to create formatting that is displayed in the onscreen version of the PDF file but not in the print version. For more information, see Appendix A, "Resources."

Cross-Reference Building Blocks

FrameMaker provides several building blocks for creating cross-reference formats. A very basic cross-reference looks like this:

```
<$paratext> on page <$pagenum>
```

It tells FrameMaker to insert the contents of the source paragraph (<$paratext>) followed by a space, the words "on page," and another space. Then, it inserts the page number of the source paragraph. The result would look something like this:

Chocolate Mousse Pie on page 27

Table 8-1 lists the available building blocks. They are grouped by function; all of the building blocks that display paragraph text are in one group, all building blocks that display paragraph numbers are in another group, and so on.

Building Block	Description
Text	
`<$paratext>`	Displays the text of the linked paragraph.
`<$paratext[paratag]>`	Works from the linked paragraph toward the beginning of the document to locate a paragraph that uses the specified paragraph tag. Displays the text of that paragraph. If no paragraph in the document matches, nothing is displayed by this building block.
`<$paratext[tag1,tag2, tag3]>` *(not shown in the dialog box)*	Displays the first instance of paragraph tag1, tag2, or tag3, whichever occurs first. Useful when referencing headings that might use a different paragraph tag later, such as a chapter that you are considering making into an appendix. For example: `<$paranumonly[ChapterTitle, AppendixTitle]>`

Table 8-1. Cross-Reference Building Blocks Grouped by Function—Not in FrameMaker Order

Building Block	Description
<$paratext[+,paratag]> *(not shown in the dialog box)*	Searches for the last paragraph using the specified paragraph tag on the page instead of the first. (This building block is also available in running header/footer variables, where it's often used for dictionary or directory headers.)
Paragraph number	
<$paranum>	Displays the paragraph number of the linked paragraph.
<$paranum[paratag]>	Works from the linked paragraph toward the beginning of the document to locate a paragraph that uses the specified paragraph tag. Displays the paragraph number of that paragraph. If no paragraph in the document matches, nothing is displayed.
<$paranumonly>	Displays the numeric portion of the linked paragraph's paragraph number. For example, if the paragraph number is "Figure 17," this building block displays "17." Chapter and volume numbers are considered numeric. The <$paranumonly> building block includes everything from the first building block to the last in the autonumber definition, including any embedded text. If the autonumber definition is Figure\ <$chapnum>\+<n+>, this building block returns 1-4 (or whatever the current figure number is). Notice that the nonbreaking hyphen between the numbers is included in the definition. Also note that other punctuation that is not part of the paragraph numbering will be removed (such as an ending period). If your complex numbering system includes punctuation, be aware that you might get unexpected results from this building block.

Table 8-1. Cross-Reference Building Blocks Grouped by Function—Not in FrameMaker Order (Continued)

Building Block	Description
`<$paranumonly[paratag]>`	Works from the linked paragraph toward the beginning of the document to locate a paragraph that uses the specified paragraph tag. Displays the numeric portion of that paragraph's number. If no paragraph in the document matches, nothing is displayed.
Page numbers	
`<$pagenum>`	Displays the page number of the linked paragraph.
`<$pagenum[paratag]>`	Works from the linked paragraph toward the beginning of the document to locate a paragraph that uses the specified paragraph tag. Displays the page number of that paragraph. If no paragraph in the document matches, nothing is displayed.
`<$chapnum>`	Displays the current chapter number.
`<$volnum>`	Displays the current volume number.
Tag names	
`<$paratag>`	Displays the name of the linked paragraph tag.
Other	
`<$filename>`	Displays the file name of the linked file.
`<$fullfilename>`	Displays the path and file name of the linked file.
`<character_tag>`	Applies the specified character tag to the items that follow in the cross-reference definition. Note that this building block does not begin with a dollar sign ($).
`<Default Para Font>` or `</>`	Removes any character formatting and returns to the regular paragraph formatting of the parent paragraph.

Table 8-1. Cross-Reference Building Blocks Grouped by Function—Not in FrameMaker Order (Continued)

Cross-Reference Examples

Table 8-2 shows cross-reference formats you might need to create. Change the italicized names in the table to match your tag names. For more information about typing special characters in dialog boxes, see "Entering Special Characters in Dialog Boxes" on page 629.

Result	Definition
see page 3-17	see page\ <$chapnum>\+<$pagenum>
see Volume II, Chapter 7	see Volume\ <$volnum>, Chapter\ <$chapnum>
Chapter 7, "The Glories of Chocolate"	Chapter\ <$chapnum>, \'<$paratext>\'
see "Tempering chocolate" in Chapter 7, "The Glories of Chocolate"	see \'<$paratext>\' in Chapter\ <$chapnum>, \'<$paratext[*ChapterTitle*]>\'
see *Tempering chocolate* in Chapter 7, "The Glories of Chocolate"	see <*Emphasis*><$paratext></> in Chapter\ <$chapnum>, \'<$paratext[*ChapterTitle*]>\'
The file name is **E:\scriptorium\data\projects \chocolate.fm**.	The file name is <*Bold*><$fullfilename></>.

Table 8-2. Cross-Reference Sample Definitions

Deleting Cross-Reference Formats

FrameMaker gives you the ability to delete cross-reference formats from your document. When you do this, any cross-references that use the format are converted to text (see page 211 for details).

To delete a cross-reference format, follow these steps:

1. Select Special➤Cross-Reference. The Cross-Reference dialog box is displayed (Figure 8-2 on page 196).
2. Click the Edit Format button. The Edit Cross-Reference Format dialog box is displayed (Figure 8-3 on page 199).
3. In the list on the left, click the format you want to delete.
4. Click the Delete button.

NOTE You can delete multiple cross-reference formats by clicking each format in turn and clicking the Delete button (you cannot SHIFT-click to select several at once).

5. Click the Done button. If the cross-reference format is used in the document, FrameMaker prompts you to confirm that you want to convert the cross-references to text. You are prompted separately for each cross-reference format that's in use. Click the OK button to delete the cross-reference format and convert it to text; click the Cancel button to retain the cross-references that use the specified format.
6. In the Cross-Reference dialog box, click the Done button to close the dialog box. (It appears in place of the Cancel button.)

Updating Cross-References

FrameMaker generally does a good job of updating cross-references. Occasionally, you may need to force an update. This section describes when updates occur and how to manage them.

By default, FrameMaker updates your cross-references when any of the following actions occur:

- Opening a file
- Saving a file
- Printing a file
- Updating a book file (cross-references are updated for all files in the book)

If you need to update a single cross-reference, the fastest way to do it is to double-click the reference to display the Cross-Reference dialog box, then click the Replace button. This works well for one or two references, but if you need to update all the references in a document (or book), the techniques described in this section are more efficient.

Automatic Updating Problems

When FrameMaker performs an automatic update, it checks each cross-reference to ensure that the paragraph or marker specified in the cross-reference still exists. For references within a single file, this works perfectly. You can run into problems, though, when the reference is one file to another. To verify the cross-reference's source, FrameMaker opens the source file and looks for the source item. If FrameMaker cannot open the source file for some reason, the updating process fails. The most common cause of this failure is that the source file uses fonts that are not installed on your system. The "missing fonts" message that's displayed when you open the file causes the cross-reference verification process to fail. FrameMaker reports that you have unresolved cross-references when in fact you merely have a cross-reference to a file that FrameMaker couldn't open. To prevent this problem, open all of the files that the current file points to, update your cross-references, and see whether the message about unresolved cross-references is displayed.

Updating Cross-References in a Book

If you are working in a document that's part of a book, whenever you update the book file, FrameMaker updates the cross-references for you. To update the book, go to the book window, then click the Update Book icon at the bottom of the window.

This process is described in detail in "Updating the Book" on page 383.

Forcing a Cross-Reference Update

Occasionally, you'll want to force FrameMaker to perform a cross-reference update. To do this, follow these steps:

1. Select Edit➤Update References. The Update References dialog box is displayed (Figure 8-4).

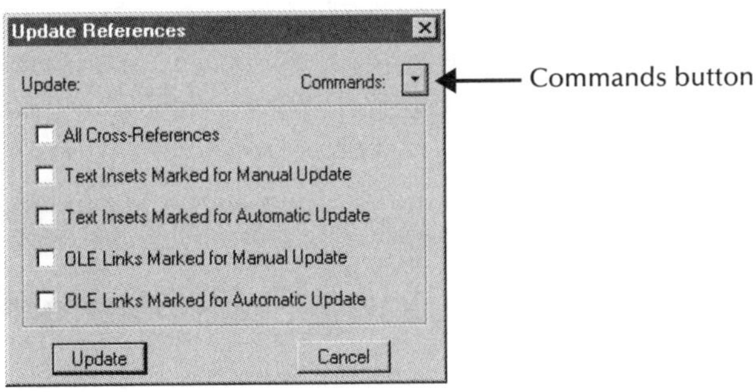

Figure 8-4. Update References dialog box

2. Check the All Cross-References check box, then click the Update button.

FrameMaker updates all of the cross-references in the current document.

NOTE The update works only if FrameMaker can open all of the source documents.

Preventing Automatic Updates

In some cases, you may need to prevent FrameMaker from updating the cross-references automatically; for example, if your FrameMaker files are in a version control system, and you've only checked out one file.

To prevent FrameMaker from trying to update your cross-references inside a file, follow these steps:

1. Select Edit➤Update References. The Update References dialog box is displayed (Figure 8-4 on page 207).
2. Click the Commands button and select Suppress Automatic Reference Updating from the pop-up menu. This displays the Suppress Automatic Reference Updating dialog box.

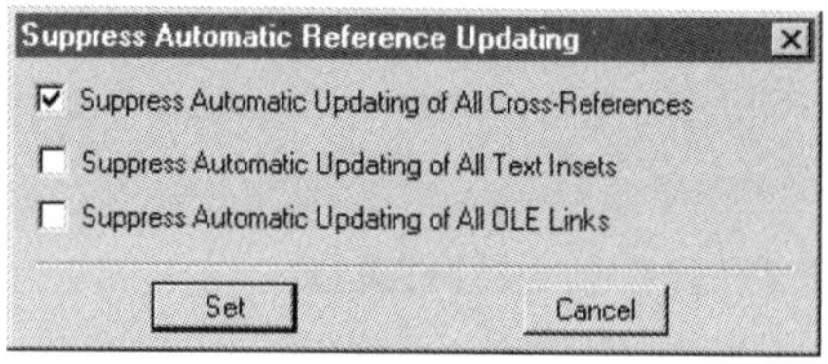

3. Check the Suppress Automatic Updating of All Cross-References check box.
4. Click the Set button.
5. In the Update References dialog box, click the Done button. (It appears in place of the Cancel button.)

NOTE You can perform the same action for an entire book by selecting Edit➤Suppress Automatic Updating when the book is the active window.

To turn automatic updating back on, repeat this procedure and uncheck the check box.

Renaming Files Without Breaking Cross-References

If you rename a file from inside the book file, FrameMaker will update the cross-references (also text insets and hypertext links) to that file.

CAUTION FrameMaker checks only the files in the current book. If the file you're renaming is used in another book, references in that book are *not* updated.

To rename a file in a book file, follow these steps:

1. *(optional)* Open all the files in the book by selecting SHIFT-File➤Open All Files in Book. This ensures that the update will work even if you have missing fonts in some of the files.
2. In the book window, click on the file you want to rename.
3. Click the file name again to make it editable. Type in the new name for the file, then press ENTER.

CAUTION Make sure you press ENTER before you click anywhere else in the book, or FrameMaker will reorder the files!

4. FrameMaker notifies you that it is going to update cross-references, hypertext links, and other items within the book file. Click the OK button to continue.

FrameMaker makes the needed updates and changes the file name.

Correcting Broken (Unresolved) Cross-References

Cross-references can break or become *unresolved.* Most often, unresolved cross-references are caused by one of the following actions:

- Renaming the file that the reference points to
- Deleting the paragraph that the reference is linked to
- Linking to text insets (for details on text insets, see Chapter 25, "Creating Modules with Text Insets")
- Deleting the cross-reference marker at the source location

Unresolved cross-references are not flagged with any special formatting. When you open a FrameMaker file, cross-references are checked. If any are unresolved, an error message is displayed.

NOTE If you suppress automatic updating, FrameMaker does not check for unresolved references when you open the file.

Cross-references are also updated when you update your book file. The book error report lists the unresolved cross-references. You can click each entry to go directly to that cross-reference so that you can fix it. (For details about the book error log, see "Troubleshooting Book Updates" on page 384.)

You can correct unresolved cross-references in two different ways:

- By changing the file that the reference points to
- By re-creating the cross-reference

Changing the Referenced File

If the cross-reference is broken because the file it's pointing to has been renamed or changed, FrameMaker provides you with a very useful way of retargeting the references to the new file name. This actually works for all of the references that are using the old file name.

CAUTION You may see "bogus" unresolved cross-reference messages. To verify references, FrameMaker attempts to open the source file. If the file-opening process fails, you get an unresolved cross-reference error. To ensure that your unresolved cross-references are not because of a file-opening error, open the source file before opening the file in which the cross-reference occurs. If this approach eliminates the message, the cross-reference is in fact resolved. The most common cause of this problem is missing fonts in the source file (which causes the automatic open to fail).

To update the file name that references are pointing to, follow these steps:

1. Select Edit➤Update References. The Update References dialog box is displayed (Figure 8-4 on page 207).
2. Click the Commands button, then select Update Unresolved Cross-References from the pop-up menu. The Update Unresolved Cross-References dialog box is displayed (Figure 8-5).

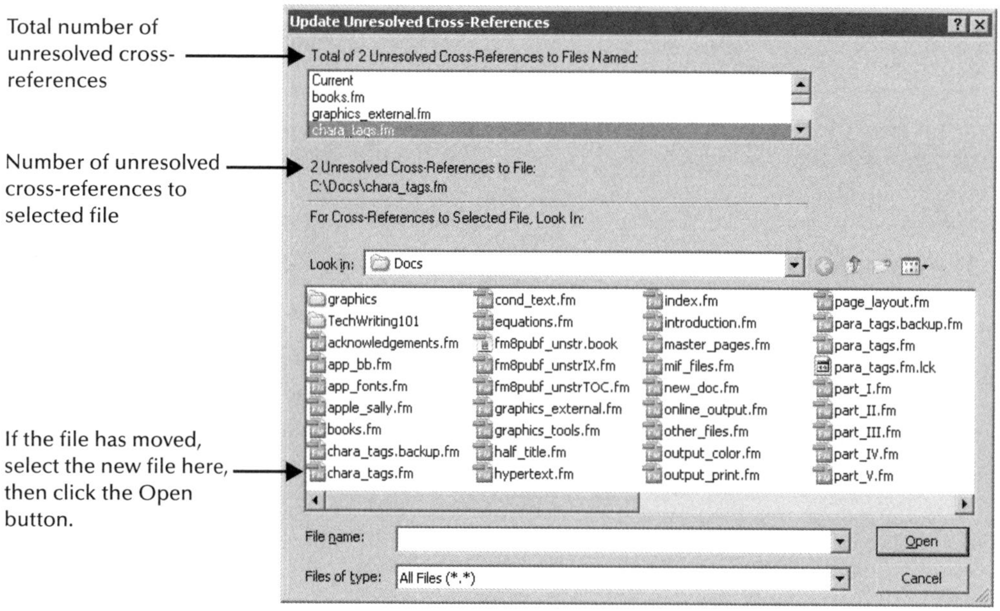

Figure 8-5. Fixing unresolved cross-references

At the top, this dialog box lists the total number of unresolved references in the file. Click on a file name in the list to see how many references to that file are unresolved.

3. For each renamed file, select the old name of the file at the top, then use the bottom half of the dialog box to locate the new file name. Click the file, then click the Open button.

NOTE The numbers at the top of the dialog box are updated.

4. When you have finished updating file locations, click the Cancel button to close the dialog box.

Re-Creating Broken Cross-References

If retargeting the new file name doesn't work (or if you didn't move or rename the file), you'll need to rebuild the cross-reference. Locate each unresolved cross-reference (use Edit➤Find and select Unresolved Cross-References in the Find drop-down list), double-click it to display the Cross-Reference dialog box, and re-create the reference.

Converting Cross-References to Text

When you convert cross-references to text, FrameMaker eliminates all of the special linking functions and changes the reference into ordinary editable text.

CAUTION If you change your mind about converting to text, you will have to re-create the cross-references. This action cannot be undone.

Changing cross-references to text means that they are no longer live links and will not appear as such in any output. It destroys the link between the cross-reference and the source paragraph or marker. *It is very rarely a good idea.* (You might consider it if for some reason you do *not* want live hyperlinks in your PDF files.)

If you need to convert some or all of your cross-references to text, follow these steps:

1. *(optional)* If you want to convert a single cross-reference to text, select it.
2. Select Special➤Cross-Reference. The Cross-Reference dialog box is displayed (Figure 8-2 on page 196).
3. Select the Convert to Text button. The Convert Cross-References to Text dialog box is displayed.

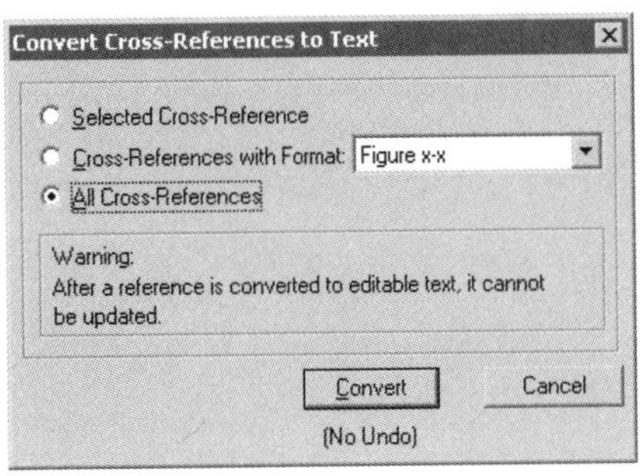

4. Specify which cross-references you want to convert:
   - To convert just the selected cross-reference, click the Selected Cross-Reference radio button.
   - To convert all cross-references of a specified format, click the Cross-References with Format radio button and, in the drop-down list, click the format you want to convert to text. All cross-references in the document that use the specified format will be converted to text.
   - To convert all cross-references in the document, click the All Cross-References radio button.
5. Click the Convert button to convert the specified cross-references to text.

   FrameMaker converts the specified formats to regular, editable text.

CHAPTER 9

Storing Content in Variables

Variables contain short pieces of information that you can use throughout your document. By inserting variables, you save time typing and don't have to remember the correct spelling or capitalization. More importantly, variables make it easy to update your documents.

FrameMaker supports two types of variables:

- **System variables.** Display information updated by your computer. Many system variables relate to the time and date. The Current Date variable displays the current system date. Other system variables apply specifically to the current file. For example, the Chapter Number variable displays a chapter number based on the location of the file in a book. As you add documents to a book file, the chapter number is updated in each file containing the variable. Although you cannot create or delete system variables or change their functions, you can edit how information from system variables is displayed.
- **User variables.** Act as placeholders for information you specify. You can create, edit, and delete user variables. A user variable can contain words that you use often, such as a book name, rough draft statement, and text for a watermark. You can also store terms that might change, such as a company or product name. Unlike system variables, which change values when you open, save, or page up and down in a document, user variables are static. You must edit a user variable definition yourself to change its value.

Variables consist of building blocks (in system variables only), character tags, and text. *Building blocks* (pieces of code that display a specific value) do much of the work in creating system variables. For example, the <$paratext> building block displays text from a specific paragraph, such as a section heading. If the section heading changes, the <$paratext> building block displays the updated text.

Character tags let you format the variable. This means you don't need to apply a character tag to the variable after you insert it in the document. For instance, you can include an italicized character tag in a book title variable, and the book title will be italicized when you insert it.

Inserting Variables

Variables are displayed in the Variable dialog box (Figure 9-1). System variables are at the top of the list (note that they're always capitalized), and user variables (which may or may not be capitalized) are toward the end. The definition for a highlighted variable is displayed below the list of variables.

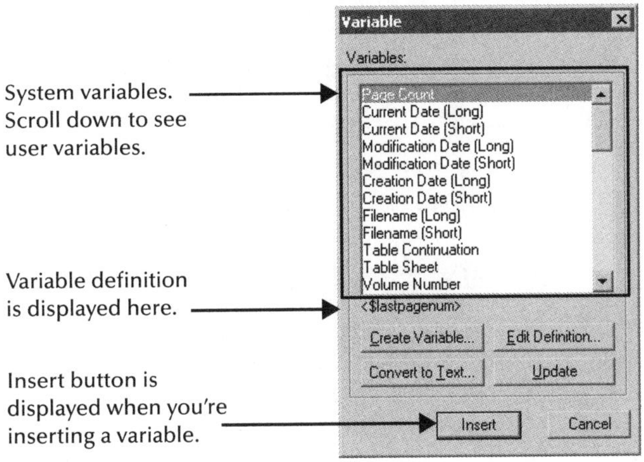

Figure 9-1. Setting up variables

Variables look like standard text on the page until you try to click in the text. Clicking highlights the entire variable. Because variable information is not actually part of the text, FrameMaker doesn't spell-check variables. If you misspell the variable definition, you can, however, correct the spelling in the variable, and each instance of the variable in your document is updated.

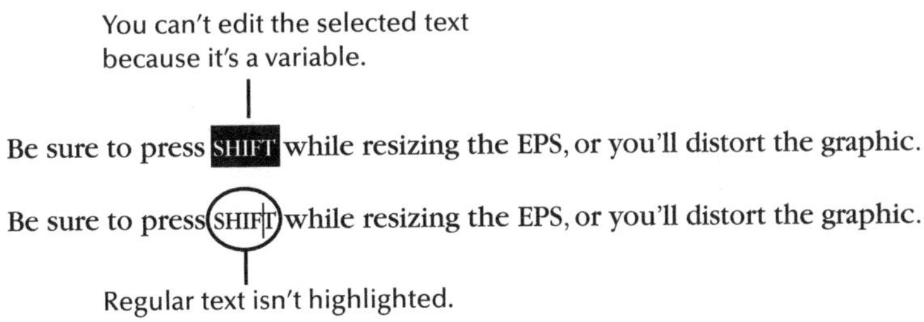

Some system variables are available only on the master pages. For example, the twelve running header/footer variables display information such as chapter and section headings in the header or footer, and you must insert them on the master pages. The Current Page Number variable inserts the page number on the master page. These variables are not available when you display the Variable dialog box on a body page.

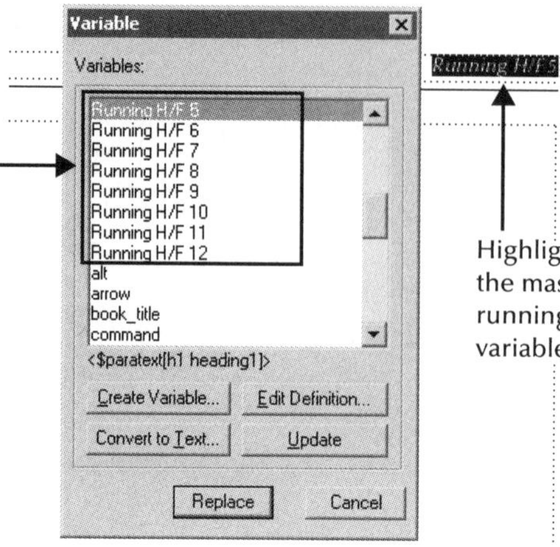

FrameMaker provides three ways to insert a variable:

- Using the menu
- Using the right-click pop-up menu
- Using a keyboard shortcut

NOTE In the Variable dialog box, the Replace button is displayed if text or a variable is selected on the page (for example, if you double-clicked a variable to display the Variable dialog box). If no text or variable is selected, the Insert button is displayed instead.

Using the Menu

To insert a variable using the Special menu, follow these steps:

1. Position the cursor on the page.
2. Select Special➤Variable. The Variable dialog box is displayed (Figure 9-1 on page 215).
3. Click the variable name, then click the Insert button.

Using the Right-Click Pop-Up Menu

You can use the pop-up menu that is displayed when you right-click to insert a variable. To use the pop-up menu to insert a variable, follow these steps:

1. Position the cursor on the page.
2. Right-click to display the pop-up menu, then select Variable.
3. Click the variable name, then click the Insert button.

Using a Keyboard Shortcut

To insert a variable using a keyboard shortcut, follow these steps:

1. Position the cursor on the page.
2. Press CTRL-0. The bottom-left status bar is highlighted.

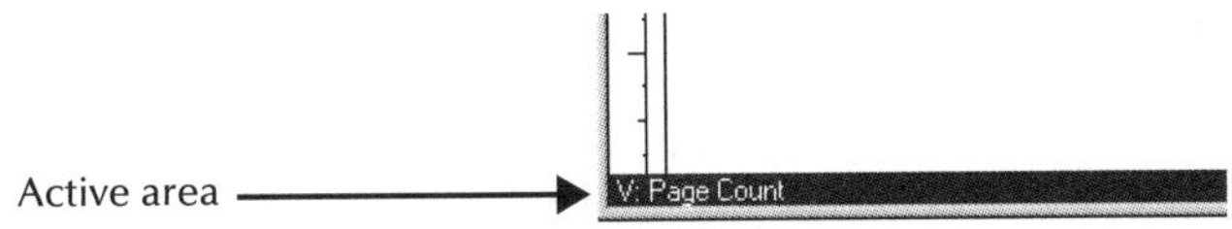

3. Display the variable you want by doing any of the following:
   - Use the arrow keys to scroll through the list of available variables.
   - Type a letter to jump to that section of the variables.
   - Type the first few letters of the variable name.
4. Press ENTER.

NOTE Some of the keys on your computer may be specially programmed. If so, one or more keyboard shortcuts may not work as described. Consult your system documentation for assistance.

Modifying System Variable Definitions

When you modify a system variable, you work with various building blocks. Different system variables allow different building blocks. For example, FrameMaker provides several building blocks that return the value of the current month, such as <$monthname> and <$monthnum>. The date-related building blocks are valid only in variables that display dates. If you type them in unrelated variables—the Filename variable, for example—an error is displayed.

System variables may not be available on all types of pages. Table 9-1 shows the locations in which system variables are valid.

Location	Available System Variables
Any text frame (body, master, or reference page)	
	Page Count Current Date, long or short Modification Date, long or short Creation Date, long or short Filename, long or short Volume Number Chapter Number

Table 9-1. Valid Locations for System Variables

Location	Available System Variables
Table title, heading, and footing rows	
	Table Continuation Table Sheet
Master pages only, in text frames with no flow tag	
	Current Page # Running H/F 1, 2, 3, 4,...,12

Table 9-1. Valid Locations for System Variables (Continued)

To modify a system variable, follow these steps:

1. Do one of the following:
   - In your document, double-click the variable that you want to modify.
   - Select Special➤Variable.

   The Variable dialog box is displayed.

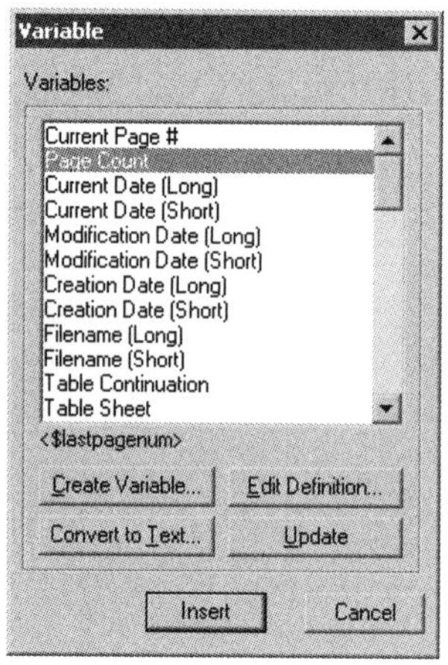

2. Click the variable you want to edit (if it's not already highlighted), then click the Edit Definition button. The Edit System Variable dialog box is displayed (Figure 9-2).

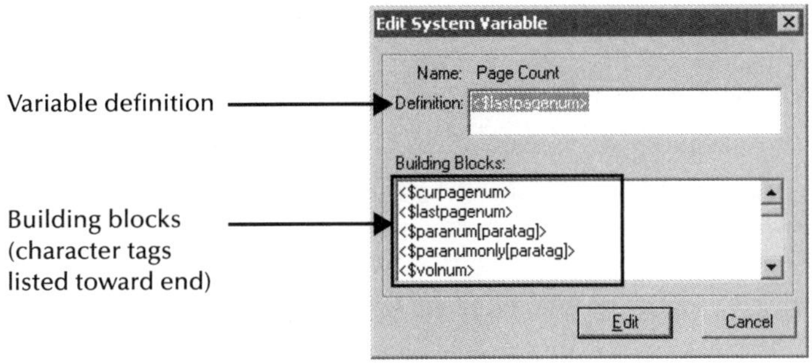

Figure 9-2. Edit System Variable dialog box

3. To add a building block or character style to the definition, click it in the Building Blocks list. You can also type building blocks, character tags, or text in the Definition field. If you use a character tag, include the <Default Para Font> character tag—which can be abbreviated </> to save space—where the character formatting should end, as shown in the following example:

   ```
   <Bold>Volume <$volnum>:</> Complete Classics
   ```

   This variable definition displays the following formatting:

   Volume IX: Complete Classics

4. Click the Edit button to save your changes, then click the Done button. The variable definition is modified, and the variable is updated where it occurs in the document.

Date and Time Variables

FrameMaker provides system variables that display the month, day, and year in long and abbreviated formats. You can access the following date- and time-related variables in any text frame:

- **Creation Date:** Displays the month, date, and year when you created the file, such as November 14, 2001 or 11/14/01.
- **Modification Date:** Displays the month, date, year, and time the document was last opened or saved, such as May 29, 2008 2:34 pm or 5/29/08. Updated when you open or save the file.
- **Current Date:** Displays the current month, date, and year, such as May 29, 2008 or 5/29/08. Updated when you change the page magnification or display a different page.

These variables consist of building blocks that display different aspects of the date and time. You can change the building blocks in each variable, but you cannot change the function of the variable. For example, you can add seconds to the Modification Date variable by inserting the <$second> building block. However, you cannot force the Modification Date variable to display the *creation* date because FrameMaker predefines the function of system variables.

NOTE If you change the language for a paragraph that includes a date or time variable, the variable is updated to use the date or time format for that language.

Table 9-2 describes the building blocks used in date variables.

Building Block	Description	Example
<$ampm>	Lowercase morning or evening abbreviation	am or pm
<$AMPM>	Uppercase morning or evening abbreviation	AM or PM
<$dayname>	Name of the day	Monday
<$shortdayname>	Abbreviated name of the day	Mon
<$daynum>	Number of the day	20
<$daynum01>	Number of the day with leading zero	09
<$hour>	Hour	1
<$hour01>	Hour with leading zero	01
<$hour24>	Hour in military format	13
<$minute>	Minute	5
<$minute00>	Minute with leading zero	05
<$monthname>	Name of the month	September
<$shortmonthname>	Abbreviated name of the month	Sept
<$monthnum>	Number of the month	9
<$second>	Seconds	8

Table 9-2. Building Blocks for Date Variables

Building Block	Description	Example
<$second00>	Seconds with leading zero	08
<$shortyear>	Abbreviated year	30
<$year>	Year	2030

Table 9-2. Building Blocks for Date Variables (Continued)

There are additional building blocks available when your system supports typing Japanese text. For more information about these building blocks, see the FrameMaker online help.

Numerical Variables

The numerical system variables display page, volume, and chapter numbers that are automatically updated when you open or save the file. You can insert a numerical variable in any text frame with the exception of the Current Page Number variable, which is available only on master pages. The following are numerical variables:

- **Current Page Number:** Displays the number of the current page.
- **Page Count:** Displays the number of the last page in the file.
- **Volume Number:** Displays the file's volume number.
- **Chapter Number:** Displays the file's chapter number.

The formats of the page, volume, and chapter numbers depend on settings in the document or book file. You can specify uppercase and lowercase Roman, alphabetic, or text-based numerals, along with standard Arabic numerals. For details, see "Managing Numbering" on page 386.

NOTE If you change the language for a paragraph that includes a numerical variable, the variable is updated to use the numerical format for that language.

Table 9-3 on page 222 describes the building blocks used in numerical variables.

Building Block	Description	Example
<$curpagenum>	Page number (only available on master pages)	735
<$lastpagenum>	Last page number in the document	758
<$paranum>	Value of autonumber field in paragraph tag	Step 2.
<$paranumonly>	Numerical value of the autonumber field (excludes punctuation and text)	2
<$chapnum>	Chapter number	9
<$volnum>	Volume number	II

Table 9-3. Building Blocks for Numerical Variables

Filename Variables

Two system variables display your document's file name. You can use the following Filename variables in any text frame:

- **Filename (Long):** Displays the system path and file name.
- **Filename (Short):** Displays only the file name.

Table 9-4 describes the building blocks used in Filename variables.

Building Block	Description	Example
<$fullfilename>	Displays the document's entire file name, including the path.	c:\Book\widget.fm
<$filename>	Displays the document's file name without the path.	widget.fm

Table 9-4. Building Blocks for Filename Variables

Table Variables

The following system variables are available only in tables:

- **Table Continuation:** Displays the definition of the variable on subsequent sheets of a table. You insert the variable into the title heading or footing row on the first sheet, but the value is not displayed on that sheet. By default, the Table Continuation variable displays "(Continued)," but you can change the text. When you insert the Table Continuation variable, a bracket (or hard space) is displayed on the first sheet. You must have the document text symbols turned on to see the character.

  Table 1: Books for Technical Communicators§ — Bracket indicates Table Continuation variable is inserted.

- **Table Sheet:** Displays the sheet number and the total number of sheets. By default, the variable displays "(Sheet # of #)," but you can edit the definition.

  Table 1: Books for Technical Communicators (Sheet 1 of 2)§

No building blocks are available in the Table Continuation variable except for character tags. Table 9-5 describes the building blocks used in the Table Sheet variable.

Building Block	Description	Example
< $tblsheetnum >	Displays the sheet number.	1
< $tblsheetcount >	Displays the total number of sheets in the table.	2

Table 9-5. Building Blocks for Table Variables

NOTE If the table's title is very long, the text from the Table Continuation variable is not displayed.

Running Header/Footer Variables

Twelve Running H/F system variables are available on the master pages of your document. You can use these variables to insert headers and footers in your document. For example, they can display the text or autonumbering from a specific paragraph tag on the right pages of a document and the book title on the left pages. In this book, the left header consists of the Running H/F 1 variable. Here's the variable definition:

```
Chapter <$paranumonly[Chapter_Number]>: <$paratext[Chapter_Title]>
```

In this example, the <$paranumonly> building block displays the value of the Chapter_Number paragraph tag, and the <$paratext> building block displays the value of the Chapter_Title tag (for example, Chapter 25: Cleaning Your Widget).

Most building blocks in Running H/F variables point to the first instance of the specified paragraph tag on the body page. If the variable points to the Heading3 paragraph tag, and the body page has two Heading3s, FrameMaker displays text from the first occurrence. If the body page lacks a Heading3, the running/header footer is determined by the previous Heading3. If one cannot be found, the running header/footer is blank. The running header/footer does not use text from master pages.

To prevent this problem, include an alternate paragraph tag in the variable definition, such as the Heading2 paragraph in the following example:

```
<$paratext[Heading3,Heading2]>
```

This variable directs FrameMaker to display text from the first Heading3 paragraph on the page. In the absence of a Heading3 paragraph, text from the first Heading2 on the page will be displayed.

The following three running header/footer building blocks have special functions:

- **<$marker1> and <$marker2>:** Display text from a marker instead of a long header or footer. For details, see "Displaying Text from a Marker" on page 225.
- **<$paratext[+,paratag]>:** Displays the last instance of the specified paragraph tag. For details, see "Displaying Dictionary-Style Headings" on page 227.
- **<$condtag[hitag,...,lotag,nomatch]>:** Searches for one or two condition tags on a page and displays the highest match. For details, see "Displaying Condition Tags" on page 228.

Table 9-6 lists the building blocks used in Running H/F variables.

Building Block	Description
Text	
<$paratext[paratag]>	Displays text from the specified paragraph tag.
<$paratext[+,paratag]>	Displays the last instance of the specified paragraph tag on the page. Often used to display dictionary-style headings.
<$paratag[paratag]>	Displays the paragraph tag rather than contents of the paragraph.
<$condtag[hitag,... lotag,nomatch]>	Displays the specified condition tag or alternate text, if the condition is not found.
<$marker1>	Displays text from the Header/Footer $1 marker in the document.
<$marker2>	Displays text from the Header/Footer $2 marker in the document.
Paragraph numbers	
<$paranum[paratag]>	Displays the autonumbering from the referenced paragraph, including punctuation.
<$paranumonly[paratag]>	Displays only the numeric portion of the referenced paragraph's autonumber.

Table 9-6. Building Blocks for Running Header/Footers

Displaying Text from a Marker

Instead of using the Running H/F variables to display text from a paragraph, you can display text from a marker. This technique is useful for displaying abbreviated headings or information that is not available in a paragraph. In the following example, the heading on the body page won't fit in the running header/footer text frame. You can type an alternate heading in a special Header/Footer marker and refer to that marker in the Running H/F variable with the appropriate building block. The abbreviated heading from the marker is displayed instead of the long heading.

Original heading on the body page → **Introduction to Programming for Nonprogrammers**

Running H/F displays long heading, but the heading is too long for the text frame on the master page. → *Introduction to Programming for Nonpro-grammers*

Abbreviated phrase is typed in a Header/Footer marker that is inserted in the heading paragraph. The short heading is displayed in the running header/footer. → *Intro for Nonprogrammers*

FrameMaker provides two building blocks (<$marker1> and <$marker2>) and two matching markers (Header/Footer $1 and Header/Footer $2) to display marker text in a running header/footer. The <$marker1> building block displays the definition of Header/Footer $1 markers; <$marker2> displays the definition of Header/Footer $2 markers. You cannot create additional markers (such as Header/Footer $3) that connect to Running H/F system variable.

To display text from a marker, follow these steps:

1. Create the marker by doing the following:
   a. Position your cursor where you want the marker (for example, in the paragraph of a long heading).
   b. Select Special➤Marker.

   The Marker dialog box is displayed.

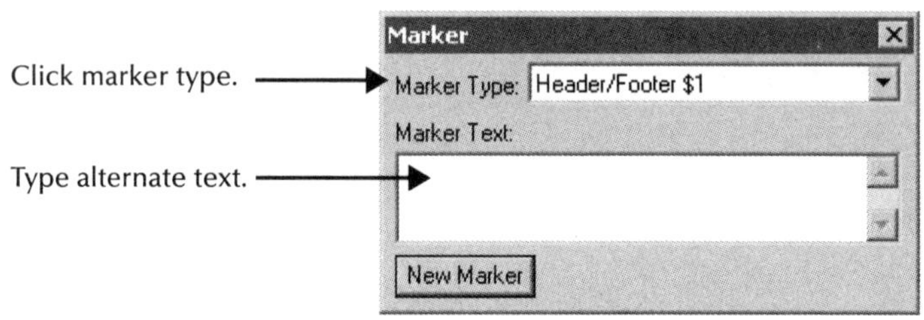

2. Click Header/Footer $1 or Header/Footer $2 in the Marker Type drop-down list.
3. In the Marker Text field, type the alternate text that you want displayed. As for all markers, the limit is 1023 characters.
4. Click the New Marker button. The marker is inserted in the paragraph.
5. View the document's master pages.
6. Do one of the following:

- In your document, double-click the variable that you want to modify.
- Position your cursor where you want the variable and select Special➤Variable.

The Variable dialog box is displayed (Figure 9-1 on page 215).

7. Click the Running H/F variable you want to edit (if it's not already highlighted), then click the Edit Definition button. The Edit System Variable dialog box is displayed (Figure 9-2 on page 219).
8. Type either **<$marker1>** or **<$marker2>** in the Definition field, depending on which Header/Footer marker you inserted.
9. Click the Edit button, then click the Insert button (or the Replace button if the variable was already on the master page).

When you display the body page, the marker text will be displayed in the running header/footer. If you define the Running H/F variable to be <$marker1> or <$marker2>, but that marker does not exist on the page with the Running H/F variable, the running header or footer will be blank.

Displaying Dictionary-Style Headings

By default, building blocks display the first instance of a paragraph tag on the page, but you can also use a variable to display the value of the last specified paragraph tag on the page. In the following example, the word at the top of the second column is also the last dictionary term on the page. The <$paratext[+,paratag]> building block in the running header refers to the Term paragraph tag.

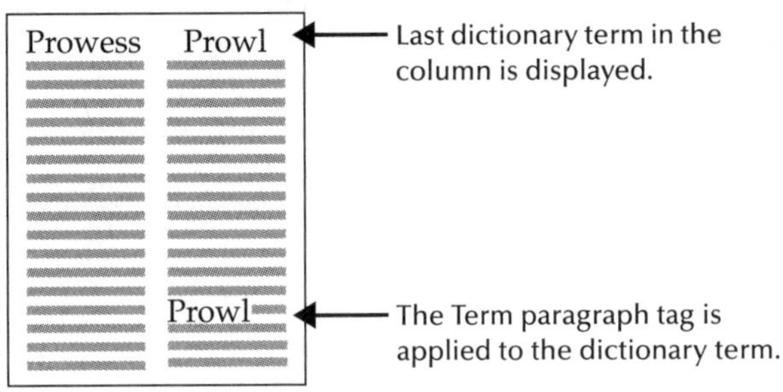

To create a dictionary-style running header/footer, follow these steps:

1. View the document's master pages.
2. Do one of the following:
   - In your document, double-click the variable that you want to modify.
   - Position your cursor where you want the variable and select Special➤Variable.

   The Variable dialog box is displayed (Figure 9-1 on page 215).

3. Click the running header/footer variable you want to edit (if it's not already highlighted), then click the Edit Definition button. The Edit System Variable dialog box is displayed.

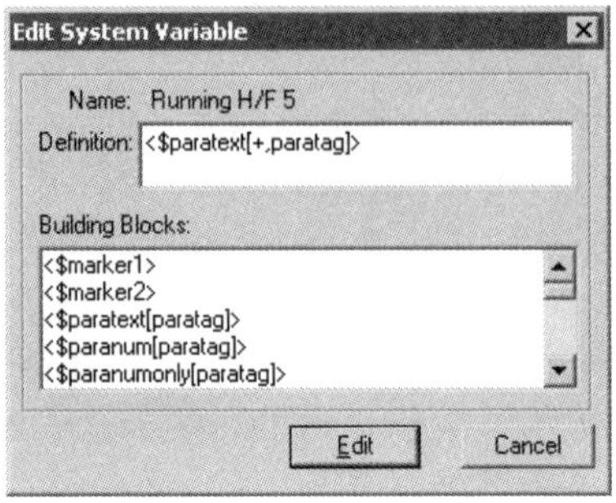

4. Type **<$paratext[+,paratag]>** in the Definition field. (This building block is not displayed in the list of building blocks, so you must type it in.)
5. Replace **paratag** with the appropriate paragraph tag.
6. Click the Edit button, then click the Insert button (or the Replace button if the variable was already on the master page).

When you display the body page, text from the last occurrence of the paragraph tag you specified is displayed in the running header/footer.

Displaying Condition Tags

In your running header/footer, you can display a condition tag applied to text on the current page. To do so, you use the <$condtag[hitag,...lotag,nomatch]> building block. This building block includes one or more condition tags and text that is displayed when the page has no condition tags, as in the following example:

```
          hitag   lotag        nomatch
            ↓       ↓             ↓
<$condtag[Print,Online,No Conditional Text]>
```

Here, FrameMaker first searches the page for the Print condition tag. If found, "Print" is displayed in the running header/footer. If not found, FrameMaker looks for the Online condition tag and displays it, if found. If it is not found, the last value is displayed. This can be either a phrase, such as "No Conditional Text," or a blank space (if you use a nonbreaking space for the last value).

The ellipsis in the <$condtag[hitag,...lotag,nomatch]> building block indicates that you can provide additional condition tags, and FrameMaker will also search for them. It's essential, however, to indicate what FrameMaker should display if no condition tags are found. Without the nomatch value, FrameMaker displays the last condition tag in the building block ("Online," in this example), even if the condition tag isn't actually on the page.

NOTE This feature is ideal for tagging pages in classified material. The conditions might be called TopSecret, Secret, Confidential, and Unclassified. Using the <$condtag[hitag,...,lotag,nomatch]> building block, you can specify that the page header or footer display the highest classification tag that occurs on the current page. As described in the previous paragraph, it is critical to provide the Unclassified tag so that pages aren't flagged as classified when they are not.

To set up a condition tag variable, follow these steps:

1. Do one of the following:
   - On the master page, double-click the variable that you want to modify.
   - Position your cursor where you want the variable and select Special➤Variable.

   The Variable dialog box is displayed (Figure 9-1 on page 215).
2. Click the variable you want to edit (if it's not already highlighted), then click the Edit Definition button. The Edit System Variable dialog box is displayed (Figure 9-2 on page 219).
3. Click the <$condtag[hitag,...lotag,nomatch]> building block to add it to the variable definition, or type it in the Definition field.
4. In place of **hitag,...lotag**, type the condition tags you want to display, for example, "Print,Online."
5. In place of **nomatch**, type one of the following:
   - The text you want displayed if no match is found, such as "No Conditional Text."
   - A nonbreaking space to display nothing if no match is found. Type \ followed by a space.
6. Click the Edit button, then click the Insert button (or the Replace button if the variable was already on the master page).
7. Display the body page. The variable text is updated.

Updating System Variables

System variables don't dynamically update their content; they must be updated by you or the system. For example, if you insert a current date variable that includes the hour, minute, and seconds, it will not be updated automatically as the time changes. The content is updated when you open or save the document. You can also force an update of the variables without saving the file.

Controlling Time Display with Building Blocks

As mentioned in "Date and Time Variables" on page 219, you can use system variables to insert the creation, current, or modification date and time in a document.

FrameMaker provides three building blocks that display time in other system variables and in running header/footer variables:

- **<$creationtime>:** Displays the creation time.
- **<$currenttime>:** Displays the current time.
- **<$modificationtime>:** Displays the time the file was last opened or saved.

These building blocks don't do anything when used alone; instead, they work with the other time building blocks to display time. For example, the <$currenttime> building block is inserted with other time building blocks in the following running header/footer variable definition:

```
<$currenttime><$hour>:<$minute> <$AMPM>
```

This variable displays the following text:

```
11:53 AM
```

The three building blocks can be used in system variables that are unrelated to time, such as Filename, but they're mostly used in running header/footer variables to create a custom header or footer.

To update system variables, follow these steps:

1. Select Special➤Variable to display the Variable dialog box (Figure 9-1 on page 215).
2. Click the Update button. FrameMaker displays a confirmation dialog box.
3. Click the OK button to update the variables.

Creating User Variables

User variables provide a way to store common terms and update words that change often. One example is a Product_Name variable. During the development process, a software program may have a code name, such as Orion. If you save the code name in a Product_Name variable and use the variable in your document, you can modify the variable when the product receives its real name. The term will be updated in each place you've inserted the variable. To update the term across an entire book, you import the variables from one document into all the documents in the book file.

In general, it is a good idea to name a variable for the type of information it contains. For example, suppose you create a variable containing the name of a book's author—Shakespeare—and name the variable Shakespeare. If the author changes to Jack Smith, the variable name becomes both hard to remember and confusing. A more generic name, such as Author, would be a better choice.

However, in some cases, you might decide to make the variable name and definition similar. If you create a variable for every product your company develops, don't use generic names, such as Product1, Product2, and so on. The variables will be easier to identify if they're named after the product.

CAUTION FrameMaker doesn't spell-check variables, so make sure you spell the definition correctly.

To create a new user variable, follow these steps:

1. Select Special➤Variable. The Variable dialog box is displayed (Figure 9-1 on page 215).
2. Click the Create Variable button. The Edit User Variable dialog box is displayed (Figure 9-3).

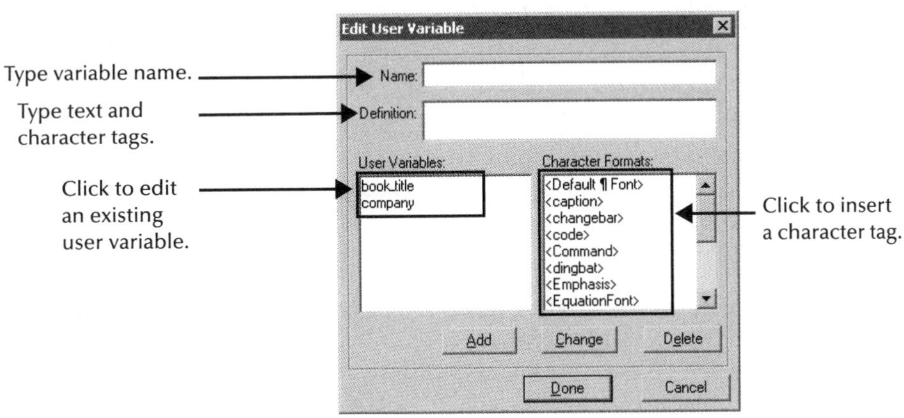

Figure 9-3. Modifying user variables

3. In the Name field, type a name for the new variable.
4. In the Definition field, type a definition for the variable. This text is displayed in the document. In addition to regular text, you can use character tags in the variable definition by clicking the tags in the Character Formats list or by typing the tags in the Definition field. The definition cannot exceed 1023 characters. Include the <Default Para Font> character tag—which can be abbreviated </> to save characters—where the character formatting should end, as shown in the following example:

```
<SmallCaps>shift</> key
```

This variable is used in the following sentence to format "shift" in small caps:

Press the SHIFT key, then select File➤Save All Open Files.

5. Click the Add button to add the variable to your list of user variables.
6. Click the Done button to close the Edit User Variable dialog box and return to the Variable dialog box.
7. Click the Done button to close the Variable dialog box. You can also insert the variable by clicking the Insert button.

Modifying User Variable Definitions

After you create a user variable, you can modify the definition by changing the text or adding character tags. The modified variable is automatically updated when you open or save the document.

To change the name or definition of an existing variable, follow these steps:

1. Do one of the following:
   - In your document, double-click the variable that you want to modify.
   - Select Special➤Variable.

   The Variable dialog box is displayed (Figure 9-1 on page 215).
2. Click the variable you want to edit (if it's not already highlighted), then click the Edit Definition button. The Edit User Variable dialog box is displayed (Figure 9-3 on page 231).
3. Change the name and definition of the variable as needed.
4. To save your changes and modify another user variable, click the Change button.
5. When you have finished modifying user variables, click the Done button.
6. In the Variable dialog box, click the Done button. The variable definition is modified, and the variable is updated where you've inserted it in the document.

NOTE In the Variable dialog box, the Replace button is displayed if text or a variable is selected on the page (for example, if you double-clicked a variable to display the Variable dialog box). If no text or variable is selected, the Insert button is displayed instead.

Converting User Variables to Text

You can convert user variables to standard text. For example, you might insert a term as a variable and decide later that the term doesn't need to be in a variable. When you convert the variable to text, character tags in the variable are applied to the converted term. For example, the Legacy Product variable is formatted by the Emphasis character tag. After converting the variable, FrameMaker applies the Emphasis character tag to the text on the page.

```
<Emphasis>Widget</>
```

↓

Widget

The converted variable can be edited and spell-checked; however, it can't be updated. For this reason, converting variables typically isn't a good idea unless you're cleaning up a template and see variables that shouldn't be there.

To convert a variable to text, follow these steps:

1. *(optional)* On the page, select the variable you want to convert.
2. Select Special➤Variable. The Variable dialog box is displayed (Figure 9-1 on page 215).
3. Click the Convert to Text button. The Convert Variables to Text dialog box is displayed.

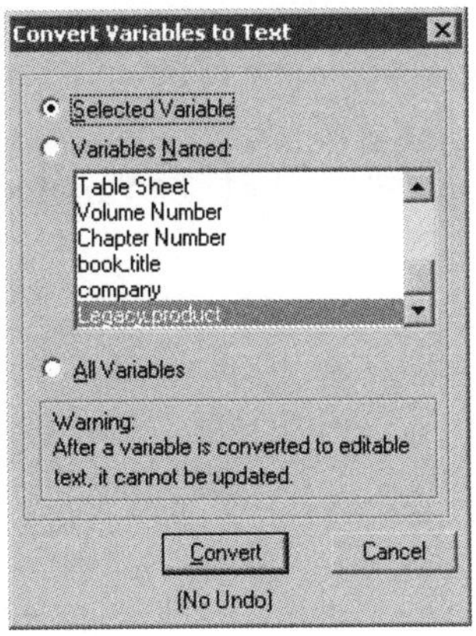

4. Do any of the following:
   - Click the Selected Variable radio button if you want to convert only the selected variable.
   - Click the Variables Named radio button, then click the name of the variable you want to convert. You can't click multiple variables.
   - Click the All Variables radio button to convert all variables in the document to text.

CAUTION At this point, you can change your mind and click the Cancel button. If you proceed to the next step, however, you cannot undo the conversion.

5. Click the Convert button, then click the Done button. The variable definition is converted to text. If you click the word, it's no longer highlighted like a variable, and character tags that were in the variable are applied to the converted text.

Deleting User Variables

You can delete user variables (but not system variables) from your document. If the variable is in use, FrameMaker displays a warning, and you can either convert the variable to standard text or cancel the action. If you're unsure whether a specific variable has been inserted in the document, search for the variable before you try to delete it. You can insert another variable in its place and then delete the variable. For details on searching for FrameMaker components, see "Searching and Replacing" on page 67.

To delete a user variable, follow these steps:

1. Do one of the following:
   - In your document, double-click the variable that you want to delete.
   - Select Special➤Variable.

   The Variable dialog box is displayed (Figure 9-1 on page 215).
2. Click the variable you want to delete (if it's not already highlighted), then click the Edit Definition button. The Edit User Variable dialog box is displayed (Figure 9-3 on page 231).
3. Click the Delete button.
4. Click the Done button to save your changes.
5. *(Skip if variable isn't in use)* A confirmation dialog box is displayed if the variable you want to delete is in the document. Click the OK button, and every instance of that variable in the document is converted to regular, editable text.

   FrameMaker warns that the variable you're trying to delete is used in the document.

   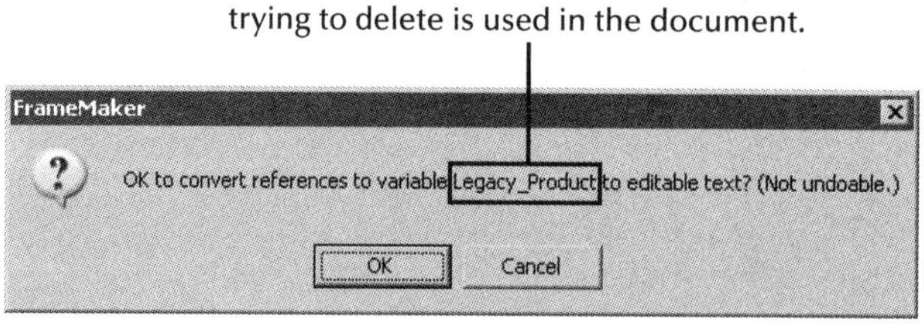

   The Variable dialog box is displayed again.
6. *(Skip if variable isn't in use)* Click the Done button to close the dialog box.

Tips for Variables

You can create your own variables to store frequently used words or phrases that often change. The variables may include character tags to format the text. Some uses of variables are as follows:

- **Software Release.** Type the software release number, as in "8.0."
- **Product Name.** Type the name of the product. During the development phase, your product might have an internal code name, such as "Pegasus." When the name is finalized, you update the variable definition. You could include the product name in the Software Release variable, but the Product Name variable can be used in several different ways with just the name.
- **Menu Item Separator.** In the variable, insert a character tag in that uses the Wingdings font, then copy the ➤ character from the Wingdings font in the Windows Character Map utility and paste it as the variable definition. Don't forget to include < / > after the variable definition to return the formatting to the default paragraph tag settings. For this example, thin spaces (\st) also enclose the symbol. The variable definition looks similar to this:

  ```
  \st<z_wingding>ä</>\st
  ```

  Separate menu items by inserting the variable, as in Format➤Paragraphs➤Designer.

  The Wingdings typeface must be installed on the computer displaying the document. If you're concerned about cross-platform compatibility, consider using OpenType fonts.

  As of FrameMaker 8.0p273, copying and pasting from the Windows Character Map utility or typing hex codes sometimes produces incorrect results. Usually (but not always), if one way doesn't work, the other way does. Entering the Unicode code point is the solution for Symbol or Zapf Dingbat characters that don't display correctly. See "Entering Special Characters in Dialog Boxes" on page 629.
- **Copyright.** Type a copyright statement. When the copyright year changes, you update the variable instead of searching for the year.
- **Company Name Long and Short.** Create two company variables: one with the full name of your company (Acme Brothers Limited Liability Company), and the other with an abbreviated name (Acme). These variables are especially useful if your company is sold to another corporation and the name changes.
- **Manual Version.** Type **First Draft** or **Second Draft** to indicate the version of your document.

PART III

Controlling Page Layout

CHAPTER 10

Understanding Master Pages

Page layout in FrameMaker is controlled by underlying pages called *master pages*. You associate master pages with the main content pages, which are *body pages*.

Master pages let you create a consistent look and feel for your content. For every body page, the assigned master page defines the location of headers and footers, background graphics, page numbers, and other items. All body pages formatted by the Left master page, for example, will have the same default layout (which you can override on the body page), and you can define a different layout for body pages formatted by the Right master page. The following illustration shows Left and Right master pages.

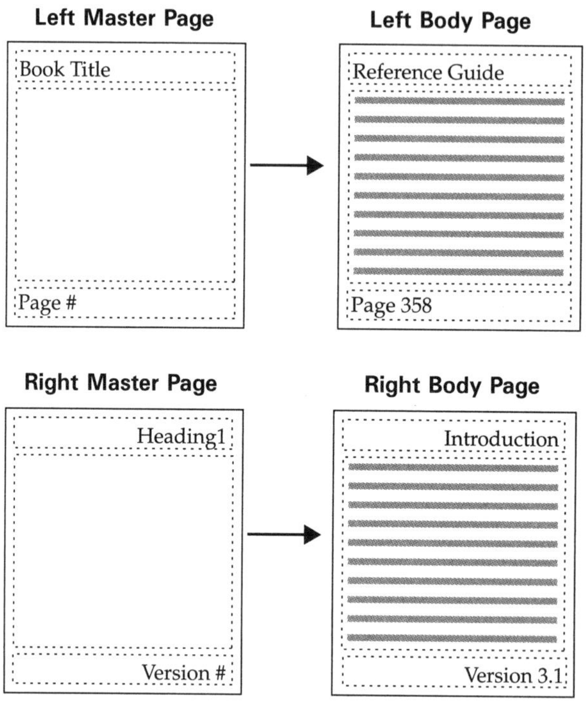

Master pages contain two types of objects:

- **Foreground objects.** Containers for the main text of the document. Many master pages have just one foreground object—the text frame in which you insert text on the body pages. Chapter 11, "Understanding Text Flows," describes how to modify foreground objects, such as adding columns and room for side heads.
- **Background objects.** Headers, footers, background graphics, page numbers, and other information that is repeated on the body pages. This chapter deals mainly with background objects.

To create foreground and background objects, you place text frames, graphic frames, and graphics on the master pages. When you draw a text frame, you are prompted to specify whether the frame is for background objects or for body page information.

Each foreground text frame has a flow tag, which controls how text fills the text frames. As you type text, FrameMaker automatically adds new pages and allows the text to flow onto those pages. (See "Understanding Text Flows" on page 272.) When you place a graphic frame or a graphic on the master page, it automatically becomes a background object. Background objects are not part of a flow.

NOTE Many page layout properties, such as margin widths or the number of columns, can be modified on either the body or master page. If you update the master page, *all* body pages formatted by the master page are updated. If you update the body page, only that page changes; you modify the body page layout when you need to customize only one page.

Displaying Master Pages

To see the master pages, select View➤Master Pages. To go to a particular master page, scroll down to find it or press CTRL-G and select the master page from the list. To return to the body pages, select View➤Body Pages.

Assigning Master Pages to Body Pages

When you add content to your FrameMaker document, the new pages are automatically set to the Right master page (for a single-sided document) or alternating Left and Right (for a double-sided document). You can, however, change the layout by assigning a different master page to one or more body pages.

To assign a master page to one or more body pages, follow these steps:

1. Display the body page you want to format.
2. Select Format➤Page Layout➤Master Page Usage. The Master Page Usage dialog box is displayed.

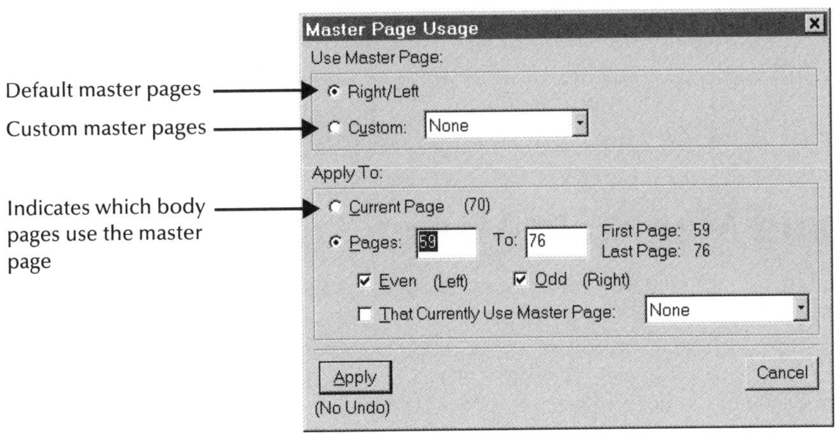

3. In the Use Master Page section, click the master page you want to assign:
   - To assign the default master page, click the Right radio button (in a single-sided document) or the Right/Left radio button (in a double-sided document).
   - To assign a master page you created, click that page in the Custom drop-down list.

CAUTION Avoid setting the master page to None. The body page will no longer be formatted by a master page even though it still looks like the previously applied master page. If the Right master page was applied before you set the custom master page to None, and you modify the Right master page, those changes are not displayed on the body page with the None setting. Setting the master page to None is a quick way to remove all headers and footers for a particular page.

4. In the Apply To section, do one of the following:
   - To assign the master page to the current body page, click the Current Page radio button (the default setting). Verify that the page number displayed next to Current Page is correct. The Current Page value is based on the page being displayed, not on the cursor location. For example, if your cursor is on page 3 and the bottom of page 4 is displayed on the screen, the current page is page 4.
   - To assign the master page to a range of pages, type the page numbers in the Pages fields.
   - To assign the master page to even or odd pages within the page range you've specified, check the Even or Odd check box.
   - To assign the master page to all pages in the document, type the page range in the Pages section and check both the Even and Odd check boxes. Note that FrameMaker provides the first and last page number in the current document to the right of the Pages fields.
   - To change all the assignments from one master page to another, specify the new master page in the Use Master Page section and the old master page in the That Currently Use Master Page drop-down list.
5. Click the Apply button. The master page is applied to the specified pages.

Creating and Managing Master Pages

FrameMaker automatically creates default master pages, which control the layout of left and right body pages. You can also create custom master pages for specialized content such as tables of contents and indexes, appendixes, and blank pages.

The following sections describe how FrameMaker creates default master pages and how you can create your own custom master pages, and how to perform tasks such as renaming or deleting master pages.

Creating Default Left and Right Master Pages

When you create a new document, FrameMaker creates default master pages for you—Right in a single-sided document, and Left and Right in a double-sided document. If you switch a single-sided document to double-sided, FrameMaker automatically creates the Left master page. You can modify the layout of default master pages, but you cannot rename, reorder, or delete them. For more information on changing the pagination of a document, see "Switching from Single- to Double-Sided Pages" on page 300.

Creating Custom Master Pages

In a typical double-sided book, you use Left and Right for regular pages, and then you create custom master pages for cover, title, landscape, rotated, and other special page layouts. You can create up to 100 master pages. All master pages in a document must be the same size; however, the pages can have different orientations. For example, you can mix 7 inch by 9 inch portrait pages with 9 inch by 7 inch landscape pages. You can change the paper size for an entire document, but to create a master page with different dimensions, you need to create a new document and define the size. See "Creating a Blank Document" on page 34 for details.

Tip You can create a master page while you're viewing a body page, but if you create a new master page while viewing the master pages, you have more design options. On the master pages, you can copy the layout of any master page or create an empty page. On the body pages, you're limited to copying the master page applied to the current page.

To create a master page based on the current body page layout, follow these steps:

1. Display the body page that looks similar to the master page you want to create.
2. Select Format➤Page Layout➤New Master Page. The New Master Page dialog box is displayed.

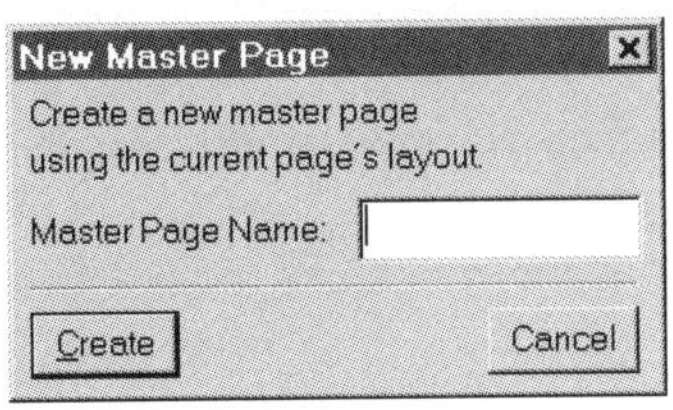

3. Type the name of the new master page in the Master Page Name field, then click the Create button. Remember that the master page name is case sensitive. A confirmation is displayed, explaining how to apply and edit the new master page.

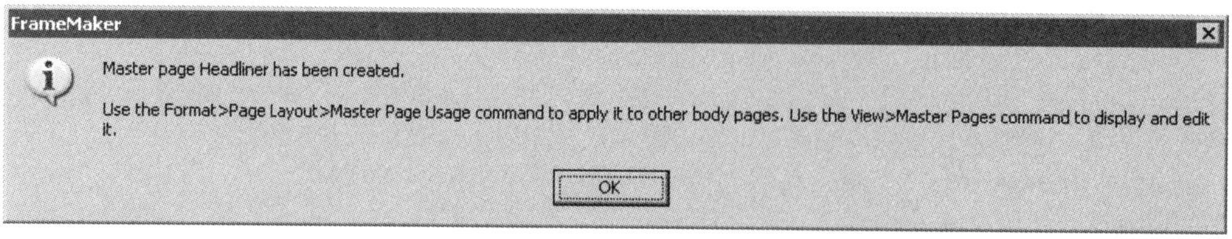

4. Click the OK button. The new master page is displayed.

To copy the layout of any master page or to create an empty master page, follow these steps:

1. Select View➤Master Pages, then select Special➤Add Master Page. The Add Master Page dialog box is displayed.

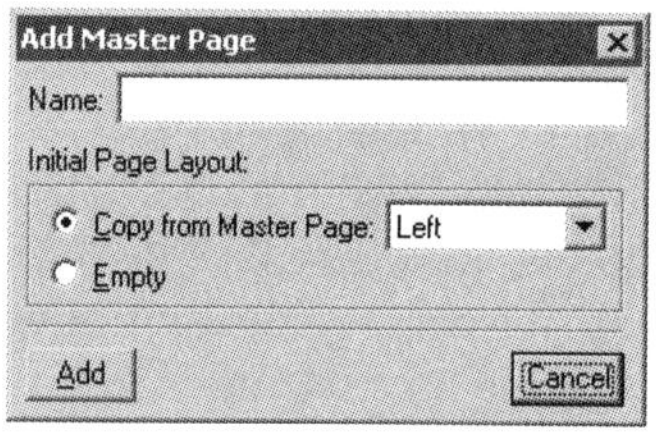

2. In the Name field, type a name for the new master page. Remember that the master page name is case sensitive.
3. Do one of the following:
   - Make a copy of an existing master page by clicking the page name in the Copy from Master Page drop-down list. Select this option if an existing master page resembles the page you want to create.
   - Create a blank page by clicking the Empty radio button. Select this option if none of the existing master pages resembles the page you want to create.
4. Click the Add button. The new master page is displayed.

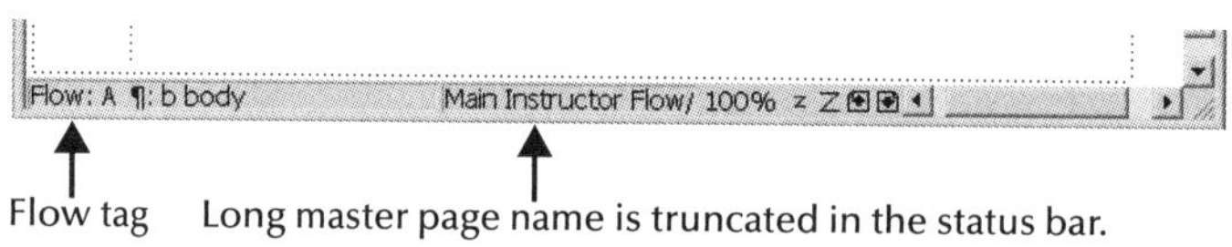

NOTE If you copy an existing master page, the new master page will use the same flow tag as the copied page. For more information about text flows, see Chapter 11, "Understanding Text Flows." If you added a blank master page, the new master page will use flow A. Make sure that the new master page you create uses the flow tag you need in your document.

Renaming Master Pages

When you rename a custom master page, the body pages that use the renamed master page automatically use the renamed page. To rename a master page, follow these steps:

1. Display the master page you want to rename.
2. Click the name of the master page in the status bar. The Master Page Name dialog box is displayed.

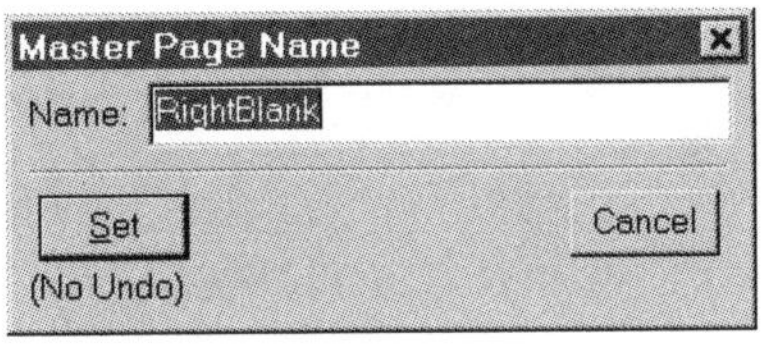

NOTE You can't rename the Left or Right master pages.

3. Type the new master page name over the highlighted name, then click the Set button. The master page is renamed.

   Any body pages that used the master page with the original name now use the renamed page. If the body pages have overrides to the master page formatting, those overrides remain. When you display the body pages again, you are prompted to keep the overrides on the body pages or remove them.

Rearranging Master Pages

Initially, master pages are displayed in the order you create them. You might prefer placing frequently used master pages at the top for easier access. You can rearrange custom master pages to display them in a different order in drop-down lists and in the master page view, as shown in the following example.

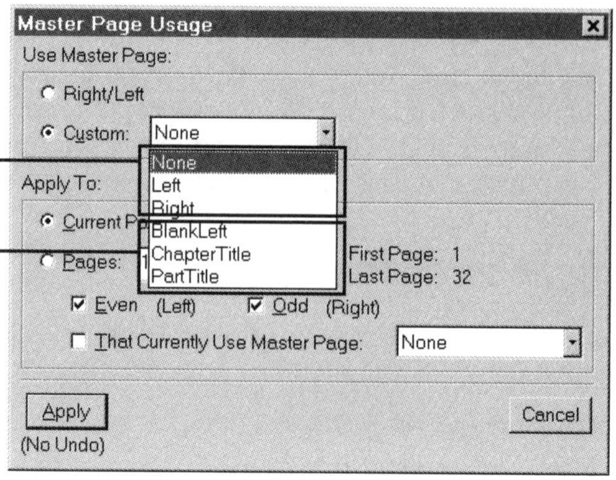

Default master pages are always displayed first.

Alphabetized custom master pages are displayed last.

The order of the master pages can't be imported into other FrameMaker files; you'll need to rearrange them in each file. (However, new files based on the file with the reordered master pages retain the order.)

To rearrange the master pages, follow these steps:

1. Display the master pages.
2. Select Format➤Page Layout➤Reorder Custom Master Pages. The Reorder Custom Master Pages dialog box is displayed.

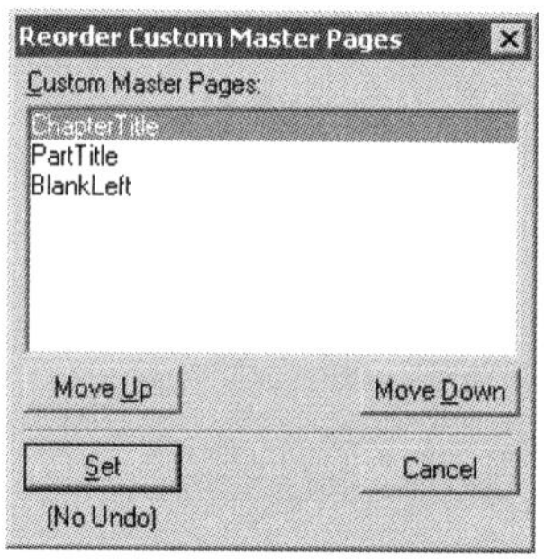

NOTE The Left and Right master pages are not displayed in the list because you can't move them; they are always displayed first.

3. Click the master page you want to move, then click the Move Up or Move Down button.
4. Click the Set button. The custom master pages are rearranged.

Modifying Master Pages

You can customize master pages to suit your document's requirements. For example, you can create multiple flows to separate text on the body pages, set up running headers and footers, and add a watermark effect. When you modify a master page that's already been assigned, the body pages assigned that master page layout are updated, and text reflows into the new layout, if necessary.

Adding Text Flows

Most master page text frames are associated with flow tags, which control how text fills text frames. In documents with more than one flow, text in each flow is displayed independently from the other flow. Newsletters often have multiple flows that continue a story from page 2, for example, to page 4. Many documents only have the default flow A, but you can add new flows. For details, see "Adding Text Flows to Master Pages" on page 276.

Setting Up Headers and Footers

Running headers and footers repeat information on body pages, such as the page number, book title, modification date, or content from a heading. Because the information in the header or footer might change from page to page or section to section, you often use variables to provide this content. For example, the page number variable represents the page number, and FrameMaker updates it automatically as you work in your document. You might use a variable to display heading text, and FrameMaker will automatically insert the heading text for the specified heading.

In the following example, the running footer displays the page number and the book title, both of which are provided by variables. For more information about using variables, see Chapter 9, "Storing Content in Variables."

The Current Page # variable is inserted in the text frame.

The Book Title variable is inserted in the text frame.

FrameMaker provides twelve variables specifically for running headers and footers, which often display the text or paragraph number of a specific paragraph. The values of these running header/footer variables are updated when content on the body page changes. For example, if the variable displays the first second-level heading on the page, and the heading changes, the new heading is displayed where you inserted the variable. For more information on running header/footer variables, see "Running Header/Footer Variables" on page 223.

FrameMaker includes running headers and footers in new documents by default. If you delete the default running header/footer or add an empty master page, you might need to add a new running header/footer.

To create a running header/footer, follow these steps:

1. Display the master page you want to change.
2. Draw the text frame where you want it on the master page. The Add New Text Frame dialog box is displayed.

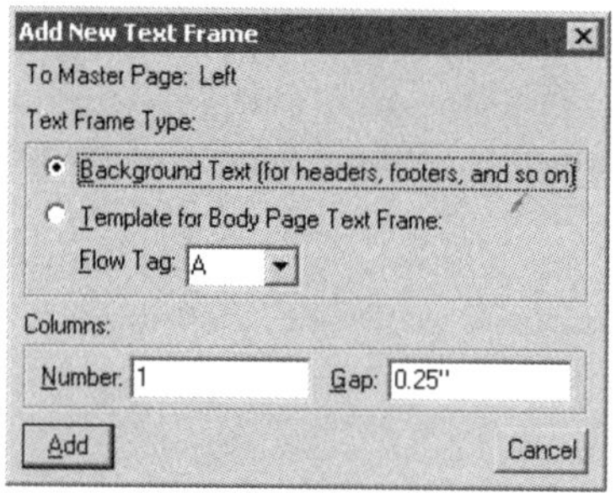

3. Click the Background Text radio button, then click the Add button. The text frame is displayed on the master page.
4. Place your cursor in the text frame, then select Special➤Variable. The Variable dialog box is displayed.
5. Click the running header/footer variable you want to insert, then click the Insert button. The variable is displayed in the text frame.

Setting Up a Watermark Effect

You can place text or graphics on the master pages to be displayed as a watermark on the body pages. Text watermarks can contain a rough draft statement or another message.

NOTE Some printer drivers also let you set up a watermark. You configure the watermark in the printer details and print the watermark only when needed.

You need to experiment with the watermark color and tint because optimum settings depend largely on your printer driver and paper. Most watermarks use a 10 percent to 25 percent gray tint. Print a page in the document to verify the color before you print the whole document. If you plan to distribute a PDF file of the document, create a test PDF file to make sure the color isn't too dark on screen.

Creating a Text Watermark

For text watermarks, you use a paragraph tag's autonumber, a variable, or text typed on the master page. Paragraph tags and variables are updated more easily than if you type text on the page—you update the watermark in the tag or variable, and each instance of the watermark is updated automatically. You can't, however, apply a condition to the autonumbered watermark. Conditions only work with text you can select.

To create a text watermark in FrameMaker, follow these steps:

1. Display the master page you want to modify.

2. Select Graphics➤Tools to display the Tools palette, then click the Text Frame icon.
3. Draw a background text frame where you want the watermark. The text frame is displayed on the page.
4. Position your cursor in the text frame and do one of the following:
   - To store the watermark in a paragraph tag, create a paragraph tag or display an existing tag in the Paragraph Designer, then type the watermark text in the Autonumbering Format field of the Numbering sheet. For a new paragraph tag, you could create a paragraph tag that formats the watermark with a 15 percent black sans-serif font set to 48 points, as shown in the following example. Print a page to make sure the color prints dark enough without reducing document readability.

     Rough Draft

   - To store the watermark in a variable, create a variable, type the watermark text in the variable, and insert the variable.
   - To type the watermark on the page, click in the text frame and type.

   The watermark is displayed on the master page.
5. *(optional)* Resize the text frame to remove white space between the watermark and text frame.

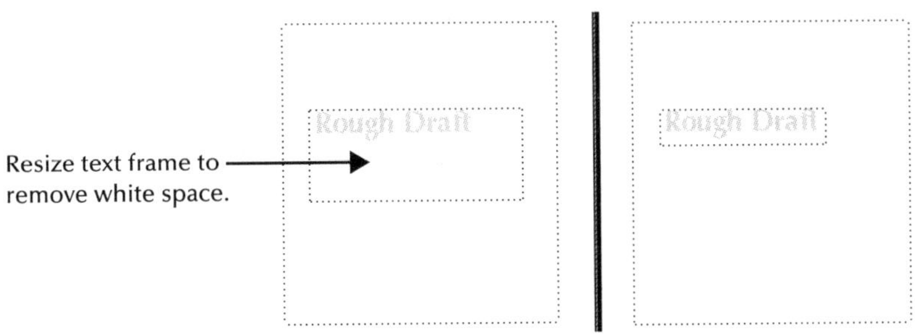

Next, you can rotate and align the watermark. See "Rotating" on page 366 for details.

If you typed the watermark text or inserted a variable, you can apply a condition tag. When you need to hide the watermark, change the Show/Hide settings for the condition tag, and the condition is updated on all body and master pages. For details, see Chapter 21, "Setting Up Conditional Text."

Creating a Watermark Graphic

For graphic watermarks, you create the graphic and import it onto the master page. If you have a specific watermark design that's difficult to set up in FrameMaker, the graphic watermark is a good alternative to text.

When you create a watermark graphic, you should make sure the color of the watermark is light enough to be displayed behind the main content without reducing readability. You might start with 15 percent to 25 percent gray tint. To angle the graphic on the page, rotate the watermark in your graphics program or within FrameMaker.

To create a graphic watermark, follow these steps:

1. Display the master page you want to modify.
2. Click outside the master page's main text frame so your cursor isn't in the text frame, then select File➤Import➤File. The Import dialog box is displayed. (If the cursor is in the text frame, the graphic will import inside an anchored frame and won't appear on body pages.)

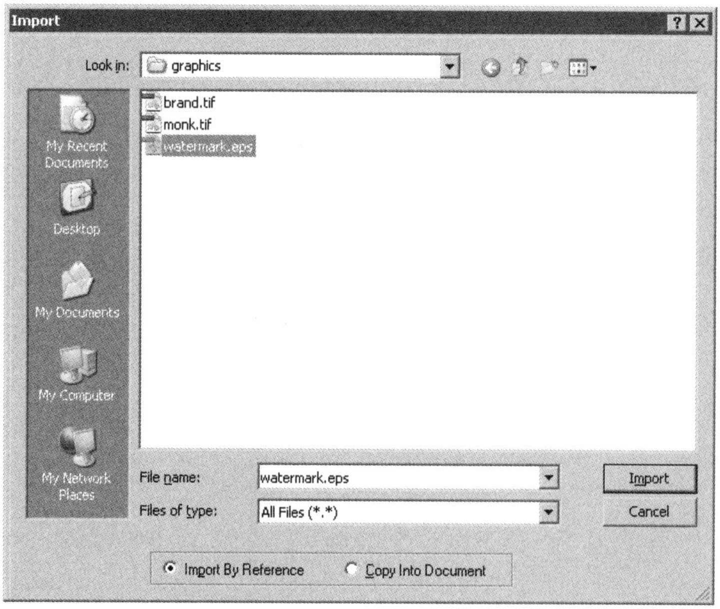

3. Import the watermark graphic as you would other graphics. The graphic is displayed in the main text frame.

You can embed a watermark graphic onto the master page or import the file by reference. If you import the graphic by reference, the file size doesn't increase from using a graphic. For more information on embedding and importing graphics, see "Importing a Graphic" on page 308.

TIP If the graphic isn't displayed, click the main text frame and select Graphics➤Send to Back. This moves the text frame behind the graphic.

Creating a Landscape Master Page

You can create pages that have portrait and landscape orientation in a single file. (You cannot, however, use different page sizes in a single file.)

Landscape master pages can contain headers and footers that are portrait- or landscape-style. The following illustration shows portrait-style footers:

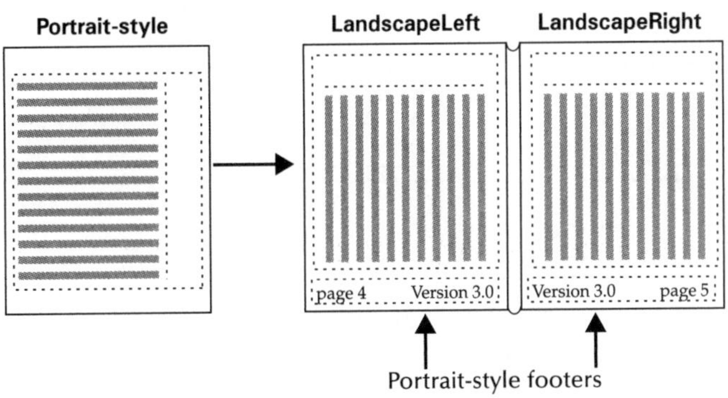

In contrast, the next illustration shows landscape-style footers:

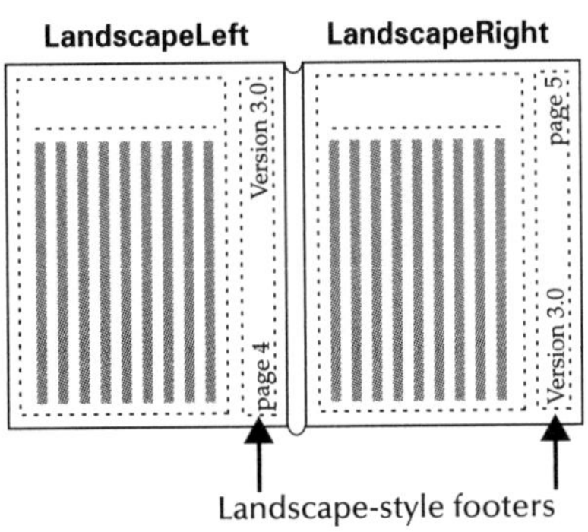

To decide which direction the headers and footers on landscape pages should face, consider the following factors:

- **Portrait-style header/footer.** The headers and footers on landscape pages match those found on portrait-style pages so the reader can see them more easily while scanning the book. Typically, this option makes more sense in terms of document readability.
- **Landscape-style header/footer.** The header and footer information is harder to read from the vertical perspective, and the book binding could cut off the text. However, in a section with several landscape pages, you can rotate the headers and footers so they all match within the group.

Creating a Landscape Master Page with Portrait Headers and Footers

To create a landscape master page with portrait headers and footers, follow these steps:

1. Create a new master page based on the Left or Right master page with a name such as LandscapeLeft or LandscapeRight.

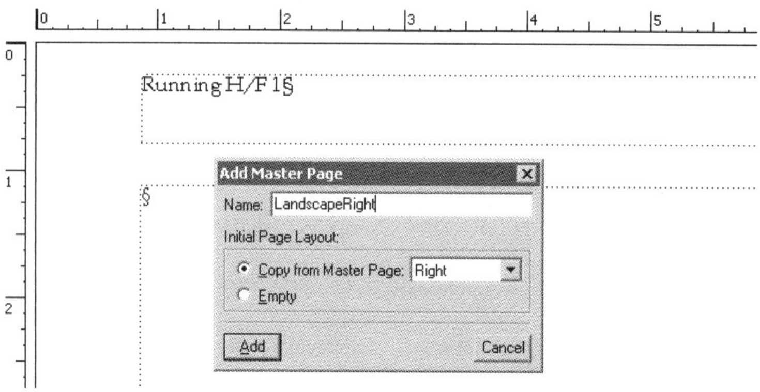

2. On the new master page, select the main text frame, then select Graphics➤Object Properties. The Customize Text Frame dialog box is displayed.

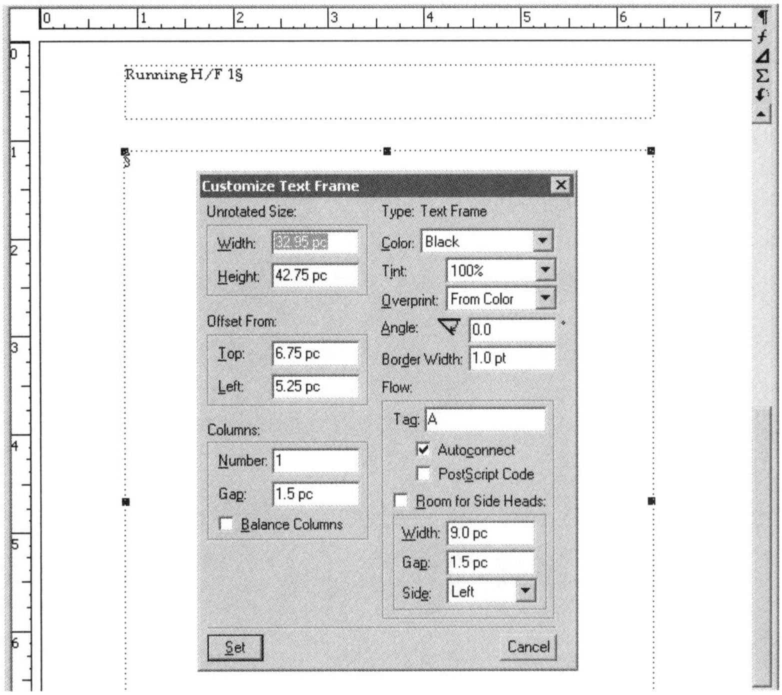

3. Write down the width and height of the main text frame, along with the top and left offset. You'll need these numbers after you rotate the page. Click the Cancel button.
4. Rotate the main text frame by selecting Graphics➤Rotate. In the Rotate Selected Objects dialog box that is displayed, specify rotation of 90 degrees counterclockwise, then click the Rotate button.

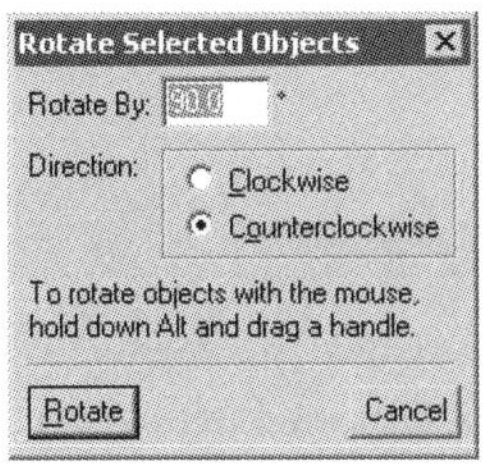

The frame looks like the following example:

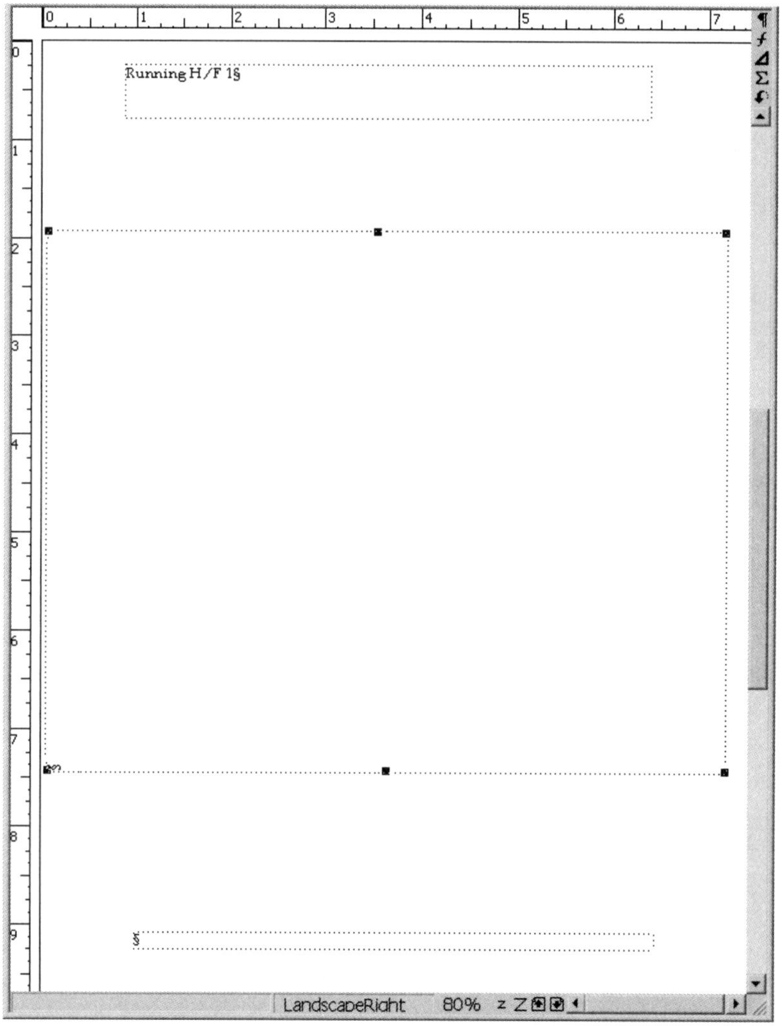

5. If not already selected, select the main text frame on the landscape master page, then select Graphics➤Object Properties. The Customize Text Frame dialog box is displayed.

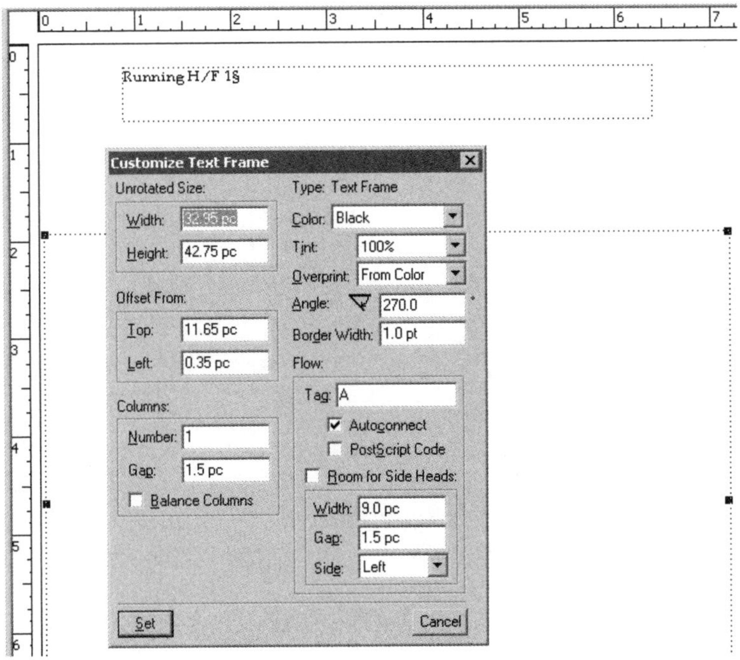

6. Refer back to the settings you wrote down in step 3 and adjust the text frame dimensions, as follows:
   a. In the Unrotated Size section, type the original height in the Width field, and type the original width in the Height field.
   b. The Offset From settings changed when you rotated the frame, so you need to change those back. In the Offset From section, type the original top offset in the Top field, and type the original left offset in the Left field.

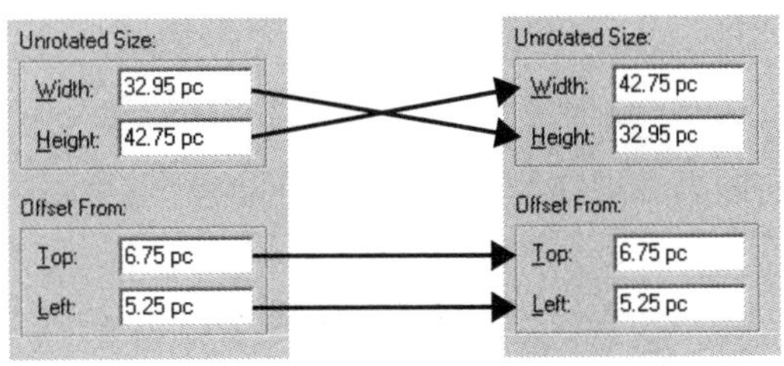

   c. You might need to adjust these values, and they might be different for right and left pages.
7. Click the Set button. The landscape master page is displayed.

8. Select Format➤Customize Layout➤Rotate Page Clockwise. The entire master page is rotated so that authors can type text from left to right (as on a portrait page) instead of typing sideways from bottom to top.

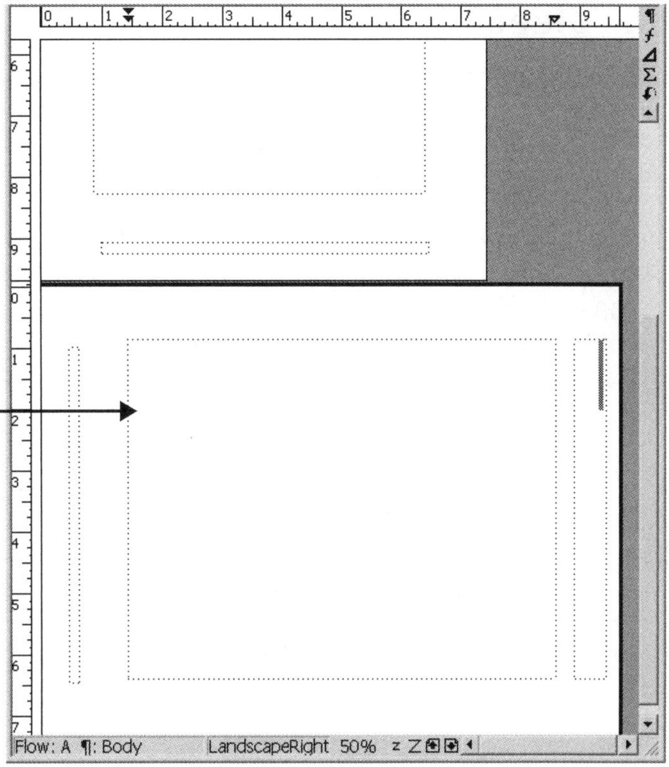

After you create the landscape page, you can rotate it so writers type into the page left to right (instead of up and down).

Creating a Landscape Master Page with Landscape Headers and Footers

To create a landscape master page with landscape headers and footers, most of the steps are similar to steps for creating a page with portrait headers and footers:

1. Repeat step 1 through step 3 in the preceding procedure for the header and footer text frames to get the information about the height of those frames. Also, make a note of the variables used in the frames.
2. Delete the header and footer frames.
3. Select the main text frame, then follow step 4 through step 8 in the preceding procedure.
4. Redraw the header and footer text frames; use the height information from step 1. For the width, you can use the width of the main text frame.
5. Reinsert the variables. You might need to adjust tab settings for the header and footer paragraph tags (or create new tags with modified tab settings) to accommodate the longer frames.

Creating Bleeding Tabs

Thumb tabs help a reader find information in a book. They can contain the chapter heading, chapter number, or other descriptive text. *Bleeding thumb tabs* are printed on the edge of the page so that the reader can easily identify section breaks while flipping through the book. In this book, all thumb tabs are stored on the Right master page. During the production edit, the unnecessary tabs were deleted, and the variable definition was updated. For example, in Part 1, all thumb tabs were deleted except for the first one. In Part 2, all thumb tabs were deleted except for the second one.

Figure 10-1 shows the page layout before and after removing tabs and updating the variable. The thumb tabs appear to be one long graphic, but they're actually several overlapping graphics. The overlap prevents gaps from printing between sections on the outside edge of the page.

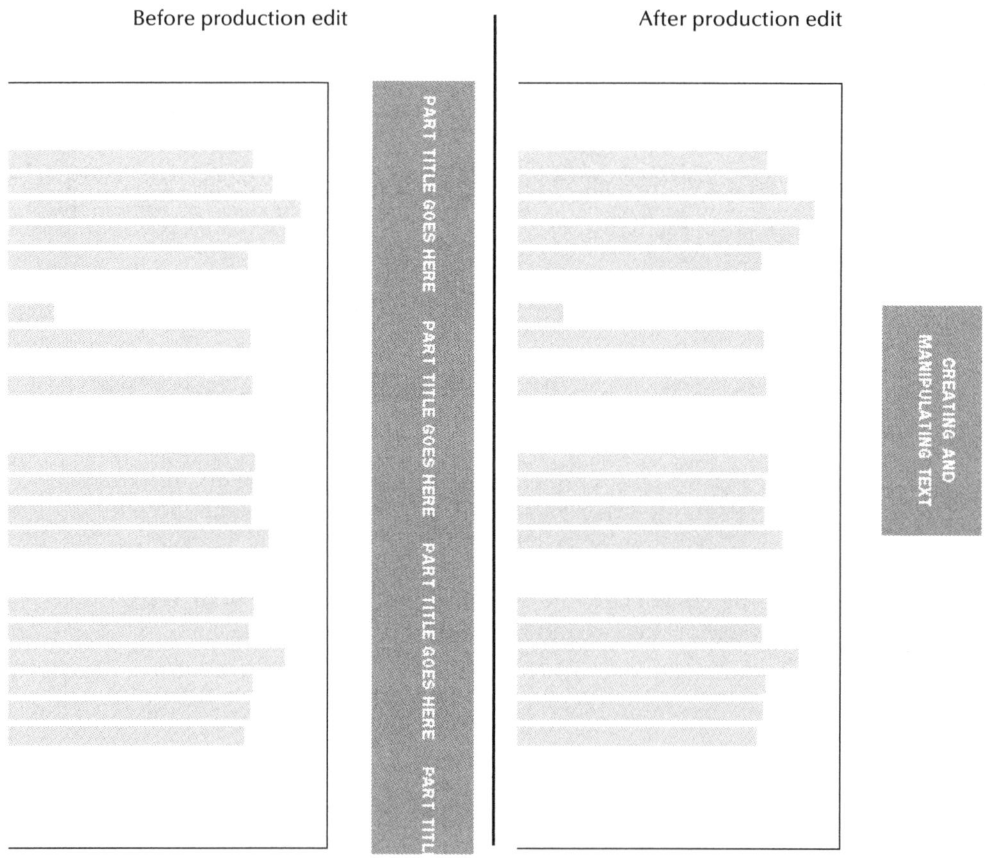

Figure 10-1. Deleting thumb tabs from the master page

Thumb tabs have four components:

- **Shaded rectangle:** Drawn on the tabs as rectangles with a solid fill.
- **Text frame:** Drawn on each tab to hold the content.

- **Variable:** Inserted into the text frames to display the content.
- **Paragraph tag:** Created to format the content in a color that displays clearly against the solid background. The tag may also center-align the text.

Consider the following factors when you plan thumb tabs:

- **Size:** How much text will be displayed on the tabs? For the chapter number and title, you'll need to create a longer tab and text frame than for just the chapter number.

TIP Your print vendor may trim the paper to reduce the finished book size. If so, you need to know which edges of the page will be cut off. If all four edges are trimmed, you need to adjust the top offset of the first and last tab on the page in addition to adjusting the left offset for all tabs. If the bottom edge of the page isn't trimmed, you don't need to adjust the top offset of the last tab.

- **Formatting:** How will you format the text? The font face, size, and color should be displayed clearly against the thumb tab. The amount of content on the tab affects the font size. The more text, the smaller the font.
- **Placement:** Will the paper be trimmed? To create bleeding tabs, the tabs must be large enough for the text, and the text frames must be placed closer to the left edge of the tab so the content isn't trimmed off.

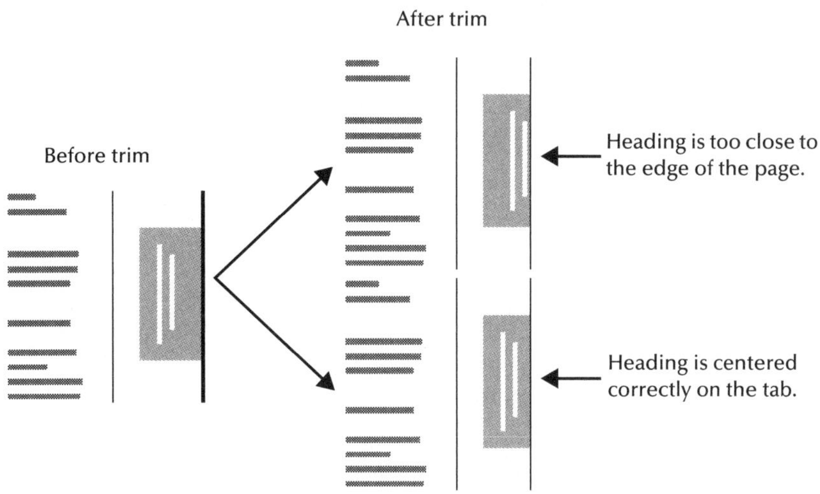

- **Master page setup:** Some users create one page for all thumb tabs, while others prefer creating a master page for each part or chapter (depending on your thumb tab setup) with the thumb tab in the correct position for that section. Creating separate thumb tab master pages saves you the step of deleting extra tabs in every section, but it also multiplies the number of master pages in your template.

The following procedure describes how to add thumb tabs to a right master page.

Drawing the Thumb Tab

Creating thumb tabs involves several stages. First, you need to draw a rectangle for the tab. To do so, follow these steps:

1. Display the master page you want to change.

2. Select Graphics➤Tools to display the Tools palette, then click the Rectangle icon.
3. Draw a rectangle against the right edge of the page. The blank rectangle is displayed. Don't worry about the position. You'll calculate the bleed and distribute the tabs later.

4. With the rectangle selected, click the Fill Pattern icon, then click the shading pattern (such as *solid*) from the Fill pop-up menu. The pattern is displayed on the tab.

The shaded thumb tab is displayed on the master page.

Adding the Text Frame

After you draw the thumb tab, you need to add the text frame. To do so, follow these steps:

1. Draw a small background text frame over the thumb tab. It shouldn't be the size of the final text frame. You're going to rotate the frame, so it will change dimensions. The background text frame is displayed on the shaded tab.
2. With the text frame selected, rotate it 90 degrees clockwise. See "Rotating" on page 366 for details.
3. Lengthen the text frame and move it closer to the left edge of the tab. This helps prevent the text from being trimmed off. You can either drag the borders of the text frame to resize it or change the size in the text frame properties.

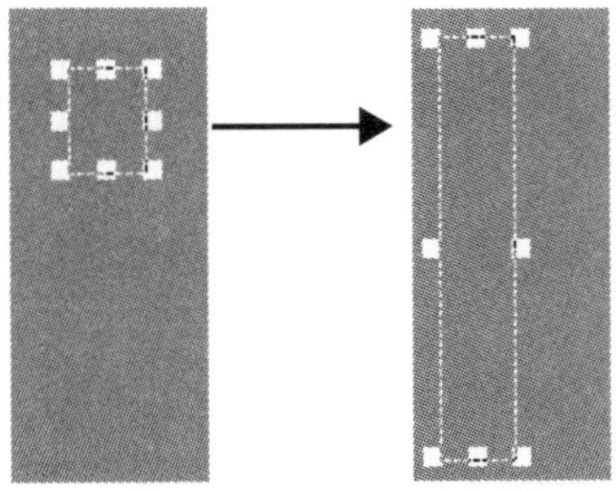

4. Insert a variable in the text frame and apply a paragraph tag. The variable is displayed on the tab, and the paragraph tag formatting is applied.

TIP To shorten long headings so they fit on the tab, you can insert a Header/Footer marker in the heading paragraph, type the shortened heading in the marker, and reference that marker in the variable. For details, see "Displaying Text from a Marker" on page 225.

5. Select View➤Body Pages to display the body pages.
6. Apply the thumb tab master page to the correct body pages, and check the position of the thumb tab text. If the paragraph is too long, you can resize the text frame or change the font size.

Creating Additional Thumb Tabs

To place additional thumb tabs down the edge of the master page and align them, follow these steps:

1. Select View➤Master Pages and page up or down to find the thumb tab page.
2. Select the thumb tab rectangle and text frame, then select Graphics➤Group. The text frame and thumb tab are grouped.
3. Copy the tab, then paste it down the edge of the page.
4. Select all tabs, then left align them. See "Aligning" on page 360 for details.

CAUTION You should wait to delete extra thumb tabs and modify any thumb tab variables until production. If you reimport the page layout properties and variable definitions from your template, the original thumb tabs are displayed, and you'll have to modify the thumb tabs and variables again.

Creating the Bleed

To make sure that the thumb tab prints to the edge of the page, follow these steps:

1. Select one of the thumb tabs, then select Graphics➤Object Properties. The Object Properties dialog box is displayed. The Offset From section is shown here.

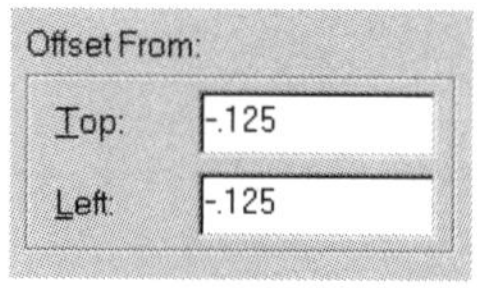

2. Change the offset values, which are different for the first and last tab. If the top or bottom edge will not be trimmed, you need to follow only step b.
   a. *(first tab only)* Type a value between -0.125 and -0.25 inches in the Offset From Top field.
   b. *(all tabs)* To calculate the Offset From Left value, subtract the tab width from the page width and add between 0.125 and 0.25 inches. Type the value in the Offset From Left field.
   c. *(last tab only)* To calculate the Offset From Top value, subtract the tab height from the page height, add between 0.125 and 0.25 inches. Type the value in the Offset From Top field.

TIP To check the page size, select Format➤Page Layout➤Page Size. The page width and height are displayed.

3. Click the Set button to save your changes. You'll need to experiment with the offset values and then trim the page to find the best location. After changing the offset, you can widen the tab to make room for text.
4. After you place all tabs on the page, you need to distribute them evenly. See "Distributing" on page 362 for details.

After you set up the tabs on the master page, you can import the page layouts into other files, apply the thumb tab master page, and delete the unnecessary tabs.

Removing Master Page Overrides

You create overrides to the master page by modifying text frame properties on the body page. For instance, when you adjust the size of the text frame to copyfit a body page, you create an override. FrameMaker warns you about the overrides when you switch from the master page to body page view. If you remove the override, FrameMaker removes all master page overrides—not just the overrides on the current page—so that the body pages match the master pages again. If you keep the override, the customized body pages are no longer formatted by the master page.

Click to remove master page overrides.

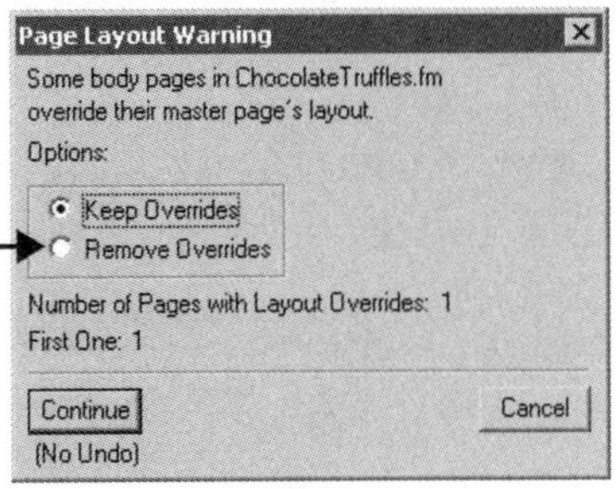

Mapping Paragraph Tags to Master Pages

FrameMaker lets you map paragraph tags to master pages. When you reapply all master pages, FrameMaker scans pages for the specified paragraph tags and assigns the correct master pages. For example, you might map the ChapTitle paragraph tag to the First master page. Instead of manually applying the master page, you apply all master pages in the document with the Apply Master Pages menu choice. The First master page is instantly applied to the page containing the ChapTitle paragraph tag. This feature also removes all page layout overrides in the document at once.

Mapping paragraph tags to master pages requires three steps: first, have FrameMaker create a master page mapping table and a reference page for it; second, set up the mappings; third, tell FrameMaker to update the master pages and apply the map. The following sections provide detailed instructions for each step.

Creating the Master Page Mapping Table

Before you set up master page mapping in a document, FrameMaker needs to generate a MasterPageMaps reference page that contains the mapping table. In a book file, you must generate the reference page for one file, and then you can import the reference pages from the updated file into the rest of the book. See "Importing Settings from a Template File" on page 615 for details. Note that you need only do this once to set up your mapping table. After the mapping table is created, you edit the existing mapping table.

To create the master page mapping table, follow these steps:

1. Select Format➤Page Layout➤Apply Master Pages.

   A confirmation dialog box is displayed.

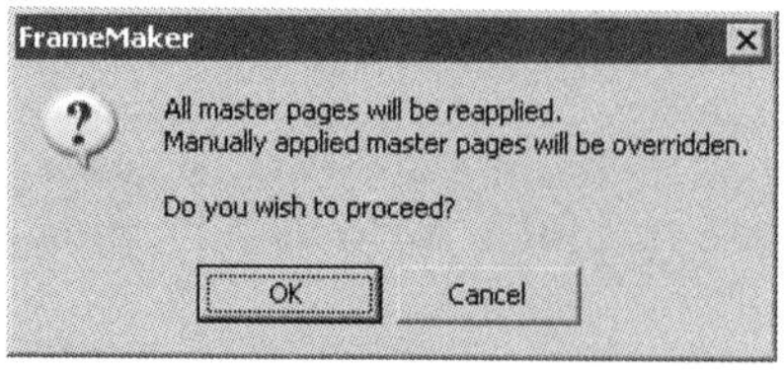

2. Click the OK button.

   A confirmation dialog box is displayed stating that FrameMaker will create the master page mapping table.

3. Click the OK button. The master page mapping table is created on a new reference page in the document.

Next, you set up the mappings using the procedure described in the following section.

Setting Up Your Mapping Table

After FrameMaker has created the mapping table, you will need to set up the mappings of paragraph tags to master pages.

To set up your mappings, follow these steps:

1. Select View➤Reference Pages to view the reference pages.
2. Go to the MasterPageMaps reference page.
3. On the MasterPageMaps reference page, there is a mapping table.

UnstructMasterPageMaps
Book Update (Yes or No): Yes

Paragraph Tag Name	Right-Handed Master Page (or Single-Sided Master Page)	Left-Handed Master Page	Range Indicator (Single, Span pages, Until changed)	Comments

4. FrameMaker allows you to reapply all master pages from your book file. If you do not want this document updated when you reapply master pages from the book, type **No** in the Book Update field.

NOTE If the Book Update field above the mapping table is blank, FrameMaker uses the default value "Yes."

5. For each paragraph tag you want to map, type the tag name in the Paragraph Tag Name column, and the master page name in the Right-Handed Master Page column. If you also want the paragraph tag mapped to a master page on left-hand pages, specify the master page name in the Left-Handed Master Page column. If you don't specify a master page for the left-hand body pages, the left-hand body pages use the setting for the right-hand body pages.
6. To assign master pages to a range of pages, type the range in the Range Indicator column. For example, the master page might be applied to a single page, a page range, or until you specify another master page. Table 10-1 lists the options available.

Field	Description
Required Fields	
Paragraph Tag Name	Paragraph that the master page is automatically applied to. Must be spelled and capitalized correctly, or FrameMaker ignores the setting and applies the default master page.
Right-Handed Master Page (or Single-Sided Master Page)	Master page applied to right body pages (in a double-sided document) or all body pages (in a single-sided document). Must be spelled and capitalized correctly, or FrameMaker displays an error when you reapply master pages and stops the process. If blank, the master page is set to None.
Optional Fields	
Left-Handed Master Page	Master page applied to left body pages. If blank, FrameMaker applies the master page mapped to the right body pages.

Table 10-1. Mapping Paragraph Tags to Master Pages

Field	Description
Range Indicator	Pages to which the master page is applied. Options are as follows: ■ **Single:** Applied only to the page with the specified tag. ■ **Span pages:** Applied to pages within the range, beginning with the specified paragraph tag. ■ **Until changed:** Applied to all pages until FrameMaker finds another mapped paragraph tag. For instance, according to the next example, the RightSL and LeftSL master pages are applied until another mapped paragraph tag is found. If the setting is blank, FrameMaker applies the master page to a single page.
Comments	Notes on the mapping.

Table 10-1. Mapping Paragraph Tags to Master Pages (Continued)

7. *(optional)* Type helpful notes in the Comments columns to document how the mappings are used.

   The following example shows sample mappings.

UnstructMasterPageMaps
Book Update (Yes or No): Yes

Paragraph Tag Name	Right-Handed Master Page (or Single-Sided Master Page)	Left-Handed Master Page	Range Indicator (Single, Span pages, Until changed)	Comments
Heading1	RightSL	LeftSL	Until changed	
ChapTitle	ChapTitle	ChapTitle	Single	
Intro	RightNonum	LeftNonum	Until changed	
Notes	NotesRight	NotesLeft	Span pages	

When FrameMaker finds more than one mapped paragraph tag on the same page, FrameMaker applies the master page for the first tag that occurs on the page.

CAUTION Make sure the mapping table has at least one paragraph mapped; otherwise, FrameMaker assigns the master page None when you apply the master pages and removes the current or default master page assignment, which is probably not what you want.

Applying the Master Page Mappings

To apply master pages you've mapped to paragraph tags, follow these steps:

1. Do one of the following:
   - *(book file)* Select Format➤Page Layout➤Apply Master Pages. Another method is to check the Apply Master Pages check box when you update the book.
   - *(single file)* Select Format➤Page Layout➤Apply Master Pages.

   A confirmation dialog box is displayed.

   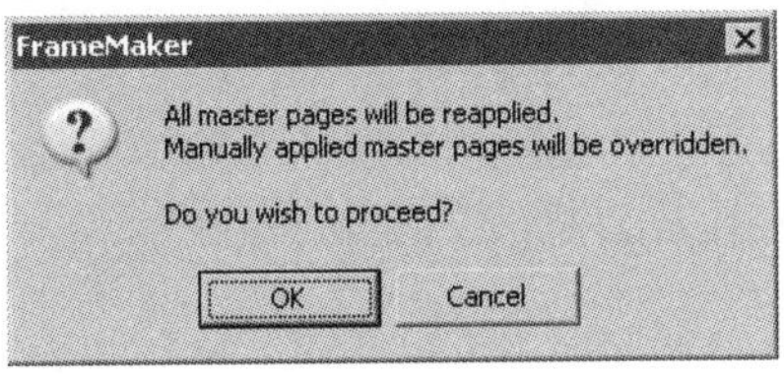

2. Click the OK button. The master pages are reapplied.

   If applying the master page would cause the mapped heading to fall on the following page, FrameMaker ignores the mapping and applies the default Right or Left master page. See the console for messages about master pages that were not applied.

   If you reapply master pages from your book file, FrameMaker displays an error if a file in the book doesn't have a MasterPageMaps reference page and mapping table. You must create a mapping table for one file in the book using the procedure in "Creating the Master Page Mapping Table" on page 263 and then import that file's reference pages into the book files (see "Importing Settings from a Template File" on page 615) before reapplying master pages from the book file.

Eliminating Page Layout Overrides

After you modify the text frame on a body page, you can update the master page applied to that page, or you can update the entire flow, as shown in the procedures that follow. When you update the master pages, all body pages to which you've applied the master page are reformatted. For example, suppose you experiment with different side head widths on a body page to see how text appears in the new layout. If you like the new size and want to modify all pages in the flow to match the current body page, you update the column layout, and FrameMaker changes the master pages in the flow according to your specifications.

Removing All Layout Overrides

To remove all layout overrides by displaying the master pages, follow these steps:

1. Select View➤Master Pages to display the master pages, then select View➤Body Pages. The Page Layout Warning dialog box is displayed (Figure 10-2).

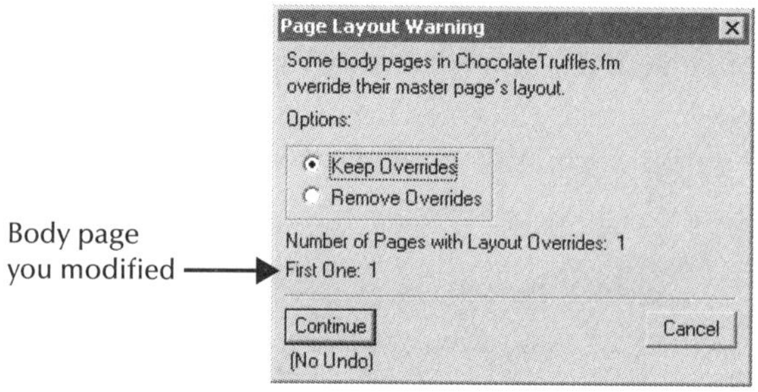

Figure 10-2. Removing page layout overrides

2. Click the Remove Overrides radio button, then click the Continue button. The page layout overrides are removed.

CAUTION Before updating master pages, make sure that the change you want is correct for all the master pages in the flow. For example, make sure the master pages that will be changed are using symmetrical layouts; if they are not and you make this change, you might get unintended results.

Updating Master Pages and Body Pages Simultaneously

To update default master pages and body pages in the same flow all at once, follow these steps:

1. Display either the master pages or the body pages.
2. Select Format➤Page Layout➤Column Layout.

   If the left and right master pages have different layouts, a warning is displayed. Click the OK button.

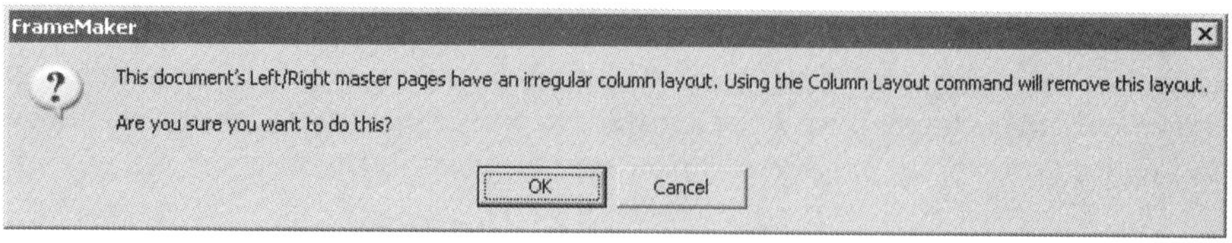

The Column Layout dialog box is displayed.

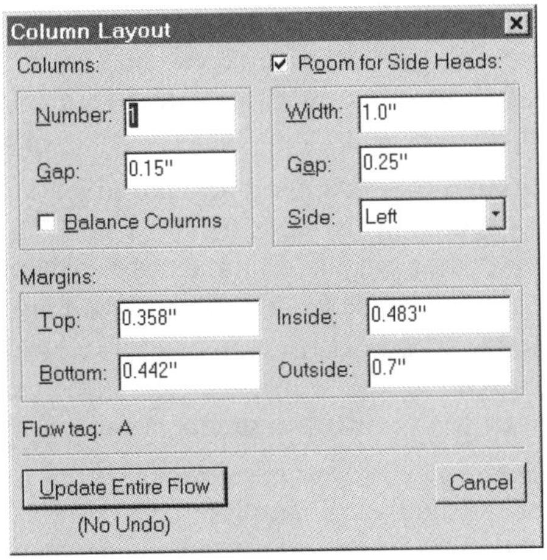

3. Change the settings you want to update. For example, to remove the side head area, uncheck the Room for Side Heads check box.
4. Click the Update Entire Flow button. The master page and body page layouts are updated.

NOTE Only the default master pages are updated. You'll need to update custom master pages individually.

Updating One Master Page

To update the master page applied to the current body page, follow these steps:

1. Display the customized body page, then select Format➤Page Layout➤Update Column Layout. The Update Column Layout dialog box is displayed.

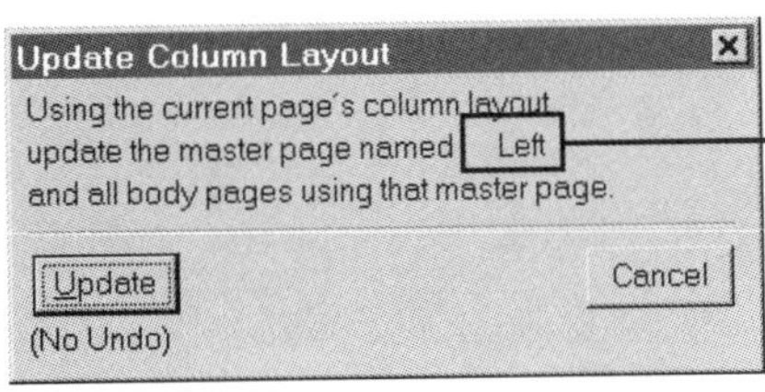

The master page applied to the current page

2. Click the Update button. The master page applied to the current body page is updated.

CONTROLLING PAGE LAYOUT

Deleting Master Pages

Although you can delete several body pages at once, you must delete master pages individually. You can delete only the master pages you create; the default master pages (Left and Right in a double-sided document and Right in a single-sided document) cannot be removed.

Before you delete a master page that has been applied to a body page, you must apply another master page to all pages that use that master page. FrameMaker warns if the master page is in use, so there's no way to delete a master page you've applied to a body page. See "Assigning Master Pages to Body Pages" on page 241 for details.

To delete a master page, follow these steps:

1. Display the master page you want to delete.
2. Select Special➤Delete Page "*master page name.*" If the master page is applied to a body page, an error is displayed. You'll need to display the body page, apply a different master page in its place, and then repeat this procedure.

Error shows which page the master page is applied to.

3. On the confirmation dialog box, click the OK button. The master page is no longer in the document.

CHAPTER 11

Understanding Text Flows

In FrameMaker, you create page layouts by placing text frames and graphics on pages. Content on the body pages flows through the document according to the structure of the frames on the master pages. For example, if you create a two-column text frame on the master page, the text on a body page based on that master page is displayed in two columns.

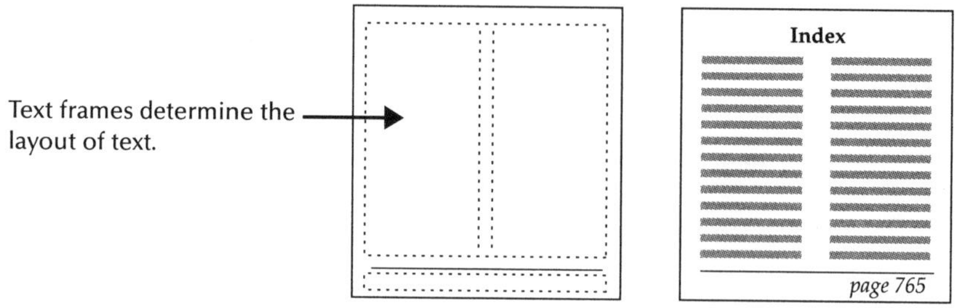

NOTE You can also create new text frames on the body pages, but text inside them does not flow from frame to frame.

Most text frames are associated with *flow tags*. Flow tags control how text fills the frames; in other words, how the frames are connected. If frames are set to *autoconnect*, when the first text frame in flow A gets full, FrameMaker generates a new page. This means you don't need to insert new pages manually.

You can define more than one flow in a document to create custom layouts, and text in each flow is displayed independently throughout the document. Take, for example, a newsletter in which the front-page article continues on page three. For this layout, you create a text flow that begins on page one and continues on page three. The article will flow automatically through from page one to page three, skipping page two, which is in another flow.

Understanding Text Flows

You define text flows on the master pages by drawing text frames and assigning a flow tag. (For information about creating master pages, see Chapter 10, "Understanding Master Pages.") By default, your documents have only one flow tag—A. As you type text, FrameMaker automatically adds new pages and allows the text to flow onto those pages. A symbol marks the end of the flow.

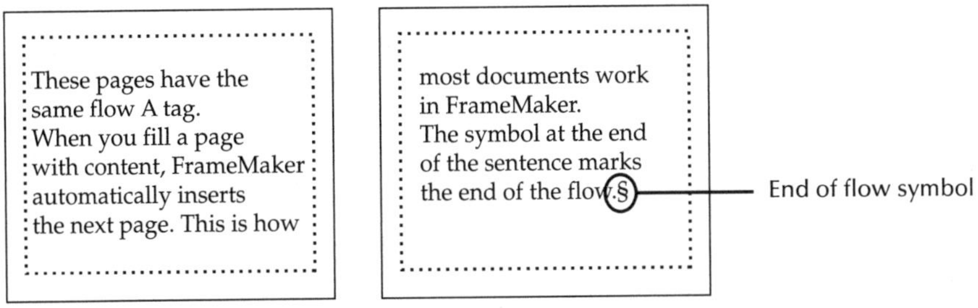

The document shown in the following example has two text flows. The text with flow tag A goes into the A columns, and the B text flow goes into the B columns. One common use for multiple flows is in creating newsletters. You can easily "jump" a story from the front page to an inside page by creating custom text flows and connecting them.

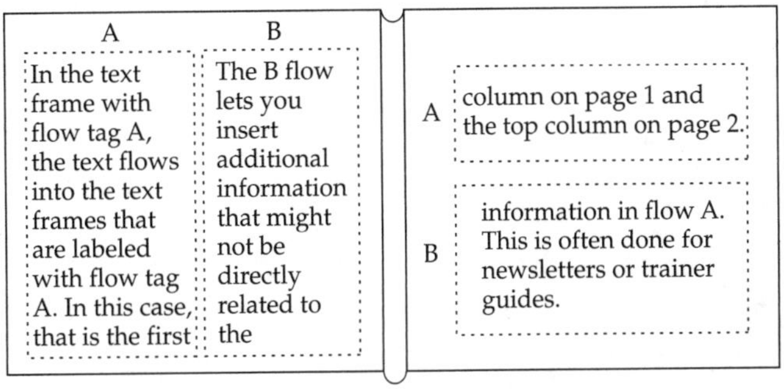

The flow tag for a text frame is displayed in the status bar next to the paragraph tag name. For example, the First master page displayed in the following example is in Flow A.

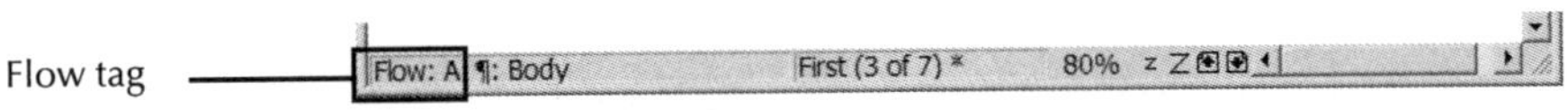

NOTE Reference pages also have text flows. These special flows help generate the index, table of contents, list of tables, and list of figures. They also contain master page mappings, graphics, and so on. See Chapter 17, "Creating Other Generated Files," for details.

Understanding Text Frame Properties

The characteristics of each text frame in a document are displayed in the text frame properties. You select the frame and select Graphic➤Object Properties to display the properties. (You can select Format➤Customize Page Layout➤Customize Text Frame to display the same properties, but using the Graphics menu is quicker.) You can modify the flow tag, text frame size, side head space, columns, and other items in the text frame properties, shown in Figure 11-1 on page 274.

If you change the text frame properties on a body page, only the selected text frame is modified. On the master page, editing a text frame updates all body pages that use that master page.

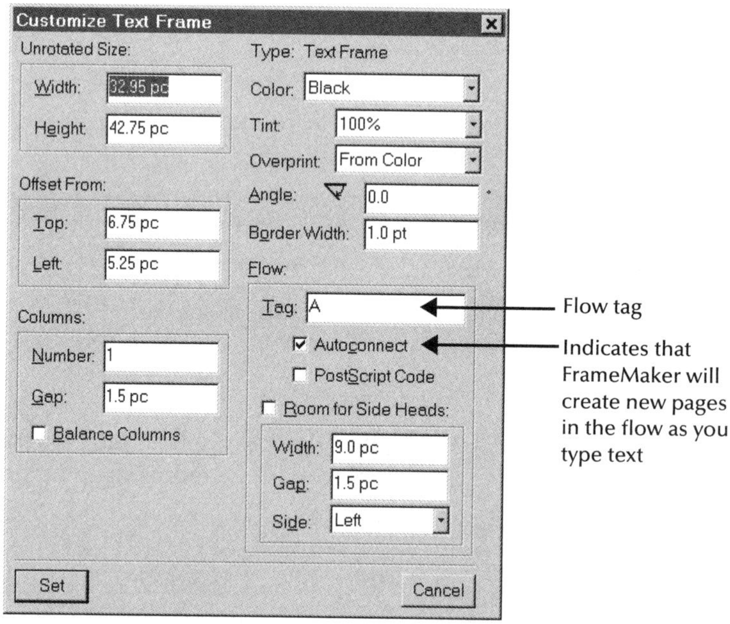

Figure 11-1. Modifying text frame properties

Table 11-1 describes the text frame properties. You can modify many graphic-related aspects, such as setting the color, tint, and border, in the Tools palette; therefore, you might prefer to set the color, tint, overprint, and other settings in that palette. For details, see "Drawing Basic Shapes" on page 338.

Property	Description
Unrotated Size	Sets the width and height of the text frame. If the text frame is rotated on the master page, the dimensions displayed are the opposite of those you see on the page.
Offset From	Indicates the space between the text frame and the top and left edges of the page or graphic frame.
Columns	Divides the text frame into equal columns and defines the space between columns. Check the Balance Columns check box to make text end on or near the same horizontal axis in all columns.
Color	Assigns a color for the fill and pen (or outline) pattern. You must select the fill and pen *style* (for example, crosshatch or solid) in the Tools palette.
Tint	Lightens the text frame color by a specific percentage. You select from 0–100 percent in 5 percent increments, or you can type another percentage in that range. For the tint to be displayed, you must select the fill style in the Tools palette.
Overprint	For four-color process printing, indicates how FrameMaker prints the colors of an overlapping text frame and object. ■ **Knock Out:** FrameMaker does not print the overlapped portion of the text frame and object. ■ **Overprint:** FrameMaker prints the overlapped portion. ■ **From Color:** FrameMaker uses the Knock Out or Overprint setting from the color definition.
Angle	Indicates the number of degrees the text frame is rotated.

Table 11-1. Text Frame Properties

Property	Description
Border Width	Specifies a border between .015 and 360 points. You must select the border (or pen) style in the Tools palette.
Flow	Associates a flow tag with the text frame and specifies the flow properties. Options are as follows: ■ **Tag:** Name of the flow tag. ■ **Autoconnect:** Indicates whether FrameMaker adds new pages to the flow automatically. If turned off, you have to add a page manually as the page fills with content and connect it with the previous page. Body flows usually use flow tag A and have the Autoconnect option selected. ■ **PostScript Code:** Indicates that the text frame contains code that a PostScript printer processes; for example, commands to create watermarks in PDF files, print an image, or print a document in landscape orientation. Embedding PostScript code is an alternative to physically altering the page. You can use PostScript code frames to embed pdfmark commands, which Acrobat can interpret. ■ **Room for Side Heads:** Creates a side head area, for which you specify the width, the gap between the side head area and in-column content, and the side head location. See "Creating Room for Side Heads" on page 285 for more information about setting up side heads.

Table 11-1. Text Frame Properties (Continued)

Adding Text Flows to Master Pages

On master pages, text frames provide layout for foreground and background items. Text frames for foreground items have an associated flow tag, identifying which text frames are related. Any content placed in text frames for foreground items is not displayed on the body pages; you provide the content on the body pages themselves. Text frames for background items, such as headers and footers, have no flow tag. Text placed in these frames on master pages is displayed on body pages. However, the text cannot be edited on body pages.

When you draw a text frame on the master page, you connect it to an existing flow on the page, or you assign a new flow tag. If the text frame is connected to an existing flow, text on the body page will flow into the new text frame. If you create a new flow, existing text will not be displayed in the new flow; you need to type new text on the body page. See "Connecting Text Flows" on page 282 for more information.

Some text frames on the master page aren't part of a flow. For example, the header and footer text frames, which contain repeated information, are considered background items. They don't need flow tags because they're not connected and don't create additional pages for content as foreground text frames do.

To draw a text frame on the master page, follow these steps:

1. Select View➤Master Pages to display the master pages, then page up or down to find the page you want to modify.

2. Select Graphics➤Tools to display the Tools palette, then click the Text Frame icon.
3. Click and drag the cursor across the page to draw a text frame. (To draw a square, press SHIFT while you draw the frame.) The Add New Text Frame dialog box is displayed.

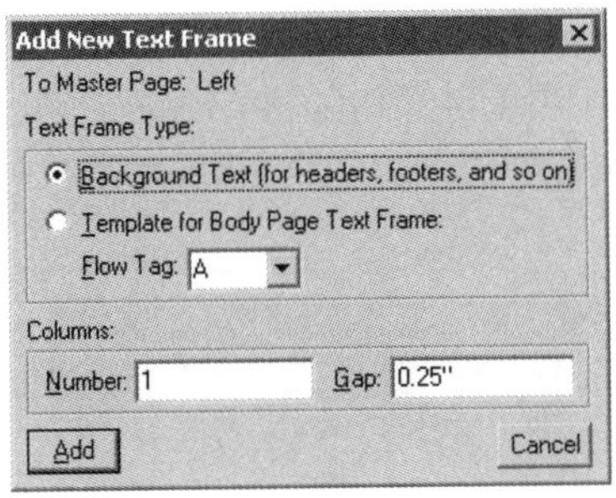

4. Do one of the following:
   - To create background text, click the Background Text radio button.
   - To create a frame for the body page, click the Template for Body Page Text Frame radio button and assign a flow tag. Although flow A is appropriate for most text frames, you can type another tag name in the Flow Tag field or change the tag later if the text frame belongs in a new flow.
5. *(optional)* To create a multicolumn text frame, type the number of columns in the Number field, then type the measurement between the columns in the Gap field. See "Adding Columns" on page 290 for more information.
6. Click the Add button. The new text frame is displayed.
7. When changes are complete, select View➤Body Pages. Your changes are displayed on the page formatted by the modified master page.

If you want to change the dimensions of the text frame, you can resize the text frame manually, using the FrameMaker rulers as a guide. (Unlike programs such as InDesign, FrameMaker does not let you drag guides from the top or side of the window to help you align objects.) You can also edit the text frame properties to assign precise dimensions. For details, see "Understanding Text Flows" on page 272.

If the document has multiple flows, text frames within each flow are connected. You create a new flow by creating the text frame first and then changing the assigned flow tag. For details, see "Changing the Flow Tag" on page 299.

Drawing Text Frames on the Body Page

Text frames added to the body pages don't belong to a flow. You can connect the text frames to a flow later, and content will fill the first frame and then flow to the second frame. If you want to reuse the layout on another page, however, you should modify the master page instead of the body page.

TIP One common use of text frames on the body page is to contain callouts for graphics in anchored frames.

To draw a text frame on the body page, follow these steps:

1. Display the body page you want to modify.

2. Select Graphics➤Tools to display the Tools palette, then click the Text Frame icon.
3. Drag the cursor across the page to draw a text frame. (To draw a square, press SHIFT while you draw the frame.) The Create New Text Frame dialog box is displayed.

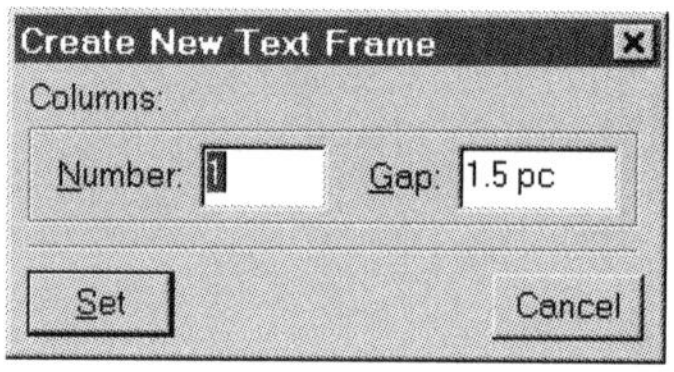

4. Type the number of columns. For multiple columns, type the space between each column in the Gap field.

NOTE In FrameMaker, you can specify the unit of measure used throughout the document—in paragraph tags, text frame properties, table tags, and so on. To change the unit of measure, select View➤Options and click a different item in the Display Unit drop-down list.

5. Click the Set button. The text frame is displayed on the page. You can position the cursor in the frame, add content, apply a paragraph tag, and modify other properties discussed in this chapter.

Selecting Text Frames

You select a text frame by CTRL-clicking the edge of the frame. Handles are displayed on the edge of the frame, indicating that the text frame is selected. You can also select objects with the Object Pointer in the Tools palette, but you'll need to select the Smart Select pointer button again to type text.

There are three ways to select several frames:

- Drag the cursor across the frames as if you're drawing a box. An outline is displayed around the frames as you hold down the mouse button. When you take your finger off the mouse button, the outline disappears, and the frames are selected.

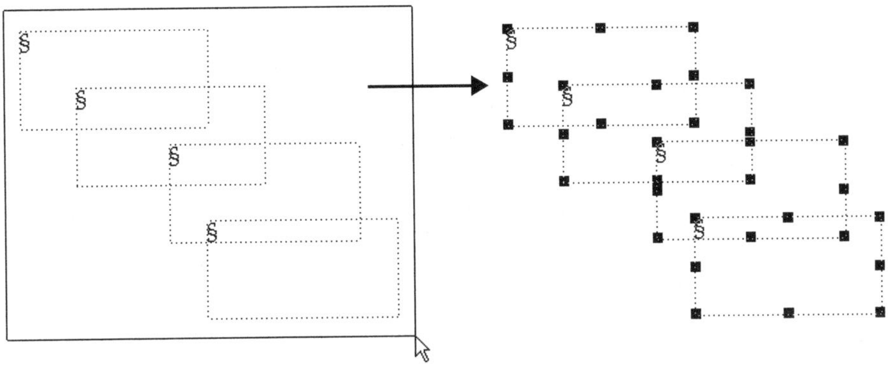

- CTRL-click the first frame, then the second frame, and so on.
- Click outside the main text frame and press CTRL-A. This selects all objects on the page, and you can CTRL-click the objects you don't want selected. Typically, you use this option if the text frames are in an anchored frame or on a page with few objects. (If your cursor is inside the text frame when you press CTRL-A, the text in the flow is highlighted instead.)

Resizing Text Frames

When you resize text frames on the master pages, the body pages formatted by those master pages are updated, and text reflows to fit the new frames. On the body page, you can resize a specific text frame, and only that body page is updated; the text frame on the master page remains unchanged. For example, you can force a line of text or a particular paragraph to move to the next page by resizing the text frame until the text is displayed on the next page.

NOTE Adjusting a text frame on the body page (instead of on the master page) creates an override. You'll get an error message when switching from the master page to body page, but you can click the Keep Overrides radio button to preserve your changes. Generally, you should avoid overrides. Adjusting text frames to copyfit text, however, may be necessary during final document production. See "Removing Master Page Overrides" on page 263 for more information.

There are two ways to resize a text frame. You can select the text frame and then drag the handles, or you can change the dimensions in the text frame properties. Typically, you manually resize text frames when copyfitting a page or modifying simple items, such as figure callouts. If you need to place the text frame at a specific location on the page, you modify the height and width in the text frame properties.

To resize a text frame manually, follow these steps:

1. Display the body page or master page containing the text frame you want to modify, then select the frame. The handles are displayed on the edges of the text frame.
2. Do one of the following to resize the frame:
   - To change the height, drag one of the middle handles on the top or bottom edge.
   - To change the width, drag one of the middle handles on the left or right edge.
   - To change the width and height at the same time, drag a corner handle.

   You can use the FrameMaker ruler or the dimensions in the left corner of the status bar as a guide. As you drag the edge of the text frame, FrameMaker updates the dimensions displayed in the status bar, and the ruler marking moves.

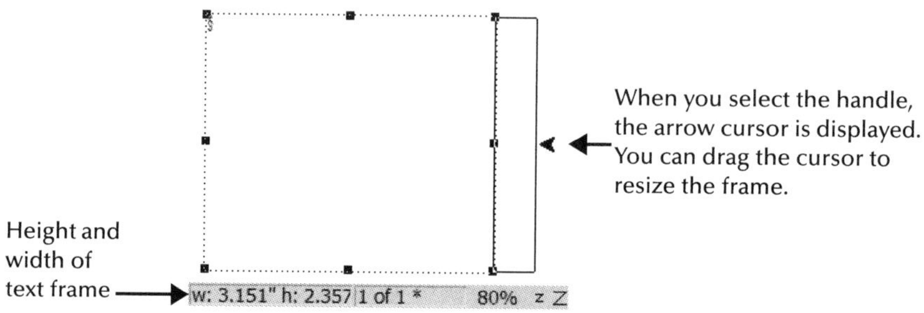

To modify the height and width of the text frame in the text frame properties, follow these steps:

1. Display the body page or master page containing the text frame you want to modify, then select the frame. The handles are displayed on the edges of the text frame.
2. Select Graphics➤Object Properties to display the text frame properties (Figure 11-1 on page 274), then change the measurements in the Height and Width fields.
3. Click the Set button. The text frame is resized.

   Notice that the top and left offset don't change when you modify the height and width of the text frame. For example, after the following text frame is resized, the left and top offsets are both still 0.5 inches.

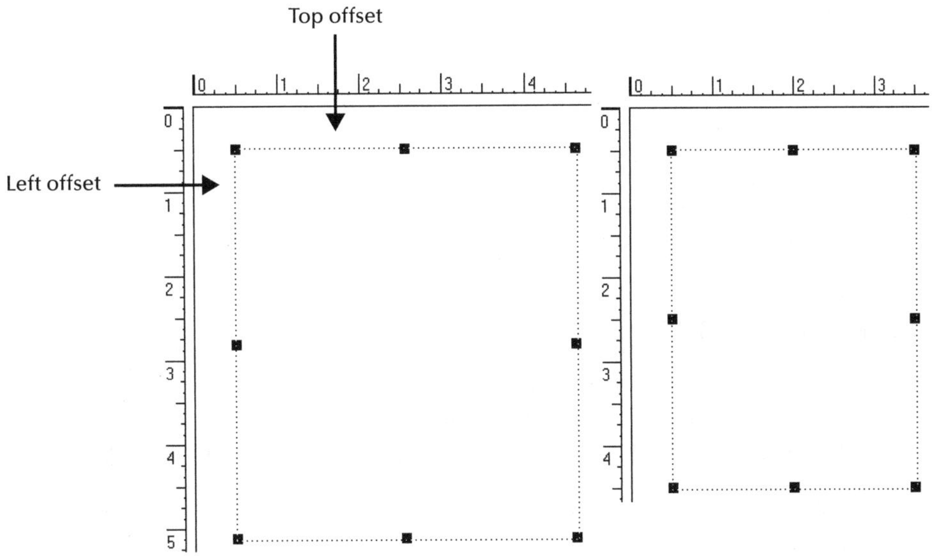

Moving and Copying Text Frames

You move and copy a text frame by dragging it on the page. To move the frame, CTRL-click the edge of the text frame and then drag and drop the frame. To copy the frame, select the frame and press CTRL while you drag and drop the frame. Alternatively, you can copy and paste a text frame, but the new frame is displayed on top of the original frame, making the new frame difficult to see.

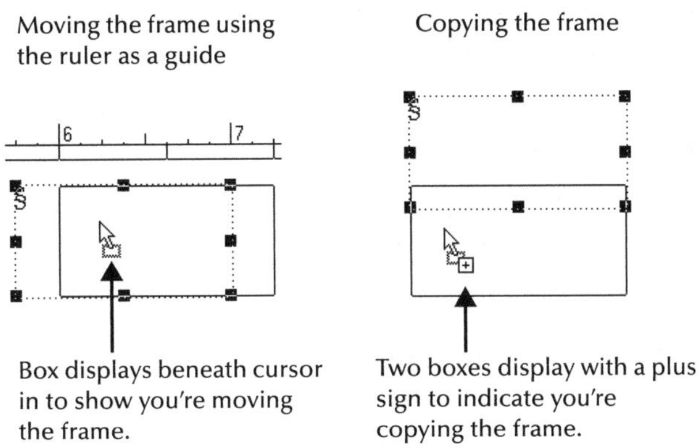

NOTE Don't select the text frame handles when you move or copy a text frame by dragging. The handles are for resizing the frame. If you try to drag the handle, you'll resize the text frame.

With FrameMaker's snap feature turned on, the edge of the text frame moves to the nearest imaginary line in the snap grid (see "Working with Grids" on page 343). In the preceding example, the text frame snapped to the 6-inch ruler marking. If you turn snap off, you can move the text frame between grid lines. For details, see "Working with Grids" on page 343.

To move a text frame to a specific place on the page, you edit the top and left offset in the text frame properties. For some text frames, such as a callout, it's easier to drag the frame where you need it.

Deleting Text Frames

After you select one or more text frames, you can delete the frames by pressing the DELETE key or selecting Edit➤Clear. If the frame you are trying to delete is autoconnected to another frame, the content of the deleted frame moves into the next frame in the connected sequence, and FrameMaker warns you that a new page may be generated to hold the displaced content. If the frame is not autoconnected, deleting the frame also deletes any content it contains.

Customizing Text Flows

You can customize text flows by adding columns, setting side head space on body pages, splitting text frames to create multiple flows, and disconnecting flows. When you modify a flow on the master page, text on the body pages formatted by that master page reflows into the new layout. You can also fine-tune the display of text in columns by balancing columns, feathering text across columns, and aligning baselines. These fine-tuning features come in handy for formatting documents such as newsletters. The following sections describe how to use these methods.

Connecting Text Flows

A master page can have text frames that are in different flows. The text frames either have different flow tags, or one of them may have no flow tag. You can connect text frames to put them in the same flow. To connect more than one frame, you must connect the first text frame you want in the flow to the second frame, then connect the second frame to the third frame, and so on.

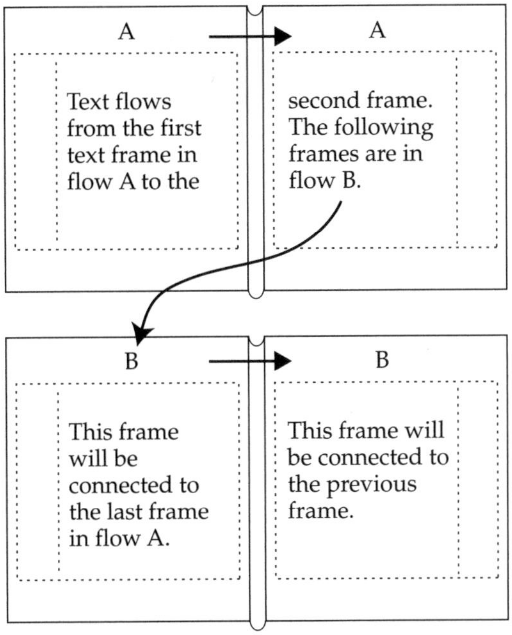

When you run out of room for text in an untagged frame, text disappears below a line, and the end of flow symbol is not displayed, as shown in the next illustration. If the text frame is not autoconnected to a flow, then a solid line is displayed at the bottom of the text frame when there is more text in the text frame than it can show.

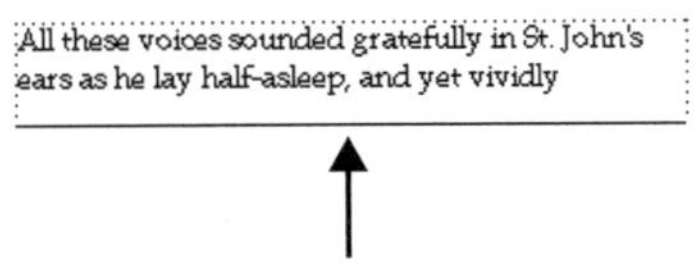

Line indicates hidden text.

In the example, the line on the bottom edge of the frame indicates that the frame should be resized to make room for the hidden text. To find out what's in the same flow, position the cursor in the top frame, and select Edit➤Select All in Flow. All content in the current flow is highlighted.

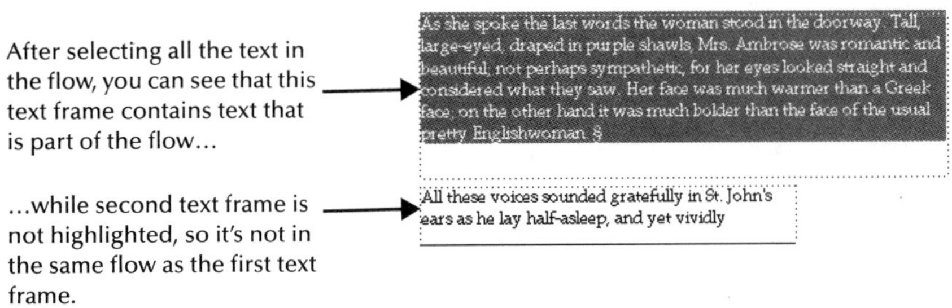

A disconnected flow can be connected to a flow that extends over more than one page. For example, suppose flow A in the next illustration is displayed on pages 1 and 2, and the disconnected flow is last on page 1. When you connect the disconnected flow to flow A, the autoconnect feature is turned off throughout flow A. This means that FrameMaker doesn't generate new pages when the existing frames fill with content. After you connect the frames, you need to turn on autoconnect in the first text frame in the flow.

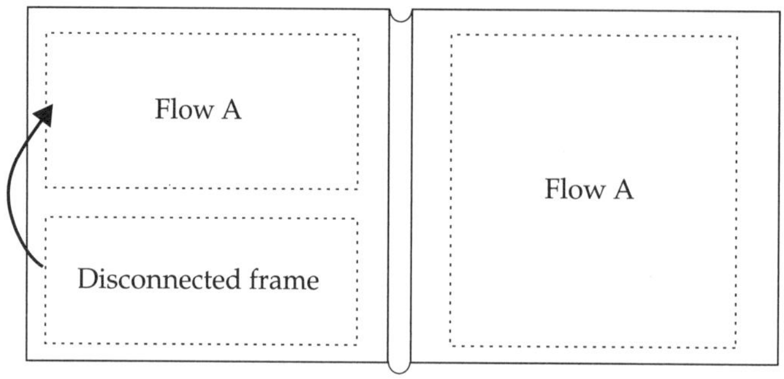

To connect text flows, follow these steps:

1. Display the master page or body page containing the flow you want to modify.
2. Select the first frame you want in the flow, then select the second frame. If the frames are on different pages, the frames aren't displayed as selected at the same time, but FrameMaker remembers which frame you selected first and makes it the first in the flow.
3. Select Format➤Customize Layout➤Connect Text Frames. One of the following occurs:
   - If you're connecting an untagged flow to a tagged flow, FrameMaker connects the frames.
   - If you're connecting two different flows, a confirmation dialog box is displayed. Click the OK button to connect the frames.
   - If one of the frames isn't visible—for example, it's on a page that's not displayed—a confirmation dialog box is displayed. Click the OK button to connect the frames.

TIP Reapply the master page to return the page layout to its original design. Text is displayed according to the master page layout; it will not be deleted.

Creating Room for Side Heads

A side head area provides an area of white space on the side of your document. You set up side head space for a flow, and the side head is displayed on all body pages in that flow.

The side head space may be on the left side, right side, side closer to binding, or side farther from binding. Figure 11-2 shows the four side head positions.

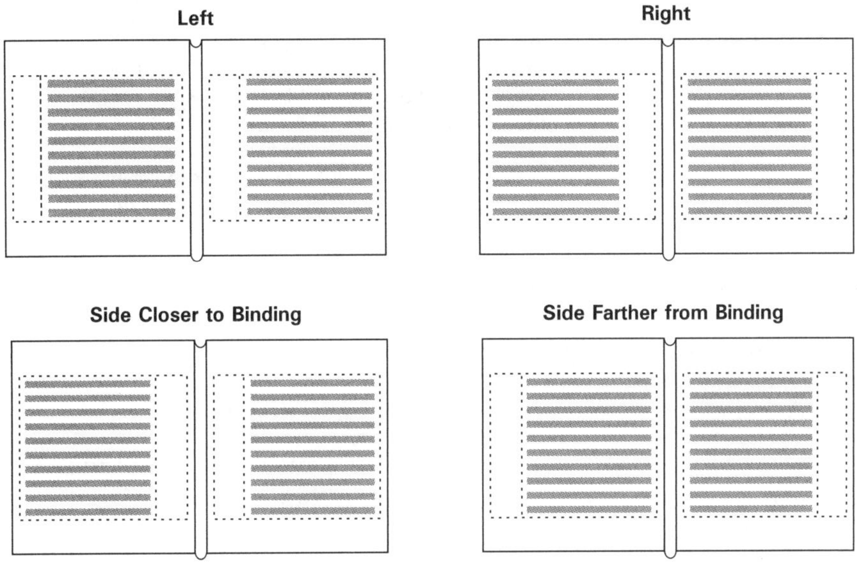

Figure 11-2. Positioning side head space

After you set up side head space, you can create tags for paragraphs that stay within the main column, stay within the side head, or flow from the main column into the side head space. Figure 11-3 on page 286 shows examples of the three types. For more information on changing the pagination settings in a paragraph tag, see "Pagination Sheet" on page 119.

In Column. The paragraphs do not use the side head area on the left.

Side Head. The black paragraph is set as a side head. It flows in the side head area.

Across All Columns and Side Heads. The black paragraph is set across all columns and side heads. It flows across the main column and the side head area.

Figure 11-3. Side head paragraph tag options

In Figure 11-4, the headings paginate across the side head space and the main column. The side head borders are displayed only for paragraphs other than side heads, and when the document borders are turned off, you won't see any borders.

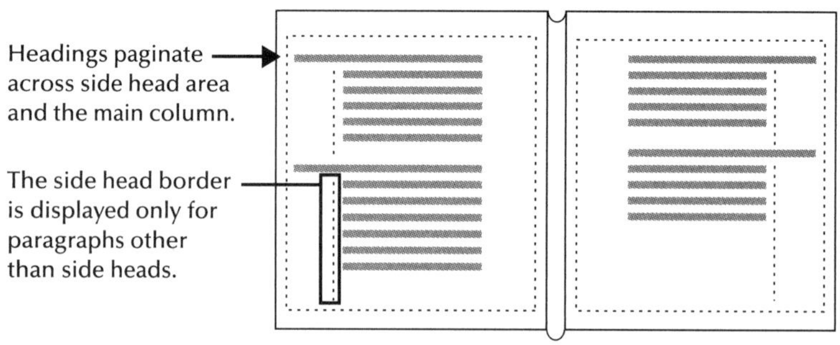

Figure 11-4. Headings across the side head space and main column

Creating Side Heads for Regular Page Layouts

If your pages use text frames that are the same size and have the same number of columns, your document has regular page layouts. If your document has irregular page layouts, follow the procedure in "Creating Side Heads for Irregular Page Layouts" on page 288.

To create space for side heads in a document or template that has regular page layouts (which means the text frames on all pages are the same width and have the same number of columns), follow these steps:

1. Back up your file. Side heads can be tricky, and you can't undo your changes.
2. On either a body or master page, position your cursor anywhere within the text flow.
3. Select Format➤Page Layout➤Column Layout. The Column Layout dialog box is displayed.

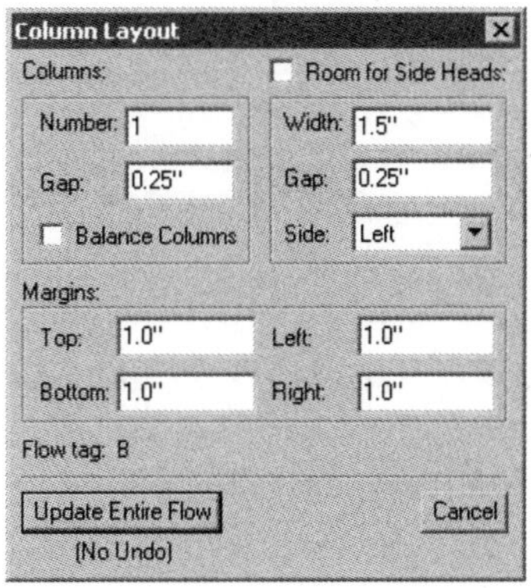

Figure 11-5. Column Layout dialog box

4. Check the Room for Side Heads check box.
5. In the Width field, type the width of the side head area.
6. In the Gap field, type the width between the side head area and the main text.

CAUTION If your document has irregular column layouts, FrameMaker displays the following message:

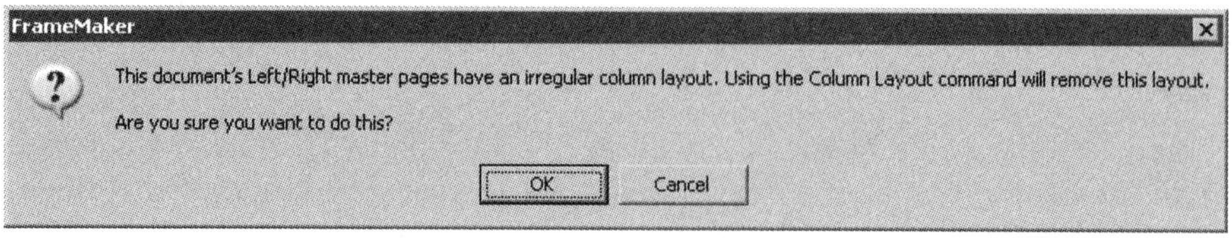

If don't want FrameMaker to change the layouts of other pages, click the Cancel button. Follow the procedure in "Creating Side Heads for Irregular Page Layouts" on page 288.

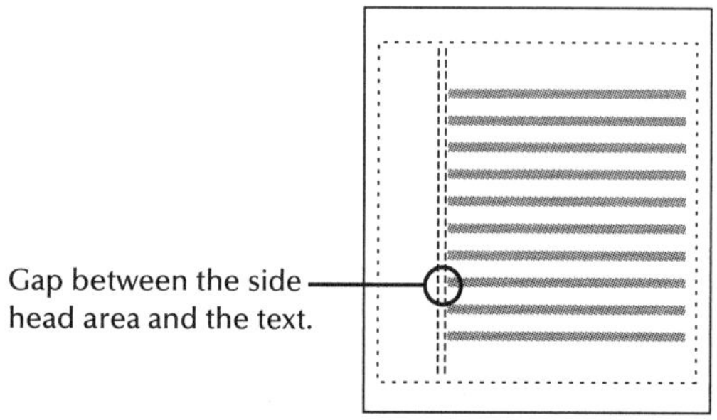

7. In the Side drop-down list, click the location of the side head (Figure 11-2 on page 285):
   - **Left:** Places the side head area on the left side of the page.
   - **Right:** Places the side head area on the right side of the page.
   - **Side Closer to Binding:** Alternates the side head area in a double-sided document. On a left page, the side head area is on the right side of the page. On a right page, the side head area is on the left side of the page.
   - **Side Farther from Binding:** Alternates the side head area in a double-sided document. On a left page, the side head area is on the left side of the page. On a right page, the side head area is on the right side of the page.
8. Click the Update Entire Flow button. Side heads are added to all pages within the flow.

Creating Side Heads for Irregular Page Layouts

If your document or template has pages with irregular page layouts (for example, some pages have one column while others have two, or some pages have narrower columns), follow these steps to add room for side heads without changing the size of the text frame or number of columns on other pages:

1. Back up your file.
2. View a body page.
3. Select the text frame, then select Graphics➤Object Properties. The Customize Text Frame dialog box is displayed.

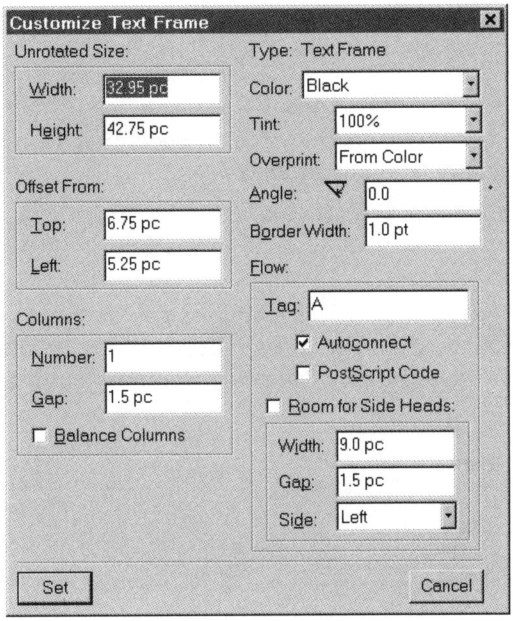

4. In the Flow section, check the Room for Side Heads check box.

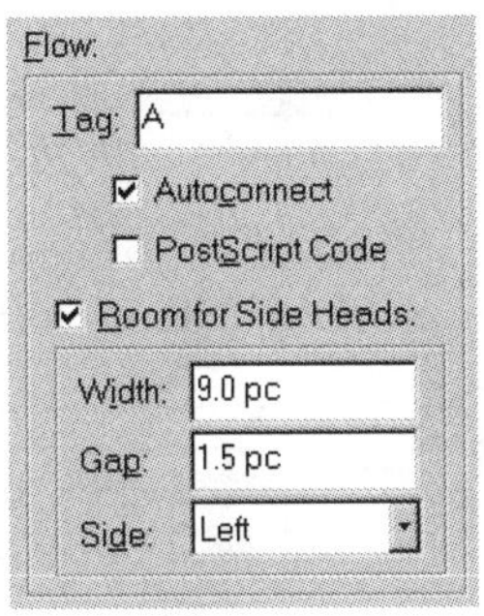

5. Follow step 5 through step 7 on page 287 to define the side head.
6. Click the Set button.
7. View the master pages.
8. Repeat this procedure to customize the text frame on all of the master pages containing the flow.

NOTE You can change the size of the side head area on the different master pages in the flow, but you cannot have some master pages in the flow that have a side head area and others that don't.

9. View the body pages. Side head changes may not be displayed on the body pages until you reapply the master pages. Select Format➤Page Layout➤Master Page Usage and reapply the master pages.

TIP If side head area is not displaying as you expect in a document, reapplying the master pages usually fixes the problem.

Adding Columns

You can add columns to a text flow and specify the gap between each column. The columns may be balanced so that text ends on or near the same line across all columns on the page. For details, see "Balancing Columns" on page 292.

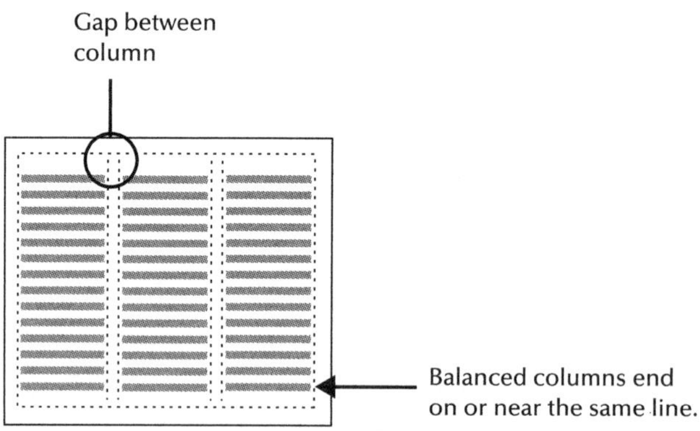

In a document with columns, you must set up paragraph tags to run across columns (such as headers) or to stay in column. See "Pagination Sheet" on page 119 for details.

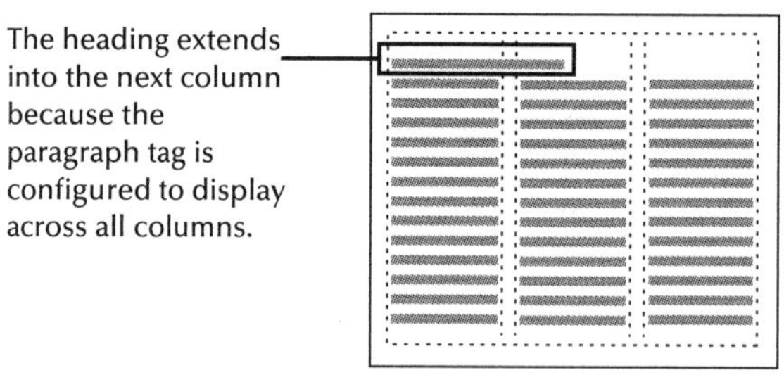

To create columns, follow these steps:

1. On either a body or master page, position your cursor anywhere within the text flow.
2. Select Format➤Page Layout➤Update Column Layout. The Column Layout dialog box is displayed (Figure 11-5 on page 287).
3. In the Columns section, type the number of columns. If you try to set the number of columns to a large number, FrameMaker might warn you that the columns will be too narrow, and if that is the case, it will not change the setting.

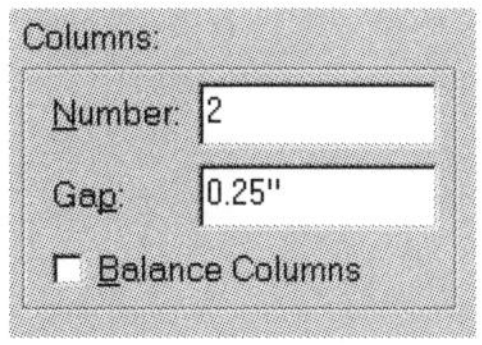

4. In the Gap field, type the space between the columns.
5. Check the Balance Columns check box for the text in all columns to end near the same horizontal line.

TIP If you set up balanced columns on the master page, all pages formatted by the master page are affected. This gives you less control over layout on specific pages, and the results can be unattractive. Instead of balancing columns on the master page, consider balancing columns only on specific body pages. See "Balancing Columns" on page 292 for more information.

6. Click the Update Entire Flow button. The master page and body pages formatted by the master page are updated.

Aligning Text Across Columns

There are three ways to align text across columns:

- **Balancing columns.** Moves the baseline of each column on the page so that text ends on or near the same horizontal axis. Does not change the amount of space between lines of text.
- **Feathering text.** Adds space between lines of text and paragraphs so that text in a column ends near the baseline. You set the maximum amount of space.
- **Synchronizing baselines.** Lines up text across columns. You specify the line spacing of the paragraphs you want to align, and you can limit how headings are aligned at the top of columns.

Though you can set up balanced columns, feathered text, and synchronized baselines on the master pages, you usually align text to copyfit specific body pages.

Balancing Columns

To balance text across columns, FrameMaker changes the line breaks so that the baseline in each column is on or near the same line. By balancing columns on a specific body page, you modify only the selected page.

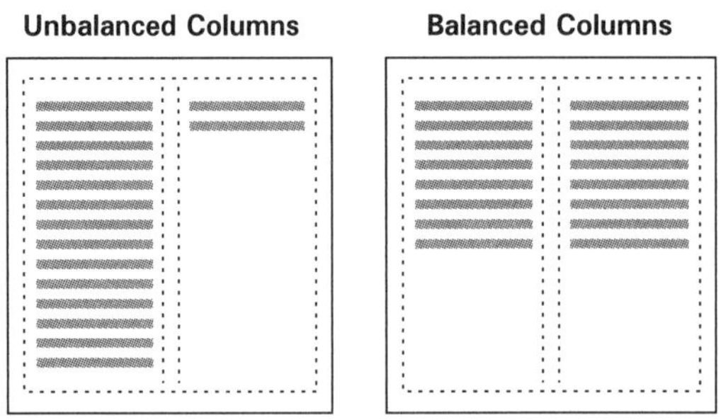

To balance columns on a body page, follow these steps:

1. Display the body page you want to modify, then select the text frame.
2. Select Graphics➤Object Properties. The Customize Text Frame dialog box is displayed (Figure 11-1 on page 274).
3. Check the Balance Columns check box, then click the Set button. Text on the body page reflows to balance across both columns.

Feathering Text

When you feather text, FrameMaker adds space, or padding, between lines of text and paragraphs to fill each page in the flow with text. You specify the maximum amount of space FrameMaker can add. There are two types of padding:

- **Interline:** FrameMaker changes the amount of line spacing on the page.
- **Interparagraph:** FrameMaker adjusts the space above and below paragraphs.

Feathering overrides the line spacing and space above and below settings from the paragraph tags. You might find feathering helpful or necessary when copyfitting pages.

In Figure 11-6, the original unfeathered page is at the top. The bottom-left page shows interline padding. The bottom-right page shows interparagraph padding. Notice that adding space between lines creates more even spacing than adding space between paragraphs. In the last column, the extra padding between the bulleted paragraphs looks awkward.

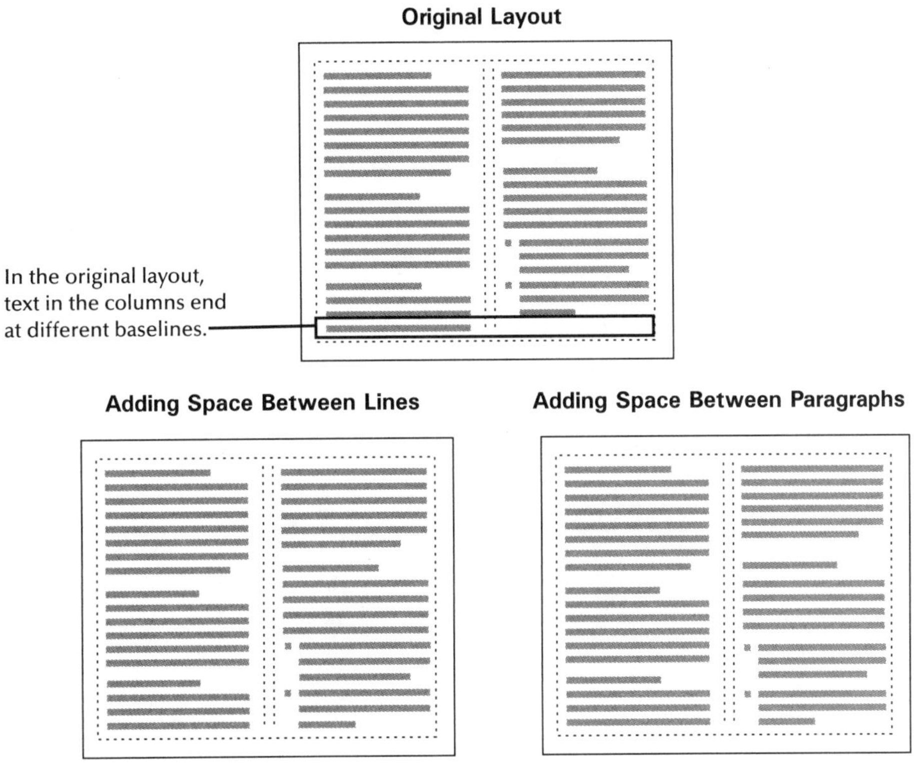

Figure 11-6. Feathering text

CAUTION Unlike balancing columns, which changes only the selected body page, feathering text affects all pages in the selected flow.

You can combine interline and interparagraph padding to get the look you want, but you should add as little space as possible so that paragraph tags control the spacing. It's also best to feather text after you're sure that the line spacing and space above and below settings in the paragraph tags won't change. For example, suppose you configure interline padding and then decrease line spacing in the Body paragraph tag. The text will move up on the page, and you might need to change the interline padding again.

To feather text, follow these steps:

1. Display a body page in the flow you want to modify, then select the text frame.
2. Select Format➤Page Layout➤Line Layout. The Line Layout dialog box is displayed (Figure 11-7).

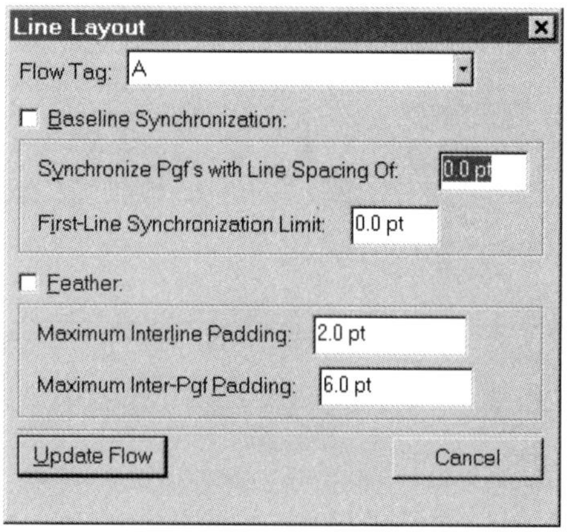

Figure 11-7. Modifying the line layout

3. Check the Feather check box.
4. Do one or both of the following:
   - To add padding between lines, type a value in the Maximum Interline Padding field.
   - To add padding between paragraphs, type a value in the Maximum Inter-Pgf Padding field.

   If you specify a value for both options, FrameMaker feathers the text between paragraphs first and then feathers between lines if necessary.

5. Click the Update Flow button. The spacing in the flow is updated. If the spacing doesn't change on the page, experiment with increasing the padding.

TIP To experiment with settings, turn on feathering, then select Edit➤Undo.

Synchronizing Baselines

To align baselines across columns, you specify the line spacing of the paragraphs you want to align, and FrameMaker snaps the text to an imaginary grid. In the following example, the body paragraphs have 12-point line spacing, so the paragraph synchronization is set to 12 points. Paragraphs that have different line spacing, such as the headings, are not aligned.

You can also limit the alignment of headings when they appear at the top of the column. For example, you might want all headings up to 12 points aligned. The headings are actually displayed above the text column, as shown in the next illustration.

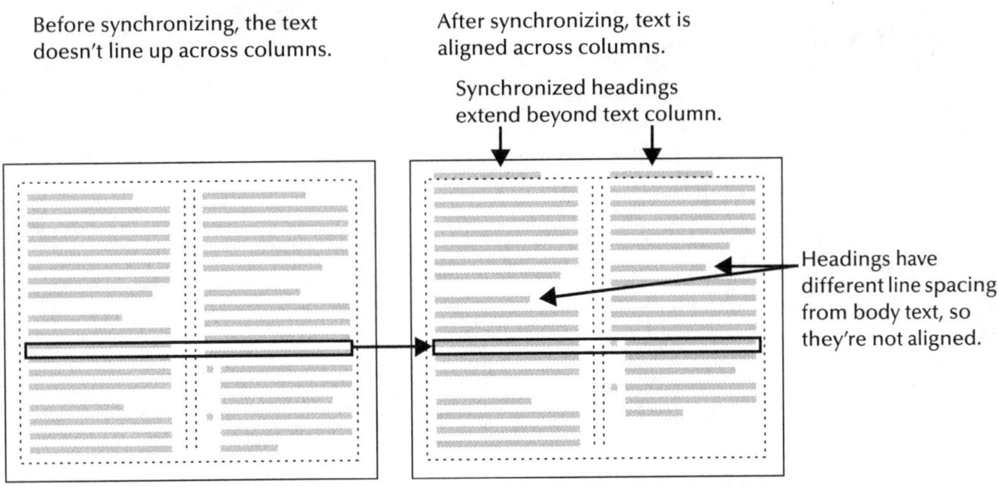

CAUTION Unlike balancing columns, which changes only the selected body page, synchronizing baselines affects all pages in the selected flow.

Synchronizing baselines is most useful when you're working with newsletters or magazine articles because the paragraphs must line up to form a pleasing layout. In technical documentation, you typically don't use this feature unless you're working with a highly customized layout. If you are using the feathering feature, you will need to turn if off for synchronizing to work correctly.

To synchronize baselines, follow these steps:

1. Display a body page in the flow you want to modify, then select the text frame.
2. Select Format➤Page Layout➤Line Layout. The Line Layout dialog box is displayed (Figure 11-7 on page 294).
3. Check the Baseline Synchronization check box.
4. Uncheck Feather if it's checked, or synchronization will not work.
5. Do one or both of the following:
   - To specify the line spacing for paragraphs, type a value in the Synchronize Pgf's with Line Spacing Of field.
   - To specify the limit for synchronizing headings at the top of a column, type the heading size in the First-Line Synchronization Limit field.
6. Click the Update Flow button. The text in the flow is updated.

TIP To compare the synchronized and unsynchronized layouts, turn on synchronization, then select Edit➤Undo.

Splitting Text Frames

You can split a text frame on the master or body pages. Content continues from the first text frame to the second frame because they're in the same flow. The insertion point determines where FrameMaker splits the frame. In the following example, the cursor is at the end of the first paragraph, so the frame is split below that line.

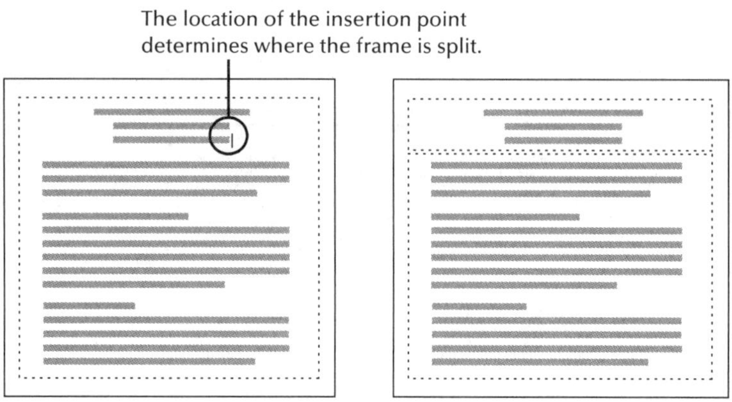

On a page with two text frames, you can make the last text frame the first in the flow by splitting and resizing the top frame and deleting the last frame.

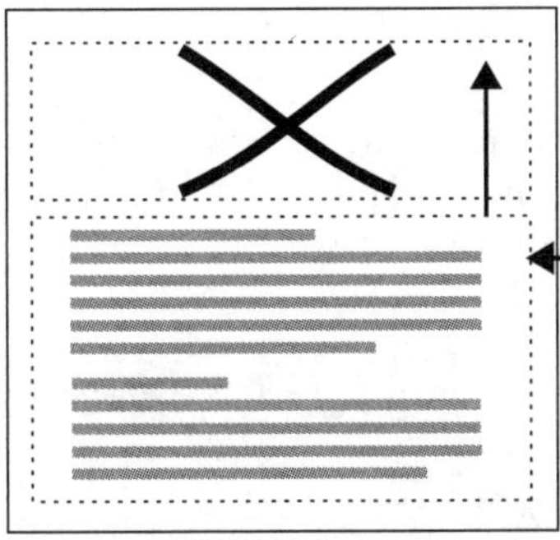

TIP If you split text frames on the body page and decide you don't need the split layout, you can reapply the master page, and the page will be reformatted by the master page.

The position of the insertion point determines the initial size of the split frames. After you split a text frame, you can adjust its dimensions in the text frame properties.

To split a text frame, follow these steps:

1. Display the body or master page you want to modify.
2. Position your cursor in the paragraph above the line where the frame will be split.
3. Select Format➤Customize Layout➤Split Text Frames. The text frame is divided into two frames. You can resize the frames to get the layout you want. See "Resizing Text Frames" on page 279 for details.

Disconnecting Text Frames

You disconnect text frames to separate content from the rest of the document. If the frames are on the same page, FrameMaker converts them to two untagged flows. If the frames are on different pages, the flow tag is preserved but the autoconnect setting is turned off in the frame on the first page. In the second text frame, autoconnect is still on, so FrameMaker adds a new page when the second page is filled.

CAUTION Disconnected text flows are autonumbered within a flow but not across flows.

Existing text remains unchanged when you disconnect text frames. You can cut and paste the text into a different text frame, but when you add new text to the disconnected frame, the text disappears under the bottom edge of the frame. To make room for the text, you can resize the bottom edge of the frame. See "Resizing Text Frames" on page 279 for details.

To find disconnected text frames in a document, place your cursor in a text frame and select Edit➤Select All in Flow. Text in the same flow is highlighted. You might need to decrease the document magnification to 25 percent or 50 percent to see the entire flow.

To disconnect text frames, follow these steps:

1. Display the body page you want to modify, then select one of the text frames you want to disconnect.
2. Select Format➤Customize Layout, then click one of the following in the pop-up menu that is displayed:
   - To disconnect the preceding text frame, select Disconnect Previous.
   - To disconnect the following text frame, select Disconnect Next.
   - To disconnect both text frames on the page, select Disconnect Both.

   One of the following occurs:

   - If the text frames are on the same page, a confirmation dialog box is displayed. Click OK to disconnect the text frames and remove them from the flow.

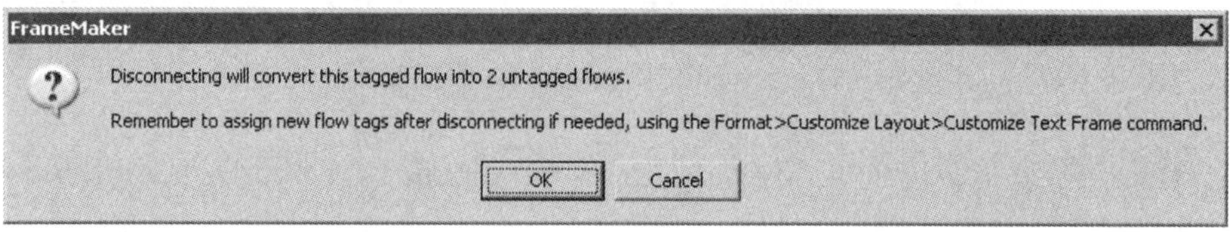

   - If the text frames are on different pages, FrameMaker disconnects the frames without warning and turns off autoconnect on the first disconnected flow.

Changing the Flow Tag

After you create a flow, you can change the flow tag. FrameMaker lets you assign a flow tag to the current frame only or to all frames in the current flow. Text on the body pages will reflow according to your changes.

To change the flow tag, follow these steps:

1. Select View➤Master Pages to display the master pages, then page up or down to find the page you want to modify. (You could also change the flow on body pages, if you needed to.)
2. Select the text frame, then select Graphics➤Object Properties. The Customize Text Frame dialog box is displayed (Figure 11-1 on page 274).
3. In the Tag field, type in a new flow tag.

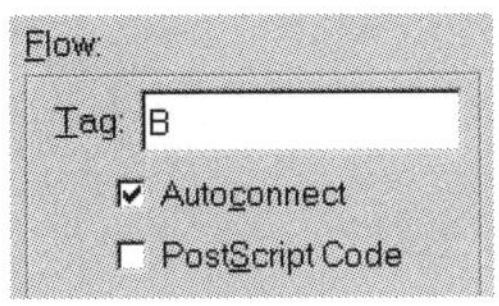

The convention is to use A, B, C, and so on for flow tags, but you can also create meaningful flow tag names. For example, a front-page newsletter article may be in the LeadStory flow and the organizational logo in the Masthead flow. You also want to keep the flow tag name short because a long flow tag name takes up more room in the status bar.

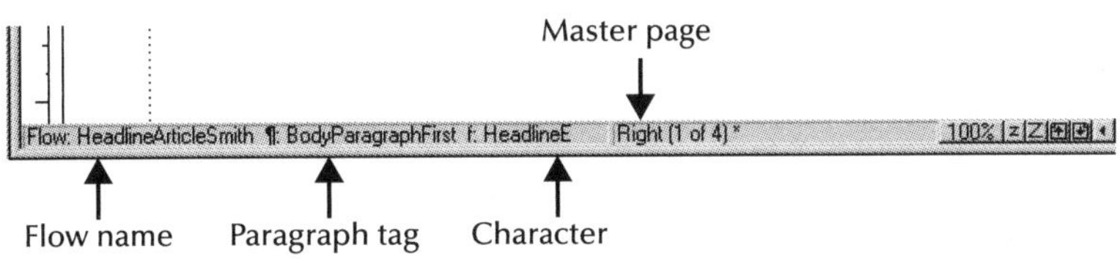

4. If you want FrameMaker to automatically create new pages when necessary, check the Autoconnect check box.
5. Click the Set button. If the text frame previously had no flow tag, the master page is updated, and you can skip the remaining steps. If you're changing the tag assigned to the text frame, the Rename Flow dialog box is displayed.

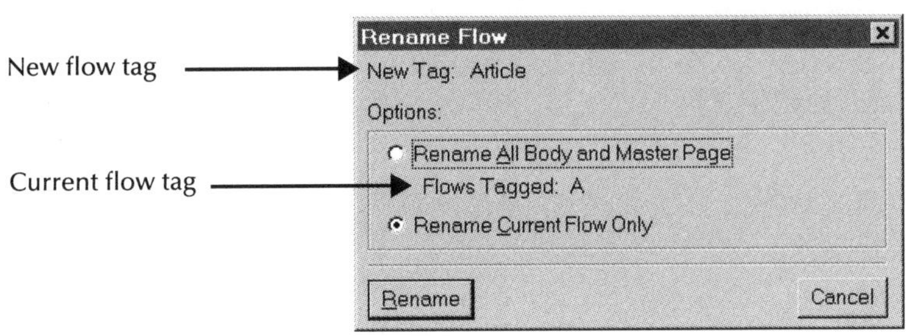

6. Do one of the following:
   - To rename all flows assigned to the current flow tag, click the Rename All Body and Master Page radio button. This doesn't create a new flow; it renames all of the existing flows with the current flow tag.
   - To rename just the current flow, click the Rename Current Flow Only radio button. This creates a new flow in the document.
7. Click the Rename button to rename the text flow.

Switching from Single- to Double-Sided Pages

The template you use to create a new document determines whether the document is single- or double-sided. For a single-sided document, FrameMaker creates a Right master page and applies it to every page. For a double-sided document, FrameMaker creates default Left and Right master pages. The Left master page is applied to the even pages, and the Right master page is applied to the odd pages by default. You can create additional master pages and apply them to create different layouts. See Chapter 10, "Understanding Master Pages," for details.

You may decide to switch a document from single- to double-sided or vice versa. Instead of requiring you to create and apply master pages manually, FrameMaker instantly adjusts the page layouts. For example, when you change a document to double-sided, FrameMaker creates a Left master page and applies it to the even pages. When you switch the document back to single-sided, FrameMaker applies the Right master page to all pages.

You can also control the page count in a document or book. For instance, in a double-sided book, you can force an even page count so that chapters always begin on the right page. FrameMaker can also delete empty pages automatically. This is particularly handy for Portable Document Format (PDF) output if you don't want to convert the empty pages in your FrameMaker book.

NOTE If your document is part of a book file, you need to set the pagination for the entire book because FrameMaker overrides pagination settings in individual files when you generate the book.

To modify pagination properties, follow these steps:

1. Do one of the following:
   - Display the book file, then CTRL-click to highlight each file you want to modify.
   - Display the document you want to modify.
2. Select Format➤Page Layout➤Pagination. The Pagination dialog box is displayed.

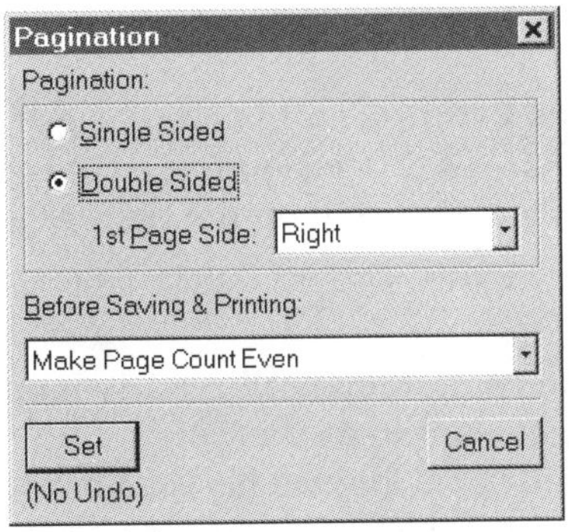

3. Set the pagination. The choices are as follows:
   - **Single-sided:** Makes the document a single-sided document that has a master page called Right and applies it to all pages by default.
   - **Double-sided:** Makes the document a double-sided document that has Left and Right master pages and applies them to the even and odd pages, respectively. You also specify the side of the document's first page:
     - **Right:** The first page is a right page (unless you've applied a custom master page to the first page).
     - **Left:** The first page is a left page (unless you've applied a custom master page to the first page).
     - **Read from File:** Begins document with the page specified in the file. Typically, you don't use this option unless you want to preserve a special layout in one document of the book. Otherwise, it can cause pagination problems.
     - **Next Available:** Begins document with the next available page and deletes the empty pages. As the illustration shows, if Chapter 1 ends on the right page, Chapter 2 will begin on the left page, despite how you've configured the page count settings. (FrameMaker changes the Before Saving & Printing setting to Delete Empty Pages.)

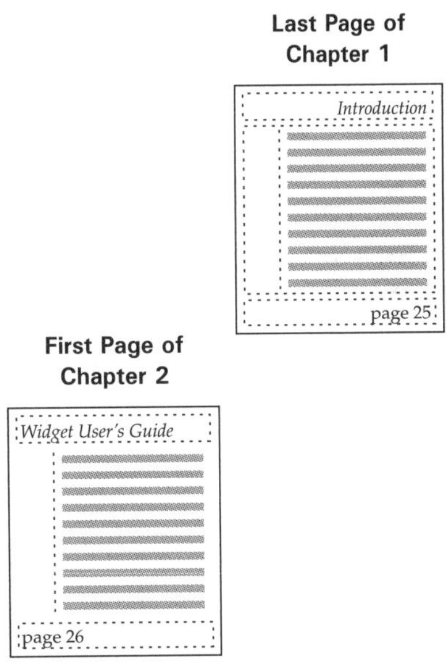

4. To set up the page count, select one of the following choices from the Before Saving & Printing list:
   - **Make Page Count Even:** Adds an empty page to files that have an odd page count. In a book file, for example, you may want to force an even page count so that all chapters begin on the right page and end on the left page.
   - **Make Page Count Odd:** Adds an empty page to files that have an even page count.
   - **Delete Empty Pages:** Automatically removes empty pages from the end of each file. You might want to do this before converting a book to PDF output. The printed book, for instance, can have an even page count. When you make a PDF file of the book, you can change the pagination to prevent empty pages from printing at the end of chapters. This applies only to left or right pages; pages formatted by custom master pages are unchanged.
   - **Don't Change Page Count:** Doesn't change the page count. If the document has several blank pages at the end, those pages are not deleted.
5. Click the Set button. The page layout is updated.

For more information on setting up numbering in book files, see "Managing Numbering" on page 386.

CHAPTER 12

Importing Graphic Content

FrameMaker supports vector graphics (line art) and bitmap images (images composed of dots, such as screen captures and photographs) in many formats. Most graphics are displayed in frames. On body pages, a graphic is usually in an anchored frame, which attaches the graphic to a paragraph. When the paragraph moves up or down on the page, the anchored frame moves with the anchoring paragraph. This lets you control the graphic alignment and position. For example, the following illustration shows a graphic anchored to the previous paragraph.

The graphic is anchored to this line.⊥

You can crop graphics with anchored frames by sizing the frame around the part of the graphic you need to crop. Graphic frames also let you mask (cover part of) graphics, but graphic frames are used primarily on reference and master pages. On reference pages, you store frequently used objects, such as icons or borders.

In FrameMaker 8, you can also import interactive content, such as Adobe Captivate files. You can also import 3D objects (U3D format) files. You can set properties for the 3D objects, such as a default view in FrameMaker. If you save the FrameMaker file as a PDF file, the 3D object becomes interactive.

Anchoring Graphics

When you import a graphic into a text frame, the graphic is automatically inserted in an anchored frame. The anchor, which looks like an upside-down T, appears on the line where you position your cursor. Alternatively, you can insert the anchored frame first, with the alignment and position you want, and then import the graphic into the frame. Inserting the frame first lets you select the alignment and position. However, importing the graphic directly into the document saves you the step of inserting the empty frame.

TIP You can change the default anchored frame properties by installing a third-party FrameMaker plug-in called ImpGraph. The plug-in saves you the step of repositioning the anchored frame each time you import a graphic. For details, see Appendix A, "Resources."

There are seven anchored frame positions. Each position has specific alignment options. Some frames can be inserted outside the text column or text frame to display, for instance, an icon in the margin. Other frames are displayed in different positions inside a text frame. Table 12-1 on page 306 describes the anchored frame options.

Inserting an Anchored Frame

You can insert an anchored frame in a document, then import a graphic or place objects in the frame. Although this adds a step to the import process, it lets you position and align the frame first.

To insert an empty anchored frame, follow these steps:

1. Select Special➤Anchored Frame. The Anchored Frame dialog box is displayed.

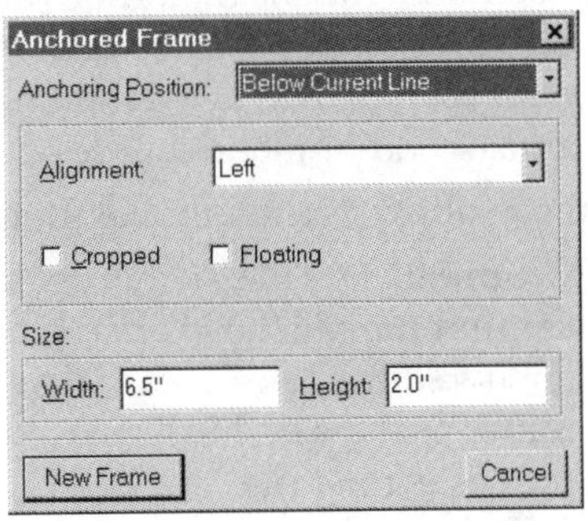

2. Click the anchored frame position in the Anchoring Position drop-down list.
3. Click the anchored frame alignment in the Alignment drop-down list. The available choices depend on the anchoring position. See Table 12-1 on page 306 for details.

<table>
<tr><th>Position</th><th>Description</th></tr>
<tr><td>

Below Current Line

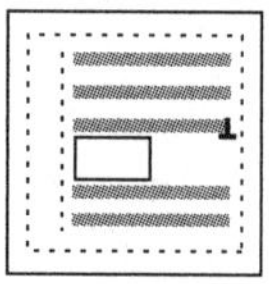

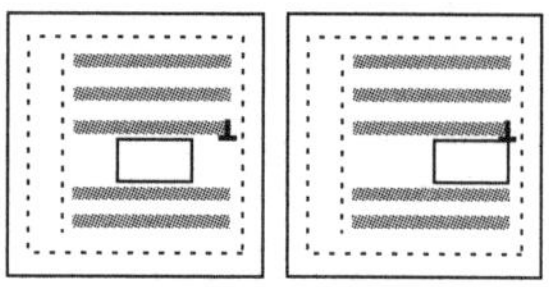

Closer to Binding   Farther from Binding

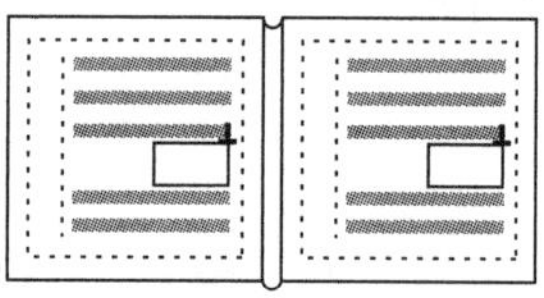

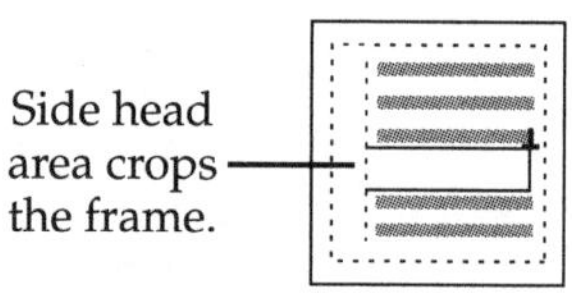

Frame floats where it fits.

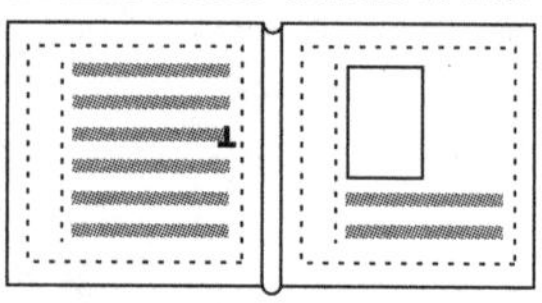

</td><td>

Places the anchored frame below the line containing the insertion point. Select the position of the frame:

- **Left:** Left aligns the frame in the text column unless the anchoring paragraph extends across the side head and columns. In that case, the graphic aligns under the anchoring paragraph.
- **Center:** Centers the frame in the text column or across the columns and side head.
- **Right:** Aligns the frame at the right edge of the column. If the graphic is wider than the column and the page has a side head area, aligns the frame on the right across both the columns and side head area.
- **Side Closer to Binding:** In a single-sided document, aligns the frame with the left side of all pages; in a double-sided document, aligns the frame with the right side of even-numbered pages or the left side of odd-numbered pages.
- **Side Farther from Binding:** In a single-sided document, aligns the frame on the right side of all pages; in a double-sided document, aligns the frame with the left side of even-numbered pages or the right side of odd-numbered pages.

You can apply two additional properties:

- **Cropped:** Fits the anchored frame within the text column (or side head area, if one exists). Cropped anchored frames are cut off by the borders of the text frame or the side head area. Uncropped anchored frames extend into the side head or margins.
- **Floating:** When there is not enough space for the anchored frame in the current column, moves the anchored frame to the top of the next column without moving the anchor.

</td></tr>
<tr><td>

At Top of Column

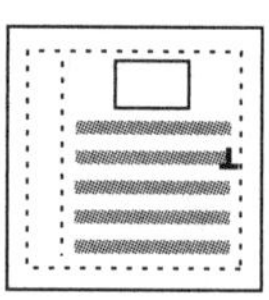

</td><td>

Places the anchored frame at the top of the column containing the insertion point. Has the same alignment and options as the Below Current Line setting.

</td></tr>
</table>

Table 12-1. Anchored Frame Options

Position	Description
At Bottom of Column 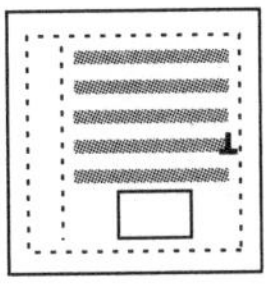	Places the anchored frame at the bottom of the column containing the insertion point. Has the same alignment and options as the Below Current Line setting.
At Insertion Point 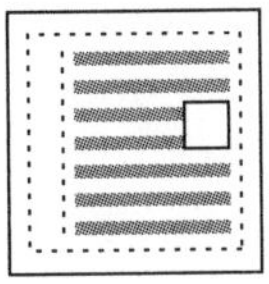	Aligns the anchored frame vertically with the bottom of the current line. The anchor is not displayed. The Distance Above Baseline option adds space between the anchored frame and the current line. For example, the illustration on the left shows a graphic placed -0.5 inches from the baseline.
Outside Column 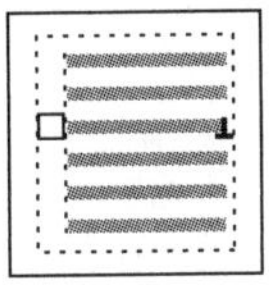	Places the anchored frame in the side head space outside the text column. Select where the frame is displayed: ■ **Left, Right, Side Closer to Binding,** or **Side Farther from Binding:** See alignment options for "Below Current Line" on page 306. ■ **Side Closer to Page Edge:** Aligns the frame closer to the edge of the page in single-sided documents. Same as Side Farther from Binding in double-sided documents. ■ **Side Farther from Page Edge:** Aligns the frame farther from the edge of the page in single-sided documents. Same as Side Closer to Binding in double-sided documents. You can also change the vertical and horizontal spacing: ■ **Distance above Baseline:** Space above or below the anchored frame. A negative setting extends the anchored frame below the baseline. ■ **Distance from Text Column:** Space to the left or right of the anchored frame.

Table 12-1. Anchored Frame Options (Continued)

Position	Description
Outside Text Frame 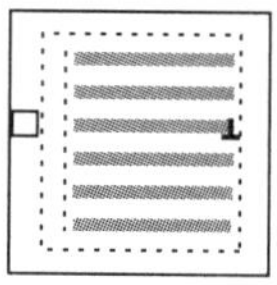	Places the anchored frame in the margin of the document outside the main text column. In a single-column document, shown in the illustration on the left, this position is the same as the Outside Column position. See alignment and spacing options for “Outside Column” on page 307.
Run into Paragraph 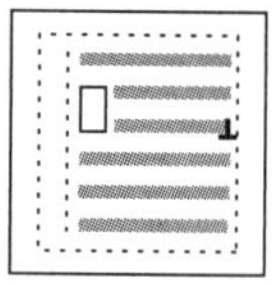	Places the anchored frame in the text column with the paragraph. Text is displayed around one side of the anchored frame. To adjust the space between the text and frame, you modify the gap setting in the anchored frame properties. Alignment options are the same for “Below Current Line” on page 306, except the center alignment is unavailable.

Table 12-1. Anchored Frame Options (Continued)

4. Complete additional fields that are displayed for the alignment you selected. Table 12-1 also describes these fields.
5. Type the size of the anchored frame in the Width and Height fields.
6. Click the New Frame button. The empty frame is inserted on the page. You can click it to import a graphic, or you can draw objects inside the frame. For details on drawing objects, see “Drawing Basic Shapes” on page 338.

TIP You can format anchored frames as you do other objects in FrameMaker. If you need a border around the imported graphic, for instance, you can add a border to the anchored frame. See “Modifying Objects” on page 346.

Importing a Graphic

When you import a graphic into a text frame, the graphic is automatically inserted into an anchored frame. You can either copy the graphic directly into the document or import the file by reference, which creates a link to the source graphic. You and your coworkers need to weigh the pros and cons before deciding which method to use. Table 12-2 describes the pros and cons of importing graphics by reference.

	Advantages	Disadvantages
Organizing	■ You maintain a central repository of graphics for your documentation, which lets coworkers insert the same graphic in multiple documents. ■ Because you can reuse the graphic, you save storage space. ■ If your FrameMaker files become corrupted, you still have the original graphics. ■ You can generate a list of graphics that shows you the location of each imported graphic and the DPI used. This list makes it easy to navigate to graphics, count the number of graphics in your book, find which folders graphics are stored in, and so on. See Chapter 17, "Creating Other Generated Files."	■ You must organize graphics clearly so that others can find what they need. ■ Anyone who opens a document with referenced graphics must have access to the location of the graphics. If the graphics are on your hard drive and the drive isn't shared, the graphics are not displayed. ■ The link to the referenced graphic will break if the graphic is renamed, moved to another directory, or deleted. ■ If cross-platform compatibility is an issue, you need to follow file naming and graphic format guidelines. See "Advice on Organizing Graphic Files" on page 320 for details. ■ If a FrameMaker file gets corrupted, you might not have the original graphic.
Updating	■ To modify a graphic, you edit the file and save it with the original name. All FrameMaker files that reference the graphic are updated when you open or save the files. ■ The name of the referenced graphic is displayed in the object properties. The file name isn't displayed with copied graphics.	You and a coworker might try to update the same graphic in different documents simultaneously.

Table 12-2. Pros and Cons of Importing Graphics by Reference

	Advantages	Disadvantages
Archiving	Your archives are smaller because the same graphic isn't placed in multiple documents.	You must be careful archiving a document with graphics that are used in other documents. To avoid breaking links in current documentation, you can generate a report of imported graphics in FrameMaker to see which graphics need to be archived.
Minimizing File Size	Files are smaller when they contain links to graphics and not the graphics themselves. Large FrameMaker files can cause memory problems, even on the most powerful computers.	None!

Table 12-2. Pros and Cons of Importing Graphics by Reference (Continued)

The graphics you import can reside on your local machine, a networked computer, the Internet, or a company intranet. If you import a graphic from the Internet or the company intranet by reference, a copy of the file is placed on your machine in your local Temporary Internet Files folder. By default, if the file on the Internet or intranet is updated, your local file is not updated until you delete the temporary file and import the graphic again.

TIP If you want FrameMaker to always update the graphic from the Internet or intranet site, edit the maker.ini file in a text editor and set the AlwaysDownloadURL flag to On. See Appendix C, "Customizing maker.ini."

FrameMaker supports both bitmap images (such as screen captures and photographs) and vector graphics (line art created with drawing tools). When you import bitmap images, which consist of pixels, you must specify the DPI (dots per inch) setting. The DPI indicates the number of pixels per inch in the imported graphic. The higher the DPI, the smaller the dimensions of the graphic. The DPI setting is crucial because it controls the image resolution. If you resize a bitmap image by dragging one of its corners, the DPI no longer determines the resolution, and the image may become distorted.

NOTE You can resize vector images, such as EPS files, by pressing SHIFT while dragging the corner or by using the Graphics➤Scale command.

For consistency's sake, you usually decide on one or two DPI settings to use in a single book. If you use different DPIs when importing screen captures of dialog boxes, for instance, the reader can't judge the true size of the images.

Most vector graphics don't have DPI settings because they consist of lines, not pixels. You do, however, need to set the DPI when you import Scalable Vector Graphics (SVGs). FrameMaker converts SVGs to bitmap images (or rasterizes them) for display in your document. The rasterization doesn't change printing or converting the graphic; it's only for FrameMaker's display of the SVG. You can even import an animated SVG, and the animation will be displayed when you export the file to HTML or XML. Although PDF files can display animated SVG if you have the appropriate plug-in, embedded SVG from FrameMaker is just a static image. The PDF specification is capable of displaying SVG directly, but there is no feature in Acrobat for doing this.

NOTE To display SVG files in a browser, you may need to download an SVG viewer plug-in. Some browsers give you this option; others may require you to download and install the viewer yourself.

FrameMaker 8 also lets you import Flash SWF ("swiff") files and Adobe Acrobat 3D files into documents. For more information, see "Providing Interactive Content" on page 333 and "Using 3D Objects" on page 335.

Importing a Vector Graphic

To import a vector graphic (other than an SVG), follow these steps:

1. Position the insertion point in the paragraph where you want to display a graphic. (If you have already inserted an anchored frame, select the anchored frame.)
2. Select File➤Import➤File. The Import dialog box is displayed (Figure 12-1).

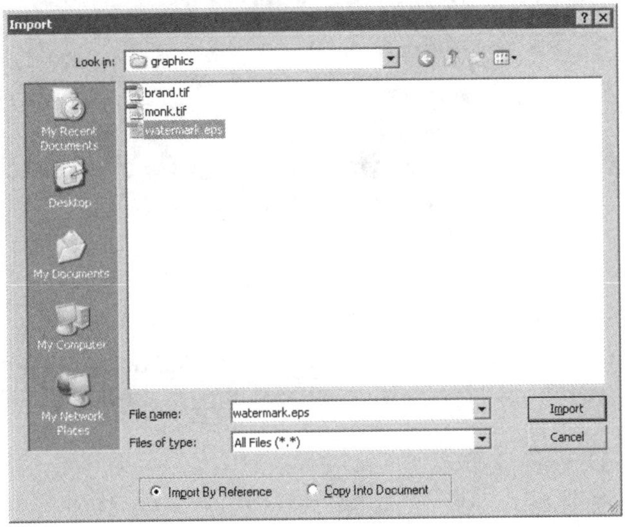

Figure 12-1. Importing graphics

3. Browse to find the file you want to import, then click the file name. Alternatively, in the File Name field, you can type a valid HTTP file path to an image, such as http://www.scriptorium.com/images/bannerowl_top.eps.
4. Do one of the following:
   - Click the Import By Reference radio button to create a link to the graphic.
   - Click the Copy Into Document radio button to embed the graphic in the FrameMaker file.

   The next time you import a graphic, FrameMaker defaults to the setting you choose.
5. Click the Import button. The file is displayed in the document within an anchored frame.

   If you have specified an HTTP file path and the file is not available, FrameMaker displays a warning:

Importing an SVG File

To import an SVG file, follow these steps:

1. Follow the previous procedure for importing a vector graphic. After you click the Import button, the Import SVG dialog box is displayed.

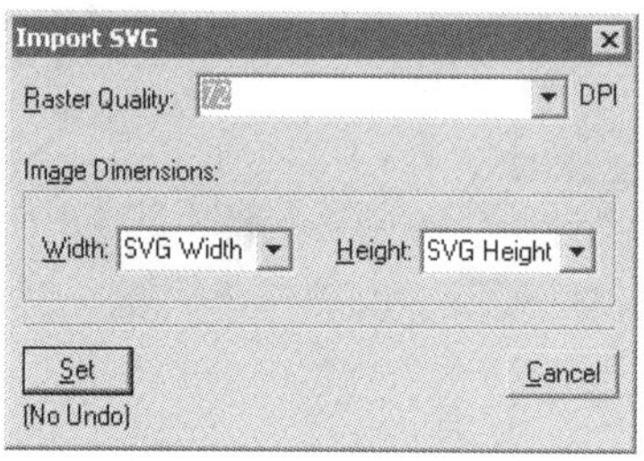

2. Do one of the following:
   - To set the DPI, click a DPI in the Raster Quality drop-down list. This resizes the graphic proportionately. (The current DPI for the graphic is displayed in this list by default.)
   - To change the specific dimensions, click a width in the Width drop-down list and a height in the Height drop-down list. This option may distort the image because you're not sizing the image proportionately.

CAUTION For the best results, resize SVGs in a graphics program. For the SVG to resize correctly when imported into FrameMaker, the SVG (which is an XML file) must have a viewBox attribute in the top-level XML element, and the units of measure must be specified in the file. Check your graphics program documentation for more information.

3. Click the Set button. The image is converted to a bitmap image and displayed in the document.

NOTE When you use FrameMaker to save a document to HTML or XML, you have the choice of converting SVG files to GIF, JPEG, or PNG—or you can pass them through unchanged in their native format.

Importing a Bitmap Image

To import a bitmap image, follow these steps:

1. Follow the steps for importing a vector graphic. (See "Importing a Vector Graphic" on page 311.) When you click the Import button, one of the following results occurs:
   - If FrameMaker can't detect the graphic format, the Unknown File Type dialog box is displayed. Click the format that matches the graphic and then click the Convert button. The Imported Graphic Scaling dialog box is displayed. Continue to step 2.
   - If FrameMaker automatically selects a graphics filter, the Imported Graphic Scaling dialog box is displayed.

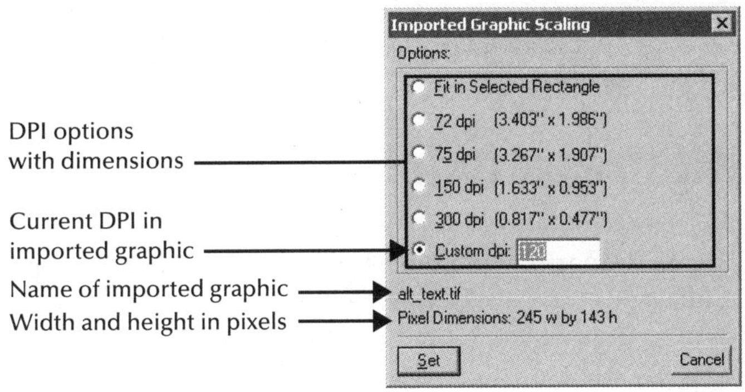

2. Select the size of the graphic:
   - To use the DPI from the graphic, don't change the setting in the Custom dpi field. The number that is displayed is the DPI of the imported graphic.
   - To change the size of the graphic, click a different radio button for the DPI, or type another number in the Custom dpi field.

CONTROLLING PAGE LAYOUT

TIP To protect the quality of the image, avoid the Fit in Selected Rectangle option. This setting resizes the object to fit inside the selected anchored or graphic frame, setting the DPI to Unknown and usually distorting the graphic in the process.

3. Click the Set button. The graphic is displayed in an anchored frame. (The following anchored frame has a border, so you can see the space between the graphic and frame.)

After you import a graphic, you can remove all white space between the graphic and anchored frame by shrink-wrapping the frame. See "Shrink-Wrapping an Anchored Frame" on page 316 for details.

Understanding Graphic Filters

During the FrameMaker installation, you install filters by default. Some filters convert text; other filters are for importing graphics. When you import a graphic, FrameMaker either detects the file type automatically or requires you to pick the correct filter. For most graphics, however, FrameMaker chooses the filter automatically. All you do is set the DPI.

If you select a filter and an error is displayed, the file might be corrupt, or your computer might not have the correct filter installed. For more information about graphics filters provided with FrameMaker, check the *Using Filters* online manual. You will find this manual, delivered as a PDF file, in the Documents folder in your FrameMaker installation folder.

NOTE The *Using Filters* online manual had not been updated for FrameMaker 8 at the time this book was written. Check the Adobe web site for the latest information.

Resizing Imported Graphics

For the best results, you resize an imported bitmap image by changing the DPI. You should avoid dragging the corner of a bitmap image to resize it. Doing so often distorts the graphic, as shown in the following example. Although you can resize objects and vector graphics proportionately by pressing SHIFT while dragging a corner, using this method on bitmap images resets the DPI to "Unknown." As a result, the graphic may not print or export properly.

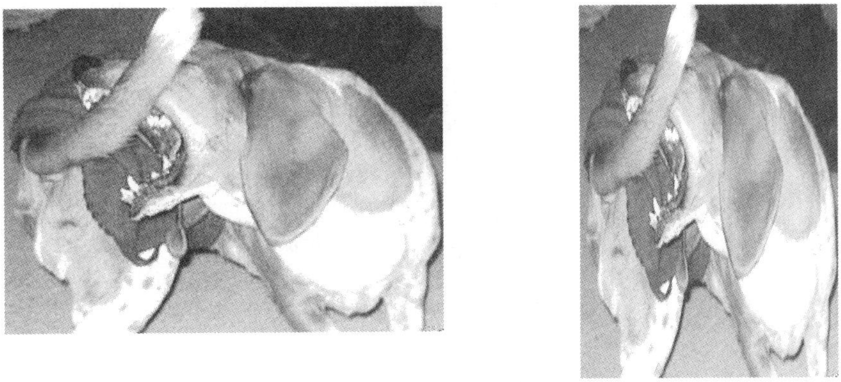

72-DPI graphic was imported at 150 DPI to decrease the dimensions of the displayed image.

150-DPI graphic was resized by dragging a corner.

Figure 12-2. Dragging the corner of a bitmap image distorts the graphic.

The DPI of the imported graphic is displayed in the object properties, which you display by selecting Graphics➤Object Properties. Next to the DPI, the scaling value shows the percentage by which the graphic was scaled when imported. For example, a 72-DPI graphic imported at 150 DPI is scaled 47.99 percent.

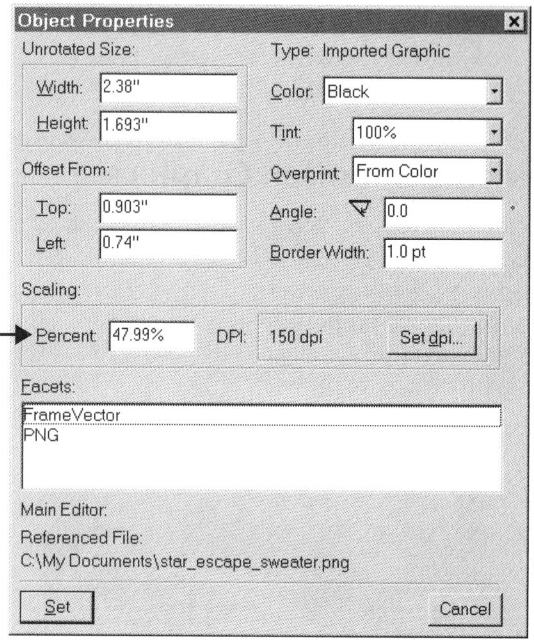

DPI for imported graphic was changed to 150 DPI, which is 47.99 percent of the original 72-DPI graphic.

To resize an imported vector graphic, you can either scale the graphic (select Graphics➤Scale and type a percentage) or press SHIFT and drag a corner of the graphic. Be sure to press SHIFT while resizing the graphic manually to maintain proportions.

Shrink-Wrapping an Anchored Frame

You shrink-wrap an anchored frame to remove the spacing between the imported graphic and its frame. Shrink-wrapping makes the anchored frame just large enough for its contents, changes the anchoring position to At Insertion Point, and displays the frame 0 points above the baseline of the text. If the anchored frame is on the same line as text, the 0-point baseline causes a problem—the graphic covers the text on the preceding lines. To prevent the problem, import a graphic on a blank line. The shrink-wrapped object doesn't cover text on blank lines. The following illustration shows the difference between inserting and shrink-wrapping an anchored frame in text and on a line by itself.

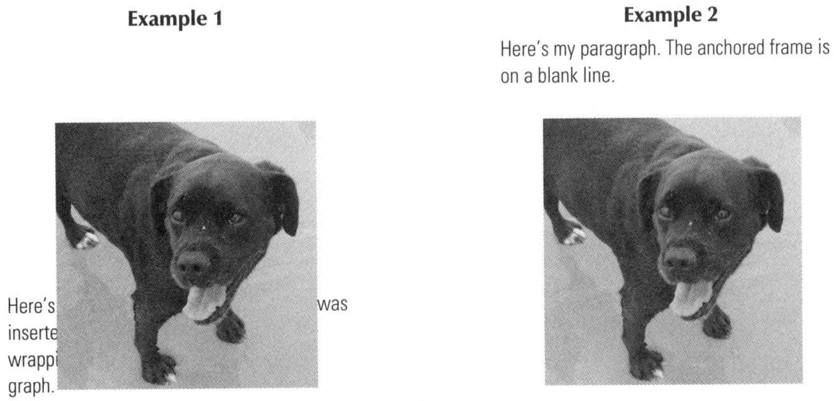

This graphic in an anchored frame set to At Insertion Point overlaps the text.

Placing the same anchored frame in its own paragraph solves the problem.

Figure 12-3. Anchored frames with the At Insertion Point setting

TIP If you want to shrink-wrap your graphics without affecting any other anchored frame properties (for example, if you want to shrink-wrap the graphic but you want the anchored frame to remain below the current line and centered), install the free plug-in shrinkwrapasis.dll from www.martinek.us/shrinkwrap.html.

When you import a graphic on a blank line, you can customize the paragraph tag applied to the line. The graphics in this book are inserted on a blank line formatted by the Figure paragraph tag. This tag has the following properties:

- **Two-point font.** Works with the space above and below the paragraph to control vertical spacing. You use the smallest supported font in FrameMaker so that the space above and below settings actually position the figure. The font family doesn't matter.
- **Eight points above and below the paragraph.** Separates the figure from the preceding and following paragraphs.
- **Line spacing must not be fixed.** Allows the paragraph spacing to expand vertically to the height of the graphic. Uncheck the Fixed check box in the Basic tab.
- **Center alignment.** Displays the figure in the center of the text column.
- **In-column pagination.** Displays the figure in the text column so that the figure is aligned consistently with in-column text. As a result, anchored frames that are wider than the column overlap the right margin, except for cropped anchored frames, which are clipped by the borders of the text frame or the side head area.

TIP If you often have wide figures, create a separate paragraph tag that displays content across all columns and side heads and apply the tag to the paragraph containing the figure. See "Pagination Sheet" on page 119 for details.

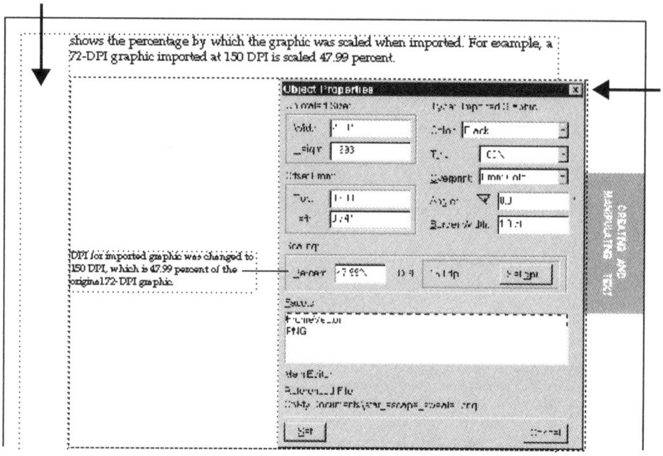

To shrink-wrap an anchored frame in an empty paragraph, follow these steps:

1. Click the anchored frame or the contents of the frame.
2. *(optional)* If the anchored frame contains several objects, select Graphics➤Group to group them.
3. Press ESC M P. The anchored frame is shrunk or expanded to fit the contents and is positioned according to the paragraph pagination settings.

NOTE There is not a menu choice or mouse action for shrink-wrapping graphics.

4. If you want to unwrap a shrink-wrapped graphic, press ESC M E.

Relinking Missing Imported Graphics

When FrameMaker displays gray boxes where you expect a graphic, it usually means FrameMaker can't locate an imported graphic. The link to the graphic can break if the graphic is renamed, moved, or deleted. When you open a document with a missing graphic, FrameMaker prompts you to find the graphic. You can either browse to find the file on your computer, or you can skip the search and fix the link later. (If the graphic was copied into the FrameMaker file rather than imported by reference, you may not be able to recover the graphic if the FrameMaker file becomes corrupted. Look for earlier copies of the FrameMaker file that may still show the graphic.)

The name of the missing graphic is also displayed in the object properties. You can use this information to reimport the graphic if you find gray boxes while working on a document.

NOTE Gray boxes can indicate missing graphics, but they are also displayed when the computer platform doesn't support the graphic and preview formats. You can tell the difference by looking at the facets in the object properties. The Facets field shows the graphic format and preview format (for graphics not supported on the platform). If there are no facets, the graphic is missing. If there are facets, the formats are not supported on the computer. For details, see "Image Facets" on page 326. Gray boxes can also indicate a corrupted imported file.

To relink a missing graphic when opening a document, follow these steps:

1. After you open the document with the missing graphic, the Missing File dialog box is displayed.

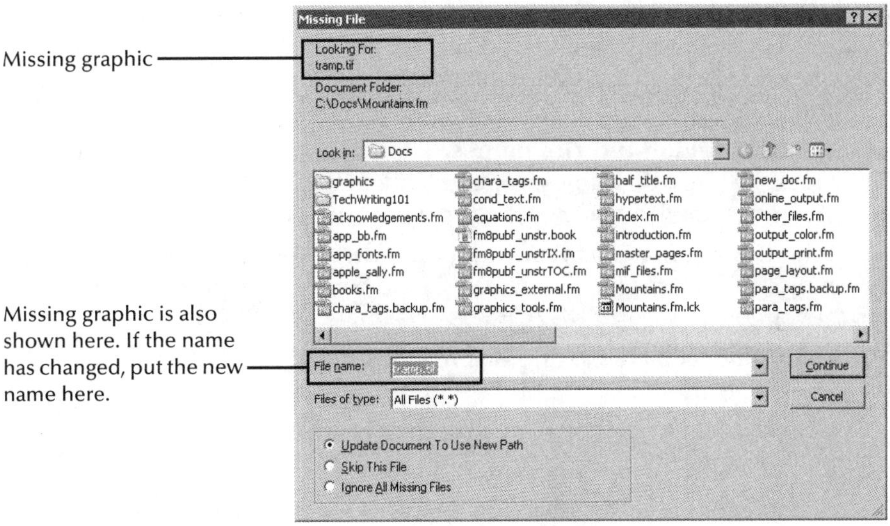

2. Do one of the following:
   - To relink the graphic, browse to find the file, and then select the file from the list of files. Make sure the Update Document To Use New Path radio button is selected.
   - If the name has changed, type the new name in the File Name field.
   - To skip the graphic, click the Skip This File radio button.
   - To skip all missing graphics, click the Ignore All Missing Files radio button.
3. Click the Continue button. The document is displayed along with the missing graphic (if you chose to relink the graphic).

Advice on Organizing Graphic Files

It's important to plan how you'll name and store graphics that are imported by reference. Lack of planning can cause organizational and computer resource problems. You might also need to follow cross-platform guidelines. Consider the following tips:

- **Decide how to organize your files.** You might group screen captures by the product or feature they depict. It's generally not a good idea to store graphics in folders named after particular chapters in a book—if you move a graphic into a different chapter, you'll have to move the graphic to the corresponding directory. To resolve missing graphics that are in different directories, you'll have to select the directory for each graphic, which is time-consuming. If graphics are in one directory, you point FrameMaker to that directory for the first graphic you're relinking, then the rest of the graphics in the directory are automatically relinked.
- **Consider a document management system.** Large corporations often use a document management system to organize files. Such systems not only track the location of files, but they also can track who modifies the files.
- **Use short folder and file names.** The Object Properties dialog box truncates long path names, so the file name of the imported graphic is sometimes not displayed. Short file names are also easier to remember.
- **Make file names platform-independent.** If your graphics files are used on multiple platforms, file names should conform to the following conventions:
  - Include file name extensions. Windows identifies files by their extensions.
  - Keep file names short. The Mac truncates file names over 32 characters.
  - Use lowercase file names. UNIX is case sensitive.
  - Exclude spaces, asterisks, quotes, slashes, question marks, colons, and other special characters from file names. Many special characters are reserved for specific functions on the Windows, UNIX, and Mac platforms. You can, however, use alphanumeric characters, underscores, and hyphens.

  For details on cross-platform graphic formats, see "Cross-Platform Images" on page 327.

Setting Anchored Frame Object Properties

In the anchored frame object properties, you can describe the contents of the frame by including the following information:

- **Alternate text.** Displayed when you place your cursor over a graphic in a tagged PDF file (or in XML produced from structured FrameMaker). Screen readers (such as the one built into Adobe Reader) will speak the alternate text.

- **Actual text.** Describes characters in the anchored frame (as opposed to graphics); exported only to tagged PDF files. For tagged PDF files saved from unstructured FrameMaker, screen readers treat alternate text and actual text the same. No text is displayed when you place the cursor over the graphic in the tagged PDF file. (This setting is more useful for structured FrameMaker.)

  See "Generating Tagged PDF Files" on page 473 for information about setting up tagged PDF files.

NOTE If you define both alternate and actual text for an anchored frame, only the alternate text is converted.

- **Attributes.** The attributes you define in the anchored frame object properties are not exported to XML or tagged PDF files. Third-party applications may process the anchored frame attributes, or you may use them for your own benefit to store notes or other information.

To define anchored frame object properties, follow these steps:

1. Click the anchored frame, then select Graphics➤Object Properties. The Object Properties dialog box is displayed.

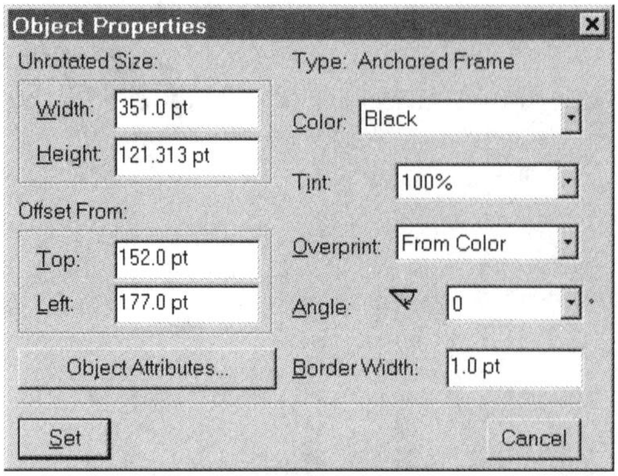

2. Click the Object Attributes button. The Object Attributes dialog box is displayed.

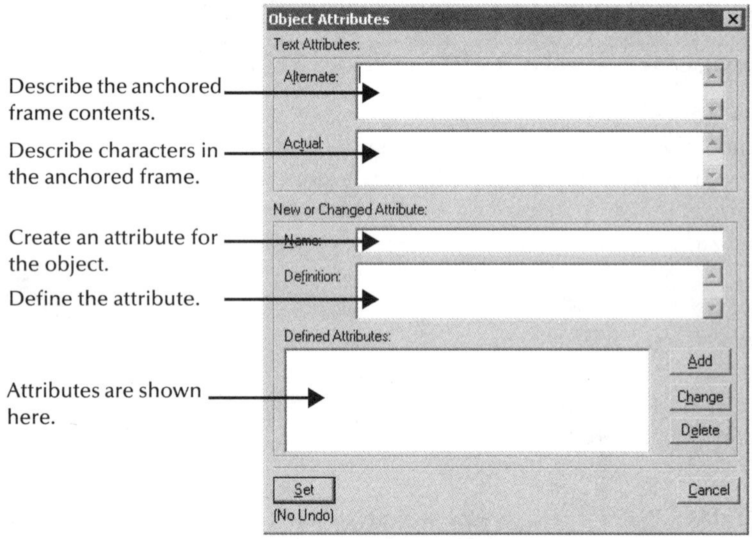

3. To describe the anchored frame contents for display in tagged PDF files (or in XML produced from structured FrameMaker), type text in the Alternate field.
4. To describe characters in the anchored frame for display in tagged PDF file, type text in the Actual Text field.

5. To add and modify attributes, do any of the following:
   - To create an attribute to describe the object, type the attribute in the Name field, type the attribute definition in the Definition field, then click the Add button.
   - To change the attribute, type the attribute in the Name field of the New or Changed Attribute section, modify the definition in the Definition field, then click the Change button.
   - To delete an attribute, click the attribute in the Defined Attributes section, then click the Delete button.
6. Click the Set button to return to the Object Properties dialog box, then click the Set button to save your changes. (If you click the Cancel button, your changes aren't saved.)

When you export the document, the alternate text or actual text is converted. For more information on creating PDF files, see Chapter 18, "Print and PDF Output."

Graphic Formats

There are two types of images—vector, which consist of lines, and bitmap, which consist of pixels. FrameMaker supports many file formats in each category. The format you choose depends largely on the final output of your document and your computer platform.

Choosing the Best Graphics Format

Your computer platform and the final output of your document determine which graphic formats you can use. Some image formats are more compatible with printed documents, while others work well in both printed and online documentation. For example, if you plan to print the document and convert a FrameMaker file to PDF, Encapsulated PostScript (EPS) graphics are a good choice because they have sharp resolution. You can also import PDF files as graphics in FrameMaker; like EPS files, PDF files also have sharp edges. For HTML or XML, screen captures are best displayed as Portable Network Graphic (PNG) files, Graphics Interchange Format (GIF) files, or SVG files. For HTMLHelp, GIF files work well for screen captures, and JPEG files work well for photographs.

Table 12-3 on page 324 lists the supported graphic formats for different kinds of output.

Graphic Format	Print	PDF	HTML and XML	HTMLHelp	DotNetHelp	WinHelp	RTF
	Final Output						
Bitmap (BMP)				✔	✔	✔	✔
CorelDRAW (CDR)	✔	✔					
Computer Graphics Metafile (CGM)	✔	✔	✔				
Enhanced Metafile (EMF)							✔
Encapsulated PostScript (EPS)	✔	✔					
Graphics Interchange Format (GIF)	✔	✔	✔	✔	✔	✔	✔
Joint Photography Experts Group (JPEG or JPG)	✔	✔	✔	✔	✔	✔	✔
Portable Document Format (PDF)	✔	✔					
Portable Network Graphic (PNG)	✔	✔	✔	✔	✔		✔
Scalable Vector Graphic (SVG)	✔	✔	✔	✔	✔		✔
Tagged Image File Format (TIFF or TIF)	✔	✔					✔
Windows Metafile (WMF)						✔	✔

Table 12-3. Choosing Graphic Formats

NOTE Third-party help authoring tools usually can convert the graphic format you are using to a supported format for online help, but it is better to choose a graphic format that is supported in your final output when you can.

Vector Graphics

A vector graphic consists of mathematical formulas that describe the drawing. EPS, PDF, SVG, CDR, and CGM are popular vector formats. If you open a vector graphic in a text editor such as TextPad or EditPlus, you'll see code like this:

```
%AI3_DocumentPreview: PC_TIFF
%AI5_ArtSize: 424.8 792
%AI5_RulerUnits: 0
%AI5_ArtFlags: 0 0 0 1 0 0 1 0 0
%AI5_TargetResolution: 800
%AI5_NumLayers: 1
```

You can decipher some of the code, but most of it is incomprehensible by any entity other than a printer. The main advantage of vector graphics is their resolution—they can be scaled drastically and maintain sharp edges. For line drawings, the files are also smaller than bitmap images. The following illustration shows an original vector graphic and another version scaled 300 percent, which looks just as crisp as the original.

Original vector graphic

Graphic was scaled 300 percent without losing resolution.

Some vector graphics have bitmap image previews that are saved with the graphic in their native application. If you use PDF files for your vector images, the preview has sharp edges instead of a blocky bitmap image.

NOTE FrameMaker supports CorelDRAW (CDR) graphics. You can save the CDR graphic as a FrameVector Image (FMV) file. The FMV file can be imported directly into a FrameMaker document.

FrameMaker uses a filter for Computer Graphics Metafiles (CGMs), which is a standard format for device-independent 2D files that is required in some industries. Although a CGM filter is installed with FrameMaker, you can make sure you have the latest version of the filter—which may be updated as often as every six months— by downloading it from www.itedo.com/E/2040.php.

Bitmap Images

Colored dots, or pixels, are arranged to create bitmap images. Bitmap images have a fixed number of pixels, and each pixel expands as you enlarge the image. The result can be a fuzzy, distorted graphic. Despite the similar name, bitmaps (BMP files) are just one possible type of bitmap image. FrameMaker also supports GIF, JPEG, EMF, PNG, TIFF, PDF, WMF, and several other bitmap image formats.

TIP PNG is a good format for both print and online output. To avoid bloating FrameMaker's color catalog, save PNGs from your graphics program with all possible colors (no subsetting or optimization). If the FrameMaker color catalog already has many colors with names like RGB 064 064 064, save the document file as MIF to remove the extra color definitions (see Appendix 24, "Maker Interchange Format"). However, the problem returns until you resave the optimized PNGs to include all colors.

For some file types, FrameMaker uses a filter to import the file. You select the appropriate filter when importing the graphic, then you set the DPI. See "Understanding Graphic Filters" on page 314 for more information.

What Are Those Gray Boxes?

Imported graphics may be displayed as gray boxes for several reasons:

- The image is missing. The referenced file might have been renamed, moved, or deleted. When you open a file with a missing image, FrameMaker prompts you to find the correct path, skip the file, or skip all missing files. Skipping the file causes the gray box to be displayed. See "Relinking Missing Imported Graphics" on page 318 for details.
- The preview format may not be supported on the current platform, or there may be no preview at all. Windows machines cannot display an EPS with a Mac preview, for instance. Graphics with PC previews, however, are displayed on the Windows platform.
- The file format isn't supported on your platform.
- The graphic file might be corrupted. Open it in a graphics editor to ensure the file is not corrupted.

To prevent the gray boxes, you should follow guidelines for cross-platform graphics (if applicable) and make sure referenced graphics are not moved, renamed, or deleted.

Image Facets

Many graphics include more than one image, although only one image is displayed. FrameMaker considers each image a *facet*, or a separate format of the same image. Facets make graphics formats compatible across computer platforms and monitors. With an EPS graphic, the TIFF facet is displayed as a preview of the graphic. The facets are listed in the imported graphic's object properties.

FrameMaker added the FrameImage facet to the SVG during import.

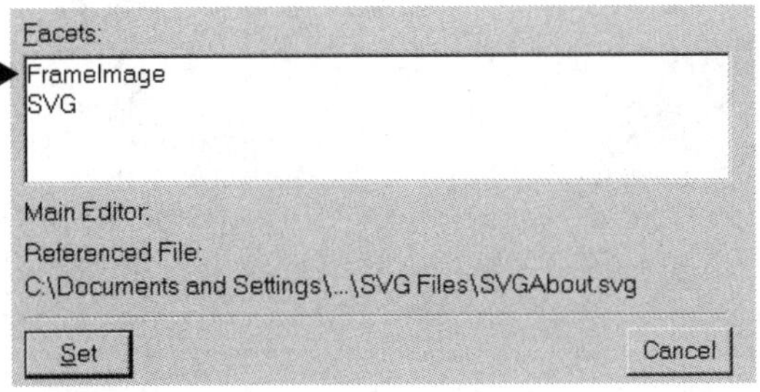

Cross-Platform Images

FrameMaker supports cross-platform graphics. This feature lets you view graphics on more than one platform. Some graphic formats, such as WMF and PICT, are displayed only on their native platforms. To view the image on non-native platforms, you copy or import the graphics into your document and set the FrameMaker preferences to create FrameImage facets (for bitmap images) and FrameVector facets (for vector graphics) when you save the document. The facet is displayed when a user, for example, views a document containing a WMF graphic on the UNIX platform. Without the facet, the WMF is displayed as a gray box on the UNIX platform.

FrameImages are saved along with the copied graphic, so the file size increases, especially with graphics-intensive documents. As a result, you might run into the following problems with FrameImages:

- If your computer doesn't have enough free memory, FrameMaker may not be able to save the document.
- Lack of free memory slows down the display of images, so scrolling through the document can take longer.
- The inflated file size can cause printing errors and problems converting the document to another format.

FrameImages are primarily for viewing the document. If you plan to do anything other than view the document, you're better off converting the graphics to a compatible format and importing them by reference.

To save FrameImage or FrameVector facets, follow these steps:

1. Select File➤Preferences➤General. The Preferences dialog box is displayed.
2. In the Compatibility Preferences section, check the Save FrameImage with Imported Graphics check box.
3. Click the Set button. The FrameImage or FrameVector will be saved in all documents that contain copied graphics until you change the preferences again.

Importing Using OLE

You can use object linking and embedding (OLE) to embed objects while maintaining the object's association with its native program. When you double-click a Visio graphic, for instance, the Visio interface is displayed inside FrameMaker. You can then edit the graphic inside the FrameMaker window instead of leaving FrameMaker and opening Visio. You can also create a number of different objects inside FrameMaker without opening the appropriate program or saving the object as a separate file. OLE has some major drawbacks. Documents are large because the OLE items are embedded, not referenced. Those who open your document must have the same version of software you used to create an OLE graphic. It's difficult to resize an OLE object—you can't set the DPI, and scaling the object often results in a distorted or pixelated image.

For best results, create graphic objects in a graphics program and import the files. For more information, see "Importing a Graphic" on page 308 and "Cross-Platform Images" on page 327.

Placing Graphics on the Reference Pages

You can store frequently used objects, such as logos or borders, on the reference pages. Some FrameMaker users maintain a library of objects on the reference pages so they can copy an object on the reference page and paste it on a body page when they need it.

By default, FrameMaker provides four line styles on the reference pages—Footnote, TableFootnote, SingleLine, and DoubleLine. You can use the line styles in paragraph tags to create a border above or below the paragraph.

Objects are displayed in graphic frames on the reference pages. Each graphic frame has a name. You can either copy graphics or import them by reference into the graphic frame. If you copy graphics, keep in mind that the graphics increase the size of the file. Most of the time, you'll import the graphics by reference to make updating the graphics throughout the book easier. See "Importing a Graphic" on page 308 for more details.

NOTE Reference pages also store definitions for the table of contents and other generated files, as well as HTML conversion information. See "Creating Paragraph-Based Lists" on page 442 for details.

Placing Graphics Above and Below the Paragraph

You can set up a paragraph that always has a line or other graphics above or below it. FrameMaker provides a few graphics; you can also create your own. For example, you can insert notes, tips, and caution paragraphs in two-column, one-row invisible tables. The TipGraphic paragraph tag is applied in the left column. This tag inserts the Tip icon above the paragraph.

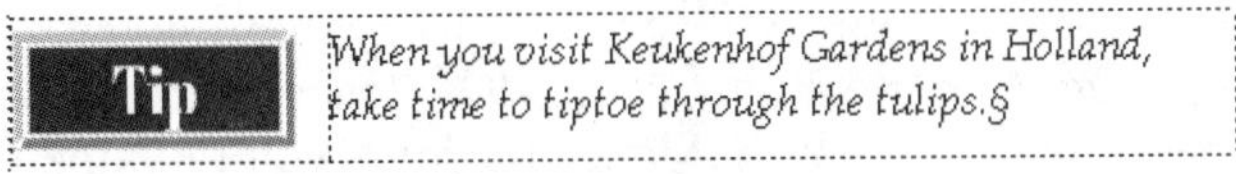

The Tip icon is displayed on the reference page. The label *tip_graphic* describes the image; the name of the actual graphic frame, which is displayed in the status bar, may differ. In the Advanced tab of the Paragraph Designer, graphic frame names are listed in the Frame Above Pgf and Frame Below Pgf drop-down lists.

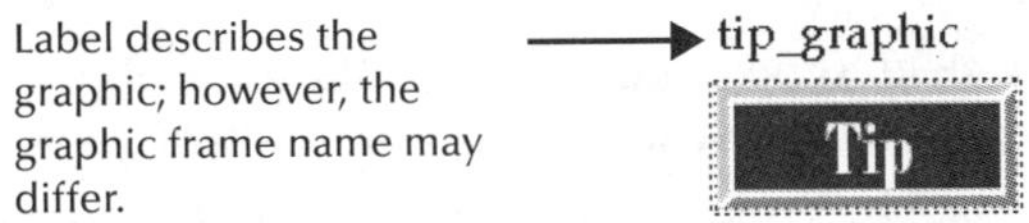

You can use grouped objects on the reference page to create bars and icons for headings. For example, you can create an H1_graphic paragraph tag that displays grouped objects above the Heading1 paragraph.

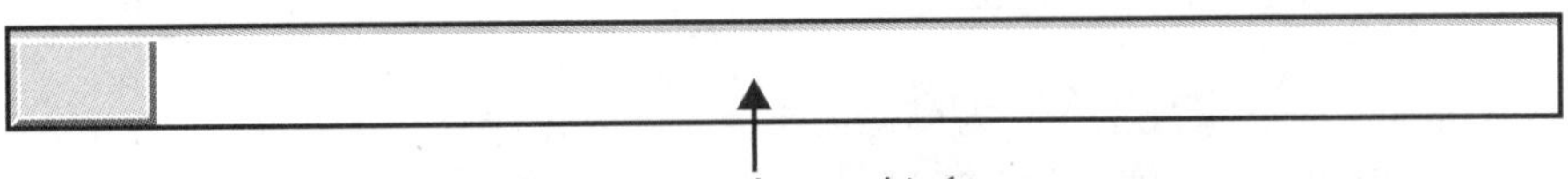

Typically, the white space in the graphic frame is displayed when you apply the paragraph tag. To display text directly over the object, however, you create another tag for the heading text and set the space above that paragraph tag to a negative number. In this example, set the Heading1 paragraph tag to have -36 points above the paragraph. You'll need to adjust the spacing based on the size of the font and of the image called by the graphic paragraph tag.

NOTE The graphic frame may appear to crop a line on the reference page, but the true dimensions of the line are displayed on master and body pages. To shorten a line, edit the object properties.

To set up a graphic to precede or follow your paragraph, follow these steps:

1. *(optional)* If you don't like any of the default FrameMaker graphics, you can create your own. Follow these steps:
    a. Select View➤Reference Pages to display the reference pages. The default FrameMaker graphics are included on the first reference page, which happens to be called "Reference."

    b. Click the Graphic Frame icon in the Graphics toolbar.
    c. Click and drag to create a new frame. The location doesn't matter. When you release the cursor, FrameMaker prompts you to name the frame.

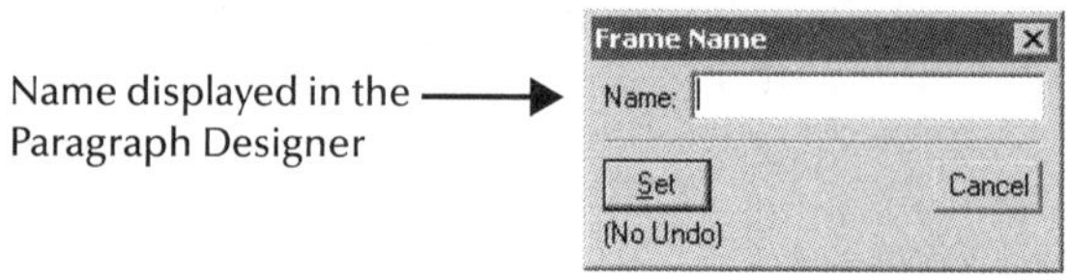

    d. In the Name field, type a name for the frame, then click the Set button. This is the name you will select later in the Paragraph Designer.
    e. Put the graphic objects you want inside the graphic frame. You can use FrameMaker's drawing tools, import an external graphic, or both.
    f. Above the frame, insert a text label (you can copy, paste, and then edit one of the existing ones) with the name of the graphic frame. This name is for identification purposes only; it's not associated with the graphic frame name.
    g. Select View➤Body Pages to return to the body pages. In the Paragraph Designer, the new frame is now available in the Frame Above Pgf and Frame Below Pgf drop-down lists on the Advanced tab.
2. Display the Paragraph Designer, then click the tag that you want to add a graphic to.
3. Click the Advanced tab.

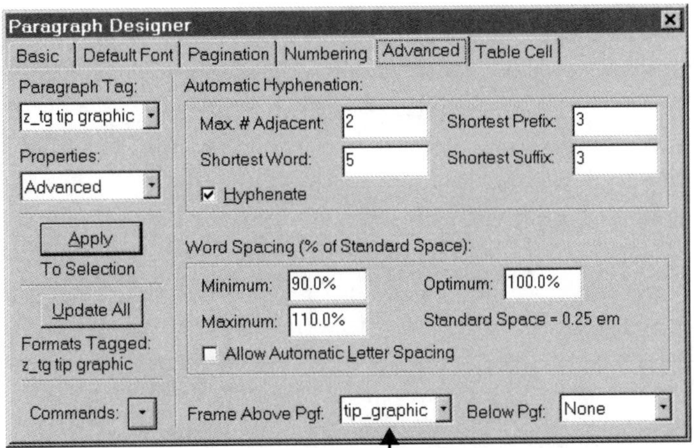

Name of the graphic frame on the reference page

4. In the Frame Above Pgf or Frame Below Pgf drop-down list, click the frame you want to use.
5. Click the Update All button to save your changes. The new graphic is displayed in each paragraph formatted by the tag.

Changing the Name of a Graphic Frame

When you add a graphic frame to the reference pages, you name the frame. You can change this name later, and the new graphic frame name will be displayed in the Frame Above Pgf and Frame Below Pgf paragraph tags.

CAUTION Don't rename graphic frames that are already referenced in paragraph tags, or you'll remove the object from the paragraph tag definition. FrameMaker doesn't provide a warning, so be sure the graphic frame isn't in use.

To change the graphic frame name, follow these steps:

1. Select View➤Reference Pages to display the reference pages.
2. Click the graphic frame, then do one of the following:
   - Click the name in the status bar. The Frame Name dialog box is displayed.
   - Select Graphic➤Object Properties. The Object Properties dialog box is displayed.

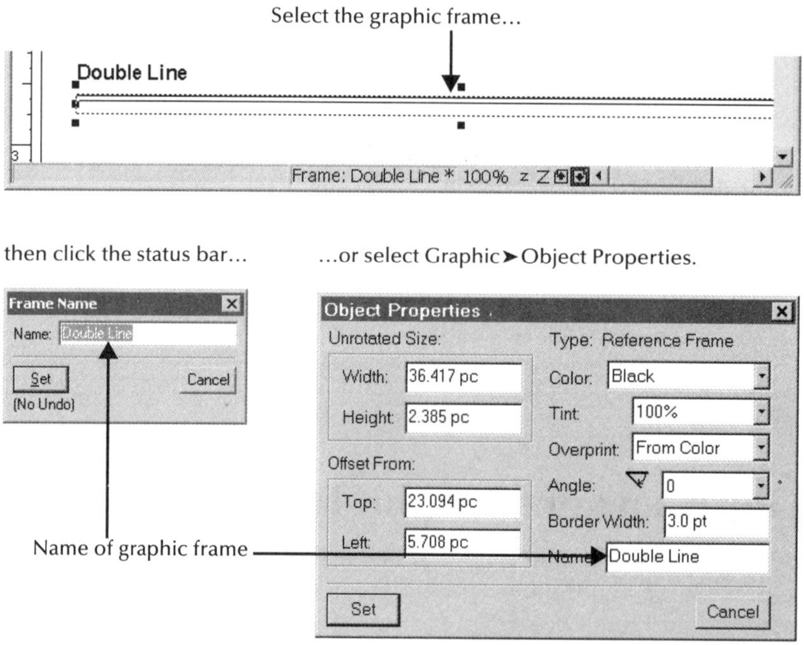

3. Modify the text in the Name field, then click the Set button. The new graphic frame name is displayed in the status bar, object properties, and paragraph tags.

Importing Graphics on a Master Page

Graphics are often placed on master pages to create special designs. Most of the time, you don't need a frame for the graphic—you just import the graphic onto the page outside the main text flow, using a graphic frame to crop the graphic, if necessary. For many graphics on the master page, you don't need an anchored frame because there's no text to displace the graphic. More importantly, if you import the graphic into the main text flow, the graphic isn't displayed on the body pages.

In this book, the title page of each chapter has a graphic. The graphic was imported by reference into a graphic frame on the ChapterTitle master page.

NOTE Objects on the master pages aren't exported to HTML or XML.

To import a graphic on the master page, follow these steps:

1. Select View➤Master Pages to display the master pages.
2. Scroll to the master page you want to edit, or select Special➤Add Master Page to create a new one.
3. Do one of the following:
   - To import the graphic into a graphic frame, click the Graphic Frame button in the Tools palette and draw the graphic frame, then click the frame and import the graphic. You can also copy and paste the object (from another master page, for instance) into the frame.
   - To import the graphic into a background object, place your cursor in the text frame and import the graphic. You can shrink-wrap the anchored frame to remove extra space.
   - If you don't need a frame for the graphic, click outside the text frame to deselect it, then import the graphic. The graphic is centered on the page. If you need to select the graphic, but the graphic is displayed behind the text frame, click the text frame, then select Graphics➤Send to Back.

After you import the graphic, you can adjust the frame or offsets to create the design you need. For details on cropping images with graphic frames, see "Cropping and Masking Graphics" on page 358.

Providing Interactive Content

You can embed interactive content such as Flash (SWF) files in your FrameMaker documents.

After you have imported or copied the SWF file into your document, FrameMaker displays the first frame of the file (or another frame, if specified as the poster frame within the SWF file), a play button, or a gray box. If you print the document, whatever appears in the document for the Flash file is what prints.

NOTE At the time this book was written, SWF files were displayed differently in FrameMaker depending on which application was used to create them. To display and print the first frame or a specified poster frame, you must use the Captivate application, which is part of the Adobe Technical Communication Suite. For more information, see www.adobeforums.com/webx/.3c06353e.

Within FrameMaker, you can double-click on the image to play the file in a supported application.

You can choose to either import the file by reference or to copy it into your document. For more information about the differences between importing by reference and copying, see "Importing a Graphic" on page 308.

If you save your document to a PDF file, you can play the SWF file in the PDF file by clicking the image in the PDF file. If you save your document as an HTML file, the SWF file is saved either to a separate folder if you imported by reference or to the same file as the HTML file if you copied it into the document.

To import a SWF file, follow these steps:

1. If you want to save your document to a PDF file and include the Flash file in your document, select File➤Preferences➤General.
2. In the Preferences dialog box, make sure that the Do not embed Adobe Flash files in PDF check box is not checked, then click Set to close the dialog box. (If this option is checked, the Flash file is displayed as a picture in the PDF, but it's no longer a movie that can be played.)
3. Position the insertion point in the paragraph where you want to display the image of the interactive file.
4. Select File➤Import➤File. The Import dialog box is displayed (Figure 12-1 on page 311).
5. Browse to find the SWF file you want to import, then click the file name. Alternatively, you can specify a valid HTTP file path to the file.
6. Do one of the following:
   - Click the Import By Reference radio button to create a link to the file.
   - Click the Copy Into Document radio button to embed the file in the FrameMaker file.
7. Click the Import button. The Imported Graphic Scaling dialog box is displayed.
8. Select the size of the graphic image to display:
   - To use the DPI from the image to be displayed, don't change the setting in the Custom dpi field. The number that is displayed is the DPI of the image to be used.
   - To change the size of the image, click a different radio button for the DPI, or type another number in the Custom dpi field. To protect the quality of the image, avoid the Fit in Selected Rectangle option. This setting resizes the object to fit inside the selected anchored or graphic frame, setting the DPI to Unknown and usually distorting the graphic in the process.
9. Click the Set button. If you have specified an HTTP file path and the file is not available, FrameMaker displays a warning.

Using 3D Objects

You can import 3D objects (U3D files) into FrameMaker files. Within FrameMaker, you can set properties for the object. After you generate a PDF file, you can change display aspects and other characteristics of the 3D object in Adobe Reader 7 or higher.

Your 3D object is rendered as a device-independent bitmap (DIB) facet in FrameMaker. Within FrameMaker, you can choose which view to display, and you can set other characteristics of how the 3D object is displayed, including background color and render mode.

The following figure is a 3D object with a custom background color. It is displayed in wireframe render mode.

To import and set up a 3D object, follow these steps:

1. Importing a 3D object is similar to importing a SWF file. Refer to step 1 through step 9 in the previous procedure. In the Preferences dialog box, make sure that the Do not embed 3D objects in PDF check box is not checked. Also, import a U3D file instead of a SWF.
2. If you want to customize the view of the 3D object in FrameMaker and the initial view displayed in the PDF file, select the 3D object in the anchored frame, and then select Graphics➤3D Menu.

3. From the 3D Menu list, you can change any of the following:
   - **Background color.** Select a background color from the Color palette. You can define a custom background color. The background color is not added to the color catalog.

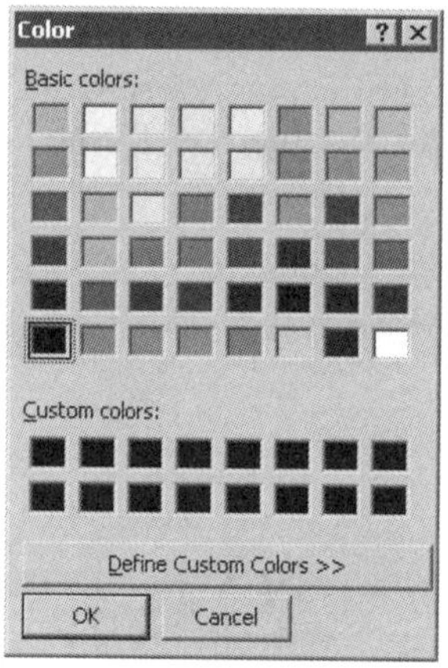

   - **Lighting.** Try out the lighting choices until you get the effect you want. The choices are Lights From File, No Lights, White Lights, Day Lights, Bright Lights, Primary Color Lights, Night Lights, Blue Lights, Red Lights, Cube Lights, CAD Optimized Lights, and Headlamp.
   - **Show Existing Views.** The person who created the 3D object may have saved views of the graphic in the U3D file. You can select these predefined views, but you can't set up new ones.

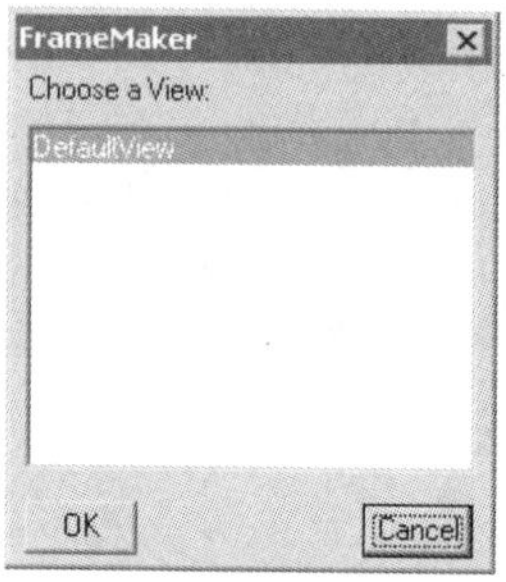

   - **Render Mode.** By default, the 3D object is rendered as a solid object. The available render modes are Bounding Box, Transparent Bounding Box, Transparent Bounding Box Outline, Vertices, Shaded Vertices, Wireframe, Shaded Wireframe, Solid, Transparent, Solid Wireframe, Transparent Wireframe, Illustration, Solid Outline, Shaded Illustration, and Hidden Wireframe.

CHAPTER 13

FrameMaker's Graphics Tools

FrameMaker includes drawing tools similar to those found in basic graphics programs. FrameMaker's tools let you draw different shapes and combine them to create objects, such as those shown in the following examples. You can change the colors and borders, apply shading, resize, rotate, layer, align, and so forth. The tools aren't appropriate for designing sophisticated magazine layouts or for detailed technical drawings, but they provide most of the features you need for illustrations in reference guides, newsletters, training manuals, or simple brochures.

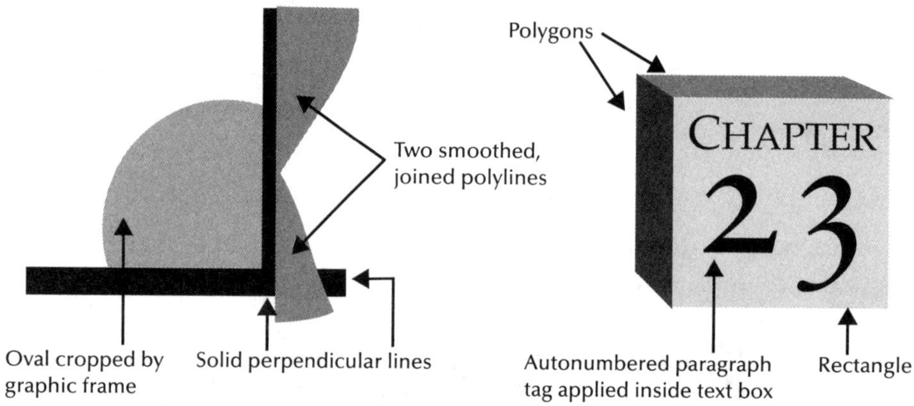

You can draw objects directly on the page, or you can place them in a frame. An *anchored frame,* which is a container for graphics and text, attaches the object to a paragraph. When the paragraph moves, the anchored frame moves as well. See "Anchoring Graphics" on page 304 for details about inserting anchored frames. *Graphic frames* can crop or mask objects. They also store frequently used items on the reference pages.

NOTE You can place imported graphics and drawn objects in the same anchored or graphic frame. In this book, for example, we imported the graphics, drew small text frames inside the anchored frame for callout text, and then drew the callout arrows.

Drawing Basic Shapes

You draw most objects by clicking a button on the Tools palette and then dragging the cursor across the page. As you draw an object, an outline appears on the page. This outline is the *path* of the object—an imaginary line that bisects the object border. When you let go of the cursor, the object border is displayed on the page, and the object is selected.

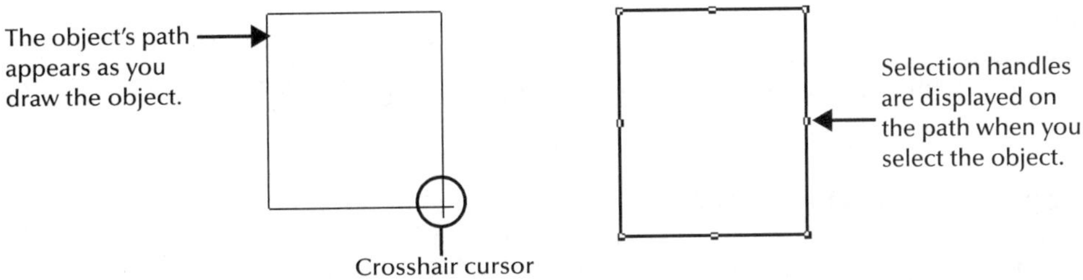

FrameMaker's drawing tools are in the Tools palette (Figure 13-1). You can format objects with a color, pattern, border, and other properties. To display the tools, select Graphics➤Tools or click the Tools palette button in the upper-right corner of your document.

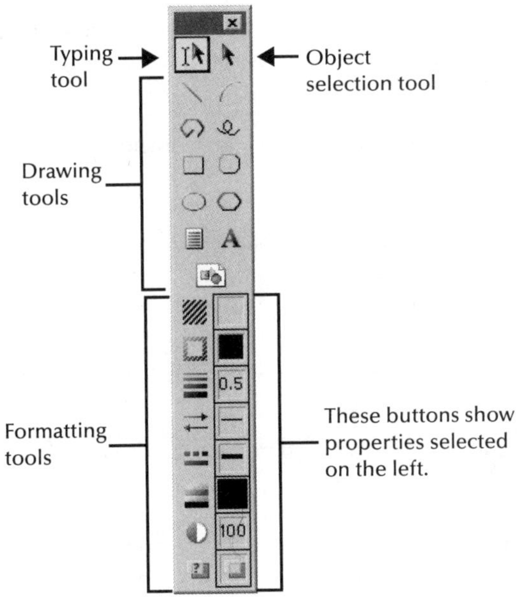

Figure 13-1. The Tools palette

Table 13-1 on page 340 summarizes the features on the Tools palette.

Button	Description
	**Smart Select.** For selecting text or objects. Press CTRL to force selection of an object.
	**Select Object.** For selecting an object but not text.
	**Line.** For drawing a straight line. To draw a line at a 45-degree angle, press SHIFT when drawing the line.
	**Arc.** For drawing a curved line. To draw one-fourth of a circle, press SHIFT when drawing the segment.
	**Polyline.** For drawing a line with several segments. To draw a polyline, click at each segment point and then double-click at the end of the line.
	**Freehand Curve.** For drawing a smoothed polyline. To draw a freehand curve, click and drag the cursor.
	**Rectangle.** For drawing a rectangle. To draw a square, press SHIFT when drawing the shape.
	**Rounded Rectangle.** For drawing a rectangle with rounded corners. To draw a square with rounded corners, press SHIFT when drawing the shape.
	**Oval.** For drawing ovals and circles. To draw a circle, press SHIFT when drawing the shape.
	**Polygon.** For drawing a closed shape composed of several line segments. To draw a polygon, click at each corner and then double-click at the end point.
	**Text Frame.** For drawing a text frame on any page in a document, including master and reference pages.

Table 13-1. Tools Palette Buttons

Button	Description
	**Text Line.** For typing lines of text. To type several lines of text, click where the text begins, type the text, and press ENTER to type another line. (Text lines don't wrap, so you must press ENTER where you want the line to break.) Each text line is a separate object that you click and move on the page. The previous cursor location determines the default font properties. For example, if your cursor was previously in a paragraph with a 24-point blue font, the text line has the same properties. You can change the text line font properties using the Format menu, object properties, character tags, or the Color button in the Tools palette. You cannot apply a paragraph tag to text lines.
	**Graphic Frame.** For drawing a frame to crop or mask objects. Also used on the reference pages to hold frequently used objects, such as note icons and borders.
	**Fill Pattern.** For choosing a fill pattern for the selected object. Some striped fill and pen patterns don't display accurately in PDF files. If you plan to convert your document to PDF, you should create a test PDF file before using a particular pattern. (If you click the fill pattern, pen pattern, or line width buttons when your cursor is in a table, the Custom Ruling and Shading dialog box is displayed.)
	**Pen Pattern.** For choosing a pen pattern, or border style, for the selected object. As is the case with fill patterns, you should create a test PDF file before using a specific pen pattern if you plan to distribute the document as a PDF file.
	**Line Width.** For choosing from four preset line widths or changing the default widths.
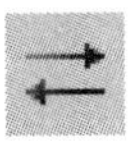	**Line End Style.** For selecting from four plain or arrowhead line ends. You can also choose from eight additional arrow styles, specify a custom arrow style, and select the shape for line ends.
	**Dashed Line Pattern.** For selecting plain or dashed line patterns. You can also choose from eight additional line patterns.
	**Color.** For setting the color of selected objects. Select from the predefined colors, plus any custom colors that you have added. See "Managing Color Definitions" on page 504 for details.

Table 13-1. Tools Palette Buttons (Continued)

Button	Description
	**Tint.** For setting the tint of a previously selected color in 5 percent increments from 0 percent to 100 percent. You can also type in a specific tint between 0 and 100 percent. The tint is reset to 100 percent if you apply a different color to the object.
	**Overprint.** Indicates how FrameMaker prints the colors of an overlapping text frame and object. When you change the color of an object, the overprint is reset to From Color. ▪ **Knock Out:** FrameMaker prints only the color of the top object. ▪ **Overprint:** FrameMaker prints both colors from the overlapped portion of the objects. ▪ **From Color:** FrameMaker prints the color using the overprint setting from the color definition. The overprint setting matters only for process printing and color separations. See Chapter 20, "Color Output," for more information on color.

Table 13-1. Tools Palette Buttons (Continued)

To draw an object, follow these steps:

1. *(optional)* Insert one of the following:
   - An anchored frame to attach the graphic to a specific paragraph.
   - A graphic frame to crop the graphic or to draw the graphic on the reference page. (See "Placing Graphics on the Reference Pages" on page 328 for more information.)
2. Select Graphics➤Tools. The Tools palette is displayed (Figure 13-1 on page 339).
3. Click the button for the object you want to draw.
4. Click where you want the object.
5. Draw the object according to descriptions in Table 13-1. For example, to draw a freehand curve, click at the starting point and drag your cursor to form the line. To draw a rectangle, rounded rectangle, or oval, click at the starting point and drag to the opposite corner or edge. To draw a polygon, click at the first point, click at the midpoints, and then double-click at the end point.

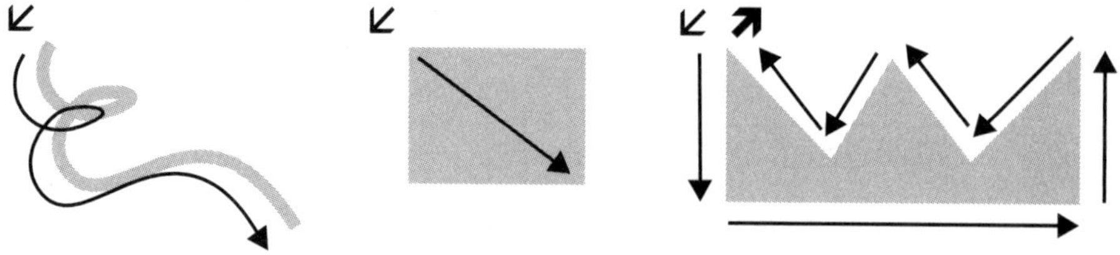

TIP To judge the size of the object as you draw, use the FrameMaker rulers or status bar dimensions as guides. The ruler markings show the size of the object as you draw, as do the dimensions displayed in the status bar. Select View➤Rulers to toggle the ruler display.

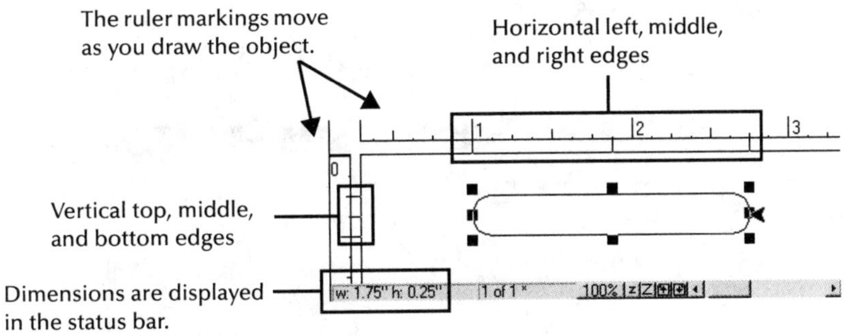

For more information on anchored frames, see "Anchoring Graphics" on page 304. See "Cropping and Masking Graphics" on page 358 for details on graphic frames.

Working with Grids

There are two types of grids in FrameMaker.

- **Snap grid.** Lets you specify spacing for an imaginary grid. Typically, you can draw, move, copy, or resize an object and drop the edge of the object at any point on the page. When snap is turned on, the edge of the object "snaps" to the imaginary grid. Snap also applies when you reshape, rotate, and align objects. To toggle the snap grid, select Graphics➤Snap.
- **Grid Lines.** Displays grid lines on the page, which may have different dimensions from the snap grid. The following example shows 0.5-inch grid lines, and the snap grid is set to 0.25 inches. When the square is resized, it snaps to the closest 0.25-inch mark on the ruler.

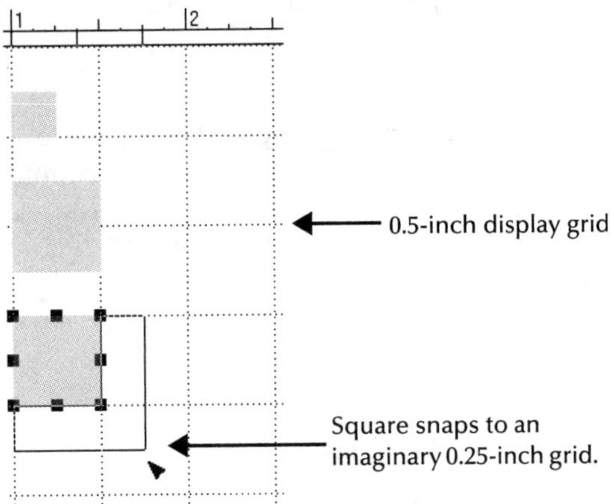

NOTE It is possible for the snap grid and the grid lines to conflict.

To toggle the grid lines, select View➤Grid Lines. To change the spacing for snap grid and grid lines, follow these steps:

1. Select View➤Options. The View Options dialog box is displayed (Figure 13-2).

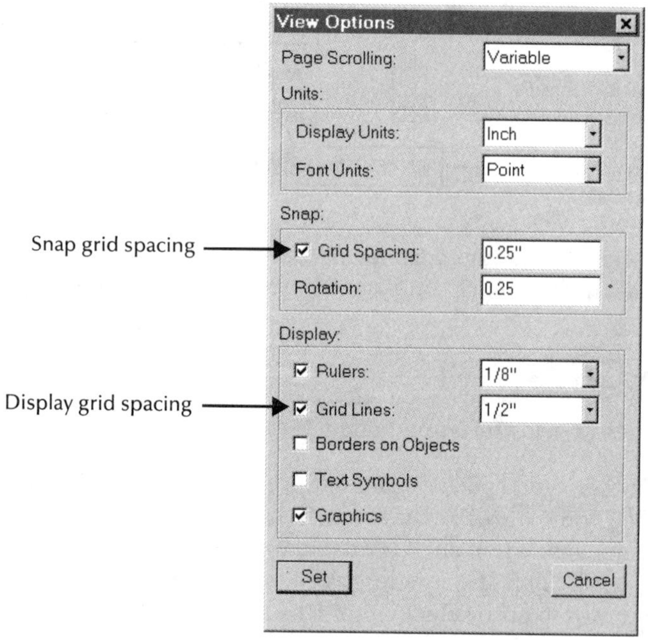

Figure 13-2. Changing the grid view settings

2. To change the snap grid spacing, type a number in the Grid Spacing field.

TIP To change the unit of measure for snap, click a different item in the Display Units drop-down list.

3. *(optional)* To apply snap to objects that you rotate manually, type the degree of rotation in the Rotation field. (Note that the setting is not in degrees proper—you type a decimal point before the number.) For instance, the following illustration shows objects rotated manually on a 45-degree snap grid. See "Rotating" on page 366 for details.

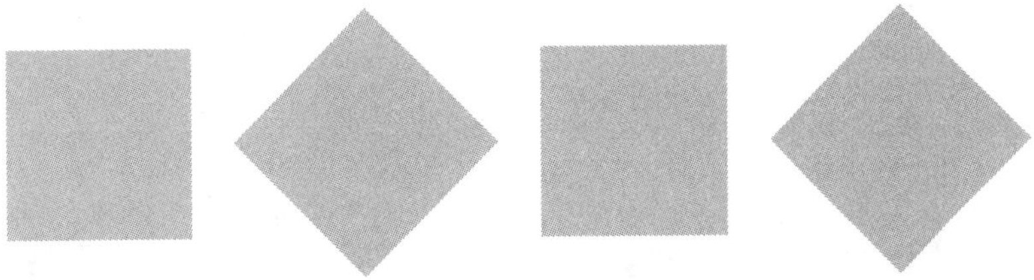

4. To change the display grid spacing, click a measurement in the Grid Lines drop-down list.

TIP After you change the grid line spacing, the Grid Lines check box is automatically checked. This means the grid lines will be displayed when you save your changes. You can uncheck the check box if you don't want to display the grid lines yet.

5. Click the Set button to save your changes.

Selecting Objects

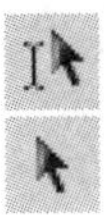

You can select objects with the Smart Select pointer, which is displayed when you edit text, or the Object Pointer, which you click in the Tools palette to select objects. Using the Smart Select pointer, you select an object by CTRL-clicking the object or border. Using the Object Pointer, you can just click the object to select it. You'll need to click the Smart Select pointer button in the Tools palette to type text again. If the object has a fill pattern, you can click anywhere in the object to select it; for hollow objects (objects without a fill pattern), you must click the border.

When an object is selected, square selection handles are displayed on the path of the object. You drag a handle to manually resize the object. See "Resizing" on page 351 for details.

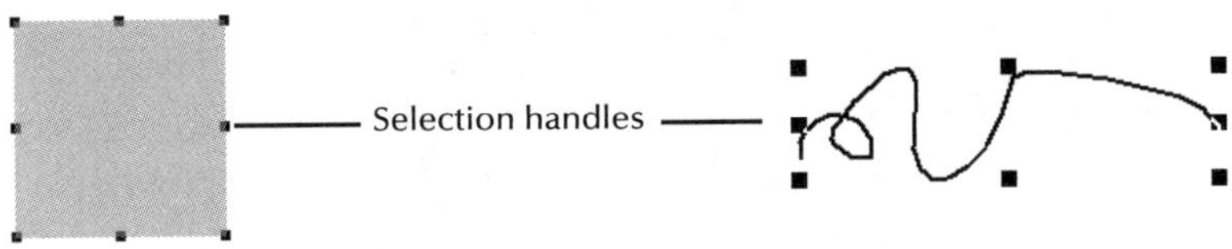

To select several objects at once, press either CTRL or SHIFT as you click each object. To select objects with a selection rectangle, press SHIFT and ALT as you drag. You can also select all objects inside an anchored or graphic frame by clicking the frame and pressing CTRL-A.

CAUTION Pressing CTRL-A with your cursor in the main flow selects all content in the flow instead of the objects.

Deleting Objects

To delete one object, select the object and press the DELETE key. To delete several objects, do one of the following:

- Select only the objects you want to delete by pressing either CTRL or SHIFT as you click each one.
- Select all objects, press either CTRL or SHIFT, and click the objects you *don't* want to delete to deselect them. Another way is to hold down SHIFT and ALT while you drag a selection rectangle around selected objects to deselect them.

Press the DELETE key to remove the selected objects.

Modifying Objects

You change basic properties such as color, tint, pattern, and border attributes in the object properties or the Tools palette. For a single object, you can use either method. To format several objects, select properties in the Tools palette. Although the Tools palette lets you change basic properties, other settings—the object dimensions, offsets from the left and top of the page, and angle—must be changed in the object properties. The following example shows the color, tint, and border width properties that are displayed in both the object properties and the Tools palette.

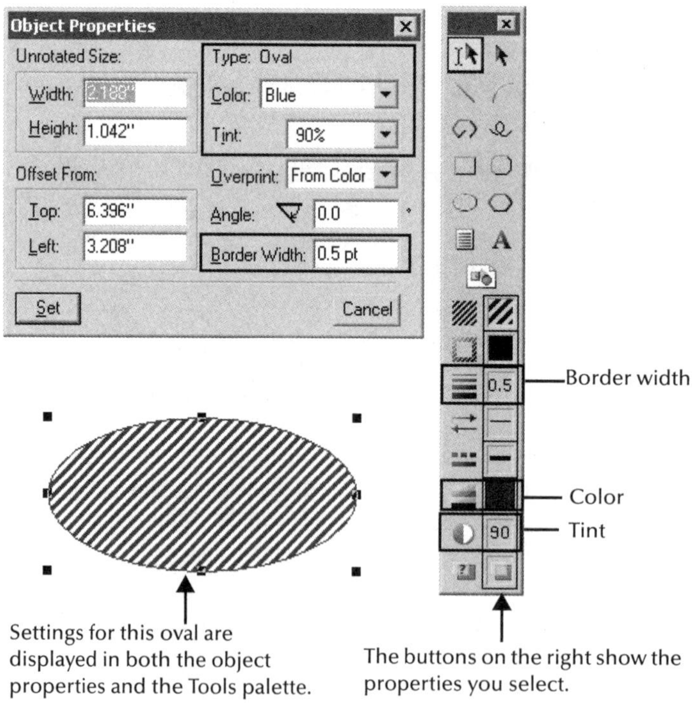

After you select a property in the Tools palette, that property is saved as a default until you change it or close FrameMaker. For example, the object in the preceding example has a 0.5-point border. This border width is saved as a default on the Line Width button until you select another line width. The property is also saved as a default when no objects are selected. To apply the same border to other objects, select the objects, then click the Line Width button.

TIP To display the properties of any object in the Tools palette, select the object, press SHIFT, and then select Graphics➤Pick up Object Properties. The formatting of the selected object is displayed on the buttons.

To format an object using the Tools palette, follow these steps:

1. Select the object or objects you want to format, then select Graphics➤Tools. The Tools palette is displayed (see the previous illustration).
2. Click the button for the property you need to change, then click an item in the pop-up menu. The properties are described in Table 13-1 on page 340. Your changes are displayed on the object, and the buttons on the Tools palette show the selected properties.

To format an item through the object properties, follow these steps:

1. Select the object you want to format, then select Graphics➤Object Properties. The Object Properties dialog box is displayed.

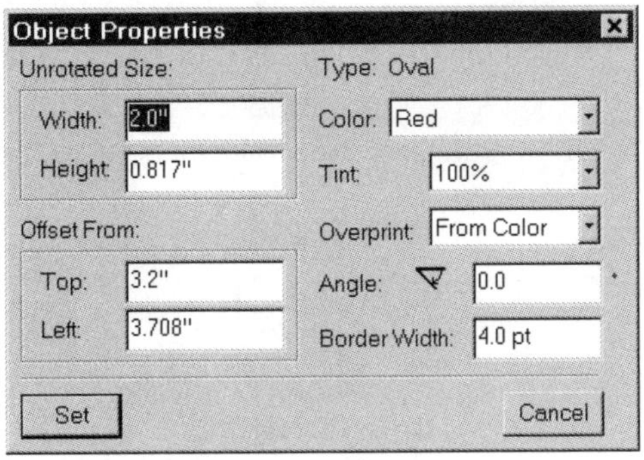

Figure 13-3. Object Properties dialog box

2. Set any of the following:
   - **Unrotated Size:** To change the size of the object, type different dimensions in the Width and Height fields. (For rotated objects, the dimensions shown are for the original, unrotated object.)
   - **Offset From:** To change the distance from the top and left edges of the page or graphic frame, type different offsets in the Top and Left fields.
   - **Color:** To change the color, click a color in the Color drop-down list.

- **Tint:** To lighten or darken the color, click a percentage in the Tint drop-down list.
- **Overprint:** To control how colors print on overlapping objects, click an option in the Overprint drop-down list. This setting is used for process printing and color separations only.
- **Angle:** To modify the orientation of the object, type the degrees in the Angle field.
- **Border Width:** To change the border, type the new width in the Border Width field.

3. Click the Set button. Your changes are applied.

Redefining Line Widths

In the Tools palette, you can change the four predefined line widths. The new line widths may be applied to objects, but they're not automatically updated in existing objects. For example, if you change the thinnest default line to 1 point, the 0.5-point lines in your document aren't updated. You have to apply the new line width to objects manually.

Unlike other properties, custom line widths are saved until you change them, even if you close FrameMaker. The chosen line width, however, defaults to the thinnest value when you close and reopen FrameMaker. So if you want the default line width to be 1 point, modify the predefined line widths to include a 1-point line as the thinnest line.

To change the default line widths, follow these steps:

1. Select Graphics➤Tools. The Tools palette is displayed (Figure 13-1 on page 339).
2. Click the Line Width button. The Line Widths pop-up menu is displayed.

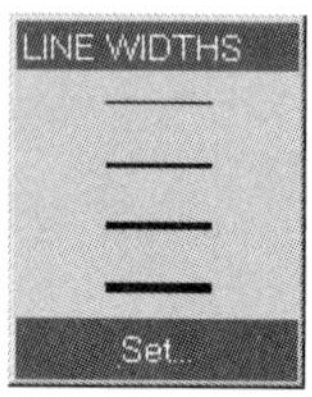

3. Click Set. The Line Width Options dialog box is displayed.

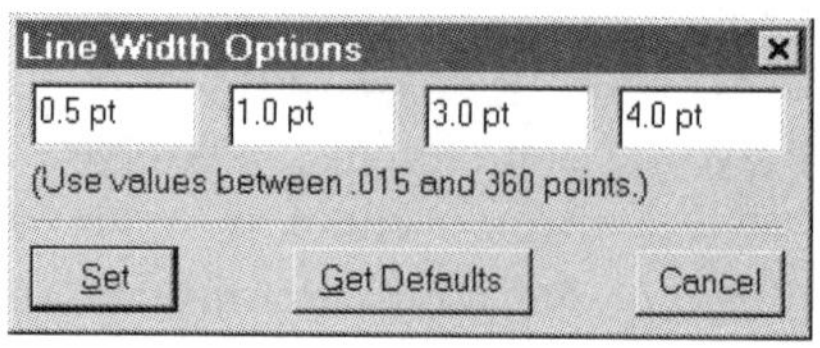

4. Type new point values in the fields, then click the Set button. The values are mapped to lines in the Line Widths pop-up menu.

TIP Using the Object Properties dialog box (Figure 13-3 on page 347), you can specify a line width that isn't in the default line widths shown in the pop-up menu in the Tools palette.

Changing the Default Arrowhead

FrameMaker provides eight predefined arrowheads. If you don't like the predefined arrowheads, you can create your own by specifying the base angle, tip angle, and length. The following example shows the settings for a custom arrowhead.

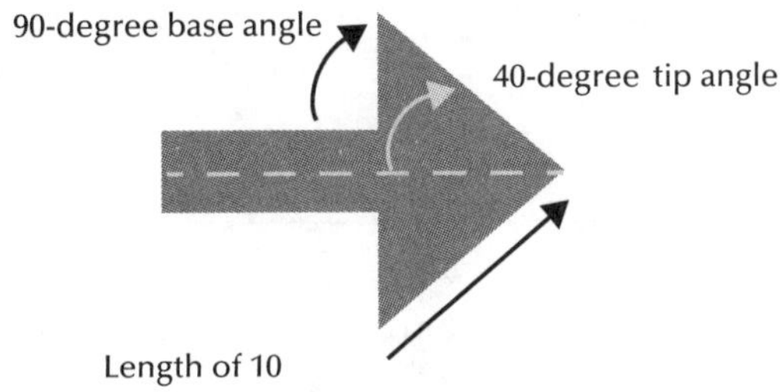

You can select a predefined or custom arrow style as the default. FrameMaker's default arrow style looks like the following:

When you close and reopen FrameMaker, the arrow style reverts to FrameMaker's default style. If you use a different arrow style in your documentation, you'll need to select it again in the Tools palette after reopening FrameMaker. Alternatively, you can click an existing arrow, press SHIFT, and then select Graphics➤Pick up Object Properties. The arrow style is selected and displayed on the Line End Style button in the Tools palette.

To change the default arrow style in a document, follow these steps:

1. Select Graphics➤Tools. The Tools palette is displayed (Figure 13-1 on page 339).
2. Click the Line End Style button. The Line Ends pop-up menu is displayed.

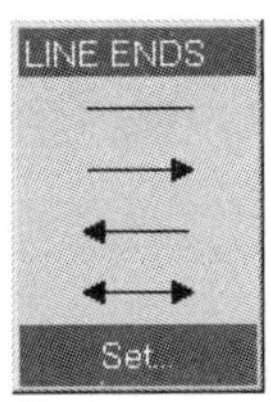

CONTROLLING PAGE LAYOUT

3. Click Set. The Line End Options dialog box is displayed.

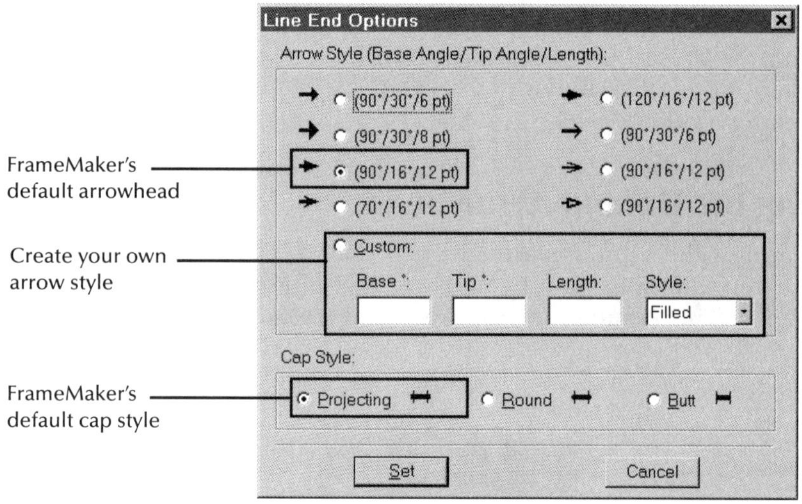

NOTE The third arrowhead on the left is FrameMaker's default arrow style.

4. Do one of the following:
   - Click a radio button for the arrow you like.
   - Click the Custom radio button, then type the base and tip angle in degrees and the length in points. Click the arrowhead style in the Style drop-down list. (The tip angle must be at least 5 degrees smaller than the base angle.)
5. To change the end of the arrowhead, click one of the radio buttons in the Cap Style section. The default is a projecting cap.
6. Click the Set button. The default arrow style is updated and can be applied to new and existing objects. (Existing objects are not automatically updated.)

Modifying the Default Dashed Line

FrameMaker provides eight default dashed lines. You can set one as the default; however, when you close and reopen FrameMaker, the line style reverts to FrameMaker's default style.

To modify the default dashed line, follow these steps:

1. Select Graphics➤Tools. The Tools palette is displayed (Figure 13-1 on page 339).
2. Click the Dashed Line Pattern button. The Line Styles pop-up menu is displayed.

3. Click Set. The Dashed Line Options dialog box is displayed.

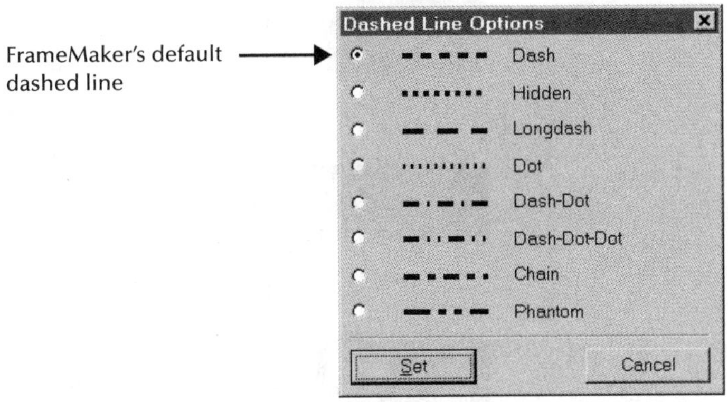

4. Click the radio button for the line you like, then click the Set button. The default dashed line is updated and can be applied to new and existing objects. (Existing objects are not automatically updated.)

Resizing

You resize objects by dragging the edge or corner of the object or providing specific dimensions. If you know the approximate size for an object, it's quicker—although perhaps less accurate—to resize the object manually and use the FrameMaker rulers as a guide. The ruler markings are updated as you resize the object, as are the dimensions displayed in the status bar. To change the specific height or width, you need to type new dimensions in the object properties or scaling properties.

FrameMaker has a handy feature called *gravity* that snaps objects together. Gravity is like "snap to object" and is called gravity because "objects attract." As you resize, reshape, or draw an object, the path or corner of the object meets the closest path or corner of the adjacent object. The centers of ovals and rectangles also have gravity. The following illustration shows how the paths of two objects meet as you resize the dark gray rectangle toward the hollow rectangle. To toggle gravity, select Graphics➤Gravity.

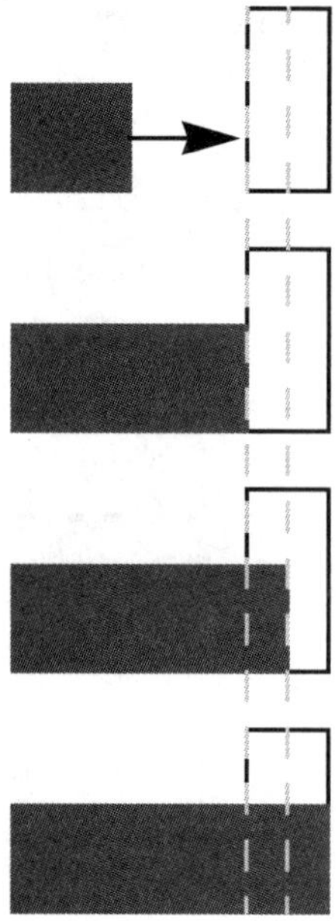

Manually Resizing an Object

To resize an object using the mouse, follow these steps:

1. Click one of the object selection handles. The cursor changes to an arrow.
2. Drag the handle to resize the object.

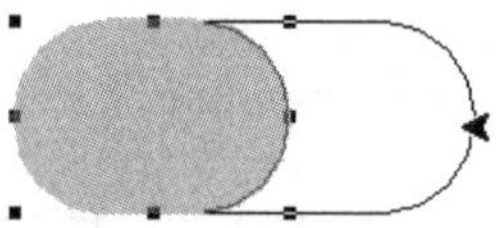

Typing a Specific Height or Width

To type a specific height or width, do one of the following:

- Select the object, then select Graphics➤Scale. The Scale dialog box is displayed. Type new dimensions in the Width or Height fields, then click the Scale button. The object is resized from the center.

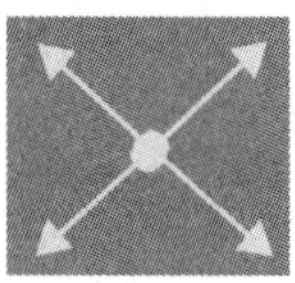

Scaled object is resized from the middle.

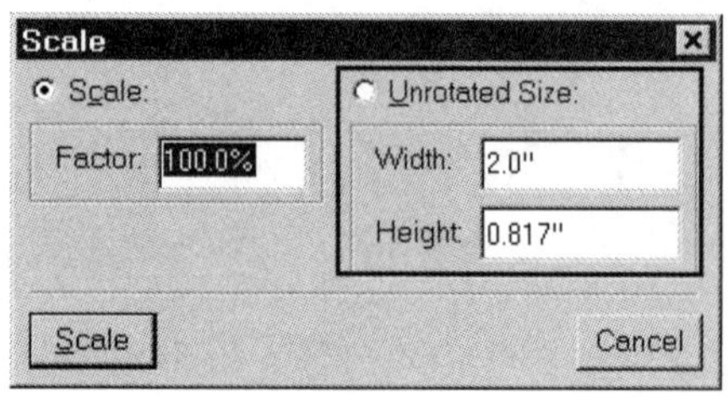

- Select the object, then select Graphics➤Object Properties. The Object Properties dialog box is displayed. Type new dimensions in the Width or Height fields, then click the Set button. The object is resized from the top-left corner.

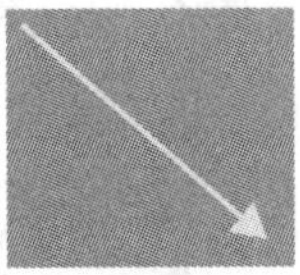

Modifying the object properties resizes from the top-left corner.

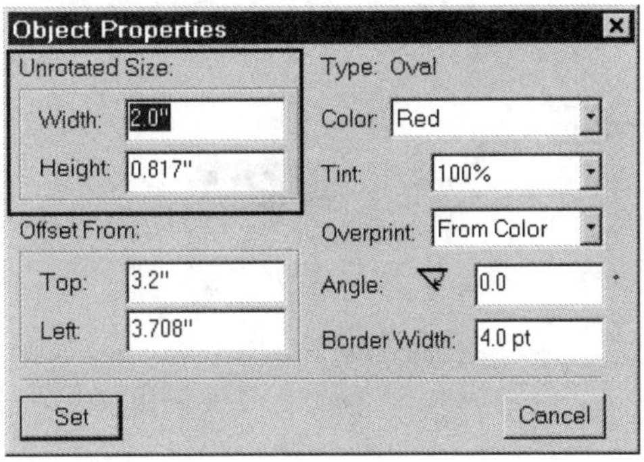

NOTE When you rotate an object, the width and height in the Object Properties don't change to reflect the rotated width and height.

Resizing Proportionately

To resize an object proportionately, do one of the following:

- Click a selection handle and press SHIFT while you drag the handle.
- Click the graphic, then select Graphics➤Scale. The Scale dialog box is displayed. Type a percentage in the Factor field, then click the Scale button.

The object is resized proportionately.

TIP To resize several objects without grouping them, select them all and then use the Scale command.

Reshaping

You can alter the shape of many objects instead of redrawing them. You reshape objects using reshape handles and control points:

- Reshape handles look like selection handles, but they appear on corners and curves. By adding, moving, or deleting the reshape handles, you modify the direction, angle, and shape of freehand curves, arcs, polylines, and polygons.
- Control points let you change the direction and curve of freehand curves.

Display reshape handles and control points by clicking the object and selecting Graphics➤Reshape. On the freehand curve, reshape handles and control points are displayed after you draw the object while it's still selected. Reshape handles and control points are no longer displayed when you deselect the object.

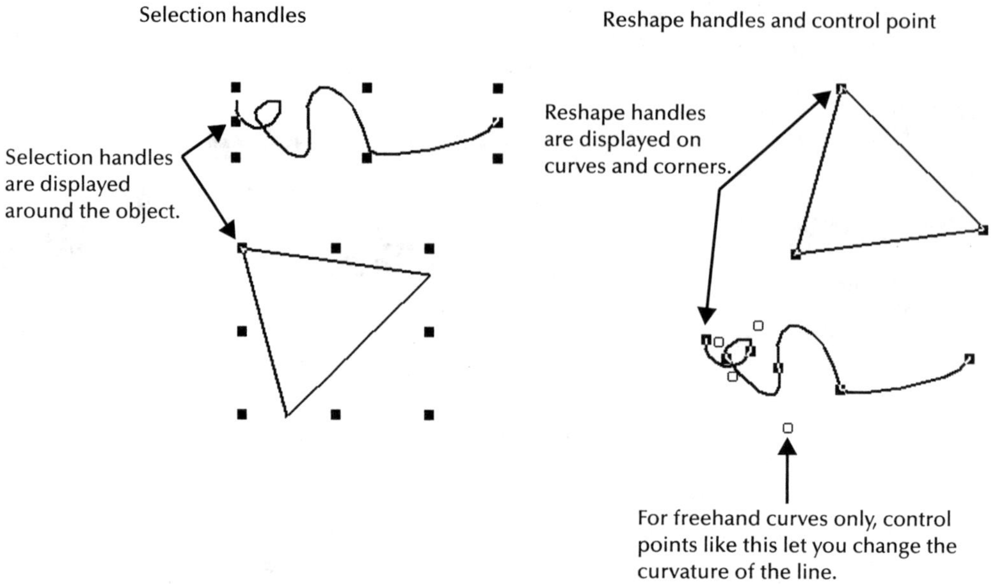

To alter the shape of a freehand curve, arc, polyline, or polygon, follow these steps:

1. Select the object, then select Graphics➤Reshape. The reshape handles are displayed.
2. Do any of the following:
   - Drag a reshape handle or control point until a solid line is displayed, then change the length and direction of the line. The crosshair pointer marks the location of the reshape handle or control point as you move it. Lengthen the line and change the direction of the line until you like the shape. In the following figure, the freehand curve has both reshape handles and control points; the example shows a reshape handle being dragged.

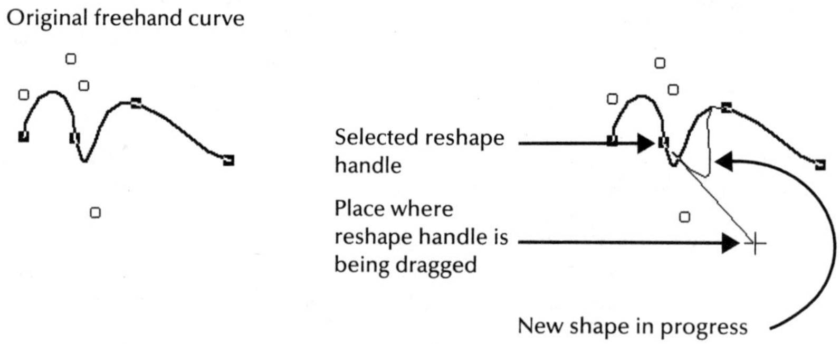

- To add a reshape handle to a freehand curve, polyline, or polygon, CTRL-click the border where you want the handle. The new handle is displayed on the object.

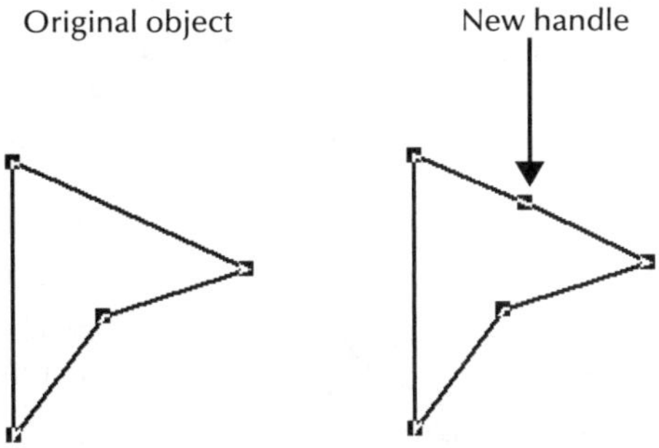

- To remove a reshape handle, CTRL-click an existing handle. The handle, which can change the shape of the object, is no longer displayed.

Smoothing Corners

On rectangles, polylines, and polygons, you can convert the corners to curves. To smooth an object, select the object, then select Graphics➤Smooth. The corners of the object are displayed as rounded edges, and the object type is updated in the object properties. To revert to the original shape, select Graphics➤Unsmooth.

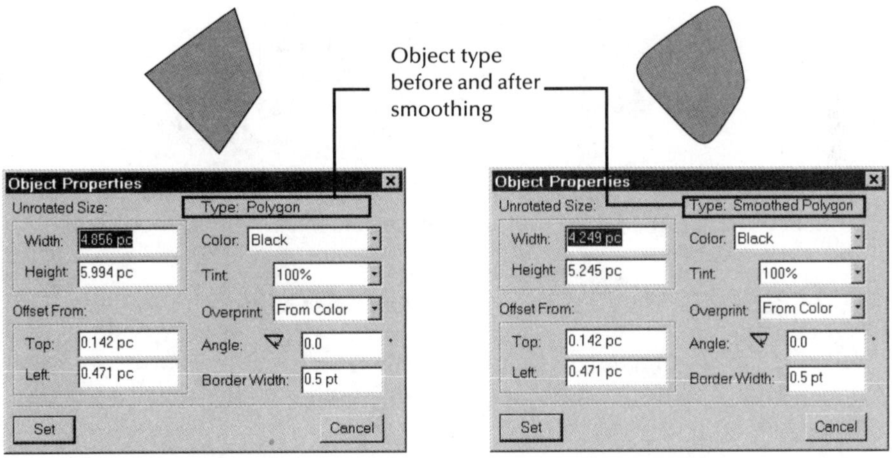

When you smooth a polyline or polygon, FrameMaker adds control points to the object. You change the curvature of the object by dragging a control point. For details on modifying a curve, see "Reshaping" on page 353.

Changing the Number of Sides

You can draw multisided objects, such as octagons and hexagons, using the Polyline or Polygon tool; however, it's quicker to draw an oval or rectangle and then change the number of sides. To configure the orientation of the object, you change the angle of the first side. For example, the following illustration shows an oval converted to an octagon with a 22-degree start angle.

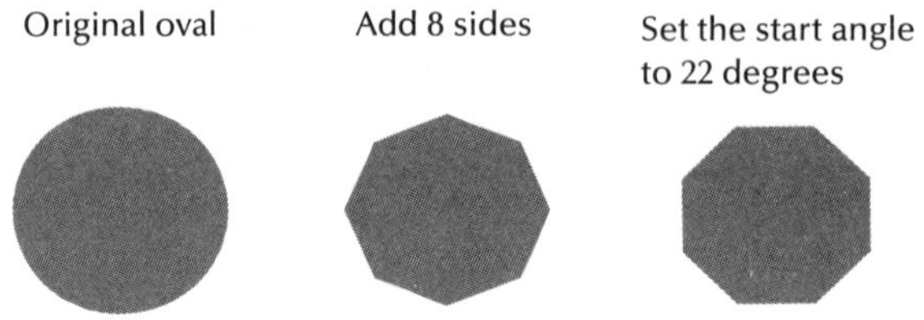

The object properties also show the angle of an object, but this angle is different from the start angle. The start angle is the degree at which the first side of the object is displayed; the angle in the object properties is the degree to which the object is rotated. If you rotate an object that has a start angle, the object is rotated from the start angle. The following illustration shows the octagon rotated 25 degrees.

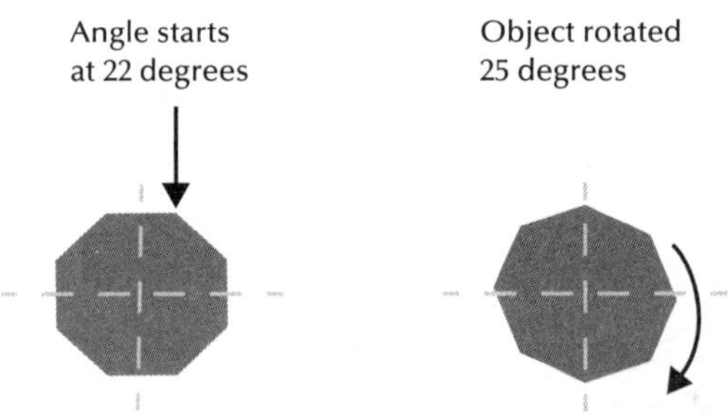

TIP You can change the number of sides on multiple objects by selecting them all at once, but a grouped or smoothed object's sides cannot be modified.

To change the number of sides on an object, follow these steps:

1. Select the oval or rectangle (not the rounded rectangle) you want to reshape, then select Graphics➤Set # Sides. The Set Number of Sides dialog box is displayed.

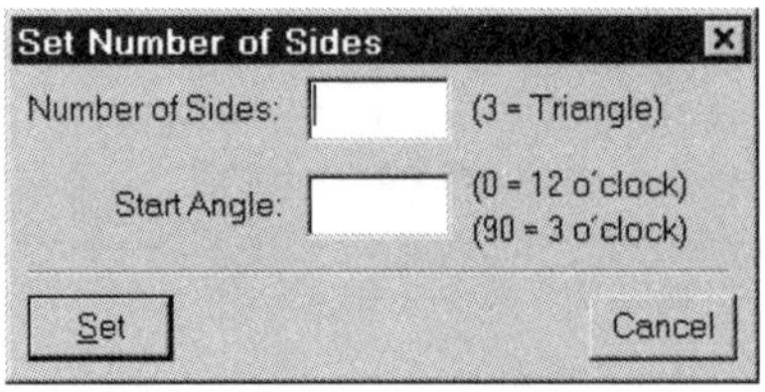

2. Type a number (3 or higher) in the Number of Sides field. For example, to convert a circle to a hexagon, type 6.

3. To change the angle of the first side, type the number of degrees in the Start Angle field.
4. Click the Set button. The object is reshaped.

Joining Lines

You can join two or more lines (straight lines, arcs, freehand curves, and polylines) to form a single object. Joining lets you create a shape from multiple lines.

When you join lines with different weights, FrameMaker assigns the width of the last selected line. The following illustration compares the result of selecting the thin or thick line last and then joining the lines.

Original lines — Thin line selected last — Thick line selected last

FrameMaker's gravity feature causes the ends of two lines attract to each other so you can join them. As you draw, resize, or reshape a line near another line, the closest paths or corners of the two lines meet. Gravity doesn't apply when you *move* a line near another line; it only works when you draw, resize, or reshape a line. If you need to move two lines together before joining them, align them and then move the lines until the edges meet. See "Aligning" on page 360 for details. To toggle gravity, select Graphics➤Gravity.

Original object doesn't line up with flipped object. — Bottom edges are aligned. — When you move one line to touch the other, the edges meet.

CAUTION There is no "unjoin" command. You must undo the joined lines after you join them, or choose a change on the History list before the lines were joined. Select Edit➤History or press CTRL-K to view the History list.

To join lines, follow these steps:

1. Drag one line toward the end of the line you want to join until the ends meet. The ends of the lines (not the paths) must touch for you to connect them.
2. Select both lines, then select Graphics➤Join. The lines form one object. If the lines weren't touching, an error is displayed. Align the objects, then try to join them again.

To create a symmetrical shape, follow these steps

1. Draw a line that's half of the shape you need.
2. With the line selected, press SHIFT, then press CTRL and drag the line to copy it. (Pressing SHIFT while you copy a line keeps the alignment.)
3. Flip the copied line by selecting Graphics➤Flip Up/Down or Graphics➤Left/Right.
4. Move the flipped line toward the original line until the ends meet.
5. Select both lines, then select Graphics➤Join. The lines form one object. If the lines weren't touching, an error is displayed. Align the objects, then try to join them again.

Draw Copy Flip   Move one line to touch the other line and then join the lines.   Apply a fill, set the pen pattern (the border), then scale the object 50 percent.

After you create the symmetrical shape, you can format the object and, if necessary, scale the object. It's easier to create small items, such as the candle flame in the preceding example, by scaling a large joined object rather than trying to work with small lines.

Cropping and Masking Graphics

Graphic frames are handy for cropping or masking objects. In the following illustration, the graphic frame on the left is placed behind the sun. This crops the bottom-right edge of the sun to fit inside the windowpane. On the right, the graphic frame is placed over the clock to mask the object and create white space. The graphic frame has a white background by default, but you can apply a color and tint to the frame.

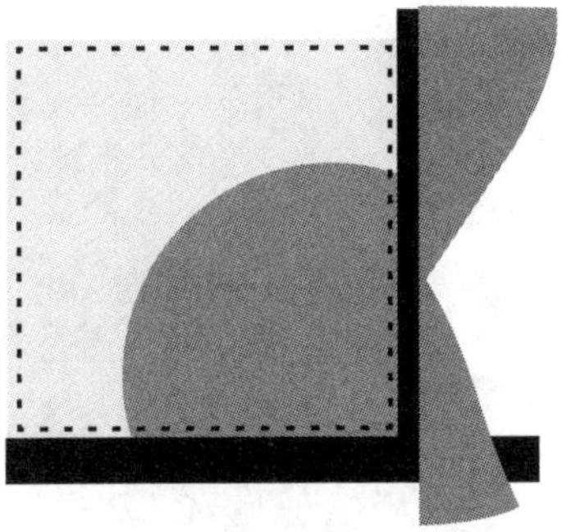

Cropped object

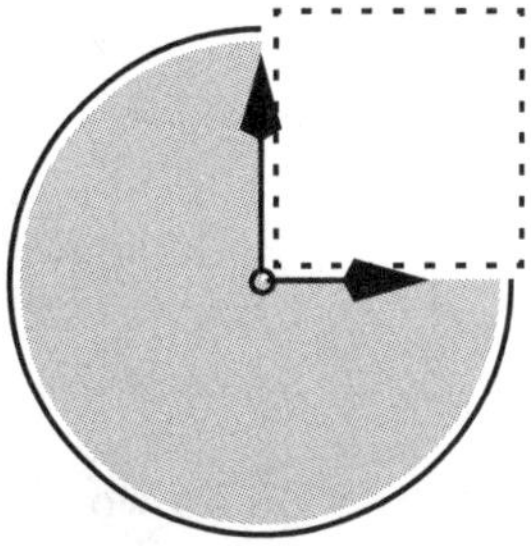

Masked object

To crop an object, follow these steps:

1. Click the Graphic Frame icon in the Tools palette and draw the frame.
2. Do one of the following:
   - Draw the object you're cropping inside the graphic frame and move the frame to crop the object.
   - Drag an existing object into the graphic frame and then adjust the frame to crop the object.

Graphic frame crops lower portion of the sun.

3. *(optional)* To apply a fill pattern and color to the graphic frame, select the frame and then click a fill pattern and color on the Tools palette.

To mask an object, follow these steps:

1. Click the Graphic Frame icon in the Tools palette.
2. Draw a graphic frame over the area of the object you want to mask. For a graphic consisting of several objects, you might need to force one of the objects to be displayed over the graphic frame. For example, placing the graphic frame over the following clock covers part of the clock hands. To display the hands on top of the frame, click the hands, then select Graphics➤Bring to Front.

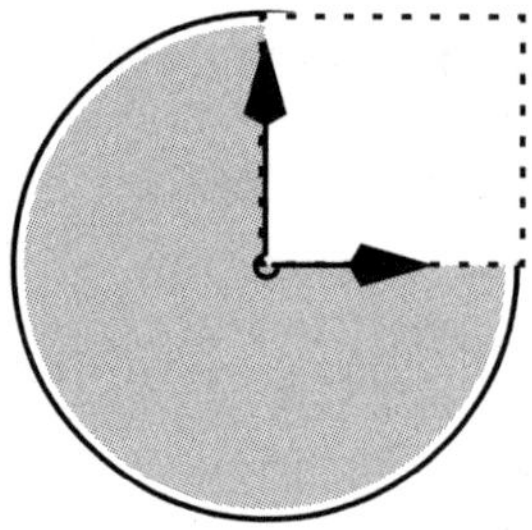

For more information on working with layered objects, see "Layering Objects" on page 365.

Rearranging Objects

Besides dragging and dropping objects to rearrange them, you can arrange objects by aligning, distributing, or moving them to the foreground or background.

Aligning

Alignment is based on the position of the last object you select. Suppose you want to align the tops of the line and triangle shown in the following illustration. If you select the line and then the triangle, the line moves down to align with the triangle. If you select the triangle first, the triangle moves up to align with the line.

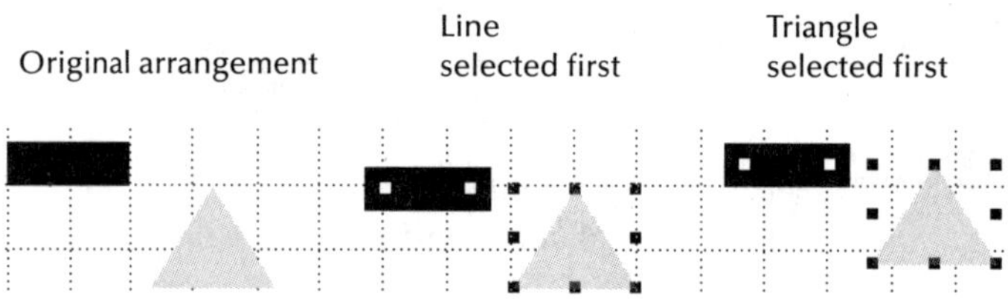

To align objects, follow these steps:

1. Select the objects you want to align.
2. Select Graphics➤Align. The Align dialog box is displayed. (If you previously aligned objects, the last settings you used are displayed.)

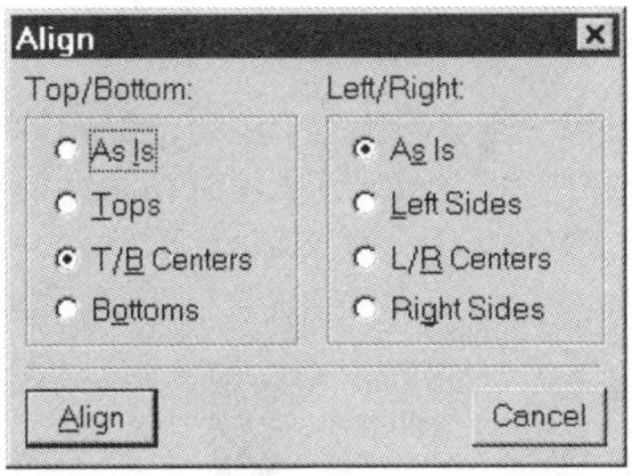

3. Do any of the following:
   - To align graphics vertically, click the appropriate radio button in the Top/Bottom section.

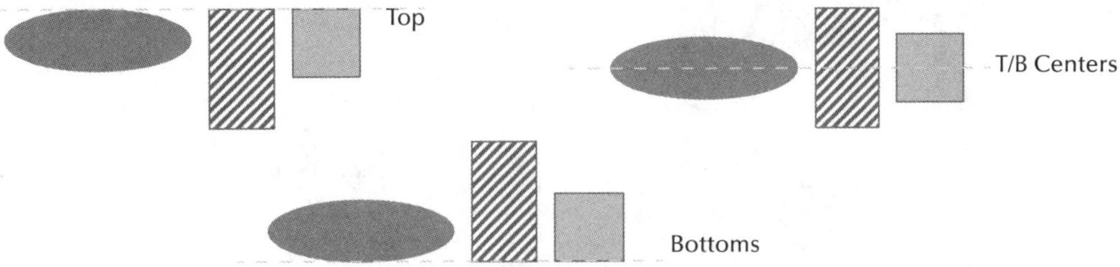

   - To align shapes horizontally, click the appropriate radio button in the Left/Right section.

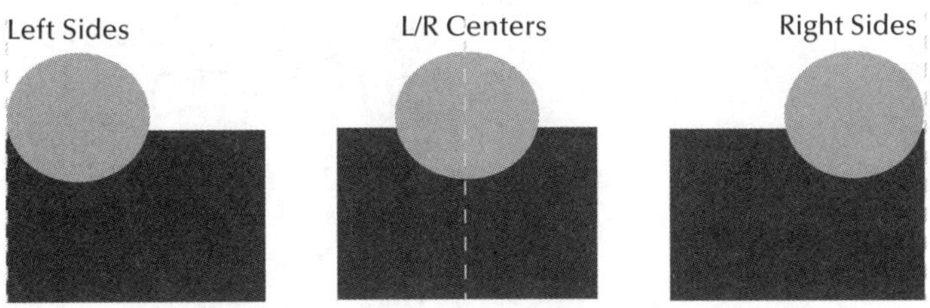

4. Click the Align button. The objects are aligned.

Distributing

You change the space among objects by distributing them. Distributing objects adds an equal amount of space vertically or horizontally. For example, if you specify a horizontal gap of 0.05 inches, FrameMaker adds 0.05 inches of space between each object horizontally.

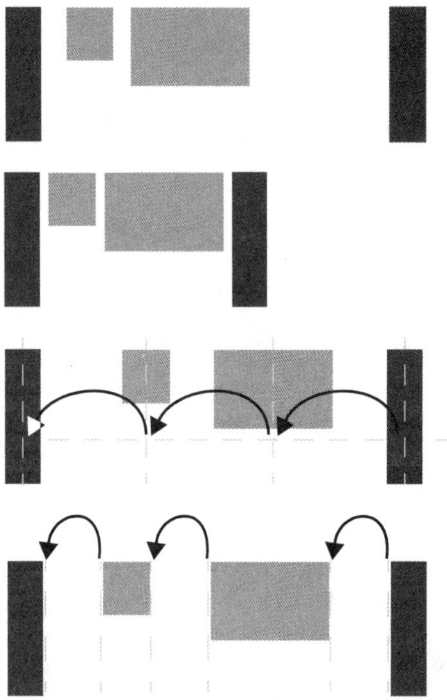

Original layout

0.05 inches between the objects

Equidistant centers

Equidistant edges

Unlike aligning, which lines up objects with the last selected object, distributing objects doesn't move the left and right objects (in horizontal distribution) or top and bottom objects (in vertical distribution); only the objects in the middle move to distribute the space. The only exception occurs when you type in the amount of space between the objects. When aligned horizontally, the objects move from the right to the left. When aligned vertically, the objects move from the bottom up.

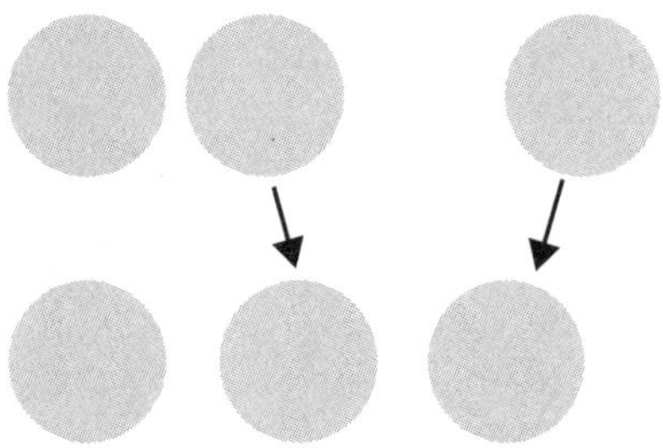

The object on the left doesn't move when objects are distributed.

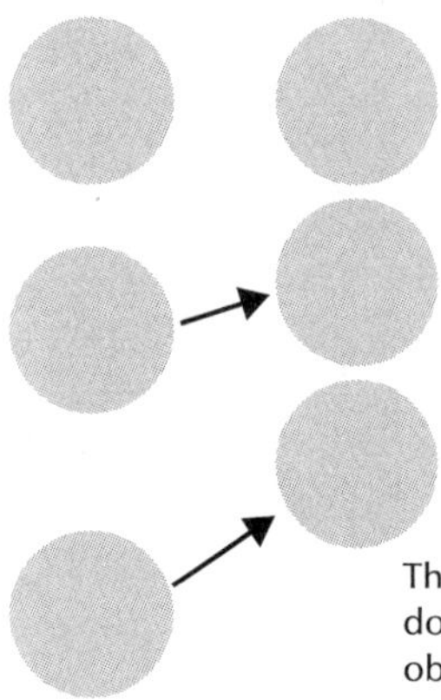

The object on the top doesn't move when objects are distributed.

To distribute spacing among objects, follow these steps:

1. Select the objects you want to distribute.
2. Select Graphics➤Distribute. The Distribute dialog box is displayed.

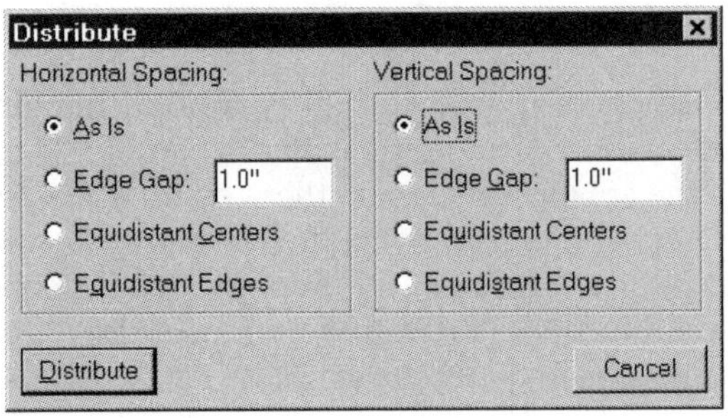

3. Do the following:
   - To align the objects horizontally, click the appropriate radio button in the Horizontal Spacing section.
   - To align the objects vertically, click the appropriate radio button in the Vertical Spacing section.

TIP To align objects so they are touching but not overlapping, set the edge gap to zero.

4. Click the Distribute button. The objects are distributed.

Grouping

Grouping is useful for creating one object from several shapes or for preventing objects from accidentally being moved on the page. You select the objects and then select Graphics➤Group to group them. After objects are grouped, you can modify, copy, move, or delete the group as one unit. For example, you can format all grouped objects with a solid fill and 5-point border. You can also flip, scale, rotate, reshape, and smooth or unsmooth; you cannot, however, change the number of sides. To ungroup a selected object, select Graphics➤Ungroup.

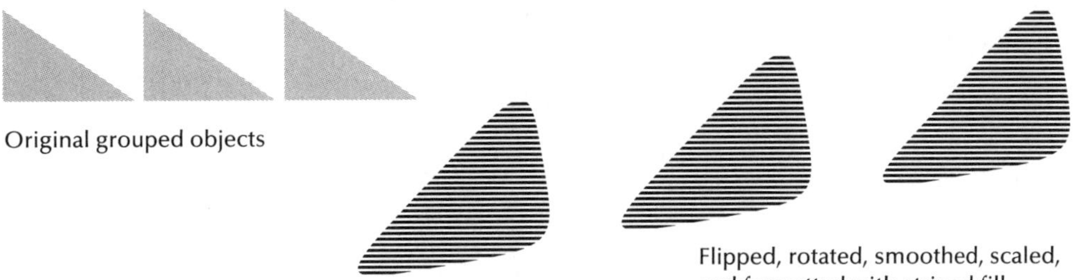

Original grouped objects

Flipped, rotated, smoothed, scaled, and formatted with striped fill

NOTE The Ungroup command is grayed out in the Graphics menu when you try to ungroup an object consisting of joined lines. See "Joining Lines" on page 357 for details.

Running Text Around an Object

You control how text is displayed around objects by configuring the object's runaround properties. The text either follows around the object's contour or the object's bounding box. (A bounding box is the smallest rectangle that contains the graphic.) You can also set the gap between the text and object. In the following illustration, the first object shows text running around the contour of the pyramid. The second object shows text that goes around the bounding box. Runaround properties aren't configured for the third object, so the text runs behind the object.

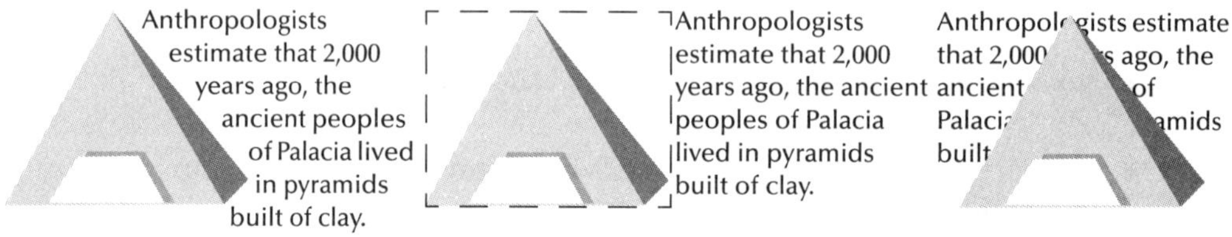

Text runs around the contour of the object.

Text runs around an imaginary box (represented by the dotted line).

Text does not run around the object.

TIP You can set runaround properties for several objects at once by selecting the objects and then changing the properties.

To configure runaround properties, follow these steps:

1. Select the object or objects, then select Graphics➤Runaround Properties. The Runaround Properties dialog box is displayed.

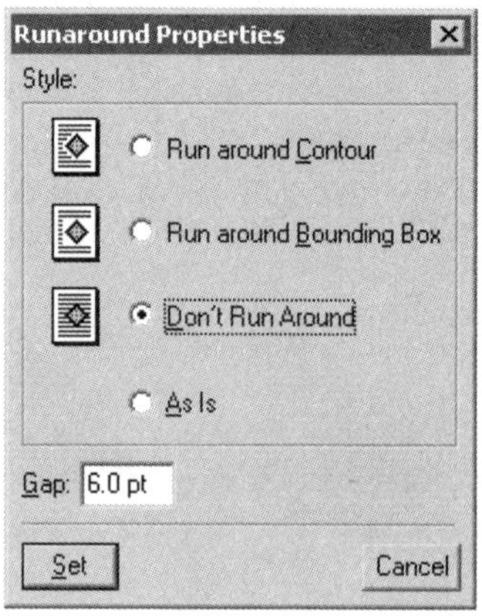

2. Do one of the following:
   - To flow text around the edges of the selected object, click the Run around Contour radio button.
   - To flow text around the bounding box, click the Run around Bounding Box radio button.
   - To avoid running text around the adjacent object, click the Don't Run Around radio button.

TIP Whenever possible, set the Don't Run Around option for your graphics and callout. If you add callouts to your graphics and the callouts won't consistently go where you want them, setting the Don't Run Around option for the graphic fixes the problem. Setting the Don't Run Around option for your graphics also prevents a long-known bug in FrameMaker where the page suddenly jumps back to the first page when you have been pressing PAGE DN to scroll through the document.

3. *(optional)* Type the number of points between the text and object in the Gap field. The default is 6 points. You cannot change the unit of measurement as you can with the default display unit.
4. Click the Set button. The text is displayed around the object as you specified.

Layering Objects

To change the order in which layered objects are displayed, you send an object to the foreground or background. Some graphics programs let you send objects forward or backward one layer at a time, which is handy when you have several layers of objects. In FrameMaker, you have two options—to move the object to the front or the back.

Objects are layered in the order you draw them. For example, in a drawing with three layers, the object you draw first is displayed on the back layer, the second object is displayed in the middle layer, and the last object is displayed on the top layer. You can only move an object to the front or the back. As a result, if you want the top layer to be in the middle, select the middle layer and bring it to the front, as shown in the following illustration.

The sky is drawn first, the pyramid is drawn next, and the sun is drawn last.

To display the sun behind the pyramid, the pyramid is sent to the front.

To rearrange layers, do any of the following:

- To display an object on the back layer, click the object and select Graphics➤Send to Back. The object is moved to the back.
- To display an object on the top layer, click the object and select Graphics➤Bring to Front. The object is moved to the front.
- To display an object on a middle layer, do one of the following:
  - Click the object you want on top, then select Graphics➤Bring to Front.
  - If you can't select the middle object, click the top layer, then select Graphics➤Send to Back. For example, the rounded rectangle in the following illustration was previously on the back layer. When the top layer is sent to the back, the rounded rectangle is displayed in the middle layer.

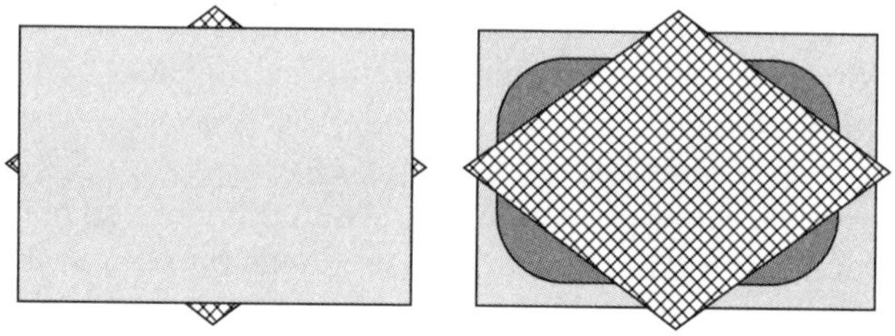

Changing the Orientation

You change the orientation of objects by rotating or flipping them. Rotating an object modifies the angle of the object; flipping creates a mirror image of the object.

Rotating

There are two ways to rotate an object. You can use the mouse to drag a corner, or you can specify the degree of rotation.

To rotate with the mouse, follow these steps:

1. ALT-click a corner of the object. The rotation arrow is displayed.
2. Drag the corner to a new orientation. (If the rotation arrow isn't displayed, you'll reshape the object instead of rotating it. Try deselecting the object and then ALT-click the corner again.)

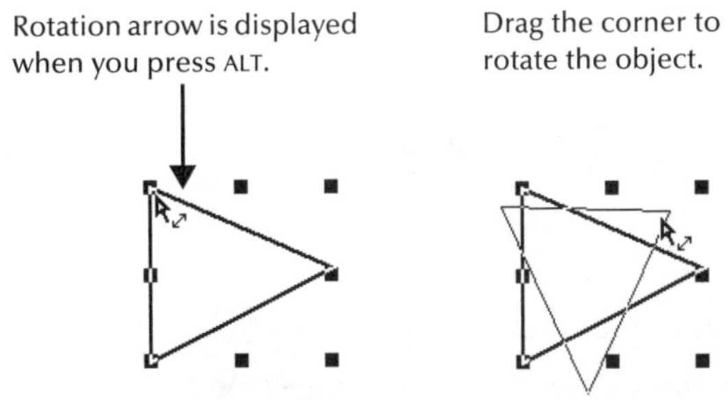

When you drag a corner to rotate the object with the graphics snap on, the degree to which you can rotate the object might be limited by the snap rotation in the View Options. For instance, a 25-degree snap rotation means that the object will snap to an imaginary grid every 25 degrees when you manually rotate the object. See "Working with Grids" on page 343 for details.

To rotate an object by specifying the degree of rotation, follow these steps:

1. Select the object you want to rotate.
2. Do one of the following:
   - To rotate the object clockwise or counterclockwise, select Graphics➤Rotate. The Rotate Selected Objects dialog box is displayed. Type the degree in the Rotate By dialog box, click the Clockwise or Counterclockwise radio button, then click the Rotate button. The object is rotated.

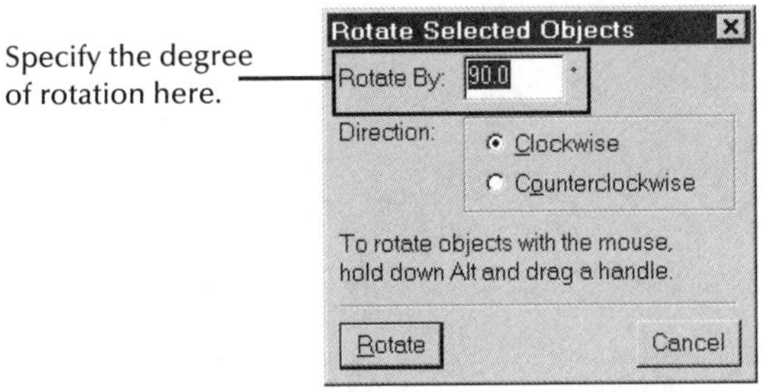

   - To rotate the object in only the clockwise direction, select Graphics➤Object Properties. The Object Properties dialog box is displayed. Type the degree of the angle in the Angle field, then click the Set button. The object is rotated.

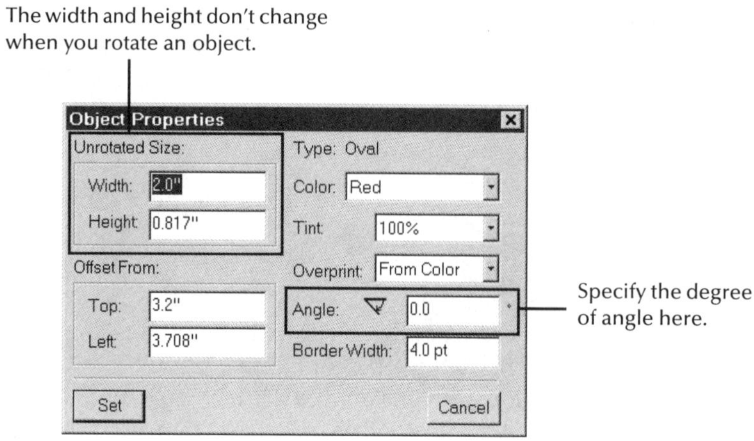

NOTE To rotate text within table cells, see "Rotating Table Cells" on page 182.

Flipping Horizontally or Vertically

When you flip an object, FrameMaker changes the object into a mirror image of itself. The object is flipped left-to-right (horizontally) or up-and-down (vertically).

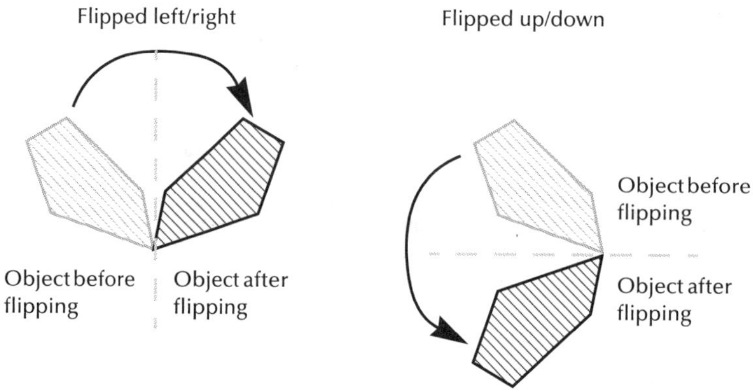

Text lines inside the object are not flipped; only the alignment of the text changes. In the following illustration, each text line is left aligned. After flipping the object horizontally, the grouped text lines are right aligned. If you ungroup the text lines and view the object properties, you'll see that the alignment has changed from left to right.

Text isn't backward after flipping.

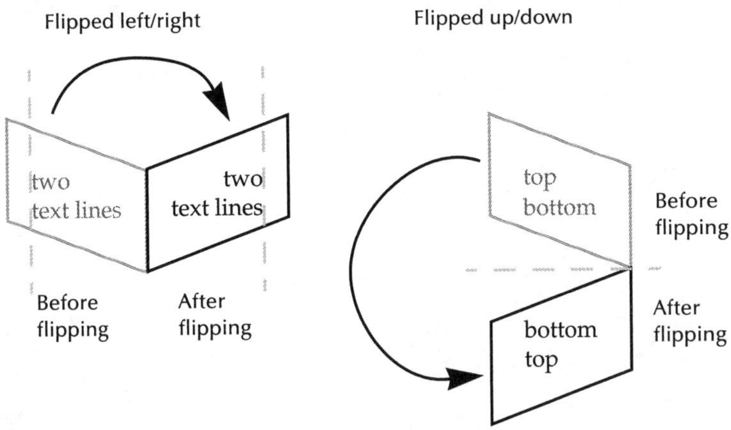

NOTE Flipping an object with a text frame does not change the text alignment because the paragraph tag applied inside the frame controls the alignment of the text.

To flip an object, follow these steps:

1. Select the object or objects you want to flip.
2. Do one of the following:
   - To flip the object horizontally, select Graphics➤Flip Left/Right.
   - To flip the object vertically, select Graphics➤Flip Up/Down.

   The object is flipped as you specified.

PART IV

Building Books

CHAPTER 14

Setting Up Book Files

FrameMaker does a good job handling short documents, but it really shines with long, complex documents. One example of this is FrameMaker's book feature, which lets you group related documents. After you put a collection of documents in a book, you can control pagination and create tables of contents (and other "generated" files), for the entire book. You can also perform many actions on the book instead of on individual files. For example, you can use the book to change conditional text settings across all the files in the book in a single step.

Creating a book file does not affect the component files; the book file is little more than a file list. Opening a file by double-clicking its icon in the book is exactly the same as using the File➤Open command. The book file contains pointers to the files—FrameMaker does not embed copies of the files in the book file.

Book files work reliably for small and large books; books with thousands of pages and hundreds of component files are not unusual. During updating, FrameMaker opens and scans each file in the book, so updating a very large book can take some time. If you have a computer with plenty of system resources, you can speed things up by opening all the files before updating.

To adjust pagination, you must update the book file. This tells FrameMaker to scan the book file and update everything. The book file does not update pagination automatically when you add a new file to the book or when you modify a component file; you must explicitly tell FrameMaker to update the files.

Creating a Book File

Before you can take advantage of all the handy management features that the book offers, you need to create a book file that contains all of your files. To create a book file, follow these steps:

1. *(optional)* Open a file that belongs in the book file.
2. Select File➤New➤Book. If you opened a file in step 1 (or started from any open file), FrameMaker asks whether you want to add that file to the book. Click the Yes button to include the file or the No button to create the book file without it. FrameMaker creates the book and displays it.

3. Save the book file.

When you save your book file, notice that the book file name is listed with a complete path. The component file is now listed with the path relative to the book file (in the example shown, the book file and the content file—a FrameMaker document—are in the same directory).

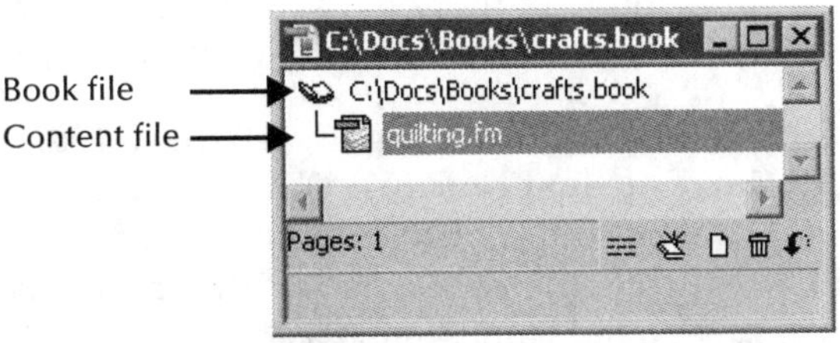

What the Book Window Tells You

FrameMaker packs a lot of information about your files into the book window (Figure 14-1).

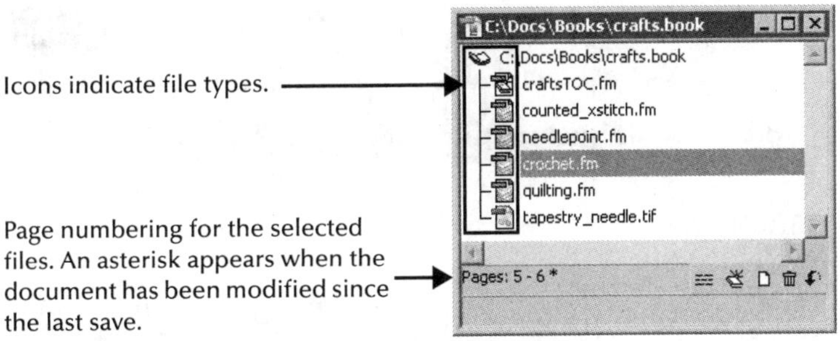

Figure 14-1. Using the information in the book window

The following items are available:

Item	Description
	**File icons:** The icons preceding the file name indicate if the FrameMaker file is a book file, a regular FrameMaker document, or a generated file. Non-FrameMaker files use their native icons . A question mark icon  indicates a missing file, which often means that the file has been deleted, moved, or renamed through Windows Explorer.

BUILDING BOOKS

Item	Description
Pages: 5 - 6 *	**Page numbering:** Select a file to see the current page numbers for that file in the status bar. If you select several files, FrameMaker lists the pagination for all of them in the status bar. A star following the page numbers indicates that the file needs to be saved.
 	**File name/paragraph text toggle (Display Filenames button/ Display Heading Text button):** Click this button to display the first paragraph of text from each document instead of the file name. Click it again to return to the file name. This is especially helpful if you must use cryptic file names, such as ch01-rev3.fm. 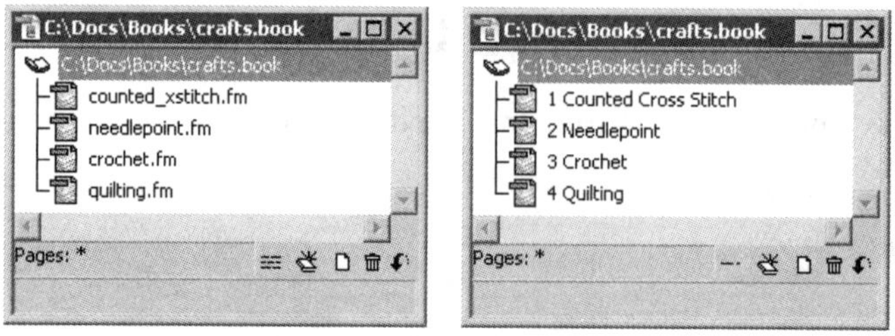
	**Update Book button:** Click to update the book.
	**Add File button:** Click to add more files to the book.
	**Delete File button:** Click to delete the selected file or files from the book.
	**History button:** Click to display the History palette, which lists previous actions that you can undo.

Managing Files in the Book

After you create a book file, you can add files to it, delete files that are listed in the book, change the order of files, and rename files. Except for renaming, these features do not affect the actual files; for example, deleting a file from the book *does not* delete it from your computer. Deleting merely removes that component from the book. (Renaming a file does rename it on the system as well as in the book file.)

Adding Files

FrameMaker makes a distinction between adding "regular" content files and adding generated files. Generated files are created from information in the book: tables of contents, indexes, lists of figures, lists of imported graphics, and others.

Regular files, often chapters or appendixes, are added to the book so that you can control file order, pagination, and the like. Generated files do not exist until you create them through the book file.

NOTE Chapter 15, "Creating Tables of Contents," Chapter 16, "Creating Indexes," and Chapter 17, "Creating Other Generated Files," describe how to add generated files to your book. This chapter focuses exclusively on managing regular files.

To add a content file (such as a chapter or appendix file), you must tell FrameMaker where the file is located and then position it in the book file, as described in the following steps:

1. Make sure the book window is the active window.
2. *(optional)* To add the file at a particular location, select the file immediately before where you want to place the new file.

NOTE By default, files are added after the selected file. It's easy to rearrange files, though, so you may want to add your files and worry about their order later.

3. Select Add➤Files (or click the Add Files icon at the bottom of the window). The Add Files dialog box is displayed.

4. Locate the file you want to add and select it. To add several files, CTRL-click them.

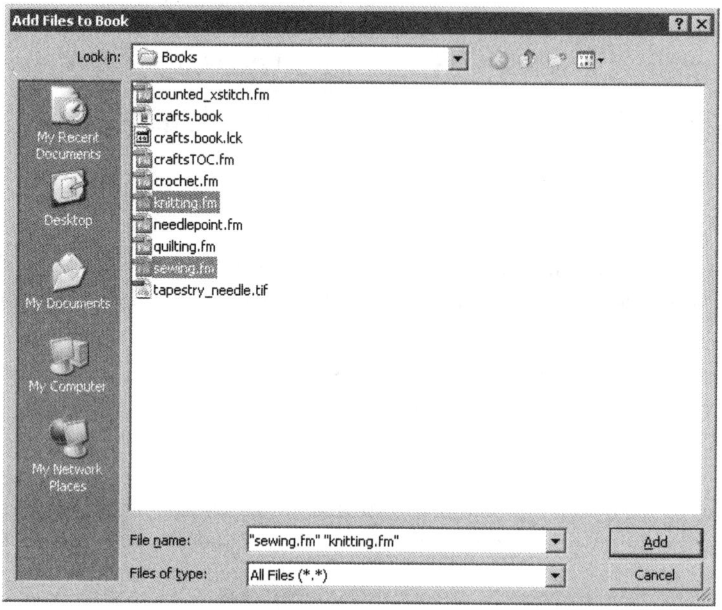

5. Click the Add button. The files are added to the book file.

If the files are not in the right order, you can move them around. See "Rearranging Files" on page 380 for details.

NOTE You can drag and drop files from the desktop or Explorer onto the book window to add them. To copy a file from one FrameMaker book file to another, open both books, select one or more files in the first book, then press CTRL and drag to the other book. (If you don't press CTRL, the files are moved instead of copied.)

Adding Non-FrameMaker Files

You can include non-FrameMaker files in your book file. Only FrameMaker files are counted in the book's pagination or numbering; however, adding a non-FrameMaker file does provide you with a few useful features, including the following:

- **Keeping track of related files.** While working on a book, you'll have many ancillary files that you need to keep track of. Adding them to the book helps to keep those files organized. Files you might want to add to the book file include outlines, style guidelines, and other "extras" that might not be in FrameMaker format.
- **Opening from the book file.** You can open the non-FrameMaker files from the book file. FrameMaker prompts you to specify whether you want to open them in FrameMaker (which probably means a conversion) or in the native application (such as Adobe Reader for a PDF file).

When you print the book, only the FrameMaker files are printed.

Opening, Closing, and Saving All Files

Manually opening each file in the book is a tedious process. Fortunately, FrameMaker provides a convenient set of shortcuts to open, close, and save all files at once. Make the book file active, hold down the SHIFT key, then select the File menu to see the global commands:

- Open All Files in Book
- Close All Files in Book
- Save All Files in Book

Regular File menu

SHIFT-File menu

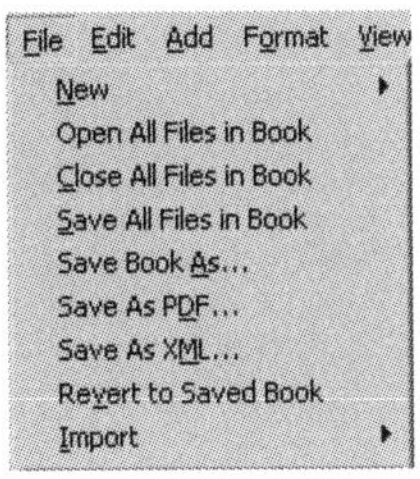

Removing Files

Removing a file from the book file does not delete the file itself from the computer; it only removes the reference to the file from the book file.

To remove a file from the book, follow these steps:

1. In the book file, select the file or files you want to remove.

2. Select Edit➤Delete File from Book, or click the Delete icon in the lower-right corner of the book window. The file disappears from the book window. There is no confirmation prompt.

NOTE The file is still available on your system.

Rearranging Files

When you add files to the book, they may not appear in the order that you want them. To correct this, you can drag and drop icons in the book window to rearrange the files. To rearrange files, follow these steps:

1. Select the file you need to move.
2. Click and drag to reposition the file. A bar shows you where the file will go.

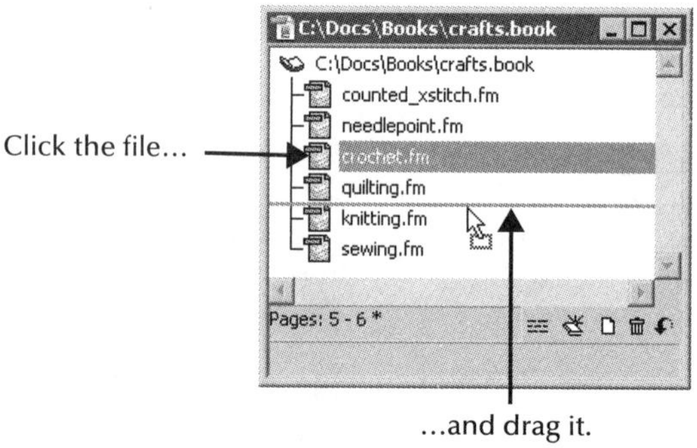

3. Release the mouse button to drop the file in its new location.

Renaming Files

You can rename files from within the book file. When you rename a file, FrameMaker updates references to that file throughout the book.

CAUTION FrameMaker updates only references within the current book file when you rename. If you rename a file that is referenced **by files outside the current book**, those references will be broken by the renaming process. As illustrated in the following figure, assume that you have a file called apple.fm. There are a number of cross-references from pie.fm and from horse_favorites.fm that point to apple.fm. The apple.fm and pie.fm files are in the book called baking.book. The horse_favorites.fm file is not part of this book. If you use the book-level renaming feature from baking.book, references between apple.fm and pie.fm will be updated correctly. However, the links from horse_favorites.fm will be broken.

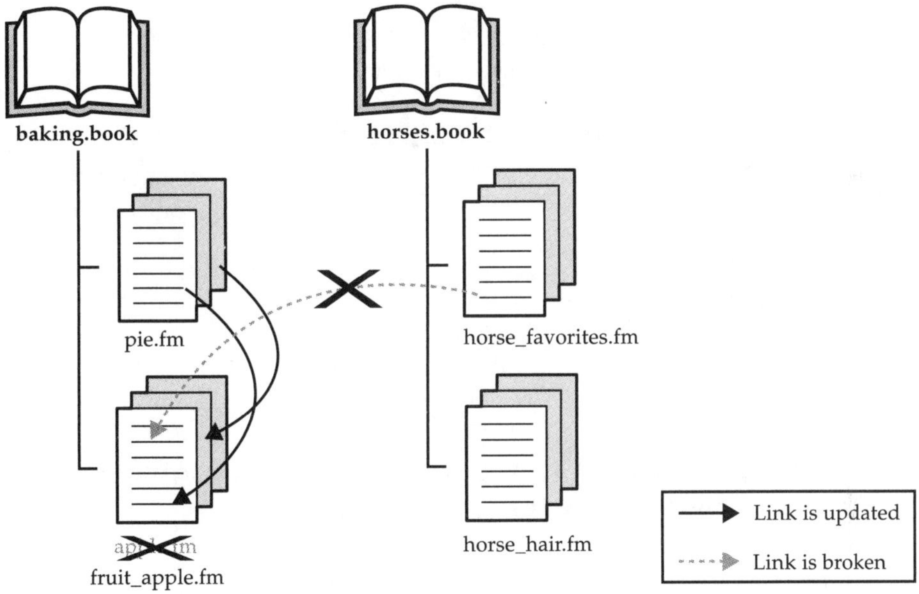

To rename a file, follow these steps:

1. *(optional, but recommended)* Open all files in the book (SHIFT-File➤Open). Opening all files speeds up the process and also ensures that any missing font problems are avoided.

CAUTION If you do not open all files, missing fonts or other opening errors (such as files in an earlier version of FrameMaker) will cause the renaming operation to fail.

2. Make sure that file names are displayed in the book window. If they are not, click the Display Filenames button to see them.

3. Click the file you want to rename. (Don't double-click because the file will open.)
4. Click on the file name to make it editable.

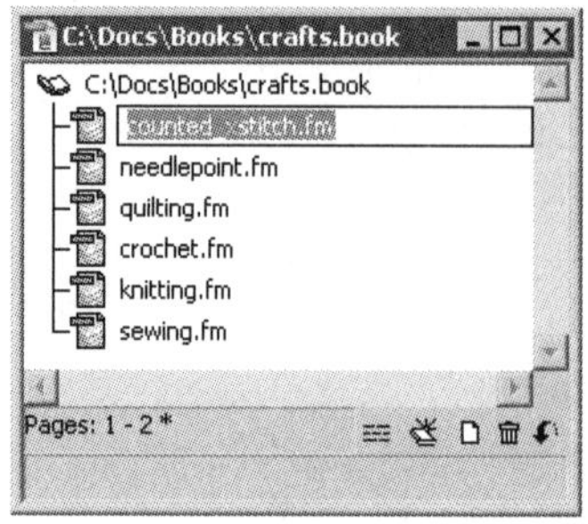

5. Type the new file name and press ENTER.

CAUTION Make sure you press ENTER before you click anywhere else in the book, or FrameMaker will reorder the files.

FrameMaker prompts you to confirm that you want to rename ("move") the file and update all references to that file with the new name.

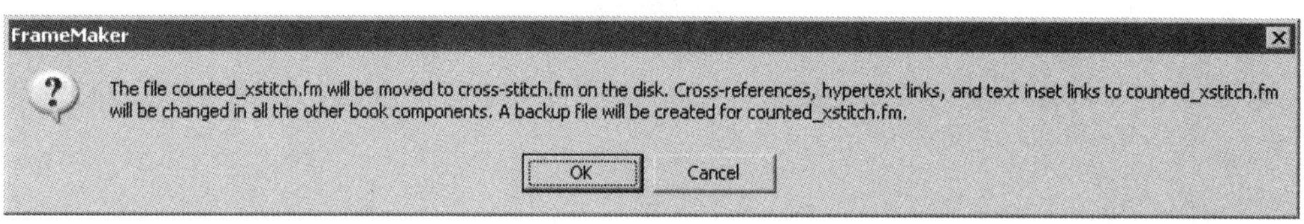

6. Click the OK button. FrameMaker scans all of the files in the book for cross-references, hypertext links, and text insets that refer to the old file name and updates them.

After completing the updating process, FrameMaker notifies you that it has updated the files.

Updating the Book

Periodically, you will need to instruct FrameMaker to update the book. During updating, FrameMaker can modify the following items:

- **Numbering.** Chapter numbers, volume numbers, and paragraph-based numbering (autonumbers) are updated.
- **Pagination.** Page numbers are updated based on the settings in the book.
- **Cross-references.** The reference page numbers and text are updated to reflect any changes.
- **Text insets.** If imported-by-reference FrameMaker files have been updated, the insets are refreshed (see Chapter 25, "Creating Modules with Text Insets").
- **OLE links.** Any OLE links are refreshed.
- **Generated files.** The entire book is scanned, and generated files are replaced with new versions.
- **Master pages.** Any master pages applied based on paragraph tags are updated.

To update your book, follow these steps:

1. Display the book file.
2. *(optional)* To speed up the generation process, and to ensure that it works even if you have missing fonts in some of the files, open all of the files in the book (SHIFT-File➤Open All Files in Book).
3.  Select Edit➤Update Book, or click the Update icon at the bottom of the book window. The Update Book dialog box is displayed (Figure 14-2).

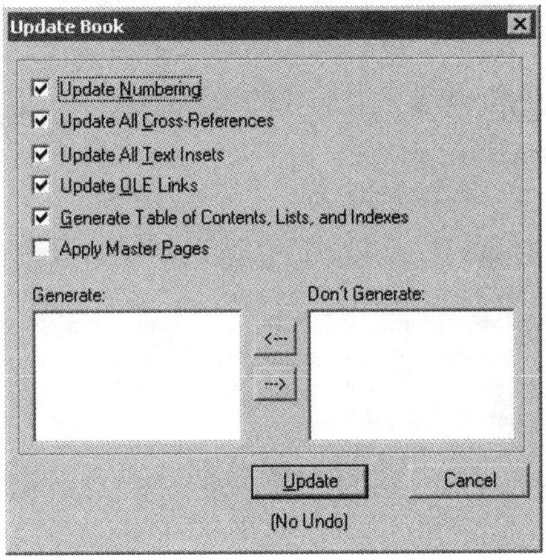

Figure 14-2. Updating a book

4. Check each of the items that you want to update. (Generally, it's a good idea to check everything except Apply Master Pages.)

Your choices are as follows:

- **Update Numbering:** If checked, all page, chapter, volume, and paragraph numbering is updated.
- **Update All Cross-References:** If checked, all cross-references are updated.
- **Update All Text Insets:** If checked, all text insets are updated.
- **Update OLE Links**: If checked, all files that are imported with OLE links are updated.
- **Generate Table of Contents, Lists, and Indexes:** If checked, FrameMaker generates the files that are listed in the Generate list. Only tables of contents, indexes, and similar generated files are available to generate or not generate.
- **Apply Master Pages:** If checked, FrameMaker updates master page assignments. For details, see "Mapping Paragraph Tags to Master Pages" on page 263.

NOTE Creating generated files is the most time-consuming part of an update. If your book is very large or your system resources are limited, you can save some time by not generating tables of contents and the like. Be sure, though, to update them before you finalize the book to ensure that the most current information appears in generated files.

Troubleshooting Book Updates

When you update your book, FrameMaker reports any problems in the book error log (Figure 14-3).

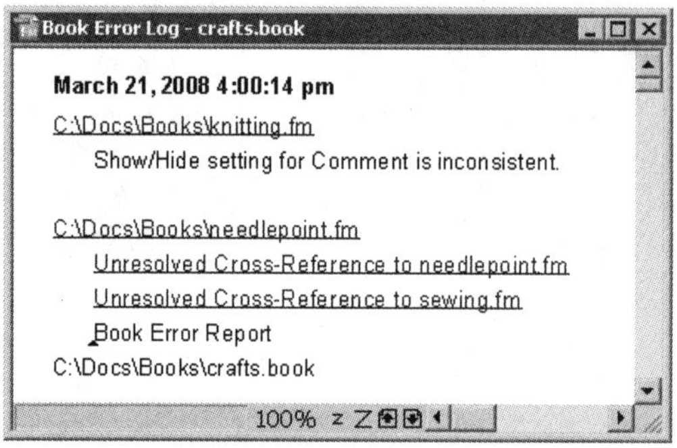

Figure 14-3. Inconsistencies in the files are listed in the book error log.

The following issues can cause the update process to fail:

- Missing fonts
- FrameMaker files from an earlier version of FrameMaker
- FrameMaker files in use by someone else
- Read/write permissions on the files

Other generation problems do not cause the process to fail but are reported in the book error log. They include the following:

- Unresolved cross-references
- Inconsistent conditional text settings
- Inconsistent color settings
- Inconsistent numbering properties

The following sections explain how to correct these problems.

Missing Fonts A missing fonts message indicates that FrameMaker attempted to open a file, but the file called for fonts that are not installed on the current system. The missing font message causes the file-opening process to fail, which in turn causes the entire book update to fail. To correct the missing fonts problem, you have three choices:

- **Install the missing fonts on your system.** This is an operating system task. Refer to your system documentation for more information.
- **Remove the missing fonts from the document.** You can change the FrameMaker preferences so that missing fonts are permanently replaced. Refer to "Handling Missing Fonts" on page 53 for instructions.
- **Open all files before updating the book.** If the files are open, FrameMaker doesn't have to open them during the update, and you avoid this error.

FrameMaker Files from an Earlier Version of FrameMaker Before updating the book, open all of the files and save them in the latest version of FrameMaker. That will eliminate this message. FrameMaker will not update a book that contains files from earlier versions of FrameMaker.

FrameMaker Files in Use This message indicates that one of the files has been opened by another user. If you attempt to open the file directly, FrameMaker will tell the machine name or user name that has locked the file. Have the other user close the file so that you can update the book.

Read/Write Permissions on the Files To open the files, FrameMaker needs read permissions. To save them, FrameMaker needs write permissions. Make sure that you have the appropriate permissions on the files. Files that are set to be read-only will not update properly. (This often happens with files that are copied from a CD.) You can also create view-only files inside FrameMaker; these will not update, either. To correct the latter problem, open the view-only file and press ESC SHIFT-F L K to make it editable.

Unresolved Cross-References This message indicates that FrameMaker has been unable to resolve cross-references in the book. This message can occur because of problems opening the file due to missing fonts in the target file or because of actual unresolved cross-references. Because there can be problems with missing fonts, either fix missing font problems or open all the files in the book before updating the book. After doing so, the listed unresolved cross-references are hyperlinked, so click the error to jump to an unresolved cross-reference. You need to fix the broken cross-references to eliminate this message.

Inconsistent Conditional Text Settings This message indicates that a particular conditional text tag is set to be shown in one file and hidden in another. The message is informational; if you need to have your files set up this way, you can ignore it (for one or all files). If the conditional text settings should be consistent across the entire book, select all the files in the book, select View➤Show/Hide Conditional Text and choose the settings you want for all the files.

Inconsistent Color Settings This message indicates that color definitions or color print settings are inconsistent. To correct the problem, apply consistent settings across the entire book (see Chapter 20, "Color Output"). You can safely ignore this message if your files do not actually use the inconsistent color.

Inconsistent Numbering Properties Indicates that the numbering set in the file conflicts with the numbering in the book. To correct this, assign consistent numbering, as described in the next section.

Managing Numbering

FrameMaker uses the order of files in the book and information you provide about numbering to control the numbering sequence for your book. You can, for example, specify that the files in the book should be numbered sequentially. When you make changes to the files, FrameMaker manages the pagination to keep everything in sequence, as shown in the following example:

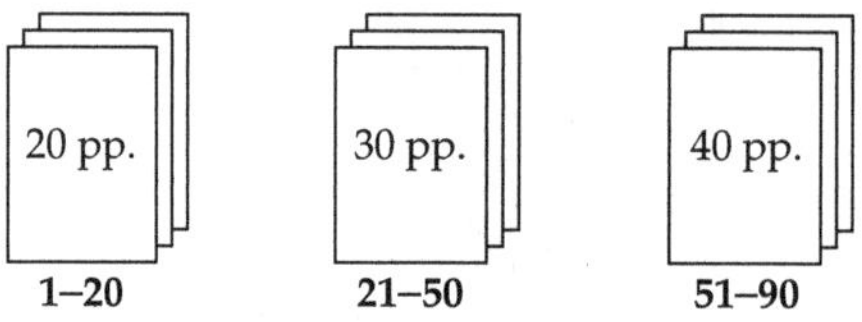

After you change the documents, the new sequence is this:

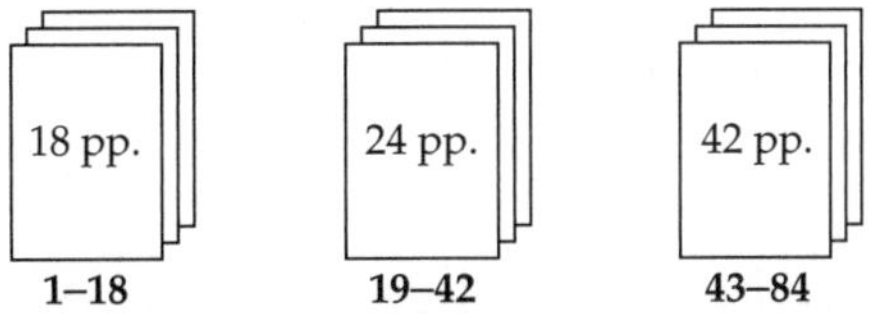

Another numbering setup might require that each chapter's page numbering restarts at 1. The page numbering would look something like this example:

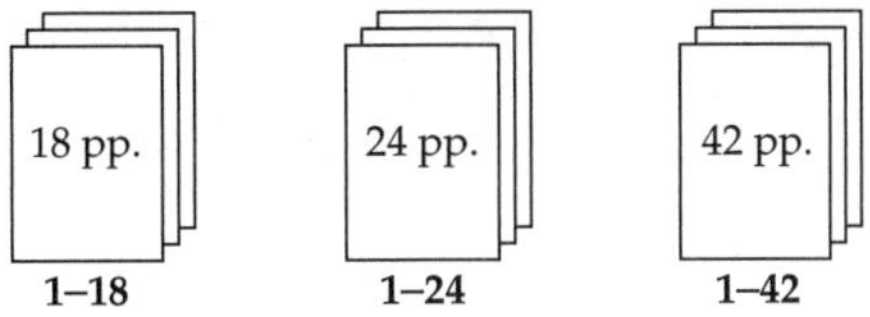

All numbering is controlled in the Numbering Properties dialog box (Format➤Document➤Numbering, shown in Figure 14-4), which provides sheets for volume, chapter, page, paragraph, footnote, and table footnote numbering.

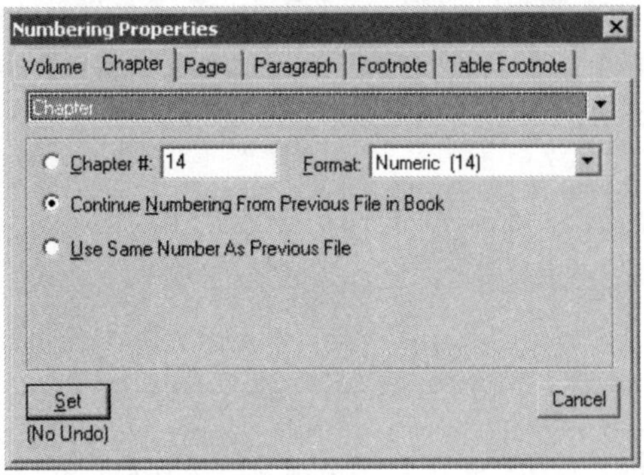

Figure 14-4. Controlling numbering properties

TIP One major point of confusion is the Continue Numbering option, which is available in most tabs. Selecting this option causes the numbering to increase by one from the previous file. To keep the same number as the previous file, select the Use Same Number option. In other words, "Continue" means that if the preceding file ends on page 57, the current file will begin on page 58.

Because FrameMaker's numbering is calculated by the file sequence, a missing file will throw off the numbering. You can eliminate this problem by assigning fixed values to a chapter (instead of letting FrameMaker calculate the value that should be there). This can make life difficult later, though, if you need to move chapters around because the hard-coded chapter number interferes with FrameMaker's ability to calculate the correct chapter numbers by position. We recommend that you resign yourself to having incorrect numbering until all of the chapters have been created. If this is unacceptable, consider creating dummy (empty) chapters and adding them to the book until the real file is ready.

Format Choices for Numbers

The Format drop-down list, available in several of the numbering tabs, lets you specify the type of numbering you want to use. Your choices are:

- Numeric (14). Creates a numeric sequence: 1, 2, 3, ...
- roman (xiv). Creates lowercase Roman numerals: i, ii, iii, ...
- ROMAN (XIV). Creates uppercase Roman numerals: I, II, III, ...
- alphabetic (n). Creates lowercase letters: a, b, c, ...
- ALPHABETIC (N). Creates uppercase letters: A, B, C, ...
- Text (volume and chapter only). Creates a custom label. If you select text, you must specify the label you want for each item. You could, for example, have a volume number of Read Me.
- Custom (footnote only). Creates a custom footnote sequence.

Each example shows the result for the number 14 in parentheses, presumably because it shows the differences clearly.

The following sections explain how to set up numbering for each of the numbering types available in FrameMaker:

- **Pages.** Controls the value of the <$pagenum> building block inside the files. Page numbers increase from page to page within a file.
- **Chapters.** Controls the value of the <$chapnum> building block inside the files. You cannot have two different values for the chapter number inside a single file; the chapter number is always the same value across the entire document. (In other words, you cannot embed both chapter 1 and chapter 2 in a single file if you want to use <$chapnum> to control the chapter numbering.)
- **Volumes.** Controls the value of the <$volnum> building block inside the files. A volume usually contains several files. Like <$chapnum>, <$volnum> can have only one value inside a file. The most common use of the <$volnum> building block is for books with multiple parts, such as this book.
- **Paragraphs.** Controls whether counters in the numbering properties for the Paragraph Designer are reset.
- **Footnotes.** Controls the value of the footnotes.
- **Table footnotes.** Controls the value of the table footnotes.

Page Numbers

FrameMaker provides three options for page numbering. The numbering can begin on a specified page (with a specified format), continue whatever numbering was specified in the previous file, or start on the page specified in the file-level numbering properties (Read from File). To set up numbering that works properly, you usually want the page numbers to continue from the previous document. Exceptions include folio-by-chapter numbering (for example, 1-12) and numbering in chapters that include multiple files per chapter.

Consider the numbering example shown in the following table. The first few files in the book (table of contents, preface, and other front matter) use Roman numerals. After that, the first chapter starts with a numeric 1. All other documents are numbered straight through.

Document	Page Numbers	Setting Needed
Title page	i–ii	Start at: 1 roman (xiv)
Table of contents	iii–vi	Continue
Preface	vii–x	Continue
Chapter 1	1–16	Start at: 1 Numeric (14)
Chapter 2	17–28	Continue
Chapter 3	29–34	Continue
Chapter 4	35–46	Continue

To match this numbering, you need to set most of the files to "continue numbering." The files will pick up the last number in the previous file and increment by 1 to continue. Set the first file in the book to start at 1 and use Roman numerals. The first chapter file needs to restart at 1 and use numerics. To set up this numbering, follow these steps:

1. Select all of the files in the book window (click in the book window and press CTRL-A or ESC E A to select all the files).
2. Select Format➤Document➤Numbering to display the numbering properties.
3. Click the Page tab to display the page numbering properties.

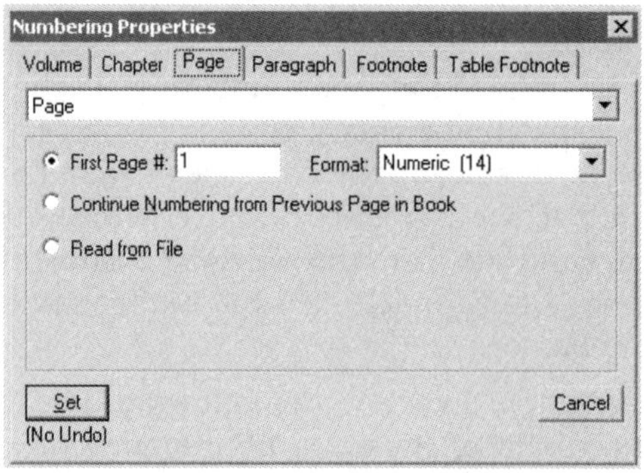

4. Click the Continue Numbering from Previous Page in Book radio button and click the Set button. FrameMaker applies the specified numbering scheme to every file in the book.
5. Now, set the numbering exceptions. Select only the table of contents file and display the Page tab in the Numbering dialog box again. In the First Page # field, type **1**. In the Format drop-down list, click roman (xiv). Click the Set button.
6. Select the first chapter file. Display the Page tab. In the First Page # field, type **1**. In the Format drop-down list, click Numeric (14). Click the Set button.
7. Update the book. Your new settings are applied throughout the book.

TIP

To set up page numbers that restart with every chapter, select all the files and set the first page number as 1 for each file. Separately, you'll need to set the chapter numbering to continue. The result will be the correct sequence:

```
1-1, 1-2, 1-3, …, 2-1, 2-2, 2-3, …, 3-1, 3-2, 3-3, …
```

You'll also need to set up the generated files and the master pages to use the chapter numbers.

Chapter Numbers

For chapter numbers, FrameMaker provides the same "restart" and "continue" settings as for page numbers. In addition, you also have the option of retaining the same chapter number as for the previous file. This allows you to split a large chapter into two files and assign the same chapter number to both files.

By default, each file in the book (including generated files such as the table of contents) is assigned a chapter number, starting with 1, unless the file already has a chapter number assigned at the file level. If the book assigns default chapter numbering, the fourth file would be chapter 4. You can reference the current chapter number in a document using the <$chapnum> building block.

You will probably need to customize the numbering to ensure that you get the correct numbers in your book. Consider the book shown in the following table. Because each file initially is assigned a chapter number, you end up with the table of contents, preface, and other front matter incrementing the chapter number.

Document	Default Chapter Number	Correct Chapter Number	Setting Needed
Title page	1	N/A	Doesn't matter
Table of contents	2	N/A	Doesn't matter
Preface	3	N/A	Doesn't matter
Chapter 1	4	1	Start at: 1 Numeric (14)
Chapter 2	5	2	Continue
Chapter 3	6	3	Continue
Chapter 4	7	4	Continue

To correct this, you need to set the chapter numbering properties so that the first chapter file starts at 1. Follow these steps:

1. Select all of the files in the book window.
2. Select Format➤Document➤Numbering to display the numbering properties.
3. Click the Chapter tab to display the chapter numbering properties.

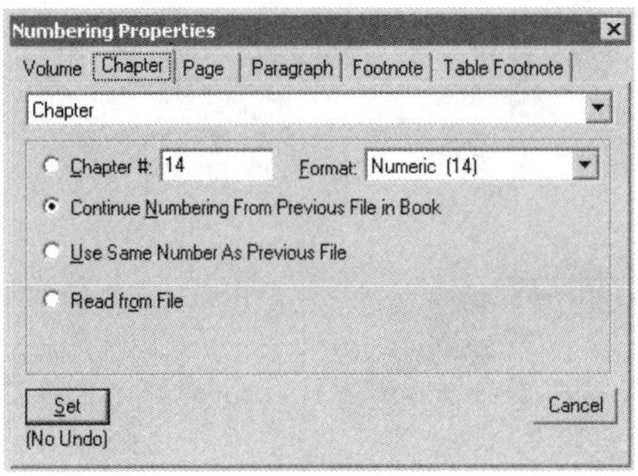

4. Select the Continue Numbering from Previous File in Book radio button and click the Set button. FrameMaker now assigns an incrementing chapter number to each file in the book.

NOTE This is the default setting for chapter numbers, but it's a good idea to reset them to ensure that any custom numbering is stripped.

5. Select only the first chapter file. Display the Chapter tab again. In the Chapter # field, type **1**, and in the Format drop-down list, select Numeric (14). Click the Set button.
6. Update the book. Your new settings are applied throughout the book. Inside the files, every reference to <$chapnum> is also updated.

The chapter number in the front matter is still incorrect, but because the front matter doesn't normally use the chapter number, you can ignore this issue.

Managing Numbering for Multifile Chapters

You may need to set up some chapters that are split across two or more files; often, because the chapters are very large or to accommodate custom master pages in the middle of a document. (If you need to assign a special master page—for example, a landscape page in a portrait document—it's helpful to split the document so that the landscape page is the first page in a file. Otherwise, you'll have to reassign master pages every time you add new information before the landscape page or use the Apply Master Pages feature to manage the master page used.)

A multifile chapter requires you to customize the book's chapter numbering handling. Make sure that the second and subsequent pieces of a chapter are set to use the same chapter number as the previous file.

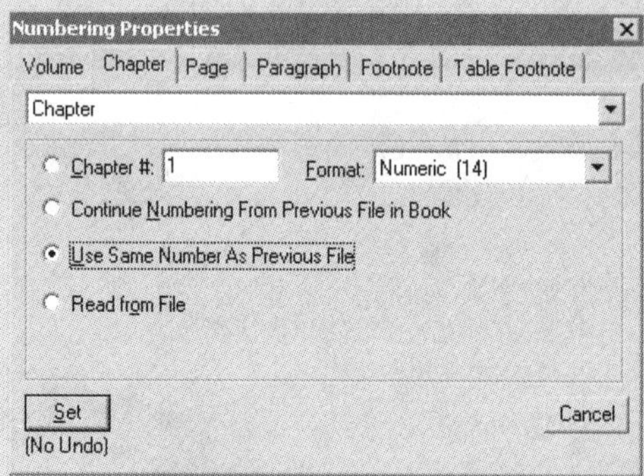

Volume Numbers

For volume numbers, FrameMaker provides the same options as for chapter numbers. FrameMaker assumes that your volumes would typically contain multiple chapters (files). To accommodate this, each file in the book defaults to using the same volume number as the preceding file (the chapter numbers increment by default), unless the volume number is set in the file.

You can reference the current volume number in a document using the <$volnum> building block.

If your book uses volume (or part) numbers, you need to customize the numbering to set the volume numbers. Consider the book shown in the following table. The book defaults to a single volume number for each file, but you need the volume number to increment with each part of the book.

Document	Volume Number	Setting Needed
Title page		Doesn't matter
Table of contents		Doesn't matter
Preface		Doesn't matter
Part I title page	I	Start at: 1 ROMAN (XIV)
Chapter 1	I	Same As Previous File
Chapter 2	I	Same As Previous File
Part II title page	II	Continue
Chapter 3	II	Same As Previous File
Chapter 4	II	Same As Previous File
Part III title page	III	Continue
Chapter 5	III	Same As Previous File
Chapter 6	III	Same As Previous File

To set the volume numbering properties, follow these steps:

1. Select all of the files in the book window.
2. Select Format➤Document➤Numbering to display the numbering properties.
3. Click the Volume tab to display the volume numbering properties.

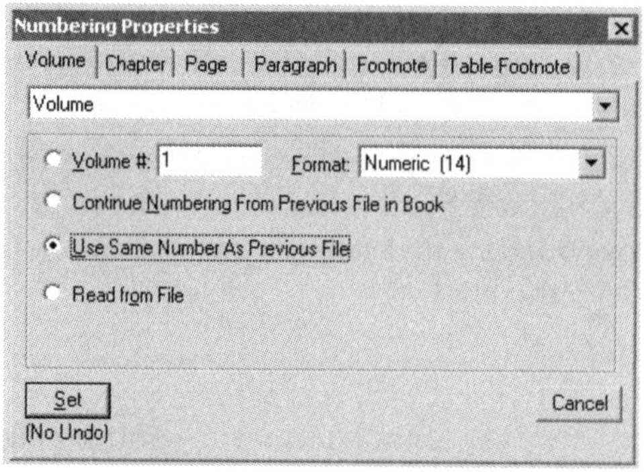

4. Select the Use Same Number As Previous File radio button, and click the Set button. FrameMaker now assigns the same volume number (1) to each file in the book.

NOTE This is the default setting for volume numbers, but it's a good idea to reset them to ensure that any custom numbering is stripped.

5. Select only the first file in the first part. Display the Volume tab again. In the Volume # field, type **1**, and in the Format drop-down list, select ROMAN (XIV). Click the Set button.
6. Select the first file in the second part. Display the Volume tab. Select the Continue Numbering from Previous File in Book radio button, and click the Set button.
7. Repeat step 6 for each additional part.
8. Update the book. Your new settings are applied throughout the book. Inside the files, every reference to <$volnum> is also updated.

Paragraph Numbers

The paragraph numbering properties determine whether autonumbering continues or restarts from one file to the next. The setting you choose here matters only if you have a numbering stream that carries over from one chapter to the next. If, for example, you have figure or table numbers that carry through the entire book (1, 2, 3, ..., 57, 58, 59, ...), make sure that paragraph numbering is set to Continue. The paragraph numbering properties control the values of the autonumbering counters.

For paragraph numbering, you have the following choices:

- **Restart Paragraph Numbering:** All counters are reset to zero at the beginning of the selected file.
- **Continue Numbering from Previous Paragraph in Book:** Counter values are carried over from the previous file.
- **Read from File:** Counter values are picked up from the current file.

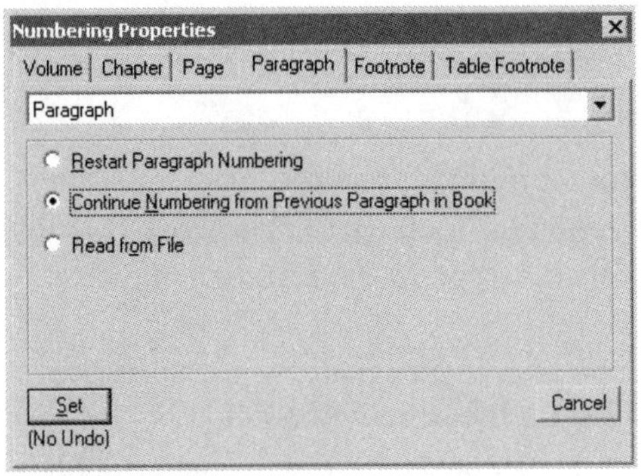

NOTE If you have set up your files to track chapter numbering in the autonumbering instead of using the book's Chapter numbering properties, changing the paragraph number settings might affect your chapter numbering.

Footnote Numbers

FrameMaker's footnote numbering gives you three alternatives. Footnotes can:

- Increment through the entire book (which means there would be only one footnote number 3 in the entire book).
- Increment starting with every chapter (footnotes would start with 1, 2, 3 in each chapter, meaning you could have several footnotes labeled 3—one per chapter).
- Restart on every page (footnotes would start with 1, 2, 3 on each page, so you could theoretically have a footnote number 3 on each page in the file).

To set up footnote numbering properties for all of the files in your book, follow these steps:

1. Select all of the files in the book window.
2. Select Format➤Document➤Numbering to display the numbering properties.
3. Click the Footnote tab to display the footnote numbering properties.

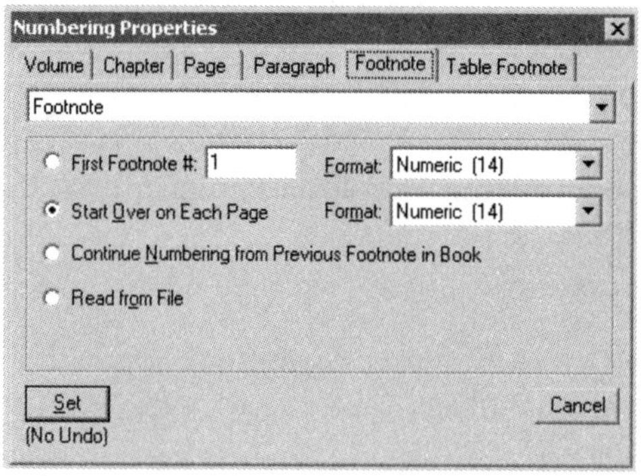

4. Select the pagination option you want:
   - To start the footnotes with a particular number (usually 1) for each file, select First Footnote, type in the number, and select a format from the drop-down list.
   - To restart footnotes on every page, select Start Over on Each Page and select a format from the drop-down list.
   - To number footnotes consecutively through the book, select Continue Numbering from Previous Footnote in Book. (If you do this, you should also set the first file to start footnotes at 1. The file *should* default to this setting, but it's safer to apply it explicitly.)
5. Click the Set button.
6. Update the book. Your new settings are applied throughout the book.

Table Footnote Numbers

Table footnotes are footnotes that are created for text inside a table. You cannot change the numbering for table footnotes; they always restart for each table. You can, however, set the format of the number at the book level.

To set the formatting for table footnotes, follow these steps:

1. Select all of the files in the book window.
2. Select Format➤Document➤Numbering to display the numbering properties.
3. Click the Table Footnote tab to display the table footnote numbering properties.

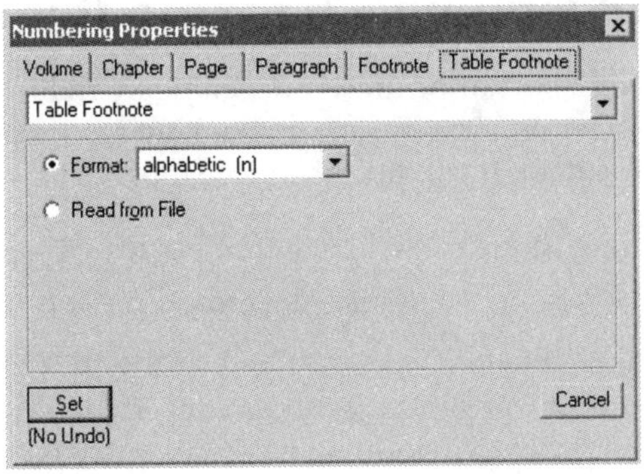

4. In the Format drop-down list, select the option you want. Click the Set button.
5. Update the book. Your new settings are applied throughout the book.

Printing a Book

From the book file, selecting File➤Print Book results in printing all the files in the book. But if you need to print just a portion of the book, you have that option, too. To print specific files in a book, follow these steps:

1. In the book window, select the files you want to print by CTRL-clicking each file.
2. Select File➤Print Selected Files.
3. Proceed as usual in selecting your print options.
4. Click the Print button to print the selected files.

Modifying Files from the Book

From the book window, FrameMaker provides a subset of the regular FrameMaker commands on the menus. These include spell-checking, find/change, conditional text settings, and more. Using these commands is equivalent to opening each file in the book and issuing the command there. The book file can save you lots of time because FrameMaker takes care of opening each file, making the change, and then saving and closing the file.

With the exception of the spell-checking and the find/change utility, the book-level commands are reversible. You can, for example, change your view settings for all the files in the book, but that change is easy to reset.

Spell-Checking and Finding/Changing Items

When you display the spell-checker or the Find/Change window from the book file, the utility begins working on the first file in the book and works through every file in order. To spell-check at the book level, follow these steps:

1. Select Edit➤Spelling Checker to display the Spelling Checker dialog box.
2. Verify that the Book radio button is selected on the left.
3. Click the Start Checking button to begin checking spelling.

   FrameMaker attempts to open each document in the book and spell-check its contents. If FrameMaker cannot open a file, an entry is made in the book error log, and the spell-checker continues with the next file. After completing spell-checking in a file, that file is saved (and closed if FrameMaker opened it), then FrameMaker moves on to the next file.
4. Use the spell-checking options as normal. See page 73 for details.
5. When FrameMaker reaches the end of the book, the spell-check is complete.

The Find/Change utility works the same way as the spell-checker. See page 67 for details.

NOTE You can start the spell-checker or find/change process at a specific location by opening that file, displaying the spell-checker or find/change dialog box, and then selecting the Book radio button to ensure that the operation is performed for all the files in the book. This works only if the book file is open when you go to a component file; otherwise, the Book option is grayed out.

Choosing Files When Performing Other Book-Level Operations

For most book-level features, you can select which files the operation is performed on. If you want to make a change to all of the files in the book, you must select all of the files in the book before applying the command.

To apply a book-level command, follow these steps:

1. In the book window, select the files that you want to make changes to.
2. Select the command you want from the menus. For example, to toggle the display of document borders, select View➤Show Borders (or Hide Borders). FrameMaker opens each file in turn and makes the change in the file.

NOTE If you open all your files before making changes, remember to save them (SHIFT-File➤Save All Open Files).

Book Features Available Inside Files

Although most book features are available only from the book window, a few are available from inside component files. To use book-level features, the book file must be open in FrameMaker while you're working inside the component file.

You can perform book-level spell-checking and find/change operations from inside the file by clicking the Book radio button in the dialog boxes for those functions.

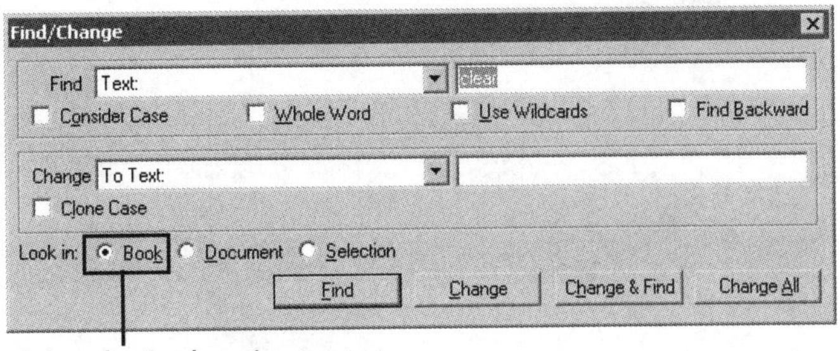

Select the Book option to start a global find/change operation.

Paging Through Files in a Book

If you are working in a file that belongs to an open book, FrameMaker understands that the current file is part of a sequence. When you scroll down through a file and reach the end of a file, you can press PAGE DOWN to go to the next file in the book. If the file is already open, FrameMaker displays the next file automatically (which can be quite disconcerting). If the file is not open, FrameMaker offers to open it.

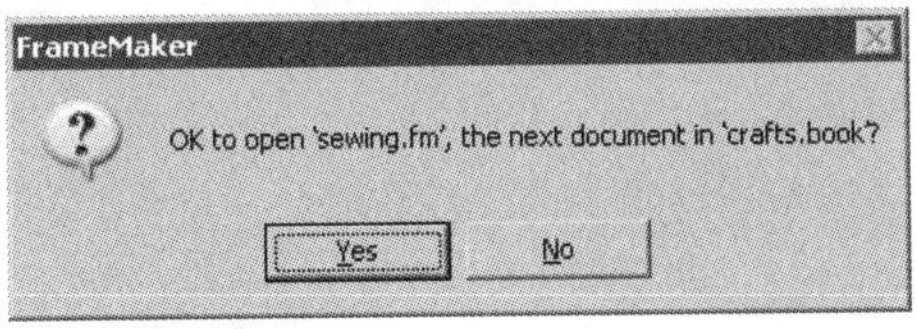

Press PAGE UP at the beginning of a file to open the preceding file.

CHAPTER 15

Creating Tables of Contents

You can automatically create and maintain tables of contents in FrameMaker. When you set up a table of contents, you specify which paragraphs should be included. FrameMaker takes care of the rest; it scans the documents to locate every instance of those paragraphs, and then lists them in the table of contents along with their page number (Figure 15-1).

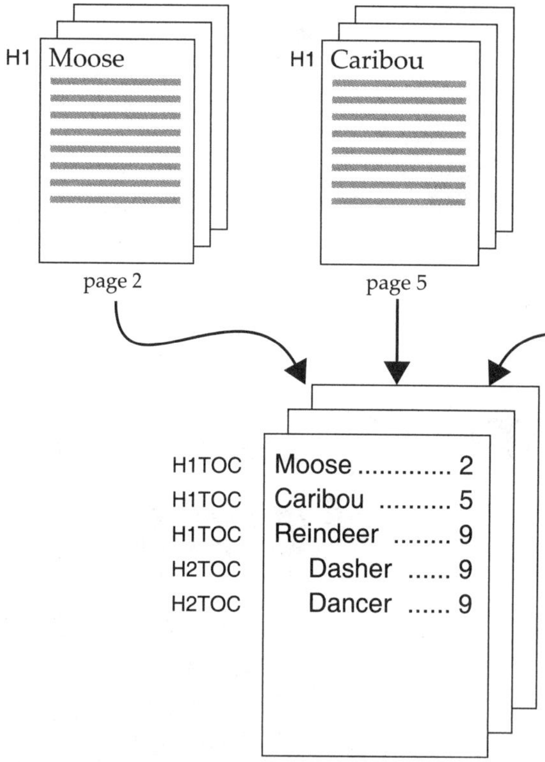

Figure 15-1. Scanning files to create a table of contents

Setting Up the Table of Contents File

When you create a table of contents, you must specify which paragraph tags you want to include in the document. This is an all-or-nothing operation—if you include the Heading1 paragraph tag, every Heading1 in the book will be included in the generated table of contents.

TIP If you want to eliminate a few headings, you must create two paragraph tags (with identical settings): Heading1 and Heading1NoTOCEntry. Tag the paragraphs as appropriate and include only the Heading1 items in your generated list.
For example, if you want to exclude the "Caribou" entry in Figure 15-1, you would tag Moose and Reindeer as Heading1 and tag Caribou as Heading1NoTOCEntry. This lets you exclude Caribou, even though it looks just like the other first-level headings.

To set up a table of contents, follow these steps:

1. Open the book file.
2. *(optional)* To add the table of contents at a particular location, select the file immediately before or after where you want the table of contents. Because you can move the table of contents after creating it, this is not a critical step.
3. Select Add➤Table of Contents. The Set Up Table of Contents dialog box is displayed.

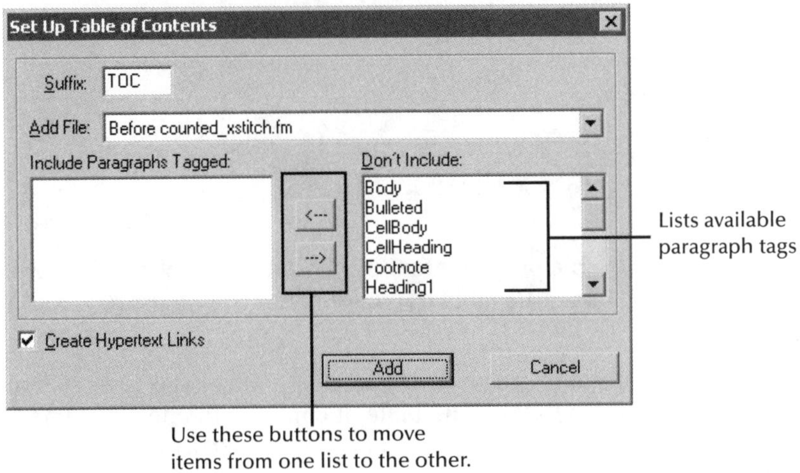

4. The default file name suffix for the table of contents is TOC. You can change it if you want to. If you create several tables of contents, the suffix increments (TOC, TOC2, TOC3, and so on).
5. *(optional)* In the Add File drop-down list, specify whether you want the table of contents before or after the file you selected in step 2.
6. Move the items that you want to include to the Include list on the left.

   You can move items by doing any of the following:

   - Select an item, then click the left or right arrow button to move it from one list to another.
   - Select an item, then double-click it to move it to the other list.
   - To move all the items from one list to another, press and hold SHIFT, then click the appropriate arrow button.
7. Make sure that the Create Hypertext Links check box is checked. This activates hyperlinks for each entry in the table of contents. It also ensures that if you convert to other formats (PDF or HTML), the links in the table of contents are preserved. If you are absolutely sure that you do not want hyperlinks, you can uncheck this box.

8. Click the Add button. FrameMaker offers to update the book immediately.

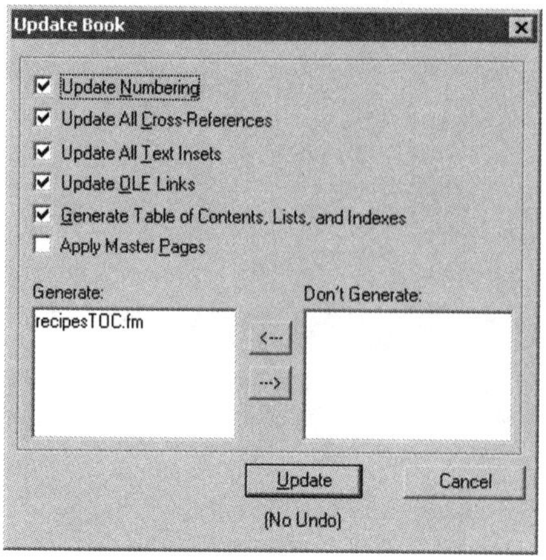

NOTE The file name of the table of contents file is based on the book file name. If your book file is foo.book, the table of contents file will be fooTOC.fm.

9. Click the Update button to create the table of contents. (See page 383 for a detailed discussion of updates.) The table of contents file now appears in the book; you can move it just like any regular file; see "Rearranging Files" on page 380.

To change the items included in the table of contents, select the table of contents file, and select Edit➤Set Up Table of Contents to display the setup dialog box again.

Embedding the Table of Contents in a File

The automatic table of contents feature always creates a separate table of contents file. This presents a problem if you want to create a table of contents that's embedded on a page; for example, a list of topics at the beginning of a chapter.

You can accomplish this in at least two different ways:

- Generate a table of contents file and then use a text inset (Chapter 25, "Creating Modules with Text Insets") to embed the information in the file.
- Create cross-references (Chapter 8, "Cross-References") or hypertext links (Chapter 22, "Creating Interactive Content with Hypertext") that point to the relevant headings.

Each approach has advantages and disadvantages. Creating a table of contents as a text inset is appealing because you update the table of contents and then update the text inset to add new information. If you use cross-references or hyperlinks, you must add or delete the entries yourself.

However, cross-references or hyperlinks have the advantage of being self-contained in the file—you don't have to create a separate table of contents file and then import it back into the source file, which is inelegant at best.

If your headings change frequently or you have a long list in each chapter, you'll probably want to use the more automated approach (inset table of contents). If you're working with shorter, more manageable lists that don't change often, the cross-reference or hyperlink approach can work well.

TIP: If you have FrameScript (www.framescript.com), the ChapterTOC script is available from Rick Quatro (www.frameexpert.com) to automatically insert cross-references to the headings you choose. The script ensures that the correct cross-references are present in the chapter (and in the correct order) without all the work of setting these up and maintaining them manually.

The Initial Table of Contents File

After creating the table of contents, you can double-click it in the book file to display it. If you used a default template, your table of contents will look something like Figure 15-2.

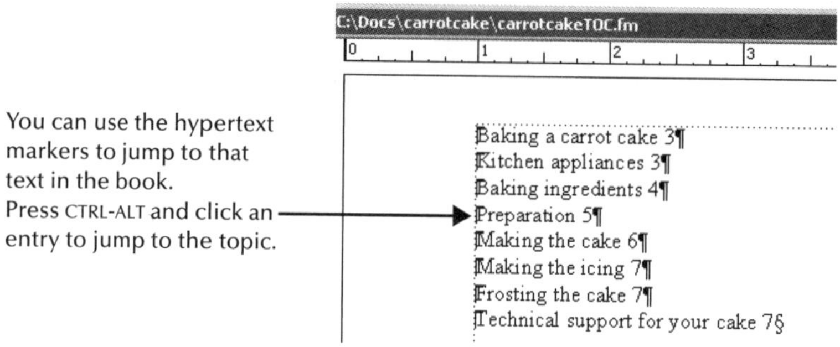

Figure 15-2. Initial table of contents (default FrameMaker TOC tags)

You can navigate to a topic from the table of contents by pressing CTRL-ALT and single-clicking the entry.

FrameMaker uses reference pages and paragraph tags to determine the appearance of the table of contents. When you create the table of contents, FrameMaker uses the first file in the book as the template for the table of contents file. If that file is set up with all the needed table of contents settings (that is, if the reference pages and paragraph tags contain the needed definitions), your work may be done. It's likely, though, that you'll want to make some changes.

If you have a table of contents template, you can import formats from that template into the table of contents file and update the book again. You should then have a table of contents that's formatted correctly.

The rest of this chapter describes how to set up the formatting in the table of contents.

TIP You can insert a title for the table of contents (such as "Contents") and apply a Title paragraph tag to it. If you do, make sure that the title is positioned before any of the generated text and before the first hypertext marker. Any information that follows the first hypertext marker in the generated file is deleted when you regenerate the file.

A Sneaky Way of Avoiding Formatting Work

If you have a template file that contains the table of contents settings you need, you can save yourself some time. Instead of generating the table of contents and then importing from the template file, try this:

1. Copy the template file to the book directory.
2. Rename the template file to match the name that FrameMaker assigns to the table of contents. For example, if your book is named long.book, the table of contents name will be longTOC.fm.
3. Open the book file and add the table of contents file as usual.
4. Update the book. FrameMaker automatically uses the file that you've snuck into the book's directory and picks up all the formatting from that file.

Customizing the Table of Contents

After creating the initial file, you have several ways to customize the table of contents. You can do any of the following:

- Include or exclude paragraphs when you set up the table of contents.
- Specify what information is included for each item (for example, paragraph text, paragraph autonumber, page number, or chapter number).
- Format the included information.

To accomplish the latter two, you must modify the reference pages and the paragraph tags in the table of contents file.

The information you set up on the reference pages depends on the paragraph tag settings, so often you have to go back and forth to get everything exactly right. You must update the book after you make changes on the reference pages before your changes are shown in the table of contents.

REMEMBER Because the table of contents generation process is based on paragraph tag names, it's important (once again) to tag your document consistently. Using blank paragraphs to provide vertical white space in a document can cause problems in the table of contents. If the blank paragraphs use a tag that's included in the table of contents, you will see empty entries in the table of contents.

To remove them, go to the source file and delete the empty paragraphs. Use the space above and space below settings in the Paragraph Designer instead (see "Avoiding Formatting Overrides" on page 111 for details).

Locating the TOC Reference Flow

The information that's displayed for each paragraph is controlled by the reference pages of the generated file. For the table of contents, the reference pages contain a reference page called TOC. On that TOC page, you will find a text frame with a TOC flow (Figure 15-3).

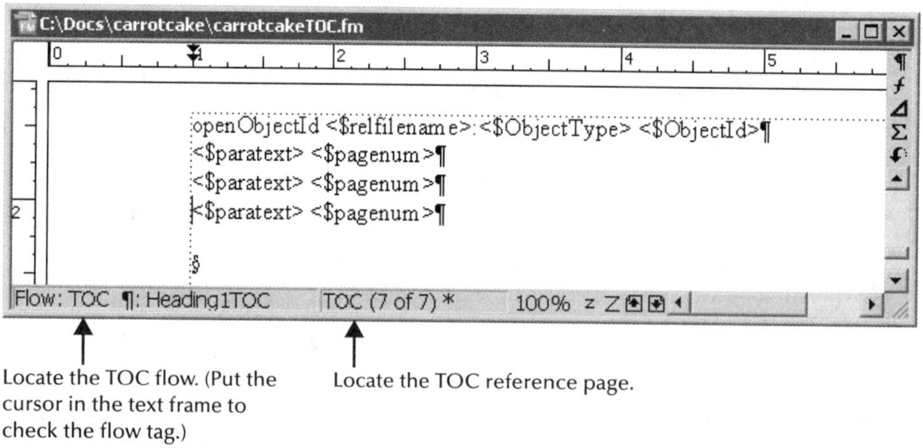

Figure 15-3. Locating the reference page information

NOTE FrameMaker has three types of pages: body pages (which are printed), master pages (which provide the templates for the body pages with headers and footers), and reference pages. Reference pages store information used ("referenced") by other parts of the document.

Each paragraph that you include in the table of contents has its own entry in the reference pages. This entry determines what information is displayed for each item.

CAUTION If you have *two* TOC flows in the file, FrameMaker uses the one that comes first in its internal sort order. If you repeatedly update the TOC flow but do not see any results when you update the book, check the reference pages for an extra TOC flow. FrameMaker might be using the other flow instead of the one you're modifying. Sort order is not necessarily the same as the page order of the reference pages, so a flow that occurs later in the document could be considered the "first" TOC flow. Check every text frame's flow tag to verify that only one text frame in the reference pages is labeled TOC. Keep in mind that the renegade extra flow might be in a very small text frame. If you do find an extra TOC flow, we recommend that you copy the information in your good flow and then delete **both** flows and regenerate. FrameMaker re-creates a TOC text frame, and you can paste the good information into this new text frame.

Book vs. Stand-Alone Table of Contents

Most of the information in this chapter focuses on tables of contents for a book. You can, however, also create a table of contents for a single file. FrameMaker calls this a *stand-alone* table of contents (presumably because the file stands alone instead of being part of a book).

Without a book file, you can't update from the book. Instead, you select Special➤Table of Contents to create a stand-alone table of contents. After you create the file, selecting Special➤Table of Contents again will update the file. Any changes you made to the list of included tags, the paragraph tags, or the reference pages in the generated file are preserved.

To locate the TOC flow on the reference pages, follow these steps:

1. Display the reference pages by selecting View➤Reference Pages.
2. Find the TOC reference page. Notice that the status bar tells you the name of each page along with the number of pages as you move from page to page (as shown in Figure 15-3).

On the TOC reference page, locate the TOC flow. Click inside the flow, and check the status bar to verify that you are in the TOC flow.

REMEMBER After changing the reference pages, you must update the book before your changes are shown in the table of contents entries.

Understanding the TOC Flow Entries

In the TOC flow, you will find a paragraph for each of the tags you've included in the table of contents. You can determine which paragraph belongs to an included item based on the paragraph tag. For example, if you included ChapterTitle in your table of contents, you will find a ChapterTitleTOC paragraph in the TOC flow.

NOTE FrameMaker does not delete paragraphs from the TOC flow. If you added a paragraph tag and later removed it from the setup dialog box, you will still see an entry on the TOC reference page. You can safely remove that line if you want to.

Each paragraph in the TOC flow determines what information is included for a specific paragraph. For instance, you might have a paragraph such as the following with a paragraph tag of Heading1TOC:

```
<$paratext> <$pagenum>
```

For each Heading1, FrameMaker will retrieve the contents of the paragraph (<$paratext>), followed by a space, followed by the page number of the paragraph (<$pagenum>).

Most TOC flow definitions consist of a mixture of text and building blocks. For instance, you could use the following definition for a chapter title:

```
Chapter <$chapnum>: <$paratext>\t<$pagenum>
```

In the chapter title tag, the word "Chapter," the colon, and the various spaces are regular, literal text. The <$chapnum>, <$paratext>, and <$pagenum> building blocks are processed every time this entry is used to determine the current values for those items. The \t is a tab (you can press the tab key to insert a tab instead of typing \t, if you choose).

Several FrameMaker features—such as cross-references and variables—use building blocks. The building blocks for the table of contents are special in a few ways:

- FrameMaker does not provide you with a way to insert building blocks by choosing them from a list. Instead, you must type the building block.
- In table of contents definitions, you cannot use building blocks that call other paragraph tags, such as:

  ```
  <$paratext[some_other_para]>
  ```

  FrameMaker can retrieve information only from the paragraph that's currently being processed.
- Because you are typing in a text frame and not a dialog box, you can use the normal keyboard shortcuts for special characters. For more information about typing special characters, see "Inserting Special Characters" on page 65.

Table 15-1 lists the available building blocks that you can type in to customize table of contents definitions.

Building Block	Description
`<$paratext>`	Inserts the text of the source paragraph (for example, "Reindeer" or "Caribou" from the example in Figure 15-1 on page 402).
`<$paranum>`	Inserts the entire autonumber (if any) of the source paragraph.
`<$paranumonly>`	Inserts the numeric portion of the autonumber from the source paragraph.
`<$pagenum>`	Inserts the page number on which the source paragraph occurs.
`<$chapnum>`	Inserts the chapter number of the source paragraph's file.
`<$volnum>`	Inserts the volume number of the source paragraph's file.
<char_tag>	Applies the specified character tag to the text that follows in the paragraph.
`<Default Para Font>` or `</>`	Removes any character tagging and returns to the paragraph's formatting.
`\t`	Inserts a tab. You can get the same result by typing a tab on the keyboard.

Table 15-1. Building Blocks for Table of Contents Definitions

Formatting the Table of Contents

For each tag you include in the table of contents, FrameMaker automatically creates a paragraph tag. The tag name is the name of the source tag with "TOC" appended. If, for example, you include Heading1 in your table of contents, all of the Heading1 entries will use the Heading1TOC paragraph tag. To format the table of contents, you modify these tag definitions in the table of contents. Refer to Chapter 5, "Formatting Text with Paragraph Tags," for details on how to format the paragraph tags.

TIP Because of FrameMaker's convention of appending "TOC" to paragraph tag names, we recommend against creating any tag names for content that end in TOC. In fact, this recommendation is for all generated files. The default file name suffix of the generated file is used for the paragraph tags that control the formatting in the generated file. (For example, in the index, the tag names end with IX; in lists of references, they end with LOR.) Different letters are appended to generated files if you are using a localized version of FrameMaker.

Using Character-Level Formatting

To format a portion of a table of contents entry differently from the rest of the paragraph, you use character tags as building blocks. For example, to make only the page number boldface, you would do something like this:

```
<$paratext> <Bold><$pagenum></>
```

NOTE The character tag you use must be defined in the character catalog of the table of contents file.

Formatting Examples

Many users are intimidated by the process of getting a table of contents to look just right. The trouble is that you have to make changes in two different places—the reference pages and the paragraph tags. Reference-page changes don't take effect until you update the book, but paragraph tag changes are immediate. In this section, you'll find explanations of two common formatting problems:

- Dot leaders
- Putting two paragraphs on a single line

Creating Entries with Dot Leaders

Setting up table of contents entries with dot leaders is a common requirement. FrameMaker can handle these automatically, but setting them up can be a bit disconcerting.

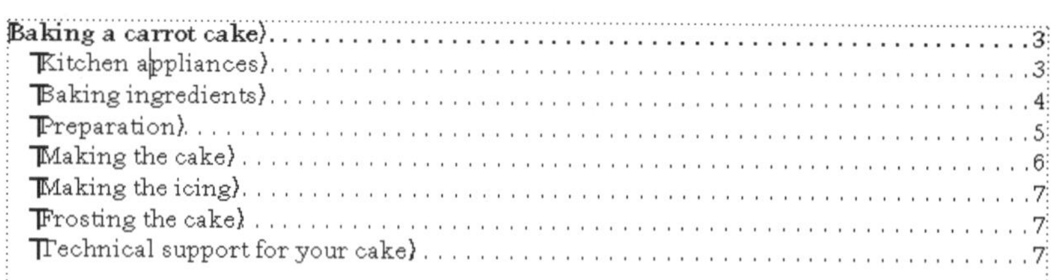

Autonumbering in the Table of Contents

Autonumbering is available for the paragraph tags in the table of contents, just like in any regular document. Therefore, you can have the same result from two different table of contents paragraph definitions.

For example, let's say you want the chapter title to look like the following sample in the table of contents:

Chapter 2: Needlepoint 33

Most of the time, the preferred method is to have FrameMaker get the numbering for the table of contents from the chapter number. You could do this using the following ChapterTitleTOC definition on the reference page:

```
Chapter <$chapnum>: <$paratext>\t<$pagenum>
```

Another way would be to set the autonumbering in the ChapterTitleTOC paragraph tag itself. For this, you would first create a ChapterTitleTOC definition on the reference page as follows:

```
<$paratext>\t<$pagenum>
```

The ChapterTitleTOC definition contains no building blocks to pick up the autonumbering from the chapters. To add the autonumbering, define the autonumbering in the ChapterTitleTOC paragraph tag (in the Numbering sheet of the Paragraph Designer), just as you would for any autonumbered paragraph:

```
S:Chapter <n+>
```

Note that the ChapterTitleTOC definition does not use <$chapnum> because FrameMaker will pick up the chapter number of the *current* file (that is, the table of contents).

In general, we do not recommend this second technique because the autonumbering stream is completely unrelated to the actual chapter number. Using autonumbering hides any possible problems with the chapter numbering sequence because you do not see the true chapter number; you see only the autonumber.

You might need to use this technique, though, if your chapter numbering and chapter titles are in separate paragraphs in your files and those paragraphs do not appear in the order you need for the table of contents. Using autonumbering in the table of contents paragraph definitions might let you create the preferred output.

To create a table of contents entry with dot leaders, follow these steps:

1. Go to the reference pages (View➤Reference Pages) and locate the TOC flow.
2. Modify the TOC definition as follows for each paragraph that should have a dot leader:

```
<$paratext>\t<$pagenum>
```

That is, place a tab between the < $paratext > and < $pagenum > building blocks. If you are using chapter numbers, your definition might look more like this:

```
<$paratext>\t<$chapnum>-<$pagenum>
```

The effect (or rather lack thereof) on the reference page is shown in the following example:

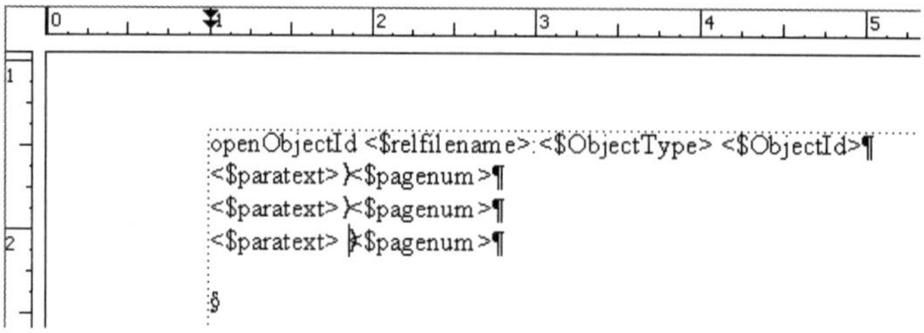

3. Update the book file, and then view the body pages for the table of contents. The tabs now appear in your table of contents entries, but they probably aren't working yet.

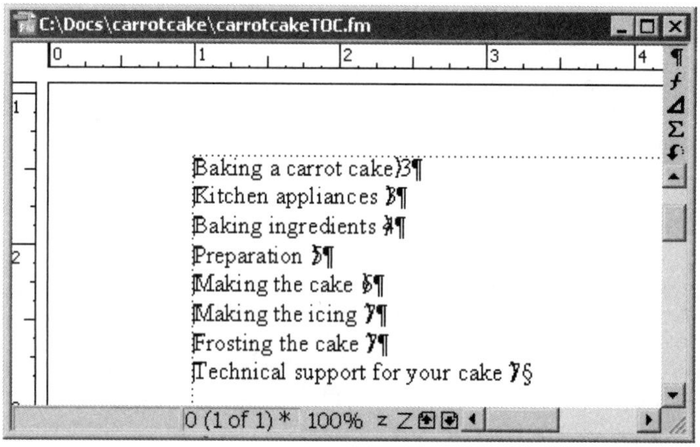

4. Modify the paragraph tags in the table of contents file to include a right-aligned tab stop with a dot leader. The following illustration shows a sample paragraph tag with the appropriate settings. You need to make this change in every TOC paragraph tag that includes a tab.

NOTE Remember to click the Update All button to save your changes for each paragraph tag you change.

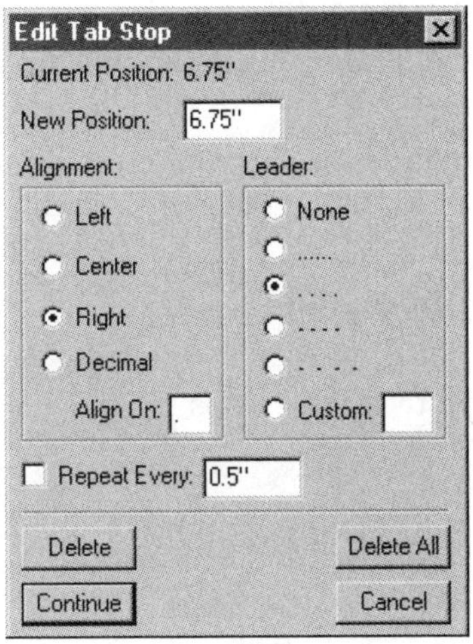

Your table of contents entries should now line up correctly.

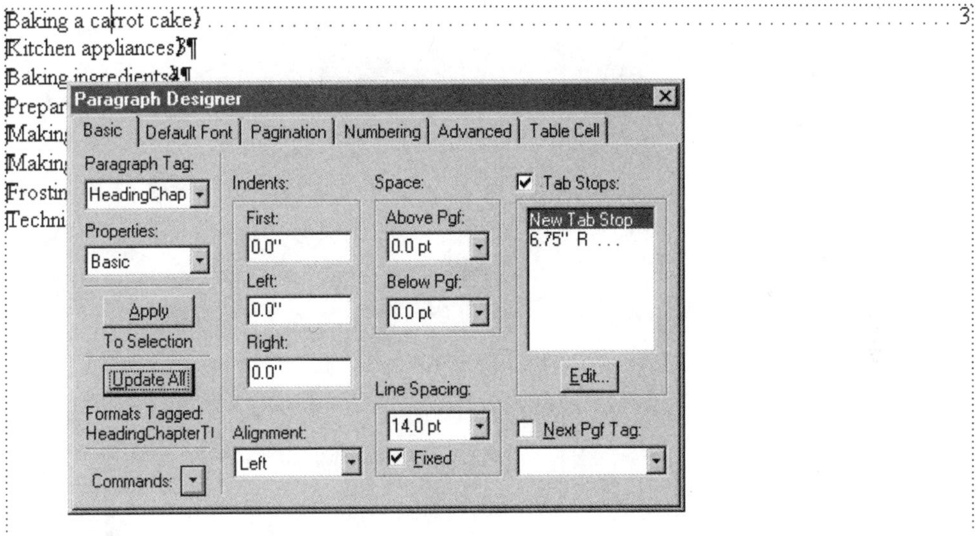

After you set up the dot leaders for each paragraph, FrameMaker generates them every time you update the table of contents.

Putting Two Paragraphs on a Single Line

A common technique used in cross-references and variables is not available inside the table of contents. In cross-references and variables, you can use building blocks that call a particular paragraph tag, such as this:

```
<$paratext[ChapTitle]>
```

These options are not available inside the table of contents definition. While generating the table of contents, FrameMaker can pick up information only from the current paragraph.

This presents a problem when, for example, your chapter number and chapter title are stored in two separate paragraphs. In the table of contents, you want something like this:

Chapter 7: Important Information

But in the document, you have two paragraphs:

- chap_number: Chapter 7
- chap_title: Important Information

If the paragraphs are in sequence, you can use a run-in heading format in the table of contents. If the chapter_numberTOC paragraph uses a run-in heading, the chapter number and title are displayed on the same line.

Managing Line Breaks in the Table of Contents

After generating the table of contents, you'll probably have a few lines that break in interesting and unfortunate ways. It's tempting to correct them by inserting forced returns (SHIFT-ENTER), but those changes are lost when you regenerate. A better strategy is to use hard spaces in the source paragraph to "glue together" the relevant pieces so that they break properly in the generated table of contents.

Baking a carrot cake 3
Kitchen appliances 3
Baking ingredients 4
Preparation 5
Making the cake 6
Preparing the ingredients 6
Putting it all together, along with some tips on how to prevent common problems with
carrot cakes 6
Making the icing 7
Frosting the cake 7
Technical support for your cake 7

Baking a carrot cake 3
Kitchen appliances 3
Baking ingredients 4
Preparation 5
Making the cake 6
Preparing the ingredients 6
Putting it all together, along with some tips on how
to prevent common problems with carrot cakes 6
Making the icing 7
Frosting the cake 7
Technical support for your cake 7

CHAPTER 16

Creating Indexes

Many readers of technical books consider the index to be the most important part of the book. A complete index lets readers locate information quickly. You can create indexes for your FrameMaker books (or files). An index, like a table of contents, is a generated file. Creating indexes, however, takes more work than creating a table of contents. Before you can generate the index, you must insert index markers (hidden text with index information) throughout the document to identify terms that should appear in the index.

FrameMaker doesn't automatically create index entries for you, but it does provide automatic sorting and concatenation of index entries (see Figure 16-1). Specifically, FrameMaker takes your index markers and does the following:

- Alphabetizes entries
- Inserts group titles (A, B, C, D, and so on)
- Groups identical entries into a single entry with multiple page numbers
- Groups secondary entries under their parent entry
- Inserts the correct page number for each entry (based on the marker location)

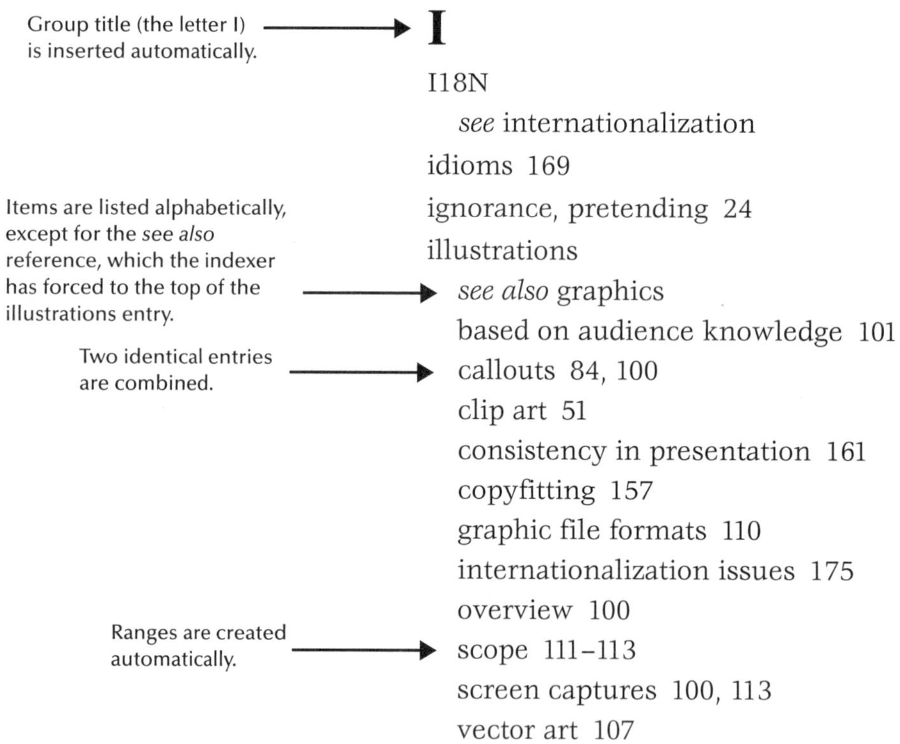

Figure 16-1. Automated index formatting features

Creating the Index File

To create an index, you must insert index markers into the document files to create content for the index. FrameMaker gathers text from the index markers and places the text in the index file.

To add an index file to a book, follow these steps:

1. Open the book file.
2. *(optional)* Click the file that will be immediately before or after the index.
3. Select Add➤Standard Index. The Set Up Standard Index dialog box is displayed (Figure 16-2).

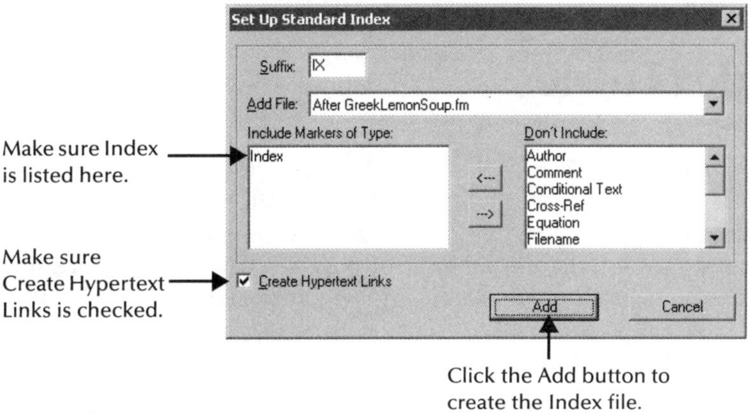

Figure 16-2. Setting up the index file

4. *(optional)* In the Add File drop-down list, select whether you want the index before or after the file you selected in step 2.
5. Verify that the Index marker is in the Include Markers of Type list.
6. Make sure that the Create Hypertext Links check box is checked. This feature creates the index entries as hyperlinks. It also ensures that if you convert to other formats (PDF or HTML), the links in the index are preserved.

CAUTION If you are generating indexes with a very large number of entries (more than 50,000 or so), don't check the Create Hypertext Links check box. With the links, the index might take a very long time to generate or fail to generate.

7. Click the Add button. The Update Book dialog box (Figure 14-2 on page 383) is displayed. The index you're creating is shown in the generated files list.
8. Make sure that the index is in the Generate list, then click the Update button. The file name of the index file is based on the book file name. If your book file is foo.book, the index file will be fooIX.fm.

   The index file now appears in the book; you can move it just like any regular file (see "Rearranging Files" on page 380).

BUILDING BOOKS

File-Level (Stand-Alone) Indexes

Although you'll probably create most indexes for a collection of files (that is, a book), you also have the option of creating an index for a single file. FrameMaker calls this a *stand-alone* index because the index stands on its own and is not part of a book.

If you're working on a very large index, consider creating a stand-alone index for each chapter as you're inserting the index markers. This lets you check the index entries chapter by chapter (instead of having to plow through the entire index).

To create a stand-alone index, open a document, then select Special➤Standard Index. Specify that you want to create a stand-alone index.

Creating Index Entries

When you insert an index marker, FrameMaker creates a corresponding index entry. The page number that appears in the index matches the page on which the index marker occurs. In addition to basic index markers, FrameMaker provides a variety of building blocks and commands that let you create secondary entries, entries with character formatting, and the like. Table 16-1 provides a quick reference for indexing commands; the sections that follow explain the commands in more detail.

Command	Marker Text Example	Result
: colon Creates a secondary reference	`apple:pie`	**A** apple pie 7

	`apple:pie:a la mode`	**A**
		apple
		  pie
		    a la mode 7

; semicolon Creates two entries in a single marker	`apple;banana`	**A** apple 7 **B** banana 7

Table 16-1. Indexing Command Examples

Command	Marker Text Example	Result
	pie:apple;cream pie:banana	**C** cream pie banana 7 **P** pie apple 7
<$nopage> Suppresses display of the page number	torte, see cake<$nopage>	**T** torte, see pie
<*character_tag*> Assigns the specified character tag to the marker text that follows	torte, <Emphasis>see</> pie<$nopage>	**T** torte, *see* pie
[*sort_order*] Sorts the entry as if it used the text shown in brackets	pie:<Emphasis>see also</>cream pie<$nopage>[pie:aa]	**P** pie *see also* cream pie apple 7
<$startrange> <$endrange> Lets you create entries with ranges	On page 8: pear<$startrange> On page 12: pear<$endrange>	**P** pear 8–12

Table 16-1. Indexing Command Examples (Continued)

Basic Entries

To create a basic index entry, follow these steps:

1. Position the cursor where the relevant information occurs in the document.
2. *(optional)* Select the term you want to index before displaying the Marker dialog box. FrameMaker automatically puts the selected text in the marker text field.

TIP Place the index marker at the beginning or end of words. If you place the marker in the middle of a word, the text will look fine in your PDF files, but PDF searches may not find the word.

3. Select Special➤Marker. The Marker dialog box is displayed.

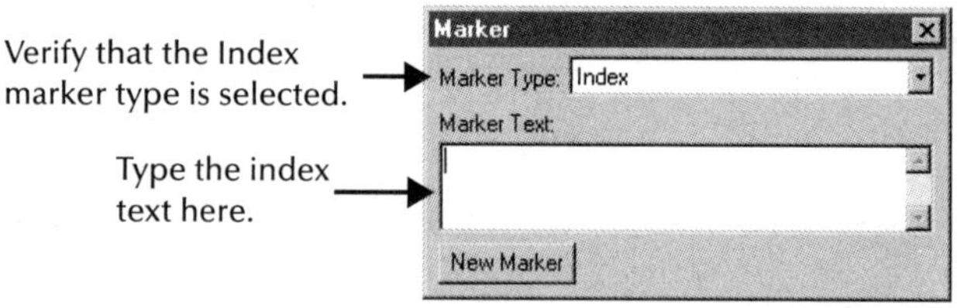

4. In the Marker Type drop-down list, make sure that Index is selected.

REMEMBER The marker type defaults to whatever type was last used, so if you just inserted a hypertext marker, you'll need to change the marker type from Hypertext back to Index.

5. In the Marker Text field, type the text you want in the index. For example, to create an entry under A for apple on page 7, go to page 7, insert a marker in the apple-related content, and type in:

```
apple
```

To insert a command character (such as colon, semicolon, or brackets) as a literal, precede it with a backslash. For example:

```
\<HTML\>
```

For information about inserting other special characters, see "Entering Special Characters in Dialog Boxes" on page 629.

6. Click the New Marker button to insert the marker. A marker symbol is displayed in your text. It looks like a boldface T, but it does not print.

Index marker symbol

7. To see the result in your index, update the book file. The new index entry is shown in the generated index.

A
apple 7

The letter A and the page number are inserted automatically. You provide only the actual index entry text.

NOTE If the entry you want appears in the text, you can insert a blank index marker immediately to the left of the relevant word. If the index marker is blank, it picks up the word to the right of the index marker during generation. However, we do not recommend this method because it makes index maintenance more difficult. You cannot search for index text; instead, you must locate the blank index markers and then check the words next to them.

Editing and Deleting Index Entries

To edit an existing marker, select the marker (or select a block of text that includes the marker). Then, select Special➤Marker to display the Marker dialog box, make your changes, and click the Edit Marker button to save them.

TIP If you are planning to do a lot of indexing, we highly recommend that you get the IXgen third-party plug-in, which helps automate a lot of index maintenance. For details, see Appendix A, "Resources."

To delete an index entry, delete the marker. However, locating index markers for editing or deleting can be tedious. Here are some tips for finding index markers:

- Use the Find command and specify that you want to locate marker text or a marker of type Index.
- Take advantage of the hypertext links in the index. When you CTRL-ALT-click on a page entry, FrameMaker opens the appropriate file, locates the index marker, and selects it.
- Leave the Marker dialog box open. When you select a marker, the marker text is displayed in the Marker dialog box automatically.

Creating Subentries

To create a subentry, separate the primary and secondary entry with a colon. For example, type the following:

```
soup:chicken noodle
```

The entry will look like this:

S

soup
  chicken noodle 27

Stacking Multiple Entries in a Single Index Marker

Use a semicolon to separate multiple, independent entries in a single index marker. For example:

```
food;drink
```

D
drink 36

F
food 36

This is equivalent to creating two separate markers, each of which contains one entry.

Creating Ranges

Page ranges in indexes tell the reader that there is a significant amount of information available about a particular topic. You indicate the beginning and the end of the range with separate, matching markers. A range looks like this:

G
gluttony 121–135

There are two ways to create ranges—you can use index markers that define ranges, or you can use the < $autorange > command. This section discusses how to create ranges with index markers; refer to page 435 for details on the < $autorange > command, which is inserted in the IX reference page flow.

To create an index entry with a range of pages, follow these steps:

1. On the first page of the range, insert an index marker with the relevant text and the < $startrange > command:

   ```
   gluttony<$startrange>
   ```

2. On the last page of the range, insert a matching index marker with the < $endrange > command:

   ```
   gluttony<$endrange>
   ```

FrameMaker matches the < $startrange > and < $endrange > commands and puts a single index entry in the index.

CAUTION The marker text must match exactly (other than the range command); otherwise, FrameMaker cannot resolve the markers. If FrameMaker cannot match the two ends of the range, you see question marks in the index:

G
gluttony ??–135

To correct this problem, make sure that every <$startrange> marker has a corresponding <$endrange> marker and that the marker text matches in those entries. A common mistake is to create one singular and one plural entry:

```
apple<$startrange>
apples<$endrange>
```

The result in the index is two entries, each with half a range:

A
apple 121–??
apples ??–125

When you insert a range command, the command is applied to the current index entry in the marker and all that follow to the right in that marker. For example, assume you have the following two markers:

```
land<$startrange>
sea;land<$endrange>
```

In this case, the "land" range resolves correctly, and you see a single page entry under "sea." However, the following will cause problems:

```
land<$startrange>
land<$endrange>;sea
```

The <$endrange> command is applied to the "land" entry and also to the "sea" entry, so the result is a broken range because you do not have a "sea<$startrange>" entry anywhere.

L
land 2–10

S
sea ??–10

To prevent this problem, which is hard to track down and correct, we recommend that you put all range commands in individual markers instead of stacking them with other entries in a single marker.

A Few Words About Good Indexing

The index provides readers with *information access points*—a way to locate the content that's of interest. Creating a detailed, useful index is critical to the success of your document. The longer the document, the more important the index becomes to the reader. A complete discussion of indexing is beyond the scope of this book, but here are a few pointers:

- Index terms where they are defined and when important information about the term is provided. Do not index every occurrence of a term (unless you're creating a specialized concordance index).
- Index actions by the action (gerund) and the item (noun). For example, for information about steeping tea, put an entry under "steeping tea" and another under "tea, steeping."
- If you have more than two or three entries for a particular item, modify the entries to create secondary entries under the primary entry.
- Use ranges to cue readers that a detailed discussion of a topic is available.
- Provide synonyms ("see" references) to help readers locate the information they want even if they don't know your terminology.

Refer to Appendix A, "Resources," for tools to help you index FrameMaker files. If you do not want to create the index yourself, consider hiring a professional indexer. The American Society of Indexers (www.asi.org) is a good place to start.

Creating References to Synonyms ("see")

In an index, *see* references or synonyms are very helpful because they point the reader in the right direction. For example, a reader might find something like this:

G
Granny Smith, *see* apple

These references are inserted just like regular index markers, except that you need to suppress the page number. For this, you need the <$nopage> command:

```
Granny Smith, see apple<$nopage>
```

If you want to italicize the word *see,* use a character tag inside the index marker and the <Default Para Font> tag or its abbreviation </> to turn off the character tagging:

```
Granny Smith, <Emphasis>see </>apple<$nopage>
```

REMEMBER The character tag you specify must be available in the index file's character catalog. It does **not** have to be available in the file where you insert the marker.

Like the range commands, <$nopage> applies to all the text that follows in the marker. You can restart pagination with the <$singlepage> building block, but it's usually easier to separate the <$nopage> entries into individual markers.

Changing Sorting Order for a Single Entry

The *see also* reference is a variation on *see* references. You generally use *see* references when you need to point readers to a different entry in an index. By contrast, *see also* references are used when the current entry has some information, but there is also another relevant possibility. In Figure 16-1 on page 420, for example, the index includes a *see also* reference (illustrations, see also graphics) and a *see* reference (I18N, see internationalization).

The problem with *see also* references is that, by default, FrameMaker sorts them under S in the subentry. Instead, you probably want them to appear at the top of the list. You accomplish this by modifying the alphabetization of that entry. Instead of using the actual text of the entry for sorting, you provide alternate text that's used when sorting the entry.

The see also entry in Figure 16-1 on page 420 uses the following syntax:

```
illustrations:<Emphasis>see also</>
graphics<$nopage>[illustrations:aa]
```

The text in brackets at the end of the entry controls where the information is sorted in the index. In the preceding example, the aa text ensures that the entry is sorted to the top of the illustrations subentries.

The text in brackets is only for the current entry in the marker. For example, consider the following:

```
Korean War;'50s[Fifties]
```

The Korean War entry appears under K, but the '50s entry shows up under F.

Formatting the Index

To format the index, you modify the index paragraph tags and the reference pages. The paragraph tags are as follows:

- **GroupTitlesIX** is applied to the lettered headings (A, B, C, and so on) that separate the alphabetical groupings in the index.
- **Level1IX** is applied to the first-level index entries.
- **Level2IX** is applied to the second-level index entries.
- If you have deeper index levels, FrameMaker creates the appropriate **Level3IX**, **Level4IX**, and so on.

You can change these paragraph tags inside the index file to create the look you want.

TIP When you generate the index, FrameMaker replaces the entire generated flow in the index. If you want to insert text preceding the index (such as the title "Index"), type this text into the index file before the generated text. Be sure that the first marker in the flow is after the title. FrameMaker will not delete any text that precedes the generated flow.

In addition to the paragraph tags, some formatting information is controlled by the IX flow on the reference pages (View➤Reference Pages). Figure 16-3 shows a sample IX flow.

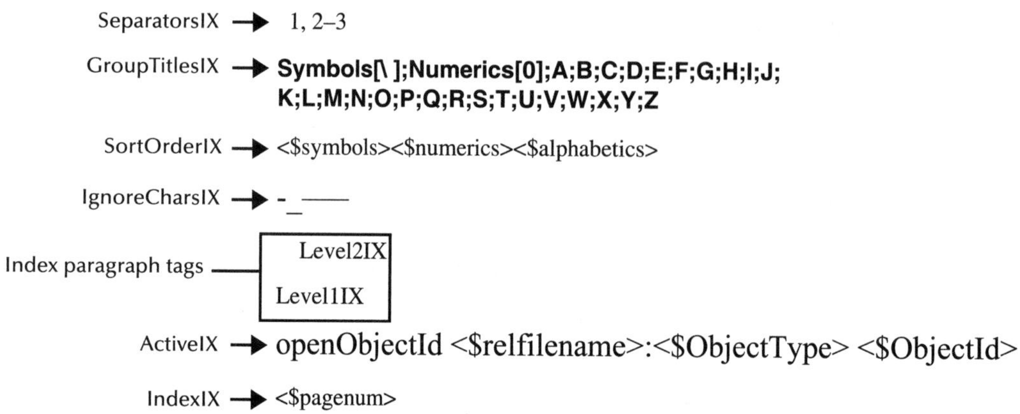

Figure 16-3. The IX flow on the reference pages controls some of the index settings.

Table 16-2 describes the function of each paragraph in the flow.

Most likely, you'll make fewer changes in the IX reference flow than you do in the TOC reference flow. The most common change that's needed is to control the formatting of the index page number (see page 434).

Paragraph Tag on Reference Page	Text in Flow	Function
IgnoreCharsIX	-_–— (hyphen, underscore, en dash, em dash)	Lists the characters that are ignored when FrameMaker sorts index entries
ActiveIX	`open ObjectId <$relfilename>: <$ObjectType> <$ObjectId>`	Inserts the hypertext markers needed to make the index markers into links

Table 16-2. IX Reference Flow Paragraphs

Paragraph Tag on Reference Page	Text in Flow	Function

Level3IX, Level2IX, Level1IX	`Level3IX`
	`Level2IX`
	`Level1IX`
		Lists the levels of index

SeparatorsIX	`1, 2-3`	Lists the characters that separate index entries and page references.
SortOrderIX	`<$symbols><$numerics>` `<$alphabetics>`	Determines the order in which symbol entries, numeric entries, and alphabetic entries are presented
GroupTitlesIX	`Symbols[\ ];Numerics [0];A;B;C;D;E;F;G;H;I ;J;K;L;M;N;O;P;Q;R;S; T;U;V;W;X;Y;Z`	Lists the group titles (usually A, B, C, and so on)
IndexIX	`<$pagenum>`	Controls the formatting of the page numbers in the index

Table 16-2. IX Reference Flow Paragraphs (Continued)

Ignoring Characters While Sorting

The IgnoreCharsIX paragraph in the IX flow controls which characters are ignored for alphabetization purposes when the index is sorted. By default, the IgnoreCharsIX contains these characters:

```
-_–—
```

The characters are hyphen, underscore, en dash, and em dash.

NOTE The default characters have changed in FrameMaker 8. In previous versions of FrameMaker, the default characters were hyphen, minus sign, en dash, and em dash.

To change which characters are considered (or not) when sorting the index, modify the items in the list. For example, to eliminate the forward slash (/) from consideration during sorting, add it to the IgnoreCharsIX line, like this:

```
-_–—/
```

When you regenerate the index, FrameMaker ignores any forward slashes while sorting index entries. The slashes and other characters listed here are still printed as part of the index entry.

By default, FrameMaker sorts index entries word-by-word. That is, the spaces between words are taken into account when sorting. To change your sort to letter-by-letter, where spaces are ignored, add a space to the IgnoreCharIX paragraph.

Modifying Page Separators

An index entry has several different components that control the overall format. The SeparatorsIX entry in the IX reference flow sets the three following parameters:

- The separator between the index entry text and the first page number
- The separator between multiple page numbers
- The separator in a range

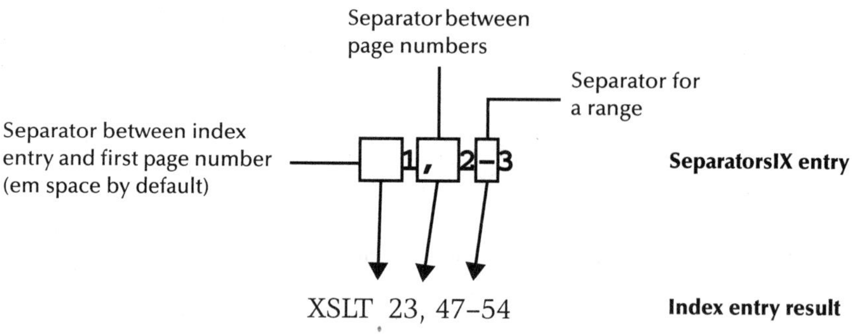

The default SeparatorsIX entry looks like this:

```
1, 2-3
```

Its settings are as follows:

- An em space between the index entry and first page number
- A comma followed by a space between separate page entries
- An en dash in ranges

To change the separators, you change the items in this line.

NOTE If you need to change the formatting of the page number, you need to modify the IndexIX entry. See "Formatting the Page Number" on page 434.

Changing the Sort Order

The SortOrderIX entry in the reference flow determines how entries are sorted. By default, it contains the following building blocks:

```
<$symbols><$numerics><$alphabetics>
```

The building blocks are placeholders for the following characters:

<$symbols>	All characters not listed under <$numerics> or <$alphabetics>, sorted by ASCII value
<$numerics>	0 1 2 3 4 5 6 7 8 9
<$alphabetics>	AÁÀÂÄÃÅaáàâäãåªBbCÇcçDdEÉÈÊËeéèêëFfƒGgHhIÍÌÎÏiíìîïJjKkLlMmNÑnñOÓÒÔÖÕØoóòôöõøºPpQqRrSsTtUÚÙÛÜuúùûüVvWwXxYŸyÿZz This is the sort order for the U.S. English interface; other languages are slightly different. You can find the specifics for other languages in the localized help.

To put the symbol characters last in the index, change the building block order:

```
<$numerics><$alphabetics><$symbols>
```

If you need finer control over the sort order, you can replace the building blocks with an expanded list. Assume, for instance, that you have a number of index entries that start with pound signs (#98). Normally, those would be sorted in the <$symbols> sections, but you want them to appear in the <$numerics> section. You can remove the <$numerics> building block and replace it with a list of characters:

```
<$symbols>0 1 2 3 4 5 6 7 8 9 #<$alphabetics>
```

The result will be that the entries that begin with a pound sign (#) are sorted after the number nine and appear in the Numerics section.

Changing the Group Titles

When you generate the index, the alphabetic group titles are inserted automatically. For sorting purposes, the titles are treated just like regular index entries; however, they use the GroupTitlesIX paragraph tag instead of one of the Level*n*IX tags. The most common modification of the group titles is consolidating entries. For example, you might have an index that contains only two or three entries under X, Y, and Z. Instead of listing them separately, you could combine them under an X–Z group title.

X X-ray 44 **Y** Yeti 36 **Z** zebra 7	→	**X–Z** X-ray 44 Yeti 36 zebra 7

The default GroupTitlesIX entry looks like this:

```
Symbols[\ ];Numerics[0];A;B;C;D;E;F;G;H;I;J;K;L;M;N;O;P;Q;R;S;T;U;V;
W;X;Y;Z
```

To consolidate titles, you must make two changes:

- Group the letters you want to combine.
- Force that title to appear at the beginning of the first letter (by customizing the alphabetization of that item).

To create an X–Z group title, modify GroupTitlesIX to look like this:

```
Symbols[\ ];Numerics[0];A;B;C;D;E;F;G;H;I;J;K;L;M;N;O;P;Q;R;S;T;U;V;
W;X-Z[X]
```

Formatting the Page Number

The information presented in the page number is set by the IndexIX entry in the IX reference flow. By default, it is set to:

```
<$pagenum>
```

If you want to include a chapter number in your index page references, modify IndexIX to include the chapter number:

```
<$chapnum>-<$pagenum>
```

TIP Use a nonbreaking hyphen (ESC HYPHEN H) instead of a regular hyphen to prevent unattractive line breaks in the index.

You can also add the volume number (<$volnum>) and the paragraph number (<$paranum> or <$paranumonly>).

The formatting of the IndexIX paragraph tag controls the appearance of page numbers in the generated files, even though the page numbers end up being part of the Level*n*IX paragraphs. If, for example, you want the page number to be italic while the index entry is regular text, you would define the Level1IX paragraph tag with the regular font and the IndexIX paragraph tag with the italic font.

Creating Ranges Automatically

FrameMaker has a little-known feature called autorange. Instead of creating matching startrange and endrange markers for each of your ranges (see page 426), you can let FrameMaker create the ranges automatically.

With autoranging activated, FrameMaker scans index entries for matching entries. When an entry occurs on two or more pages in sequence, a range is created in the index.

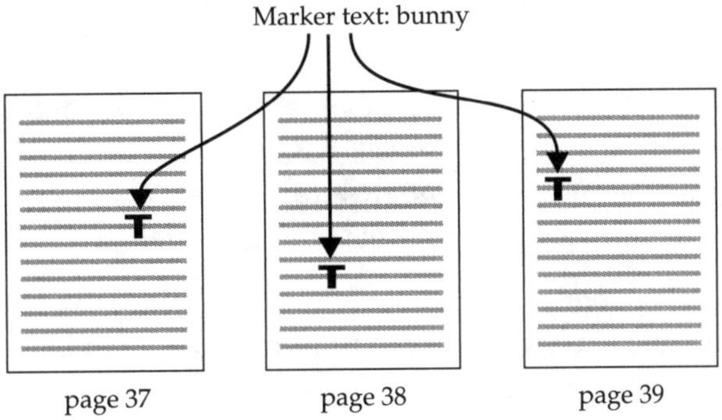

<$pagenum> ⟶ **B**
bunny 37, 38, 39

<$pagenum><$autorange> ⟶ **B**
bunny 37–39

To activate autoranging, modify the IndexIX paragraph in the IX reference flow to contain the <$autorange> command:

```
<$pagenum><$autorange>
```

Autorange lets you avoid creating startrange and endrange markers. The disadvantage of autorange is that you must insert identical index markers on every page in the sequence. If the range is more than two or three pages, inserting all those markers will become quite tedious. Inserting a startrange and an endrange command is suddenly much more appealing.

Eliminating Unwanted Chapter Numbers

Including the <$chapnum> building block in the IndexIX definition is much faster than the old way of setting up page numbers, which involved using chapter prefixes that had to be set individually for each chapter. There is, however, a problem with the new feature if your files are set up as follows:

- The main body text has multipart page numbers with chapter and page number (3-1, 3-2, and so on).
- The front matter (or back matter) uses a different numbering scheme without a chapter number (for example, i, ii, iii, iv, and so on).

If you insert index entries into both numbering streams, you end up with the following numbers for the front matter entries: 1-iv, 1-x, and so on.

The problem occurs because the reference page flow requires a <$chapnum> building block to be inserted for every index entry. There are two solutions for this problem:

- Eliminate index entries from the front matter (this is known as "avoidance").
- Use a special marker type (for example, IndexRoman) for all of the index entries in the front matter.

To set up the special entries, follow these steps:

1. In the files that use Roman numerals, create an IndexRoman marker type by following these steps:

   a. Select Special➤Marker. The Marker dialog box is displayed.

   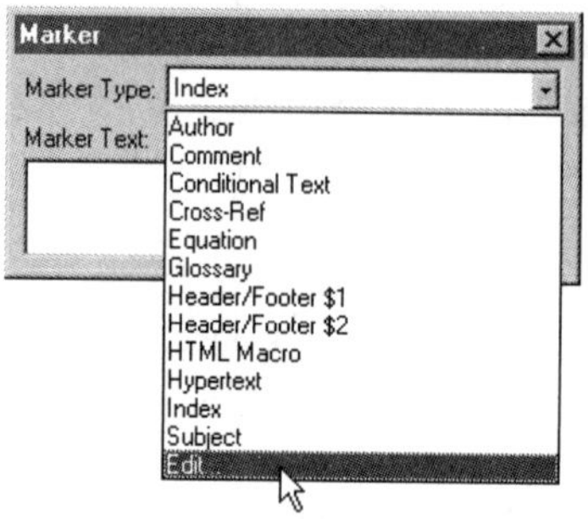

   b. In the Marker Type drop-down list, click Edit. The Edit Custom Marker Type dialog box is displayed.

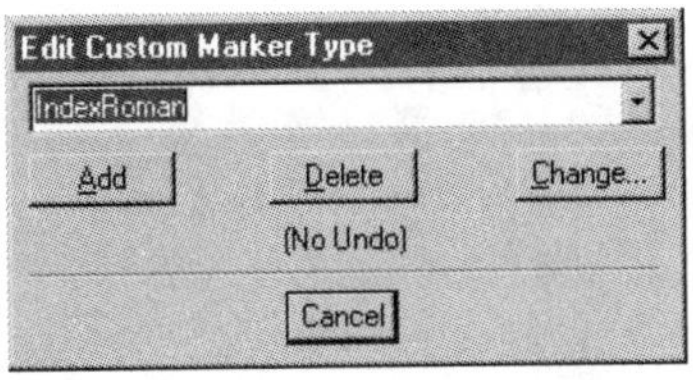

c. In the marker type field, type **IndexRoman**, the name of the new marker.

d. Click the Add button.

e. Click the Done button to close the Edit Custom Marker Type dialog box and return to the Marker dialog box. The new marker type is now shown in the Marker Type list.

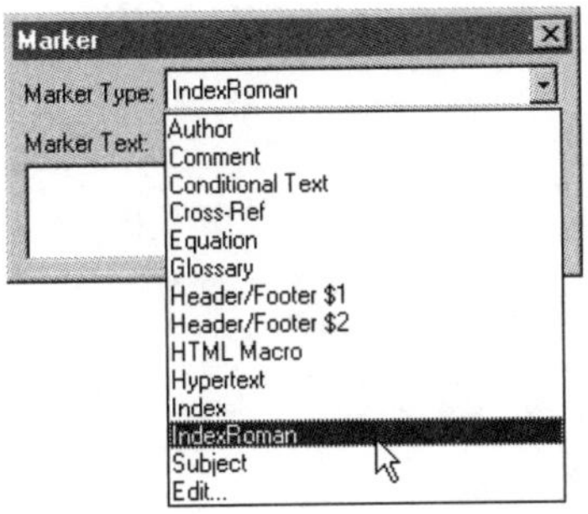

TIP Custom marker definitions are stored as part of the document properties, so you can import formats from one file to another to copy over the new marker type.

2. Make sure that all of the index entries in the front matter use the IndexRoman marker type.
3. Go to your book file, click the index, then select Edit➤Set Up Standard Index.
4. Add IndexRoman to the list of markers that are included when this file is generated.
5. Update the book.
6. Open the index and go to the reference pages. Locate the IndexRomanIX entry in the IX flow and make sure it includes only the page number:

```
<$pagenum>
```

7. Update the book again to see the results.

CHAPTER 17

Creating Other Generated Files

Tables of contents and indexes—discussed in Chapters 15 and 16, respectively—are the most common generated files, but you can also generate several other types of files. They are divided into generated lists and generated indexes.

Broadly, generated lists display information in the order that it occurs in the document; indexes list information in alphabetical order with separators (or "group titles") for each letter in the alphabet. (Just to confuse matters further, two lists are available in page order *or* alphabetical order.) Figure 17-1 shows how the same information is organized differently in a generated list and a generated index.

Like indexes and tables of contents, you can customize other generated lists by controlling the formatting and by using reference page flows to determine what information is included.

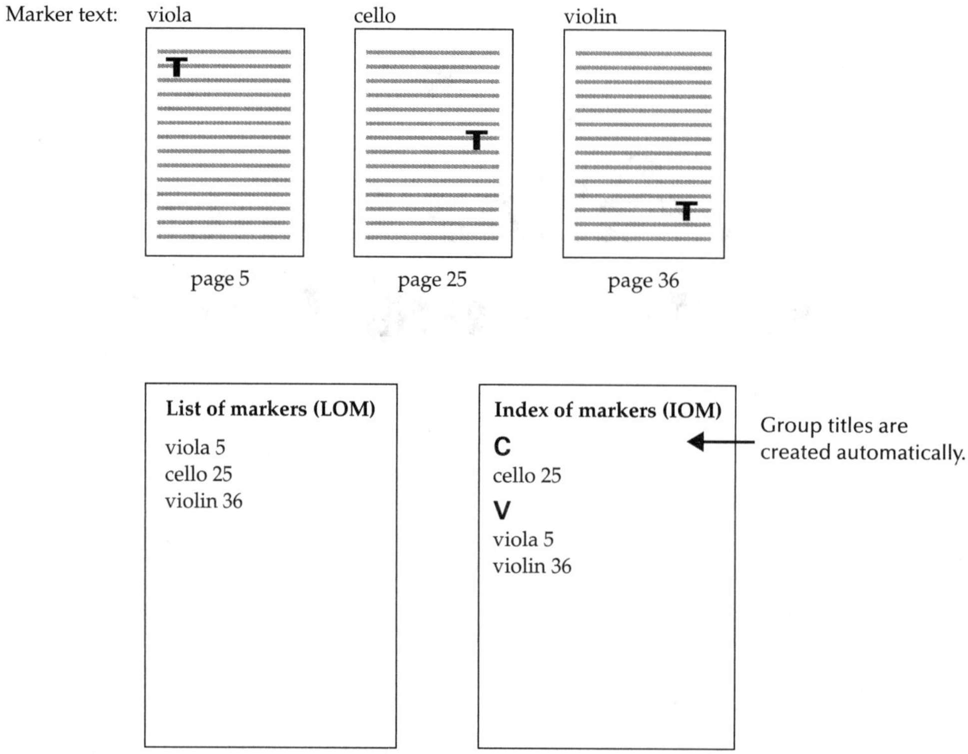

Figure 17-1. Generated lists and indexes can include the same information, but they organize it differently.

Each generated file has a unique suffix, which is used for the file name, the paragraph tags in the generated file, and the reference page flow tag. For example, a list of markers uses the LOM suffix by default. If the book file you start from is named foo.book, the list of markers file will be fooLOM.fm, and the reference page flow tag is LOM. The paragraphs tags in the generated file will end with LOM (for example, if you include Cross-Ref markers, they will be formatted by the Cross-RefLOM paragraph tag).

Generated File	Suffix
List of figures	LOF
List of tables	LOT
List of paragraphs	LOP
Alphabetical list of paragraphs	APL
List of markers	LOM
Alphabetical list of markers	AML
List of references	LOR
Index of authors	AIX
Index of subjects	SIX
Index of markers	IOM
Index of references	IOR

The steps you follow to create a generated list or index are similar for each type of generated file.

To create a generated list or index, follow these steps:

1. Open the book or file for which you want to create a list.
2. Select Special➤List Of *or* Index Of➤and the appropriate item. A setup dialog box is displayed for the list or index.
3. Make sure that the Create Hypertext Links check box is checked. This creates a hyperlinked generated list. If you do not want the list to be linked, or if you do not need links in any PDF or HTML files you might create, you can uncheck this option.
4. Select the settings you want for the generated file, then click the Set button to create it.

TIP If the item you want does not appear in the list, try updating the book.

5. *(for file-level generated files)* Confirm that you want to create a file-level, stand-alone generated file.
6. *(for book-level generated files)* Click the Update button to create the new file.

The following sections discuss how to set up and customize each type of generated file.

Creating Paragraph-Based Lists

Several of the generated lists are based on selecting items from a list of available paragraphs. They are as follows:

- List of figures
- List of tables
- List of paragraphs
- Table of contents

There is no functional difference between these four lists. In each case, you select various paragraph tags, and FrameMaker generates a list of those items in the order they occur in the documents.

Chapter 15, "Creating Tables of Contents," describes in detail how to set up table of contents files. You can apply the information provided there to the list of figures, list of tables, and list of paragraphs.

TIP Keep in mind that you can use the list of figures and list of tables for generated lists other than those implied by the titles. You could, for example, generate a list of syntax examples by including the CodeExampleTitle tag instead of the FigureTitle tag for a so-called "list of figures."

List of Figures

When you create a list of figures, the Set Up List of Figures dialog box provides a list of paragraphs to select from, as shown in Figure 17-2.

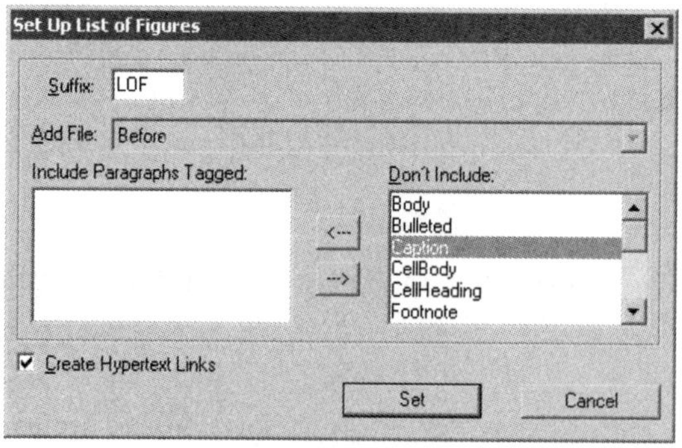

Figure 17-2. Setting up the list of figures

To create a simple list of figures, select your figure caption paragraph tag (for example, Caption) and generate the list. To display the figure number along with the caption, format the CaptionLOF entry in the reference page flow similar to this example:

```
Figure <$paranumonly>: <$paratext>\t<$pagenum>
```

REMEMBER You must define a tab stop in the Paragraph Designer for the tab.

List of Tables

When you create a list of tables, the Set Up List of Tables dialog box provides a list of paragraphs to select from. The dialog box is identical to the Set Up List of Figures dialog box (shown in Figure 17-2), except for the window title and the default suffix.

To create a list of tables, select your table title paragraph tag (for example, TableTitle) and generate the list. To display the table number along with the caption, format the TableTitleLOT entry in the reference page flow similar to this example:

```
Table <$paranumonly>: <$paratext>\t<$pagenum>
```

REMEMBER You must define a tab stop in the Paragraph Designer for the tab.

List of Paragraphs

The list of paragraphs works just like the table of contents. The Set Up List of Paragraphs dialog box provides a list of paragraphs to select from. Except for the window title and the default suffix, the dialog box is identical to the Set Up List of Figures dialog box shown in Figure 17-2.

To create a list of paragraphs, select the items you want to include and generate the list. The reference page LOP flow will provide entries for each included item, which you can format just like table of contents entries.

The list of paragraphs is very useful for review comments. If you have a review comment paragraph tag, you can generate a hyperlinked list of all review comments in the file or book.

Alphabetical List of Paragraphs

The alphabetical list of paragraphs contains the same information as the regular list of paragraphs, but instead of listing the items in the order they occur in the book, they are listed in alphabetical order. To set up the list of paragraphs, specify the paragraphs you want to include in the Set Up Alphabetical Paragraph List dialog box. Except for the dialog box name and the default suffix, the dialog box is identical to the Set Up List of Figures dialog box shown in Figure 17-2.

Creating Lists of Other Items

In addition to the paragraph-based lists, you can create lists of markers and of references. Within the list of references, you can select from several items, including imported graphics, conditional text tags, and fonts.

List of Markers

The generated list of markers is a page-by-page list of markers in a document or book. When you set up the list of markers, you can include one or all of the marker types, including custom markers, as shown in Figure 17-3.

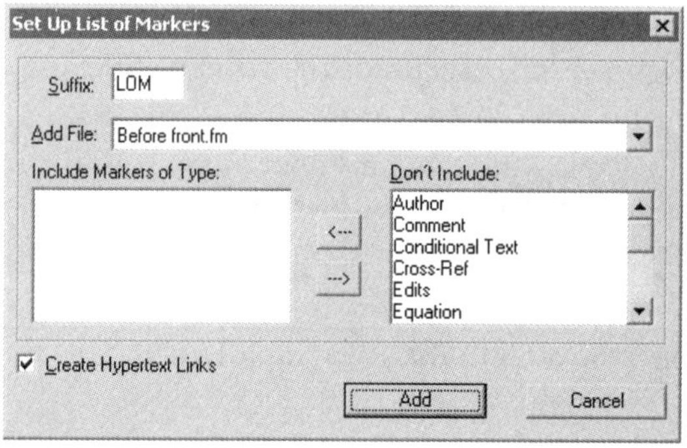

Figure 17-3. The list of markers lets you select any or all marker types, including any custom markers you've created.

For each marker you select, the LOM flow on the reference page will contain a corresponding entry. For example, if you include the Index marker type, the LOM flow will contain an IndexLOM entry.

By default, the definition for each entry is:

```
<$markertext> <$pagenum>
```

The <$markertext> building block retrieves the information in the marker text field for each marker.

Alphabetical List of Markers

Like the list of markers, the alphabetical list of markers lets you select which marker types you want to include. Except for the dialog box name and the default suffix, the dialog box is identical to the Set Up List of Markers dialog box shown in Figure 17-3.

The resulting list, however, is sorted alphabetically by marker text rather than in page order.

NOTE The only difference between the alphabetical list of markers and an index is how the entries are organized. The index provides group titles along with primary and secondary entries. See Figure 17-1 on page 440 for an example.

List of References

The list of references feature lets you create generated lists that include the following items:

- Condition tags
- External cross-references (that is, cross-references that point outside the current file)
- Fonts
- Imported graphics
- Text insets
- Unresolved cross-references
- Unresolved text insets

When you set up the list of references, you can choose to include any or all of these items in the Set Up List of References dialog box:

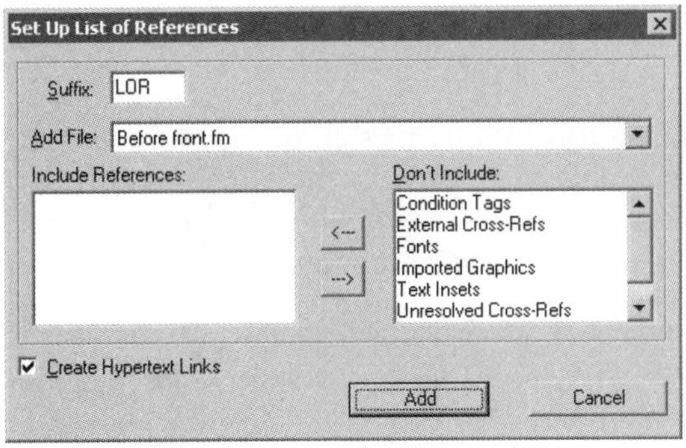

For each item, FrameMaker creates an entry in the LOR flow on the reference pages. The entry's name is the included item with an LOR suffix; for example, Text InsetsLOR. The same building blocks are used for each item:

```
<$referencename> <$pagenum>
```

The <$referencename> building block, however, results in different information for each type of reference.

Condition Tags

Select condition tags to create a list of every occurrence of *shown* conditional text in the document. FrameMaker will ignore any conditional text that is currently hidden. The generated file lists the name of the condition tag and the page on which it is used, such as:

```
Comment 47
Draft 58
```

TIP If you need a list of all conditional text, show all the conditional text tags before you create this list.

External Cross-References

Select external cross-references to create a list of references from the current file to other files. If you create this list for a book, the list will include references from one file in the book to another as well as references to files outside the current book. The resulting list will show the name of the referenced file (including any path name that FrameMaker has stored) and the text of the Cross-Reference marker that identifies the cross-reference's target. For example:

```
toc.fm (cn chapter_number: Chapter 5) 214
index.fm (cn chapter_number: Chapter 9) 214
```

Lists of external cross-references are very useful for locating cross-references that point to local files instead of network files and the like.

Fonts

Select Fonts to create a list of all the fonts that occur in the document. FrameMaker lists the font, the font size, and the page on which the font occurs. The font list is based on the fonts that occur on each page, so you'll see the same font listed multiple times. The following is a short excerpt from a generated list of fonts.

```
Univers 57 Condensed @ 12.0 pt 213
Palatino Linotype @ 75.0 pt 213
Univers Condensed @ 40.0 pt 213
Univers 57 Condensed @ 10.0 pt 214
Univers 57 Condensed @ 12.0 pt 214
Times @ 12.0 pt 214
```

TIP To create an alphabetical list of fonts, convert the listings to a table (each paragraph should be a cell) and sort the table. Better yet, generate an index of references for your fonts, which will automatically create one entry per font. See page 449.

Imported Graphics

The list of imported graphics lists only graphics that are imported by reference—not graphics that were copied (embedded) into the document. For each graphic, FrameMaker lists the file path, the DPI setting being used (for bitmap images only), and the page number on which the graphic occurs, as shown in the following example:

```
graphics/para_cat_button.tif @ 48 dpi 6
```

```
graphics/status_bar_para.tif @ 96 dpi 7
graphics/formatting_bar.tif @ 125 dpi 8
graphics/override_para.tif @ 96 dpi 10
graphics/para_des.tif @ 125 dpi 11
graphics/para_des_pagination.tif @ 125 dpi 12
graphics/tabs.tif @ 125 dpi 15
graphics/no_indent.eps 16
graphics/all_indent.eps 16
```

The list of imported graphics is useful for verifying any or all of the following items for a file:

- Checking DPI settings to ensure that graphics are sized consistently.
- Verifying file locations to ensure graphics are in the correct directory. (In the preceding example, all graphics are stored in a graphics subdirectory; an entry that doesn't begin with `graphics/` would indicate a graphic that needs to be moved.)
- Checking file names to ensure that they follow naming conventions established by your company or client.
- Verifying that all graphics are copied instead of embedded. (If all graphics are copied in, the generated list of imported graphics should be empty.)

Text Insets

Generating a list of text insets has a similar purpose as generating lists of imported graphics; it lets you verify that external files are being imported properly. For each text inset, the generated file lists the file name and path, and the page number on which it begins, as shown in the following example:

```
segment1.fm 222
segment2.fm 255
```

The list of text insets lets you quickly review a list of files that are being imported into the book or file you generated from.

Unresolved Cross-References and Text Insets

When you generate a book file, the book error log creates a list of unresolved cross-references and text insets that occur in the documents. When you use the list of references to create a list of unresolved cross-references or text insets, you get the same information. If you created the list with hyperlinks (highly recommended), you can use the generated list to jump directly to the unresolved item and fix it.

Generated Indexes

The various "other" indexes are all quite similar to the standard index (IX) discussed in Chapter 16, "Creating Indexes." In addition to the standard index, the following indexes are available:

- Index of authors
- Index of subjects
- Index of markers
- Index of references

Each index creates an alphabetical list of entries, with matching entries grouped into a single index entry with multiple page numbers.

Although the standard index defaults to using only the Index marker type, you can use other (or additional) markers in the standard index. The index of authors and index of subjects default to including the matching index markers to create the index, but you can choose to include other marker types instead (or in addition to the default Author and Subject markers).

Index of Authors

The index of authors creates an index of the Author markers in the document or book. The index lets the reader look up information based on the original author. To set up an index of this type, you would first go through your document and identify the sections where different authors are involved. For each entry you want to create, set up an Author marker by following these steps:

1. Click in the text where the author's material occurs.
2. Create an Author marker (Special➤Marker; make sure that Author is selected in the Marker Type drop-down list).

NOTE For detailed instructions on inserting markers, see "Creating Index Entries" on page 422.

3. In the marker text field, type in the author's name. For example:

```
Sayers, Dorothy
```

Repeat this process for every item that you want to mark for a particular author. Then, generate the index of authors to see the result:

J
James, P. D. 35

M
Marsh, Ngaio 22
Maron, Margaret 45

R
Reichs, Kathy 12

S
Sayers, Dorothy 100

Index of Subjects

By default, the index of subjects creates an index from all of the Subject markers in the documents. You can customize them just like any other index entries.

Index of Markers

The index of markers lets you create an index of any marker type. You might, for instance, create an index of hypertext markers to verify that the syntax and path names are correct for each. If you use spot cross-references extensively in a document, you could use an index of Cross-Reference markers to verify that each marker's text is unique.

Index of References

The index of references lets you create an index for each of the items that are available for the list of references. Instead of sorting items by page number, an index sorts them alphabetically, and matching items are grouped. That can make the index version much more manageable and usable than the list version. The index of fonts, for example, would look something like the following example:

```
Courier @ 9.0 pt 185-189, 192
Palatino Linotype @ 10.0 pt 178-193
Palatino Linotype @ 4.0 pt 178-180, 182-187, 189, 191-193
Palatino Linotype @ 75.0 pt 177
Palatino Linotype @ 8.0 pt 179, 182, 184
Times New Roman @ 2.0 pt 178-182, 184, 189-192
Univers @ 10.0 pt 178-180, 182, 184, 186, 189, 191
Univers @ 11.0 pt 186
Univers @ 16.0 pt 178, 181-183, 185, 187-188, 193
Univers 57 Condensed @ 10.0 pt 178-194
Univers 57 Condensed @ 12.0 pt 177-194
Univers Condensed @ 40.0 pt 177
ZapfDingbats @ 10.0 pt 180-181, 183, 187-188
```

You can quickly scan this list to find renegade fonts in your document.

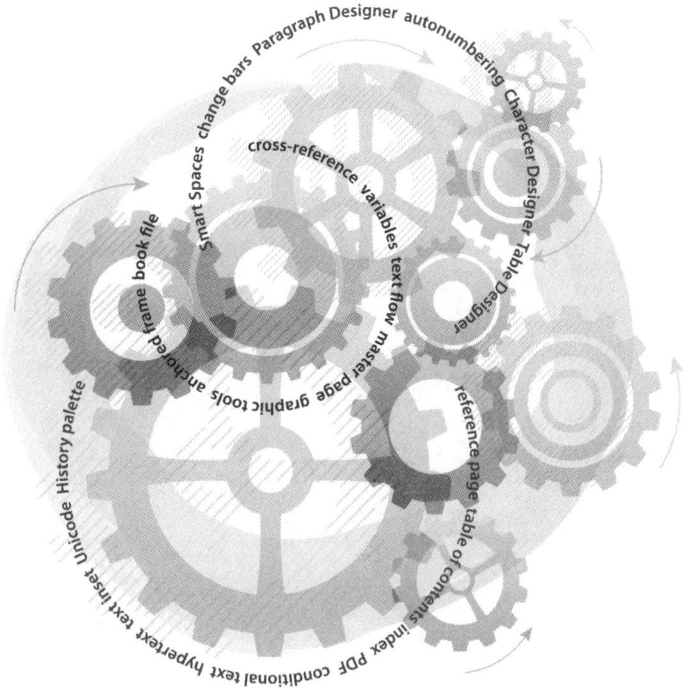

PART V

Creating Output

CHAPTER 18

Print and PDF Output

You can create many kinds of output from FrameMaker documents. The most common output formats are print and Portable Document Format (PDF) files. Users following procedures in a guide might prefer to read a printed document rather than an online PDF file; however, if the user only occasionally refers to the document, the PDF file often suffices.

The print and PDF formats both have advantages. The advantages to printed documents are as follows:

- Users who don't work at a computer station—for example, when repairing equipment at a customer's office—can read the document and write notes.
- When the user is installing software, the installation often covers the entire screen. In many cases, the installer will not permit other applications to run, so the user cannot read a file online. (Furthermore, the online books or online help are often not available because they haven't been installed yet.) Installation documents need to be available separately.
- Many end users (and salespeople) consider printed documentation an integral part of a product. The documentation helps them understand the product and also enhances the quality of their experience with the product.
- Many users don't want to use their own paper to print a document.
- You choose the size of the printed document and the binding method. This increases the usability of the document. For example, it's easier to flip through a small spiral-bound document than a PDF file the user prints on letter-sized paper.
- Print resolution is higher than screen resolution, so screen captures that are reduced to fit better on the page are clearer in print than those displayed in PDF files.
- Some users can locate printed documents more quickly than browsing their computers or a web site for the PDF file.

The main advantages of PDF files are as follows:

- The PDF file preserves formatting from the FrameMaker file, unlike formats such as HTML.
- PDF files can include clickable hyperlinks.
- PDF files can embed rich media such as 3D files and Flash movies that the user can manipulate and play.
- Many companies post PDF versions of their documentation on an intranet or on the Internet, which gives users and employees easy access to the information.

- PDF files are easy to create. Configuring conversion to online formats can be quite challenging.
- The user can search the PDF file in Adobe Reader or Acrobat. In print, you have to rely on a comprehensive index and table of contents to find information.
- The user can print only the pages he or she needs, which conserves paper.
- Compared to the printing and packaging costs of a book, PDF files are far less expensive.
- Producing PDF files is quicker than printing a book. This gives you more time before a product release to complete the documentation because you don't have to send the documentation to a print vendor.
- The PDF file can be updated more easily and economically than printed documents, which require you to print change pages or reprint the entire book.
- You can create tagged PDF files, which lets you repurpose the document for screen readers and small displays.
- You can release the documentation immediately with no shipping costs.

Your company or documentation group usually decides which format works best for you or your customers. Based on the situation, you might choose print versus PDF files or produce both formats.

NOTE In this chapter, the terms "print vendor" and "printer" have different meanings. A print vendor is a commercial printer that prints books on offset or digital presses. The print vendor may bind the books, or the binding may be outsourced to an external bindery. The term "printer" refers to a physical printer, such as the one in your office or home.

Printing Your Documents

FrameMaker provides numerous printing options. You probably use many of the basic features, such as outputting page ranges or printing several copies, every day. Other options, such as printing registration marks, are used primarily in preparing your document for final printing. You can print a single document, specific chapters in a book file, or an entire book. The print options for document files and book files are nearly the same. The printer you select provides additional features, such as support for special paper sizes, sophisticated color matching, and high-resolution printing. You should make sure the printer is set up correctly before printing. See your printer's documentation for details.

Printing an Individual Document

To print a single document outside the book window, follow these steps:

1. Open the document you want to print, then select File➤Print. The Print dialog box is displayed (Figure 18-1 on page 456).

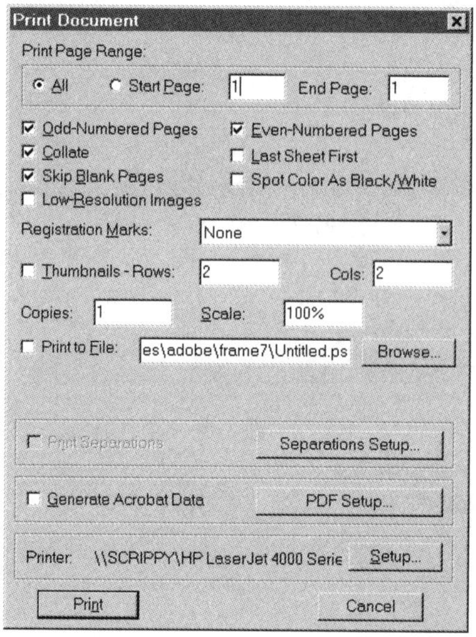

Figure 18-1. The Print dialog box

2. Change the printer options based on the following sections, then click the Print button. Your document prints.

Printing from the Book File

In a book file, you can print one file, specific pages in the book, or the entire book.

TIP When printing a book, open all files in the book to prevent missing font and other error messages from stopping the process. The file will also print more quickly because FrameMaker doesn't have to open each file in the book. Before you print, you should also regenerate the book to update the cross-references, page numbers, autonumbering, text insets, OLE links, and generated files (the table of contents, list of figures, and list of tables). For more information, see "Printing a Book" on page 397.

To print from the book file, follow these steps:

1. Open the book file, then specify the file or files you want to print by doing one of the following:
   - To print the entire book, select File➤Print Book. The Print Book dialog box is displayed. The book and standard Print dialog boxes are identical. See Figure 18-1.
   - To print specific chapters in a book, CTRL-click the files in the book window, then select File➤Print Selected Files. The Print Selected Files in Book dialog box is displayed.
2. Change the printer options based on the following sections, then click the Print button. The book or selected documents are printed.

Specifying Pages

You can print one page, a range of pages, or the entire document. This section describes how to specify the pages you want to print in a document or book.

Selecting All Pages

To select all pages in the document or book, display the Print dialog box (Figure 18-1), and click the All radio button in the Print Page Range section.

Selecting Specific Pages in a Document

To select specific pages in a document, display the Print dialog box (Figure 18-1), and follow these directions:

1. In the Print Page Range section, type the first page in the Start Page field and type the last page in the End Page field.
2. Click the Print button to print the selected range. (The current page number is displayed in both fields by default.) Note that you cannot specify multiple ranges in one step.

NOTE You must specify Roman or Arabic numbers that match the file's numbering.

Selecting Specific Pages in a Book

To select specific pages in a book, follow these steps:

1. CTRL-click the file or files in which the pages occur.
2. Display the Print dialog box (Figure 18-1).
3. Select File➤Print Selected Files.
4. Type the first and last page in the Start Page and End Page fields, respectively.

If Your Document Doesn't Print

There are several reasons why a document might not print. Before reprinting, verify the following:

- You could have inadvertently printed the document to file. In the Print dialog box, make sure the Print to File check box is unchecked before printing.
- If the document is long or graphics-intensive, check the print job dialog box to see if the document is displayed. The document might still be spooling to the printer.
- There could also be a problem with the printer. Check for a paper jam or an empty paper tray.
- If you are seeing odd characters in the file, it may be that you are printing to a printer that does not include the correct fonts for your document. Select Save As PDF, then print the resulting PDF file to the printer.
- Shut down your computer, then restart only FrameMaker.

Printing Several Copies

You can print several copies of one page, a range of pages, or the entire document, and you can print the copies one set at time. To specify copies, follow these steps:

1. Display the Print dialog box (Figure 18-1 on page 456), then indicate the pages you want to print. See "Specifying Pages" on page 457 for details.
2. Indicate the number of copies to print by typing the number of copies to print in the Copies field.
3. To print one set at a time (for example, pages 1–15) instead of all copies of page 1, all copies of page 2, and so on, check the Collate check box.
4. If your printer places the printed page face-up, check the Last Sheet First check box.

Changing the Paper Size

You can change the paper size in your printer driver. You might print a document on a larger paper size to make room for registration marks. FrameMaker displays a warning if the paper isn't large enough for the text or registration marks to print completely.

To change the paper size, follow these steps:

1. Display the Print dialog box (Figure 18-1 on page 456).
2. Click the Setup button. Depending on your printer driver, the paper options might be displayed in this dialog box.
3. If the paper options are not displayed, click the Properties button, then click the Advanced button. Click a different paper size in the Paper Size drop-down list.

Printing Double-Sided Documents

Some printers have duplexing units that automatically print odd pages on one side of the paper and even pages on the reverse side. You can print a double-sided document on a printer that only prints single-sided by printing all odd pages first, flipping the paper in the printer, and printing the even pages. Before you print an entire document this way, test a few pages to make sure the paper is in the right direction. After printing one side of the document, you might need to print the other side in reverse order depending on your printer. Refer to your printer documentation for instructions on feeding the paper correctly.

To print a double-sided document on a printer without a duplexing unit, follow these steps:

1. Display the Print dialog box (Figure 18-1 on page 456), then check the Odd-Numbered Pages check box and uncheck the Even-Numbered Pages check box.
2. Click the Print button. The odd-numbered pages (1, 3, 5, 7...) are printed.
3. Flip over the paper in the paper tray. If you're printing to the manual feed paper tray, change the paper setting in your printer driver.
4. Select File➤Print to display the Print dialog box again, then uncheck the Odd-Numbered Pages check box and check the Even-Numbered Pages check box.
5. If your printer requires it, check the Last Sheet First check box to print the other side in reverse order.
6. Click the Print button. The even-numbered pages (2, 4, 6, 8...) are printed on the back of the odd-numbered pages.

Skipping Blank Pages

You can skip printing blank pages. This is handy for printing a double-sided document as a single-sided document. Many double-sided documents have blank pages to force chapters to begin on a right page. When you print rough drafts, you can save paper by skipping the blank pages.

To suppress blank pages, display the Print dialog box (Figure 18-1 on page 456), and check the Skip Blank Pages check box. Another way to avoid printing blank pages is to convert a double-sided document to single-sided before you print, and then convert it back to double-sided. See "Switching from Single- to Double-Sided Pages" on page 300 for more information.

NOTE A page is considered blank if the main text flow is empty. The running headers and footers and other background objects don't count.

Printing Thumbnails

You can print several pages as mini-images on a single page. This option is useful for checking the pagination of an entire document. You indicate the number of rows and columns you want printed (for instance, the 2-row by 4-column layout shown in the following illustration). The document is double-sided, so the thumbnails begin with the first right page.

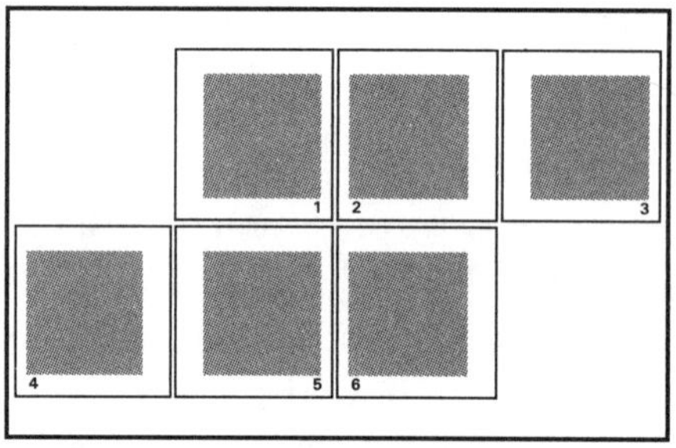

CAUTION Some printers don't support thumbnails. Refer to your printer documentation for details.

To print thumbnails, follow these steps:

1. Display the Print dialog box (Figure 18-1 on page 456), then check the Thumbnails check box.
2. In the Rows field, type the number of rows to print across the page.

3. In the Cols field, type the number of columns to print. Keep in mind the orientation of the paper. You can print more thumbnails on a landscape page than a portrait page. Refer to your printer documentation for details on specifying landscape pages.
4. Click the Print button.

Printing Spot Color in Black and White

You can save color ink by printing *spot color* as black and white. You may want to do this when printing to use less color ink, because black ink is often cheaper. If your printer prints only in black and white, you may want to print spot color as black so that the areas that use spot colors print as a deep black instead (for example, if you use spot color for the lines and arrows in your graphics).

When you send your book to the print vendor, spot color is premixed before the printing process and printed on one printing plate. *Process color* mixes shades of cyan, magenta, yellow, and black (CMYK), with each color printing on a different plate. To see which colors in your document are spot colors, select View➤Color➤Definitions, then click a color in the Name drop-down list. The setting is displayed in the Print As drop-down list. For more information, see Chapter 20, "Color Output."

To print spot color in black and white, follow these steps:

1. Display the Print dialog box (Figure 18-1 on page 456).
2. Check the Spot Color as Black/White check box.

Printing Low-Resolution Images

You can speed up the printing of graphic-intensive documents by printing the images at low resolution. The images print as gray boxes.

To turn on low-resolution printing, follow these steps:

1. Display the Print dialog box (Figure 18-1 on page 456).
2. Check the Low-Resolution Images check box.

Printing Registration Marks

Registration marks provide instructions for printing color separations, which are the individual pages that describe how to mix color for four-color printing. Information about the document is also displayed outside the registration marks—the date, time, file name, and page number. When you print registration marks in FrameMaker, *crop marks* also print in each corner of the page to indicate where to trim the paper after the book is printed. Registration marks are automatically added to color separations, and the color and halftone information is displayed outside the registration marks.

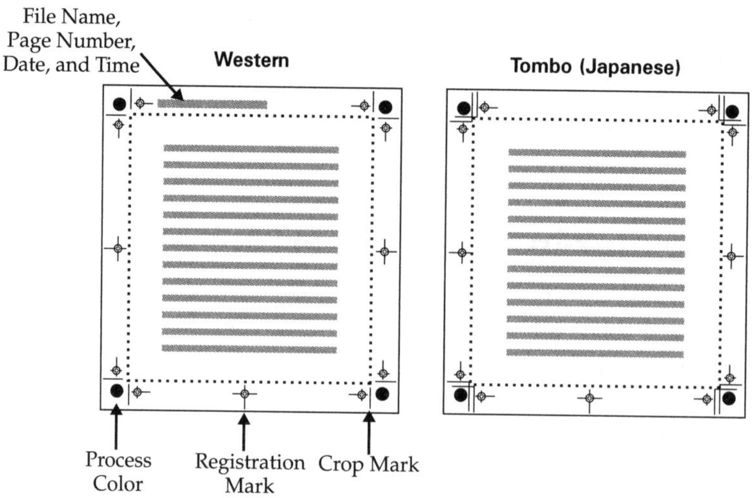

CAUTION To provide room for registration marks, you must print on paper that is at least one inch taller and wider than the paper size. If, for example, your document is 7 inches wide by 9 inches tall, you must use paper that's at least 8 inches wide by 10 inches tall to ensure that registration marks are displayed. In practice, this means that if your page size is a standard letter size (US Letter or A4), you cannot print registration marks for your document—unless you output the pages onto larger paper.

Many print vendors require registration marks in the PDF file, but some printers add registration crop marks automatically. Be sure to consult with your print vendor. FrameMaker supports both Western registration marks and Tombo (Japanese) registration marks.

To select registration marks, follow these steps:

1. Display the Print dialog box (Figure 18-1 on page 456).
2. Click Western or Tombo in the Registration Marks drop-down list.

CAUTION To print registration marks in a PDF file, you must increase the page size in the PDF setup because the Adobe PDF Creation Add-On (or Acrobat Distiller) crops the page. See "Setting Up Registration Marks in a PDF File" on page 473 for details.

Changing the Printer

Initially, the printer displayed in the Print dialog box is the default printer for your system. You can, however, change the printer used in FrameMaker without changing the default printer. Many times, you need to switch to the Adobe PDF printer to ensure that what you see on screen matches what you will deliver in the PDF files. Also, if some characters are not displaying correctly, selecting the Adobe PDF printer may fix the problem. If you print to a non-PostScript printer, any Encapsulated PostScript (EPS) images print as blocky bitmap images instead of as smooth lines. To print the EPS images correctly, create a PDF of the file, then print the PDF on your non-PostScript printer. (See "Vector Graphics" on page 324 for more information about EPS files.)

TIP It's good practice to keep Adobe PDF as your default printer because special characters such as arrows and check marks are displayed correctly. You can install SetPrint.dll from Sundorne Communications to make the Adobe PDF printer the default printer for FrameMaker while allowing your other applications to use the default printer selected in the Windows Control Panel. For more information, see Appendix A, "Resources."

When you switch printers, a warning is displayed, indicating that the fonts for your system have changed. These fonts are the *printer-resident fonts* (described in "Printing Fonts Accurately" on page 468). If the required fonts are installed on your computer, the document should print correctly.

CAUTION Don't change drivers after you copyfit a book because the line breaks might change. If you do need to change the printer, you'll need to skim the pages for bad page and line breaks and regenerate the book file to update cross-references and generated files.

To change the printer, follow these steps:

1. Display the Print dialog box (Figure 18-1 on page 456).
2. In the Printer section of the Print dialog box, click the Setup button. The Print Setup dialog box is displayed.
3. Click a printer in the Name drop-down list, then click the OK button. The new printer is displayed. (If the resident fonts change, a warning is displayed. Click the OK button.)

About Color Separations

FrameMaker running on Windows does not support the creation of color separations. The Windows Graphics Device Interface (GDI) that FrameMaker uses to create output supports only the RGB color model, not the CMYK color model needed for color separations. You don't need color separations if you deliver your documentation to your customers as PDF files or if your print vendor uses a digital printing process. If you do need color separations, your print vendor can use preflighting software to correct the colors and create color separations from your PDF files. Discuss color printing requirements with your print vendor before you send the PDF files.

Adobe PDF Creation Add-On

FrameMaker 8 no longer includes the full version of Acrobat Distiller. Instead, FrameMaker includes the Adobe PDF Creation Add-On, which is a version of Acrobat Distiller that runs in the background when you select File➤Save As PDF.

NOTE The Adobe Technical Communication Suite includes FrameMaker and Adobe Acrobat 3D, so the suite includes Adobe Distiller instead of the Adobe PDF Creation Add-On.

The biggest difference between the Adobe PDF Creation Add-On and Acrobat Distiller is that you can create PDFs only from FrameMaker (not from other applications) with the Add-On. Also, Acrobat Distiller is part of the full Adobe Acrobat program, which lets you edit your PDF files, enable online reviews, create forms, and more. Whether you use the Adobe PDF Creation Add-On or Acrobat Distiller, the process for creating PDF files from FrameMaker is the same.

CAUTION The Adobe PDF Creation Add-On is included with FrameMaker on its own separate CD. If you have Adobe Acrobat Professional or 3D, you should not install the Adobe PDF Creation Add-On when you install FrameMaker 8. If you have already installed the Adobe PDF Creation Add-On, you will be prompted to uninstall it before installing Adobe Acrobat.

Setting PDF Job Options

PDF job options files (.joboptions) specify a group of settings for PDF output. These settings include which version of PDF to produce (later versions let you create smaller files but users need the latest Adobe Reader), whether fonts are embedded in the PDF, how graphics are compressed, and many other settings. The Adobe PDF Creation Add-On includes several predefined PDF job options files that have names that indicate how they are intended to be used—High Quality Print.joboptions and Smallest File Size.joboptions, for example. You can also define your own PDF job options files.

TIP Ask your print vendor which PDF job options to use for best results. Some print vendors will send you a customized PDF job options file they want you to use.

To create your own customized PDF job options file, do the following:

1. Select File➤Print Setup, then select Adobe PDF from the list.

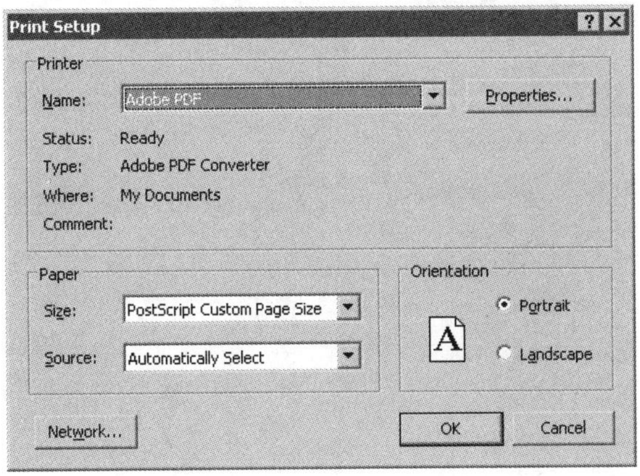

2. Click the Properties button. The Adobe PDF Document Properties dialog box is displayed.

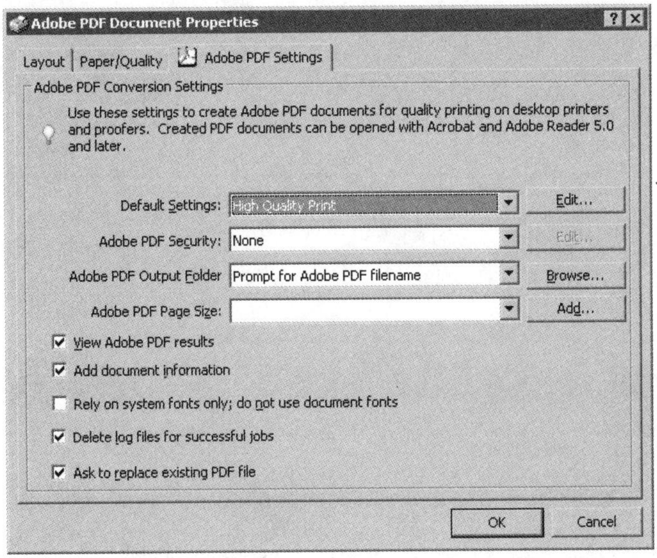

3. From the Default Settings list, select the PDF job options that are closest to what you want (for example, High Quality Print).

4. Click the Edit button. The Adobe PDF Settings dialog box for the PDF job options file you selected is displayed.

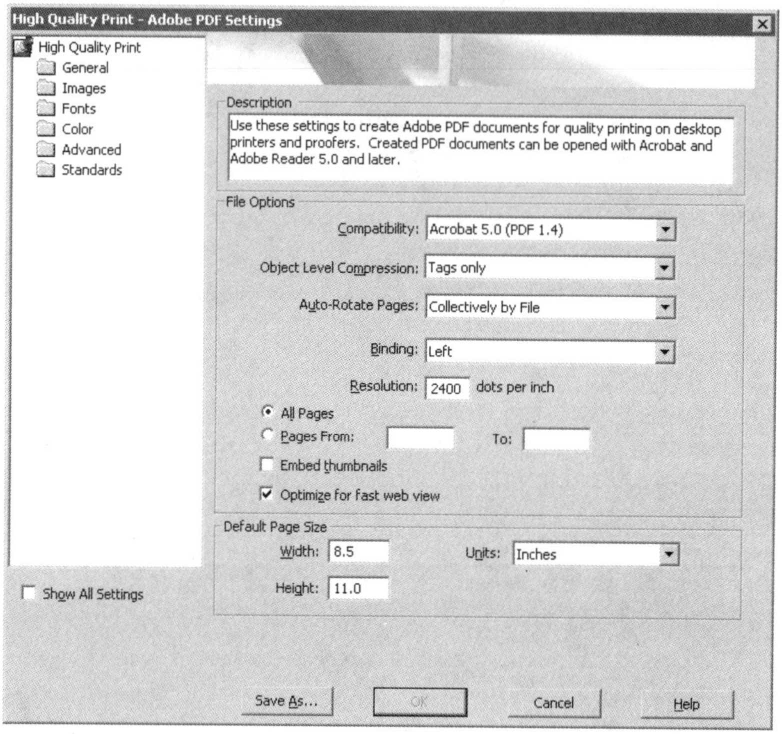

The Adobe PDF Settings dialog box has six sheets, which are listed on the left:

- General
- Images
- Fonts
- Color
- Advanced
- Standard

5. Click each folder on the left to display its sheet. Change any options you choose. Refer to the online help for details on the numerous settings. See the sidebar "Printing Fonts Accurately" on page 468 for more information about the Fonts sheet.
6. Click the Save As button. The Save Adobe PDF Settings As dialog box is displayed.
7. Type a name for your job options file, then click the OK button.

FrameMaker stores the custom job options file in your application data folder (for example, C:\Documents and Settings*user_name*\Application Data\Adobe\Adobe PDF\Settings). When you create a PDF file (described in the next section), you can choose your custom PDF job options file, as shown in Figure 18-3 on page 470.

Creating PDF Files

You create a PDF file from FrameMaker using the Save As PDF function. This starts either the Adobe PDF Creation Add-On that is included with the FrameMaker product or the Adobe Distiller product that is included with Adobe Acrobat, depending on which you are using.

To save a FrameMaker file as a PDF file, follow these steps:

1. Select File➤Save As PDF. The Save Document dialog box is displayed.

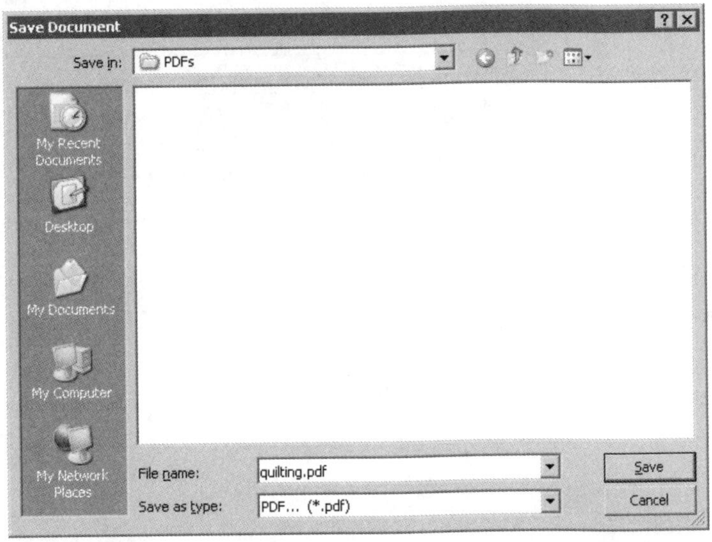

2. *(optional)* Navigate to the directory where the PDF file will be created. By default, the PDF file is stored in the same folder as the FrameMaker file.
3. *(optional)* Specify the PDF file name.
4. Click the Save button. The PDF Setup dialog box (Figure 18-3 on page 470) is displayed. (The same options are displayed by selecting Format➤Document➤PDF Setup.)
5. Choose the settings you want in the PDF Setup dialog box, then click the Set button. You must click the Set button even if you don't customize the settings.

FrameMaker creates a temporary PostScript file (.tps) and starts the Adobe PDF Creation Add-On (or Adobe Distiller) to convert the file to a PDF file. A log file is placed in the same directory as the PDF file, with the same name as the PDF file but with a .log extension. You can open the log file in a text editor to check for any errors.

Printing Fonts Accurately

You should embed fonts in your PDF files to avoid font substitution problems. By embedding fonts, you can be sure that the print vendor has all of the fonts used in the document. To ensure that fonts print as you expect, do the following:

- Buy professional fonts whose licensing allows you to embed them in the PDF files.
- Use the Adobe PDF printer driver (which is always used when you select Save As PDF).
- In the PDF job options file, make sure that the option to embed all fonts is selected. To make the PDF smaller without loss of quality, select the option to subset the fonts when the percent of characters used is less than 100%.

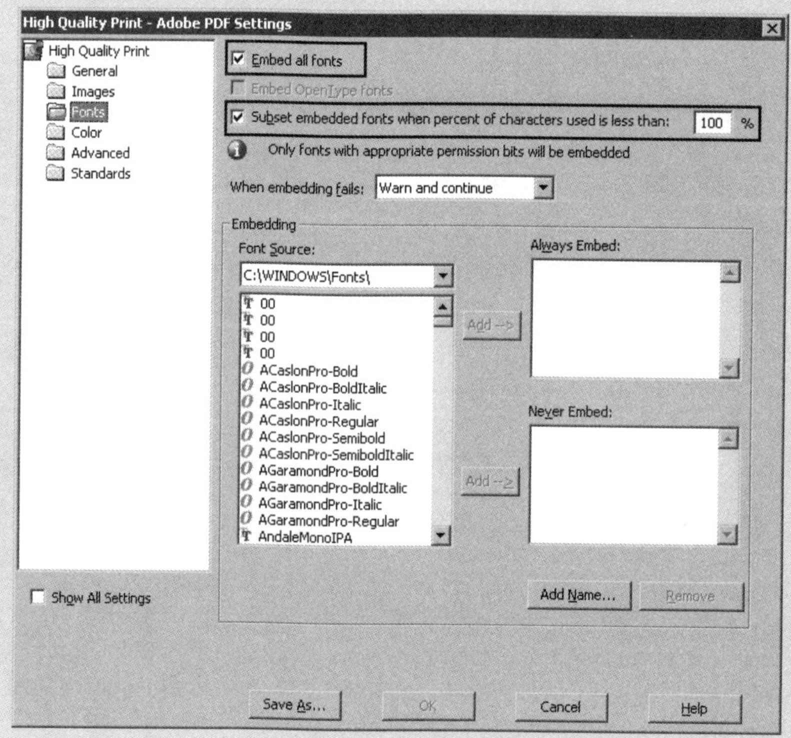

Generating Bookmarks

A *bookmark* is a link available in the left pane of the Adobe Reader or Acrobat window. The user can click the bookmark to view a specific topic in the PDF file. (Actually, bookmarks can also link to web sites, other files, or even perform actions—but when you set up bookmarks from the PDF Setup dialog box, you are setting links within the PDF file.)

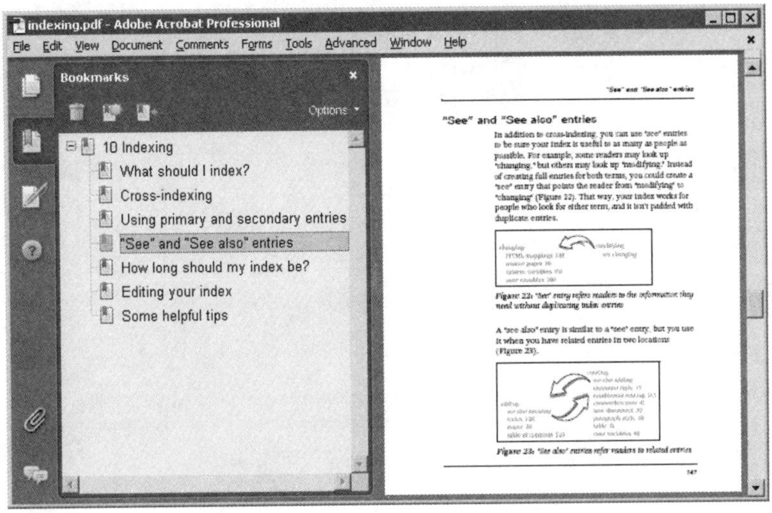

Figure 18-2. Bookmarks in PDF File

You can create bookmarks automatically from FrameMaker content. To do so, you specify which paragraph tags to include and their hierarchial relationship. Top-level bookmarks are displayed flush left. The second-level bookmarks are indented once, the third-level bookmarks are indented twice, and so on.

In the bookmark setup, you decide whether the bookmarks are expanded or collapsed by default when the user opens the PDF file. If all bookmarks are expanded, the user doesn't need to click each collapsed bookmark to display the list. But if the document has many bookmarks, and they're all expanded, the user will have to scroll down to search through all of the bookmarks.

To specify the paragraph tags you want to convert to bookmarks in a document, follow these steps:

1. Select Format➤Document➤PDF Setup. The PDF Setup dialog box is displayed (Figure 18-3 on page 470).

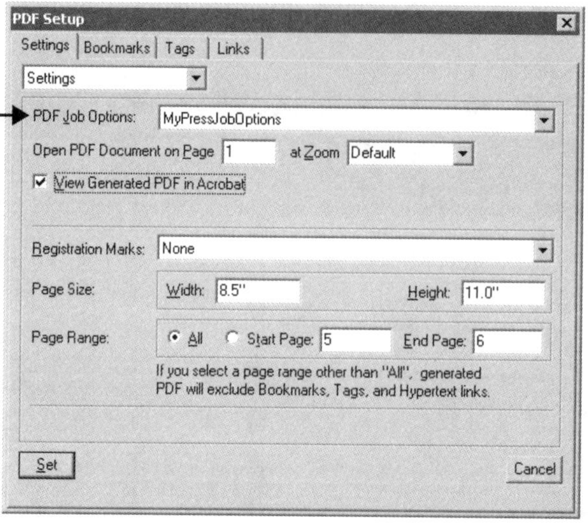

Figure 18-3. Setting up the PDF conversion in FrameMaker

2. Click the Bookmarks tab. The Bookmarks sheet is displayed.

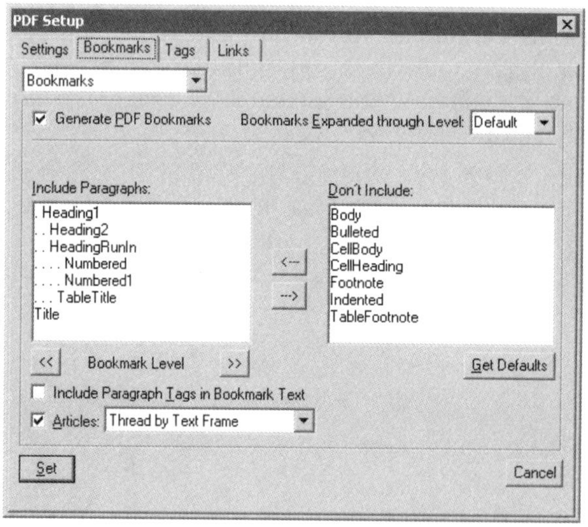

3. Check the Generate PDF Bookmarks check box.
4. Move the items that you want to bookmark to the Include Paragraphs list on the left.

   You can move items by doing any of the following:

   - Select an item, then click the left or right arrow button to move it from one list to another.
   - Select an item, then double-click it to move it to the other list.
   - To move all the items from one list to another, press and hold SHIFT, then click the appropriate arrow button.
5. To specify the hierarchy of the bookmarks, click a tag in the Include Paragraphs column, then click the Bookmark Level (< < and > >) buttons until the tag is indented correctly. A dot is displayed next to the tag to indicate the level of indentation—one dot indicates the first indented paragraph tag, two dots indicates the second indented paragraph tag, up to the sixth level. After the sixth level, a number is displayed instead of the dots.
6. To include the paragraph tag name in the bookmark, check the Include Tags in Bookmark Text check box. This option can help you verify bookmark levels in draft PDF files.
7. To expand or collapse bookmarks in the PDF file, do one of the following in the Bookmarks Expanded through Level drop-down list:
   - Accept Default to use the Acrobat settings specified in the user's Adobe Reader or Adobe Acrobat program.
   - Click None to collapse all bookmarks.
   - Click All to expand all bookmarks. A maximum of 25 bookmarks can be expanded.
   - Type a number to indicate the number of levels to expand. For example, to expand three levels of bookmarks, type **3**.

Threading Articles

Documents such as newsletters and magazine layouts often have articles that are in separate text flows. In a PDF file, you can thread articles by their text flow. When you reach the bottom of the article in flow A on page 1, the continued article at the bottom of page 2 is displayed.

Threaded by Text Flow

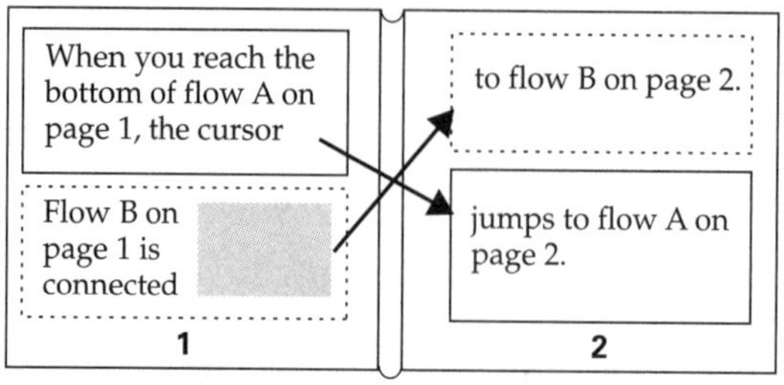

Threaded by Text Frame

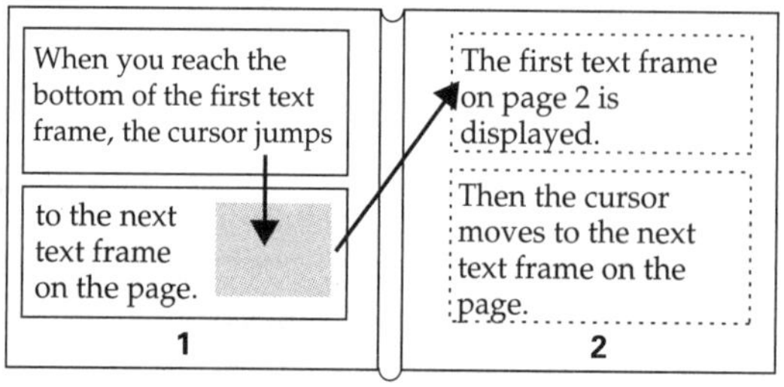

In a single-column document, articles are usually threaded by text frame, so the cursor moves from text frame to text frame instead of from flow to flow. This is the default value in the PDF setup.

To indicate how the articles will be threaded, follow these steps:

1. Select Format➤Document➤PDF Setup. The PDF Setup dialog box is displayed (Figure 18-3 on page 470).
2. Click the Bookmarks tab, then do one of the following:
   - To read the articles in a multicolumn document, click Thread by Column in the Articles drop-down list.
   - To read the articles in a single-column document, click Thread by Text Frame in the Articles drop-down list.

Specifying the Default Zoom Level and First Displayed Page

When the user opens a PDF file, the first page from the FrameMaker file is usually displayed. You might want another page displayed first if, for example, the user probably won't care about viewing the title page or front matter. You can also control the zoom level at which the PDF file is displayed. This zoom level overrides the default magnification in the user's Adobe Reader or Acrobat settings.

To specify the default zoom level and first displayed page, follow these steps:

1. Select Format➤Document➤PDF Setup. The Settings sheet of the PDF Setup dialog box is displayed (Figure 18-3 on page 470).
2. To change the first displayed page, type the page number in the Open PDF Document on Page field.
3. To change the zoom level, click an item in the Zoom drop-down list:
   - **Default:** Uses the Acrobat settings specified in the user's Adobe Reader or Adobe Acrobat program.
   - **Fit Page:** Displays the entire page in Adobe Reader or Acrobat.
   - **Fit Width:** Displays the width of the page.
   - **Fit Height:** Displays the height of the page.
   - **10% to 400%:** Specifies the magnification level.

Setting Up Registration Marks in a PDF File

By default, when you convert a document to a PDF file, the Adobe PDF Creation Add-On or Acrobat Distiller removes any extra space to maintain the page size of the FrameMaker file. Removing the extra space also removes registration marks because they fall into the area that's deleted. To prevent this, you must increase the page size in the PDF setup and uncheck the Generate Acrobat Data option in the Print dialog box.

To set up registration marks in a PDF file, follow these steps:

1. Display the Print dialog box, then click Western or Tombo in the Registration Marks drop-down list (see Figure 18-1 on page 456).
2. Click the PDF Setup button. The PDF Setup dialog box is displayed (Figure 18-3 on page 470).
3. Click the Settings tab, then click the type of registration marks in the Registration Marks drop-down list.
4. Add 1 inch to the width and height, respectively, in the Page Size section.

Generating Tagged PDF Files

Tagged PDF files display a logical hierarchy of the document so you can repurpose the PDF file for alternate displays, such as screen readers and small devices. For example, you can make sure any header or footer paragraph tags are not included in the tagged PDF file, so screen readers (such as the one built into Adobe Reader) know to skip them when reading the PDF file aloud.

The tree structure shows paragraphs in the document. The contents of anchored frames may be displayed if you assigned text attributes to the anchored frame object properties (see "Setting Anchored Frame Object Properties" on page 321).

To set up a tagged PDF file, follow these steps:

1. Select Format➤Document➤PDF Setup. The PDF Setup dialog box is displayed (Figure 18-3 on page 470).
2. Click the Tags tab. The Tags sheet is displayed.

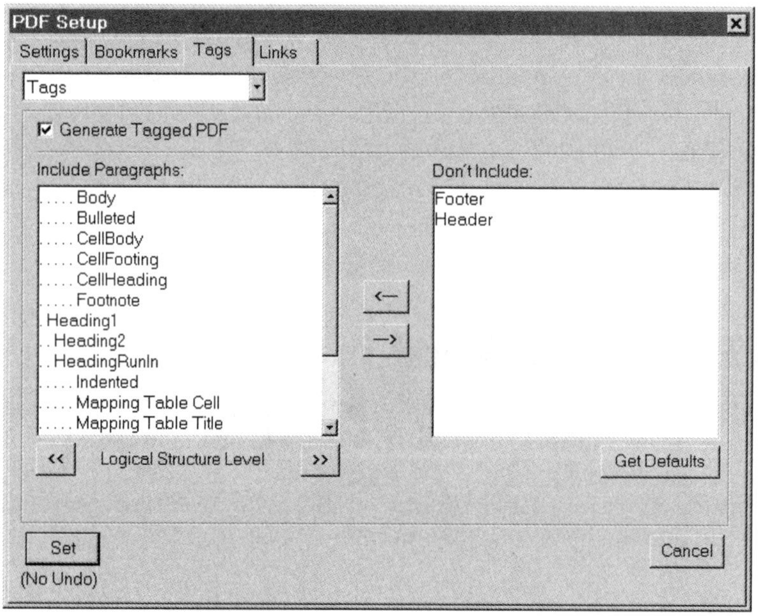

3. Check the Generate Tagged PDF check box.
4. Move the items that you want to include in the logical hierarchy to the Include Paragraphs list on the left.

   You can move items by doing any of the following:

   - Select an item, then click the left or right arrow button to move it from one list to another.
   - Select an item, then double-click it to move it to the other list.
   - To move all the items from one list to another, press and hold SHIFT, then click the appropriate arrow button.

   It is not critical that you include the logical hierarchy if your primary concern is making the PDF file accessible for screen readers. Just make sure you include the paragraphs you want screen readers to speak aloud and omit those you don't.

NOTE You must include at least one paragraph tag or the resulting PDF file will be untagged. If you include only one paragraph tag, that is the only paragraph that screen readers will read.

For information on describing the contents of anchored frames in tagged PDF files, see "Setting Anchored Frame Object Properties" on page 321.

Optimizing PDF Files

If you specify that you do not want FrameMaker to create named destinations for all paragraphs for a file was created in FrameMaker 6 or earlier, some hyperlinks in the PDF file may not work. If this occurs, an error message is displayed in the console window to let you know that the file must be optimized to take advantage of this feature.

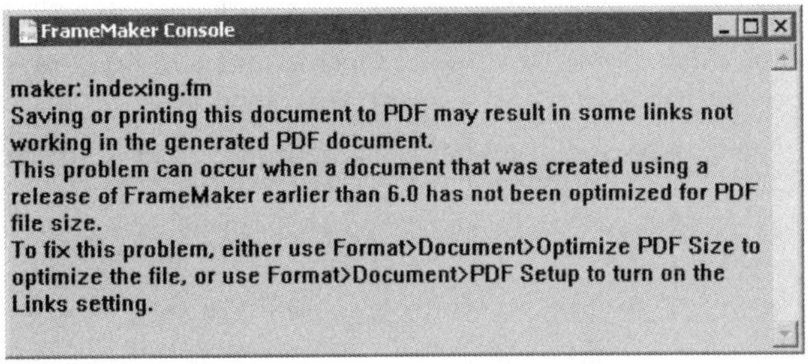

TIP Unless an error message is displayed in the console window, you can ignore this section on optimizing.

To set the optimization options, do the following:

1. Select Format➤Document➤Optimize PDF Size➤Options. The Optimization Options dialog box is displayed.

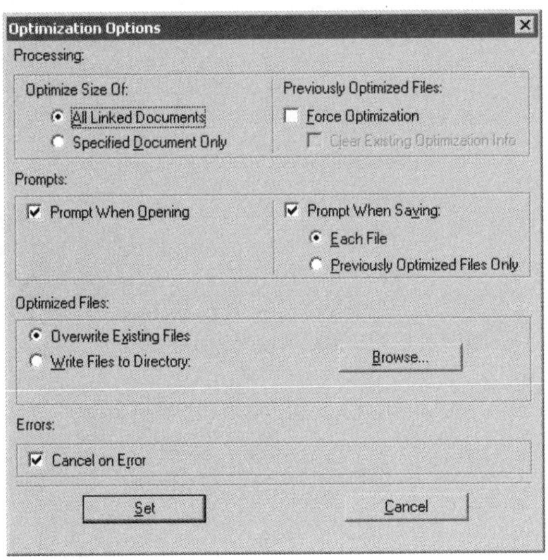

2. Set the following options (but you can leave the default settings, which provide good results):
   - Optimize Size Of: Select whether you want FrameMaker to optimize only the file and all of the FrameMaker files it links to.
   - Previously Optimized Files: If the file has already been optimized, FrameMaker does not try to optimize it again. If you select Force Optimization, also select Clear Existing Optimization Info.
   - Prompts: FrameMaker displays a prompt before opening the linked files.
   - Prompt When Saving: If you selected Prompt When Opening, specify whether FrameMaker should display a prompt for each file or only for files that were previously optimized.
   - Optimized Files: Select whether FrameMaker should overwrite the existing files or write the files to a different directory.
   - Errors: Select whether you want FrameMaker to stop optimizing the file if an error occurs.
3. Click Set.

To optimize a file, do the following:

1. Format➤Document➤Optimize PDF Size➤Optimize File.

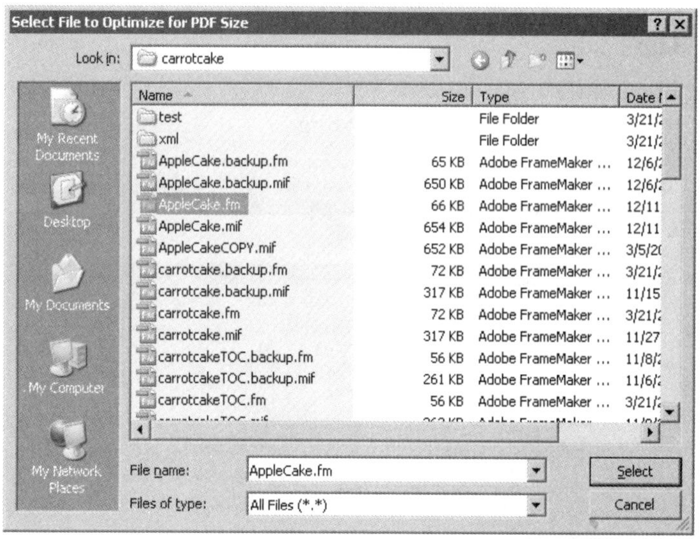

2. Select the file you want FrameMaker to process.
3. FrameMaker optimizes the file and optionally any files it links to. Progress and error messages are displayed in the console window.

TIP If you still have broken links in the PDF file, try creating all named destinations, as explained in the next section. That makes the PDF file larger, but it usually fixes any unexpected broken links. For the best results, use the FrameMaker-To-Acrobat TimeSavers product (www.microtype.com), create all named destinations, and let TimeSavers select which named destinations to preserve.

Creating Hyperlinks to Other PDF Files

You can hyperlink paragraphs from one PDF file to another by creating the PDF files with *named destinations.* For example, this option lets you add cross-references or hypertext links from one FrameMaker document to another without resaving the documents as PDF files. Keep in mind that named destinations increase PDF size.

To generate named destinations, follow these steps:

1. Select Format➤Document➤PDF Setup. The PDF Setup dialog box is displayed (Figure 18-3 on page 470).
2. Click the Links tab, then check the Create Named Destinations for All Paragraphs check box.

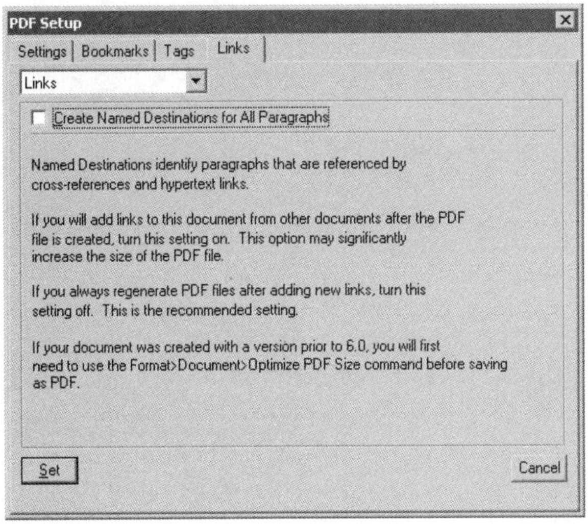

3. Click the Set button. FrameMaker will generate named destinations when you create the PDF file.

If You Can't Create a PDF File

Some PDF files are inexplicably troublesome to create and print. Here are possible solutions:

- Delete the FNTCACHE.dat file (found in the Windows\System32 folder), then reboot your machine.
- If the Adobe PDF Creation Add-On crashed, delete any .tps or .log files created by the software.
- If you are using Save As PDF, create the PDF twice (same file name, same settings). This often works.
- Open the properties for the Adobe PDF driver, then uncheck the "Rely on system fonts only; do not use document fonts" check box.
- If some text is not displaying in the PDF file, try deleting any temporary FrameMaker files. These are named frm*.tmp.

See your network administrator for additional assistance.

CHAPTER 19

Producing Online Output

This chapter describes creating online output. (For details about PDF files, see Chapter 18, "Print and PDF Output.") There are several ways to create HTML, online help, or XML from FrameMaker files. Some options give you "quick-and-dirty" conversions—easy to set up but with limited control over the output. Other choices (which usually require additional software) are more difficult to configure but provide better customization options.

FrameMaker provides a Save As HTML feature that was first included in FrameMaker 5.5 and has not changed significantly since. This feature uses mapping tables stored on the reference pages and provides limited output customization. Most of this chapter explains how to use the Save As HTML feature.

NOTE Avoid the related Save As XML feature. See the sidebar "Exporting XML Output" on page 495 for more information about the limits of Save As XML in unstructured FrameMaker. If you want to produce XML from FrameMaker, use structured FrameMaker. Refer to *Publishing Fundamentals: Structured FrameMaker 8*.

Third-Party Tools for Online Output

The following third-party tools provide much better online output than the Save As HTML feature:

- Adobe RoboHelp/Adobe Technical Communication Suite
- Madcap Flare
- Quadralay ePublisher Platform
- Omni Systems MIF2GO

Unlike ePublisher Platform and MIF2GO, RoboHelp and Flare are authoring environments, not conversion tools. That is, they can accept FrameMaker files as input or be used as standalone authoring tools.

ePublisher Platform and MIF2GO have very different interfaces, but they are conceptually similar: they read the tagging information in the FrameMaker files and replace it with HTML, RTF, or other markup.

All of these applications are more powerful and more configurable than the built-in Save As HTML feature. Consider using one of these tools for converting longer files or for environments where you need to convert lots of files frequently. See "Online Output Conversion Tools" on page 667 for web sites for these tools.

Saving as HTML

You can use the Save As command to create HTML from document and book files. FrameMaker uses mapping settings that are stored on the reference pages to export content into HTML files.

The Save As HTML feature lets you customize mappings and output to some degree. The conversion settings are saved on the reference pages; depending on whether you are saving a single document file or a book file, the reference pages are called HTML or BookHTML, HTML(cont) or BookHTML(cont), Headings or BookHeadings, and Headings(cont) or BookHeadings(cont). If these pages are not included in the original document, FrameMaker creates the needed pages the first time you save to HTML.

Saving a Single Document File as HTML

To save a single document file as HTML, follow these steps:

1. Select File➤Save As. The Save Document dialog box is displayed.

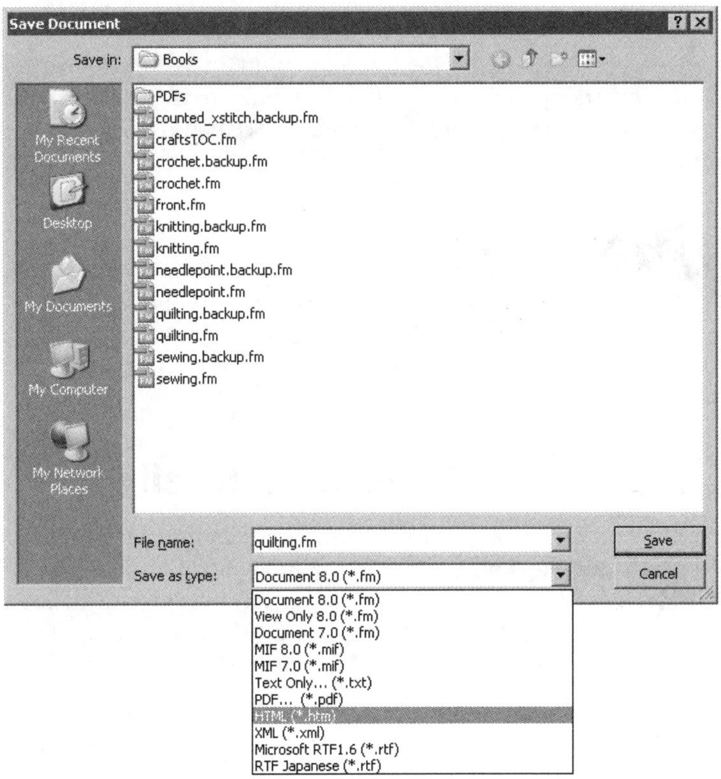

2. In the File name field, specify a name for the output file.

3. In the Save as type field, select HTML.
4. Click the Save button to save the file in the specified format.

The first time you convert a file, FrameMaker creates several new HTML reference pages. These reference pages store the conversion settings for your files. See "Customizing HTML Output" on page 482 for information about customizing these settings.

Saving a Book as HTML

To save a book file as HTML, open the book file, select File➤Save Book As, and choose HTML as the format, just as you do with a document file. FrameMaker processes each file in the book in turn and creates one (or more) HTML output files for each FrameMaker file. The conversion settings for the book are stored on reference pages in the first file in the book; the pages are named BookHTML and BookHeadings. To modify conversion settings, open the first file in the book, locate these reference pages, and change them just as you would file-level HTML and Headings reference pages.

TIP If you have already set up file-level conversion and want to use those settings for a book conversion, copy the mapping tables from the HTML and Headings reference pages onto the BookHTML and BookHeadings reference pages of the first file in the book.

Customizing HTML Output

You can customize some aspects of the HTML output from FrameMaker. To do so, you can set mappings through a graphical interface or through the mappings table on the HTML, BookHTML, Headings, and BookHeadings reference pages. The following sections describe both methods.

Modifying Conversion Settings Graphically

For HTML conversion, FrameMaker provides a graphical interface in which you can perform some basic mapping. The HTML Setup dialog box is somewhat useful in establishing initial conversion settings, but you will almost certainly need to fine-tune settings by modifying mapping tables on the HTML reference pages.

CAUTION Do not attempt to make changes in the HTML Setup dialog box while displaying the HTML reference pages. This can cause file corruption.

You can customize the paragraph, character, and cross-reference mappings in the HTML Setup dialog box.

Paragraph Mappings

You can customize file conversion (but not book conversion) using the HTML Setup dialog box. To customize your paragraph mappings, follow these steps:

1. Open the file you want to convert. Make sure the reference pages are *not* displayed.
2. Select File➤Utilities➤HTML Setup. The HTML Setup dialog box is displayed.

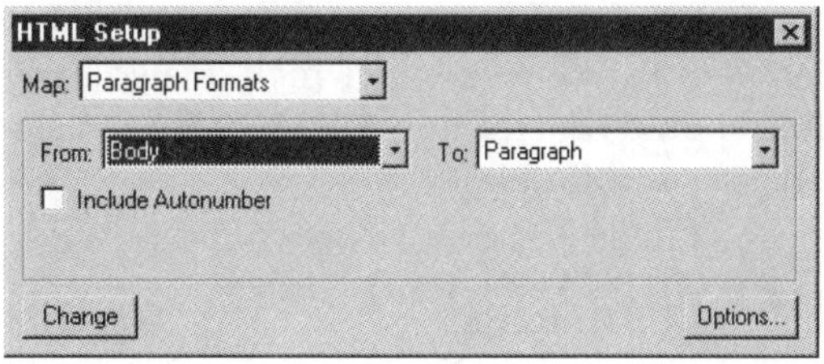

3. In the Map drop-down list, make sure that Paragraph Formats (the default) is selected.
4. The From drop-down list includes all of the paragraph tags in this document. For each paragraph tag, click the corresponding mapping in the To drop-down list. The options are as follows:

Mapping Style	Description
Heading (Auto Level)	Use for headings in your document. The heading level is determined by a mapping table on the reference pages. For details, see "Assigning Heading Levels" on page 488.
Paragraph	Use for body paragraphs in your document.
Preformatted Text	Use for monospaced paragraphs, such as code examples, in your text.
Address	Use for an address block.
Block Quote	Use for an indented quotation.
List Item	Use for bulleted and numbered lists.
List Item (Continued)	Use for paragraphs inside a bulleted or numbered list that do not have a bullet or number.
Data Term	Use for terms.
Data Definition	Use for definitions.

Mapping Style	Description
Data Definition (Continued)	Use for a continuation paragraph in a definition.
Throw Away	Use for paragraphs you want to eliminate from the HTML output.

Some mappings provide additional options. Headings, for example, include a Start New, Linked Web Page check box, which lets you specify whether a particular heading should cause a new HTML page to begin in the output. The additional options are as follows:

Available in...	Option	Description
All styles	Include Autonumber check box	If checked, the paragraph autonumber is included in the output. If unchecked, the paragraph autonumber is discarded.
Heading (Auto Level)	Start New, Linked Web Page check box	If checked, the specified paragraph tag starts a new web page.
List Item List Item (Continued)	*Item will be in a bulleted/numbered list*	FrameMaker automatically sets either a bulleted or numbered list for list items.
List Item List Item (Continued)	Nest List at Depth...	Determines the indentation level of the list item.

5. When you have finished, click the Change button.

Character Mappings

You can set up initial character tag mappings in the HTML Setup dialog box. To map your character tags, follows these steps:

1. Open the file you want to convert. Make sure the reference pages are *not* displayed.
2. Select File➤Utilities➤HTML Setup. The HTML Setup dialog box is displayed.

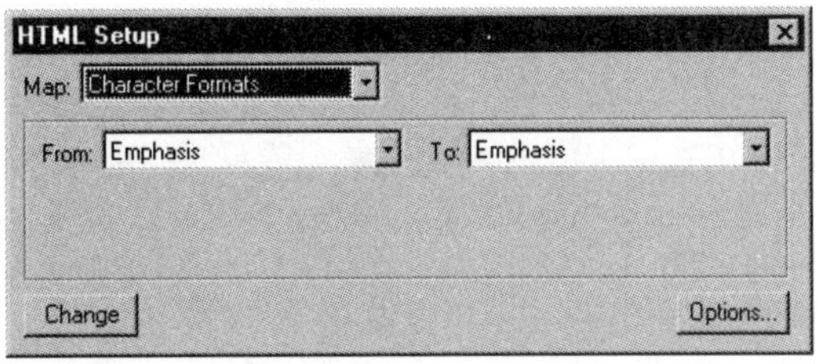

3. In the Map drop-down list, make sure that Character Formats is selected.
4. The From drop-down list includes all of the character tags in this document. For each character tag, click the corresponding mapping in the To drop-down list. The options are as follows:

Mapping Style	Description
Blink	Use to create blinking text.
Citation	Use for inline citations or quotes.
Code	Use for monospaced text, such as programming commands in text.
Definition	Use for inline definitions.
Emphasis	Use for emphasized text.
Keyboard	Use for text you type in (similar to Code).
Language (Intl.)	Specifies the language of the enclosed text.
Sample	Use for monospaced text.
Short Quotation (Intl.)	Use for inline quotes.
Span (CSS)	Use to reference formatting in a CSS file.
Strong Emphasis	Use for heavy emphasis.
Typewriter	Use to produce monospaced text; similar to Code.
Variable	Use for variables in programming code.
Plain Text	Use to output text with no additional formatting.
Throw Away	Use to delete text from the output.

5. When you have finished, click the Change button.

Cross-Reference Mappings

You can set up initial cross-reference mappings in the HTML Setup dialog box. After this initial setup, you can further tweak these settings on the reference pages.

To set up cross-reference formats, follow these steps:

1. Make sure that the reference pages are *not* displayed.
2. Select File➤Utilities➤HTML Setup. The HTML Setup dialog box is displayed.

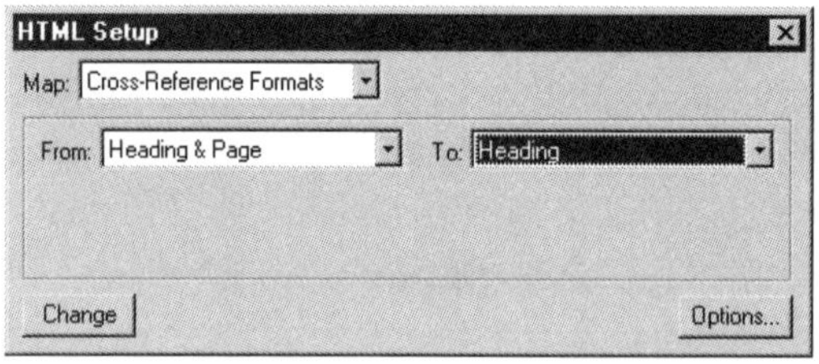

3. In the Map drop-down list, click Cross-Reference Formats. The dialog box now displays a list of cross-reference formats in the From drop-down list.
4. For each cross-reference format, assign a cross-reference mapping in the To list. Your options are as follows:

Mapping Style	Description
Figure All	Figure <$paranumonly>, <$paratext> Displays the figure number and title.
Figure Number	Figure <$paranumonly> Displays the figure number only.
Heading	<$paratext> Displays the paragraph text only. Appropriate for most online references.
See Also	See <$paratext> Displays the paragraph text with “See.”
Table All	Table <$paranumonly>, <$paratext> Displays the table number and title.
Table Number	Table <$paranumonly> Displays the table number only.

Mapping Style	Description
Original Cross-Reference Format	Processes the cross-reference without changing the format.
Throw Away	The cross-reference is deleted during conversion.

5. When you have finished, click the Change button.

Setting the Format of Output Graphics

You can convert graphics into one of three formats: GIF, JPEG, or PNG. Flash movies (SWF) are converted to static GIF graphics. If graphics were imported by reference in FrameMaker and the source files are in a web-ready format, you can copy the graphics instead of converting them.

To set your graphic conversion options, follow these steps:

1. Make sure that the reference pages are *not* displayed.
2. Select File➤Utilities➤HTML Setup. The HTML Setup dialog box is displayed.
3. Click the Options button. The HTML Options dialog box is displayed.

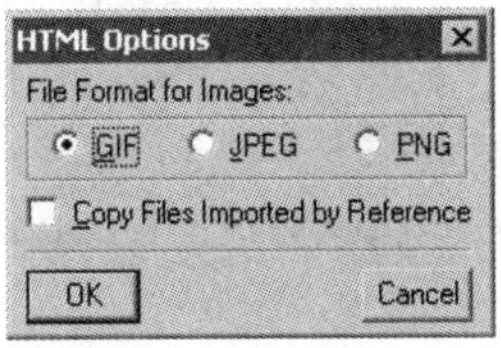

4. In the File Format for Images section, choose an output format for your graphics.
5. If you want to use source files instead of converting files for the items imported by reference, check the Copy Files Imported by Reference check box.
6. Click the OK button.

Modifying the Reference Pages

For better control over your HTML output, you can make changes to the mapping tables on the reference pages.

Assigning Heading Levels

The heading levels in your output are determined by the Headings mapping table found on the Headings reference page.

§

Headings Table§

Heading Level§	Paragraph Format§	Comments§
1§	**Title§**	§
2§	**Heading1§**	§
3§	**Heading2§**	§
4§	**HeadingRunIn§**	§
4§	**TableTitle§**	§

NOTE For a book conversion, this table is on the BookHeadings reference page.

The columns in this table are as follows:

- **Heading Level:** Determines the level of the output heading.
- **Paragraph Format:** Lists the heading paragraph tags in the document. In the preceding example, the paragraphs use the listed paragraph tags (for example, the Title listing is formatted using the Title paragraph tag), but this is not required.
- **Comments:** You can provide comments to explain the information in the table. By default, the Comments column is blank.

FrameMaker provides a default set of mappings, shown in the preceding example. If your document contains other paragraph tags, they are listed alphabetically by default. You can rearrange them in hierarchical order to make the table easier to maintain.

Setting Up Paragraph Mappings

The paragraph mappings are stored in the HTML Mapping Table on the reference pages:

§

HTML Mapping Table§

FrameMaker Source Item§	HTML Item§		Include Auto#§	Comments§
	Element§	New Web Page?§		
P:Body§	P§	N§	N§	§
P:Bulleted§	LI¶ Parent = UL¶ Depth = 0§	N§	N§	§
P:CellBody§	P§	N§	N§	§
P:CellHeading§	P§	N§	N§	§
P:Footnote§	P§	N§	N§	§
P:Heading1§	H*§	N§	N§	§
P:Heading2§	H*§	N§	N§	§
P:HeadingRunIn§	H*§	N§	N§	§
P:Indented§	P¶ Parent = UL¶ Depth = 0§	N§	N§	§
P:Mapping Table Cell§	P§	N§	N§	§
P:Mapping Table Title§	P§	N§	N§	§
P:Numbered§	LI¶ Parent = OL¶ Depth = 0§	N§	N§	§

You can modify settings here instead of working through the HTML Setup dialog box. Notice that the paragraph mappings start with a P: prefix.

FrameMaker creates an initial listing of tags in this table. If you add paragraph tags to your document, those tags are added into the table, but they may be added at the bottom of the table, not in the paragraph tag section. Keep in mind that paragraph tags, character tags, and cross-reference formats are all listed in this table, but may not be grouped together.

Mapping Character Tags

The HTML Mapping Table lists character tags with a C: prefix, as shown in the following example:

HTML Mapping Table§

FrameMaker Source Item§	HTML Item§		Include Auto#§	Comments§
	Element§	New Web Page?§		
P:Numbered1 §	LI¶ Parent = OL¶ Depth = 0§	N§	N§	§
P:TableFootnote§	P§	N§	N§	§
P:TableTitle§	H*§	N§	N§	§
P:Title§	H*§	N§	N§	§
C:Emphasis§	EM§	N§	N§	§
C:EquationVariables§	EM§	N§	N§	§
X:Heading & Page§	Heading§	N§	N§	§
X:Page§	Heading§	N§	N§	§
X:See Heading & Page§	See Also§	N§	N§	§
X:Table All§	Table All§	N§	N§	§
X:Table Number & Page§	Table Number§	N§	N§	§

Character mappings (C:Emphasis§ and C:EquationVariables§ rows)

In this example, the Emphasis and EquationVariables character tags are both mapped to the EM element.

Emphasis character tag

This paragraph uses *Emphasis.*

```
<p>This paragraph uses <EM>Emphasis</EM>.</p>
```

HTML output uses <EM>.

You could change the mapping table to produce different output. The code you enter is used to create opening <*xxx*> and closing </*xxx*> tags. Keep in mind that you must supply a tag that HTML can interpret.

Mapping Cross-Reference Formats

The mappings you establish in the HTML Setup dialog box are saved in the reference pages as part of the HTML Mapping Table. The cross-reference formats are listed with X: prefixes, as shown in the following example:

HTML Mapping Table§

FrameMaker Source Item§	HTML Item§		Include Auto#§	Comments§
	Element§	New Web Page?§		
P:Numbered1 §	LI¶ Parent = OL¶ Depth = 0§	N§	N§	§
P:TableFootnote§	P§	N§	N§	§
P:TableTitle§	H*§	N§	N§	§
P:Title§	H*§	N§	N§	§
C:Emphasis§	EM§	N§	N§	§
C:EquationVariables§	EM§	N§	N§	§
X:Heading & Page§	Heading§	N§	N§	§
X:Page§	Heading§	N§	N§	§
X:See Heading & Page§	See Also§	N§	N§	§
X:Table All§	Table All§	N§	N§	§
X:Table Number & Page§	Table Number§	N§	N§	§

Cross-reference mappings

Unlike the paragraph and character tags, the elements listed for the cross-references (such as Heading and See Also in the preceding example) are not translated directly into HTML tags. Instead, the cross-reference formats use cross-reference macros. For example, Heading is defined as a macro in the Cross-Reference Macros table on the HTML reference pages, shown here:

Cross-Reference Macros§

Macro Name§	Replace With§	Comments§
Heading§	<$paratext>§	§
See Also§	See <$paratext>.§	§
Table All§	Table <$paranumonly>, <$paratext>§	§
Table Number§	Table <$paranumonly>§	§

The Heading macro is defined as:

```
<$paratext>
```

The cross-reference macros are used to replace the original cross-reference format definition during conversion. FrameMaker automatically converts cross-references to HTML links, and that conversion is not reflected anywhere in the mapping tables.

Modifying Style Sheet Information

When you save to HTML, FrameMaker creates a cascading style sheet (CSS) file based on the tag settings in your document. This file controls the formatting of the items in the HTML file. You can make changes to the CSS file to control the look and feel of each item in the HTML output.

The following example shows a CSS formatting specification:

```
P.Body {
    display: block;
    text-align: left;
    text-indent: 0.000000pt;
    margin-top: 0.000000pt;
    margin-bottom: 0.000000pt;
    margin-right: 0.000000pt;
    margin-left: 0.000000pt;
    font-size: 12.000000pt;
    font-weight: medium;
    font-style: Regular;
    color: #000000;
    text-decoration: none;
    vertical-align: baseline;
    text-transform: none;
    font-family: "Times New Roman";
}
EM.Emphasis {
    font-style: Italic;
}
```

By default, FrameMaker updates the CSS file every time you Save As HTML. If you make changes to the CSS file, be sure to copy the file to another directory. After creating the output (and overwriting the CSS file), you can then copy your updated CSS file back into the HTML output directory.

Modifying Page Opening and Closing Code

The opening and closing tags in the output HTML are set by the System Macros table, shown here:

System Macros§

Macro Name§	Replace With§	Head§	Comments§
StartOfDoc§	§	<TITLE> <$defaulttitle></ TITLE>§	§
EndOfDoc§	§	§	§
StartOfSubDoc§	§	<TITLE> <$defaulttitle></ TITLE>§	§
EndOfSubDoc§	§	§	§
StartOfFirstSubDoc§	§	<TITLE> <$defaulttitle></ TITLE>§	§
EndOfFirstSubDoc§	§	§	§
StartOfLastSubDoc§	§	<TITLE> <$defaulttitle></ TITLE>§	§
EndOfLastSubDoc§	§	§	§

The available macros distinguish between documents (Docs) and subdocuments (SubDocs). If you break up a FrameMaker file into multiple output files, the first output file is considered the main document. The additional output files are subdocuments. The macros available to customize these output files are defined as follows:

- **StartOfDoc:** Beginning of the main document.
- **EndOfDoc:** End of the main document.
- **StartOfSubDoc:** Beginning of the subdocuments (except the first and last).
- **EndOfSubDoc:** End of the subdocuments (except the first and last).
- **StartOfFirstSubDoc:** Beginning of the first subdocument.
- **EndOfFirstSubDoc:** End of the first subdocument.
- **StartOfLastSubDoc:** Beginning of the last subdocument.
- **EndOfLastSubDoc:** End of the last subdocument.

Several building blocks are available for use in these macros to help you customize the output. You could, for instance, use the <$nextsubdoc> and <$prevsubdoc> macros to create a navigation bar. The following table lists the building blocks available to customize the system macros:

Building Block	Description
`<$paratext>`	The text of the current paragraph.
`<$paratag>`	The name of the current paragraph tag.
`<$paranum>`	The autonumber of the current paragraph tag.
`<$paranumonly>`	The numeric portion of the autonumber of the current paragraph tag.
`<$variable[`*`variablename`*`]>`	The definition of the *variablename* variable.
`<$defaulttitle>`	The text of the most recent paragraph tag that is tagged as a heading. (That is, it must be identified as a heading in the HTML Mapping Table.)
`<$nextsubdoc>`	The file name of the next document in the output.
`<$prevsubdoc>`	The file name of the previous document in the output.
`<$parentdoc>`	The file name of the document that is at the next higher level in the HTML output hierarchy.

CREATING OUTPUT

Processing Special Characters

Special characters require special handling during conversion. The Character Macros table lets you define how special characters are processed:

Character Macros§

Character§	Replace With§	Comments§
¢§	¢§	§
©§	©§	§
®§	®§	§
°§	°§	§
—§	--§	§
–§	-§	§
…§	...§	§

For characters that don't work in the HTML files, you need to set up a replacement by adding a line to this table. For instance, the trademark symbol, ™, doesn't translate properly, so you would add a line to the mapping table, as shown in the following example:

Character	Replace With	Comments
™	™	

Defining Macros

During conversion, you can further customize your output with macros. A *general macro* lets you define HTML code, which you can then use for mappings. You set up these macros in the General Macros table, shown in the following example:

General Macros§

Macro Name§	Replace With§	Head§	Comments§
BodyBold§	<p><b>§	§	§

After you define a general macro, you can reference it in the HTML Mapping Table:

HTML Mapping Table§

FrameMaker Source Item§	HTML Item§		Include Auto#§	Comments§
	Element§	New Web Page?§		
P:Body§	P§	N§	N§	§
P:BodyBold§	BodyBold§	§	§	general macros§

Instead of assigning the general macro to a particular mapping, you can also insert arbitrary HTML code in your document. To do so, define the code as a general macro, then insert a custom marker called HTML Macro in your document where you want the code to appear. In the marker, insert the name of the macro as the marker text.

Exporting XML Output

FrameMaker includes a Save As XML feature that works differently depending on whether you are using unstructured or structured FrameMaker. From unstructured FrameMaker, you customize the XML output by customizing reference pages called XML and XML(cont) that are almost identical to the reference pages described in this chapter for the Save As HTML feature. There is no dialog box to help you set up the XML export as there is for HTML export.

Because of the simplistic nature of the XML mapping, however, it's best to avoid the Save as XML option. Mapping paragraph and other tag names to element names does create *well-formed* XML-tagged files, which means the XML has the necessary opening and closing XML tags. However, the XML files that it creates are probably not going to be very useful. Because the mapping moves data from a flat, unstructured file, the output has minimal hierarchy. In addition, unless you have chosen your FrameMaker tag names very carefully and with structure in mind, using tag names as element names will probably not convey the meaning of the information appropriately. To create *valid XML*, which has a hierarchy and can be validated against a document type definition (DTD) that provides the rules for the elements in the XML, you need to use structured FrameMaker to set up a structured application.

For more information about converting unstructured files to structured files, refer to *Publishing Fundamentals: Structured FrameMaker 8*.

Going Beyond Basic Customization

It's likely that your HTML conversion requirements will go beyond what the Save As feature can provide. In that case, you need to consider other options:

- Third-party converters give you much more flexibility.
- Scripting utilities (such as Perl) could allow you to write code that post-processes your output to produce exactly what you need.
- With structured FrameMaker, you can create XML that is transformed with XSL into HTML. Refer to *Publishing Fundamentals: Structured FrameMaker 8* for information on creating XML from structured FrameMaker files.

Each option requires a significant amount of setup time and some scripting expertise. Alternatively, many consultants are available who can help set up “push-button” conversion environments.

CHAPTER 20

Color Output

FrameMaker lets you create full-color documentation using a rich set of tools. The available colors are stored in a color catalog, which is available through the Paragraph Designer, Character Designer, and many other dialog boxes.

You assign color to text or objects by applying tags that contain references to color definitions. For example, to create a purple first-level heading, you assign purple to the Heading1 paragraph tag.

My Purple Paragraph

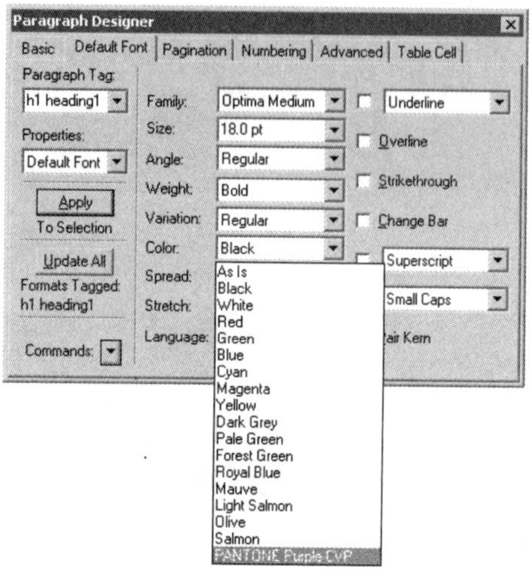

To create blue, underlined cross-references that stand out in PDF files, you create a character tag that applies blue and underlining, then insert the character tag in your cross-reference formats. In the PDF file, the hyperlink will be underlined and displayed as blue text.

See "Life and How to Live It" on page 1200.

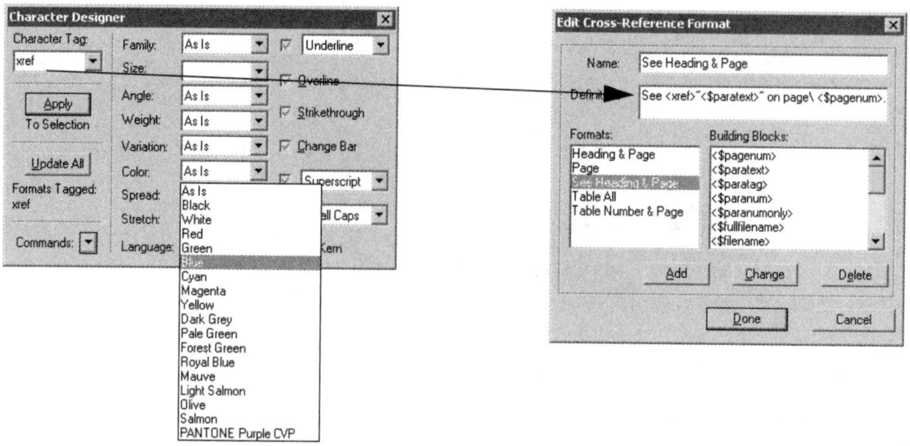

You assign color to some items, such as borders or FrameMaker drawings, by choosing a color in the Tools palette or object properties.

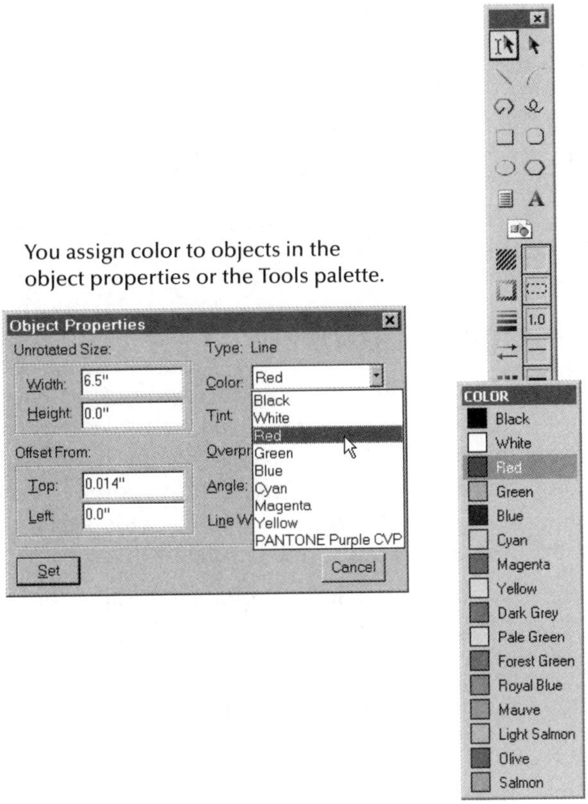

You assign color to objects in the object properties or the Tools palette.

Understanding Types of Color

In FrameMaker, color definitions are based on one of three color models:

- **RGB.** Defines colors in percentages of red, green, and blue; usually for onscreen display. Colors are displayed in PDF files as RGB colors, and when you convert a FrameMaker document to an online format, images are converted to RGB images.
- **CMYK.** Defines colors in percentages of cyan, magenta, yellow, and black inks (black is the *key* color, thus the "K"). CMYK is for color printing. The four colors are used to print *color separations*—individual pages that describe how to mix cyan, magenta, yellow, and black for four-color printing. Because your computer monitor uses RGB to display colors, the colors you see onscreen do not match colors in print. Ask your print vendor to run a test document or get a swatch book to ensure that you pick the right colors.
- **HLS.** Defines colors by their location on a color wheel (hue), lightness, and saturation. The amount of red, green, yellow, and blue determines the hue. The intensity of the color determines the lightness. The amount of gray

determines the saturation. HLS color should be used only for documents that you plan to convert to online formats, although the color is translated to RGB upon conversion.

RGB, CMYK, and HLS colors are available in *color libraries.* If you plan to print the document, your print vendor typically recommends a color library based on paper quality and texture, ink color accuracy, lamination, and other printing factors. Most color libraries provide CMYK color; however, a few consist only of RGB or HLS color. See "Managing Color Definitions" on page 504 for details.

Understanding Process Color

When you send a document to be printed on a printing press (called *offset printing*), you can use two types of color: *process color* and *spot color.* Process color, or four-color printing, is mixed on the press from cyan, magenta, yellow, and black (CMYK) inks; spot color (described in the next section) is mixed before going to press. Using process color lets you combine the inks on the press to create a wide variety of colors. Process color works well for printing photographs and gradiated images.

To print process color, you create color separations. Each separation describes how to print a single color on the page. For a four-color document, you need four separations for each page:

- The cyan separation shows only cyan portions of the page.
- The magenta separation shows only magenta portions of the page.
- The yellow separation shows only yellow portions of the page.
- The black separation shows only black portions of the page.

TIP For more economical four-color printing, leave blank pages out of your color separations. See "Skipping Blank Pages" on page 460 for details.

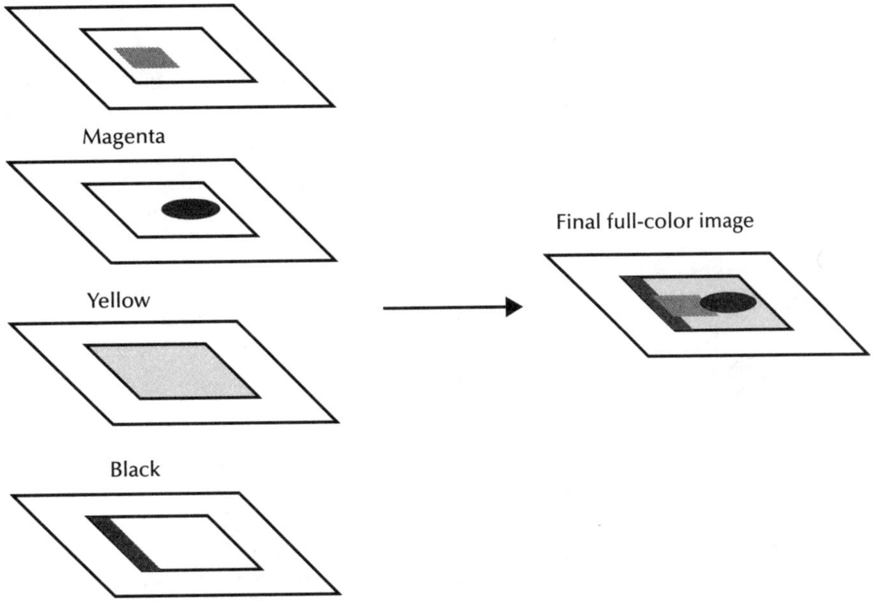

Separations are burned onto individual plates. Each plate is used to print a single color onto a page. Registration marks allow the print technician to line up the separations correctly. Slight deviations in alignment can cause the color to print in the wrong place, and if the separations aren't aligned, the color combinations do not produce the colors you need. See "Modifying Existing Colors" on page 505 for information on preventing registration errors.

Separations were accurately aligned.

Separations were misaligned, so there is a gap between the overlapping objects.

Separations also define *halftones*—the overlapping grids of dots by which process color is printed. The more dots you include in the halftone, the darker the color. You also specify the angle of the grids, which helps print color smoothly instead of in a checkerboard pattern. Your print vendor might prefer to set up the halftones before going to press, so consult with them before changing halftone screens in FrameMaker.

FrameMaker can create separations only for imported EPS line art, CMYK TIFFs, and Desktop Color Separation (DCS) images. If you have a CMYK bitmap image in an EPS file, FrameMaker can create separations if the EPS can also be separated in Adobe Illustrator.

TIP To make sure your colors print correctly before going through the expense of printing to plate, ask the print vendor to print a color proof from a color laser printer. The colors won't be exact, but they'll be close.

Understanding Spot Color

In contrast to process color, spot color is mixed before your job goes to press. Instead of filling the ink wells on the press with CMYK, you use the premixed spot colors on the press. For print jobs that use only two or three colors, using spot colors cuts the cost of printing (because printing three colors is less expensive than printing four colors—fewer separations, fewer plates, fewer layers to keep in registration). If you use process color to produce those same two or three colors, you must set up plates for all four CMYK colors, even though you're mixing them to produce just a few colors.

Spot colors are also useful for printing colors that are outside the CMYK *gamut*; that is, colors that you cannot create by mixing CMYK inks. Metallic or fluorescent inks (neon colors) usually require a spot color because they are outside the CMYK gamut.

If you are using one spot color (plus black) to reduce costs, you can create the impression of additional colors by using *tints,* or lighter versions of a base spot color. Instead of printing a color at full strength, you print only a percentage of the color. For example, 50 percent of a deep blue produces a light slate blue. Because tints use the same base color as the spot color, they are set up on the same separation.

If you're printing images with solid patches of color and can create the necessary color with a few inks, consider using spot color. If your document contains color photographs, though, you'll need to use process color. See "Understanding Process Color" on page 500 for more information.

NOTE Spot colors in EPS files come into FrameMaker as spot, but spot colors from PDF files (even if produced in Adobe Illustrator) do not. If you need to preserve spot colors within imported graphics, use either EPS or a third-party tool such as Grafikhuset Publi PDF (www.grafikhuset.net/PubliPDF) to correct the colors in the PDF file.

Applying Color to Text and Objects

You format text and objects with color by deciding on a color in the color catalog and assigning the color in one of the following items:

- Paragraph tags
- Character tags
- Table tags
- Condition tags
- Custom table ruling and shading
- Change bars
- Object properties
- Tools palette

You apply the appropriate tag, edit the object properties, or select the color in the Tools palette. If you modify a color in the color catalog, each item that uses that color is automatically updated. Suppose you create a custom color but decide to reduce the amount of red in the color. You update the color definition, and the color is updated globally—in existing text and objects and those you create later.

Table 20-1 summarizes assigning color to text and objects.

Item	How to Assign Color	More Information
assigning color to text		
Paragraph	Select the color in a paragraph tag.	"Modifying Paragraph Tags" on page 112
One or more words	Select the color in a character tag.	"Modifying Character Tags" on page 146
Conditional text	Select the color in the conditional tag definition.	"Creating Condition Tags" on page 529
Variable (all instances)	Type the character tag in the variable definition.	"Creating User Variables" on page 230
Cross-reference style (all instances)	Type the character tag in the cross-reference format definition.	"Formatting Cross-References" on page 201

Table 20-1. Assigning Color to Text and Objects

Item	How to Assign Color	More Information
Assigning color to objects		
One object	Select the color in the object properties.	"Modifying Objects" on page 346
One or more objects	Select the color in the Tools palette.	"Modifying Objects" on page 346
Table border	Select the color in the custom ruling style definition.	"Changing Ruling Options" on page 178
Change bars	Select the color in the change bar properties, or select the change bar in a character tag.	"Using Change Bars" on page 91 and "Modifying Character Tags" on page 146

Table 20-1. Assigning Color to Text and Objects (Continued)

Managing Color Definitions

FrameMaker documents contain 16 basic colors by default. The color catalog lists them in the following order: Black, White, Red, Green, Blue, Cyan, Magenta, Yellow, Dark Grey, Pale Green, Forest Green, Royal Blue, Mauve, Light Salmon, Olive, and Salmon. (Color names are case sensitive.) You add more colors by doing one of the following:

- Modifying existing colors (except default colors)
- Creating custom colors
- Adding colors from a color library
- Renaming colors

TIP When you paste an object from one document to another, the color of the object is added to the color definitions if it doesn't already exist. Colors defined in imported EPS files are also added to the color catalog. If you import a PNG file that uses an optimized palette—which means the palette uses fewer than the maximum number of colors available—the color catalog includes all the colors defined in the PNG. (Saving as MIF, reopening the file in FrameMaker, and saving as an FM file fixes the problem.) In addition, colors are imported when you open a Microsoft Word document in FrameMaker. The new colors are named "Color n," where "n" equals the location in the color catalog. You can give the colors descriptive names. See "Renaming Colors" on page 512 for details.

Modifying Existing Colors

To modify an existing color (other than the default colors), you move the sliders in the color definition or type a specific value until the color you want is displayed, as shown in Figure 20-1. You can experiment with values and update the color definition when you get the right color. This updates the color throughout the document.

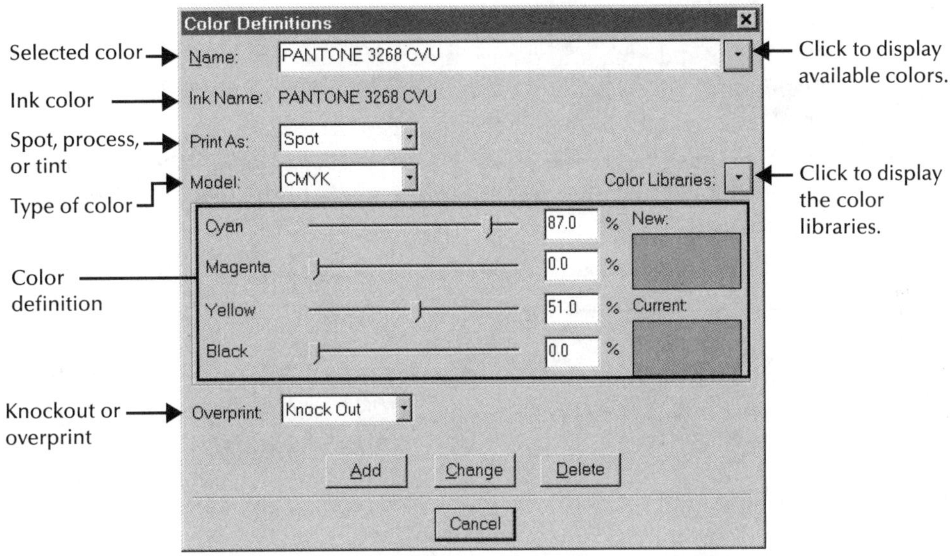

Figure 20-1. Managing color definitions

To modify a color definition, follow these steps:

1. Select View➤Color➤Definitions. The Color Definitions dialog box is displayed (Figure 20-1).
2. In the Name drop-down list, click the color you want to modify. You cannot modify a default color—the sliders are grayed out, and the color value fields aren't displayed.
3. To change how the color will be printed, click one of the following in the Print As drop-down list:
   - **Spot:** Premixes the color.
   - **Process:** Mixes the color on the press. (Print CMYK colors as process for the best results.)
   - **Tint:** Prints a percentage of the selected color. (Be sure to test the tint. Those lighter than 10 percent don't display accurately and might not print correctly.)
   - **Don't Print:** Prevents colors such as white from printing.

4. To change the type of color, click one of the following in the Model drop-down list:
   - **CMYK:** Prints each color in percentages of cyan, magenta, yellow, and black.
   - **RGB:** Prints the color in percentages of red, green, and blue.
   - **HLS:** Prints the color in terms of the hue, lightness, and saturation.
5. To adjust the color values, do one of the following:
   - Click a slider and drag it to the right or left until the color you need is displayed in the New section. Remember that the color will look different in print, so refer to a swatch book.
   - Type a specific value in the fields. Most values are percentages, but in the HLS color model, the Hue represents the angle of the color on a color wheel.

Click the slider and drag it to the right or left to change color values.

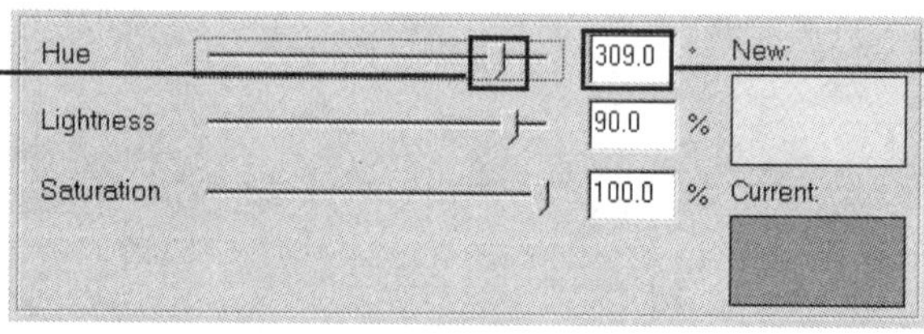

Type the degree at which the hue is displayed on the color wheel.

6. To indicate how FrameMaker prints the overlapping color of two objects, click one of the following in the Overprint drop-down list:
   - **Knock Out:** The overlapped portion looks white and doesn't print. Helps prevent the colors of a light object on top and a dark object on bottom from mixing, although the separations must be lined up correctly, or the knocked out piece may appear in the printed copy.

The color of the top object is set to "knock out."

The overlapped portion of the square is cut out so that it looks white and won't print.

If separations aren't lined up correctly, the knocked out piece might print.

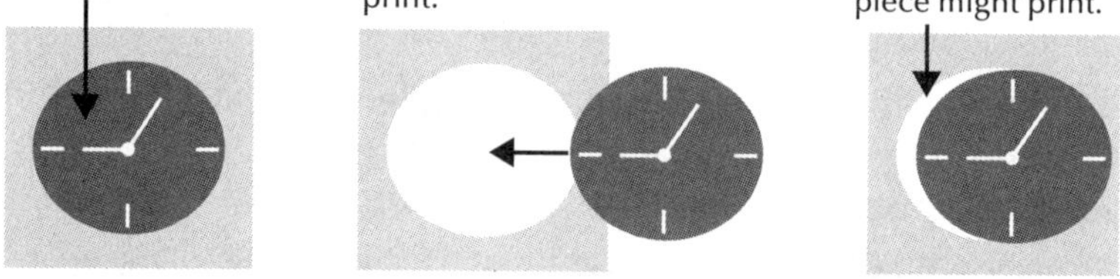

   - **Overprint:** Both colors from the overlapped portion of the objects are printed. Helps prevent a gap from printing between objects; however, if the top object is lighter than the bottom object, the two colors might mix.

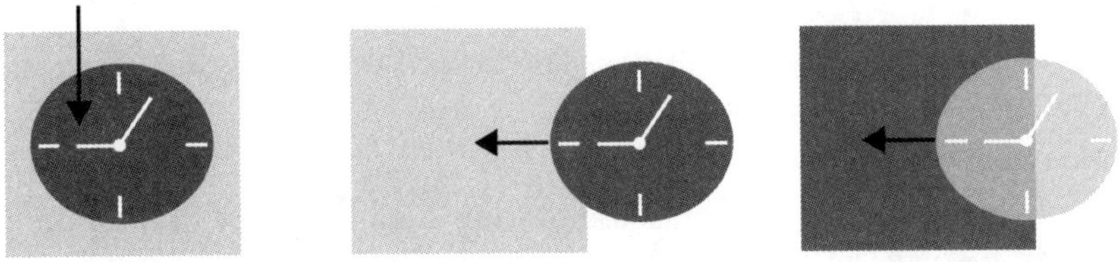

7. Click the Change button. The color definition is updated, and all items formatted with the color are reformatted. (If you modified the definition of a library color, a warning is displayed. Unless you intended to change the library color, click the Cancel button, then click the color in the Name drop-down list to restore the definition.)

CAUTION Unless you use a library color as a basis for a new color, you shouldn't modify the definition of a library color. This changes the composition of the ink, so the color won't match the color you chose from the library. If you accidentally change a library color but don't save your changes, you can restore the original definition by clicking the color in the Name drop-down list. The original color definition and ink name are displayed.

Naming Colors

When you add new colors, you need to name the colors consistently. Most colors you choose from a library have an official ink name, but the name doesn't indicate that Pantone 252 CVU, for example, is a shade of pink. You can rename the color before adding it to your color definitions, and the ink name is still displayed in the color definitions.

Colors are easier to manage if you name them based on their function, not their color. Your company's logo color is a good example. Instead of naming the color "Aqua," name it "Logo." If the color changes from aqua to teal, you can update the Logo color definition, import the new color definition into all your files, and the Logo color is instantly updated throughout your documents. If you had named the color "Aqua," you would need to rename the color after changing the definition. See "Renaming Colors" on page 512 for details.

Creating Custom Colors

Instead of choosing a predefined color, you can create your own colors. To do so, follow these steps:

1. Select View➤Color➤Definitions. The Color Definitions dialog box is displayed (Figure 20-1 on page 505).
2. Do one of the following:
   - To base the color on an existing color, click the color in the Name drop-down list.
   - To create a unique color, click New Color in the Name drop-down list. "New Color" is displayed in the Name field, followed by a number. The number increments with each new color if you don't change this default name; however, you should name the color something descriptive.
   - To type specific RGB values, click the Color Libraries pop-up menu, then click Common Color Picker. Type the values in the RGB percentage fields, or click and drag the slider, then click the Done button.

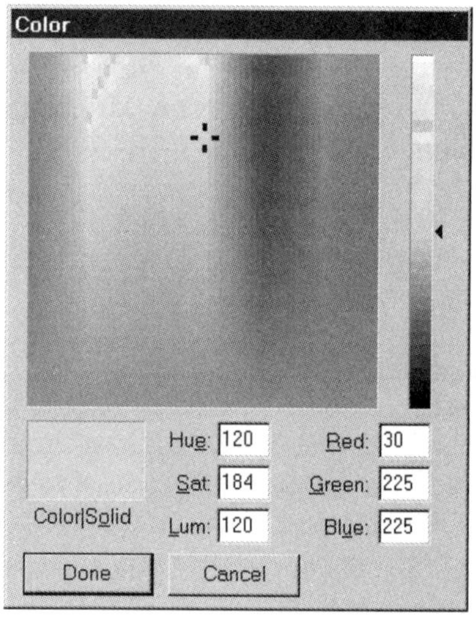

3. Type the name of the new color in the Name field. If you based the color on a default color, the Add button is no longer grayed out.
4. Click the Add button. The new color is added to the document's color catalog.

CAUTION Do not click the Change button (which is displayed only if you based the color on an existing nondefault color), or you'll rename the existing color definition. See "Renaming Colors" on page 512 for details.

Adding Colors from a Color Library

The color libraries provide predefined colors. Table 20-2 describes the color libraries available in FrameMaker.

Color Library	Description
RGB Color	
Common Color Picker	Lets you select a color using the operating system's color picker. You can also type specific RGB or HLS values.
Crayon	Developed by Adobe to provide access to common RGB colors using everyday names in alphabetical order. Do not use Crayon colors as spot colors.
MUNSELL High Chroma Colors and Book of Color	Provides RGB colors in terms of hue, value, and chroma. ■ **Hue:** Shades of red, yellow, green, blue, and purple in ten hue sectors: R, YR, Y, GY, G, BG, B, PB, P and RP (red, yellow-red, yellow, green-yellow, and so on). ■ **Value:** Lightness of the color from 0 (for pure black) to 10 (for pure white). ■ **Chroma:** Saturation level, or the degree of gray in the color, from 0 to infinity.
Online	Provides 216 "web-safe" colors that have a consistent appearance on all platforms when viewed with a web browser. The colors have a sequential number and a hexadecimal code.
CMYK Color	
DIC COLOR GUIDE SPOT	Provides spot colors; used mostly in Japan.
FOCOLTONE	Provides 860 process colors; helps prevent trapping and registration problems by showing the overprints that make up the colors.
Greys	Developed by Adobe; provides both process and spot shades of gray in 1 percent increments.

Table 20-2. Color Libraries in FrameMaker

<table>
<tr><th>Color Library</th><th>Description</th></tr>
<tr><td>PANTONE Coated, PANTONE Uncoated, PANTONE ProSim, PANTONE ProSim EURO, PANTONE Process CSG, and PANTONE Process Euro</td><td>Define ink colors in CMYK equivalents.
▪ PANTONE Coated: For printing on coated paper. The paper coating affects how you perceive the color—color on coated paper looks lighter than color on uncoated paper.
▪ PANTONE Uncoated: For printing on uncoated paper.
▪ PANTONE ProSim and PANTONE ProSim EURO: For simulating Pantone spot colors onscreen. (ProSim stands for "process simulation.") Use the Euro library for documents printed in Europe.
▪ PANTONE Process CSG and PANTONE Process Euro: For printing process colors. Use the Euro library for documents printed in Europe.</td></tr>
<tr><td>TOYO COLOR FINDER</td><td>Provides more than 1,000 colors based on the most common printing inks in Japan.</td></tr>
<tr><td>TRUMATCH 4-Color Selector</td><td>Provides more than 2,000 computer-generated colors that predictably match the CMYK color spectrum.</td></tr>
</table>

Table 20-2. Color Libraries in FrameMaker (Continued)

TIP You can add a color library to FrameMaker if the library file is formatted in ASCII Color Format (.acf) version 2.1 or earlier, or in Binary Color Format (.bcf) version 2.0. Place the file in the FrameMaker8\fminit\color directory, and restart FrameMaker. The library will be displayed with the default color libraries.

To add a color from a color library, follow these steps:

1. Select View➤Color➤Definitions. The Color Definitions dialog box is displayed (Figure 20-1 on page 505).
2. Click the Color Libraries button. The Color Pickers pop-up menu is displayed.

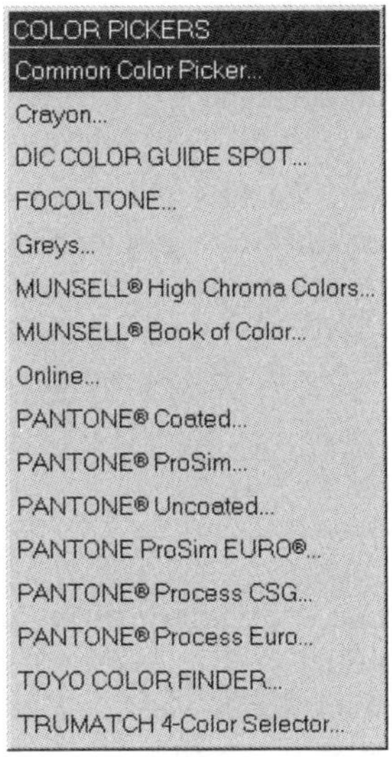

3. Click the library you want to display, then do one of the following:
   - Type the first few characters of the color name or number in the Find field.
   - Click and drag the slider.
4. Click the color you need. The name or number of the color is displayed in the top field.

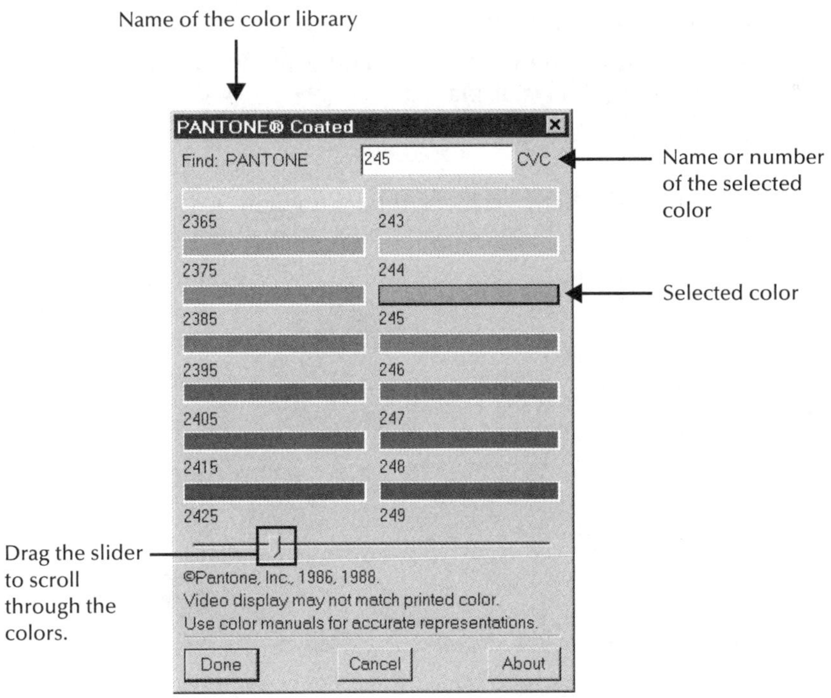

5. Click the Done button. The Color Definitions dialog box is displayed.
6. Click the Add button. The new color is added to the document's color catalog.

CAUTION Unless you use a library color as a basis for a new color, you shouldn't modify the definition of a library color. This changes the composition of the ink, so the color won't match the color you chose from the library. If you accidentally change a library color but don't save your changes, you can restore the original definition by clicking the color in the Name drop-down list. The original color definition and ink name are displayed.

Renaming Colors

When you rename a color, the name is updated throughout the document. For example, if you rename "Ocean Blue" to "Ocean Green," the new name is displayed instead of the original name where you can assign color—paragraph tags, object properties, and the like.

You cannot rename the 16 basic colors; however, color names are case-sensitive, so you can create "green" in addition to the default "Green."

To rename a color, follow these steps:

1. Select View➤Color➤Definitions. The Color Definitions dialog box is displayed (Figure 20-1 on page 505).
2. In the Name drop-down list, click the color you want to rename.
3. Type a new name in the Name field, then click the Change button.
   A confirmation dialog box is displayed.
4. Click the OK button. The color is renamed throughout the document.

NOTE If you tried to rename the color using the name of an existing color, that color is displayed. Redisplay the original color and then assign a name that's not in use.

Viewing Colors

You can configure up to six color views that show and hide specific colors in your document. View 1, the default color view, displays all colors used in the document. You should not modify this view. Each of the remaining views displays specific colors and hides others. For example, you can preview color separations before printing them by creating color views that each display only one color. In the following illustration, a different color view is displayed in each document:

View 1: All colors are displayed in this document.

View 2: The process color of the curtain is displayed in this document.

View 3: The spot color of the windowpane is displayed in this document.

You also set up color views to customize overlapping objects, such as those in the following example. In View 1 on the left, the text color is set to Normal, so the color of the dark object mixes with the lighter overlapping text. In View 2 on the right, the text color is set to Cutout, so the color is displayed accurately. Because View 1 is displayed most of the time, you could set the color of the text to Cutout in View 1.

View 1

View 2

The overlapping text looks slightly darker than the true color in the Normal view.

When the text color is set to Cutout, the color is displayed accurately.

Selecting a Color View

To select a color view, follow these steps:

1. Select View➤Color➤Views. The Define Color Views dialog box is displayed (Figure 20-2).

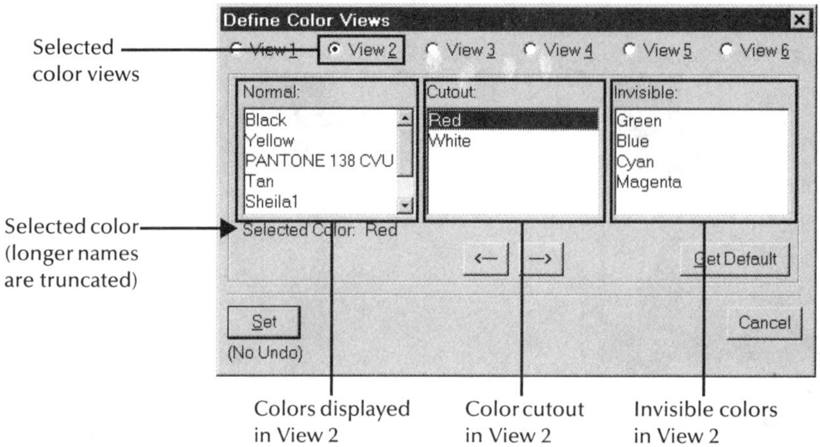

Figure 20-2. Selecting a color view

2. Click the radio button for the view you want to display, then click the Set button. The correct colors are displayed, cutout, or hidden in your document.

Setting up Color Views

To set up color views, follow these steps:

1. Select View➤Color➤Views. The Define Color Views dialog box is displayed (Figure 20-2).
2. Click the radio button for the view you want to modify.
3. Click the color you want to move, then click the left arrow or right arrow button until the color is displayed in the correct section. Your choices are as follows:
   - **Normal:** The color prints as normal.
   - **Cutout:** The color prints as white on overlapping objects.
   - **Invisible:** The color doesn't print.

TIP Press SHIFT while clicking an arrow to move all colors from one section to the other.

4. Click the Set button. The color view is updated.

Deleting Colors

You can delete any color except the 16 default colors. If the color has been assigned in the document and you delete the color, a warning is displayed. You must substitute black for the deleted color or cancel the action.

To delete a color, follow these steps:

1. Select View➤Color➤Definitions. The Color Definitions dialog box is displayed (Figure 20-1 on page 505).
2. In the Name drop-down list, click the color you want to delete.
3. Click the Delete button. Do one of the following:
   - If the color is in use, a warning is displayed. Click the OK button to delete the color and reassign black to the items, or click the Cancel button if you don't want to delete the color.
   - Click the OK button to delete the color.

Color for Online Output

Many FrameMaker documents are converted to an online format, such as PDF, HTML, or HTML Help. Conversion often changes the color you chose in FrameMaker—aqua may look more teal onscreen, for example. To avoid this problem, make sure you choose RGB or HLS color for online documentation. If you need to print color separations *and* create online documentation, you can use RGB colors for most FrameMaker graphics and use CMYK only when necessary. You'll need to test the conversion to see if you like the onscreen color. See "Understanding Types of Color" on page 499 for more information.

NOTE All default FrameMaker colors are RGB colors, and the Online, Crayon, MUNSELL, and Common Color Picker libraries also provide RGB colors.

The colors you specify in FrameMaker might not convert correctly. Some conversion processes alter color or replace it with a completely different color. Table 20-3 on page 516 describes how to prevent color conversion problems.

Problem	Solution
Windows converts CMYK color to RGB when the file is converted or printed.	■ Apply CMYK colors in EPS graphics only, because EPS graphics preserve the original colors. ■ Check converted colors; if unacceptable, convert the color to RGB in FrameMaker.
Distiller might alter color during PDF conversion (for example, it can convert RGB color to sRGB, the RGB color standard optimized for onscreen display).	If you own Adobe Acrobat, create your own Distiller job option profile that leaves the color unchanged. Refer to the Adobe Acrobat documentation for more information.
Colors in different browsers don't match.	Apply colors from the Online color library. They're designed to display uniformly in web browsers.

Table 20-3. Common Online Color Problems

Part VI

Advanced Techniques

CHAPTER 21

Setting Up Conditional Text

Conditional text lets you identify sections as belonging to a particular version of a document. By assigning condition tags to various sections and then showing and hiding the condition tags in different combinations, you change the information that is displayed. You can maintain two or more versions of the same document in a single file. For example, an instructor could set up a file that includes the questions and the answers for an exam. In this scenario, the condition tag ExamAnswers is applied to the answers. The instructor hides the ExamAnswers information to print out the exam for students and then displays ExamAnswers to print out the answer key.

Exam

Question 1: What is Avogadro's number? What is it for?

Question 2: What is the Pythagorean theorem?

Answer Key

Question 1: What is Avogadro's number? What is it for?

Answer: 6.023×10^{23}
Extra credit for describing its use in chemistry. Extra extra credit for using the word "mole."

Question 2: What is the Pythagorean theorem?

Answer: In a right triangle, the square of the hypotenuse is equal to the sum of the squares of the other sides.

How Conditional Text Works

When you show and hide conditional text, FrameMaker automatically repaginates the document. A section of hidden conditional text is collapsed into a single (nonprinting) marker, and the text that follows automatically moves up into the space that the hidden conditional text occupied. When you show hidden conditional text, the text that follows automatically moves down to make room for the newly displayed information.

Conditional text is showing.

Conditional text is hidden.

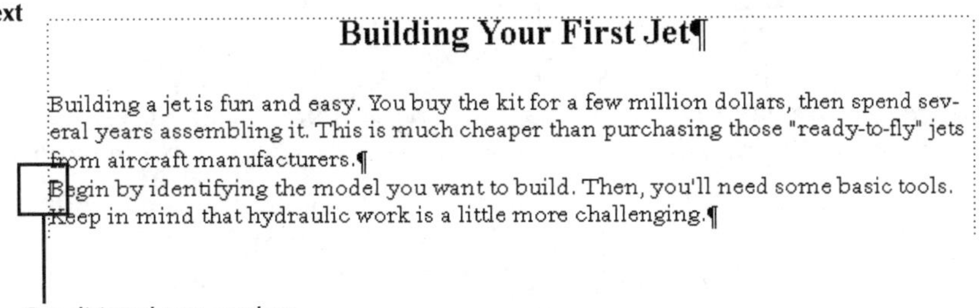

Conditional text marker indicates hidden text.

CAUTION Do not delete the conditional text marker; this will delete the entire section of hidden conditional text! Fortunately, FrameMaker warns you when you are about to delete a conditional text marker.

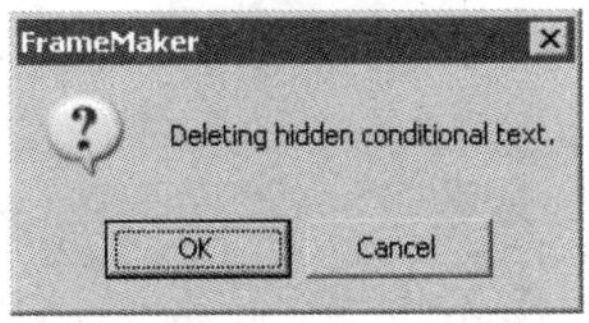

Some Conditional Text Examples

To create two versions of a document, you usually need two condition tags—one for information that's unique to version A and one for information that's unique to version B. (If only one version has unique information, you need only one condition tag.) Any information that's common to both versions is not tagged (that is, you leave it unconditional).

CAUTION A common mistake is to apply all available condition tags to information that's used in all versions. If the information is never hidden, it does not need a condition tag.

If you're creating FrameMaker documents for print and online delivery, you could create two condition tags: Print and Online. Conceptual information and graphics could be tagged Print; lists of related topics could be Online. Typically, the Print and Online condition tags are mutually exclusive—you would not apply both tags to the same information.

When you create additional condition tags, the complexity of managing the versions increases. Consider a situation where you need to document two versions of a single product—a Light version and a Professional version. The two products are used by different people, so you've decided to create two books: *Widget Light User's Guide* and *Widget Professional User's Guide*. The content of the two books is quite similar; the Professional guide just contains more information than the Light version. For this, you could create a single Pro condition tag. But in addition to that, you need to manage the printed and online information, so you also need Print and Online condition tags.

Previous versions of FrameMaker required you to create multiple condition tags, some of which incorporate multiple forms of output (for example, ProPrint for information that's intended for the printed *Widget Professional User's Guide*). FrameMaker 8 lets you create condition expressions, which are statements that include and exclude combinations of condition tags to create the intended output. (See "Showing or Hiding Conditional Text Using Expressions" on page 539 for details on this new feature.)

With FrameMaker 8, you can use either of two methods to show or hide conditional text. Show as per Condition uses the Show and Hide fields. Show as per Expression lets you build expressions that process combinations of condition tags.

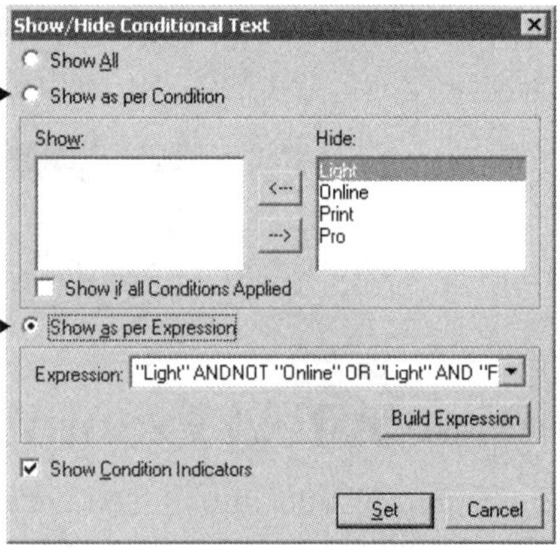

Applying Condition Tags

Although the feature is called conditional *text*, you can apply condition tags to many different items in your documents, including the following:

- Text in the main flow, in text frames, or inside table cells
- Anchored frames
- Table rows
- Markers
- Cross-references

- Variables
- Equations

A few items *cannot* be made conditional. They include the following:

- Text lines or text inside a text line
- Graphic (unanchored) frames
- Graphics that are not in frames
- Table cells or columns (but you *can* conditionalize text inside a table cell)

To apply a condition tag, follow these steps:

1. Select the information that you want to make conditional.
2. Select Special➤Conditional Text➤Apply Conditional Text. The Conditional Text dialog box is displayed (Figure 21-1).

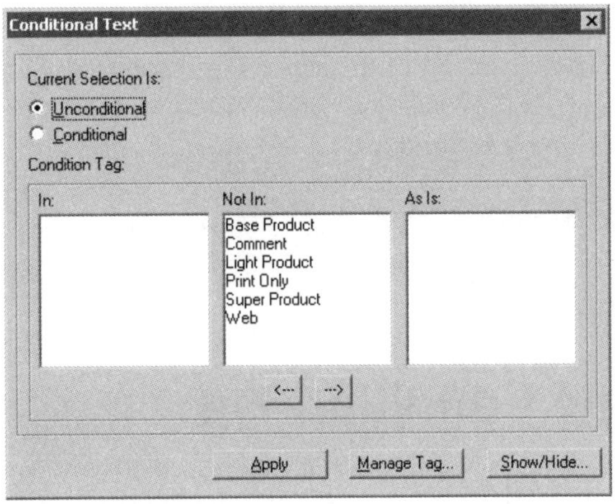

Figure 21-1. Applying conditional text

   All of the condition tags that are defined in the document are listed in the Not In list, indicating that the selected text does not have a condition tag applied to it.

3. Click the condition tag you want to apply to the selected items, then click the left arrow button to move it to the In list.
4. Make sure that all other condition tags are in the Not In list—unless you want to apply multiple condition tags.
5. Click the Apply button. The selected information is now tagged with the condition tag you chose. You can verify this in two ways:
   - Many condition tags have colors or special formatting (such as an underline or a strikethrough) associated with them (see page 529). If the formatting of the selected text changes, you know that you applied the

condition tag successfully. Keep in mind, though, that this formatting change occurs only if your condition indicators (discussed on page 526) are turned on.

- The status bar indicates the condition tag for the selected text.

In this example, conditional text is red and underlined.

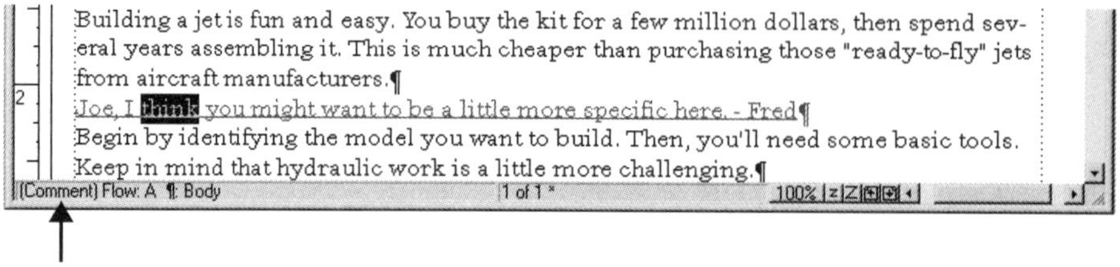

The status bar shows the current condition tag in parentheses.

You can use keyboard shortcuts to apply condition tags. To do so, follow these steps:

1. Select the items that you want to make conditional.
2. Press CTRL-4. The lower left of the status bar displays a `?:` prompt.
3. Type in the first few letters of the condition tag, or use the arrow keys to scroll through the list of condition tags.

4. When the tag you want is displayed in the status bar, press ENTER to apply it to the selected text.

Removing a Single Condition Tag

If you change your mind about a condition tag assignment, you can remove it. This process removes a single condition tag from the selected content. If you have several condition tags applied to the selected content and want to remove all of them at once, it's faster to remove all condition tags from the text, as described in the next section.

To remove a condition tag, follow these steps:

1. Select the item from which you want to remove the condition tag.
2. Select Special➤Conditional Text➤Apply Conditional Text. The Conditional Text dialog box is displayed (Figure 21-1 on page 523).
3. Move the condition tag that you want to remove into the Not In list.
4. Click the Apply button.

Applying Condition Tags to Tables and Graphics

In tables, you can apply condition tags to entire rows, or you can apply condition tags to text inside a table cell. You *cannot* apply condition tags to any of the following:

- A column in a table
- A cell or a group of cells in a table

For graphics, you can apply a condition tag to the anchored frame, which makes the entire graphic conditional, and to text inside the anchored frame, provided that the text is in a text frame. You *cannot* apply condition tags to any of the following graphic elements:

- An actual graphic—you must apply the condition tag to the anchored frame that surrounds the graphic. If the graphic is not inside an anchored frame, you cannot make it conditional.
- A text line or part of a text line.
- An unanchored frame.

You can accomplish the same thing using keyboard shortcuts. Follow these steps:

1. Select the item from which you want to remove the condition tag.
2. Press CTRL-5. The lower left of the status bar displays an upside-down question mark.
3. Type in the first few letters of the condition tag, or use the arrow keys to scroll through the list of condition tags.
4. When the tag you want to remove is displayed in the status bar, press ENTER.

Removing All Condition Tags from Text

To remove all condition tags from text, follow these steps:

1. Select the text you want to make unconditional.
2. Select Special➤Conditional Text➤Apply Conditional Text. The Conditional Text dialog box is displayed (Figure 21-1 on page 523).
3. Click the Unconditional radio button.
4. Click the Apply button.

There is also a keyboard shortcut available. Follow these steps:

1. Select the text you want to make unconditional.
2. Press CTRL-6.

TIP If you want to remove *all* condition tags throughout a document, show all of the conditional text, and then select all the content in the document and press CTRL-6. If you do not display all of the condition tags, pressing CTRL-6 removes condition tags from all of the currently shown text but does not change the hidden conditional text.

Using Condition Indicators

The style and colors that your condition tags use are called *condition indicators*. When you edit a file on screen, they make it easy to see which information uses which condition tag. When you finalize your content, though, you probably want conditional text to blend into the surrounding text.

You can turn off condition indicators, which control whether the condition tags provide color and style cues. Turning off condition indicators *does not* change, remove, show, or hide conditional text.

To turn the condition indicators on or off, follow these steps:

1. Select Special➤Conditional Text➤Show/Hide Conditional Text. The Show/Hide Conditional Text dialog box is displayed.

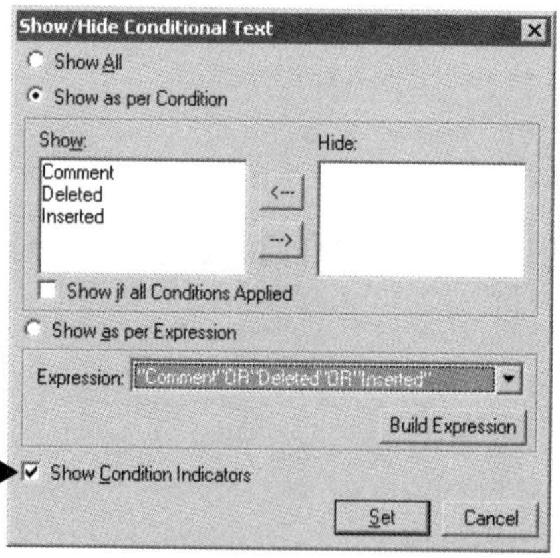

Show Condition Indicators check box

2. Check the Show Condition Indicators check box to display your condition indicators. Check the check box again to remove the condition indicators.
3. Click the Set button to apply your changes. Notice that although the text looks like regular text, the status bar still indicates that the text is conditional.

Planning Conditional Text

Before you create condition tags and start making your document conditional, some planning is advisable:

- **Analyze the information and identify the versions that are needed.** Determine which information is common to all versions (unconditional) and what information is needed in a specific version. Set a up a condition tag for each version.
- **Use distinct condition tag names.** Using names that are easily distinguished alphabetically makes maintenance easier. For example, instead of using "revision_3" and "revision_4," try "3rev" and "4rev." The latter two tags are much easier to distinguish in an alphabetical list. Even better would be something like "Dec2007" and "April2008."
- **Limit the number of condition tags to the bare minimum.** FrameMaker can handle a large number of tags, but the number of styles available as indicators makes smaller numbers more convenient. You can also use custom colors as indicators. If content has multiple condition tags applied, FrameMaker displays a mix of the colors. Often, these colors mix to brown or grayish black, especially as you apply more condition tags. The limiting factor in creating condition tags is not FrameMaker; it's the user's ability to manage and apply the condition tags correctly.

TIP In a department or workgroup, avoid "tag creep" by ensuring that condition tags are set up and maintained as part of the template. Generally, you do not want personal tags—such as JoesFirstDraft—to remain in your documents.

You may need more (sometimes many more) condition tags depending on how you specify which conditional text shows in the output. If you show by condition, each condition tag is either shown or hidden. If you show by expression, you can specify more complicated processing (for example, you might specify that content with the Online condition tag applied is shown only when the Pro condition is also applied). See "Choosing the Method for Showing Conditional Text" on page 533 for more information.

- **Assign condition tags based on whether you select Show as Per Condition or Show as per Expression.** The best way to tag your document varies depending on how you show the conditional text:
  - If you show by condition, avoid assigning multiple condition tags to the same information. Multiple condition tags are very difficult to maintain.
  - If you show by expression, assigning layers of all relevant tags to the content makes it much easier to use expressions for filtering. See "Examples of Expressions" on page 542 for details on how layering condition tags affects expressions.

When you begin applying condition tags, try to keep the tagging as simple as possible. Here are two recommendations:

- **If possible, tag entire paragraphs as conditional.** Conditional paragraphs are much easier to maintain than conditional sentences or words. If you must tag inside paragraphs, tag entire sentences. If your content is translated, sentence structure varies across languages, so tagging sentence fragments can cause serious translation problems.
- **Tag spaces consistently.** If you are tagging sentences, be consistent in whether you tag the space before and after the conditional part. If you are not consistent, when you hide the conditional text, you will have difficulties with missing spaces or two spaces in a row in your document. The same is true when tagging individual words or phrases.

If you need to transfer information from the database, save the information to a tab-delimited text file; then import that file into the new application. You can set several options, such as the line ending format, when you export the file. Just about every database should be able to accept tab-delimited text.

Common Condition Tags

The most difficult part of implementing conditional text is figuring out how to organize your information and set up the condition tags. Here are a few common uses for condition tags:

- **Different product levels.** If your product has multiple versions (such as Light, Standard, and Professional versions), you can break out the differences with conditional text.
- **Information that's under development.** Use conditional text to hide information that isn't appropriate for the current release of the documentation but needs to be included in the next version.
- **Review comments.** You can embed queries to reviewers or comments from reviewers using conditional text. This lets you hide the information and print out a clean draft. (Another alternative is to use a paragraph tag that's hard to miss—such as 14-point bold italic blue text.)
- **Platform differences.** Use Windows, Mac, and UNIX condition tags to manage platform-specific information.
- **Audience levels.** For a training manual, you might need Student and Instructor versions. Use condition tags to manage that information.
- **Delivery medium.** Conditional text is an important component of any single-sourcing effort. Use it to identify information that is delivered in a particular medium; you might have Print, PDF, and Online condition tags.

Alternatives to Conditional Text

In addition to conditional text, a few other techniques are available that let you set up different versions of information inside a document. Consider using these instead of—or in addition to—conditional text:

- **Variables.** For company names, product names, and other short pieces of text that are repeated throughout the document, consider using a variable. See Chapter 9, "Storing Content in Variables," for details.
- **Marker types.** You can use custom marker types for different types of indexed information. You can then include or exclude those markers when you generate the index. For example, you could use the Index marker type for most index entries and then use a custom RangeIndex marker for ranges (which you want to exclude from the online version of the index).

REMEMBER If hidden conditional text contains a marker, the information in that marker is not available. This means, for example, that an index entry is not generated for a marker inside hidden conditional text.

- **Graphics.** If you need to create two different versions of each graphic, one approach is to create two anchored frames and make them conditional. Perhaps a more efficient idea is to set up two sets of source graphic files and swap out the directories as needed. To make this work, you must have the same file names and three graphics directories—the directory in use, the directory for version A and the directory for version B. To swap files, you overwrite the content of the "in use" directory with the files from version A or version B.

Creating Condition Tags

When you have analyzed your content and figured out what condition tags you need, you're ready to create those tags.

To add a condition tag, follow these steps:

1. Select Special➤Conditional Text➤Manage Condition. The Manage Condition Tag dialog box is displayed.

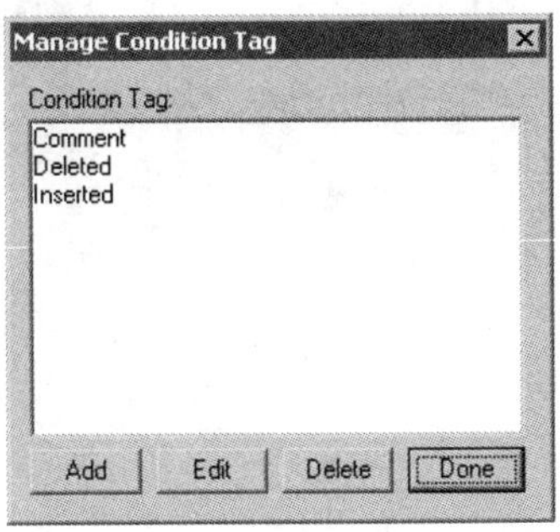

2. Click the Add button.

The Add Condition Tag dialog box is displayed.

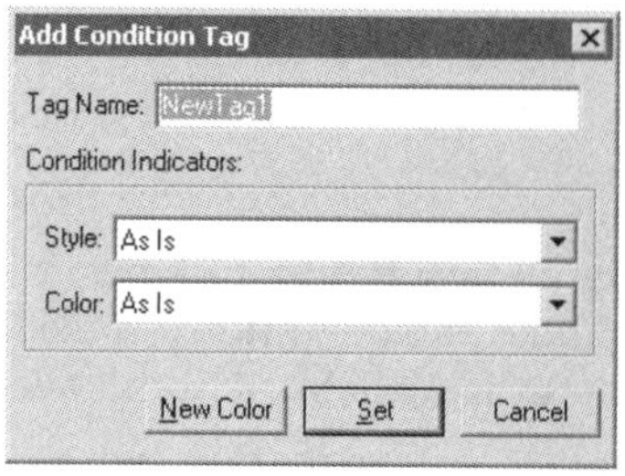

3. Type the new condition tag's name in the Tag Name field.
4. Set the condition indicators. You can set this condition tag to use a style (such as an underline), a color, or both.
   a. In the Style drop-down list, select a style for this condition tag. If you do not want to use a style, select As Is.
   b. In the Color drop-down list, select a color for this condition tag. If you do not want to use a color, select As Is.

   The colors listed are taken from the color catalog. If the color you want isn't available, click the New Color button to add a new color to the color definitions, and then select it from the drop-down list for your condition tag.

   The colors and styles you assign to your condition tags can be hidden before you print the document. See "Using Condition Indicators" on page 526.
5. Click the Set button to add the new the condition tag.
6. Click the Done button to close the Manage Condition Tag dialog box.

After you create the condition tag, it is listed in the Conditional Text dialog box, and you can apply it to content in your document.

Modifying Condition Tags

To edit a condition tag, follow these steps:

1. Select Special➤Conditional Text➤Manage Condition. The Manage Condition Tag dialog box is displayed.

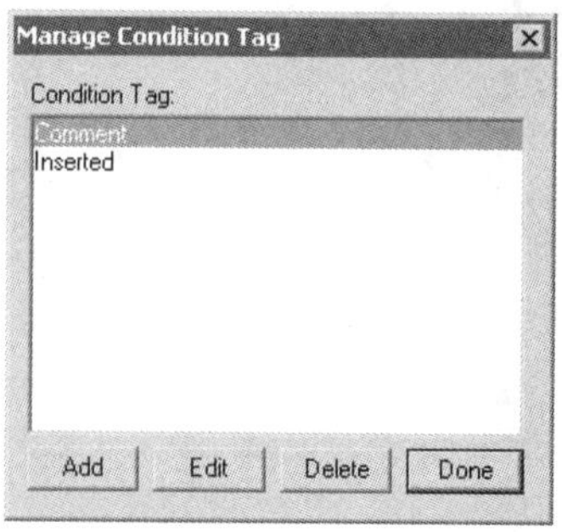

2. Click on the tag, then click the Edit button.

   The Edit Condition Tag dialog box is displayed with the settings for the selected tag.

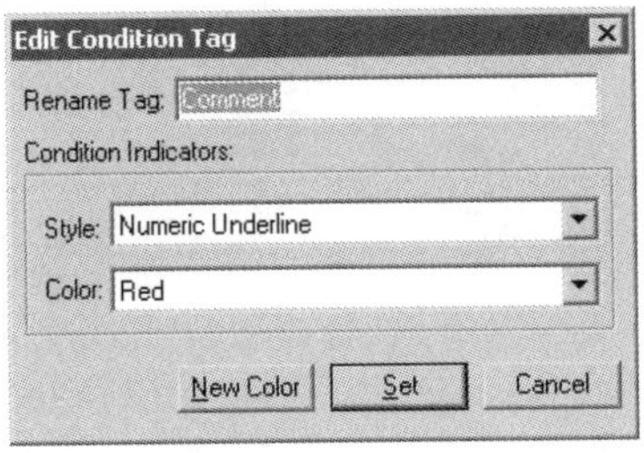

3. *(optional)* To rename the tag, type a new name in the Rename Tag field. Any text with the original condition tag applied uses the new condition tag name.

   A message is displayed to let you know that expressions may be affected if you have defined any. (The expressions stay as they are, so if you have used the condition tag within an expression, the expression still includes the old name. See "Building Expressions" on page 540 for more information.)
4. Set the condition indicators as described in "Creating Condition Tags" on page 529.

Deleting a Condition Tag

You can delete condition tags from your document. If some text has one condition tag applied to it and you delete that condition tag, you can either delete that text (along with the condition tag itself) or make the text unconditional. If a particular piece of text uses more than one condition tag, the deleted tag is removed from your file, but the text stays in your file with the remaining condition tags still applied.

To delete a condition tag, follow these steps:

1. Select Special➤Conditional Text➤Manage Condition. The Manage Condition Tag dialog box is displayed.
2. Select the tag that you want to delete.
3. Click the Delete button. A dialog box is displayed telling you that deleting condition tags can affect expressions. Click the OK button to continue.

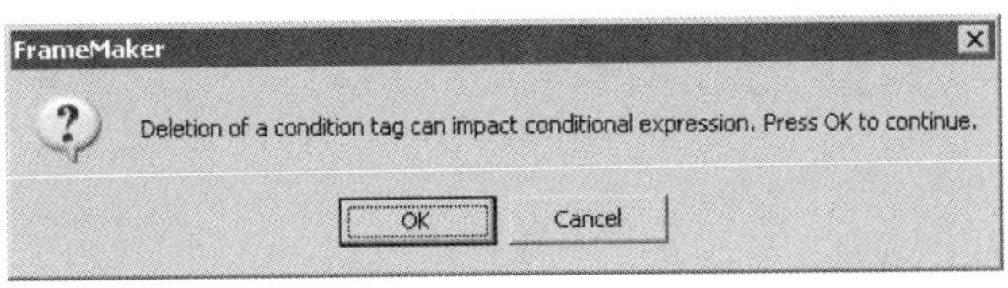

4. If the specified tag is applied to some text in your document, a dialog box is displayed:

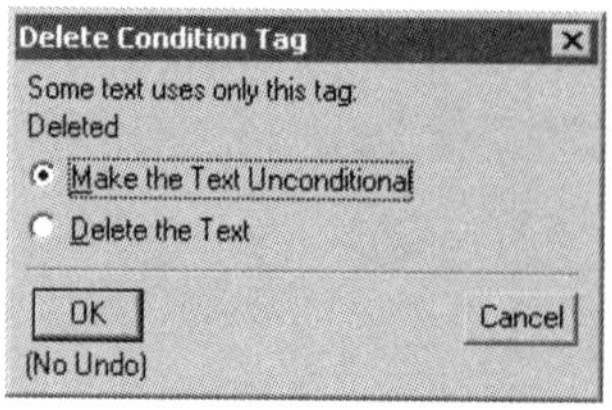

To delete the text that uses only this condition tag, click the Delete the Text radio button. To remove the condition tag and make the text unconditional, click the Make the Text Unconditional radio button.

5. Click the OK button to delete the condition tag.

Showing and Hiding Conditional Text

After you have assigned condition tags in your document, you can show and hide each condition tag individually, or you can create expressions to show or hide sets of conditional text. FrameMaker dynamically repaginates your document whenever you show or hide information.

CAUTION If you hide a cross-reference marker and a cross-reference that points at the marker is still shown, the cross-reference becomes unresolved. To prevent this problem, be sure that the cross-reference and the cross-reference marker always have the same condition settings. You can also make all cross-reference markers unconditional. After changing show/hide settings, update the book so that the generated files are correct.

Showing All Conditional Text

To show or hide all the conditional text in your document, follow these steps:

1. Select Special➤Conditional Text➤Show/Hide Conditional Text. The Show/Hide Conditional Text dialog box is displayed (Figure 21-2).
2. Click the Show All radio button.
3. Click the Set button. The document displays all conditional text.

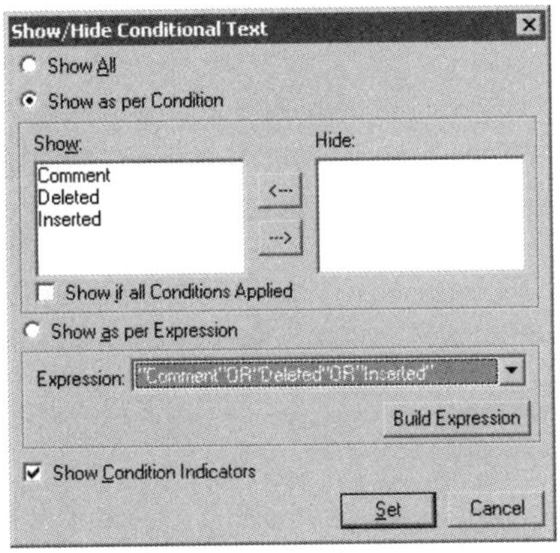

Figure 21-2. Showing or hiding conditional text

TIP Show all conditional text while you are revising a document to be sure you don't miss anything.

4. Update the book that the file belongs to so that pagination and cross-references are updated.

TIP To show or hide all conditional text in a book, go to your book file, select all of the files in the book, then select View➤Show/Hide Conditional Text.

Choosing the Method for Showing Conditional Text

You can show conditional text either using the traditional Show/Hide box (Show as per Condition) or, beginning with FrameMaker 8, using expressions you create (Show as per Expression). The number of condition tags that you have in a document affects how you choose to show your conditional text, but the biggest factor is how many different groupings (or *dimensions*) of condition tags there are.

Here are some examples:

- One dimension: Each condition tag identifies a different product (for example, Light, Standard, and Pro).
- Two dimensions: The document has condition tags for both products (Light, Pro) and output types (Print, Online).
- Three dimensions: The document has condition tags for products, output types, and platforms (Windows, Mac, and UNIX).

Figure 21-3 on page 534 shows three dimensions of conditional text.

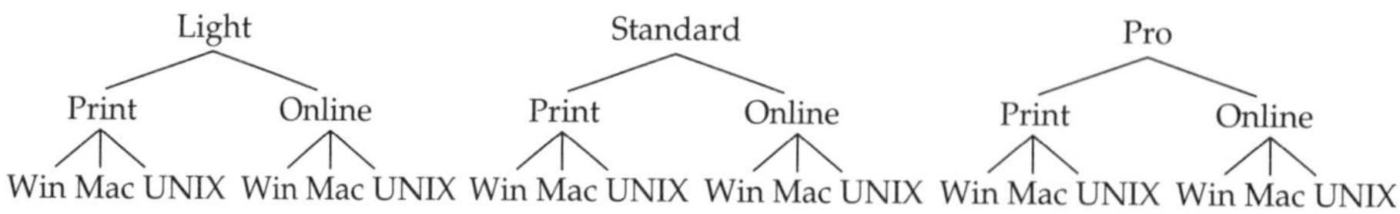

Figure 21-3. Three dimensions of conditional text

In general, show as per condition is easier if you have a single dimension of conditional text or only a few dimensions. Showing by expression is probably worth the trouble if you have many dimensions to your conditional text. You can also use expressions to create new output from existing content that already has condition tags applied (although it won't be easy).

As you add other dimensions of conditional text, the number of condition tags you need increases, especially if you are showing by condition. For example, if you want to create a print version of the document for the Light product on the Windows platform, you may need extra conditions for LightPrint, LightWindows, and even LightPrintWindows. Using an expression, you would need only the Light, Print, and Windows condition tags. Even so, expressions are difficult to create, test, and maintain, so consider whether creating the extra tags and showing by condition may still be worthwhile.

NOTE If you need to use complex combinations of condition tags, consider setting up a workflow in the structured interface of FrameMaker. Structured documents allow you to create versions based on attributes, which are easier to use and more powerful than expressions. For more information, refer to *Publishing Fundamentals: Structured FrameMaker 8*.

The number of tags you need to have (and the number you need to apply to the text) varies depending on the conditional text methods you use. The following sections provide details.

Tags Needed for Show as Per Condition

If you are using the Show as per Condition method, you can avoid applying layers of conditional tags to your content, or you can do the opposite and use layered tags. Both have advantages and disadvantages.

NOTE Discussions of conditional text become complicated quickly. To illustrate the concepts clearly, the examples that follow in this section assume that you always apply either a single condition tag or layers of condition tags. Of course, you could mix these methods to have some conditional text with a single tag and other chunks with layered tags.

Text tagged with a single condition tag When you apply condition tags to your content, the status line shows the names of the condition tags that are applied to the selected text. If you apply only one condition tag to a piece of content, the status line has enough space to display the name of that one condition tag. Also, the colors you define for your condition tags are easy to distinguish when you apply individual tags (as opposed to blended colors). Because it's easier to manage condition tags when you can see which ones are applied, the traditional advice has been to avoid layering condition tags whenever practical.

NOTE Before FrameMaker 8, any text that had two or more condition tags was always displayed in magenta. FrameMaker 8 blends the colors (often producing brown or gray).

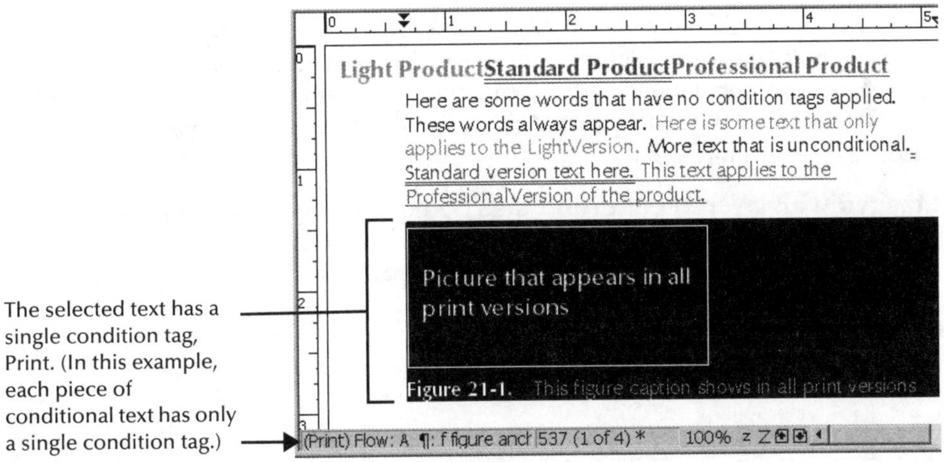

Figure 21-4. Using a single tag for text that appears in all print editions

The downside of avoiding layered condition tags is that you need more tags. For example, suppose that you have only the three dimensions shown in Figure 21-3, and you don't want to layer any condition tags. Assuming that there is no overlapping content within a dimension (for example, all content is unique among Light, Standard, and Pro, between Print and Online, and among Win, Mac, and UNIX), then you need the 32 condition tags shown in Figure 21-5 on page 536.

Light Standard Pro			
Print Online	LightPrint StandardPrint ProPrint	LightOnline StandardOnline ProOnline	
Win Mac UNIX	LightPrintWin StandardPrintWin ProPrintWin LightOnlineWin StandardOnlineWin ProOnlineWin	LightPrintMac StandardPrintMac ProPrintMac LightOnlineMac StandardOnlineMac ProOnlineMac	LightPrintUNIX StandardPrintUNIX ProPrintUNIX LightOnlineUNIX StandardOnlineUNIX ProOnlineUNIX

Figure 21-5. Condition tags needed for Show as per Condition with no layered tags

If there is some text that appears across a dimension (for example, some text appears in both Light and Standard, so you would need tags like LightStandard, LightStandardPrint, LightStandardPrintWin, and so on), then you need even more tags: up to 47 instead of 32. If you need other dimensions, the number of required condition tags is far more.

Text tagged with layered condition tags Another choice is to apply layers of condition tags. In this case, you only need 18 tags, which doesn't seem bad in comparison to 32 or 47 tags. The condition tags are all hybrid tags such LightPrintWin, as shown in Figure 21-6.

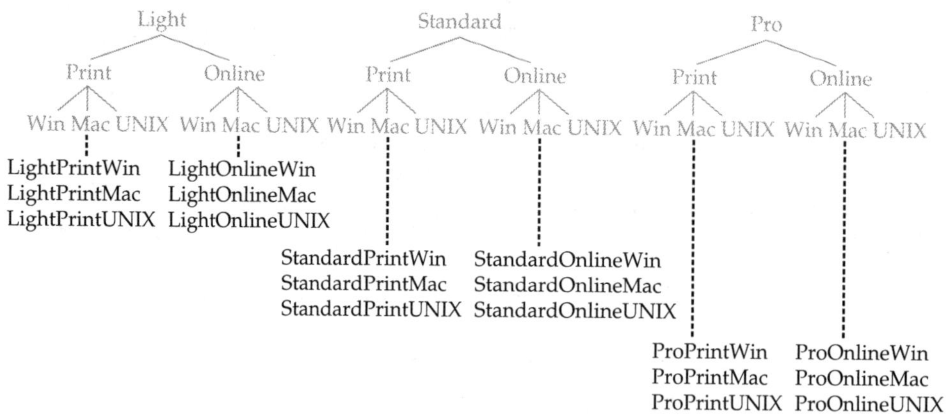

Figure 21-6. Condition tags needed for Show as per Condition with layers

In Figure 21-4 on page 535, text that appeared in all printed output—but not in the online output—had a single condition tag (Print) applied. If you use layered condition tags, you must apply all nine condition tags that are used for the different printed versions of the document (Figure 21-7).

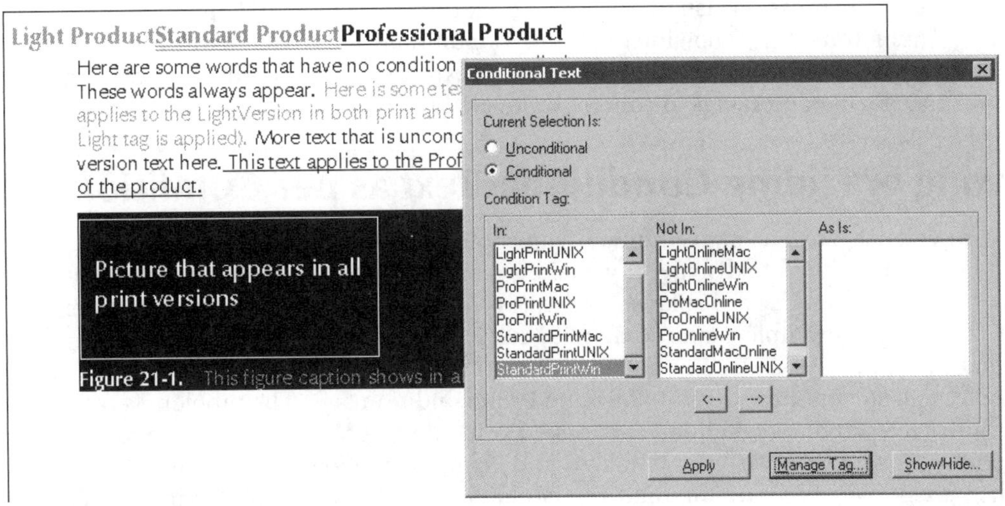

Figure 21-7. Layered condition tags for print versions

If you have a piece of text that appears in every version except, for example, LightPrintMac, you must apply all 17 of the other condition tags to exclude that one condition tag. To make sure you include all needed condition tags, display the Conditional Text dialog box instead of using the keyboard shortcuts like CTRL + 4. You can't see that many condition tags displayed in the status line. Also, after you apply a few condition tags, the blended colors will look muddy, so you can't rely on color to reveal whether you have applied all the tags.

Tags Needed for Show as per Expression

If you are using the Show as per Expression method to create output for the example shown in Figure 21-3, you again have the choice of applying either single or layered condition tags. In both cases, you need only eight condition tags (Figure 21-8).

Light
Standard
Pro

Print
Online

Win
Mac
UNIX

Figure 21-8. Show as per Expression requires fewer condition tags.

NOTE Using expressions isn't necessarily easier than creating and applying numerous tags. "Showing or Hiding Conditional Text Using Expressions" on page 539 provides detailed examples of expressions required when you apply single condition tags to content or layers of condition tags.

Showing or Hiding Conditional Text as per Condition

When you use Show as per Condition, you show or hide conditional text by selecting which condition tags to display. If you show a specific condition tag, all text marked with that condition tag is displayed, regardless of what other condition tags are applied to the text. For example, suppose that you have Windows, Mac, Print, and Online condition tags in your document. You want to create a Windows/Print version of the document, so you show the Windows and Print condition tags. The problem is that text that has the Windows condition tag applied could be tagged with any of the following combinations: Windows only, Windows and Print, or Windows and Online. If you show the Windows condition, then you could potentially display text that is intended for both the print and online versions. To solve the problem, create and apply additional condition tags as needed.

To show or hide conditional text by condition, follow these steps:

1. Select Special➤Conditional Text➤Show/Hide Conditional Text. The Show/Hide Conditional Text dialog box is displayed.

All text that has the Light, LightPrint, or Print condition tags is displayed.

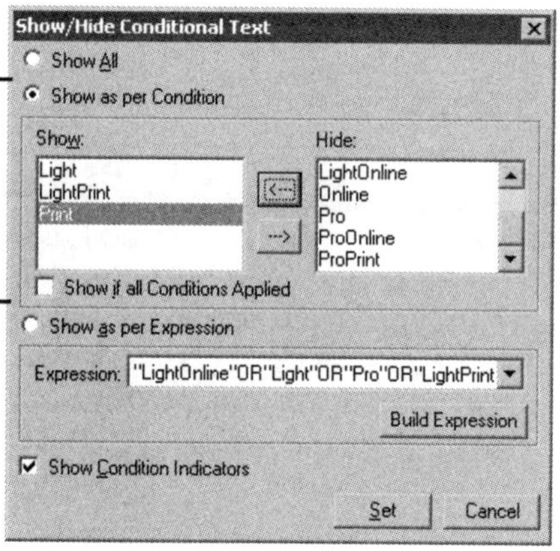

2. To change which condition tags are displayed, do any of the following:
   - To show a condition tag, select it, then click the left arrow button to move it to the Show list on the left.
   - To hide a condition tag, select it, then click the right arrow button to move it to the Hide list on the right.
   - Select the Show If All Conditions Applied check box if you want text to show (as if it were unconditional) when every condition tag is applied to the text—even if you have moved all of the condition tags into the Hide list on the right.

3. Click the Set button. The document displays the condition tags you've specified.
4. Update the book that the file belongs to so that pagination and cross-references are updated.

Showing or Hiding Conditional Text Using Expressions

To show or hide conditional text by creating an expression, follow these steps:

1. Select Special➤Conditional Text➤Show/Hide Conditional Text. The Show/Hide Conditional Text dialog box is displayed (Figure 21-9).

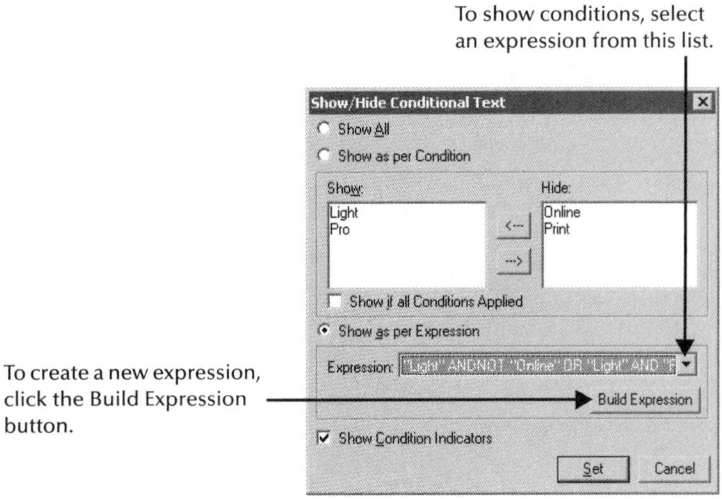

Figure 21-9. Show/Hide Conditional Text dialog box

2. To change which conditional text is displayed, do one of the following:
   - Select an expression from the Expression drop-down list in the Show as per Expression area.
   - Click the Build Expression button, create your expression in the Build Expression dialog box, then click Set to close the Build Expression dialog box. For more information about how to build expressions, see "Building Expressions" on page 540.
3. Click the Set button. The document displays the conditional text you specified.
4. Update the book that the file belongs to so that pagination and cross-references are updated.

Building Expressions

To show or hide text using an expression, first create the expression in the Build Expression dialog box:

1. Select Special➤Conditional Text➤Show/Hide Conditional Text. The Show/Hide Conditional Text dialog box is displayed (Figure 21-9 on page 539).
2. Click the Build Expression button. The Build Expression dialog box is displayed.

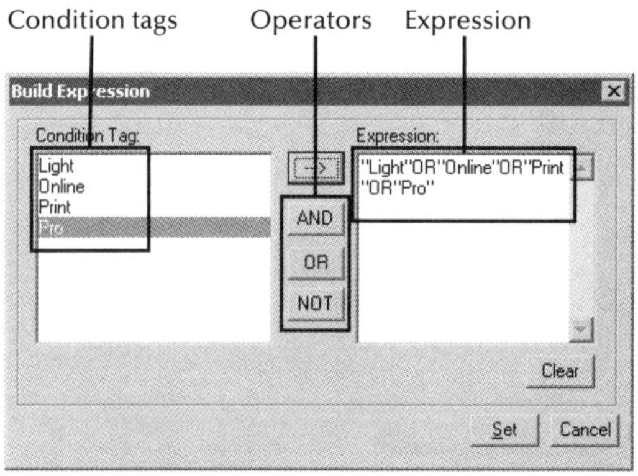

The Build Expression dialog box lists the defined condition tags on the left. The operators (AND, OR, NOT) that let you combine condition tags are located on buttons in the center. The expression is displayed on the right.

NOTE Within the expression, condition tags are enclosed in straight double quotes, which ensures that condition tags with spaces in their names are processed correctly.

When you build expressions, you specify an operator or a condition tag, then provide additional operators and tags to create your expression.

3. To start a new expression, click the Clear button. (To edit an existing expression, see "Modifying Expressions" on page 542.)
4. To build expressions, specify an operator or a condition tag and then provide additional operators and tags to create your expression:
   - To add a condition tag to the end of the expression, click the condition tag in the Condition Tag list on the left, then click the arrow --> button. Double-clicking the condition tag also works.
   - To add operators to the end of the expression, click operator buttons:

Operator	Usage
AND	The AND operator connects two or more two condition tags; both condition tags must be applied to the text for it to be displayed. For example, `"Light" AND "Print"` means that the content is shown when it has *both* the Light and Print condition tags applied. (Text that has only one of the condition tags applied is hidden.) The AND operator can connect more than two condition tags; for example, `"Light" AND "Print" AND "Windows"` means that all three condition tags must be applied to the text for it to be shown.
OR	Like the AND operator, the OR operator connects two condition tags; if either of the condition tags is applied, the text is displayed. For example, `"Light" OR "Print"` means that any content that has either of these condition tags applied is shown. OR is the default operator, so specifying only `"Windows"` means that all the text with the Windows condition tag is displayed. (Note that using Show as per Condition produces the same results as specifying an expression using only the OR operator.)
NOT	NOT excludes the condition tag that immediately follows it from what is shown. For example, `NOT "Online"` means that all conditional text that does not have the Online condition tag applied is displayed.
ANDNOT	Click the AND button and then click the NOT button to create the operator ANDNOT. The ANDNOT operator connects two operators to limit what is shown. For example, "Light" ANDNOT "Mac" shows all the content with the Light condition tag applied except the content that has both the Light and Mac condition tags applied.

NOTE Unconditional text is never affected by expressions.

5. Click the Set button.

TIP Expressions can be challenging. Create test documents that use all your defined condition tags and test creating all the output variations you will need with the expressions you create.

Modifying Expressions

To edit an existing expression, display the expression in the Build Expression dialog box and type your changes. You can use the buttons in the Build Expression dialog box to add the condition tags or operators only to the end of the expression.

You can type spaces between the condition tags and operators to make it easier to read the expressions (for example, `"Light"AND"Online"` produces the same result as `"Light" AND "Online"`).

Often, it is easier to keep track of your expressions if you paste them from the Build Expression dialog box into a text document where you can add notes that explain what the expression is used. If you then paste text from that text document into an expression, make sure that there is no space at the beginning of the expression or FrameMaker will reject the expression as invalid. Also, line breaks aren't accepted, so don't paste those in.

Be sure to use straight double quotes around the condition tag names. These are inserted automatically when you use the Build Expression dialog box to build the expression, but be sure you don't paste any curly quotes into the expression.

You cannot add parentheses to the expressions, so test thoroughly to make sure you are getting the results you expect.

Deleting Expressions

As you are testing and creating new expressions, the list of expressions grows quickly. FrameMaker includes at least one expression by default (an OR expression that includes all the tags and is equivalent to Show All). If you rename any condition tags, FrameMaker also adds some expressions to the list of expressions, but it doesn't update the expressions you have already created. It is difficult to keep track of the expressions, so you will want to delete the extraneous ones.

To delete expressions, you must save the file as MIF, search on Condition, find the expressions, and delete the ones you don't need. See Chapter 24, "Maker Interchange Format," for information about editing MIF files.

Examples of Expressions

As described earlier in the chapter, you can create condition tags for the different versions you want to produce. For the following examples, there are two dimensions of condition tags: product (Light and Pro) and output type (Print and Online).

Expressions are powerful, and you can use them to include or exclude almost all possible combinations of condition tags. Depending on how the condition tags are applied in the document, the expressions you need to create can be very simple or very complex. In previous versions of FrameMaker, it was good practice to avoid using many layers of condition tags, but using multiple layers can greatly simplify the expressions you need. The following sections show two ways to apply the four condition tags (Light, Pro, Print, and Online) and to build the resulting expressions that produce identical results for Light/Print, Light/Online, Pro/Print, and Pro/Online output.

Example of Layered Condition Tags and Resulting Expressions

For this example, there are four condition tags: Light and Pro are the tags for one dimension (product), and Print and Online form another dimension (output type). If you always layer at least two condition tags (one from each dimension) on all conditional text, the expressions you need are straightforward.

In the following sample document, none of the conditional text has fewer than two condition tags applied (Figure 21-10). For this example, some content applies only to the Light or Pro product. The print version includes pictures and figure captions that aren't included in the online version. The online version includes a list of related topics that doesn't appear in print.

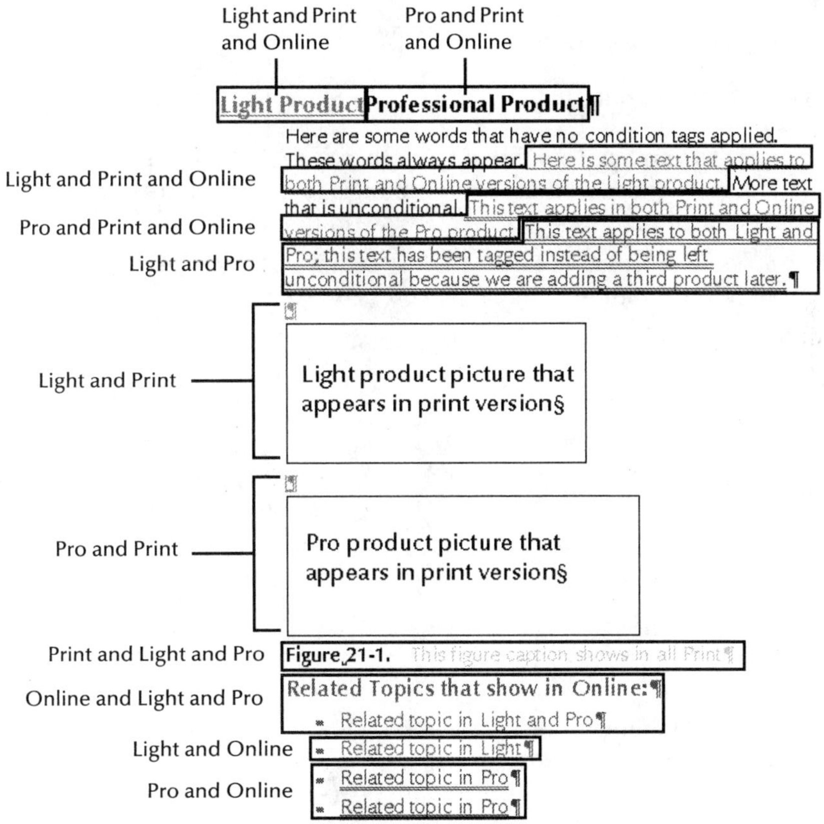

Figure 21-10. All conditional text has condition tags from each dimension applied.

If you apply condition tags from each possible dimension to all the conditional text, you need to use only the AND operator when you build the expressions. For example, to create the Light product's print version, create an expression that shows all the text that has both the Light and Print condition tags applied:

```
"Light" AND "Print"
```

Figure 21-11 shows the resulting output for Light/Print.

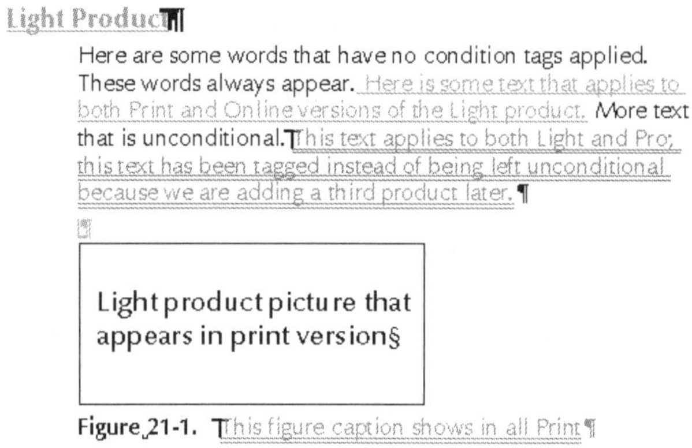

Figure 21-11. Light/Print output

The conditional text can have condition tags other than Light and Print applied and that won't affect the output. The important thing is to make sure that both Light and Print are applied to all the text you want to show in this version.

The expressions for the other versions are just as simple. To create the online version for the Light product, build the following expression:

```
"Light" AND "Online"
```

Figure 21-12 shows the resulting output for Light/Online.

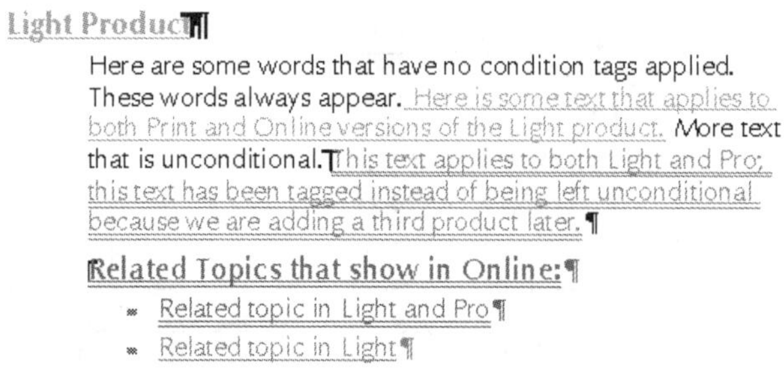

Figure 21-12. Light/Online output

To create the print version for the Professional product, build the following expression:

```
"Pro" AND "Print"
```

Figure 21-13 shows the resulting output for Pro/Print.

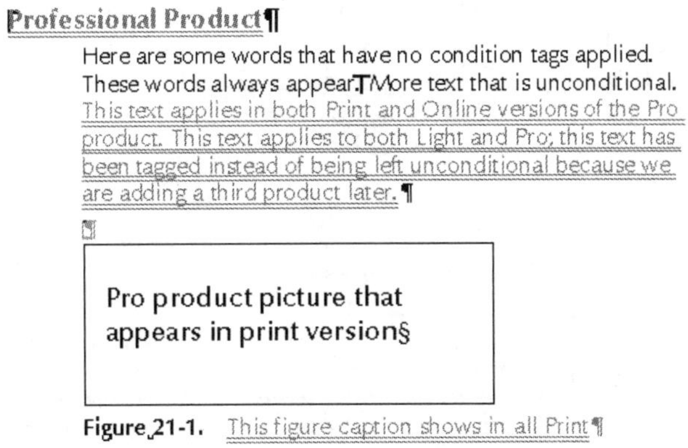

Figure 21-13. Pro/Print output

To create the print version for the Professional product, build the following expression:

```
"Pro" AND "Online"
```

Figure 21-14 shows the resulting output for Pro/Online.

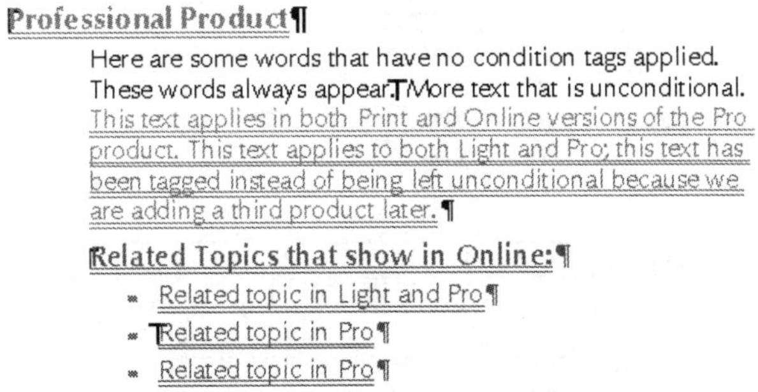

Figure 21-14. Pro/Online output

REMEMBER Applying multiple condition tags to all conditional text isn't required, but it allows you to use much simpler expressions.

Example of Traditional Condition Tagging and Resulting Expressions

Traditionally, it has been considered a best practice to avoid layering condition tags when possible. For example, if a piece of content appeared in all print versions, writers would apply only the Print condition tag. You can still write expressions to process content that is tagged this way, but the expressions can become extremely complicated, because the expression must exclude any content that has the Print condition tag applied but doesn't belong in the output you are trying to create.

The sample document shown in Figure 21-15 is similar to Figure 21-10 on page 543, but the conditional text doesn't always have layers. The conditional text sometimes has only a single condition tag. Also, the conditional text may not include condition tags from both the product dimension (Light or Pro) and the output type dimension (Print or Online).

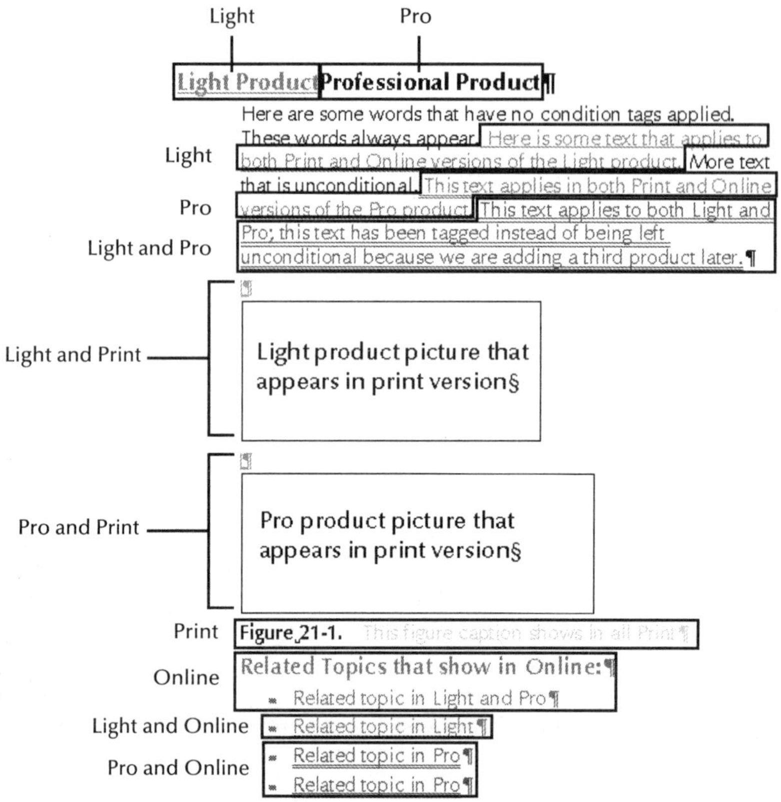

Figure 21-15. Much of the conditional text in this example does not include condition tags from all dimensions.

This following expression produces the same Light/Print output previously shown in Figure 21-11 on page 544:

```
"Light" ANDNOT "Online" OR "Light" AND "Print" OR "Print" ANDNOT
"Pro"
```

Logically, you can break the expression at the OR operators to separate the expression into understandable pieces (but omit the line breaks when you build the expression).

Here is an explanation of what this expression is doing:

`"Light" ANDNOT "Online"`	Shows all the conditional text that has the Light condition tag applied *except* for the content that has both the Light and Online condition tags applied. Because this expression produces Light/ Print version, we want to exclude any content that is intended only for the Light/Online version.
`OR "Light" AND "Print"`	Shows conditional text tagged with both Light and Print. This part of the expression might not be needed, but if there are pieces that have Light, Print, and Online condition tags all three applied, this line includes those.
`OR "Print" ANDNOT "Pro"`	Shows conditional text with only the Print condition tag applied, but excludes content that has both the Print and Pro condition tags applied. If you apply only the Print condition tag to content, you are logically marking that content as being Print, but not Light, not Pro, and not Online. You need this line to process any content that is marked with only the Print condition tag.

The expressions that create the other outputs are similar:

- **Light/Online.** This expression produces the output shown in Figure 21-12 on page 544:

  ```
  "Light" ANDNOT "Print"
  OR "Light "AND" Online"
  OR "Online "ANDNOT" Pro"
  ```

- **Professional/Print.** This expression produces the output shown in Figure 21-13 on page 545:

  ```
  "Pro" ANDNOT "Online"
  OR "Pro" AND "Print"
  OR "Print" ANDNOT "Light"
  ```

- **Professional/Online.** This expression produces the output shown in Figure 21-14 on page 545:

  ```
  "Pro" ANDNOT "Print"
  OR"Pro" AND "Online"
  OR"Online" ANDNOT "Light"
  ```

As you can see, conditional text lets you maintain multiple versions within a single document, but implementing conditional text can get messy. If you need to use conditional text extensively, consider setting up structured documents. For more information, refer to *Publishing Fundamentals: Structured FrameMaker 8*.

CHAPTER 22

Creating Interactive Content with Hypertext

Hypertext refers to online documents that are connected with links. In a printed document, you can supply links by instructing readers to "see page 88." The reader then turns to page 88 to find the relevant information. In online documents, hypertext lets you create a live link; to go from one topic to another, the reader clicks on the link and immediately jumps to the new information.

The term *hypertext* is also used for the features that make documents interactive (such as links). FrameMaker provides hypertext commands—for items such as links, pop-up alerts, and image maps—that let you create interactive online documents.

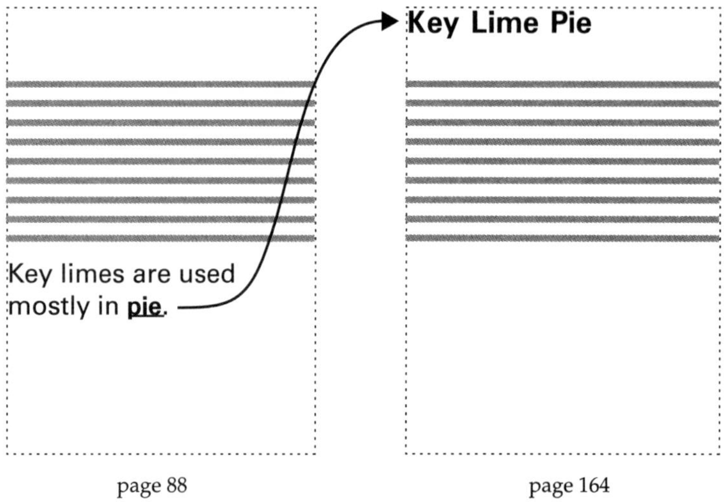

Initially, FrameMaker hypertext was developed for use in view-only FrameMaker documents. The FrameViewer and FrameReader products allowed others to read FrameMaker documents and use hypertext features. These document readers never really took off, though. Today, most online documents created from FrameMaker are distributed as PDF (Portable Document Format, also called Adobe Acrobat format) or HTML files.

Hypertext is irrelevant in print but available when you convert FrameMaker files to PDF or HTML files. Several of the FrameMaker hypertext commands, however, are only available in native FrameMaker documents. The FrameMaker-only commands are generally refinements of commands that work in other media; for example, the "jump to link" command works in all media but the "jump to link and open in a new window" works only in native FrameMaker files.

FrameMaker hypertext has become a critical part of a single-sourcing strategy because you can embed commands that are ignored in the print version but make the online files interactive.

Hypertext uses hypertext markers extensively. First, you insert a marker to identify a target, or *named destination,* with a keyword. To create a jump to that location, you insert a second marker that points to the named destination.

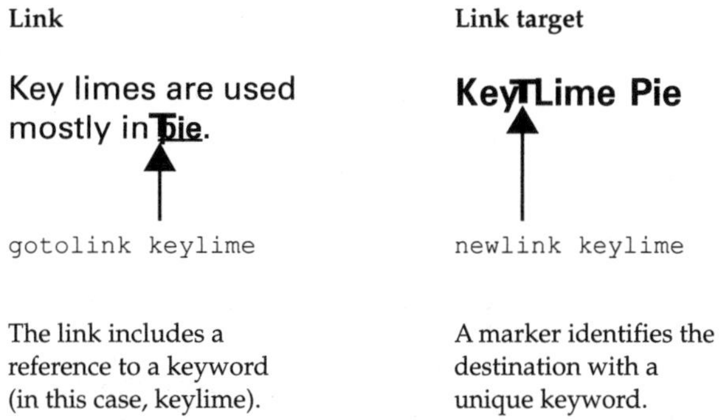

Cross-References vs. Hypertext

Cross-references are a specialized form of hypertext. When you create cross-references, FrameMaker automatically creates links for you, and these are also preserved in PDF or HTML files. In many cases, you can use both cross-references and hypertext to accomplish the same goal, and you can use both features in the same document. Here are some things to consider when you decide which feature to use for a particular link:

- You can automatically format cross-references by embedding character tags in the cross-reference definitions. For hypertext, you must apply character tags separately.
- Hypertext lets you make any area of text (or a graphic) a link. With cross-references, you generally need to use the text of the destination or a page reference.
- It's easier and faster to create cross-references. Hyperlinks are more time consuming.

As a general rule, it's a good idea to use cross-references whenever you can and to reserve hyperlinks for those situations where cross-references aren't flexible enough for the job. For example, assume that you have some information about rowing a boat. You can easily create cross-references that look like this:

- see "Rowing a boat" on page 77
- see page 77
- Rowing a boat

You need hypertext commands to create links with wording that doesn't exactly match the text of the heading:

- Before you begin, make sure you know how to row.
- Learn all about rowing.

When creating documents for online distribution, a very common requirement is a navigation bar. Users click a button in the bar to go to the next page in the document. You can set up hypertext links on the master pages of your document—like page numbers, their result changes for each body page. For example, you can set up a hyperlink with the nextpage command on a master page. On the body pages, the result is a link that takes the reader to the next page. When clicked on page 4, the link goes to page 5; from page 88, it goes to page 89.

This chapter describes how to create interactive hypertext features in your documents.

Hypertext Links in Generated Files

When you set up indexes, tables of contents, and other generated files, you can specify that entries become hypertext links by checking the Create Hypertext Links check box. (For complete instructions, see "Setting Up the Table of Contents File" on page 402.) After the generated file is created, the reader can jump from a page number in the file to the referenced item like any other hypertext link.

Setting Up a Basic Hypertext Link

A hypertext link lets the reader click an item and jump to another document or a different part of the current document. To create a hypertext link in FrameMaker, you need to complete three steps (described in detail in the sections that follow):

- Identify the target of the link
- Create a link to the target
- Create the link's active area in text

Identifying the Target of a Link

To identify a target, you must insert a hypertext marker that creates a *named destination*. A named destination serves as a unique label or identifier for a location in the document.

NOTE The named destination is equivalent to the cross-reference marker (with a unique numeric identifier) automatically inserted when you create a cross-reference.

To create a named destination for a link, follow these steps:

1. Click at the location where you want the target. That is, you need to set up a named destination where you want the link to end up.
2. Select Special➤Hypertext. The Hypertext dialog box is displayed (Figure 22-1).

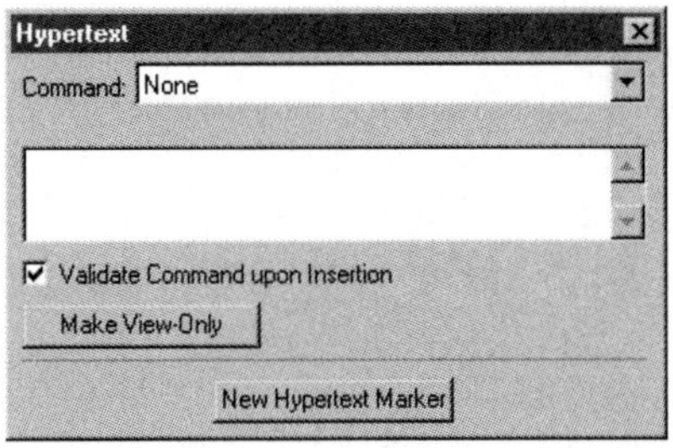

Figure 22-1. Creating a new hypertext marker

3. In the Command drop-down list, click Specify Named Destination. This inserts the newlink command into the text field.

TIP You can type **newlink** into the text field instead of selecting the command.

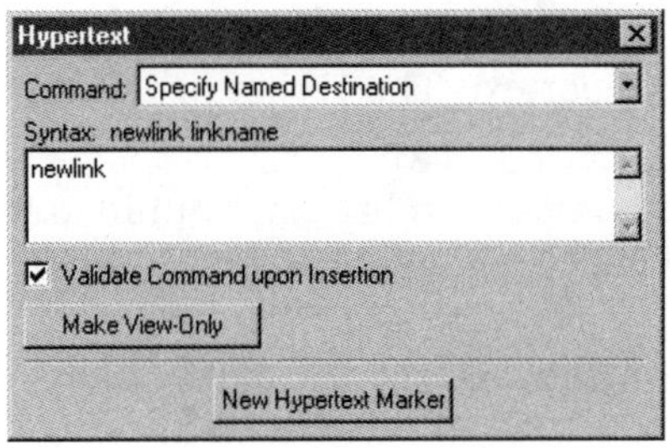

4. Type a name for this destination after newlink. To make maintenance easier, use alphanumeric, lowercase characters. We recommend avoiding spaces and keeping the names as short as possible; however, each named destination within a FrameMaker file must have a unique name. The marker text should look like this:

   ```
   newlink linkname
   ```

5. By default, the Validate Command Upon Insertion check box is checked. We recommend leaving it checked; FrameMaker will check the syntax of your hypertext command when you create the marker. (If you want to create the gotolink command before the newlink command, validation fails because the destination doesn't exist yet. In that case, you might want to uncheck the validation check box.)

CAUTION Clicking the Make View-Only button changes the entire document to view-only. This could be useful if you want to check hypertext links, but to change the document back to an editable state, you must type ESC SHIFT-F L K.

6. Click the New Hypertext Marker button to insert the new named destination. A new hypertext marker is created at the cursor location. The marker stores the named destination information for you.

Creating a Link to the Target

After identifying the link's destination, you create the link itself. You can create links within a single file or from one file to another.

If you create cross-file links, you must deliver all of the files to the customer. If FileA links to FileB, you must ship FileA and FileB to your readers. If you forget to send FileB, readers will encounter a broken link.

To create a hypertext link, follow these steps:

1. Position your cursor in the text where you want the link to occur. If the files are going to be sent out for translation, the translators will appreciate markers at the beginning or end of a word instead of in the middle of words.
2. Select Special➤Hypertext. The Hypertext dialog box is displayed (Figure 22-1 on page 553).
3. In the Command drop-down list, click Jump to Named Destination. This inserts the gotolink command into the text field.

TIP You can type **gotolink** into the text field instead of selecting the command.

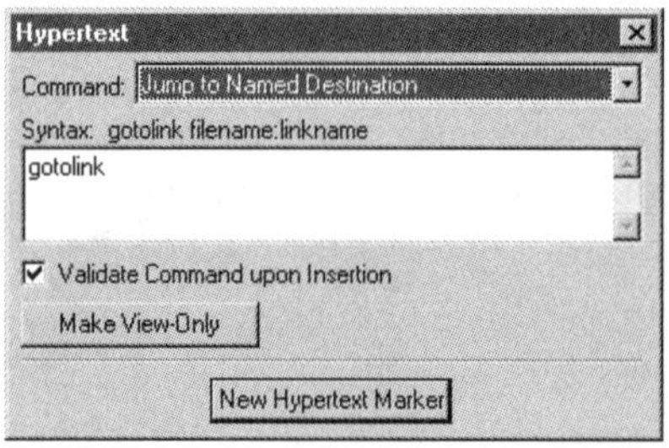

4. Type in the destination after gotolink. The *linkname* corresponds to the keyword you set up in the preceding section with the newlink command.

   For links within a file, use this syntax:

   ```
   gotolink linkname
   ```

   For links to another file in the same directory, use this syntax:

   ```
   gotolink file.fm:linkname
   ```

For links to a file in a different directory, use this syntax (be sure to use forward slashes and not backward slashes in the path name):

```
gotolink path/file.fm:linkname
```

5. Click the New Hypertext Marker button to insert the hypertext marker.

Creating the Active Area in Text

The active area is the "clickable" section of text that lets you use the hypertext link.

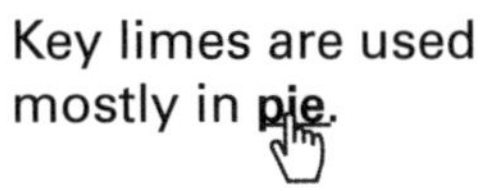

The word "pie" is the active area.

When you create a hypertext link, FrameMaker creates an active area in the paragraph where the link occurs. By default, the active area is the entire paragraph, but if you have any character tag formatting inside the paragraph, the active area stops where the character tag changes. If you want an entire paragraph to be active, the paragraph cannot contain any character tags or formatting overrides.

If you're delivering your files as PDF files for online viewing, consider setting up a special Hyperlink character tag, which sets the text to blue and underlined.

To specify an active area for a hyperlink, follow these steps:

1. Select the text you want to make active. The selected area must contain the hypertext marker you set up in the preceding section.
2. Apply a character tag to the text. If you do not want the appearance of the text to change, create a character tag in which every attribute is set to As Is and apply that.

TIP If you want to create active areas on a graphic, see "Creating Image Maps" on page 556.

Testing Links

To verify that links are working, you can test them. To do so, press and hold CTRL-ALT and move the cursor over the link. The cursor turns into a hand. Click the link.

If you need to test a large number of links, you may want to convert the document to a view-only document. In view-only documents, you click on links without holding down additional keys. To convert a document from editable to view-only, press ESC SHIFT-F L K. Repeat the key sequence to convert from view-only back to a regular, editable document.

Creating Image Maps

You can set up rectangular active areas over a graphic to create image maps for your PDF and HTML files. An image map links to different locations based on where the reader clicks on the image. One use for image maps in PDF files is a navigation bar with graphic elements that link to the next, previous, first and last pages in the document. You can create active areas on graphics of any shape, but the active areas you create in FrameMaker are always rectangles.

To set up this type of active area, you must set up the destination with a newlink command as described on page 552. Then, you activate the graphic (or a portion of the graphic) with a text frame that contains the corresponding gotolink command.

To create an active area on a graphic, follow these steps:

1. Draw a text frame on top of the graphic. The dimensions of the text frame will become the active area on the graphic.

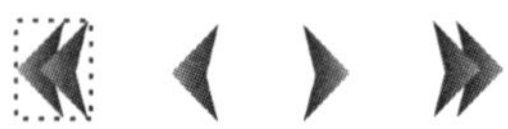

2. Position your cursor inside the text frame.
3. Create a hypertext marker in the text frame as described in "Creating a Link to the Target" on page 554.

NOTE When you create an active area on a graphic, you insert only the hypertext marker in the text frame. You do not need any text in the frame.

Creating a Link to a Web Address

You can create links that point to a web address. When the link is displayed in FrameMaker, clicking it starts the default web browser. In PDF files, web links require that the Adobe Reader or Acrobat be configured to handle web links. If the Reader is configured properly, clicking a web link displays the web page.

To create a web link, follow these steps:

1. Create an active area for the link, either with character tagging or by creating a text frame on top of a graphic.
2. Position your cursor in the active area.
3. Select Special➤Hypertext. The Hypertext dialog box is displayed (Figure 22-1 on page 553).

4. In the Command drop-down list, click Go to URL. This inserts the message URL command into the text field.

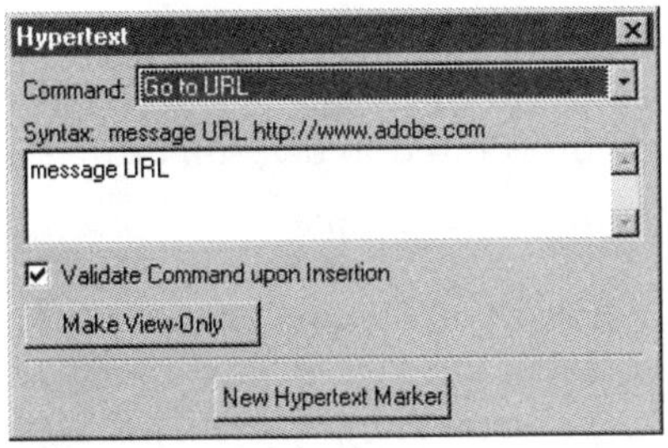

5. Type in the web address after message URL. For example:

```
message URL http://www.scriptorium.com
```

6. Click the New Hypertext Marker button to insert the marker.

Creating an Email Link

You can add links that create an email message. The email opens in the default email program when the link is clicked in the PDF or HTML file.

To create an email link, do the following:

1. Create a Go to URL hypertext link, as described in steps 1 through 4 of the previous procedure, "Creating a Link to a Web Address."
2. For the web address, type a mail URL such as:

   ```
   mailto:sales@scriptorium.com
   ```

   You can also type extra information to populate the message. For example, you can add a predefined subject:

   ```
   mailto:sales@scriptorium.com?subject=Comments%20for%20FM8%20book
   ```

NOTE Some punctuation marks have to be specified as hex values (for example, a space is %20). See www.blooberry.com/indexdot/html/topics/urlencoding.htm for more information about using hex values in HTML.

3. Click the New Hypertext Marker button to insert the marker.

Creating Notes in PDF Files

FrameMaker provides hypertext commands that let you create notes in PDF files. Alert messages are not supported in HTML.

For example, you could include alert messages in a draft document where information is not yet available, or where you wanted to flag something in the PDF file.

To create an alert message, follow these steps:

1. You do not need to create an active area for an alert. Position your cursor where you want the note in the PDF file.
2. Select Special➤Hypertext. The Hypertext dialog box is displayed.
3. In the Command drop-down list, click Alert. This inserts the alert command into the text field.

TIP Ignore the Alert with Title command. The title isn't supported when you create a PDF file. In effect, Alert and Alert with Title do the same thing.

4. Type the alert message in the marker text field. The limit is 1023 characters. For example, to create an alert with the message "Not yet available", use this syntax:

```
alert Not yet available
```

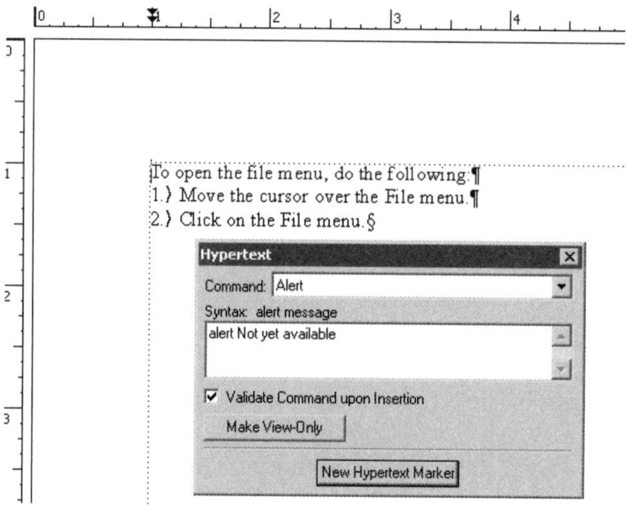

5. Click the New Hypertext Marker button to insert the hypertext marker.

   In the PDF file, the alert becomes a note.

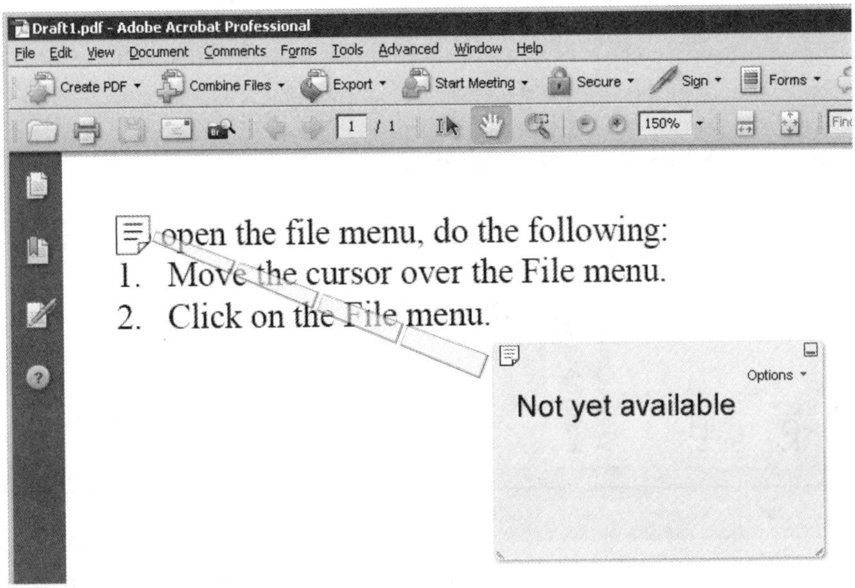

Locking and Unlocking View-Only Documents

You may sometimes want to make a FrameMaker file view-only so it can't be changed automatically or so you can test hypertext links. More often, you may need to unlock a file has been saved to the view-only format accidentally.

To toggle between view-only and editable formats in an open document, press ESC SHIFT-F L K.

Hypertext Command Reference

Table 22-1 lists the available hypertext commands and specifies whether the commands work in PDF files, HTML output, and view-only FrameMaker files. Commands marked "Obsolete" apply to view-only FrameMaker files and have no effect on PDF or HTML output.

NOTE If you are creating HTML output, you probably use the procedures that your third-party tool requires to create links.

Command	PDF	HTML	View-Only FrameMaker	Description and Syntax
Alert	✔		✔	Displays an alert box. `alert` *`message of up to 1023 characters`* See "Creating Notes in PDF Files" on page 558 for details.
Alert with Title	✔		✔	Displays an alert box (and a title in FrameMaker view-only documents). `alerttitle` *`title text`*`:`*`message of up to 1023 characters`* No title is displayed in PDF files. The Alert command is preferred. See "Creating Notes in PDF Files" on page 558 for details.
Specify Named Destination	✔	✔	✔	Defines a name used to create a link to the marker location. `newlink` *`linkname`* `newlink` *`filename:linkname`* See "Identifying the Target of a Link" on page 552 for details.
Jump to Named Destination	✔	✔	✔	Displays content that contains the named link. `gotolink` *`linkname`* `gotolink` *`filename:linkname`* See "Creating a Link to the Target" on page 554 for details.

Table 22-1. Hypertext Commands

Command	PDF	HTML	View-Only FrameMaker	Description and Syntax
Jump to Named Destination & Fit to Page	✔	✔	✔	Displays destination (and fits to page in FrameMaker view-only documents). `gotolinkfitwin` *`linkname`* `gotolinkfitwin` *`filename:linkname`* Does not fit to page for PDF and HTML files. The Jump to Named Destination command (`gotolink`) is preferred.

Jump to First Page	✔		✔	Displays first page of specified document.
				`gotolink firstpage`
				`gotolink` *`filename:`*`firstpage`

Jump to Last Page	✔		✔	Displays last page of specified document.
				`gotolink lastpage`
				`gotolink` *`filename:`*`lastpage`

Jump to Page Number	✔		✔	Displays specified page. `gotolink` *`pagenumber`* `gotopage` *`filename`*`:`*`pagenumber`* Page numbers are hard to maintain. The Jump to Named Destination command (`gotolink`) is preferred.
Jump to Previous Page	✔		✔	Displays previous page viewed. `previouspage`
Jump to Next Page	✔		✔	Displays next page of current document. `nextpage`
Jump Back	✔		✔	Displays location last viewed. `previouslink`
Jump Back and Fit to Page	✔		✔	Displays location last viewed (and fits to page for FrameMaker view-only documents). `previouslinkfitwin` Does not fit to page in PDF files. Jump Back command (`previouslink`) is preferred.

Table 22-1. Hypertext Commands (Continued)

Command	PDF	HTML	View-Only FrameMaker	Description and Syntax
Open Document	✔	✔	✔	Displays another page of current or different document. `openlink` *`linkname`* `openlink` *`filename:linkname`* The Jump to Named Destination command (`gotolink`) is preferred.
Open Document & Fit to Page	✔	✔	✔	Displays another page of current or different document and fits to page in FrameMaker view-only documents. `openlinkfitwin` *`linkname`* `openlinkfitwin` *`filename:linkname`* Does not fit to page in PDF or HTML files. The Jump to Named Destination command (`gotolink`) is preferred.

Open Document at First Page	✔	✔	✔	Displays first page of current or different document.
				`openlink firstpage`
				`openlink` *`filename:`*`firstpage`
				The Jump to First Page command (`gotolink firstpage`) is preferred.

Open Document at Last Page	✔	✔	✔	Displays last page of current or different document.
				`openlink lastpage`
				`openlink` *`filename:`*`lastpage`
				The Jump to Last Page command (`gotolink lastpage`) is preferred.

Open Document at Page Number	✔	✔	✔	Displays specific page number of current or different document. `openpage` *`pagenumber`* `openpage` *`filename pagenumber`* Page numbers are hard to maintain. The Jump to Named Destination command (`gotolink`) is preferred.

Table 22-1. Hypertext Commands (Continued)

Command	PDF	HTML	View-Only FrameMaker	Description and Syntax
Open Document as New			✔	Obsolete. Opens file as untitled FrameMaker document from FrameMaker view-only document. `opennew` *`filename`*
Popup Menu			✔	Obsolete. Displays a pop-up menu containing hypertext links as choices in the FrameMaker view-only file. `popup` *`flowname`*
Button Matrix			✔	Obsolete. Allows reader to select from a matrix to run hypertext commands in FrameMaker view-only document. `matrix` *`number_of_rows number_of_columns flowname`* To create an image map instead of a button matrix, see "Creating Image Maps" on page 556.
Go to URL	✔	✔	✔	Opens a web address. `message URL` *`web_address`* See "Creating a Link to a Web Address" on page 556 and "Creating an Email Link" on page 557 for details.
Message Client	✔		✔	Starts other programs. `message openfile` *`filename`*
Close Current Window			✔	Obsolete. Closes current viewer window in FrameMaker view-only document. `quit`
Close All Hypertext Windows			✔	Obsolete. Closes all windows in FrameMaker view-only document. `quitall`
Exit Application			✔	Obsolete. Exits application in FrameMaker view-only document. `exit`

Table 22-1. Hypertext Commands (Continued)

Implementing Additional Interactive Features in PDF Files

If you plan to deliver your document as a PDF file, interactivity is not limited to creating cross-references and hypertext commands. You can also use pdfmark commands to further customize your documents. Detailed information about pdfmark is available in Adobe's online user documentation (installed in the help directory of your Adobe Acrobat folder).

Briefly, pdfmark is a special command for embedding information in PostScript files. When Acrobat Distiller processes the PostScript files, it reads the pdfmark commands and adds special features to the resulting PDF files. Using pdfmark, you can implement movies, sounds, annotations, forms, and much more.

You can embed pdfmark commands in FrameMaker using PostScript text frames. Follow these steps:

1. On the page where you want the pdfmark command to occur, draw a text frame.
2. Insert the pdfmark code into the text frame. Refer to Adobe's documentation for details about pdfmark commands.
3. CTRL-click to select the text frame.
4. Select Graphics➤Object Properties. The Customize Text Frame dialog box is displayed.
5. In the Flow section, check the PostScript code check box. This tells FrameMaker to interpret the contents of the frame as PostScript code.

After setting up the PostScript text frame, you cannot edit the contents. Uncheck the PostScript code check box to make any changes.

For more details about advanced FrameMaker-to-Acrobat conversion techniques, we recommend that you consult www.microtype.com.

CHAPTER 23

Writing Equations

In FrameMaker, you can write complex equations, such as those found in scientific or mathematical documents. Equations consist of operators, alphanumeric characters, symbols, text strings, and other math elements.

$$(x \times y)^2 = y \qquad \text{area} = \pi r(\ )^2 \qquad \frac{(9+3)}{6}$$

To write an equation, you type the math elements or use the Equations palette to insert the items. For example, consider the following equation:

$$\log_a \Delta = \frac{\ln \Delta}{\ln a}$$

To write this equation, you first create a high-level approximation of the equation, as shown here:

$$? = \frac{?}{?}$$

You then replace the question marks with symbols, functions, and other math elements.

Equations are displayed in anchored or graphic frames. You can move an equation inside the frame by selecting the equation and using keyboard shortcuts or commands in the Equations palette. You can also shrink-wrap anchored frames to remove extra space between the frame and equation.

Understanding the Equations Palette

Σ Symbols, operators, delimiters, and other math elements are displayed in the Equations palette (Figure 23-1). Select Special➤Equations or click the Equations icon in the upper- right corner of the FrameMaker window to display the Equations palette. The palette is divided into nine pages for each type of math element or command. You click one of the buttons to display the appropriate page, and then you click a button in the palette.

Table 23-1 describes each page in the Equations palette.

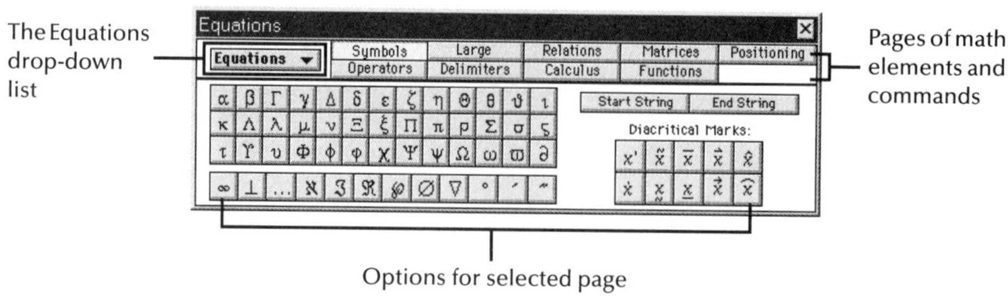

Figure 23-1. Understanding the Equations palette

Category	Description	Page
Symbols	Greek characters, atomic symbols, diacritical marks, and strings	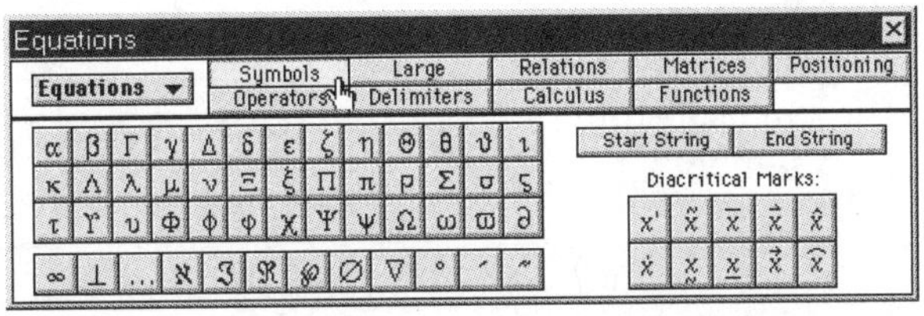
Large	Sums, products, integrals, intersections, and unions	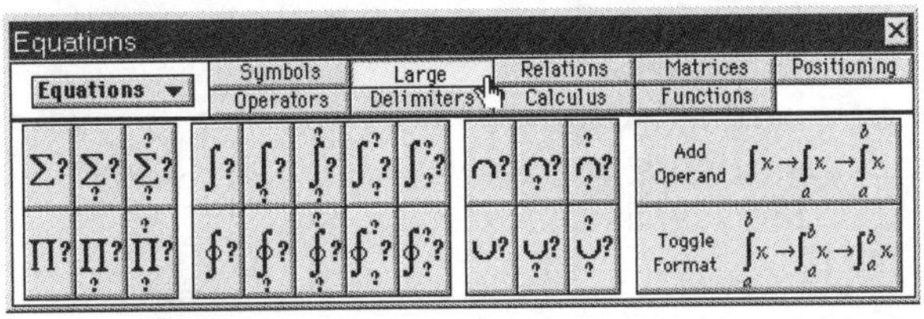
Relations	Equal, less than, greater than, similar to, subset of, and proportional to symbols	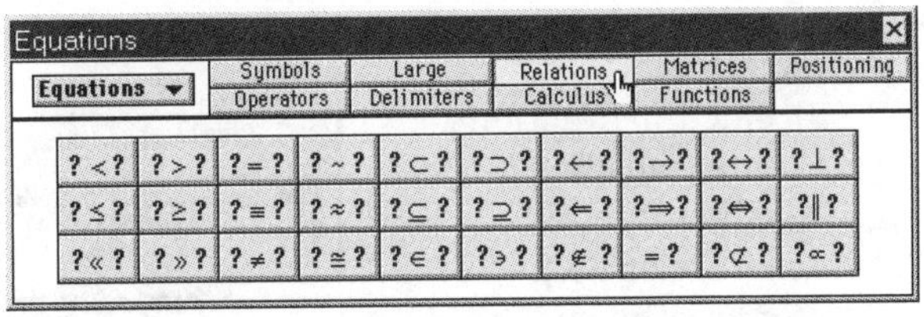
Matrices	Matrices and matrix commands	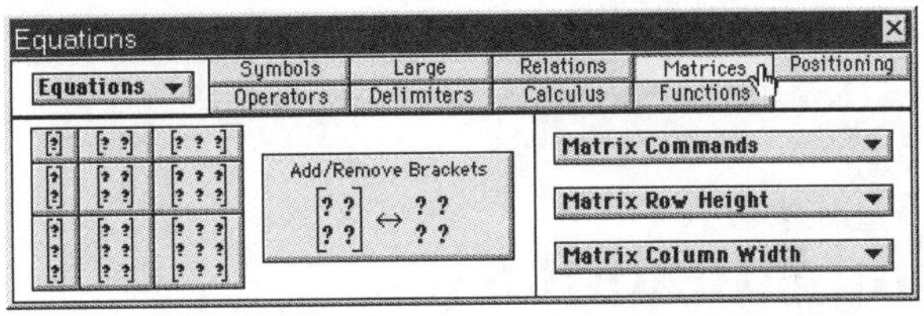
Positioning	Micropositioning, alignment, line breaks, and spacing options	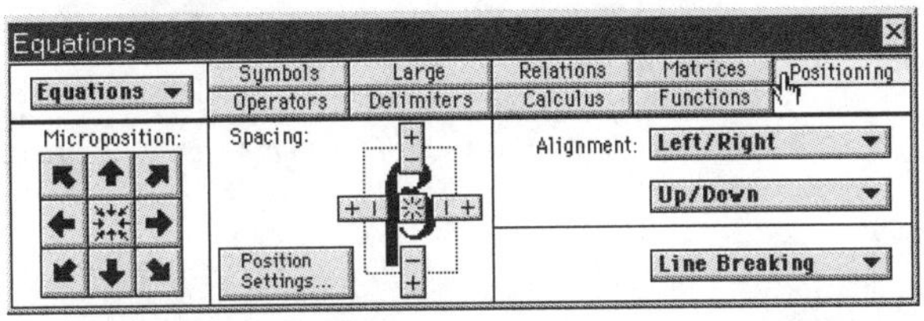
Operators	Roots, powers, signs, subscripts, superscripts, and logic symbols	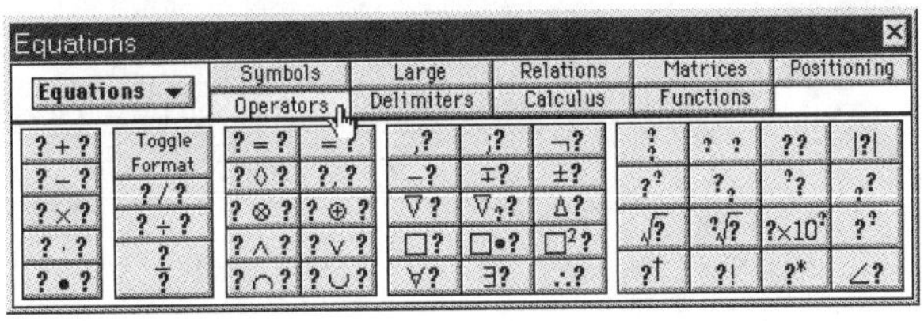

Table 23-1. Equations Palette Pages

Category	Description	Page
Delimiters	Parentheses, brackets, braces, and substitution symbols	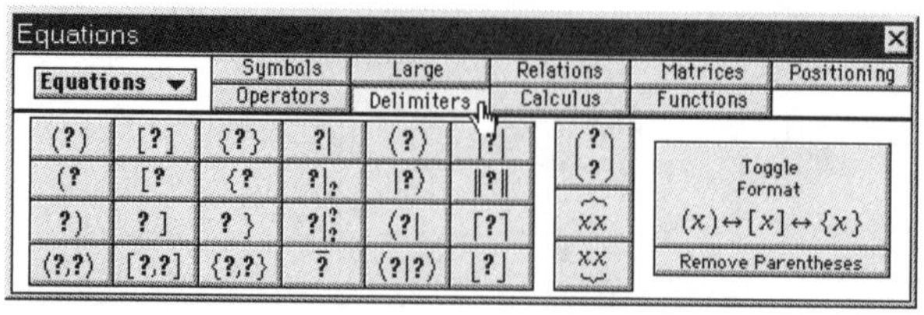
Calculus	Integrals, derivatives, partial derivatives, gradients, and limit symbols	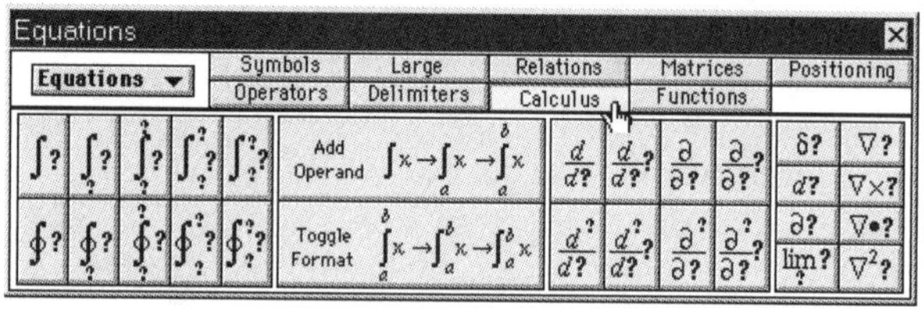
Functions	Trigonometric, hyperbolic, and logarithm functions; commands for evaluating expressions and for creating and applying rules	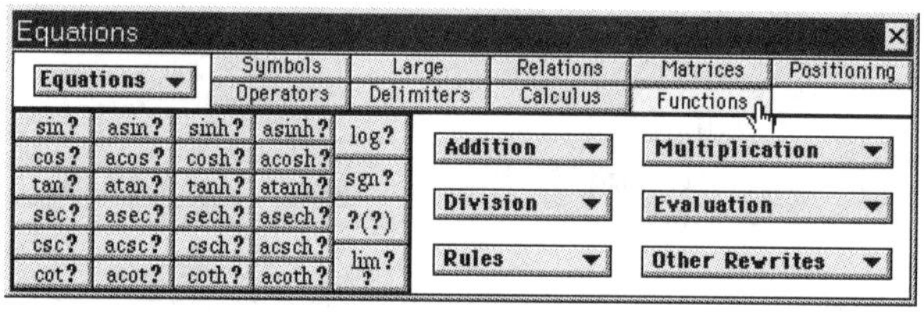

Table 23-1. Equations Palette Pages (Continued)

Inserting Equations

Equations inserted in empty paragraphs, as shown in the following example, are called *display equations.*

Figure the square footage by solving the following equation:

$$l \times w = h$$

When inserted in sentences, as shown in the following example, equations are called *inline equations.*

Figure the square footage by calculating $l \times w = h$

To insert an equation, follow these steps:

1. Do one of the following:
   - To create a display equation within an anchored frame, position your cursor in an empty paragraph:

     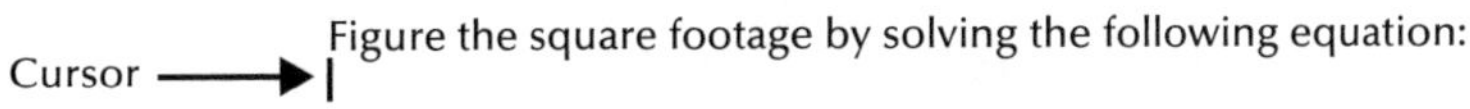

   - To create an inline equation within an anchored frame, position your cursor where the equation should begin:

     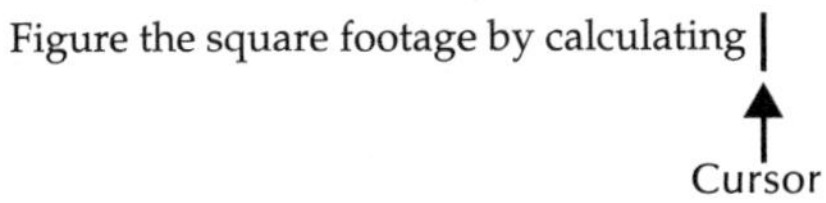

   - To create an equation in a graphic frame, select Graphics➤Tools to display the Tools palette, click the Graphic Frame icon, then draw a frame on the page. Select the frame before proceeding.

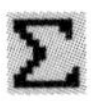

2. Select Special➤Equations, or click the Equations icon in the upper-right corner of the FrameMaker window. The Equations palette is displayed (Figure 23-1 on page 566).
3. In the Equations drop-down list, click the size of the equation you want to insert. The equation size is determined by the default font size and spread in the Equations Sizes dialog box. See "Changing Equation Font Sizes" on page 578 for details. Choices are as follows:
   - New Small Equation
   - New Medium Equation
   - New Large Equation

NOTE You can change the size of the equation later in the object properties if you don't like the size you selected. See "Changing the Equation Size" on page 580 for details.

An *equation object* is displayed as a highlighted question mark. (The outline in the next example shows the location of the anchored frame or graphic frame.)

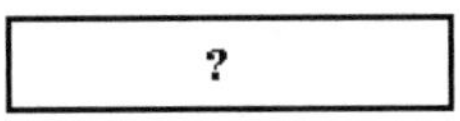

4. Do one of the following:
   - Click math elements and commands in the Equations palette to replace the equation object with your equation.
   - Type the equation in place of the equation object.

The next sections show how to write the following equation using each method:

$$? \longrightarrow \frac{8}{2} + \frac{10}{5} = 6$$

Using the Equations Palette

To use the Equations palette to write the preceding equation, follow these steps:

1. CTRL-click the equation object, or press the SPACEBAR. The equation object is selected.

   $$?$$

2. Click the Operators button in the Equations palette, then click the [?=?] button. The object is updated.

   $$? = ?$$

3. With the question mark on the far left selected, click the [?+?] button. The object is updated.

   $$? + ? = ?$$

4. With the question mark on the far left selected, click the [?/?] button. The object is updated.

   $$\frac{?}{?} + ? = ?$$

5. Press the TAB key until the next single question mark is selected, then click the [?/?] button. The object is updated, and the final form of the equation object is displayed.

   $$\frac{?}{?} + \frac{?}{?} = ?$$

6. Type the numbers in the equation; press the TAB key to move between objects.

   $$\frac{8}{2} + \frac{10}{5} = 6$$

NOTE Though you must calculate equations, FrameMaker can transform selected expressions to alternate formats. See "Evaluating Equations" on page 581 for details.

7. For equations in anchored frames, remove extra space between the frame and equation by selecting Shrink-Wrap Equation in the Equations drop-down list or by pressing ESC M P. If you change the size of the equation fonts, the shrink-wrapped equations are automatically shrink-wrapped again to fit the new font sizes.

$$\frac{8}{2}+\frac{10}{5}=6$$

NOTE When you shrink-wrap an anchored frame, the anchoring position changes to At Insertion Point. You might need to reposition the frame based on where you want the equation displayed. See "Anchoring Graphics" on page 304 for details.

Typing an Equation

If you're writing a simple equation or know the keystrokes, you might want to type the equation instead of using the Equations palette. To do so, follow these steps:

1. CTRL-click the equation object. The equation object is highlighted.

2. Type **8/2**. The fraction is displayed.

$$\frac{8}{2}$$

3. Press the SPACEBAR twice to select the equation, then type **+ 10/5**. The object is updated.

$$\frac{8}{2}+\frac{10}{5}=?$$

4. Press the SPACEBAR twice to select the equation, then type **= 6**. The final equation is displayed.

$$\frac{8}{2}+\frac{10}{5}=6$$

TIP To type text in an equation, click the Symbols page in the Equations palette, and then click the Start String button. Quotes are displayed, and when you type text, the text replaces the quotes. Click the End String button to close the text string.

Selecting Equations and Math Elements

You can select an entire equation as you do other objects, or you can select specific math elements. In individual equations, the location of the insertion point determines which characters are selected. For example, if a fraction is selected, and you press the DOWN ARROW key, the numerator in the equation is selected.

$$\frac{10}{2}+\frac{6}{3}=7 \qquad \frac{10}{2}+\frac{6}{3}=7$$

To select one or more characters in an equation, do one of the following:

- To select an equation, CTRL-click the equation. The selection handles are displayed around the object.

$$\log_a\Delta = \frac{\ln\Delta}{\ln a}$$

- To select part of an equation, drag the cursor across the text, or use one of the shortcuts in Table 23-2.

CAUTION You must use your cursor to select a text string; the keyboard shortcuts don't work.

Keystroke	Description
SPACEBAR	Expands the selection. $\frac{10}{2}+\frac{6}{3}=7$ $\frac{10}{2}+\frac{6}{3}=7$ $\frac{10}{2}+\frac{6}{3}=7$
LEFT ARROW	Selects the next character on the left. $\frac{10}{2}+\frac{6}{3}=7$ $\frac{10}{2}+\frac{6}{3}=7$ $\frac{10}{2}+\frac{6}{3}=7$ $\frac{10}{2}+\frac{6}{3}=7$
RIGHT ARROW	Selects the next character on the right. $\frac{10}{2}+\frac{6}{3}=7$ $\frac{10}{2}+\frac{6}{3}=7$ $\frac{10}{2}+\frac{6}{3}=7$ $\frac{10}{2}+\frac{6}{3}=7$

Table 23-2. Selecting Items in Equations

Keystroke	Description
DOWN ARROW	Selects the numerator in a fraction when the whole fraction is selected. $\boxed{\frac{10}{2}}+\frac{6}{3}=7$ $\frac{\boxed{10}}{2}+\frac{6}{3}=7$
CTRL-A	Selects all objects in an anchored or graphic frame. Before using this shortcut, you must select the frame or click an item inside the frame; otherwise, you'll insert a new equation object above the insertion point.

Table 23-2. Selecting Items in Equations (Continued)

Navigating Through Equations

To move the cursor between math elements in an equation, you use the arrow keys. Table 23-3 shows how the insertion point moves when you press the arrow keys.

Key	Description
LEFT ARROW	Moves the cursor to the left. $\frac{10}{2}+\frac{6}{3}=7|$ $\frac{10}{2}+\frac{6}{3}=|7$ $\frac{10}{2}+\frac{6|}{3}=7$ $\frac{10}{2}+\frac{|6}{3}=7$ $\frac{10}{2|}+\frac{6}{3}=7$
RIGHT ARROW	Moves the cursor to the right. $|\frac{10}{2}+\frac{6}{3}=7$ $\frac{10}{2}|+\frac{6}{3}=7$ $\frac{10}{2}+|\frac{6}{3}=7$ $\frac{10}{2}+\frac{6}{3}|=7$
DOWN ARROW	Moves the cursor from the side of a fraction to its numerator. $|\frac{10}{2}+\frac{6}{3}=7$ $\frac{|10}{2}+\frac{6}{3}=7$
UP ARROW	Moves the cursor from the numerator to the entire fraction. $\frac{|10}{2}+\frac{6}{3}=7$ $|\frac{10}{2}+\frac{6}{3}=7$

Table 23-3. Moving the Cursor Through Equations

Moving Equations

After you select an equation, you can move it on the page by one of three methods. To move an equation, select the equation, and then do one of the following:

- Drag the selected equation to a new location.
- Press ALT while pressing one of the arrow keys.
- Right-click the equation, then select Graphics➤Object Properties. The Object Properties dialog box is displayed (Figure 23-2). Type new left or top offsets, then click the Set button.

Position of object from the top and left edges of the text frame

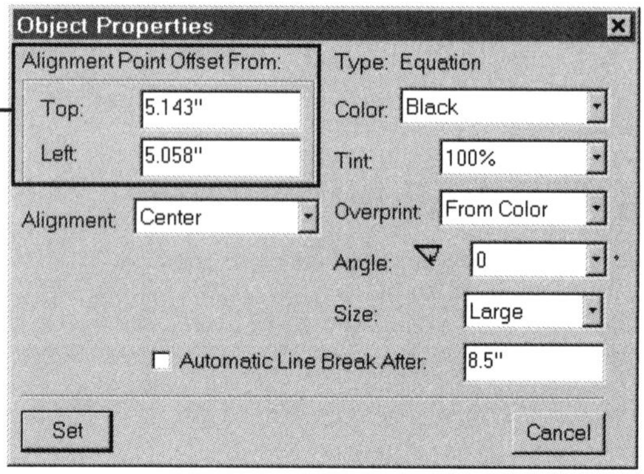

Figure 23-2. Modifying the offsets

For more information on modifying the position and alignment of objects, see "Rearranging Objects" on page 360.

CAUTION You can move the equation outside the anchored frame; however, the equation is no longer linked to the paragraph, and text added or deleted above the equation may be displayed over the equation.

Modifying Equations

After you write an equation, you can modify the spacing and alignment in several ways. For example, you can tighten the spacing or add a line break. You should wait to modify spacing and alignment until the equation is final, or you might need to make additional adjustments.

Moving Text Using Keyboard Shortcuts

You can move selected text up and down, left-to-right, and diagonally using keyboard shortcuts. To do so, select the text you want to move, and use keyboard shortcuts in the following table to microposition the text. (The point values apply to documents displayed at 100 percent.)

Direction	Shortcut
Left one point	ALT-LEFT ARROW
Right one point	ALT-RIGHT ARROW
Up one point	ALT-UP ARROW
Down one point	ALT-DOWN ARROW
Left six points	ALT-SHIFT-LEFT ARROW
Right six points	ALT-SHIFT-RIGHT ARROW
Up six points	ALT-SHIFT-UP ARROW
Down six points	ALT-SHIFT-DOWN ARROW

NOTE Some of the keys on your computer may be specially programmed. If so, one or more keyboard shortcuts may not work as described. Consult your system documentation for help.

Moving Text Using the Equations Palette

In addition to using keyboard shortcuts, you can reposition an equation using commands in the Positioning page.

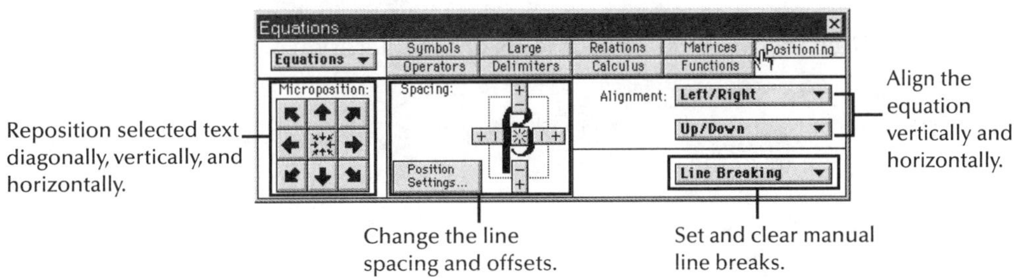

The following list describes some of the most common ways to modify equations using the Equations palette:

- **Adjusting the spread.** Add or remove space between characters in an equation by selecting the characters and clicking the appropriate Spacing arrow. (The middle button resets the alignment.)

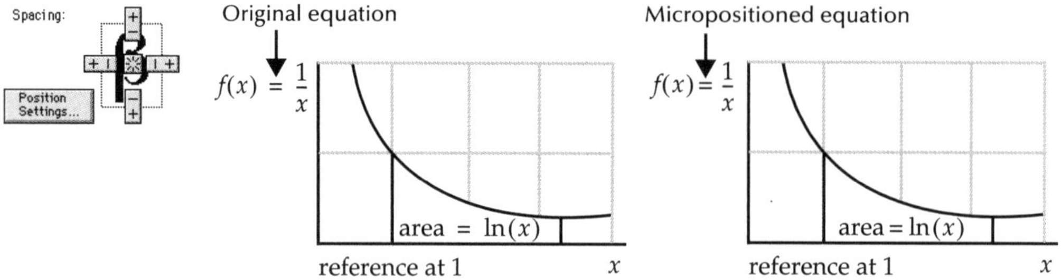

- **Adjusting the line spacing.** Add or remove space between lines of a multiline equation by editing spacing in the Position Settings dialog box.

Original equation

$$(10-2)+6+x^4+2y$$
$$+y^2+3+10+2$$

0.35 picas was added to the line spacing.

$$(10-2)+6+x^4+2y$$
$$+y^2+3+10+2$$

- **Repositioning text.** Move selected text up and down, side-to-side, and diagonally by clicking one of the Microposition arrows. (The middle button resets the alignment.)

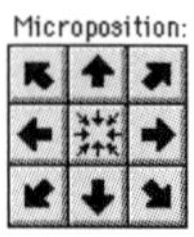

$$\log_a\Delta = \frac{\ln\Delta}{\ln_a}$$

CAUTION If you add math elements after using the Microposition commands, the repositioned text will move back to its original location.

- **Aligning.** Line up equations at specific points (for example, along the equal signs or centers of the equations).

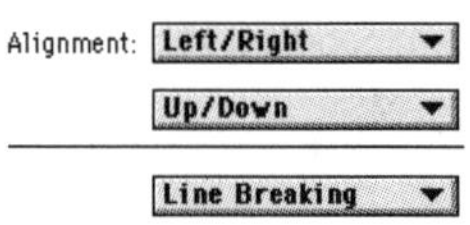

$$a(x)\frac{dy}{dx}+b(x)y = c(x)$$
$$\frac{dy}{dx}+p(x)y = q(x)$$

Manual alignment point is set to the right of the equal signs.

$$a(x)\frac{dy}{dx}+b(x)y = c(x)$$
$$\frac{dy}{dx}+p(x)y = q(x)$$

Equations are centered.

- **Adding a line break.** Sets a manual line break in an equation. (You can set up an automatic line break in the equation's object properties.)

$$x - 3y + (10 \times 350) + 9 - 2 \longrightarrow \begin{array}{l} x - 3y + (10 \times 350) \\ +9-2 \end{array}$$

For more information on modifying the spacing and alignment of equations, see the FrameMaker online help.

Deleting Equations

You can delete specific math elements in an equation or the entire equation. When you delete a math element, a question mark is displayed in place of the element. You can insert another item in place of the question mark or continue to delete more of the equation.

To delete items in an equation, follow these steps:

1. Do one of the following:
   - Select the item you want to delete.
   - Position the cursor on the right side of the item.
2. Press the BACKSPACE key. The item is deleted, and the question mark is displayed in its place.
3. Repeat to delete additional items.

To delete an entire equation, select the equation, then press the DELETE key.

Formatting Equations

FrameMaker lets you set the global font properties for equations. You customize equation fonts by assigning a character format. For example, you might create a character tag with a sans-serif typeface and assign the format in the Equations palette. You can also modify the font sizes in small, medium, and large equations and adjust the default spread of each equation. When you modify global font settings, new and existing equations are updated, and shrink-wrapped equations are rewrapped, if necessary.

You reformat individual equations in the equation's object properties. In addition to modifying the typical object properties—color, tint, overprint, and angle—you set up automatic line breaks or change the size of the equation. To reformat certain characters in an equation, you must use character tags.

Changing Equation Fonts

In equations, alphanumeric characters, including functions, are formatted with the Times or Times New Roman typeface. You change the font properties by assigning a character tag. The five types of equation characters—math symbols, functions, numbers, strings, and variables—may use different character tags.

To modify default equation fonts, follow these steps:

1. Create a character tag for each kind of formatting. For example, you can create a separate tag for functions and numbers. See "Creating Character Tags" on page 149 for details.
2. Display the Equations palette, then click Equation Fonts in the Equations drop-down list. The Equation Fonts dialog box is displayed.

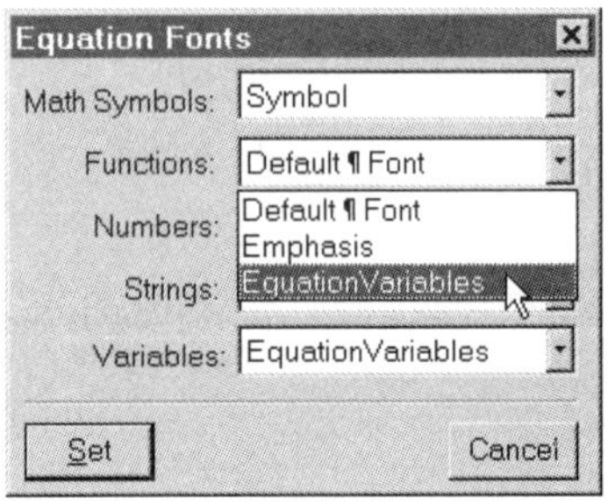

3. To change the math symbol font, click a font in the Math Symbols drop-down list. Only math fonts are displayed.
4. To apply a character tag to other math elements, click the character tag in the appropriate drop-down list.

CAUTION The EquationVariables character tag is assigned to variables to italicize the characters. Don't delete this character tag from your template if you insert equations in your document.

5. Click the Set button. The default font properties in new and existing equations are updated.

Changing Equation Font Sizes

When you insert an equation, you choose a small, medium, or large equation. The default font sizes determine the size of the equation. Certain types of characters within each equation also differ in size. For example, integral and sigma symbols are larger than other characters, and there are three font sizes for different levels of alphanumeric characters. You can change the default font sizes for equations, and all existing equations are also updated.

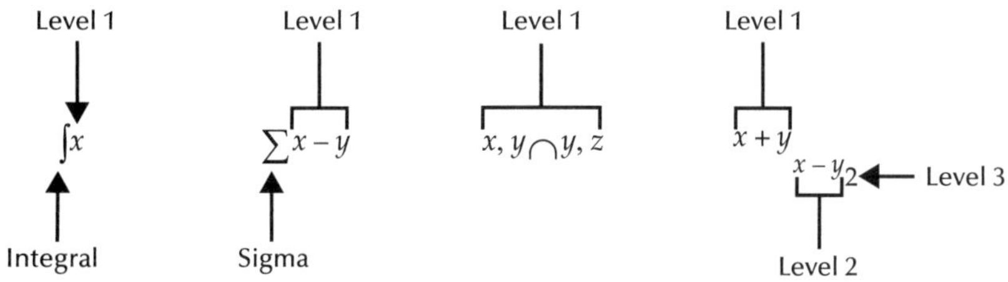

In addition to editing font sizes, you can change the equation's vertical or horizontal spread. The spread setting functions the same as spread in a paragraph tag. See "Default Font Sheet" on page 117 for more information.

To change the default font sizes and spreads, follow these steps:

1. Display the Equations palette, then click Equation Sizes in the Equations drop-down list. The Equation Sizes dialog box is displayed.

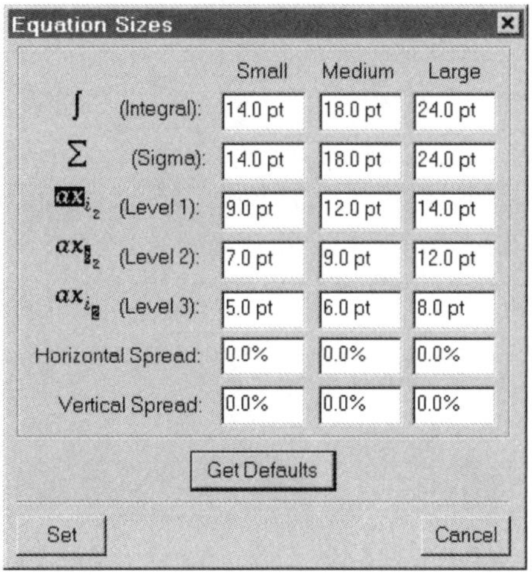

2. To change the font sizes for equations, type new values in the Small, Medium, and Large fields.
3. To change the spacing between characters, do any of the following:
   - To modify space horizontally, type new values in the Horizontal Spread values.
   - To modify space vertically, type new values in the Vertical Spread values.

NOTE To restore the default font sizes, click the Get Defaults button. (The defaults are displayed in the previous graphic.)

4. Click the Set button. The default font sizes in new and existing equations are updated.

Inserting Automatic Line Breaks

You can set up automatic line breaks in individual equations. When an equation reaches a certain length, the equation wraps to the next line. To insert an automatic line break, follow these steps:

1. Select the equation, then select Graphics➤Object Properties. The Object Properties dialog box is displayed (Figure 23-2 on page 574).
2. Check the Automatic Line Break After check box, type the length at which the line break occurs, then click the Set button. The equation properties are updated.

Changing the Equation Size

After you insert an equation, you can change the size. For example, you might insert a small equation and decide the font is too small. Instead of modifying the size of the font globally, you can assign a different size to the equation. To change the equation size, follow these steps:

1. Select the equation, then select Graphics➤Object Properties. The Object Properties dialog box is displayed (Figure 23-2 on page 574).
2. Click a size in the Size drop-down list, then click the Set button. The equation size is updated.

For details on changing equation sizes globally, see "Changing Equation Font Sizes" on page 578.

Applying Character Tags

You can reformat specific characters in an equation by applying character tags. This overrides the global character formatting specified in the Equation Fonts dialog box. For details, see "Changing Equation Fonts" on page 578.

To apply a character tag, select the text, and click a tag in the character catalog. You cannot use the keyboard shortcut for applying character tags because the shortcut is mapped to one of the operators in the Equations palette. For more information, see "Applying Character Tags" on page 144.

Evaluating Equations

FrameMaker can evaluate a selected expression and either display an alternate format or correct the syntax. The following example shows an expression before and after evaluation. In the numerator of the first expression, the parenthetical values were transformed to display the values in the correct order. The denominator was converted to its simplest expression. The second expression was also converted to its simplest value.

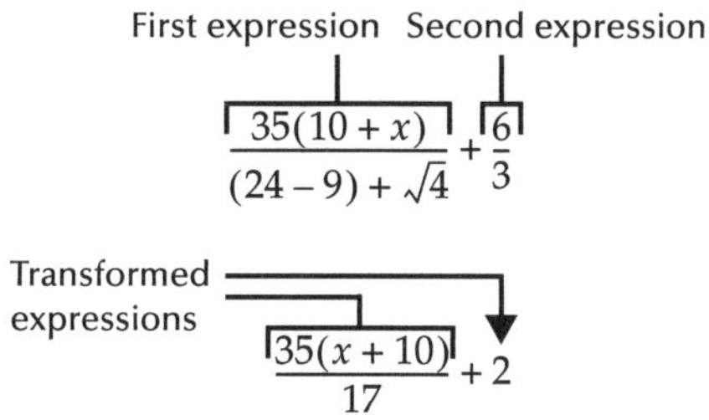

To evaluate an equation, follow these steps:

1. Display the Equations palette, then click the Functions button. The Functions page is displayed.

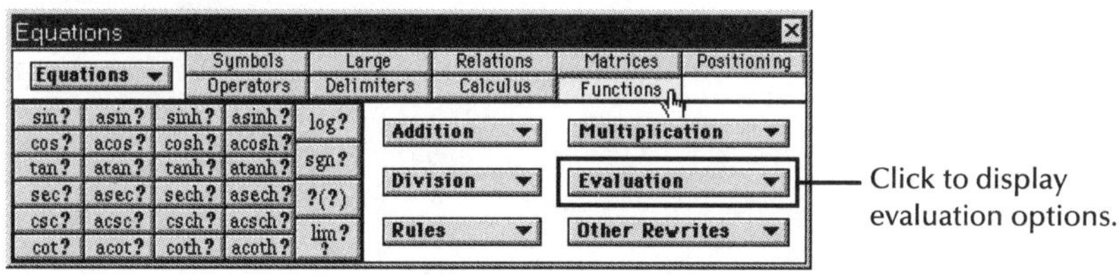

2. Select the expression you want to evaluate.
3. Click the Evaluation drop-down list, then click the appropriate command for your expression. Your equation is evaluated, and the alternate values are displayed.

For more information on evaluating equations, see the FrameMaker online help.

CHAPTER 24

Maker Interchange Format

Normally, FrameMaker files are stored in a binary format. In some cases, though, it's useful to have a text version of FrameMaker files. For this, an alternate Maker Interchange Format (MIF) is available. A MIF file contains the same information as a regular, binary FrameMaker file, but it's encoded in a plain text file instead of a binary file.

Editing MIF files directly provides an alternative to working in FrameMaker's graphical interface. For some issues, this is the most efficient way to work. For example, you can use MIF files to perform global search-and-replace operations on fonts. This is much faster than editing each tag in the paragraph catalog—even the global update options aren't as fast as editing MIF.

A MIF file contains all of the information that your FrameMaker file does in a markup format. The following MIF fragment shows one short paragraph of text:

What's displayed in FrameMaker

> Cross-stitching is easy to learn, fun, and relax-
> ing. Best of all, it doesn't require a computer!

Corresponding MIF markup

Paragraph tag BodyFirst is assigned to the paragraph. → `<PgfTag `BodyFirst'>`

```
<Para
  <Unique 998321>
  <PgfTag `BodyFirst'>
<ParaLine
   <TextRectID 19>
   <String `Cross-stitching is easy to learn,
fun, and relax'>
   <Char SoftHyphen>
  > # end of ParaLine
  <ParaLine
   <String `ing. Best of all, it doesn't require
a computer!'>
  > # end of ParaLine
> # end of Para
```

In addition to the text, graphics, markers, and so on, the MIF file also contains a complete listing of your formatting catalogs. The following code excerpt shows the definition for the BodyFirst paragraph tag referenced in the preceding example. Notice that each item available in the Paragraph Designer has its own entry in the list.

```
<Pgf
 <PgfTag `Body'>
 <PgfUseNextTag No>
 <PgfNextTag `'>
 <PgfAlignment Left>
 <PgfFIndent  0.0">
 <PgfLIndent  0.0">
```

```
<PgfRIndent  0.0">
<PgfFIndentRelative No>
<PgfFIndentOffset  0.0">
<PgfTopSeparator `'>
<PgfTopSepAtIndent No>
<PgfTopSepOffset  0.0">
<PgfBotSeparator `'>
<PgfBotSepAtIndent No>
<PgfBotSepOffset  0.0">
<PgfPlacement Anywhere>
<PgfPlacementStyle Normal>
<PgfRunInDefaultPunct `'>
<PgfSpBefore  0.0 pt>
<PgfSpAfter  0.0 pt>
<PgfWithPrev No>
<PgfWithNext No>
<PgfBlockSize 2>
<PgfFont
 <FTag `'>
 <FPlatformName `W.Times New Roman.R.400'>
 <FFamily `Times New Roman'>
 <FVar `Regular'>
 <FWeight `Regular'>
 <FAngle `Regular'>
 <FEncoding `FrameRoman'>
 <FSize  12.0 pt>
 <FUnderlining FNoUnderlining>
 <FOverline No>
 <FStrike No>
 <FChangeBar No>
 <FOutline No>
 <FShadow No>
 <FPairKern Yes>
 <FTsume No>
 <FCase FAsTyped>
 <FPosition FNormal>
 <FDX  0.0%>
 <FDY  0.0%>
 <FDW  0.0%>
 <FStretch  100.0%>
 <FLanguage USEnglish>
 <FLocked No>
 <FSeparation 0>
 <FColor `Black'>
> # end of PgfFont
```

```
    <PgfLineSpacing Proportional>
    <PgfLeading  2.0 pt>
    <PgfAutoNum No>
    <PgfNumTabs 0>
    <PgfHyphenate Yes>
    <HyphenMaxLines 2>
    <HyphenMinPrefix 3>
    <HyphenMinSuffix 3>
    <HyphenMinWord 5>
    <PgfLetterSpace No>
    <PgfMinWordSpace 90>
    <PgfOptWordSpace 100>
    <PgfMaxWordSpace 110>
    <PgfMinJRomanLetterSpace 0>
    <PgfOptJRomanLetterSpace 25>
    <PgfMaxJRomanLetterSpace 50>
    <PgfMinJLetterSpace 0>
    <PgfOptJLetterSpace 0>
    <PgfMaxJLetterSpace 10>
    <PgfYakumonoType Floating>
    <PgfPDFStructureLevel 6>
    <PgfLanguage USEnglish>
    <PgfCellAlignment Top>
    <PgfCellMargins  0.0 pt 0.0 pt 0.0 pt 0.0 pt>
    <PgfCellLMarginFixed No>
    <PgfCellTMarginFixed No>
    <PgfCellRMarginFixed No>
    <PgfCellBMarginFixed No>
    <PgfLocked No>
  > # end of Pgf
```

After reviewing this, it's probably no surprise to find out that MIF files are generally larger than FrameMaker files. On average, MIF files are about 10 times larger than the corresponding FrameMaker file, so saving a 100KB FrameMaker file to MIF results in a 1MB MIF file.

Almost every third-party utility that can read or write FrameMaker files uses MIF as an intermediate format. HTML converters such as ePublisherPro and MIF2GO save FrameMaker files to MIF, and then process the resulting MIF files to produce HTML or other markup. Most database publishing applications generate MIF markup files, which can then be opened in FrameMaker.

NOTE In addition to MIF format, a second markup format, Maker Markup Language (MML), is also available. MML is no longer being developed, so it's not nearly as rich as MIF. MML, however, is much easier to create than MIF. For this reason, MML is used for some applications because creating a complete MIF file would be too much work. For details on MML, refer to the MML Reference, found in the Documents folder in your FrameMaker installation directory.

FrameMaker comes with the *MIF Reference*, found in the Documents folder in your FrameMaker installation directory. The *MIF Reference* describes MIF syntax and options in great detail. We strongly recommend that you consult this manual for detailed information about MIF syntax. In addition, the MIF file format has changed from version 7 (now called MIF 7 or MIF-Classic). Consult the *MIF Reference* for a detailed description of the changes for version 8 (now called MIF 8 or MIF-Unicode).

At the highest level, the MIF file is organized into the following sections:

- **MIFFile:** Identifies the file as a MIF file and provides the FrameMaker version from which the file was created. Every MIF file must start with this statement.
- **Units** and **CharUnits:** Specify measurement units for this file.
- **ColorCatalog:** Lists the color definitions.
- **ConditionCatalog:** Lists the conditional text tag definitions.
- **BoolCondCatalog:** Lists the defined conditional expressions.
- **DefAttrValuesCatalog:** Lists the default attribute values, used for filtering structured documents. Empty for unstructured documents.
- **AttrCondExprCatalog:** Lists defined conditional expressions for filtering structured documents. Empty for unstructured documents.
- **CombinedFontCatalog:** Lists combined fonts (used in double-byte languages such as Japanese).
- **PgfCatalog:** Lists the paragraph tag definitions.
- **FontCatalog:** Lists character tag definitions.
- **Ruling Catalog:** Lists table rule definitions.
- **TblCatalog:** Lists table definitions.
- **KumihanCatalog:** Provides line composition rules for Japanese text.
- **Views:** Lists color view definitions.
- **VariableFormats:** Lists variable definitions.
- **MarkerTypeCatalog:** Lists available custom marker types.

- **XRefFormats:** Lists cross-reference format definitions.
- **Document:** Lists document defaults, including volume, chapter, page, paragraph, and footnote numbering; document window size and location; text options; track text edits settings; change bar properties; and view options.
- **BookComponent:** Lists settings for generated files.
- **InitialAutoNums:** Lists default starting numbers for autonumbered paragraphs.
- **Dictionary:** Lists words not in the dictionary but allowed in this document (added when you click the Allow in Document button in the spell-checker).
- **AFrames:** Lists the anchored frames that occur in this document. The frames' unique identifiers are used to reference the frames in the text flow where they are anchored.
- **Tbls:** Lists the tables that occur in this document. The tables' identifiers are used to reference the tables in the text flow where they are anchored.
- **Page:** Lists the master pages, reference pages, and body pages that occur in this document.
- **Text Flow:** Lists the text flows that occur in this document and their contents.

Creating a MIF File

To create a MIF file from a regular FrameMaker file, you need to save the FrameMaker file to MIF format. Follow these steps:

1. Open the file you want to save as MIF.
2. Select File➤Save As. The Save Document dialog box is displayed.
3. In the Save as type drop-down list, click MIF 8.0.
4. In the File name field, specify a name for the file. Be sure to change the file extension to MIF; FrameMaker doesn't always do this automatically.
5. Click the Save button.

FrameMaker creates the MIF file.

Opening a MIF File in FrameMaker

To open a MIF file and convert it back to regular FrameMaker format, follow these steps:

1. Select File➤Open. The Open dialog box is displayed.
2. Locate the MIF file on your system and select it.
3. Click the Open button to open the file.

FrameMaker reads the MIF file and displays it as a FrameMaker file. During conversion, a console window may display error messages. FrameMaker will skip any information it cannot process in the MIF file. For example, if you save a FrameMaker 8 file to MIF and then open that MIF file in version 7 (or earlier), error messages will be displayed.

Viewing a MIF File

You can view a MIF 8 file in any text editor that supports UTF-8 character encoding. If you don't have a text editor available, you can use FrameMaker as a text editor.

To open a MIF 8 file as text in FrameMaker, follow these steps:

1. Select File➤Open. The Open dialog box is displayed.
2. Locate the MIF file you want to open, hold down the CTRL key, and double-click the file or hold down the SHIFT key and click the Open button.
3. In the Reading Text File dialog box, from the Encoding drop-down list select UTF-8, then click Read.

FrameMaker reads the file as a text file instead of interpreting the MIF commands.

CAUTION Do not save the text file as a FrameMaker file. You could inadvertently overwrite your source FrameMaker file with text.

If you see unusual text within the MIF file in your editor, such as the following,

```
<String `ing. Best of all, it doesnâ€™t require a computer!'>
```

make sure your editor provides UTF-8 encoding for viewing and working with text files.

Cool Stuff You Can Do with MIF

There are numerous scenarios in which a MIF file can be helpful. Before you begin working in a file, assemble your arsenal; you will need the following items:

- A text editor that can handle MIF files and provides UTF-8 encoding support. One we like is PSPad. (Notepad and SimpleText cannot open most MIF files because they are too long.)
- A powerful search-and-replace engine. Some text editors offer advanced search-and-replace options; you can also use a scripting language such as Perl.
- A basic understanding of MIF syntax and the items you need to modify. If, for example, you want to work with index markers and aren't sure how the index markers look in MIF format, create a small sample file, insert an index marker with some unique text, save the file to MIF, and search for your sample text.

- Access to character code references. For MIF 8 files, you can use the Windows Character Map utility to find the Unicode code points, if needed.
- A backup of your file, just in case.

The following sections describe a few common uses for MIF files.

Eliminating File Corruption Problems

FrameMaker files are usually quite stable. Every now and then, though, a file goes haywire for no apparent reason. One technique that can sometimes eliminate the problem is to save the file to MIF, open the MIF in FrameMaker, and save it back to FrameMaker format. You're not making any changes in the MIF file, so this operation is relatively safe.

There are a couple of problems that occur frequently that saving to MIF solves:

- If Find/Change won't recognize words that you know are present in the file, the problem is often hidden characters that were imported from Microsoft Word files.
- The color catalog becomes bloated with colors you didn't define that have names starting with RGB if you import PNG graphics that use an optimized palette. Of course, you must save the PNG with the maximum number of colors or the colors will show up in the color palette again.

Making a File Available to an Older Version of FrameMaker

Older versions of FrameMaker cannot open files created in newer versions. For example, a file created in FrameMaker 6 cannot be opened in any release of FrameMaker 5. In version 8, Adobe does include a "save as FrameMaker 7" option, so that you can write FrameMaker 8 files to a format that's compatible with FrameMaker 7. If, however, you need to transfer files back to an older version, you must go through MIF format.

In FrameMaker 8, save your file to MIF 7 format, open the older version of FrameMaker, and open the MIF file there. You will see a number of error messages in the console window, but this technique should allow you to open files all the way back to FrameMaker version 3.

Keep in mind that any features that aren't available in the earlier version will be stripped from your file, which can cause formatting problems, especially if you are going back to a very old version of FrameMaker.

Creating a Character Tag for a Vertical Baseline Shift

Some settings are available as MIF file settings but are not accessible through the graphical interface. Vertical baseline shift is one of those items. In the Character Designer, you can set up a character tag that uses a superscript, but you cannot use multiple vertical offsets in a single file—you only have superscripts available, and they always use the same vertical offset.

There is, however, a vertical offset setting available in FrameMaker. In a MIF file, you can assign this offset using the <FDY> token. You can create a character tag definition in a MIF file. You can then use that file as a template and import the tag into a document.

To create a character tag with a vertical baseline shift, follow these steps:

1. Create a text file and insert the following text:

   ```
   <MIFFile 8.00>
   <FontCatalog
   <Font
    <FTag `VerticalOffset'>
    <FDY -60>
    <FLocked No>
    > # end of Font
    > # end of FontCatalog
   ```

   The offset value can range from -100 to 100; negative values move the text up, and positive values move the text down. The quotes surrounding the words VerticalOffset are the backtick character for the opening quote and a straight single quote for the closing quote.

2. Save the file with a .MIF extension.
3. In FrameMaker, open the MIF file and display the document that you want to import the character tag into.
4. Select File➤Import➤Formats. The Import Formats dialog box is displayed.

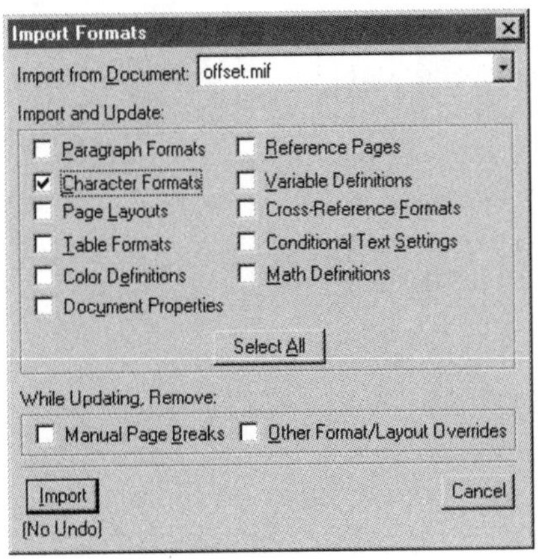

5. In the Import from Document drop-down list, click the MIF file to select it.
6. In the Import and Update section, check the Character Formats check box; make sure all other items are unchecked.
7. Click the Import button. The VerticalOffset character tag is displayed in the character catalog. When you apply it, a vertical offset results.

CAUTION You cannot access the vertical offset setting from the Character Designer. However, if you make changes to the VerticalOffset character tag in the Character Designer and click the Update All button, the baseline offset setting will be deleted.

Using MIF Fragments to Update Catalog Settings

You can use the technique described in the previous section to add information to other catalogs. This is especially useful if you want to import only user variables.

When you import variables from one FrameMaker document to another, both the system variables and the user variables are imported. Often, you may want to update only the user variables. There are probably a few variables—such as book title or copyright date—that you update frequently. Also, you may need to import only the user variable if the system variables conflict across the book. For example, if the templates for the chapter files and the index use the same system variable for different purposes (such as redefining the Running H/F 1 variable on the master pages), then importing the system variables would break the headers in some of the files.

You can update only the user variables by doing the following:

1. In a text editor, create a MIF file that contains definitions for the user variables you want to import:

```
<MIFFile 8.00>
<VariableFormats
<VariableFormat
 <VariableName `book_title'>
 <VariableDef `Troubleshooting My Document'>
 > # end of VariableFormat
<VariableFormat
 <VariableName `version_number'>
 <VariableDef `6.2.5beta'>
 > # end of VariableFormat
> # end of VariableFormats
```

2. Save the MIF file and close the text editor.
3. Open the MIF file in FrameMaker. Do not save the MIF file.

CAUTION If you save the MIF file, FrameMaker automatically adds pages of default information to the MIF—including default system variables.

4. Import the variables from the MIF file. Only the user variables you defined are imported.

NOTE After you import the variable definitions, they are available in the Variables dialog box. You can edit them just like any other variable.

5. Save the FrameMaker files, but close the MIF fragment without saving it.

Performing Global Search-and-Replace Operations

Inside FrameMaker, you have a significant number of Find/Change options available, but sometimes, you'll run across a problem that can't be automated in the Find/Change dialog box.

For example, you might have a situation where you were working on an index. After several hours of work, you realize that you inadvertently inserted markers with a Subject type instead of an Index type.

Here's how to fix this using the find/change feature in FrameMaker:

1. Select Edit➤Find/Change. The Find/Change dialog box is displayed:

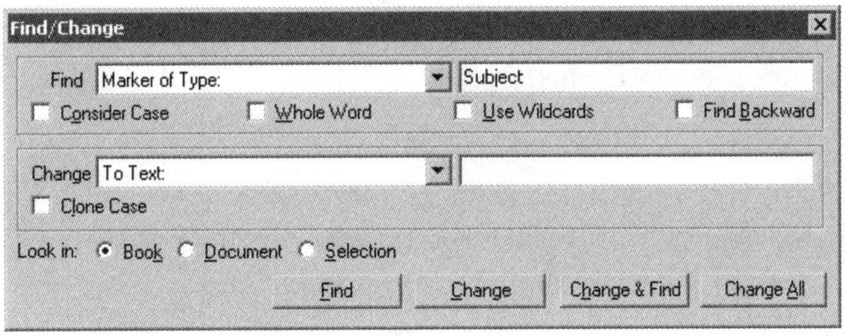

2. In the Find drop-down list, click Marker of Type; in the field to the right of Marker Type, type in **Subject**.
3. Click the Find button. FrameMaker locates the first Subject marker.
4. Select Special➤Marker. The Marker dialog box is displayed.

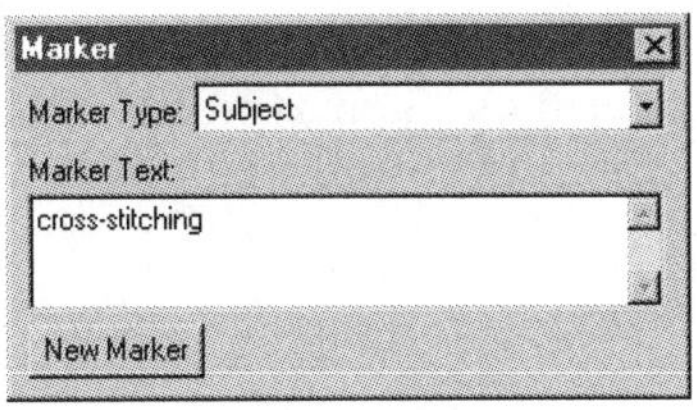

5. In the Marker Type drop-down list, click Index.
6. Click the Edit Marker button.
7. Repeat steps 3–6 for each problem marker.

The MIF alternative is much more appealing:

1. Save the problem files to MIF format.
2. Write a script that locates the Subject markers, or just use search and replace in your editor. The items that are the same for each marker are shown in boldface in the following example:

```
<Marker
 <MType 4>
 <MTypeName `Subject'>
 <MText `cross-stitching'>
 <MCurrPage `87'>
 <Unique 1075663>
 > # end of Marker
```

3. Globally change the <MType> to 2 and the <MTypeName> to Index, as shown in the following example:

```
<Marker
 <MType 2>
 <MTypeName `Index'>
 <MText `cross-stitching'>
 <MCurrPage `87'>
 <Unique 1075663>
 > # end of Marker
```

4. Save your modified MIF files.
5. Open the files in FrameMaker, and save them back to regular FrameMaker format.

These types of global search-and-replace operations can save you hours of work.

Writing Your Own Conversion Tools

If you are required to convert information in FrameMaker to other formats and third-party converters are not doing the job, you may want to consider writing your own conversion tool. With some Perl scripting knowledge, you could, for example, write a converter that takes a MIF file as input and creates help pages for a UNIX program.

The MIF file contains all of the information needed to display and print a file, so converting it to online markup formats, such as troff, HTML, or XML, almost always involves throwing away large amounts of information.

Using MIF in Configuration Management Environments

Many configuration management or source control systems are designed for software development environments. Their support for text files is very good and includes the ability to compare two versions of a file side by side and see what changes were made.

FrameMaker's binary files can be stored under source control, but you will not be able to use many of the features that make source control so useful—the source control software cannot run a useful comparison on binary files. (A few source control systems, such as Documentum, do have direct support for FrameMaker.)

MIF provides one way to work around this problem. Instead of storing FrameMaker files, store MIF files under source control. There are, however, a number of problems with this technique:

- **File size.** MIF files are much larger than FrameMaker files, so file storage requirements are increased. However, storing 10 versions of a binary file may require just as much space as storing one copy of a MIF file and a list of changes for each version.
- **Workflow.** A MIF-based storage scheme requires that authors save files out to MIF before checking them in to the storage system. This can be automated with scripts, but it still adds an extra step to your workflow.

MIF files offer you a powerful alternative to working in the FrameMaker interface. The next time you face hours of manual reformatting or other tedious, repetitive work in FrameMaker, consider whether editing the MIF files might be quicker.

CHAPTER 25

Creating Modules with Text Insets

Most desktop publishing applications let you link graphics—you set up a pointer from a document to a particular graphic file. If that file is updated, the graphic in the document is updated automatically. FrameMaker supports linked graphics (they are discussed in Chapter 12, "Importing Graphic Content"), but in addition to graphics, FrameMaker also lets you link text into a document. Instead of importing a graphic, you import a file that contains text. If you update the file, its content is also updated where it is linked.

The imported-by-reference text fragments are called *text insets.* A development process based on assembling text fragments into larger documents is referred to as creating *modular documentation* or modular text—your final document is made up of smaller text chunks or *modules.* The composite document that's assembled from modules is called a *container document.*

TIP Text insets are used most commonly to import one FrameMaker file into another, but you can also import other supported file formats, such as Word files, as text insets. This works best if the file is relatively simple and if the styles used in Word match paragraph tags in the FrameMaker file.

Breaking up documents into modules lets you create small, reusable topics. This modular approach makes sense if you must write documentation for several related products. By dividing information in small chunks, you can maximize reuse of common information and write separate modules where the products differ.

Consider the example shown in Figure 25-1. You have two installation documents, one for Product A and one for Product B. The two products have identical system requirements and licensing agreements, but other information in the installation instructions is different. To take advantage of reuse, you created a system requirements document (reqs.fm) and a licensing agreement document (license.fm) and imported these as text insets. Any updates to the inset files will be reflected in both installation documents. Because you only have one copy of the license.fm and reqs.fm files, it doesn't make sense to put them in a specific product's directory; instead, many authors set up a shared directory, as shown in the following example:

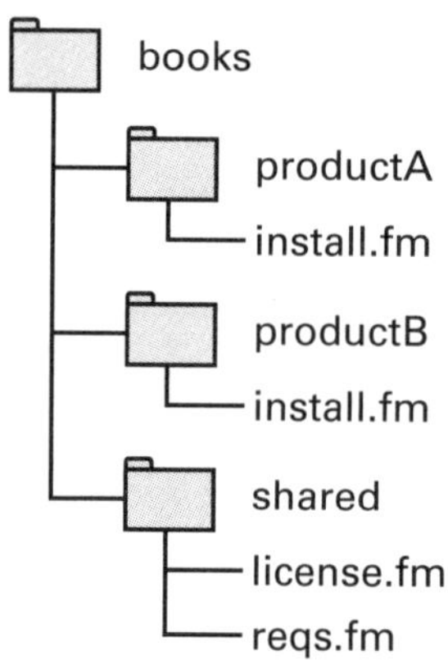

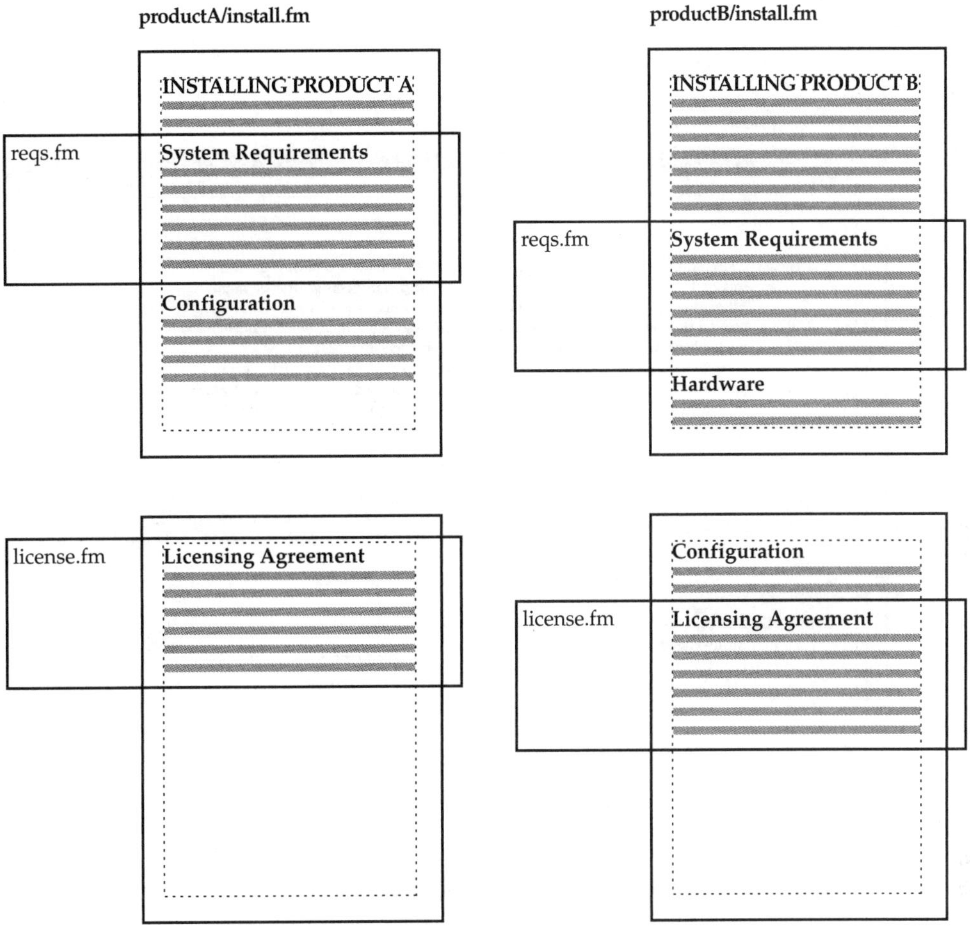

Figure 25-1. Text insets let you reuse information, which simplifies maintenance.

A Text Inset Example

Although FrameMaker refers to text insets as importing files, that isn't completely accurate. When you create a text inset, you import a specific *flow* from a file; most often, the main body flow (flow A). However, in some cases, you might set up a document that contains several different flows that you might want to import. This would be especially useful if you have a series of standard warnings that you need to repeat throughout a book. Instead of copying and pasting, you could create text insets in the book so that you don't have to worry about consistency.

In the following example, the author has set up separate text flows for each standard warning:

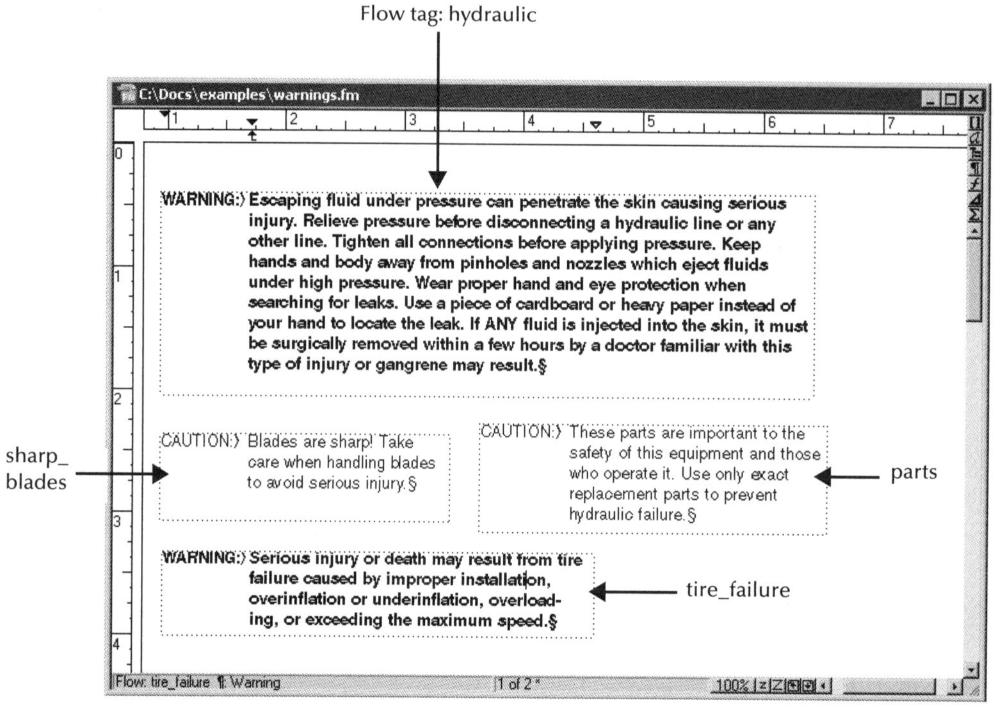

When you specify that you want to import text from the warnings file, you are prompted to choose a flow.

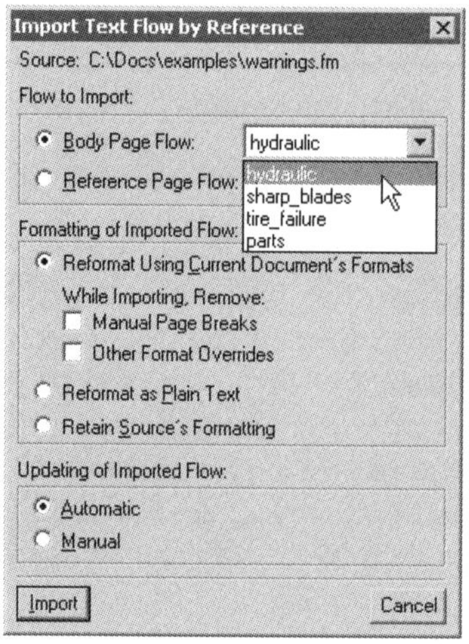

After selecting a flow, that information is included in the container document.

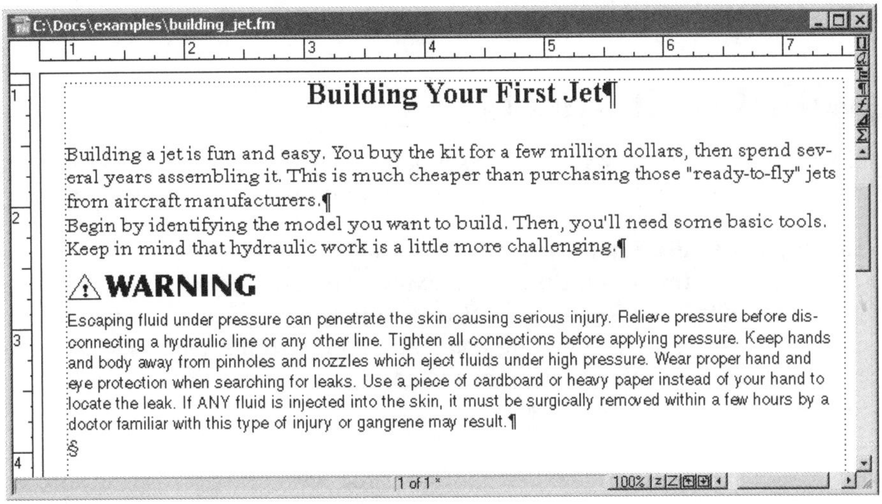

NOTE In the example shown here, formatting of the warning paragraph is quite different in the source (warnings.fm) than it is when used in a container. The paragraph tag definition in the container document is overriding the information provided in the source document. You can control this with the Formatting of Imported Flow section when you import the text flow.

You cannot edit text insets in the container document. Selecting them results in the entire text inset being selected, just like a cross-reference or a variable (except that the text inset could be many pages long).

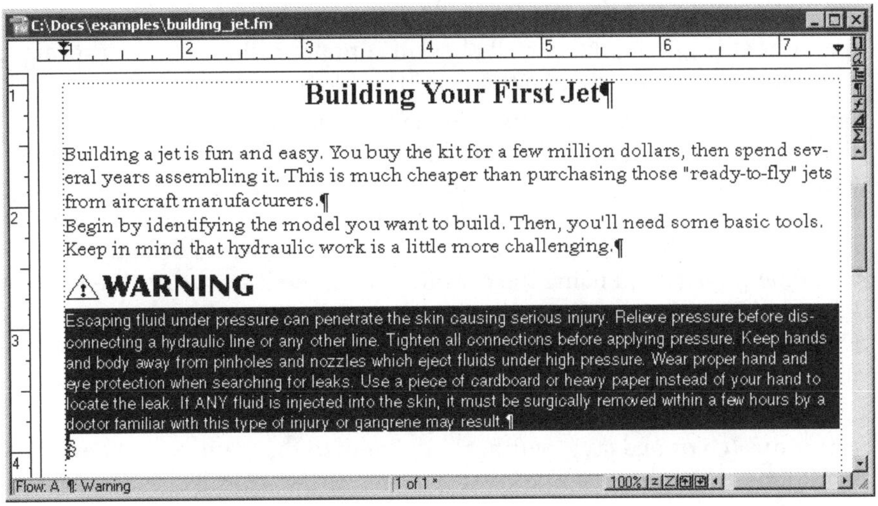

Instead, you must open the source document and make any changes there. After you save the file and update your text insets, the new information is displayed wherever that text inset is used.

Working with Text in Insets

For some features, content inside a text inset behaves like regular text. In some cases, though, there are differences between regular text and text in a text inset:

- **Adding cross-references.** If you want to add a cross-reference to a heading that is part of a text inset, there is an extra step that isn't obvious. Before you cross-reference anything in the text inset, open the text inset and add a cross-reference marker to the heading you want to cross-reference. Save the text inset. To add cross-references to headings in the text inset, point to the container file, not the text inset.

Tip

If you add a cross-reference to a container file without first making sure the text inset has the necessary cross-reference marker saved in it, the cross-reference breaks when you update the cross-references. The cross-reference often looks fine (although it won't be updated if the text or page number changes), but the broken cross-reference message keeps reappearing. It's not unusual for authors to redo the cross-references repeatedly and then finally give up on text insets in frustration.

- **Finding unresolved cross-references.** Text insets are checked for unresolved cross-references when you open the container file.
- **Finding and replacing information.** The Find/Change command does not work inside text insets when searching a container file. To search inside a text inset, you must open the text inset file.
- **Spell-checking.** When you spell-check a container file, its text insets are not spell-checked. You must open the text inset file to spell-check it.
- **Variable definitions.** If you use a variable inside a text inset, the container file may display the variable definition from the text inset or the variable definition from the container file, depending on your settings. If you specify that you want to retain the formatting from the source file, the variable definition from the text inset file is used. If you specify that the text inset should be reformatted using the container document's settings, the variable definition from the container document is used, *provided that the variable is defined in the container document.* If it is not, the original value from the inset file is used.
- **Conditional text settings.** Show/Hide settings and conditional text definitions (color and style settings) are handled the same way that variable definitions are. If you retain formatting from the source document, settings

from the text inset are used. If you reformat with the container document's settings, the container document overrides tags with matching names.

- **Generated lists.** When you create a generated list from the container file, information from the inset file is included.
- **Separating stacked text insets.** After a text inset, make sure you insert a blank paragraph (as regular text in the container document) with a space in it before beginning the next text inset. Stacking text insets without the "separator" paragraph causes formatting problems. The second text inset takes on the formatting used by the first line of the first text inset. (You can define the separator paragraph with a two-point font size and negative space above or below so that it doesn't take up any space on the page.)
- **Converting text with insets to HTML.** When you convert to HTML, text insets are treated like regular text.

Considering Text Insets and Other Reuse Options

Text insets are not the only way you can reuse information. As you begin to plan your physical file organization, consider using any or all of the following techniques:

- **Cross-references.** With cross-references, you can link to a paragraph of text. This works well for standard, repeated information, such as a copyright statement or standard warnings. However, you cannot create a cross-reference that picks up more than a paragraph of text at one time, so if you need to insert more than one paragraph of text, cross-references won't work.
- **Conditional text.** Conditional text lets you label information as belonging to a particular version of a document. You can use conditional text to embed two (or more) versions of the same document in a single file. Text insets, by contrast, let you reuse information in multiple files.
- **Multiple books.** You can create two versions of a document by creating two book files. You include the files that the two versions have in common in both files; the specific files are in only one book or another. The main disadvantage to this approach is that each file must start on a new page. If your product differences are at the chapter level, this approach usually works quite well. Text insets do not have to start a new page.
- **Text insets.** Lets you embed chunks of text from one file in another. Chunks can include any type of content—paragraphs, character tags, anchored frames, equations, and so on—and can be a paragraph or several pages long. When you create a text inset, the information is integrated into the container file without requiring a page break. To create different versions of content, you must create two or more container files and import different sets of text modules into those files.

Planning Modular Text

Like conditional text, text insets are much easier to create than to plan. Assigning a condition or importing a text inset is the easy part; deciding what conditions to use and what information should go in which text inset is much more difficult. Without careful planning, you're likely to encounter serious frustration with text insets.

Breaking Text Down into Modules

Breaking down information into modules can be a bit of a black art. Headings are a logical starting place. Some highly hierarchical documents are easy to break up. For example, an alphabetical list of programming commands is easy to break into modules where each module contains one command, its explanation, code example, and the like. For task-oriented user's guides, a logical starting point for creating modules would be procedures. The most difficult part in creating modular procedures is the transition information from one procedure to the next. Instead of trying to write generic transitions in the text inset, consider inserting that content in the container document as you assemble the documents.

File Storage

File storage requirements will depend on the number of modules. If you are sharing just a few modules—such as a copyright page, system requirements list, and document conventions—across a few books, you may be able to create a simple file organization with a shared folder for the modules.

As the number of modules increases, however, it becomes more difficult to manage the module files. If you have hundreds or thousands of module files, you will probably need to set up a version control system, which lets you check in and check out files.

Information Retrieval

Setting up a storage system for files can be complicated, but establishing a system that ensures you can find relevant modules is an even bigger challenge. To locate files, you need to track some or all of the following information about each module:

- Main topic/title
- Keywords
- File location
- Author
- Last revision date
- Used in which books

For a small group of modules, a simple table or spreadsheet could suffice:

Topic	Keywords	File	Author	Revised
copyright	copyright, legal statements, trademarks	shared/ copyright.fm	SSO	6/5/02
system requirements	system requirements, hardware, software, RAM, memory	shared/reqs.fm	SAL	5/20/02
document conventions	boldface, italic, conventions, menu selection	shared/ conventions.fm	ASP	1/16/02

If you have hundreds or thousands of modules, consider setting up a database to keep track of them.

Controlling Formatting in Text Insets

Like any other FrameMaker file, a file used as a text inset contains tagging information. The text inset file also includes formatting information that specifies how a paragraph tag should be displayed.

When you import a file as a text inset, you can use the formatting specified in the text inset file. But more often, you specify that the container file's formatting should override the information in the text inset. This results in a situation where the appearance of information in the text inset file may be significantly different from the appearance in the text inset because the formatting templates are different.

The following example shows a warning in the original file. Notice the word "WARNING:" and the hanging indent.

WARNING: **Escaping fluid under pressure can penetrate the skin causing serious injury. Relieve pressure before disconnecting a hydraulic line or any other line. Tighten all connections before applying pressure. Keep hands and body away from pinholes and nozzles which eject fluids under high pressure. Wear proper hand and eye protection when searching for leaks. Use a piece of cardboard or heavy paper instead of your hand to locate the leak. If ANY fluid is injected into the skin, it must be surgically removed within a few hours by a doctor familiar with this type of injury or gangrene may result.§**

After that text flow is imported into a container document, the appearance of the warning changes significantly. The warning paragraph tag in the container document uses a frame above the paragraph (see page 125) to insert the exclamation mark icon and the word warning. The font is different, and there is no hanging indent.

> ⚠ **WARNING**
>
> Escaping fluid under pressure can penetrate the skin causing serious injury. Relieve pressure before dis-connecting a hydraulic line or any other line. Tighten all connections before applying pressure. Keep hands and body away from pinholes and nozzles which eject fluids under high pressure. Wear proper hand and eye protection when searching for leaks. Use a piece of cardboard or heavy paper instead of your hand to locate the leak. If ANY fluid is injected into the skin, it must be surgically removed within a few hours by a doctor familiar with this type of injury or gangrene may result.¶

TIP In addition to modifying paragraph styles, the inset items also inherit other settings, such as variable definitions and conditional text settings. That means you can set a variable for a product name in the text inset, and display different product names depending on the variable definition in each container document. You do not have to update the text inset's variable definition. The inset is displayed in different containers with different values for the variable.

If you are overriding formatting in the source files, the actual paragraph tag settings in the source files are irrelevant. It is important, though, to ensure that each text inset uses the correct set of tags. When you update your template, you must import those formats into each text inset file. To help make this task easier, consider creating a book to manage text insets. The book contains a link to each of the text inset files, so you can update formats definitions for each text inset by importing formats to all of the files in the book.

Using a dummy book also lets you perform global search-and-replace operations across text insets—remember that search and replace on a container file does *not* look inside the inset files.

Creating a Text Inset

To create a text inset, you need at least two documents: the module file and the container file into which you plan to import the module.

To set up the text inset, follow these steps:

1. Open the container document.
2. Position your cursor where you want the text inset to start.

TIP Use a blank paragraph before the inset to ensure that the text inset doesn't get mashed into the previous paragraph.

3. Select File➤Import➤File, just as if you were getting ready to import a graphic. The Import dialog box is displayed.

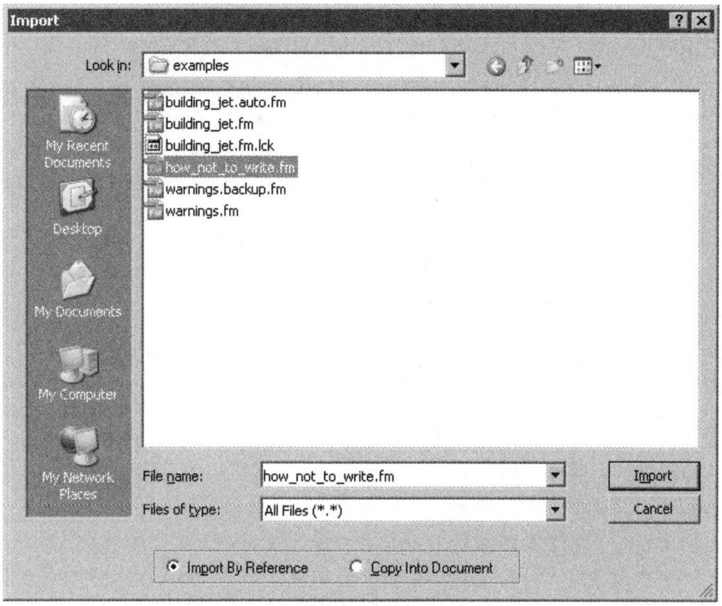

4. In the Import dialog box, locate and select the file you want to use.
5. Make sure that the Import by Reference radio button is selected, then click the Import button. The Import Text Flow by Reference dialog box is displayed (Figure 25-2).

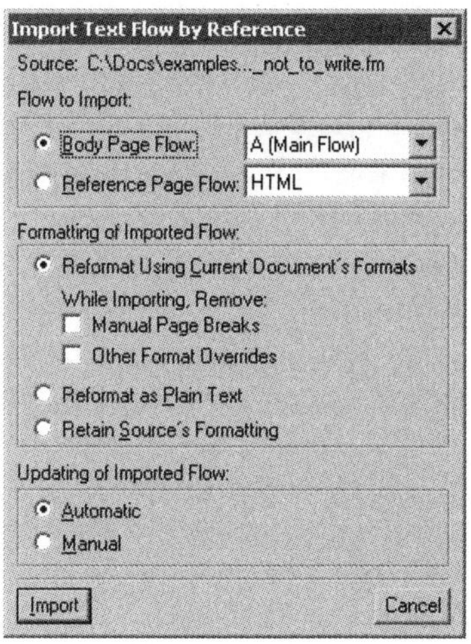

Figure 25-2. When importing, you can choose a particular flow and how the inset should be formatted.

6. Select a flow to import. The main body page flow is usually A.

7. In the Formatting of Imported Flow section, specify whether you want to apply the current document's template. Your choices are as follows:
   - **Reformat Using Current Document's Catalogs:** Inserts the content and applies the paragraph and other tags from the current document. Any matching tags are overwritten, so if the text inset uses a Body tag that's defined with Helvetica, and the container document has a Body tag that's defined with Garamond, all of the Body tags in the text inset will be displayed with the Garamond tag.
   - **Reformat as Plain Text:** The entire imported text flow is formatted using the format of the paragraph tag into which you are inserting the text.
   - **Retain Source's Formatting:** The inset retains the formatting specified in the inset document.
8. Specify how you want the imported flow updated:
   - **Automatic:** The text inset is updated when you open or print the container document and when a book that includes the container document is updated with an update for text insets specified.
   - **Manual:** The text inset is updated only when you select Edit➤References and specify that you want to update text insets set for manual updates or when you update the book and specify that you want to update text insets.
9. Click the Import button. The specified flow is imported into the container file.

Managing Text Insets

Text insets are updated differently from imported graphics. When you change a graphic file that's imported by reference, FrameMaker immediately picks up the change in the graphic and updates the version displayed in the FrameMaker file. With text insets, updating is similar to cross-references; it occurs when you open a file, update the book, and the like. However, unlike cross-references, you can set text insets for two different types of updates—manual or automatic. This setting determines when the text insets are updated.

When you first import a text inset, you are prompted to specify whether the inset should be updated manually or automatically (see step 8 in the preceding section).

To change a text inset's update status, follow these steps:

1. Double-click the text inset. This displays the Text Inset Properties dialog box (Figure 25-3).

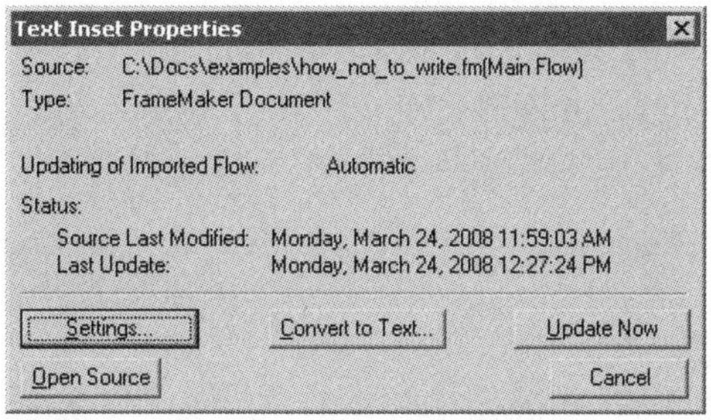

Figure 25-3. FrameMaker keeps track of the file name and the flow of the selected text inset.

2. Click the Settings button. This displays the Import Text Flow by Reference dialog box (Figure 25-2 on page 607).
3. In the Updating of Imported Flow section, select Automatic or Manual.
4. Click the Import button to update the text inset's settings.

FrameMaker provides several different ways to update text insets. Some methods update only the insets set up for automatic updates; some update both.

Text insets set for manual updates are refreshed only when you explicitly request an update.

TIP To update a single text inset, double-click it to display the Text Inset Properties dialog box (shown in Figure 25-3), then click the Update Now button. To update all the text insets in a file, complete the next procedure.

To update text insets, follow these steps:

1. In the container document, select Edit➤Update References. The Update References dialog box is displayed.

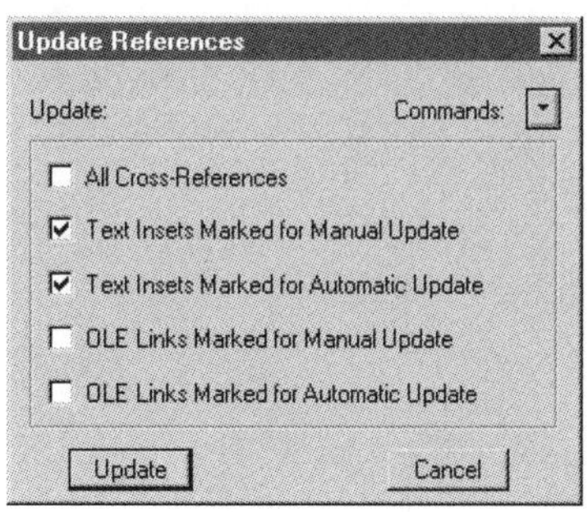

2. Check the items you want to update. To update all text insets, make sure that both the Text Insets Marked for Manual Update and the Text Insets Marked for Automatic Update check boxes are checked.
3. Click the Update button to update the specified items.

There are a number of other ways to update text insets; they are shown in the following table.

Action	Automatic Updates	Manual Updates
Open file	Yes	No
Edit➤Update References	Yes, if Text Insets Marked for Automatic Update check box is checked	Yes, if Text Insets Marked for Manual Update check box is checked
Update book	Yes, if Update All Text Insets is selected	Yes, if Update All Text Insets is selected
Print file	Yes	No
Save file	Yes	No
Double-click text inset, then click Update Now button	Yes	Yes

Opening the Source File

You can open the text inset source file by selecting File➤Open, locating the text inset, and opening it just like any other FrameMaker file. To edit a text inset that's displayed in the document window, double-click it, and then click the Open Source button in the Text Inset Properties dialog box (Figure 25-3 on page 609).

Converting Text Insets to Text

If necessary, you can convert text insets to regular text. Doing so destroys the link from the container file to the text inset file.

To convert text insets to text, follow these steps:

1. Double-click a text inset to display the Text Inset Properties dialog box (Figure 25-3 on page 609).
2. Click the Convert to Text button. This displays the Convert Text Insets to Text dialog box.

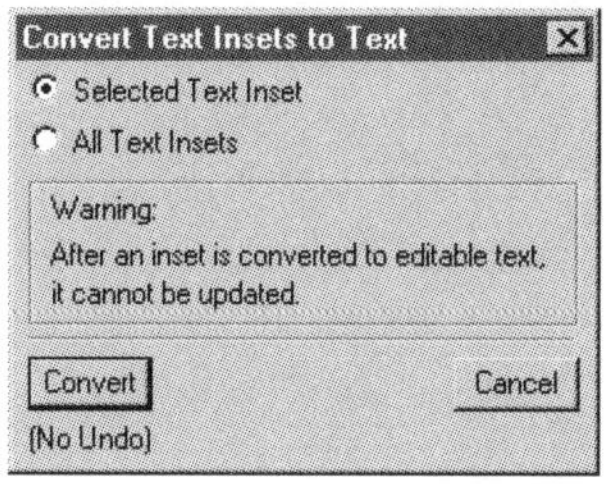

3. Do one of the following:
   - To convert only the current text inset, click the Selected Text Inset radio button.
   - To convert all text insets in this file to text, click the All Text Insets radio button.

CAUTION Converting text insets to text destroys the links. The information is no longer linked to the source file, so updating the source file doesn't change anything in the container files.

4. Click the Convert button. The specified text insets are converted to text.

CHAPTER 26

Templates

FrameMaker workflow relies on style sheets. By importing formats from a template file, different authors can create documents with consistent formatting. FrameMaker files do not refer to an external template file; instead, once the template is set up, you must import formatting information from the template file into the document files. Doing so creates a complete copy of all of the template information in the document files. Any document can theoretically be used as a template, but it's a very good idea to create a single, official template file and keep it in a safe place. All style sheet changes or additions should be made in that file. Without an official template, documents will eventually start to diverge as you or others add tags to individual files. (This phenomenon is known as "tag creep.")

Setting up FrameMaker templates requires much more detailed knowledge about the product than using templates after they are developed. Many organizations employ specialists or hire an outside consultant to set up their templates. Generally, the responsibilities in a writing group are divided into a number of different roles:

- **Template designer:** The template designer needs advanced FrameMaker skills. The designer creates FrameMaker templates.
- **Content creator (author):** The author needs basic-to-intermediate FrameMaker skills. Authors use established FrameMaker templates to create and edit information. Authors need to know how to apply style sheets and create special entities, such as cross-references.
- **Production editor:** The production editor needs advanced FrameMaker skills. The production editor prepares documents for printing or other final output. Production editors check formatting, ensure that pages and lines break in appropriate places, and usually create the final version of tables of contents and indexes.

A larger publications group may also include technical editors, indexers, and the like; their level of FrameMaker knowledge needs to be similar to that of the authors. In a small publications group, one person often performs all of these roles.

This chapter describes some of the issues you must consider as a template designer.

Why You Should Care About Templates

A well-designed template increases productivity greatly because it supports the authors, editors, and production editors in creating a document that's formatted correctly. Table tags, for example, let you define ruling and shading properties in a table so that when an author inserts a table, the table automatically uses the correct settings. Without a table tag, authors or production editors would have to spend time formatting each table manually. Running headers and footers save a lot of work by picking up information from the main body text, such as the current first-level heading, and automatically displaying it at the top or bottom of the page.

Reference page definitions control how generated tables of contents and indexes are formatted. Predefined cross-reference formats anticipate references that the author might need to insert and provide various options for the cross-reference text.

It's *possible* to create consistent documents without templates, but it's not efficient. In an environment where you are producing hundreds or thousands of pages of documents every year, working without an established template is a lot like walking a tightrope without a safety net—and wearing clown shoes.

Getting Started with Templates

The easiest way to begin creating templates is to start with an existing template and modify it to suit your requirements. When you install FrameMaker, several templates are put in your installation directory in the templates folder. These templates are also available when you select File➤New➤Document.

Adobe has also created a number of additional templates, which you can download from their web site. At the time of this writing, the templates are located at www.adobe.com/products/framemaker/tempseries/.

If that link doesn't work, try searching adobe.com for "framemaker templates." If you don't have the time to create your own templates, many FrameMaker consultants offer template design services.

Importing Settings from a Template File

When you import formats from a template file to a document, you can specify which catalogs you want to update. In each catalog, FrameMaker performs an additive merge—that is, tags with matching names are updated, and any tags that exist in the template but not in the document are added to the document.

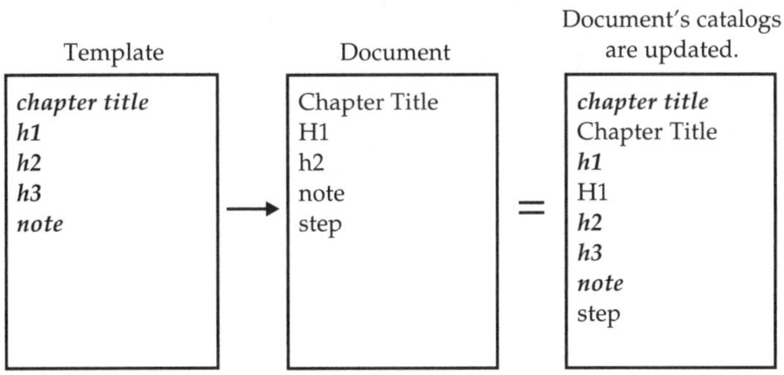

To apply a template, follow these steps:

1. Open the template file.
2. Open your working file (the file you want to apply the template to).

TIP To import formats into several files in a book file, open the book, then select the files you want to update.

3. Select File➤Import➤Formats. The Import Formats dialog box is displayed (Figure 26-1).

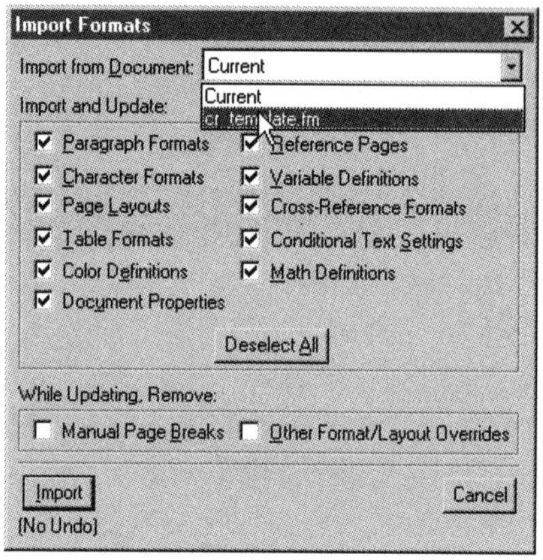

Figure 26-1. Importing formats from one file to another

4. In the Import from Document drop-down list, click the template file. Only open files are shown in this list.

TIP One quick way to remove overrides from a document is to import formats from the current file and check all the available check boxes.

5. In the Import and Update section, check all of the items you want to update from the template. Generally, you will want to update everything, but you can also perform selective updates. Click the Deselect All button to uncheck every option; click the Select All button (which replaces the Deselect All button) to check every option.
6. *(optional)* To remove page breaks that were set with overrides, check the Manual Page Breaks check box.
7. *(optional)* To remove overrides other than page breaks, check the Other Format/Layout Overrides check box.
8. Click the Import button to import the specified items from the template.

What's Imported?

Each check box in the Import and Update section of the Import Formats dialog box (Figure 26-1) controls a specific set of formatting catalogs. They are as follows:

- **Paragraph Formats:** Imports the contents of the paragraph catalog.
- **Character Formats:** Imports the contents of the character catalog.
- **Page Layouts:** Imports the master pages.
- **Table Formats:** Imports the table catalog; the list is in the Table Designer.
- **Color Definitions:** Imports the color catalog.
- **Document Properties:** Imports several miscellaneous settings. They include custom marker definitions, change bar settings, numbering properties, text options, and PDF settings.
- **Reference Pages:** Imports the reference pages.
- **Variable Definitions:** Imports the variables and their definitions.
- **Cross-Reference Formats:** Imports cross-reference formats.
- **Conditional Text Settings:** Imports conditional text tags, conditional expressions, and show/hide settings.
- **Math Definitions:** Imports custom math element definitions (used in equations).

What Makes a "Good" Template?

Because templates involve making design decisions, beauty may well be in the eye of the beholder. There are, however, features that can make some templates more functional than others. The purpose of a template is to enable authors to create documents that have a consistent look and feel. A good template will assist in this process and help automate some tasks.

Consider, for example, the use of paragraph tags. It's possible to create two pages that look the same without using paragraph tags—the author could use the Format menu's Font selections and create two identical pages. It is, however, a tedious, manual, and time-consuming process. It would be much more efficient to create a couple of paragraph tags to format the items on the page. The paragraph tags, however, are useful only if the authors choose to use them.

Designing a good template requires more than just implementing paragraph tags. It also requires you, the template designer, to balance complexity and completeness. A *complete* template is a file that contains all of the tags needed to format documents consistently. But if that template is too *complex,* authors will face a steep learning curve in figuring out all the available tags and how to use them. Authors generally respond to an overly complex template by ignoring it.

Perhaps the best definition of a good template is any template that authors are willing and able to follow consistently, and can use to produce consistent results.

Understanding Template Interactions

There is no single correct way to build a template. Some template designers start with master pages and page settings, and then they add paragraph tags to get the overall page design set up. Others insist that you must start with character tags because they are used by other features (such as paragraph autonumbering, variables, and cross-references). Still another approach is to create lots of different items as needed—if a paragraph tag needs a character tag for autonumber formatting, the designer jumps over to the Character Designer, creates the character tag, and returns to the Paragraph Designer to complete the paragraph definition.

We do recommend that you make a list of all of the needed formats and check them off as you build them so that you can keep track of what's needed and what's been created.

As you create your template, keep in mind that most of the template features are interdependent. Variables use character tags for formatting. Paragraph tags use the color catalog for available colors. Cross-references can call paragraphs. The configuration of master pages affects how paragraph tags appear on the page. Master pages use system variables for headers and footers. All of these interactions can make designing a template a rather disconcerting experience because it's impossible to design in a linear process. See Figure 26-2.

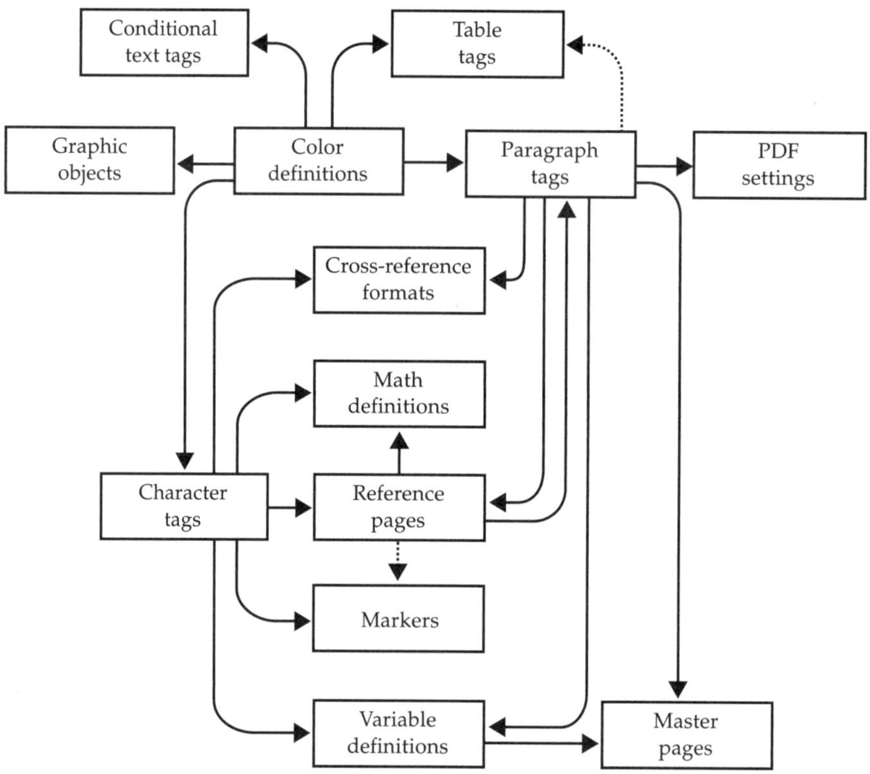

Figure 26-2. Template items have significant interdependencies.

The following sections explain how the template components interact.

Color Definitions

The color catalog is rarely the first item created in a template, but perhaps it should be. The color definitions are accessible to a number of other items, but color definitions do not have any dependencies on other template items. By default, 16 are provided.

Character Tags

Character tags have only one dependency; the colors available in the Color drop-down list are taken from the color catalog. To assign a custom color to a character tag, you must first define the color in the color definitions.

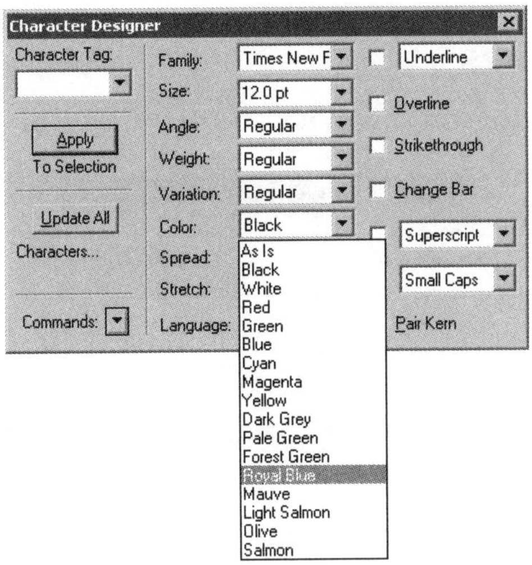

Character tags are widely used in other template components, including paragraph tags, variables, cross-references, and reference pages. They are also used in markers to assign formatting.

Graphic Objects

When you create various graphic objects using FrameMaker's drawing tools, the colors you can assign are determined by the color catalog.

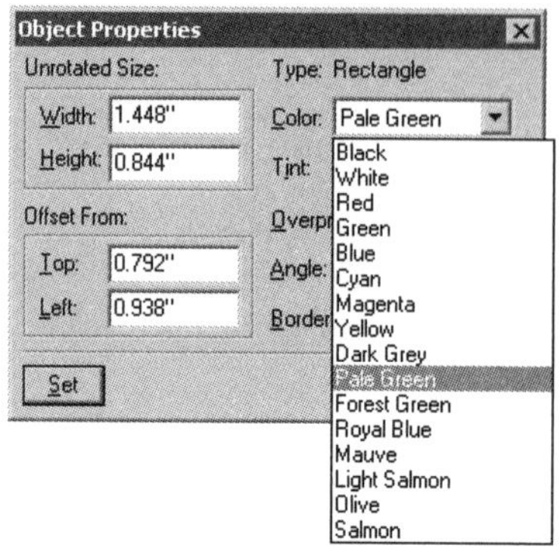

If your drawing includes text lines, they are formatted with character tags. Text in text frames is formatted with paragraph tags. Because not every graphic includes text, these relationships are not shown in Figure 26-2.

Conditional Text Tags

The colors available for conditional text tags are determined by the color catalog.

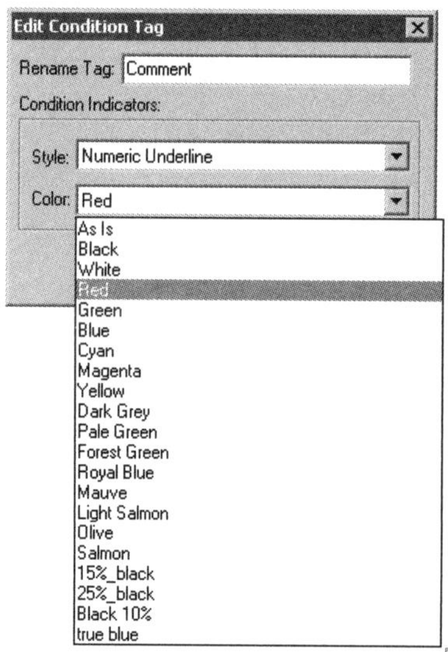

You might want to set up conditional text in the template, perhaps to include certain items in online output that don't show in print, or to insert comments that you can show in drafts and hide in the final output. Plan which conditions you need and how you want them to interact. You can choose whether you want conditions to Show as per Condition or Show as per Expression, which is as confusing as it sounds. See Chapter 21, "Setting Up Conditional Text," for details about conditional text.

Paragraph Tags

Settings in the Paragraph Designer have three dependencies: color, reference pages, and character tags. For color, the situation is identical to the Character Designer; you can only assign colors that are defined in the color catalog. Character tags are available to format autonumbering. On the Advanced properties sheet, the reference pages are involved because the options available in the Frame Above and Frame Below drop-down lists correspond to the named graphic frames defined in the reference pages.

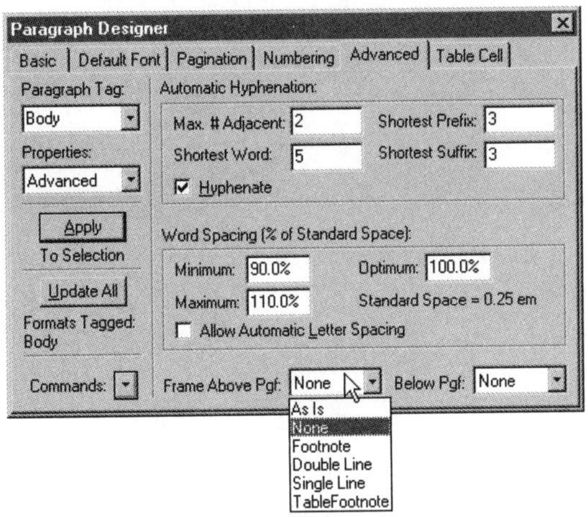

Paragraph tags are used by several other template components. Master page maps on reference pages use paragraph tags to determine which master page should be assigned to which page, variables call paragraph tags and use their text for running headers and footers, and so on.

Table Tags

Table tags use the color catalog and, under the covers, paragraph tags. The color definitions are available in several locations.

When you define shading colors, the Table Designer uses the color catalog:

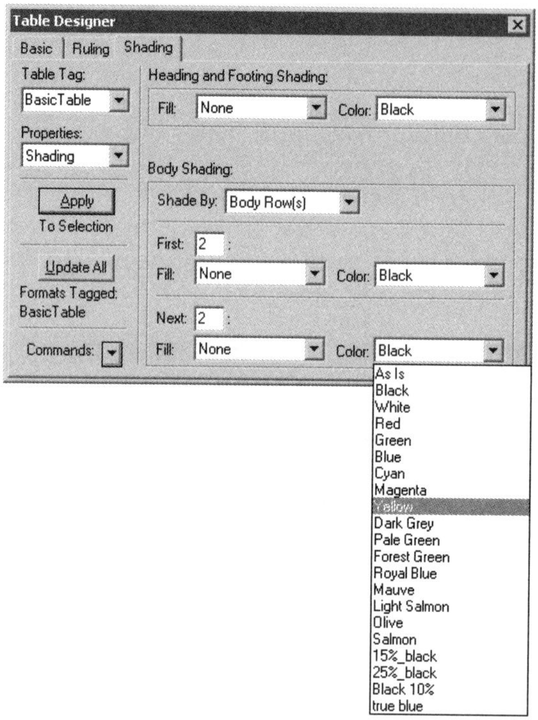

If you apply custom ruling and shading (Table➤Custom Ruling & Shading), the color catalog is also accessed. Finally, if you edit a ruling style (click the Edit Ruling Style button on the Custom Ruling and Shading dialog box), you again have to use information from the color catalog.

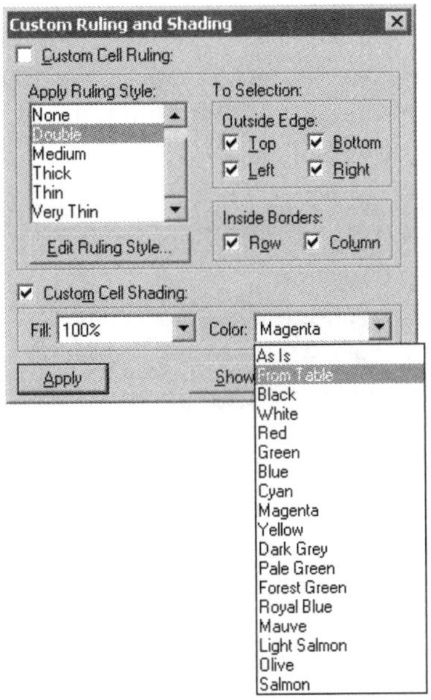

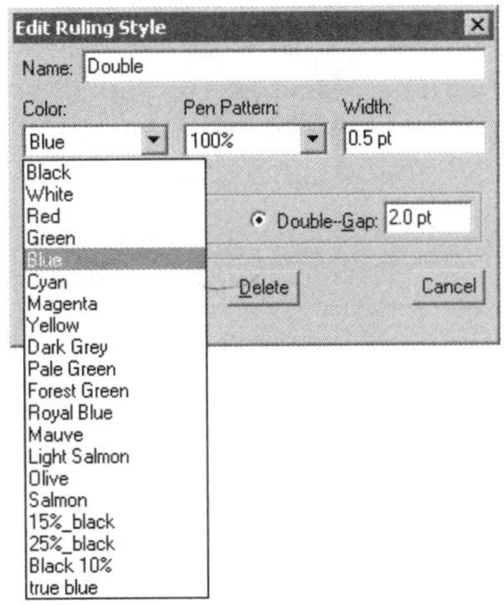

The relationship between table tags and paragraph tags is more subtle. The table definition stores a list of default paragraph tags used when you create new tables. For details, see "Applying Paragraph Tags" on page 175.

Cross-Reference Formats

Cross-references use character tags for formatting and paragraph tags to get information. When you set up a cross-reference definition, character tags are available in the list of building blocks. The items available are taken from the document's character catalog.

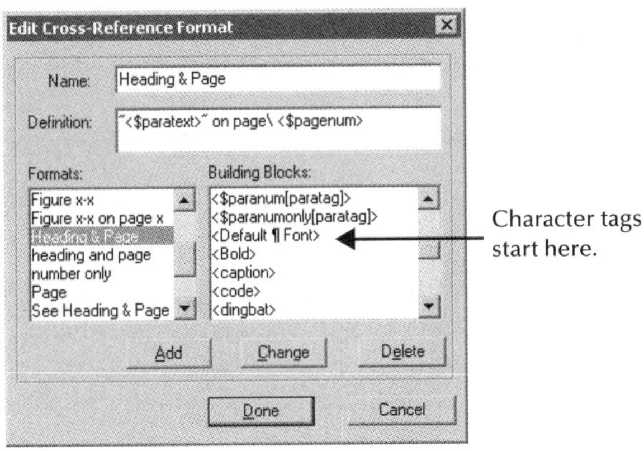

Several of the building blocks, such as <$paratext>, can be set up to refer to a specific paragraph tag.

Variable Definitions

Variable definitions, like cross-reference formats, use character tags for formatting and paragraph tags to determine what information to display. When you edit a system or user variable definition, you can assign character tags:

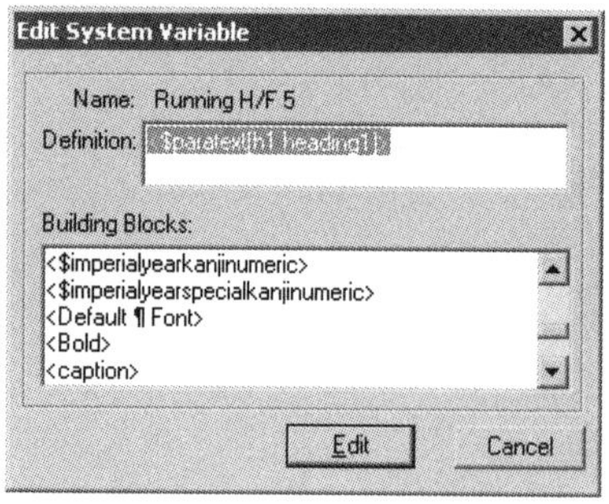

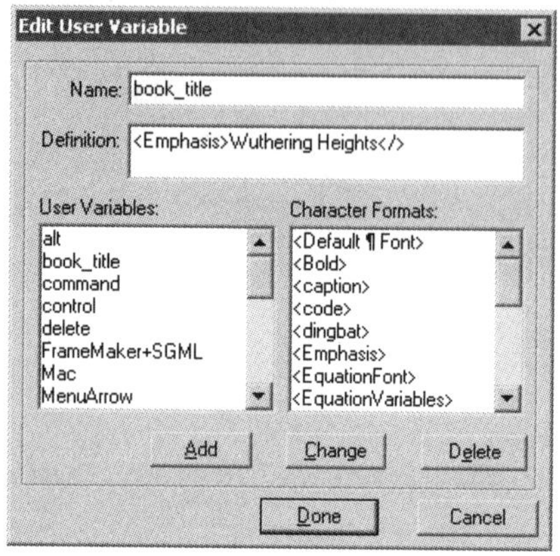

TIP The </> building block is equivalent to <Default Para Font>, but takes up much less space.

Some variables, such as running headers and footers, let you reference specific paragraph tags with syntax such as:

```
<$paratext[ChapterTitle]>
```

If you import variables from another FrameMaker document, both the system variables and user variables are imported together. Although you can use a MIF snippet or a third-party plug-in to get around this (see "Using MIF Fragments to Update Catalog Settings" on page 592), we recommend that you use the same system variables across all the files in the book. For example, define the system variable Running H/F 1 the same across all the files in your book. Otherwise, when you import variable formats, the headers or footers in some of the files may be wrong.

Reference Pages

Reference pages use information from the character tags and paragraph tags, and in turn are used by paragraph tags. There is also a relationship between reference pages and markers. When you set up flows for generated files, you work on the reference pages. These flows use character tags for formatting and refer to paragraph tags and sometimes markers.

The Paragraph Designer uses reference page information for Frame Above and Frame Below settings.

Markers

When you create marker text, such as index entries, you can use character tags to control the formatting of the file generated with the marker information. The appearance of the marker text is further governed by the information set on the reference pages in the generated file.

Math Definitions

Math definitions are custom components for equations. For the most part, equations stand on their own separately from other document objects. Equations do, however, use character tags for formatting.

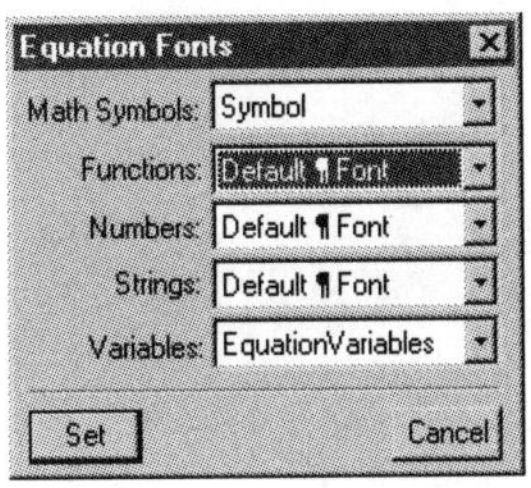

Equations can also use information from reference pages. You can define a custom equation object on a FrameMath reference page. This object is then available in the Equations Palette.

Master Pages

When you create master page definitions, you almost always use variables. The Current Page # system variable, for example, is on almost every master page definition. Running header and footer variables are also common.

You can assign master pages based on paragraph tags that occur on the body pages. This makes the master pages dependent on paragraph tags.

NOTE The mapping table that establishes these links is stored on the reference pages.

PDF Settings

When you configure the PDF Setup dialog box (Format➤Document➤PDF Setup), the bookmarks and tags are set based on available paragraph tags. PDF Setup is probably one of the last items you'll configure in your template.

The Bookmarks sheet lets you specify which FrameMaker paragraph tags should be displayed as bookmarks in the PDF file; you also specify their hierarchy.

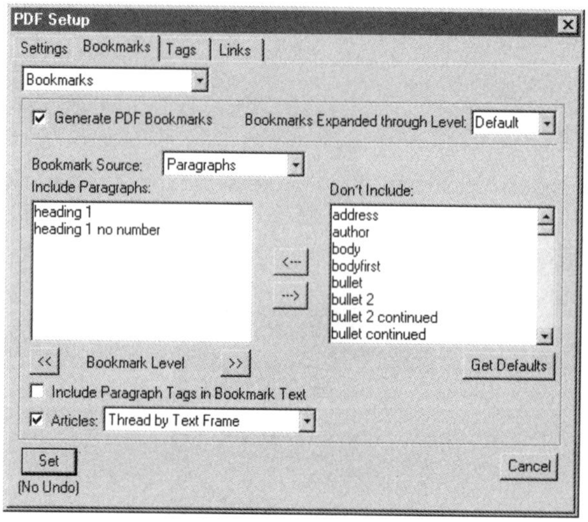

The Tags sheet lets you specify which FrameMaker paragraphs to include to create tagged PDF files. See "Generating Tagged PDF Files" on page 473 for more information about tagged PDF files.

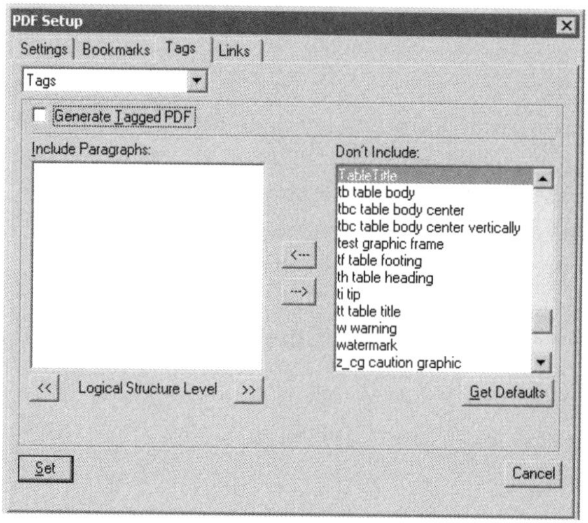

Tips and Tricks

This section describes some design tricks that automate certain features and make templates easier to use.

Paragraph Tags

When creating paragraph tags, pay close attention to naming conventions. Users spend more time using paragraph tags than any other item in the template.

Here are some issues to consider as you create paragraph tags:

- How many heading levels does the document need?
- How many types of body text does the document need?
- How many levels of indent?
- What kind of numbered lists?
- What kind of bulleted (unordered) lists?
- Do you need to set up header and footer styles? Are they different on left and right master pages?
- Does the document require an overall numbering scheme? Will you use <$volnum> and <$chapnum>? How will these integrate into the autonumbering you need to define?
- Do you need notes, cautions, warnings, tips, and other asides?
- Do you need formats for sidebars?
- What about table, figure, or example captions?

The following items will make your tags more useful:

- **Use Keep with Next (Pagination properties) to avoid awkward page breaks.** Headings usually belong with the paragraph beneath them, so set heading formats to keep with the next paragraph. This eliminates unsightly headings hanging at the bottom of a page. Consider whether other paragraph tags have similar requirements.
- **Control spell-checking with the Language setting (Default Font properties).** A language of None causes a paragraph to be skipped by the spell-checker, which is useful for code. If you have multiple languages in a single document, create paragraph tags for each language and set the Language attribute for each one. FrameMaker will use the dictionary and hyphenation settings of the specified language as it spell-checks each paragraph.
- **Set Widow/Orphan Lines (Pagination properties) to reduce awkward page breaks.** Use a widow/orphan setting of at least 2 throughout the paragraph tags to prevent solitary lines at the beginning or end of a page. If you want to keep an entire paragraph on the same page, use a very high number (for example, 99 or 999).

- **Use autonumbering for bullets, steps, notes, cautions, and any other repeated text.** Autonumbering is wonderful for numbered headings, figure captions, and tables, but don't forget the "text-based" autonumbering, which can also save significant amounts of time.
- **Use the Start setting (Pagination properties) to set up paragraph tags that should always start at the top of a page or column.** Most often, this will be your chapter title (Start Top of Right Page) and your first-level headings (Start Top of Page).
- **Use the Next Pgf Tag setting (Basic properties) where you can predict a likely paragraph tag.** Most heading paragraphs are followed by a body or firstbody paragraph. Most step 1 paragraphs are followed by step 2. By setting the default, you'll save your users a step—they won't have to assign the tag manually.

Character Tags

In addition to providing character-level formatting in regular text, character tags are referenced by several other features. Refer to this preliminary checklist as you build your list of required character tags:

- Character-level formatting
- Variables
- Formatting for autonumbers
- Cross-references
- Generated files
- Markers, especially index markers
- Math definitions
- Reference pages
- Text lines

As you create your character tags, keep in mind the following issues:

- In general, it's best to use the As Is setting throughout the character tag and assign specific settings only to the items you want to change.
- The Language attribute in the character tag overrides the Language attribute assigned by the paragraph tag.
- Consider creating special one-letter character tags that make inserting formatting in markers faster. For example, you could italicize a word in an index entry with this syntax:

```
cross-stitching needle: <Emphasis>see<Default Para
Font> tapestry needle<$nopage>
```

But if you define an "i" character tag, you could use this syntax for the same result:

```
cross-stitching needle: <i>see</>tapestry
needle<$nopage>
```

These shorter tags will also be very helpful on the reference pages. (Notice that these tags do break the rule against naming tags by their formatting.)

Table Tags

In addition to the ruling and shading attributes, keep in mind that you can set several properties as defaults (although not in the Table Designer). The defaults are saved based on the settings in the selected table when you click the Update All button in the Table Designer. The settings saved as defaults are the number of rows and columns, the column widths, and the default paragraph tags for the heading rows, body rows, and footing rows.

Reference Pages

When you create a graphic frame on the reference pages, you must assign a name to the graphic frame. The graphic frames are not, however, labeled by default, so to figure out which frame has which name, you must click each graphic frame so see its name. To avoid this, add a text label next to each graphic frame as you create it.

Entering Special Characters in Dialog Boxes

If you need to enter a special character that isn't on your keyboard into a dialog box, you cannot use keyboard sequences or the Symbols list available from the toolbar. Usually, the easiest way to enter special characters into dialog boxes is to copy and paste them from a document, but there are other methods you can use:

- Windows Character Map utility
- Unicode code points or hexadecimal codes
- Special escape sequences that FrameMaker provides
- ANSI codes

Pasting into Dialog Boxes from the Windows Character Map Utility

You can cut and paste from the Windows Character Map utility into a dialog box. See "Pasting from the Windows Character Map Utility" on page 66 for information about starting the utility.

For example, if you are adding a variable in which you want to use the Symbol font, you can define a character tag named Symbols for the font. The variable definition includes the character tag, the special character, and the building block for the default paragraph font. The definition looks like this in the dialog box for editing the variable:

```
<Symbols>§</>
```

The formatting from the character tag is not applied until you insert the variable in your document. In this example, the variable looks like this in the text:

♣

REMEMBER Characters pasted into dialog boxes such as the Find/Change dialog box retain their formatting. Characters in variables, character tag autonumbering, and markers display in the default system font until you insert them in your document.

Using Unicode Code Points or Hexadecimal Codes

You can type Unicode code points or a hexadecimal codes into dialog boxes. You can find the codes in the Windows Character Map utility. Supported hexadecimal codes are also listed in the *Adobe FrameMaker 8 Character Sets* online manual, which is in the Documents folder in the FrameMaker 8 installation directory.

To insert a character using a Unicode code point or hexadecimal code, follow these steps:

1. Open the Windows Character Map utility (see "Pasting from the Windows Character Map Utility" on page 66) and locate the code for the special character you want to insert:
   a. In the Font drop-down list, select the font.
   b. Check the Advanced View check box.
   c. If the Character Set drop-down list is available, select Unicode. (The Character Set is selectable when the font has Unicode code points associated with it. Selecting Unicode ensures that the correct characters are displayed in the dialog box. If the field isn't selectable, you can ignore this setting because the field has no effect on the characters shown in the dialog box.)

d. Click the special character you want to use. Its code is displayed at the bottom of the window. The code is a Unicode code point if it begins with a U (such U+1EBB). The code is a hexadecimal code if it doesn't have a U at the beginning (such as 0x65).

2. In the FrameMaker dialog box, type the code:

- **Unicode code point.** Type the Unicode code in the format \uXXXX. where XXXX is the code point. For example, to enter the Arial character ẻ (U+1EBB), type **\u1EBB**.

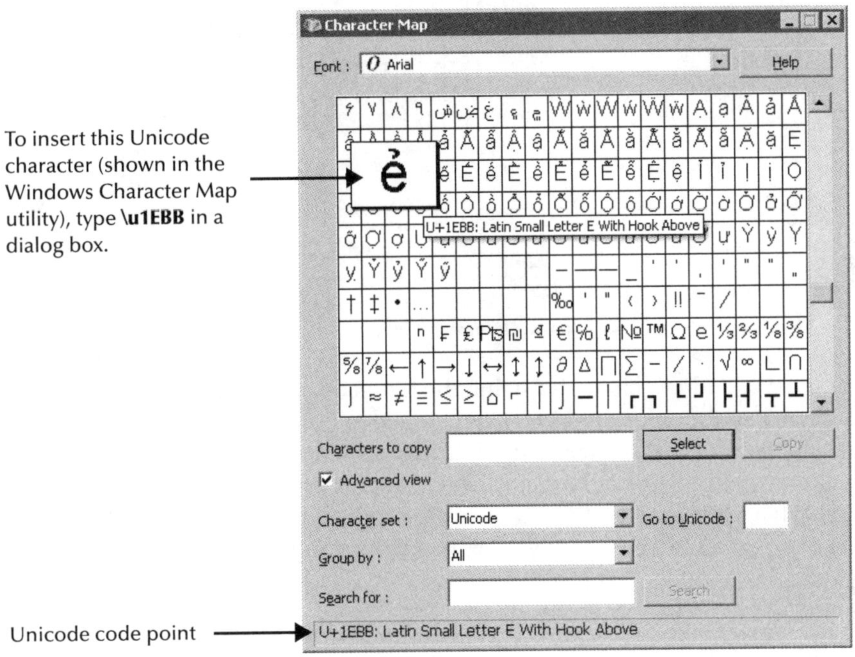

- **Hexadecimal code.** Type the hexadecimal code preceded by \x. (The *Adobe FrameMaker 8 Character Sets* online manual includes the \x with the codes.) If you found the code in the Windows Character Map utility, exclude the leading zero. For example, to enter the WP IconicSymbolsA character ✤ (065), type **\x65**.

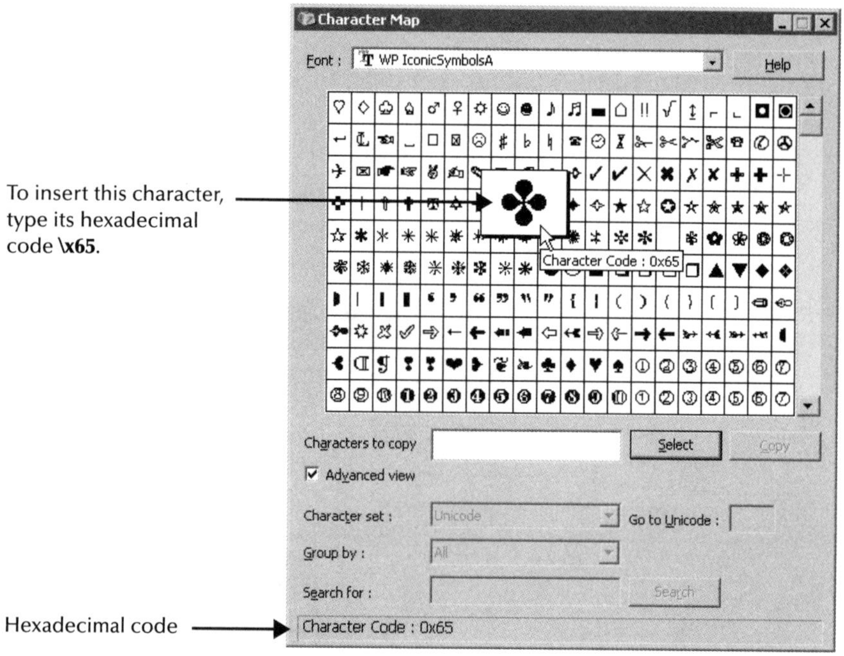

After you have added the character using the Unicode code point or hexadecimal code into a dialog boxes (such as the Find/Change dialog box), the dialog box displays the character itself instead of the code. In dialog boxes where you can specify the character's formatting with a character—such as cross-reference definitions, variables, and paragraph autonumbers—the character is displayed with the system's default font, so the character may not look like you expect until you insert it in the document with the character tag applied.

NOTE If the text uses a non-Unicode font, a question mark (?) is displayed in the text instead of the character. Apply the correct Unicode font to fix the problem. You may also see an unexpected character if the Adobe PDF printer is not selected in print setup.

Using Escape Sequences

FrameMaker provides escape sequences for typing some special characters. To use the escape sequence, you type a backslash and an additional character or characters. For example, to type an em dash in a dialog box, you type:

```
\=
```

The escape sequences for typing special characters in dialog boxes are documented in the FrameMaker online help.

For most special characters, the actual character (and not the backslash and other characters you typed) is displayed when you reopen the dialog box. For example, if you type \=, the dialog box contains the actual em dash character (—). However, for characters that would be invisible or confusing if the actual character were displayed in the dialog box, the escape sequences (such as \sm for an em space, \+ for a nonbreaking hyphen, or \t for a tab) continue to be displayed when you reopen the dialog box.

Using ANSI Codes in Dialog Boxes

You can use ANSI codes to insert special characters in dialog boxes just as you would within your FrameMaker document. See "Inserting Special Characters" on page 65. After you have added the character using either the ANSI code, you will no longer see the ANSI code in the dialog box. The dialog box will display the character itself.

Naming Conventions

The names you assign to tags can make your template significantly more or less usable. A carefully chosen set of tag names will be easy to understand and lend themselves to using keyboard shortcuts.

Capitalization

For the most part, the capitalization you choose for tags can be left to your personal preference. There are, however, a few things to consider:

- FrameMaker's default tags have an initial capital letter (Heading1, Body, and so on). If you plan to use the default tags, you may want to match other tags to use similar capitalization.
- If you do not plan to use FrameMaker's default tags, consider creating only lowercase tag names in your template so that you can easily distinguish your tags from any "renegade" tags.
- Default Word template styles use initial capital letters. When you convert Word files to FrameMaker, the style names are converted to paragraph tag names, and similar considerations apply as for the default FrameMaker templates.

Special Characters

FrameMaker *will* generally allow you to use special characters, such as asterisks (*), question marks (?), and pound signs (#), as part of your tag names. These characters can cause major problems, though, when you attempt to reference the tags. We strongly recommend that you use only alphanumeric characters (a–z, A–Z, and 0–9), underscores, and spaces.

Taking Keyboard Shortcuts into Account

Authors can apply many tags using keyboard shortcuts. In general, you press a key sequence to display the tag list in the status bar, and press a letter to jump to that part of the list. To accommodate authors who use this shortcut, it's very helpful to create tag names whose first few letters are unique. A good example of how *not* to do this are the default heading names in FrameMaker: Heading1, Heading2, and HeadingRunIn. Instead, you might use 1Head, 2Head, and 3Head. Some template designers start each tag name with a short, unique prefix, as shown in the following example:

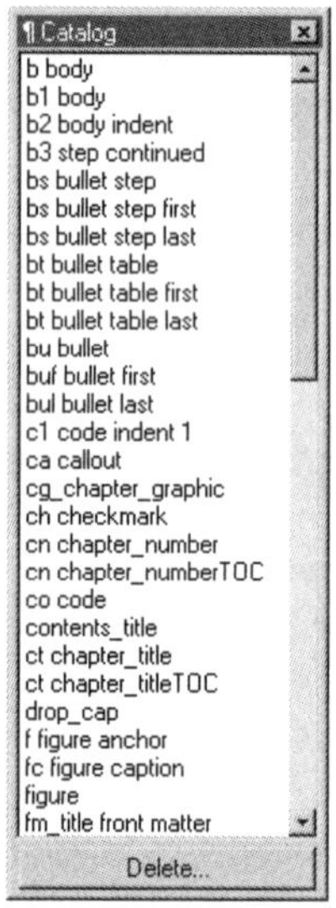

Format vs. Function Names

Most tag names are based on the format or function of the tag. For example, an Italics character tag is a format-based name; a PrintOnline conditional text tag is a function-based name.

Template designers generally recommend that you use names that describe function. There are several reasons for this:

- **Tags named by function are easier for an author to learn.** For example, if a book title occurs in a document, the author has an easier time remembering to apply the BookTitle character tag than remembering that italics are required and then locating the Italics character tag.
- **You can change formatting associated with functional tags without making the tag name obsolete.** Consider a character tag that indicates menu selection. In the past, your style guide indicated that the menu choice must be boldface; the new standard is to make the menu choice italic. You can change a

MenuItem character tag from boldface to italics; if your tag was named Bold, changing it to actually apply italics would cause great confusion.

- **Functional names are better suited to outputting structured documents.** A paragraph tag labeled Helv10pt would need to be mapped to an HTML tag of <p> or an XML tag of <para> or something similar. Using functional names in both FrameMaker and XML makes it easier to understand the relationship between the two formats.

There are a few occasions where a combination of functional and formatting names might be useful. For example, you might create a Body paragraph tag (functional) and a second BodyBold paragraph tag (functional and formatting). BodyBold tells the author very quickly what the difference is between the two paragraph tags. A more functional name, such as BodyImportant, might not deliver the message as quickly.

When implementing functional names, keep in mind that tag duplication can become a problem. You might, for example, have several different functional items that need to be italicized:

- BookTitle
- ForeignWord
- Emphasis
- FileName
- URL

Some authors will learn quickly that BookTitle creates italics, and will use BookTitle any time they need italics, even though other tags are more appropriate. Again, the key is to balance the need for functional labels against the overall usability of the template.

Separating Out "Housekeeping" Tags

Every template will have a number of tags that are intended for use "under the covers" and should not be applied by authors. These might include paragraph tags for the header and footer paragraphs and other information that occurs on the master pages. Consider using a special prefix for those tags. For example, naming them with a z_ prefix ensures that these tags are sorted to the bottom of the paragraph catalog, which makes it less likely that an author will accidentally use one of those tags.

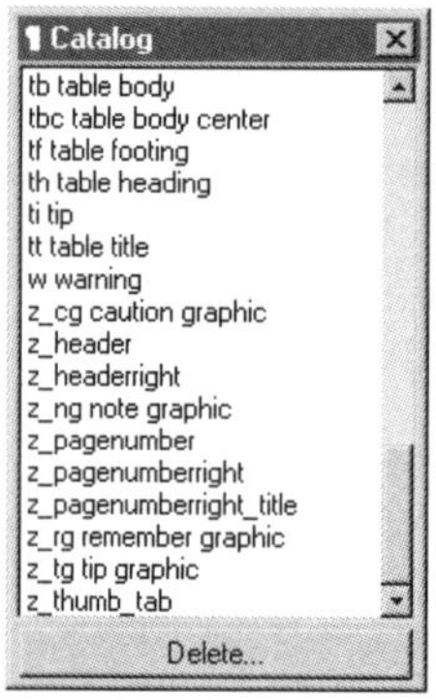

Documenting Your Template

Please document your templates. Documentation doesn't have to be elaborate, but a basic list of tags and how they are used will be extremely helpful to authors. It also helps to enforce consistency.

The best place to provide documentation for the template is in the template file itself. You can list paragraph tags in one table, character tags in another, conditional text settings in a third, and so on. Providing an example of each tag to show what it looks like is helpful.

Template documentation is a good place to list autonumbering streams. This helps you keep track of which series labels have been used and avoid collisions. For example, you might have something like the following table:

Tag	Autonumbering Definition
ChapterTitle	H:<$chapnum>
Heading1	H:<$chapnum>.<n+>
Heading2	H:<$chapnum>.<n>.<n+>
Figure	F:Figure <$chapnum>-<n+>
Table	T:Table <$chapnum>-<n+>
Step1	S:Step <n=1>
Step2	S:Step <n+>
SubStepA	U:<a=1>.
SubStepB	U:<a+>.

We recommend providing a list of tags for each type of formatting item. You may also want to provide additional documentation, such as standard settings for graphics (what resolution should be used when importing bitmap images?), instructions for creating books, tables of contents, and indexes, and perhaps even some basic style guidelines.

REMEMBER When you add new tags to the template, don't forget to update the template documentation.

Using Single-Purpose Templates

Some publishing applications have special documents that manage settings called *control files*. When you make a change in the control file, it is automatically applied to all of the files in the book.

FrameMaker does not have actual control files. You can, however, mimic this feature by using a single-purpose template, a document that contains a limited number of settings. You might, for example, create a document that contains no paragraph tags, character tags, or cross-references but has a full set of variable definitions. When you create a new book, all of the component files use the default settings for variables. When you are ready to set the variables to the values needed for this book, you follow these steps:

1. Open the variable control file and set the variables to the values needed for this book.
2. Open the book file.
3. Select all of the files in the book.
4. Select File➤Import➤Formats. The Import Formats dialog box is displayed.

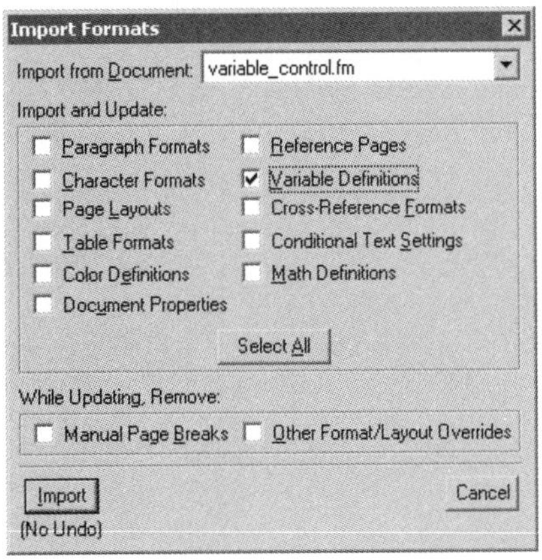

5. In the Import from Document drop-down list, click your variable control file.
6. In the Import and Update section, click the Deselect All button to uncheck all the boxes. (The button label toggles between Deselect All and Select All.)

7. Check only the Variable Definitions check box.
8. Click the Import button to import variable definitions from the selected file into all of the files in the book.

You could accomplish the same thing by modifying the variables in a chapter file and importing the formats from that file to the others in the book. Maintaining a separate variable-only file makes it easier, though, to segregate the changes you want to make (variable definitions) from any other changes that might have crept into the other chapter files.

TIP If you want to be extra-cautious (paranoid?) about accidentally copying in settings you don't want, you can create a MIF fragment that contains only the variable definitions instead of using a full-blown FrameMaker file. For details, see Chapter 24, "Maker Interchange Format."

CHAPTER 27

Sharing and Managing Files Using WebDAV

Web-based Distributed Authoring and Versioning, or *WebDAV,* is a technology that lets you share and manage documents over the Internet. Using WebDAV, you can take advantage of basic content management features without buying a separate software package. The documents you want FrameMaker to manage are stored on a server running the WebDAV protocol. To access the files, you set up a *workgroup* in FrameMaker that points to the WebDAV server. To edit files, you check out the files, which means working copies of the files are placed in a folder on your hard drive. FrameMaker also locks files to prevent users from modifying the same documents simultaneously. Other users can open the files you checked out and can download the last version saved on the server, but they can't modify the files. When you have finished, you check in the files.

FrameMaker files can be managed in a workgroup along with non-FrameMaker files, such as imported graphics or PDF files. Applications other than FrameMaker also support WebDAV, so you can open a managed graphic in Adobe Illustrator, for example, or open a managed PDF file in Adobe Acrobat.

NOTE You can turn off the workgroup feature if you're not working with files on the WebDAV server. As a result, the WebDAVLinks palette isn't displayed when you open FrameMaker. However, if you open a managed document when workgroup functionality is off, the document is opened in read-only mode. See "Modifying Workgroup Preferences" on page 644 for details.

Managing Workgroups

Before you begin sharing files, a WebDAV server must be installed and configured. Many WebDAV servers are available for free from www.webdav.org. Typically, your system administrator (or an eager coworker) handles the installation. The server can be difficult to configure, and security policies must be set up to provide for secure transfers over the Internet. You'll probably have a user name and password to download and upload files.

To create a workgroup in FrameMaker after the WebDAV server is installed, follow these steps:

1. Click in the text flow of a FrameMaker document
2. Select File➤Workgroup➤Workgroup Servers. The Workgroup Servers dialog box is displayed.

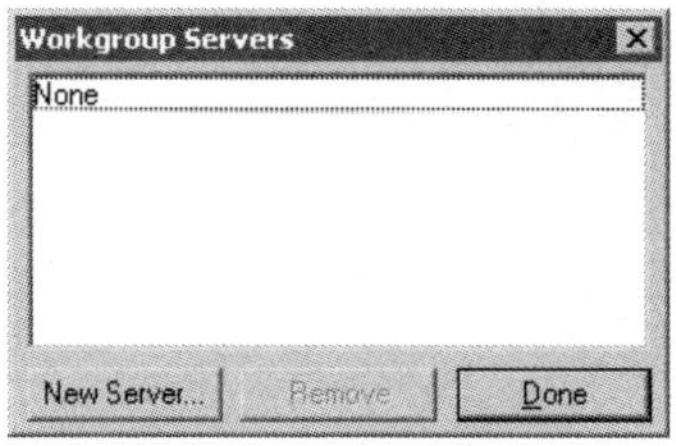

NOTE If your cursor isn't in the text flow, the Workgroup menu choices are grayed out.

The New Server button changes to an Edit Server button if you select a server other than None.

3. Click the New Server button. The Server Setup dialog box is displayed.

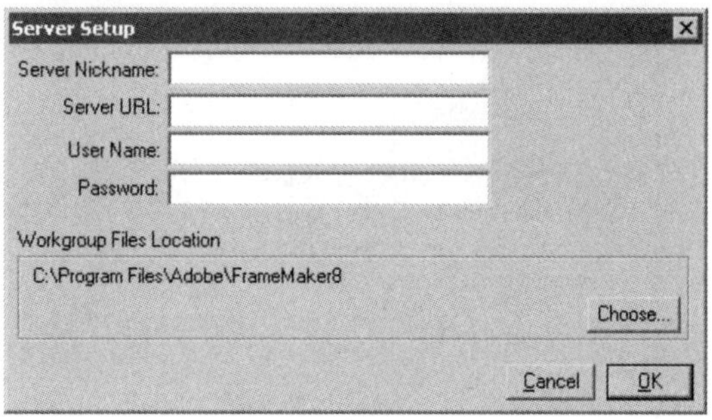

4. Type in a name for the workgroup in the Server Nickname field.
5. Type the Uniform Resource Locator (URL) for the workgroup in the Server URL field.

NOTE Include the full URL for the workgroup server. After you click the OK button to save the workgroup settings, an error is displayed if you leave out "http://" or type an invalid URL. Consult with your system administrator for the correct information.

6. *(optional)* Type your user name in the User Name field and your password in the Password field. This gives you access to files on the WebDAV server.

CAUTION Typically, you shouldn't add your user name and password. If you do, anyone who uses your computer will have access to files on the workgroup server.

7. To select the folder where you will download files, follow these steps:
   a. Click the Choose button. The Browse for Folder dialog box is displayed.

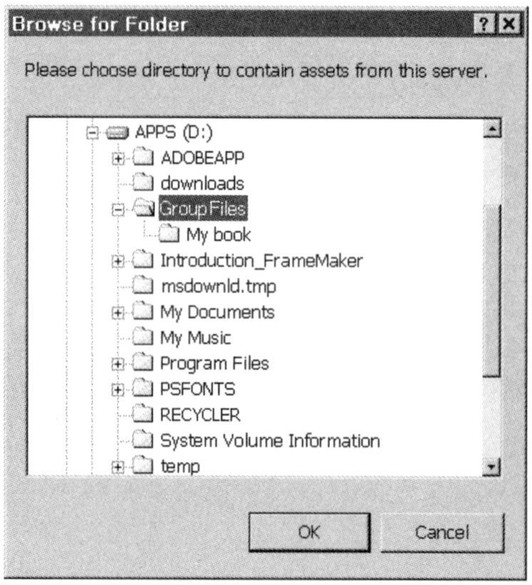

   b. Click the folder, then click the OK button. The Server Setup dialog box is displayed again (Figure 27-1).

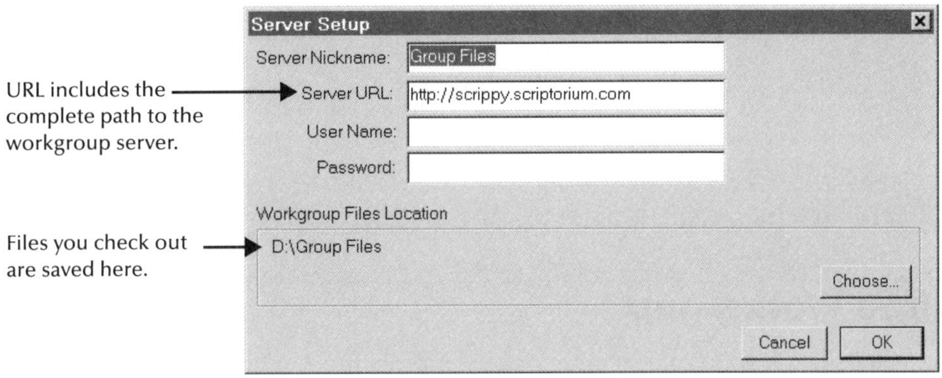

Figure 27-1. Displaying and setting up workgroups

8. Click the OK button, then click the Done button. You've configured your workgroup server. If an error is displayed, verify that the server is working and you have the correct URL.

Editing a Workgroup

After you create a workgroup, you can edit your workgroup settings. For example, you can change your local workgroup directory. After you change the directory, files you download and check out are saved to the new directory, and files in the old directory remain in the same location. To edit the workgroup settings, follow these steps:

1. Select File➤Workgroup➤Workgroup Servers. The Workgroup Servers dialog box is displayed (Figure 27-2).

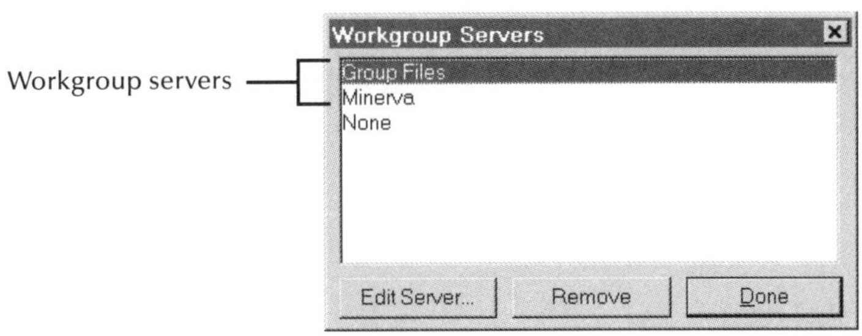

Figure 27-2. Selecting a workgroup server

2. Click the server you want to modify, then click the Edit Server button. (The New Server button reads "Edit Server" when you click a workgroup.)

3. Modify the settings, then click the OK button. The Workgroup Servers dialog box is displayed again.

CAUTION Typically, you shouldn't add your user name and password. If you do, anyone who uses your computer will have access to files on the workgroup server.

4. Click the Done button. Your changes are saved.

Deleting a Workgroup

When you delete a workgroup, FrameMaker removes the workgroup from your list of configured servers; the files on the server or in your local directory are not deleted. You need to delete obsolete workgroups—servers that no longer exist or to which you don't have access. If you don't delete them, a warning is displayed each time you display the list of workgroups. You can click the OK button to ignore the warning, but this gets tedious.

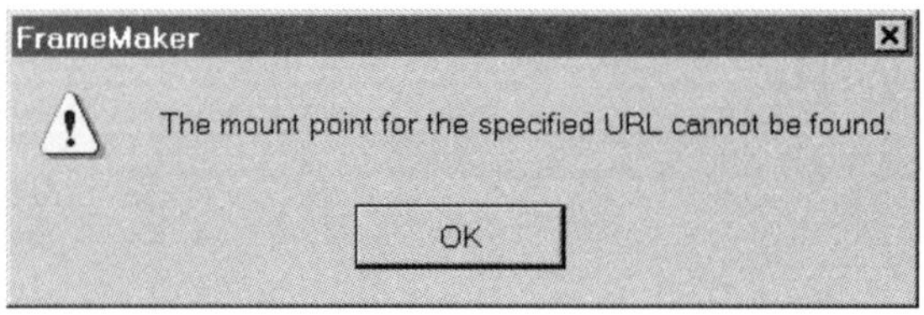

To delete a workgroup, follow these steps:

1. Select File➤Workgroup➤Workgroup Servers. The Workgroup Servers dialog box is displayed (Figure 27-2).
2. Click the workgroup you want to delete, then click the Remove button. A confirmation dialog box is displayed.
3. Click the Yes button to delete the server. The server is removed from your workgroup setup in FrameMaker.

Modifying Workgroup Preferences

The workgroup preferences provide options for managing documents and links. You can also turn off the workgroup feature. Table 27-1 describes the preferences.

To modify the preferences, follow these steps:

1. Select File➤Preferences➤Workgroup. The Workgroup Preferences dialog box is displayed.

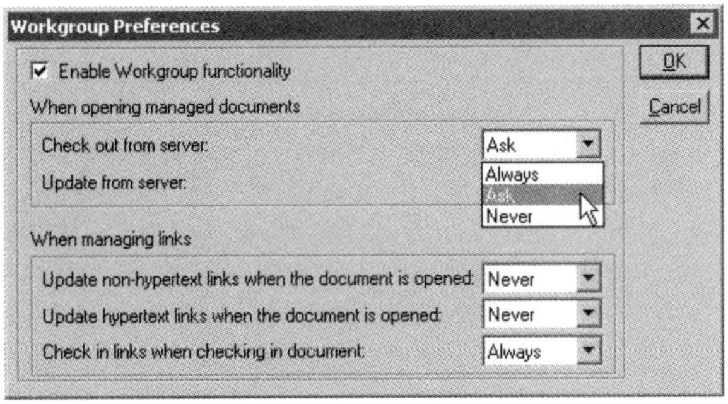

2. In each drop-down list, click Always, Ask, or Never. See Table 27-1 for details.
3. Click the OK button. The preferences are updated.

Option	Description
Enable Workgroup functionality	Turns the workgroup feature on or off. When turned off, the Workgroup menus are grayed out, and the WebDAVLinks palette isn't displayed when you open FrameMaker. Turning the feature off doesn't affect your managed files. When you turn the feature on again, the Workgroup menus are displayed, and the WebDAVLinks palette is displayed when you open FrameMaker.
When opening managed documents	
Check out from server	**Always:** Checks out a file automatically when you open it. **Ask:** Asks if you want to check out the file. If you click the No button, a read-only version is displayed. **Never:** Never checks out the file. A read-only version is displayed. Because you might want to open a file only for reading (not for modifying), it's usually best to select Ask or Never. Never is the default setting. See "Checking Out Files" on page 652 for details.

Table 27-1. Modifying Workgroup Preferences

Option	Description
Update from server (affects only documents that are checked in)	**Always:** Opens the latest version from the server instead of from your local directory. **Ask:** Asks if you want to open an updated version from the server. If you click the No button, your local copy is displayed. **Never:** Opens your local copy. To make sure you're always working from the most up-to-date file, keep the default setting, Always. See "Updating Local Documents" on page 655 for details.
When managing links	
Update non-hypertext links when the document is opened	**Always:** Automatically downloads the latest imported graphics, text insets, links to files in a book, and other non-hypertext links from the server when you open the file. **Ask:** Asks if you want to download the latest non-hypertext links from the server. **Never:** Never downloads the latest non-hypertext links. The links saved in your local copy of the document are displayed. See "Updating Managed Links" on page 662 for details.
Update hypertext links when the document is opened	**Always:** Automatically downloads the latest cross-references, table of contents entries, index entries, and other hypertext links from the server when you open the file. **Ask:** Asks if you want to download the latest hypertext links from the server. **Never:** Never updates hypertext links. The links saved in your local copy of the document are displayed. See "Updating Managed Links" on page 662 for details.
Check in links when checking in document	**Always:** Automatically checks in links when checking in a document. **Ask:** Asks if you want to check in links. **Never:** Never checks in links. You have to check them in manually. See "Checking In Links" on page 662 for details.

Table 27-1. Modifying Workgroup Preferences (Continued)

TIP Keep in mind that if a document is large or has many links, updating the links every time you open the file might cause your file to open slowly. In addition, the imported items don't need to be updated every time if they aren't modified frequently. You can later update the links all at once after opening the document. See "Updating Managed Links" on page 662 for details.

Working with Managed Documents

Files on the workgroup server are *managed* documents. You create managed documents by saving them from FrameMaker to the workgroup server. From there, you can work with the managed documents. Features include the following:

- **Saving a file on the workgroup server.** When you save a FrameMaker file onto the workgroup server for the first time, you create a managed document. A working copy is saved to your local workgroup directory, and you choose whether to check out the file. If you don't check out the file, a read-only version is displayed.
- **Opening a managed file.** When you open a file from the workgroup server, a read-only copy is displayed. You must check out the file to gain write access.
- **Checking out a file.** To modify a managed document, you check out the file. A copy is saved to your local workgroup directory. Others can't modify the file on the WebDAV server until you check it in. They can, however, open the file in read-only mode or update their local copy.
- **Saving a file.** To give others access to your changes while you have the document checked out, you can save the document to the workgroup server. Both your local copy and the server versions are updated.
- **Canceling a check out.** After checking out a document, you might decide that you don't need to modify it. To release the lock on the file and let others check it out, you cancel your check out.
- **Checking in a file.** To let others modify a managed document, you check in the file. You can also check in the managed links so that others may modify the linked items (such as imported graphics). When you check in a file, your local copy is displayed in read-only mode.
- **Updating your local copy.** While someone has a document checked out, you can update your local copy to view the latest version.
- **Reverting to the last saved copy.** To discard your changes to a file, you can revert to the last saved version.
- **Renaming a file.** You can rename files on the workgroup server; however, the file still exists under the original name until you delete it.
- **Uploading and downloading non-FrameMaker files.** FrameMaker lets you manage non-FrameMaker files on the workgroup server.

Adding Files to the Server

To add a file to the server, follow these steps:

1. Select File➤Open, then open the file you want to upload.
2. Select File➤Workgroup➤Save As. The Save To Server dialog box is displayed.

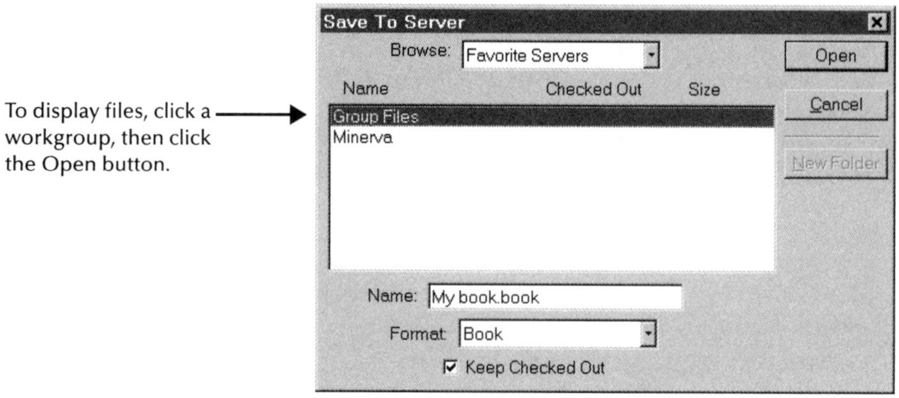

3. To display the correct folder on the server, do one of the following:
   - Click a workgroup or folder, then click the Open button.
   - Click the workgroup or folder in the Browse drop-down list.

   The contents of the server or folder are displayed (Figure 27-3).

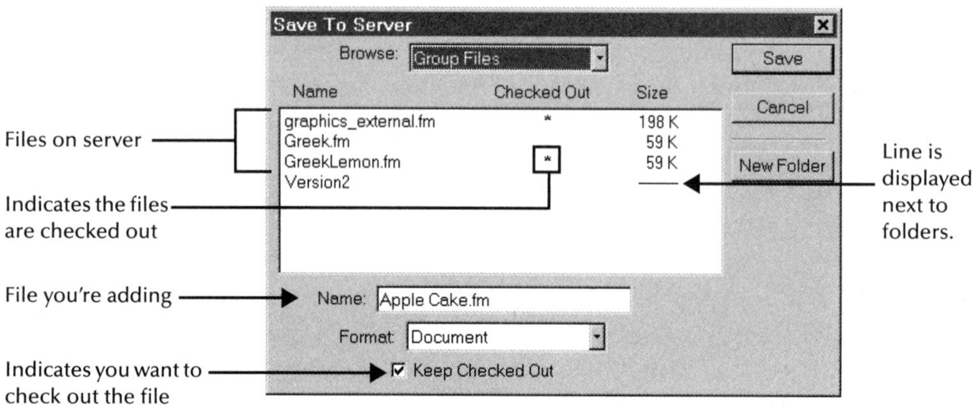

Figure 27-3. Adding files to the workgroup server

4. *(optional)* To create a new folder on the server, follow these steps:
   a. Click the New Folder button. The New Folder dialog box is displayed.

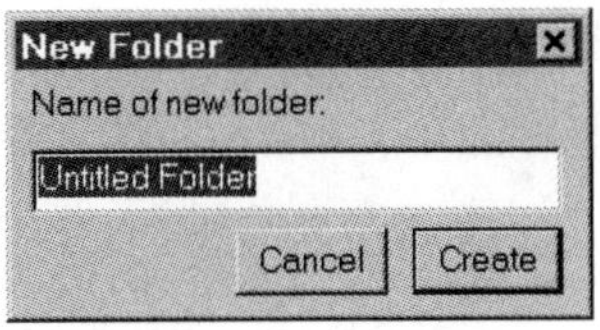

b. Type the name of the folder, then click the Create button. The new folder is added to the drop-down list, and the Save To Server dialog box is displayed.

New folder (The new folder isn't always displayed after you create it, so you might need to select the folder in the drop-down list.)

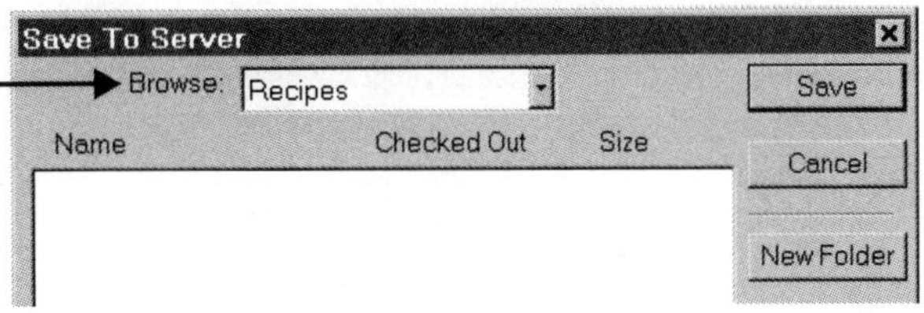

c. Click the new folder (scroll down if necessary), then click the Open button. (The name of the button is either Open or Save, depending on what you're doing.) The name of the new folder is displayed in the Browse field.

5. *(optional)* To save the file with a different name, type the name in the Name field.

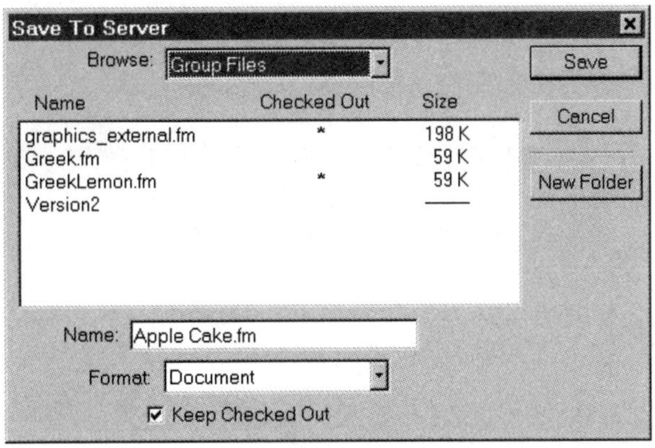

6. *(optional)* To save the file as a Maker Interchange Format (MIF) file, click MIF in the Format drop-down list.

CAUTION The file is saved in MIF 8 format, so the file cannot be opened in previous versions of FrameMaker if the MIF file has any Unicode characters in it.

7. *(optional)* To check out the file, check the Keep Checked Out check box. This means that others cannot modify the file until you check it in.
8. Click the Save button. A confirmation dialog box is displayed.

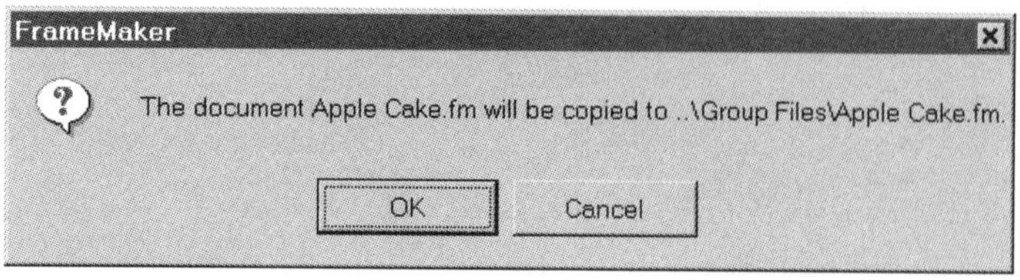

9. Click the OK button. If your user name and password are not specified for the server, the Authentication dialog box is displayed.

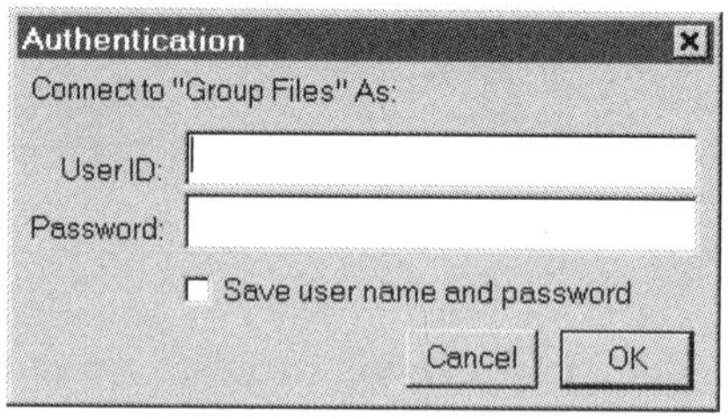

10. Type your user name and password, then click the OK button. The file is copied to your local directory and the workgroup server. One of the following might occur:
    - If the file is already in your local directory, a confirmation dialog box is displayed. To replace the existing file, click the Yes button.

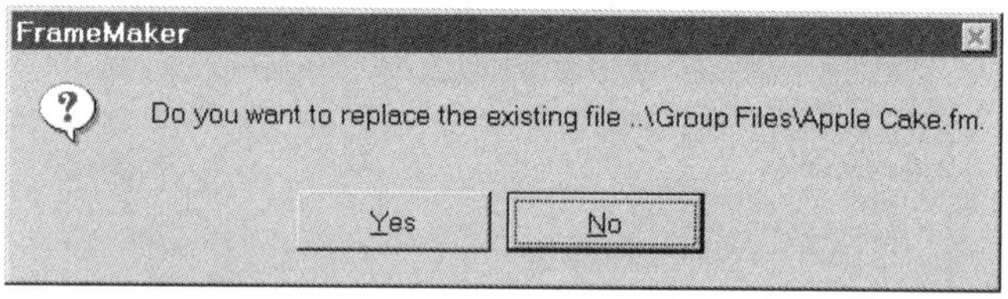

    - If the file is already in the workgroup directory, a confirmation dialog box is displayed. To replace the existing file, click the Yes button.

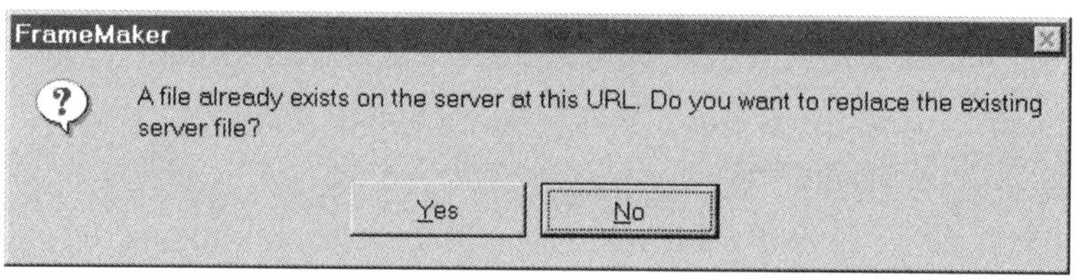

If you didn't check out the file, the following occurs:

- The file reverts to a read-only version.
- Only the file name is displayed in the title bar.
- The menus change.

You need to check out the file to modify it. See "Checking Out Files" on page 652 for details.

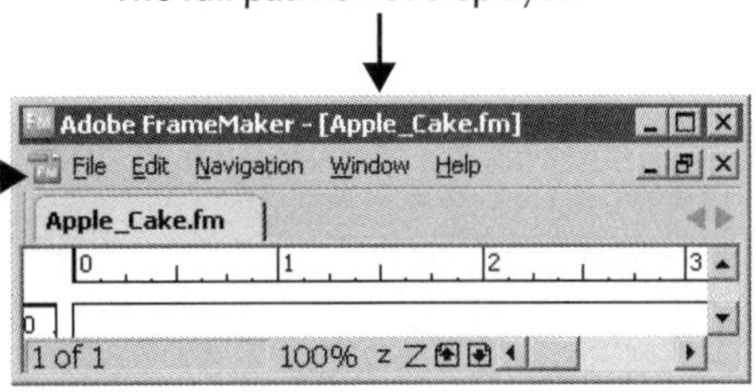

Opening Files

You can open a file on the server and check it out, or if it's already checked out, just view the document. To open a file, follow these steps:

1. Select File➤Workgroup➤Open. The Open From Server dialog box is displayed (Figure 27-4).

NOTE Files marked with stars are already checked out. A warning is displayed if you try to check them out.

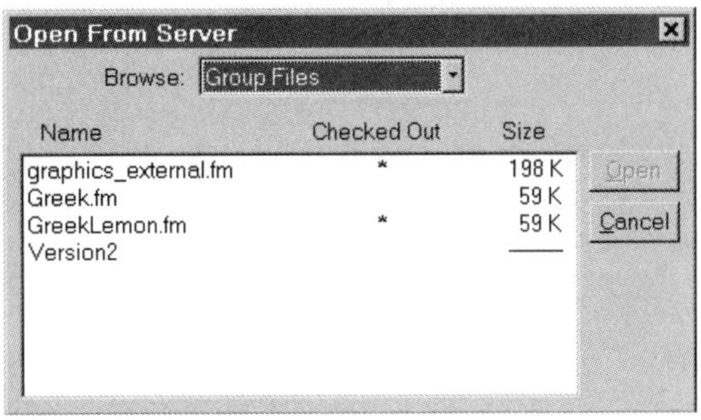

Figure 27-4. Opening a file on the server

2. To display the folder that contains the file, click the folder in the Browse drop-down list.
3. If you need to enter your user name and password, the Authentication dialog box is displayed. Type the information, then click the OK button. The Open From Server dialog box is displayed again (Figure 27-4).
4. Click the file, then click the Open button. One of the following occurs:
   - If your preferences are set up to update hyperlinks automatically, the links are updated.

- If your preferences are set up to ask if you want to update hyperlinks, dialog boxes are displayed for updating hypertext links and non-hypertext links. Click the Yes buttons in both boxes to update links or the No buttons to avoid updating them. In a document with many links, the update may take some time. You can update the links later if you want to. See "Updating Managed Links" on page 662 for details.

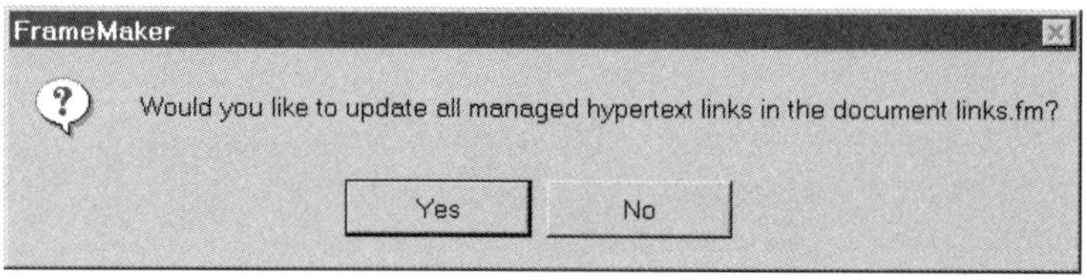

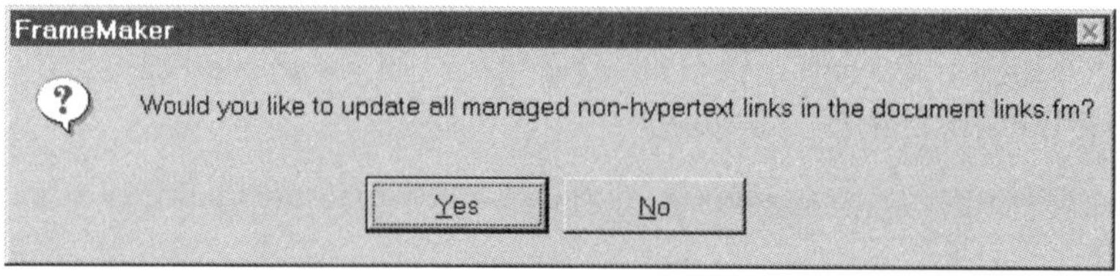

5. Next, one of the following occurs:
   - If your preferences are set up to check out files automatically when you open them, the file is copied to your local directory, and the file on the server is locked to prevent others from making changes.
   - If your preferences are set up to ask if you want to check out a file when you open it, a confirmation dialog box is displayed. Click the Yes button to check out the file and copy it to your local directory or the No button to display the file in read-only mode.
   - If your preferences are set up to never check out files automatically, the file is displayed in read-only mode.

Checking Out Files

After you open a file, you can check it out to make changes. FrameMaker locks the file and saves a copy to your local directory in the same directory organization as the server. For example, files are usually stored in subdirectories on the server. If the file is in the "Group Files/Recipes" subdirectory, FrameMaker creates the "Group Files/Recipes" folder in your local directory and copies the file into the new folders.

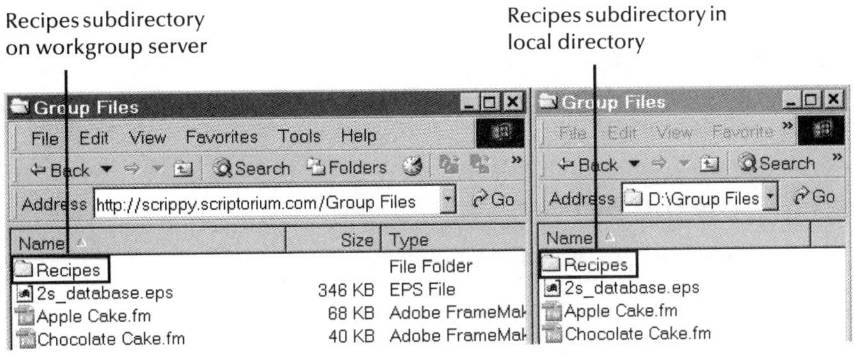

In the Open From Server dialog box (Figure 27-4 on page 651), the Checked Out column indicates which files are checked out. If checked out, a star is displayed next to the file name. You can open one of these files, but an error is displayed if you try to check out the file.

NOTE By default, FrameMaker prompts for a confirmation when you try to check out a file. You can configure the workgroup preferences to check out files automatically or never check out files when you open them. See "Modifying Workgroup Preferences" on page 644 for details.

To check out one or more open files, do one of the following:

- **Check out one open file.** Select File➤Workgroup➤Check Out.
- **Check out all open files.** Press SHIFT and select File➤Workgroup➤Check Out All Open Files.

The files are checked out, copied to your local workgroup directory, and locked.

Saving Managed Documents

You can save managed files in your local directory or on the server. If you save documents in your local directory, other users can't see your changes or update their local copies until you save the file on the server or check in the file. However, by saving the file on the server, you give others access to your changes without releasing your lock on the file.

Saving Files Locally

To save one or more files on your hard drive, save them as you do unmanaged documents. You can also save a file in a different directory as you normally do. See "Opening, Saving, Closing, and Printing Documents" on page 36 for details.

Saving Files on the Server

To save files on the server, do one of the following:

- **Save one open file.** Select File➤Workgroup➤Save.
- **Save all open files.** Press SHIFT and select File➤Workgroup➤Save All Open Documents.
- **Save an open file to another folder.** Select File➤Workgroup➤Save As. The Save To Server dialog box is displayed (Figure 27-3 on page 648). Browse to find the correct folder, then click the Save button.

NOTE When you check in files, FrameMaker saves the files on the server before checking them in.

Canceling Check Outs

You can decide you only want to view a file after you check it out. If so, you cancel the check out. FrameMaker unlocks the file and discards your changes.

To cancel check outs, do one of the following:

- **Cancel check out on one file.** Select File➤Workgroup➤Cancel Check Out. A confirmation dialog box is displayed. Click the Yes button.

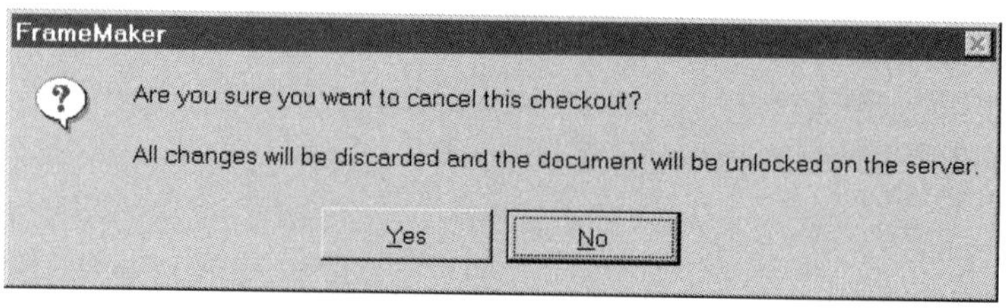

- **Cancel check out on all open files.** Press SHIFT and select File➤Workgroup➤Cancel Checkout of All Open Documents. A confirmation dialog box is displayed for each document. Click the Yes button for each document.

The files are unlocked, and read-only versions are displayed.

Checking In Files

After you modify a managed file, you check in the file. FrameMaker lets you check in all managed links and unlocks the file. To check in files, do one of the following:

- **Check in one open file.** Select File➤Workgroup➤Check In.
- **Check in all open files.** Press SHIFT and select File➤Workgroup➤Check In All Open Files.

If the document contains managed links, a confirmation dialog box is displayed. Click the Yes button to check in all managed links. The files are saved, unlocked, and read-only versions are displayed. See "Managing Links" on page 659 for more information on updating links.

Updating Local Documents

You can update your local copy of a managed document while another user has the file checked out. This lets you read the latest version of the document. To update local documents, do one of the following:

- **Update one open document.** Select File➤Workgroup➤Update.
- **Update all open documents.** Press SHIFT and select File➤Workgroup➤Update All Open Documents.

Reverting to the Last Saved Document

Before you save changes to a document, you have the option of reverting to the last saved copy on the server. When you revert, the changes you made are discarded (whether or not you saved them to your local workgroup), but the file remains checked out. To revert to the last saved copy of a document, do one of the following:

- **Revert one document.** Select File➤Workgroup➤Revert. A confirmation dialog box is displayed. Click the Yes button.

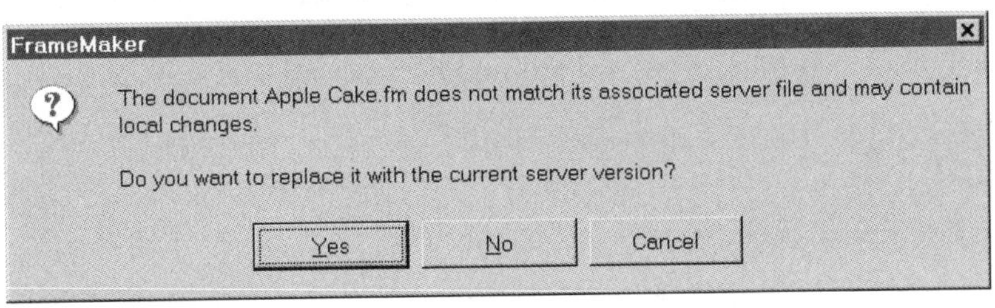

- **Revert all open documents.** Press SHIFT and select File➤Workgroup➤Revert All Open Documents. A confirmation dialog box is displayed for each file that doesn't match the server version. Click the Yes button for each document.

Your changes are discarded, and the last-saved version of the document is displayed.

Renaming Files

You can rename a managed document, and the contents of the document are copied into a new document. If another user opens the document with the old name, FrameMaker does not display a warning, so you'll need to delete the old file or notify other users that you've changed the name.

To rename an open file, follow these steps:

1. Select File➤Workgroup➤Save As. The Save To Server dialog box is displayed (Figure 27-3 on page 648).
2. Type a new name in the Name field, then click the Save button. A confirmation dialog box is displayed.

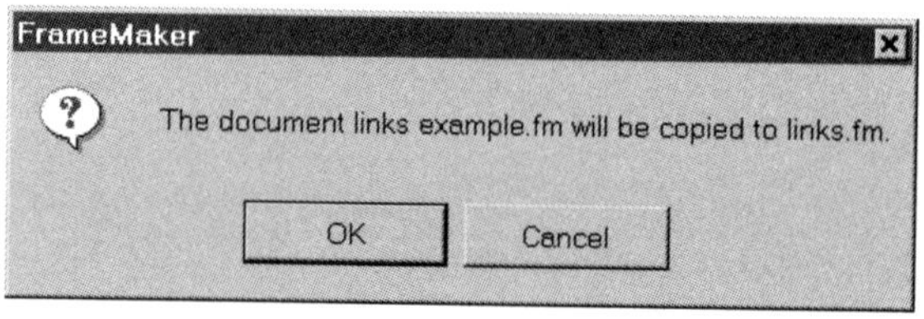

3. Click the OK button. The contents of the document are copied into a new file.

Closing Files

You close managed files just as you do unmanaged files—by selecting File➤Close or pressing SHIFT and selecting File➤Close All Open Files. Make sure you save or check in the file before closing it; otherwise, your changes will be discarded. If you don't check in the file, the file is still checked out to you, and other users will be unable to modify the file. See "Saving Managed Documents" on page 653 and "Checking In Files" on page 655 for details.

Uploading and Downloading Files

FrameMaker lets you download and upload files to the server without opening the files. For example, you can upload a graphic or spreadsheet. These files can be imported into managed files or opened in another program that supports WebDAV.

Uploading Files

To upload a file, follow these steps:

1. Select File➤Workgroup➤Put File on Server. The Please select a file to be uploaded dialog box is displayed.

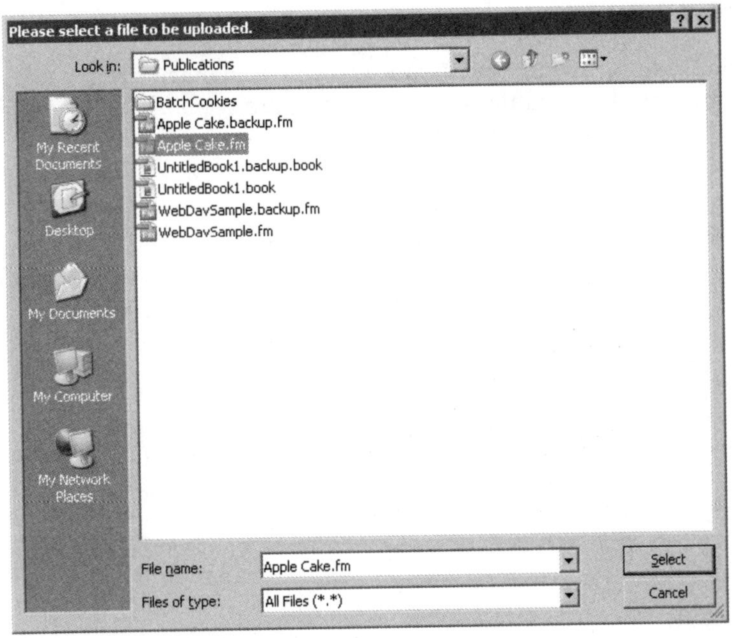

2. Click the file (you can select only one at a time), then click the Select button. The Save To Server dialog box is displayed (Figure 27-3 on page 648).
3. *(optional)* To rename the file, type a new name in the Name field.
4. *(optional)* To prevent others from modifying the file, check the Keep Checked Out check box.
5. Click the Save button. A confirmation dialog box is displayed, stating that the file will be copied to your local directory.
6. Click the OK button. The file is uploaded to the server.

Downloading Files

To download a file to your local directory, follow these steps:

1. Select File➤Workgroup➤Get File from Server. The Open From Server dialog box is displayed (Figure 27-4 on page 651).
2. Click the Open button. The file is copied to your local directory.

Adding and Managing Links

In addition to managing documents, FrameMaker can manage the links in a document. Both hypertext and non-hypertext links are supported. Hypertext links include items such as cross-references, table of contents entries, and index entries. Non-hypertext include items such as imported graphics, text insets, and links to files in a book.

Link management options are similar to document management options. You can check in and out, save, cancel check outs, update, and revert hyperlinks to the last saved versions on the server.

Importing Files

You can import files into a managed document from your local directory or the server, either by creating a link to the file or copying the file into the document. When you check out a document that has imported files, those files aren't automatically checked out. You must check them out separately. See "Managing Links" on page 659 for details.

Importing Unmanaged Files

To import a file from your computer, import them as you do in an unmanaged document. See "Importing a Graphic" on page 308 for details. If you decide later that you want to manage the file, you can save the link to the server from the WebDAVLinks palette. See "Saving Unmanaged Links" on page 660 for details.

Importing Managed Files

To import a managed file into an open document, follow these steps:

1. Select File➤Workgroup➤Import. The Import From Server dialog box is displayed.

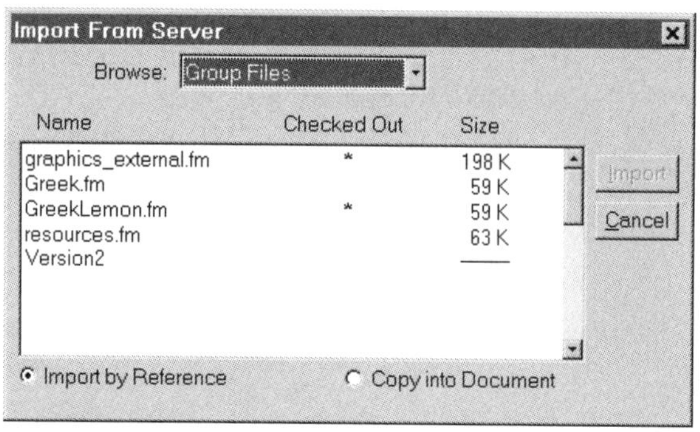

2. Click the file, then click one of the following:
   - To create a link to the file, click the Import by Reference radio button.
   - To copy the file into the document, click the Copy into Document radio button.
3. Click the Import button. The file is displayed in the document and copied into your local directory.

Managing Links

After you import files into a document or add files to a book file, you manage their links in the WebDAVLinks palette. Select File➤Links to display the palette. Basic information about links in the document is displayed, such as whether links are unmanaged, checked in, or checked out. The name and location of a selected link is also displayed.

In the Links drop-down list, you select options to manage your links. For example, you can save links to the server, check links in and out, revert to the last saved link on the server, updating links that are checked in, and cancel checked-out links.

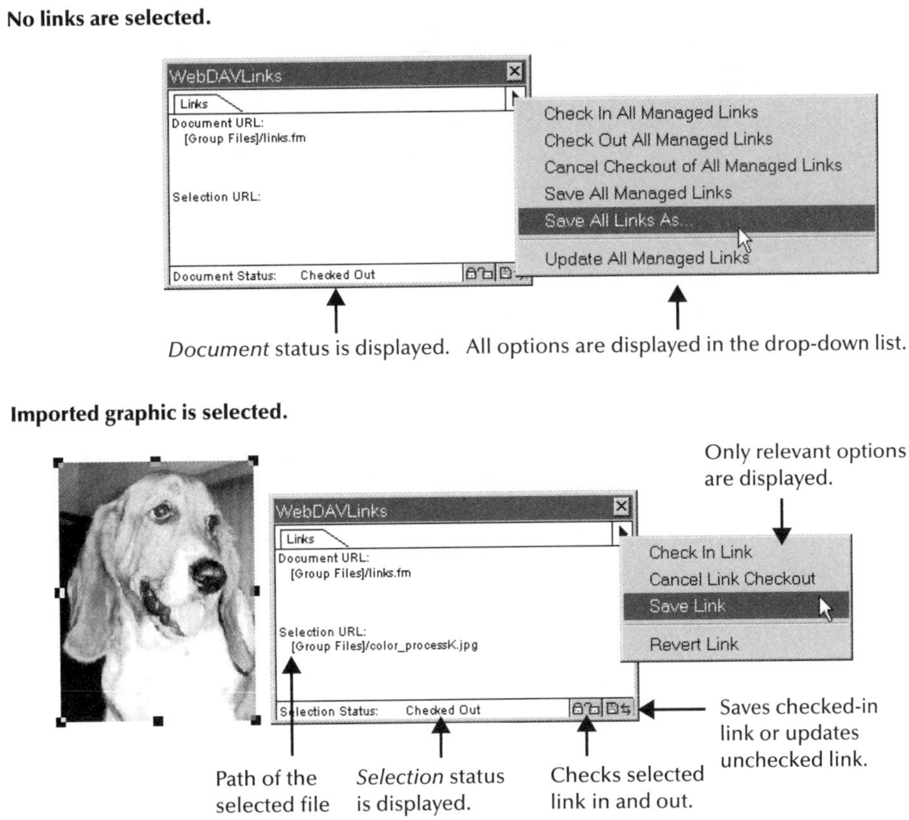

Figure 27-5. Working with managed links

Saving Unmanaged Links

You save unmanaged links on the server to begin managing them. FrameMaker prompts you to name each link and gives you the option of checking them out. To save links in a file you've checked out, follow these steps:

1. Select File➤Links. The WebDAVLinks palette is displayed (Figure 27-5 on page 659).
2. Indicate which links you want to save, then click an item in the Links drop-down list. The choices are as follows:
   - **Save one link.** Select the link, then click Save Link As.
   - **Save several links.** Select the links, then click Save Selected Link As.
   - **Save all links:** Deselect all links, then click Save All Links As.

   The Save To Server dialog box is displayed (Figure 27-3 on page 648).
3. *(optional)* To rename the file, type a new name in the Name field.
4. *(optional)* To check out the file, check the Keep File Checked Out check box.
5. Click the Save button. A confirmation dialog box is displayed.

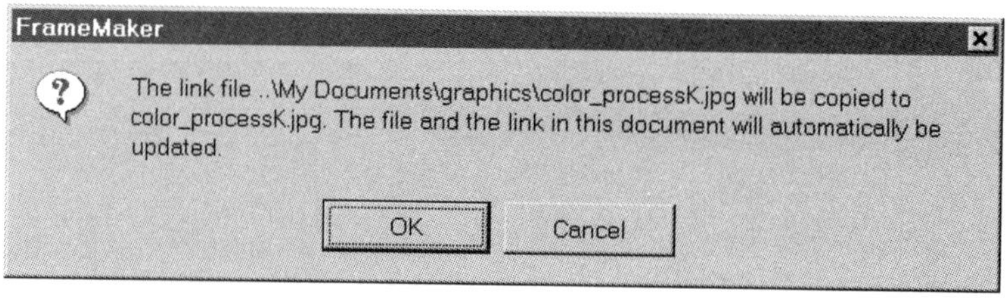

6. Click the OK button. The file is saved and checked out (if chosen).

If there are additional unmanaged links, the Save To Server dialog box is displayed again. Repeat the procedure.

Checking Out Links

You check out links to prevent others from making changes while you're working with them. To check out links, follow these steps:

1. Select File➤Links. The WebDAVLinks palette is displayed (Figure 27-5 on page 659).
2. Indicate which links you want to check out, then click an item in the Links drop-down list. The choices are as follows:
   - **Check out one link.** Select the link, then click Check Out Link or click the button in the lower-right corner of the Links palette.

- **Check out several links.** Select the links, then click Check Out Selected Links or click the button in the lower-right corner of the Links palette.
- **Check out all managed links.** Deselect all links, then click Check Out All Managed Links.

The links are checked out.

Saving Checked-Out Links

You save checked-out links to give other users access to your changes without checking in the links. To save checked-out links, follow these steps:

1. Select File➤Links. The WebDAVLinks palette is displayed (Figure 27-5 on page 659).
2. Indicate which links you want to check out, then click an item in the Links drop-down list. The choices are as follows:
   - **Save one checked-out link.** Select the link, then click Save Link, or click the button in the lower-right corner of the Links palette.
   - **Save several checked-out links.** Select the links, then click Save Selected Links, or click the button in the lower-right corner of the Links palette.
   - **Save all checked-out links.** Deselect all links, then click Save All Managed Links.

   The checked-out links are saved.

Canceling Check Outs

To cancel links you checked out and discard your changes, follow these steps:

1. Select File➤Links. The WebDAVLinks palette is displayed (Figure 27-5 on page 659).
2. Indicate which checked-out links you want to cancel, then click an item in the Links drop-down list. The choices are as follows:
   - **Cancel link checkout.** Select the link, then click Cancel Link Checkout.
   - **Cancel checkout of several links.** Select the links, then click Cancel Checkout of Selected Links.
   - **Cancel checkout of all managed links.** Deselect all links, then click Cancel Checkout of All Managed Links.

   The check outs are canceled, and your changes are discarded.

Checking In Links

To save and check in links, follow these steps:

1. Select File➤Links. The WebDAVLinks palette is displayed (Figure 27-5 on page 659).
2. Indicate which links you want to check in, then click an item in the Links drop-down list. The choices are as follows:
   - **Check in one link.** Select the link, then click Check In Link or click the button in the lower-right corner of the Links palette.
   - **Check in several links.** Select the links, then click Check In Selected Links or click the button in the lower-right corner of the Links palette.
   - **Check in all managed links.** Deselect all links, then click Check In All Managed Links.

   The links are saved and checked in.

Updating Managed Links

To update the links in a local copy of a checked-in document, follow these steps:

1. Select File➤Links. The WebDAVLinks palette is displayed (Figure 27-5 on page 659).
2. Click Update All Managed Links. The links are updated in your local document.

NOTE You can't select or modify a link until you check out the document.

Reverting to the Last Saved Version

To revert to the server version of a link and discard your changes, follow these steps:

1. Select File➤Links. The WebDAVLinks palette is displayed (Figure 27-5 on page 659).
2. Select the link on the page, then click Revert Link in the drop-down list. A confirmation dialog box is displayed.

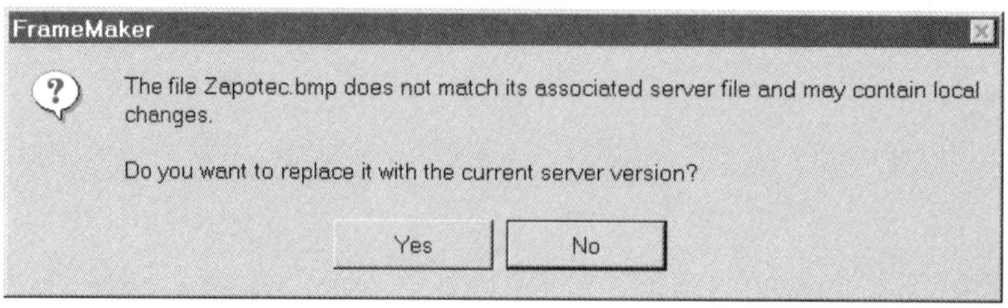

3. Click the Yes button. The server version of the link is displayed.

PART VII

Appendixes

APPENDIX A

Resources

This appendix lists FrameMaker-related resources, including add-on software, web sites, and mailing lists. Please keep in mind that web sites do change; we have verified all of these sites at the time of printing, but web site addresses become obsolete very quickly.

NOTE These tools worked with FrameMaker 8 when this book was written, but FrameMaker updates might affect them, so check before you install. Also, this appendix lists just some web sites and tools; there are many good tools that are not listed here.

FrameMaker-Related Web Sites

Adobe Systems. Adobe Systems makes FrameMaker software. The web site contains product information, support information, printer drivers, and more.

www.adobe.com

FrameUsers. An unofficial FrameMaker resource site. It contains information about FrameMaker service providers, add-on software, and more.

www.frameusers.com

Frame User (German). Another unofficial FrameMaker resource site. If you speak German, this is the site for you.

www.frame-user.de

Scriptorium Publishing. Scriptorium Publishing develops complex publishing systems and provides training and consulting on FrameMaker. It is also the publisher of this book. The web site contains useful white papers and a collection of links to other FrameMaker resources.

www.scriptorium.com

Mailing Lists

Framers. A mailing list for FrameMaker users. The framers list has been around for years; its membership includes both new FrameMaker users and experts, some of whom have subscribed to the list for many years. List traffic is heavy but generally fairly well-focused on issues related to FrameMaker.

lists.frameusers.com/mailman/listinfo/framers

Free Framers. Similar to the framers list based at frameusers.com, but it has less traffic. In the past, many topics were posted to both lists. The archives of the framers@omsys.com list through 2005 are searchable. To subscribe, send email to majordomo@omsys.com. In the body of the message, type: **subscribe framers**.

www.freeframers.org

HATT. A high-volume list for help authoring tools and technology.

groups.yahoo.com/group/hatt

techwr-l (Tech whirlers). A high-volume list for technical writers.

www.techwr-l.com/techwhirl/index.php3

wwp-users (WebWorks and ePublisher). A mailing list for ePublisher Platform users. Discussions are usually highly focused on ePublisher Platform topics.

groups.yahoo.com/group/wwp-users

Online Output Conversion Tools

The following are powerful tools that create high-quality, customized HTML, online help, and other outputs from FrameMaker files.

Adobe RoboHelp. www.adobe.com/products/robohelp

NOTE RoboHelp is available as a standalone product or as part of the Adobe Technical Communication Suite.

MadCap Flare. www.madcapsoftware.com/products/flare

Quadralay ePublisher Platform. www.quadralay.com

Omni Systems MIF2GO. www.omsys.com/dcl/mif2go_main.htm

Third-Party Tools and Plug-Ins

FrameMaker offers lots of features, but every now and then you run across something you really wish it had. In many cases, a third-party plug-in or add-on software can accomplish what you want. This section lists some sites for software that extends FrameMaker's features.

Bruce Foster Tools. The ImpGraph plug-in lets you specify the default settings for the anchored frames around inserted figures. The Archive tool gathers all the files for your book into a single folder, with text insets and graphics in their own subfolders. There are other tools here as well.

home.comcast.net/%7Ebruce.foster/products.htm

Carmen Publishing. Rick Quatro of Carmen Publishing writes custom scripts and plug-ins. If you convert Microsoft Word files to FrameMaker, consider TableCleaner, which removes overrides to formatting in tables imported from Word documents. Other tools available here include ImportFormatsSpecial, BookPageCount, RunaroundNone, PageLabeler (which makes your FrameMaker numbering and PDF file numbering match), FindChangeSpecial, and PageBreaks.

www.frameexpert.com

CudSpan Tools. Cudspan is a set of tools that generates a list of paragraph overrides, lets you delete unused paragraph tags, runs batch processes on documents or book files, provides bookwide searches, remembers page and line breaks in generated files, and associates icons with paragraphs.

www.freeframers.org/freeware/cud

IXgen. This tool places all of the index markers across a book file's documents in one list, where you can edit them.

www.fsatools.com

Filtrix. This filtering tool converts files from one format to another; it has bidirectional MIF filtering capability.

www.blueberrysoftware.com

FrameScript. FrameScript lets you automate tasks inside FrameMaker. Writing in FrameScript can be daunting; however, many scripts are available for download, and you can hire experts to write powerful custom scripts.

www.framescript.com

Leximation. Scott Prentice maintains this site, which has a comprehensive list of many Framescript scripts and FrameMaker plug-ins (including some of his own). If there is a tool you need for FrameMaker, it is likely you can find it by looking here. His MarkerTools plug-in makes it much easier to edit markers that are stacked on top of each other, lets you use variables within markers, and lets you create templates for marker text (which are handy for all those "see also" index entries).

www.leximation.com/toolsearch

MicroType. Shlomo Perets offers tools that let you automate many FrameMaker-to-PDF items (colored bookmarks, page transitions, hyperlink highlights that show up online but don't print, setting cropping to mix different size pages within a single file, and more). This site has a list of past and current FrameMaker bugs and annoyances. The main tool is FrameMaker-to-Acrobat Timesavers, which has a number of add-ons available for specialized PDF tasks like adding custom navigation and setting additional options for displaying 3D files.

www.microtype.com

Silicon Prairie Software. The Auto-Text plug-in lets you associate keystrokes or menu choices from a custom menu with text or graphics. Your menu can contain graphics, text, formatted tables, paragraphs with pictures beside them, symbols, and other items you use frequently. To change the menu, you update a single FrameMaker file.

Other tools from this site include Alert Tool, Character Tools, Index Tools, Index Tools Professional (which includes instructions for creating a master index for a set of FrameMaker books), LEP Tools for creating Lists of Effective Pages (often required for military documents), Master Page Tools, Outline Tools, Paragraph Tools, Readability Tools, and Table Tools.

www.siliconprairiesoftware.com

Setprint. This plug-in makes the Adobe PDF printer (or whichever printer you choose) the default printer for FrameMaker while allowing your other applications to use the default printer selected in the Windows Control Panel.

www.sundorne.com/FrameMaker/Freeware/setPrint.htm

ShrinkwrapAsIs DLL. Preserves the anchored frame settings when you shrink-wrap a graphic. FrameMaker normally changes the anchored frame to At Insertion Point. If you have already set your anchored frame how you want it—for example, centered below current line—ShrinkwrapAsIs resizes the anchored frame without changing the anchored frame settings.

www.martinek.us/shrinkwrap.html

SnagIt. This screen capture tool lets you take screen captures, preview and edit them, and then import them by reference without leaving FrameMaker. The FrameMaker add-in is not installed by default, so be sure to select the Custom installation choice to add it.

www.techsmith.com

Database Publishing from FrameMaker

The following tools retrieve information from databases and use FrameMaker to apply complex formatting. For example, these tools can create catalogs of information stored in a database.

Miramo. Miramo lets you bring database content into FrameMaker.

www.miramo.com

PatternStream. PatternStream lets you bring database content into FrameMaker.

www.fml.com

Online Manuals

FrameMaker comes with several manuals in PDF format, which are in the Documents folder in the FrameMaker 8 installation directory. The online manuals include the *User Guide* and the *MIF Reference Guide*. You can also download additional manuals and tutorials from the Adobe web site:

www.adobe.com/support/documentation/en/framemaker

Reporting Bugs

If you have a FrameMaker problem you want to report to Adobe Systems, use this bug report form:

www.adobe.com/misc/bugreport.html

APPENDIX B

Building Blocks

Building blocks are placeholders in FrameMaker. When FrameMaker encounters a building block, it replaces the building block with a real value. Building blocks are used in cross-reference formats, variables, autonumbered paragraph tags, reference pages, and master pages. For example, the cross-reference format called "See Heading & Page" displays the heading and page of the referenced paragraph tag as:

See "Managing Color Definitions" on page 504.

The cross-reference definition is:

```
See "<$paratext>" on page <$pagenum>.
```

When the document is opened or saved, the heading and page number are updated automatically. If the heading changed to "Editing Color Definitions," the cross-reference would include the updated heading.

Building blocks are enclosed by angle brackets and are often preceded by a dollar sign (<$year>, for example). The following table describes FrameMaker building blocks and indicates where each building block is valid. The table is sorted by symbols and then alphabetical entries, so you'll find building blocks beginning with "$" toward the top and building blocks such as "<R>" at the end.

FrameMaker provides Japanese building blocks for sorting symbols and generated lists and displaying the date and time; however, they're not covered here. Refer to the FrameMaker help for details.

NOTE Some building blocks don't do anything when used alone; instead, they work with other building blocks to display information. For example, <$creationtime> doesn't display the creation time; it causes the building blocks that follow (such as <$hour>:<$minute> <$AMPM>) to display the creation time. Building blocks that don't produce output have "(undisplayed)" in the description.

		Used In					
Building Block	**Displays**	Autonumber	Cross-Reference	Index Marker	Variable	HTML Reference Page	Other Reference Pages
;	Separates entries in an index marker			✔			
:	Separates levels in an index marker			✔			
[ ]	Indicates sort order for an index entry			✔			

Building Block	Displays	Autonumber	Cross-Reference	Index Marker	Variable	HTML Reference Page	Other Reference Pages
\t	Tab	✔					✔
• or\b	Bullet	✔					
< =0>	Resets value to zero or another specified number (undisplayed)	✔					
< >	Keeps value of first counter (undisplayed)	✔					
<$alphabetics>	Sort order for alphabetic entries						✔
<$ampm>	Lowercase morning or evening designation (am)				✔		
<$AMPM>	Uppercase morning or evening designation (AM)				✔		
<$autorange>	Automatic page ranges						✔
<$chapnum>	Chapter number	✔	✔		✔	✔	✔
<$condtag[*condtag*]>	Specified condition tag				✔		
<$creationtime>	Causes any following time building block to display the creation time (only in running h/f and non-time system variables; undisplayed)				✔		
<$curpagenum>	Page number (used only on master pages)						✔
<$currenttime>	Causes any following time building block to display the current time (only in running h/f and non-time system variables; undisplayed)				✔		
<$dayname>	Name of the day (Monday)				✔		
<$daynum>	Number of the day (1)				✔		
<$daynum01>	Number of the day with leading 0 (01)				✔		
<$defaulttitle>	Text of the first document heading					✔	
<$endrange>	End of a page range			✔			
<$filename>	Name of the file example: widget.fm		✔		✔	✔	

Building Block	Displays	Used In: Autonumber	Used In: Cross-Reference	Used In: Index Marker	Used In: Variable	Used In: HTML Reference Page	Used In: Other Reference Pages
`<$fullfilename>`	Name of the path and file example: c:\Book\widget.fm		✔		✔	✔	
`<$hour>`	Hours (1)				✔		
`<$hour01>`	Hours with leading 0 (01)				✔		
`<$hour24>`	Hours in 0–24 military format (13)				✔		
`<$lastpagenum>`	Last page number in document				✔		
`<$marker1>`	Header/Footer $1 marker text				✔		
`<$marker2>`	Header/Footer $2 marker text				✔		
`<$minute>`	Minutes (1)				✔		
`<$minute00>`	Minutes with leading 0 (01)				✔		
`<$modificationtime>`	Causes any following time building block to display the time the file was last opened or saved (only in running h/f and non-time system variables; undisplayed)				✔		
`<$monthname>`	Name of the month (January)				✔		
`<$monthnum>`	Number of the month (1)				✔		
`<$monthnum01>`	Number of the month with leading 0 (01)				✔		
`<$nextsubdoc>`	URL of the next document					✔	
`<$nopage>`	Suppresses the page number			✔			
`<$numerics>`	Sort order for numeric entries						✔
`<$ObjectId>`	Numeric identifier assigned to the linked object						✔
`<$ObjectType>`	Numeric identifier indicating the type of link						✔
`<$pagenum>`	Page number of the linked paragraph		✔		✔		✔

Building Block	Displays	Used In: Autonumber	Cross-Reference	Index Marker	Variable	HTML Reference Page	Other Reference Pages
<$paranum[*paratag*]>	Autonumber of first matching paragraph tag on page, including text (Chapter 1)		✔		✔	✔	✔
<$paranum>	Autonumber of the linked paragraph, including text		✔		✔		✔
<$paranumonly [*paratag*]>	Autonumber of first matching paragraph tag on page, excluding text (1)		✔		✔	✔	✔
<$paratag[*paratag*]>	Name of first matching paragraph tag on page (ChapterTitle)		✔		✔	✔	✔
<$paratext[+,*paratag*]>	Text of last paragraph on page matching the tag		✔		✔	✔	✔
<$paratext[*paratag1*, *paratag2*,*paratag3*]>	Text of first paragraph on page matching the tag		✔		✔	✔	✔
<$paratext>	Text from the source paragraph		✔		✔	✔	✔
<$parentdoc>	URL of the first document					✔	
<$prevsubdoc>	URL of the previous document					✔	
<$relfilename>	Relative path to linked file example: Book\widget.fm					✔	✔
<$second>	Seconds (1)				✔		
<$second00>	Seconds with leading 0 (01)				✔		
<$shortdayname>	Name of the day (Mon)				✔		
<$shortmonthname>	Name of the month (Jan)				✔		
<$shortyear>	Year (30)				✔		
<$singlepage>	Designates single page number after <$nopage>			✔			
<$startrange>	Beginning of page range			✔			
<$symbols>	Sort order for symbolic entries						✔

Used In

Building Block	Displays	Autonumber	Cross-Reference	Index Marker	Variable	HTML Reference Page	Other Reference Pages
`<$tblsheetcount>`	Total number of table sheets				✔		
`<$tblsheetnum>`	Number of current table sheet				✔		
`<$variable[`*varname*`]>`	Text of the variable					✔	
`<$volnum>`	Volume number	✔	✔		✔	✔	✔
`<$year>`	Year (2030)				✔		
`<a+>`	Lowercase alphabetic numbering; value increased by 1	✔					
`<A+>`	Uppercase alphabetic numbering; value increased by 1	✔					
`<a=1>`	Lowercase alphabetic numbering; value set to 1 (or another number)	✔					
`<A=1>`	Uppercase alphabetic numbering; value set to 1 (or another number)	✔					
`<a>`	Lowercase alphabetic numbering; value unchanged	✔					
`<A>`	Uppercase alphabetic numbering; value unchanged	✔					
<*char_tag*>	Applies the specified character tag to the items that follow in the definition	✔	✔	✔	✔	✔	✔
`<Default Para Font>` or `</>`	Removes any character formatting and returns to the regular paragraph formatting of the parent paragraph	✔	✔	✔	✔	✔	✔
`<n+>`	Numeric numbering; value increased by 1	✔					
`<n=1>`	Numeric numbering; value set to 1 (or another number)	✔					
`<n>`	Numeric numbering; value unchanged	✔					

Building Block	Displays	Used In: Autonumber	Cross-Reference	Index Marker	Variable	HTML Reference Page	Other Reference Pages
<r+>	Lowercase Roman numeral numbering; value increased by 1	✔					
<R+>	Uppercase Roman numeral numbering; value increased by 1	✔					
<r=1>	Lowercase Roman numeral numbering; value set to 1 (or another number)	✔					
<R=1>	Uppercase Roman numeral numbering; value set to 1 (or another number)	✔					
<r>	Lowercase Roman numeral numbering; value unchanged	✔					
<R>	Uppercase Roman numeral numbering; value unchanged	✔					

APPENDIXES

Appendix C

Customizing maker.ini

The default settings and paths for FrameMaker are stored in the maker.ini file. In general, you won't need to edit maker.ini often, but there are a few FrameMaker defaults that you should probably change. For example, you should change the clipboard paste order so that Unicode characters are included and not displayed as question marks when you paste from Microsoft Word. Also, some plug-ins for FrameMaker require that you edit maker.ini.

The following lists some of the information stored in maker.ini:

- FrameMaker version and license information
- Preferences such as whether to create backup files, remember missing fonts, and so on
- Recently opened files
- Pen thicknesses and patterns
- Directories for templates and samples
- The location of dialog boxes on the screen
- Information needed for plug-ins
- Spelling options
- Default font information
- Filters

Editing maker.ini

To edit maker.ini, do the following:

1. Close FrameMaker.
2. There are two maker.ini files. Find maker.ini in the following folders:
   - If all users on your computer have the same FrameMaker preferences, open maker.ini from:
     \Program Files\Adobe\FrameMaker8
   - If users have different FrameMaker preferences, open maker.ini from:
     \Documents and
     Settings*username*\ApplicationData\Adobe\FrameMaker\8.0
     (Windows XP),
     or
     username\AppData\Roaming\Adobe\FrameMaker\8.0 (Windows Vista)

   Edit only one of the maker.ini files.

NOTE If a setting appears in both maker.ini files, the settings in maker.ini in the Documents and Settings folder take precedence over the settings in the FrameMaker folder.

3. Create a backup of maker.ini.

4. Open the original maker.ini file in a text editor such as Notepad or PSPad.
5. Scroll down until you find the setting you want to change. The sections that follow describe some recommended changes.
6. Edit the text, then save maker.ini. Your changes are saved and applied the next time you open FrameMaker.

Making Onscreen Text Align Like It Prints

By default, FrameMaker tries to align characters so they look good on screen. It's preferable to have the text on screen look like it does when you print it. To make the alignment of the text on screen and in print the same, find this line in maker.ini:

```
DisplayUsingPrinterMetrics=Off
```

Change it to On:

```
DisplayUsingPrinterMetrics=On
```


Setting Clipboard Pasting Order

When you paste into FrameMaker, FrameMaker looks at the content of the clipboard and tries to determine how the text should be pasted. For example, if you paste a paragraph from one FrameMaker file into another, FrameMaker maintains the formatting, markers, and so on. However, if you paste from an application like Microsoft Word, the result may be an OLE object or text that displays gray boxes or question marks that indicate missing characters. For better results, find this line in maker.ini:

```
ClipboardFormatsPriorities=FILE, OLE 2, EMF, META, DIB, BMP,
MIFW, MIF, RTF, UNICODE TEXT, TEXT
```

Change the pasting order:

```
ClipboardFormatsPriorities=FILE, UNICODE TEXT, TEXT, EMF,
META, DIB, BMP, MIFW, MIF, RTF, OLE 2
```

Updating Graphics from Web Addresses

(optional) If you import graphics from the Internet or an intranet site, you can have FrameMaker always update the graphic. Find the following line in maker.ini:

```
AlwaysDownloadURL flag=Off
```

Change it to On:

```
AlwaysDownloadURL flag=On
```

Changing the Substitution Fonts

The fonts that FrameMaker substitutes for missing fonts are defined in maker.ini. For example, you might open a document that uses the Minion Pro font. If your system doesn't have the font, FrameMaker substitutes the default font, which is Times New Roman or Times Roman. If you know ahead of time that a document uses a font you don't have, you can map the font to a more appropriate font. Find the default font mappings:

```
; Default used to map unknown fonts:
;
DefaultFamily=Times New Roman, Tms Rmn
DefaultAngle=Regular
DefaultVariation=Regular
DefaultWeight=Regular
DefaultSize=12
```

TIP When you create a new FrameMaker document using one of the predefined FrameMaker templates, the default fonts defined in maker.ini are selected in paragraph and character tags.

Change the default family setting. You might also want to change the default size. In the following example, the default font is Veljovic and the size is 11:

```
; Default used to map unknown fonts:
;
DefaultFamily=Veljovic
DefaultAngle=Regular
DefaultVariation=Regular
DefaultWeight=Regular
DefaultSize=11
```

INDEX

Symbols

Numerics

A

E

N

S

T

Y

Z

SCRIPTORIUM
press